Contemporary Business Writing:

A Problem-Solving Approach

Contemporary Business Writing:

A Problem-Solving Approach

Terry McNally

Peter Schiff

Northern Kentucky University

Wadsworth Publishing Company
Belmont, California
A Division of Wadsworth, Inc.

English Editor: **John Strohmeier**
Editorial Assistant: **Holly Allen**
Production Editor: **Sandra Craig**
Print Buyer: **Ruth Cole**
Designer: **Paula Shuhert**
Copy Editor: **Charles McNally**
Technical Illustrator: **Donna Salmon**
Compositor: **Boyer & Brass, Inc.**
Cover Designer: **Mark McGeoch**

Printed in the United States of America
3 4 5 6 7 8 9 10–90 89 88

ISBN 0-534-05784-5

Library of Congress Cataloging-in-Publication Data
McNally, Terry, 1937–
    Contemporary business writing.
    Includes index.
    1. Business report writing.   I. Schiff, Peter,
1948–   . II. Title.
HF5719.M39   1986   808'.066651   85-20314
ISBN 0-534-05784-5

For
Joan Eling McNally,
Aileen Nora McNally,
Carolyn Joan McNally,
and Timothy Eling McNally
with love and gratitude.

To
Adam Schiff,
Marla Schiff,
and especially Phyllis Schiff
with love and thanks for their support, patience,
understanding, and assistance.

CONTENTS

Preface

ontemporary Business Writing: A Problem-Solving Approach is written for anyone planning a business-related career. Students in diverse fields will easily understand it, whether they are from business, the humanities, the physical or social sciences, or programs such as information systems or hospital administration. While it draws examples and exercises from many areas of business—management, accounting, marketing, and finance—it requires only a lay knowledge of business. The book will also serve business-related professionals as a desktop reference work.

This book integrates three elements—a process approach to writing, problem solving, and computer technology—all in the context of business writing. Our goal is not only to teach students the many forms of business communication but also to teach a process approach to writing. We use this process approach to solve the rhetorical problems involved in business writing. We also teach the new computer technology that has become a part of writing in business through dictation and word processing.

Often when they begin to write, students try to accomplish too much at one time—organizing, writing, and polishing simultaneously. Few of them realize the amount of time professional writers devote to planning and revising. We therefore emphasize a process approach to writing, stressing the importance of planning before writing, and revising after writing.

This process approach analyzes business writing in four steps. The first step is defining the writing problem—setting goals and developing a reader profile. The second step is analyzing the writing problem—finding out more about it through research and analysis, and considering organizational and strategic options. The third step is selecting an organizational strategy and developing at least one rough draft of a document. The final step is revising and editing—making the large- and small-scale changes required to meet the writer's specifications.

We regard problem solving as the adaptation of this process approach to business writing tasks. These techniques blend well because every business writing task can be viewed as a problem to be solved. Moreover, as a technique familiar to many students, problem solving translates the writing process into language that students understand and with which they feel comfortable.

We distinguish, however, between business problem solving and rhetorical problem solving. Solving a business problem involves the application of business knowledge, experience, and insight. Solving a rhetorical problem involves the application of writing principles, techniques, and imagination. The province of this text is not business, but rhetorical problem solving.

Computer technology, through dictation and word processing, is the third element integrated into this text. We adapt these technologies to the writing process. For example, we show how effective dictation requires planning and revising and how word processing actually accelerates these two steps. We keep writing paramount at all times, and we explain technology not as an end but as a means to better writing.

The text is divided into three parts. Part 1 explains the four problem-solving steps to writing. We devote a full chapter to each step, clarifying with examples and exercises.

Part 2 applies this problem-solving method to the forms of business communication commonly used today. We cover not only the usual forms, such as the memo, report, proposal, and letter, but also forms that, though seldom treated in textbooks, are often written in business—the job description, performance appraisal, procedure, policy statement, warning, commendation, and feasibility report.

Although the text covers these "new" topics, it covers all traditional subjects as well, devoting a chapter each to the formal report and to writing as a part of the job search process. The text introduces the student to a greater variety of resume options than do most texts and devotes considerable space to the job interview and follow-up communications.

Part 2 also devotes separate chapters to such supports to the writing process as research (including opinion sampling, interviews, government documents, and computer searches), graphs and illustrations (including computer graphics), and oral presentations.

Part 3 devotes a chapter each to three contemporary methods of writing—word processing, dictating, and collaborative writing—all from a process point of view.

The Handbook at the end of the book covers numerous conventions in grammar, usage, and punctuation and serves as a valuable reference tool.

Most chapters feature continuing cases exemplifying the principles explained in the chapter. Every chapter concludes with writing exercises in which students apply the techniques learned in the chapter to business cases ranging from sales to finance, from management to accounting.

Special Features at a Glance

- Four chapters devoted to the writing process as a means of solving business writing problems.

- Step-by-step application of problem-solving techniques to virtually every form of business writing.

- Inclusion of all common business writing forms, including many seldom covered, such as feasibility reports, job descriptions, and performance appraisals.

- Writing samples showing progressive drafts of a document.

- Coverage of analytical tools such as flowcharts, decision trees, and matrices.

- A research chapter covering databases, questionnaires, interviews, and library research.

- Continuing cases woven into the chapters showing writers making decisions and producing drafts.

- Instructions on writing nonsexist prose.

- A complete chapter on writing with a word processor.

- A chapter integrating dictation and the process approach to writing.

- A chapter on collaborative writing.

- A chapter that teaches students how to produce graphs, with and without a computer, and how to integrate them with text.

- A job search chapter with alternate resume options and questions to ask an interviewer.

- A Handbook that covers students' most common grammatical and stylistic problems.

Acknowledgments

We would like to thank the acquisitions editor, John Strohmeier, and the production editor, Sandra Craig, for their efforts, concern, and expertise in the preparation of this book. We would also like to acknowledge the reviewers: Kathy Bell, University of Miami, Coral Gables; Anita Brostoff, University of Pittsburgh; Eileen B. Evans, Western Michigan University; Sarah Liggett, Louisiana State University; George Miller, University of Delaware; Paul Reuben, California State University, Stanislaus; Patricia Thomas, California State University, Fullerton; and Thomas Willard, University of Arizona.

We thank Kevin Howat and Cedric Crocker for guidance in the earlier stages of the project.

Terry McNally appreciates the assistance of Dr. Charles Barrett, chairman of the board and chief executive officer of Western-Southern Life Insurance Company, and that of Mr. Ronald Humphrey of the same company. He thanks Professor William McKim, Jr., for help in getting a sabbatical.

Peter Schiff acknowledges the moral support of his parents, Rudolph Schiff and Lillian Schiff. He wishes also to thank Professor Leonora Woodman of Purdue University, who first stimulated his interest in writing instruction.

Terry McNally

Peter Schiff

Introduction

I n this introduction, we will discuss four topics: what writing can do for your career, how business and academic writing differ, why problem solving and a process approach to writing can help you write more effectively, and how this text is organized.

What Writing Can Do for Your Career

We make no exaggerated claims for writing. By itself, writing will not get you to the top. Few chief executive officers will lean back in their chairs, grin, and confess, "I owe it all to my college business writing course."

But most business executives at any level will admit that, other things being equal, the manager who writes well has an edge over the one who does not. Executives also agree that as you climb the corporate pyramid, communication skills become increasingly important. If managers succeed or fail largely by the quality of their decisions, those decisions can be the best ones only if they are based on timely, accurate, and highly intelligible letters, memos, and reports.

Because of this close relationship between good decisions and communication, good communicators are invaluable assets to upper management. In fact, a prime way to gain the attention of higher management is through your writing. In your early years with a large corporation, you may have no direct contact with upper management. But if you write a well-organized, highly readable document, copies of which move up the chain of command—with your name on them—you will have a chance to impress the leaders of your company.

Writing well can make you an indispensable aid to someone higher up who does *not* write well. Such a person is often looking for subordinates who will compensate for his or her deficiencies.

Moreover, the competition for better jobs in business becomes keener each year for the thousands of applicants entering the job market. Among these job seekers, those who can demonstrate communication skills have the edge over those who cannot. The person who can point to a good grade in a business writing course has demonstrated that skill.

Taking this course will add to your confidence in writing. The text will acquaint you with the major forms of business writing and supply useful exercises in each. With this study and practice, you can begin to think of yourself as a skilled writer, with the confidence that stems from knowledge and experience. Most college graduates can write a well-organized memorandum, but not many can write one that is both well-organized *and* readable. That's the difference between a skilled and an unskilled writer, between memos we hate to read and those we wish we had written.

That's what this text is about—teaching you the techniques that differentiate the skilled from the unskilled writer. As you learn and master those techniques, you should simultaneously cultivate a sense of pride and workmanship in your writing.

How Business and Academic Writing Differ

By *academic writing,* we mean the kind of writing you do in your college courses, for example, the essays in composition class, the term paper in economics, or the report in political science. Technically, the memos and reports you write for this course are a form of academic writing. *Business writing*—the kind of writing people do on the job—has much in common with academic writing, but it differs in time pressure, length, and subject.

Few students can imagine their instructor telling them at 10:14 A.M. that a writing assignment is due at 5:00 P.M. that same day. But in the business world, it is not uncommon for your boss to ask for a written report to be on his or her desk before you leave the office. This is pressure.

Another difference has to do with the length of written documents. In college, the instructor will often specify the length of an assignment—for example, 5,000 words. Finding material that can be stretched into 5,000 words can present a major problem. In business, however, finding material to flesh out the letter, memo, or report is seldom desirable. The reader of the business document will generally prize conciseness—the shorter the document, provided it is complete, the better.

Still another difference is subject matter. The author of the academic paper often must choose a subject. The author of the business report usually has a subject but must choose the best way to present that subject to the audience.

These differences should not obscure the similarities between academic and business writing. The universal goals of meeting the needs of the reader, organizing the material most effectively, and choosing the most appropriate style and tone are constants in all writing. In this book, however, we have tried to emphasize the kinds of writing common to the business world—for example, memorandum reports, letters, proposals, procedures, guidelines, and appraisals.

Why Problem Solving and a Process Approach to Writing Can Help You Write More Effectively

The most distinctive feature of this text is its application of the problem-solving technique to business writing. This is especially true in that the text provides an unusually thorough application of the problem-solving technique to most of the kinds of writing *actually* done in business.

How do you determine the best solution to a problem with many possible solutions? You do so by establishing criteria for the best possible solution and by applying those criteria to all available solutions. For example, if your problem is to determine which electronic typewriter is best for your office, you may establish criteria which will identify the "best" model, such as its quality of type, speed, affordability, dependability, and the availability of good service.

The Concept of Problem Solving

Problem solving therefore requires a progression that can be broken down into steps. The number of steps in the problem-solving process will vary, from as many as eight to as few as three. The number of steps is arbitrary; what matters is that they describe all the important stages of the process.

We have divided the problem-solving technique itself into four steps. The first step is to define the problem: what are you trying to do and what are your goals? The second step is to analyze the problem. You find out as much as you can about the problem, using formal analytical methods. The third step is decision making. Having defined your goals and analyzed the problem and potential solutions, now you decide on the best available solution and commit yourself to a course of action. The fourth step is the follow-up stage. Having chosen a solution, you check its efficacy, adjust it to the situation, and work out the details.

This method of problem solving can be applied in almost any field, writing being only one of them. Business uses the problem-solving technique, as do engineering, architecture, design, and data processing, to name a few.

Accordingly, we distinguish two applications of the technique. We are not distinguishing two *kinds* of problem solving but two applications of one technique: rhetorical problem solving and business problem solving.

Rhetorical refers to decision making about writing. It means (1) being aware of the various styles of language, the forms of organization, and the variations in tone, and (2) choosing a style, a plan, and a tone, all of which will communicate your message to your intended reader. A rhetorician studies the impact of style, the interrelationship of style and patterns of organization, the effect of tone, and the choice of words to gain an intended effect.

Rhetorical Versus Business Problem Solving

The term *rhetorical* suggests the need to choose the best available alternative. Thus we will be focusing on rhetorical problem solving in a business context.

But do not confuse rhetorical problem solving with *business* problem solving, which is the application of the technique to business problems such as how to cut production costs, reduce absenteeism, or improve morale. Business problems can concern, among other things, finance, production, inventory, management, cash flow, personnel, or advertising. So the difference between rhetorical and business problem solving lies not in the *way* you solve the problem but in the *kind* of problem you solve.

Often, though, business and rhetorical problems can intertwine. Take the example of the sales representative who sells dictation equipment. The business problem is first to determine the best dictation system for the customer and then to convince the customer that this system is superior to any from the competition.

To sell the customer on the product, the sales representative may decide to write a sales letter, which now poses a rhetorical problem. What, for instance, should be the main appeal of the letter—the product's special features, versatility, affordability, or dependability? What is the overall approach best suited to this customer—direct or indirect? How technical should the presentation be? So it is evident that a rhetorical problem can be part of a business problem—that is, writing a successful sales letter can contribute to closing the sale.

Let's take another example, the case of the small public accounting firm of Cahill, Rosen, Walton and Associates, which needs to cut costs. The partners feel they can do little at present to increase the volume of their practice, so they meet and agree to certain cost-saving measures:

1. Instituting a new automated billing system
2. Leasing smaller cars for all professionals
3. Replacing private secretaries with a typing pool
4. Introducing the use of dictation units for all correspondence
5. Employing part-time clerical help
6. Using more economical but inferior photocopy machines

The partners decide that in these six measures they have probably arrived at the best available solution to their business problem of cutting costs. Next they must communicate their decision to their employees. For strategic reasons, they decide to write a memorandum rather than to call a meeting. Now they have a rhetorical problem, namely, how to frame the memo so as to gain as much support for their measures as possible and to reduce, as far as possible, the resistance to change.

Here is a classic interrelationship of a business and a rhetorical problem. Often after the business problem is considered solved, the rhetorical problem arises! The manager now becomes a writer, thinking, "Well, that's probably going to solve the problem of cutting costs; now, how do I sell my solution to this group?"

For example, the partners wonder whether the memo should be direct, stating only the essential facts behind the decision. Or should they give reasons? If they do, what should those reasons be? Should they focus on motives for cooperation? Should the memo mention alternative measures? The right answers to such questions should help the partners solve their writing problem and thus, of course, the business problem.

The business problem—how to cut costs—and the rhetorical problem— how to convey the "bad news" of the cost-cutting measures to the professional staff—are clearly *different* kinds of problems. And yet they interrelate. Solving the rhetorical problem—writing a good memo—may gain acceptance for the cost-cutting measures, increasing their chances of success. Failing to solve the rhetorical problem—writing the memo ineptly—may contribute to employees' resistance to the unpopular decision.

We can therefore draw two conclusions. First, problem solving as a technique is fairly standard, but it can be applied to the clearly distinct business and rhetorical problems. Second, rhetorical and business problems can intertwine, and when they do, the rhetorical problem will often be a part of the larger business problem, and its solution can contribute to the solution of the business problem.

The purpose of this book is to give advice on solving rhetorical problems that occur in business. Consider it a bonus when you discover that in some cases solving a rhetorical problem helps solve a business problem.

A final point: many people who do a great deal of writing will tell you, if you haven't already found out for yourself, that writing is one of the best ways to learn about a topic. Writing forces you to research a topic, organize that research, draw conclusions, and express those conclusions clearly. Writing forces you to define ideas. Thus, when you write about a business problem, you will probably begin to understand it better.

Having defined rhetorical problem solving, we would like to clarify its relationship to another important concept, the process approach to writing. The process approach breaks composing into stages, usually the three stages of pre-writing, writing, and post-writing.

Rhetorical Problem Solving and the Process Approach to Writing

Pre-writing is the planning stage, in which the writer gathers information about the subject, decides on a tone, a level of style and technicality, and a plan of organization. **Writing** is the drafting stage, in which the writer produces one or more drafts of the document. **Post-writing** is the stage in which the author takes a critical look at the document in the light of the original pre-writing specifications and makes revisions to bring the document into closer compliance with those specifications. In this stage the author also edits the document for word choice, sentence variety, and grammar.

The process approach to writing is an ongoing process. Authors constantly look for ways to improve their writing. We maintain that problem solving applied to writing in a four-step process as follows can help students improve their writing in general, and business writing in particular.

1. *Defining the writing problem.* You develop a profile of your reader, identifying what you know or can learn about your reader, your relationship to the reader, and the reader's likely preconceptions and needs. You also define your goals, specifying the kind of response you want from your reader, defining the image you wish to project, and planning to meet your deadline.
2. *Analyzing the writing problem.* You use any of a broad spectrum of analytical tools to help you understand the writing problem and its solutions. These tools include outlines, note card decks, flow charts, decision trees, and matrices.
3. *From decision making to drafting.* You decide about information, ideas, organization, and style. Then you try out those decisions by writing a draft of the document.
4. *Revising and editing.* You review the draft to see whether you need to make large-scale revisions in ideas and organization. You then reexamine the draft to make any necessary small-scale editing changes in such matters as sentence structure, wording, and spelling.

These four steps embody the process approach explained earlier. However, we divide pre-writing, the first stage in the process approach, into two steps: (1) defining the writing problem and (2) analyzing the writing problem. The last two elements in each method are the same. The writing stage corresponds to step 3, from decision making to drafting; the post-writing stage corresponds to step 4, revising and editing. We will use the problem-solving steps throughout this text.

Finally, we must add two important provisos to this four-stage division of the rhetorical problem-solving process. First, the process is recursive. You can and often must go back to an earlier step in order to be ready to tackle a subsequent one. For example, while writing the draft of a document, you may wish to go back and revise the outline. You should not hesitate to return to and revise any step already completed, because the change will probably improve the document.

Second, you can expand or contract this problem-solving technique. If you are writing a one-page letter, for example, you may complete the four steps in 30 minutes. If you are writing a lengthy formal proposal, finishing all four stages may take weeks. Rhetorical problem solving allows you to be flexible.

How This Text Is Organized

The book is divided into three parts, followed by a Handbook. Part 1 explains the four steps to solving a writing problem. Chapter 1 explains how to define the writing problem; chapter 2 explains how to analyze it; chapter 3 discusses decision making and writing the first draft; chapter 4 covers revising and editing.

Part 2 applies the four problem-solving steps to common business writing forms and discusses crucial supports to the writing process. Specifically, chapter 5 explains the major strategies of memos and short reports (writing to inform, persuade, or direct). Chapter 6 examines the qualities of good business letters, their organization, and major kinds. Chapter 7 discusses the process of getting a job (researching the job market, writing the resume and cover letter, and interviewing). Chapter 10 details the process of writing a formal report. Chapter 11 examines the process of writing the feasibility report and the proposal.

Part 2 also explains three supports of the writing process. Chapter 8 details the techniques of research and information gathering; chapter 9 presents the use of graphs and illustrations; chapter 12 discusses the techniques of oral presentation.

Part 3 explains three contemporary developments that have become increasingly integral to writing. Chapter 13 discusses word processing from the writer's viewpoint; chapter 14 examines dictation as a part of the writing process; chapter 15 details collaborative writing—writing as a team.

Writing problems follow each chapter. Each problem appears in the context of a business case and offers practice in applying the strategies discussed in the chapter.

The Handbook at the end of the text explains the essentials that a business writer needs to know about style, grammar, and punctuation.

Finally, throughout this text, as you have probably noted, we will use the word *document* to apply to any kind of business writing, whether it is a one-page memo or a long formal report.

PART 1

Four Steps to Solving a Writing Problem

art 1 presents a sequence of steps for solving rhetorical problems in business and industry. Chapter 1, "Defining the Writing Problem," shows you how to develop a profile of your reader. This chapter also illustrates how to define your writing goals by specifying the response you want from your reader, defining the image you wish to project, and planning to meet your deadline.

Chapter 2, "Analyzing the Writing Problem," explains how to apply techniques for understanding a writing task so that you can proceed with it efficiently. These techniques include outlines, note card decks, flow charts, decision trees, and matrices. The chapter also shows you how to refine such analyses so they can help you prepare to draft.

Chapter 3, "From Decision Making to Drafting," discusses important choices you must make about your information and main idea before drafting your document. This chapter then takes you through the complete drafting process to a first version of your document.

Chapter 4, "Revising and Editing," shows you how to make the large-scale revisions and small-scale editing changes that turn your document from a rough draft to a polished piece of writing.

From time to time in part 1, we remind you that it may be necessary to go back to an earlier problem-solving step before you can continue with a subsequent one. For instance, you may write a rough draft only to find that you have to revise your analysis to accommodate new information about your topic. Because the problem-solving sequence is flexible, you *can* go back to improve what you have done before. By following the problem-solving steps sequentially and returning to earlier ones if necessary, your writing process will become more efficient and your finished documents more effective.

CHAPTER 1

Defining the Writing Problem

*I*n the Introduction to the book, we stressed that the province of this book is *rhetorical* problem solving, and we explained the four steps in rhetorical problem solving, namely, (1) defining the writing problem, (2) analyzing it, (3) decision making and drafting, and (4) revising and editing. In this chapter we will explain in detail the first step—defining the writing problem.

We divide defining the writing problem into two substeps that you take *before* writing. First, you must develop a reader profile. That means defining such items as your reader's probable needs, reactions, and preconceptions. Second, you must define your goals for writing. That means specifying, before writing, how you want your reader to react to your document, to be informed or persuaded, for example. It means defining the kind of image you wish eventually to project in the document. Finally, it means planning to meet your deadline.

Developing a Reader Profile

To define as accurately as possible the reactions of your reader, you must be able to answer the following five questions:

1. For whom are you writing?
2. What do you know or can you learn about your reader?
3. What is your relationship to your reader?
4. What are the reader's likely preconceptions?
5. What are the reader's needs?

To communicate effectively, you must identify with your reader: see with his or her eyes, think as the reader does, even feel, for a time, as the reader feels. Doing so will enable you to shape your message in forms and terms acceptable to the reader. All good writing requires this creative leap into another person's mind.

If you have taken a college composition course, you may already know about audience analysis, which we equate with reader profile. In composition class, your instructor may have insisted that you write first for a generalized, educated reader, and second for the instructor. Perhaps your classmates formed a third audience. That was good practice because your early writing assignments in college challenged you to write for more than one audience, which business people often have to do.

In business you will sometimes write for a large, diversified audience. For example, you might write a policy statement for the entire firm, an appeal to your coworkers to contribute time or money to a fund drive, or a sales letter to potential customers. But in most of the writing you do in business, your audience will be a specific person or group. Often you will personally know your reader and will have dealt with him or her in the past. Therefore you will be able to target your message more accurately than you could in composition class.

We're going to focus on the five questions that shape your reader profile in detail and supply examples of each. Throughout this book, we ask you to refer to this list of questions before you write any major assignment. Answering each of these questions will require you to define your reader's needs, reactions, and expectations. Answering these questions, however, is no more than a valuable exercise. On the job you will seldom have time to answer such questions formally before writing. Nonetheless, focusing on these questions now will heighten your awareness of your reader as you plan and write in the future.

Learning the steps in writing is comparable to learning how to ride a bike. You concentrate on one step at a time—pedaling, balancing, steering, and braking—until you put it all together. So with writing: in the practice stages you concentrate on separate skills that become almost second nature as you gain experience. Today it may take a while to develop a reader profile; later you will probably do it in minutes or even seconds.

Let's examine the questions in detail.

For Whom Are
You Writing?

You might at first think the answer to this question is obvious, but business people, as we said, often write for more than one reader. Almost everything you do in an organization ties in somehow with the work of your department or your division. The people most directly involved with your present task may receive copies of the memorandum or letter you write.

Therefore we use the terms *primary* and *secondary* reader. The primary reader is the one to whom the document is addressed. The secondary reader is any person other than the primary reader who might read the document. Often the name or names of secondary readers are listed at the end of the document, for example:

Copy: Ann Slavensky, Vice-President, Finance

Imagine that you work for a large insurance company called Ontario Life and Casualty Company and your title is senior claims analyst. One of your duties is to answer the letters policyholders write to the company when they think they have a claim, that is, the right to a payment under the terms of their policy. Your job is to determine whether such a payment is justified and either to forward payment or to explain why the company will not pay the claim. You write dozens of these letters in a day, most of them fairly standard letters.

The policyholder is the primary reader; there will probably be more than one secondary reader. First, you will write your letter knowing that your boss will probably read it, especially if the claim is for a large amount of money. A company attorney may get a copy. On the receiving end, the policyholder may show the letter to his or her attorney. All these people have an interest in the settlement of the claim.

Yet each of these readers has a different viewpoint. For example, the policyholder is interested in having his or her claim paid in full. If the company decides not to pay or to pay a lesser amount than the policyholder expects, he or she will probably be interested primarily in the reasons for the decision. The policyholder's attorney, if consulted, will read the letter to see whether the company has met its obligations as stated in the policy.

On the company's side, your manager will read the letter to determine whether or not you exercised good judgment and followed the proper procedures. In addition, the manager will probably want to make sure that the letter will be clear to the policyholder and that the tone is courteous. If a company attorney reads the letter, he or she will want to be assured that the amount of the settlement is no larger than it need be legally.

Writing to satisfy the different readers of your document may sound like a difficult task. We are not saying that it is possible to satisfy all of them, but that you must write with their different viewpoints in mind. The goal is to identify your primary and secondary readers and to answer the following questions about each. (We suggest that you answer the questions in writing.)

1. Who is (are) my primary reader(s)?
2. Who is (are) my secondary reader(s)?

    a. _____

    b. _____

    c. _____

To help you apply the points we are making about defining a writing problem, we will use the following case, in which we give you a role to play and the information you need to define the writing problem.

Case: Belmont Industries

You graduated from college a few years ago and are presently employed in your second job, working for a middle-sized company called Belmont Industries, located in Chicago, Illinois. We're not going to specify what goods and services the company produces because we want the simulation to typify a variety of companies. For two years you have been an assistant to the president of the company, Donald J. Poole. You perform a variety of services for Poole. Sometimes you ghostwrite for him, listen to him as he thinks out loud, gather information for him, explain his directives to his subordinates, and explain the views of his subordinates to Poole. You are in one sense his alter ego, but you do not make decisions for him.

This morning Poole explains your next assignment. He wants to explore the advantages and disadvantages of word processing for Belmont Industries. Poole has just completed a one-day seminar given by a consultant on word processing; therefore, he is generally aware of what word processing does, and he knows that it is not useful for every company. He also knows that a company considering word processing usually commissions a feasibility study to determine whether the advantages of such a system outweigh the disadvantages for that company.

You are Poole's choice to head up this project. Why you? First, because you previously worked for a company that installed word processing, so you have some familiarity with it, although you were not involved in that company's feasibility study. Second, you work well with people, having chaired at least one special task force for Poole in the past year. Finally, you write well. (Remember, you had this course.)

Poole outlines the task. First, without actually doing a feasibility study, he wants you to anticipate potential advantages and problems in switching over to word processing. Second, you are to find out what makes a good feasibility study. Who does the study? What questions should it answer? How much time will it take? How many company employees will it involve? Above all, how much will the study cost? Poole makes a final request. He does not want to read articles about word processing, for which he has no time. He wants a written report from you answering these questions. He wants copies of the report sent to three of his vice-presidents: Inez Garcia of Marketing, Freeman Werner of Finance, and Bert Jankowski of Human Resources. Poole wants the report in two weeks.

Your initial step is to define the writing problem: first, to develop a profile of your reader, and, second, to define your goals for writing. Beginning the profile, you list your readers as follows:

Primary reader: Don Poole, president

Secondary readers:

1. Inez Garcia, vice-president, Marketing
2. Freeman Werner, vice-president, Finance
3. Bert Jankowski, vice-president, Human Resources
4. "Ghostreaders"

The last category requires explanation. Ghostwriters, of course, are people who write anonymously for someone else; "ghostreaders" are the people who may read your report without your knowledge. For example, each of the vice-presidents listed may show a copy of your report to one or more subordinates. Or the president might pass on a copy to the chairperson of the board of directors. You cannot predict exactly who will read your report, but you are aware that you may be writing for a larger audience.

We'll come back to the case after we take up each major point in this chapter.

The more you know about a person, the more effectively you can write for him or her. You probably learned that rhetorical principle in your college composition class. There you were on the first day of the semester, seated in the class of a total stranger, for whom you would have to write several themes upon which your final grade depended. What was this person like?

What Do You Know or Can You Learn about Your Reader?

Liberal or conservative, religious or agnostic, Democrat or Republican? As the semester progressed and the instructor became less of a stranger, it probably became easier to write your essays.

When you are writing for someone you know, you have insights into the person's professional and personal style, an impression of his or her intelligence and knowledge. You may know, for instance, that Mike Stacy in the Accounting Department will appreciate a touch of humor, but Clarence Ryan of the same department will not. You may know that Bob Ortega likes detail, but Cindy Kaplan wants only the salient points.

When you write for someone you do not know well, you must estimate his or her level of intelligence and education. If you judge your reader to be intelligent and well educated, you may use longer, more involved sentences and a sophisticated vocabulary. If you judge your reader to be of average intelligence and modest education, you may wish to use shorter sentences and simpler words.

In writing for a large group of people of different educational, economic, and social backgrounds, a writer determines the least common denominator and writes at that level. If your group contains psychiatrists and waiters, write for the waiters and the psychiatrists will understand. If you write for the psychiatrists, you might lose the waiters—and the taxi drivers, bartenders, and mechanics.

No matter who your reader is, ask yourself what this person does not know about the situation or subject. Concepts and procedures that seem evident to you may be new to your reader. Except in special circumstances, no writer deliberately chooses to be unclear, but the writer may still select wording or concepts that are ambiguous to the reader. The result is that the reader feels shut out.

Take an example one of your authors experienced. He purchased a storm door and was preparing to install it when he discovered that the manufacturer had provided three sets of installation directions. One set explained how to install the storm door frame in the house door frame; another described how to assemble the latch mechanism on the storm door; and the third explained how to assemble the automatic door-closing mechanism. But none explained the sequence of these three steps. For example, should assembly of the latch mechanism precede or follow assembly of the automatic door-closing mechanism? Or perhaps the order of assembly made no difference? Whoever put together the packet of instructions assumed that the reader knew something he in fact did not.

If you do not know much about your reader, perhaps you can learn more, especially if your document will be important. For example, if the professor in your economics class assigns a written report that is to account for 25 percent of your final grade, you may want not only to follow the professor's stated guidelines for the report but also to ask the professor's former students what he or she expects in a report. For example, does the professor welcome opinions or does he or she want students to be completely objective? Does the professor lower the grade for lapses in style?

At the office, you may ask your coworkers about your readers' expectations and preferences, or you can ask the readers themselves. You may learn about their taste in writing either directly or through documents they consider well written. You can infer from such reports or proposals in the files something about the style that most appeals to them. You might study the prose of others in the office whom your readers admire, and draw conclusions from such study.

If you're writing for strangers with whom you have no channels of communication, try other ways to research the reader. For example, has anyone else done any research on this kind of person? If you're writing a letter to a particular group of consumers, there may be marketing studies on this group done by your own firm, or demographic studies done by the United States government or consumer research firms.

Case: Belmont Industries (continued)

You have the built-in advantage of most people who write for their boss—you know Don Poole fairly well. He is intelligent and well educated, having earned an M.B.A. at Michigan State University. You consider him open to new ideas and progressive; like many company presidents, he hates to be left behind while others seem to be moving ahead. Your instincts tell you that he is probably leaning toward the implementation of word processing at Belmont Industries, perhaps even hoping that your research will endorse the move.

Also, choosing you to head up the project may contain a clue about his attitude, since he knows you are generally positive about word processing. On the other hand, his choosing you may reflect only the reasons already given—your previous experience, ability to work with people, and writing expertise. Therefore you must be careful not to display bias in favor of word processing.

You realize that Poole knows well enough what computers do, since many operations at Belmont are already computerized, from inventory to billing, from payroll to records. And he has just returned from a seminar on word processing, so he is familiar with the concept of the word processing feasibility study. Much of the jargon he already knows, for example, terms like *CRT*, *software*, *disk*, and *hard copy*. Other terms, however, will probably need explanation, such as *scrolling*, *WordStar*, and *toggle switch*.

Poole values directness in writing, getting to the point. He prefers a succinct report, supported by solid reasons, that offers a recommendation. Ordinarily he does not like detailed reports; if data are to be included, he wants them presented as a graph.

Among the secondary readers, Poole has a high regard for the opinions of Inez Garcia, vice-president of Marketing. In her tenure at Belmont, the firm has made impressive advances in product development and advertising. She has also recruited a group of bright young sales and product managers. Any recommendation you make about the feasibility study will carry more weight if it has the backing of Inez Garcia. Therefore the study must take her concerns into account.

But while Inez Garcia may be the most influential of your secondary readers, she is not the only one you must consider as you plan and write. Freeman Werner, the vice-president of Finance, will be interested in the potential of word processing for controlling costs and maximizing the use of personnel and equipment. Another secondary reader, Bert Jankowski, the vice-president of Human Resources, will be interested in implications for personnel in word processing, for example, new roles and career paths for clerical employees.

What Is Your Relationship to Your Reader?

As you know, position in the company is the most obvious determinant of relationships between individuals. For example, your position can influence your response to another person's suggestion, determining whether you consider it only briefly or accept it immediately. Organizationally, others will be above you, on the same level, or on a lower level. Therefore we speak of communication as upward, lateral, or downward.

Figure 1.1 shows these three directions of communication in an organizational chart depicting the chain of command in the sales division of a company. The chart moves upward from the sales representatives to the sales managers and then to the district sales manager. The chart could have continued up the line to the regional sales manager and the vice-president of sales, but the part shown will illustrate our points.

The arrows in the center of the chart indicate the direction of the communication. A document from one sales representative to another is lateral communication, one from manager to representative is downward, and one from sales representative to manager is upward.

Each of these three modes of communication has an appropriate tone, and using the wrong one can cost you some goodwill and deprive you of the cooperation you seek. For example, if you address your boss in an overly casual manner, he or she may resent it. If you use a commanding tone with a peer, he or she will almost surely resent it. And if you use a collegial tone with your subordinates, they may feel you are being phony. The goal is to match the tone to the relationship. That might sound easy, but you'd be surprised how often people blunder with tone.

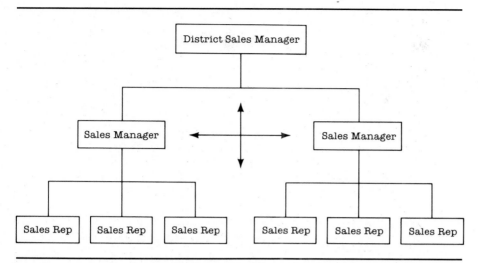

Figure 1.1   Upward, downward, and lateral communication

Although tone is often as important as what you say, the concept is elusive. In conversation, we speak of the tone of voice a person uses. Vocal intonation and inflections can completely change the meaning of a statement. For example, you might say "Dr. Wong is an outstanding teacher" in a bored, sarcastic voice. Of course, facial expressions underscore the meaning that tone of voice conveys.

Tone is thus the attitude you project toward your subject and your listener or reader. In writing, this attitude can be revealed by your choice of wording. For example, when you ask different people to react to a new idea, you might seek *advice* from your boss, an *opinion* from your peer, and a *suggestion* from your subordinate. Tone can also be controlled by sentence length, the level of diction, the use of the active versus the passive voice, and the use of contractions and other aspects of conversational language.

The three memos in figure 1.2 make the same request, but the relationship between reader and writer is different in each case. The writer of all three memos, Vern Markle, is a staff accountant in a CPA firm. He is asking Ms. Patricia Olivas to critique a report he has written, but in each memo she plays a different role. In the lateral memo, she is another staff accountant; in the upward memo, Markle's boss; and in the downward memo, his assistant. Each memo adjusts its tone to the relationship. The word choice, attitude, and length of the memos differ and account for the modulation in tone.

By asking you to adjust your tone to particular circumstances, we're not suggesting that you fawn on superiors or treat subordinates disrespectfully.

Lateral

Date: January 5, 1986

To: Pat Olivas

From: Vern Markle

Subject: My Report to the Partners

I realize how busy you are, Pat, but I wondered whether you would go over my enclosed report to the partners on accounting software packages. I'm especially concerned about the vocabulary I've used--whether it's too technical for them. Would you read it from the perspective of execs who do not know the nitty-gritty of computer terminology? See whether it seems as though I'm talking over their heads. Jot comments in the margin, phone me, or both.

Hope I can return the favor, maybe in kind.

Upward

Date: January 5, 1986

To: Ms. Patricia Olivas

From: Vern Markle

Subject: A Request for Your Advice

I hope you will not think me presumptuous if I ask you to read the enclosed report I've written. I would value your critique because you know the audience better than I and you're a better writer.

The report deals with the viability of three different accounting software packages. I need your advice on whether or not I have written above the heads of my readers, who, as you know, have a limited background in computer terminology. If you have any other pointers, please include them.

If you would, please phone me at Extension 5509 or pen your comments in the margins. I will appreciate the guidance.

Downward

Date: January 5, 1986

To: Pat Olivas

From: Vern Markle

Subject: My Report to the Partners

Run through the enclosed report, will you? I'm afraid I may be talking over the heads of the partners, who have only a limited background in computer terminology. See whether any passages strike you as unclear and mark them in the margins. Drop it off before you leave this afternoon, OK? Thanks!

Figure 1.2 Lateral, upward, and downward communication

We are urging you to meet the reasonable expectations of your reader. Generally, your managers will expect a respectful tone from you, your peers an informal one, and your subordinates a confident, authoritative one.

Whatever tone you adopt, it should be the result of a conscious choice based on your relationship with the reader. For example, if you are on cordial terms with a peer, you will probably adopt a friendly, conversational tone. If you are writing to a peer whom you do not know well, adopting a friendly, conversational tone might seem slightly forward.

Case: Belmont Industries (continued)

> Now to define your relationship to the reader of your report. You will be writing for a wider audience than just the president, Don Poole. In addition to the three vice-presidents, you may be writing for other employees and even the board of directors. Obviously you cannot define your relationship to every reader in these circumstances, so you must concentrate on the most important relationships. That means concentrating on the upward communication line to Poole and the vice-presidents, so your document must be objective and slightly formal, but not stuffy, in tone.[1]

Try to anticipate the preconceptions of your reader toward your message. As far as you can tell, how will he or she react to your message? We can distinguish three general categories of reader reaction: positive, neutral, and negative. Figure 1.3 shows a scale illustrating these three categories and the degrees of emotional reaction the reader might feel. Of course readers are rarely completely positive, neutral, or negative. A typical reaction falls somewhere between two categories. (Can you imagine *total* neutrality?)

A particular reader may be expected to feel fairly neutral toward your idea but inclining toward positive, so you might place that reader at 6 or 7 on the scale. You could judge another reader to be negative with only slight leanings toward neutral, so you might place that reader at 1 or 2. It's more important to gauge the reader's general reaction than to make fine distinctions—between 1 and 2, for instance.

What Are the Reader's Likely Preconceptions?

---

[1]For examples of the tone you will strive for, you might note the style of articles in periodicals such as *Management World, Business Week, Administrative Management,* and *Communication World.*

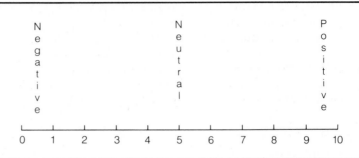

Figure 1.3   Reader reaction scale

Anticipating the preconceptions of the reader is important so that you can organize your message effectively. For example, if you anticipate that your reader will be highly skeptical (that is, negative) about any claims you make (possibly 2 or 3 on the scale), you will go to greater lengths to support those claims with solid evidence. On the other hand, if you anticipate that the reader will regard your proposal favorably (probably at least 8 on the scale), you can spend less time justifying the proposal and more time developing other aspects, such as a consideration of the financing or the schedule of the project.

Imagine that you manage a small graphics department for a company and believe that it needs its own copier because your people waste considerable time taking copy to and from the nearest copier and waiting in line to use it. You write a budget request for the copier to the controller of the company. If you anticipate a generally negative response, you will carefully build your case, perhaps using a time-and-motion study to support your request. But if you anticipate a generally positive response, you can state your reasons for the request and then discuss your department's specific copying needs, perhaps indicating the brand of copier you judge would do the best job.

Ask yourself how your reader will probably react to your message. Be especially careful with bad news: a refusal, a negative value judgment, inconvenience to the reader, a potential or real threat to someone's authority or status. We will explain how to deal with bad-news messages later in the text, but for now it is important that you anticipate possible negative reactions from your reader, so that you will be better able to deal with them effectively.

Another preconception we refer to is occupational. Unfortunately, it is easy to stereotype strangers on the basis of their occupation. Think of the stereotypes many people have of salespersons, attorneys, real estate agents, professors, accountants, and consultants. The reader who does not know the writer personally may tend, even unconsciously, to expect stereotypical reactions or behavior. You may have to go out of your way to offset these preconceptions. For example, in writing to potential clients, the management professor who does consulting in addition to his or her academic duties may stress his or her practical qualities, the track record of past consulting jobs, rather than academic credentials.

Case: Belmont Industries (continued)

You have already considered the possibility that the president may be favorably disposed toward word processing at Belmont Industries. Nevertheless, Don Poole must be sure that the move to word processing is supported by solid reasons and is right for Belmont's long-range welfare. He must be convinced that word processing will enhance the already high quality of Belmont's correspondence, that the cost of the proposed system versus the cost of the present one will be justified, and that Belmont's employees will accept the change.

The secondary readers, the vice-presidents, must be convinced of these same conclusions. But here is a critical difference: each of these must also be reassured that the advantages of word processing outweigh the disadvantages to his or her division. For example, the vice-president of finance may consider primarily the costs of the change and the potential savings involved; the vice-president of marketing may consider the advantages in sales and promotion. Therefore sections of the report may have to point out advantages to both the primary and the secondary readers. You will jot notes to yourself about aspects of the study to be emphasized in the light of your different readers' preconceptions.

At this stage you must also anticipate problems your readers may detect in a change to word processing. For example, Bert Jankowski, vice-president of Human Resources, will realize that his responsibilities will clearly increase if word processing is adopted. For example, it is conceivable that the majority of Belmont's secretaries will experience a significant change in their roles and the nature of their work. Consequently, Bert must insure that these changes take place evenly and efficiently. He must lead the project that will redesign the secretary's function and career path at Belmont. Job descriptions will change; new performance standards will be developed; new supervisory roles will emerge. Because Bert and his subordinates will guide many of these changes, you must try to anticipate his reactions and shape parts of the report to address his concerns.

Others may feel threatened by word processing. Many executives who now have private secretaries may lose them to the word processing center and thus feel less important. You may reassure them by suggesting that they are leaders unafraid of change and by showing that their correspondence will continue to be typed accurately and efficiently.

What Are the Reader's Needs?

Anticipating and meeting the needs of the reader provide a major guarantee of success in any writing project. Generally, your reader will have three kinds of needs. First, you must use terms the reader understands; second, you must provide the information the reader needs; and third, you must sometimes provide emotional support for the reader.

First, you must be careful to use language that the reader will understand without difficulty. The type of language known to any reader depends on his or her experience and knowledge of the subject under discussion. Assessing that knowledge leads to three possibilities: the reader may know the subject less well than, as well as, or better than you know it.

Of these three, writing for a reader who knows less about the subject than you do requires the most attention. Writing for readers whose knowledge is equal to or superior to your own poses fewer problems because you can presume a familiarity with technical terms and concepts that you cannot presume in the first case.

When your reader knows less about the subject than you do, you must make sure that you have not used any terms he or she will not understand. If you are writing to the controller of your company to justify the purchase of a new microcomputer for your department, you had better be certain that he or she understands such terms as *megabyte, CPU,* and *X-Y digitizer.*

Many writers assume that it is the reader's responsibility to learn any technical terminology used, either by looking it up or asking someone else to explain the term. The reader will more likely become frustrated and give up. That's understandable, since it is *not* the reader's obligation to understand the writer's language; it is the writer's obligation to use language the reader understands.

Second, the reader needs the right kind and amount of information, and no more. Ask yourself what kind of background information the reader may need to understand your message, or whether the reader needs an explanation of any concepts that form the basis of your thinking. Often the kind of information your reader needs is determined by the response you want. For example, you might write a report on the income statement in accounting—a summary of the net income, expenses, and receipts of a specific company over a specific period of time. If you merely want the reader to *understand* what goes into an income statement and its purpose, your report will be short, probably two or three pages. But if you want someone to *produce* an income statement for a company, your report will be longer and more detailed and will be accompanied by figures illustrating procedures. Later in the chapter we will discuss how the intended reader response affects the amount of information you need to include in a document.

What special needs will the reader have? Will visual aids be helpful, such as photographs, drawings, maps, or graphs? One example of meeting the special needs of the reader occurs in the instructions provided with a certain brand of pocket calculator. The instructions are printed in English, French, German, and Spanish. The firm that makes this calculator thus meets the need of its customers to read instructions in their own language. You must also ask yourself what information the reader does not need and exclude such material from your message. That sounds easy, but often writers provide their readers with unnecessary information, perhaps because they are eager to demonstrate their expertise or because they worked hard at accumulating the information and are reluctant to discard it. Using the example of the report on the income statement, mentioned previously, we can observe that if your purpose is merely to inform someone about the contents and use of the income statement, instructions on how to produce one are unnecessary and will only bog the reader down in needless details.

Third, you must, in some cases, provide the emotional support your reader needs. Everyone has a built-in need for self-esteem, respect, and courtesy. Look at the many common acts of courtesy that we extend to total strangers. You won't get very far with a reader if you say or imply anything that diminishes his or her self-esteem. For example, when you propose a measure that will deprive an executive of his or her private secretary, you are probably diminishing that executive's self-esteem, since to be assigned a private secretary has long been considered a mark of prestige.

You must deal with such threats to your reader's self-esteem, perhaps by stressing advantages in your proposal that will reassure your imaginary executive that he or she has not lost prestige or status. You might dwell on the priority handling of executive correspondence, for example. If what you say reinforces that person's sense of worth, your message is more apt to succeed.

Case: Belmont Industries (continued)

Remember, Don Poole is your primary reader, and his most obvious need is for conciseness. As a busy executive, he must sometimes read dozens of reports in a day, so he wants you to take up as little of his time as possible but still communicate all important points. You must judge on a point-by-point basis what information Poole needs or does not need to make a good decision.

Poole also needs a report expressed in terms he understands. You place his knowledge of computer terminology about midway between the extremes of technical and lay familiarity. He will understand terms like *software, monitor, keyboard,* and *peripheral* but not such terms as *microjustification* or *wordwrap.* Therefore you will write the report just below the technical level.

The needs of your secondary readers will be more varied. They have the same need as Poole for grasping the important ideas without unnecessary words or details. The same level of technicality should suit most of them, but you must check that point with them or their secretaries, as opportunity permits.

You decide to make detailed notes on the implications of word processing for the division of *each* of the secondary readers—Garcia, Werner, and Jankowski. You list both potential advantages and disadvantages as far as you can anticipate them. Thus you can shape the report to stress the advantages and to come to grips with the potential disadvantages, such as reorganization and transfers.

Defining Your Goals

Defining—and achieving—your goals in writing involves using the reader profile at almost every point, since you can achieve your goals only through effective communication with your reader. Defining your goals involves three decisions on your part. First, you must specify the response you want from your reader (to be informed or persuaded). Second, you must define the image of yourself that you wish to project to your reader. Third, you must plan to meet your deadline.

Specifying the Response You Want from the Reader

We define two broad categories of response a writer may wish to elicit from a reader. The first response is the reader's *understanding* of the information the writer wishes to convey. The second response is the reader's *agreement* to decide or act as the writer wishes. Of course, these two kinds of responses may overlap, since the reader may need to be informed before he or she can be persuaded. For clarity's sake, however, we will treat the two kinds of reader response (being informed or persuaded) separately.

Writing to Inform the Reader   Sometimes your purpose in writing is to inform rather than to persuade. Before writing, you should define your purpose and make a conscious effort throughout the project to stick to it unless you go back and revise it. Otherwise, if you unconsciously drift away from your purpose of informing and begin to persuade, you run the risk of overstepping your boundary, a switch that your reader might not welcome.

Your boss, for example, has decided to purchase several memory typewriters for the office clerical staff. Since she does not have the time to investigate the various brands and models on the market, she wants you to write a report describing the most affordable ones. You are to explain both the standard equipment of all these typewriters and the special features of each. You are also requested to cover such items as maintenance and service contracts.

Note that she is asking you for information, not for a recommendation of a specific model for the office. If you include a recommendation, she may be appreciative and follow your advice. Or she may feel that you have infringed upon her right to make the decision. It's your choice, but we suggest that you stick to the instructions.

At times, however, a document cannot be exclusively informational. Some opinion will inevitably enter. For example, in the case above, one brand of typewriter may have many attractive features and yet be flimsily constructed. Probably your manager will then welcome an opinion, but the point is to stick to the overall purpose of the document.

Many forms of business writing, including status reports, procedures, policy statements, and job descriptions, call for this informational kind of writing. Later in this text we will cover each of these forms and make specific suggestions on how to achieve the goals of each form.

Case: Belmont Industries (continued)

Here your goal is primarily to give information to a decision maker, Don Poole. In his instructions, he clearly delineated the goals of your report. Your first goal is to determine the potential advantages and disadvantages to Belmont Industries of word processing. In doing so, you are to anticipate rather than preempt the feasibility study that will presumably follow your report in the future. (The feasibility study will ultimately answer the question of advantages and disadvantages.) Your second goal is to answer these five questions:

1. What makes a good feasibility study?
2. What questions should it answer?
3. How much time will it take?
4. How many employees will it involve?
5. How much will it cost?

Often when you write for the boss, he or she will define your goals for you; however, you may set yourself additional goals. For example, you might stress points of interest to key subordinates of Poole, the vice-presidents of Marketing and Human Resources.

Writing to Persuade the Reader   At other times your goal is to persuade the reader to believe as you do or to act as you wish. When we use the verb *to act* in this context, we include not only physical action but mental action as well, such as a decision. In this sense, if you have persuaded a person to make a certain decision, you have convinced that person to act.

Because persuasion is an integral part of decision making, business people must know how to convince others. Forms of business writing that emphasize persuasion are proposals, sales letters, letters of application for jobs, equipment justifications, feasibility reports, performance appraisals, and customer-service letters. At various points in this book, we will make specific suggestions on how to be persuasive in these different forms.

Since forms of persuasion can vary, you should define the overall thrust of your appeal. What will you stress? It is usually a good idea to relate whatever it is you propose to the satisfaction of some reader need. For example, if you wish to persuade the boss to buy dictation equipment, you could stress its role in improving productivity and cutting clerical costs, two objectives that satisfy a manager's needs. The appeal you make will depend on your sense of your reader's preconceptions and needs. Your reader profile therefore largely determines which appeals you will stress.

Defining the
Image You Wish
to Project

Communication is usually a two-way street. Just as you must develop a profile of your reader to communicate effectively, your reader will form an image of you. Not that your reader will guess your height or the color of your hair, but, almost unconsciously, the reader will gain an impression of your attitude, competence, and professionalism.

In fact, you cannot avoid projecting *some* image in your writing, and, accurate or not, the reader cannot avoid forming one. This image derives from all aspects of a document, from its tone to its organization. If your letters are courteous and pleasant or curt and impersonal, your reader will form an impression of you as sharing the same traits. Similarly, if your letters or reports are illogical and disorganized, your reader will judge them to be the products of an illogical and disorganized mind.

Even the physical appearance of the document contributes to the image of its author. A letter neatly typed on good bond paper makes a favorable impression; a letter carelessly typed on cheap paper with dirty typewriter keys makes a less favorable impression. Make sure that every document creates the image that you wish to project.

Sometimes the only contact between a firm and a potential client is a piece of writing, for example, a letter, report, or brochure. Consulting firms, for instance, report that winning a contract often depends on the potential client's reaction to their written proposal. While such cases are not typical, we all at times write documents that can have a significant effect on our working lives. For example, when we apply for a job, the letter of application and our resume are usually all the company has by which to judge us, and these documents determine whether or not we get an interview.

In every case you should project a positive image in your writing, an image that will vary according to the direction of the communication—upward, downward, or lateral. For example, if you're writing to a client to collect money owed to your company, the image you project will be courteous but firm, especially if you have tried in the past to collect on the overdue account. If the client has ignored your requests for payment, you must temper your courtesy with determination.

Here is a list of image-related terms that suggest the varied possibilities in your image-making attempts:

Image-Related Terms

assertive	dynamic	objective
astute	enthusiastic	professional
authoritative	fair	progressive
cautious	firm	prudent
concerned	formal	reliable
conciliatory	generous	reserved
confident	helpful	respectful
considerate	innovative	skeptical
cooperative	knowledgeable	tireless
decisive	noncommittal	understanding

If you define in advance how you want the reader to see you, you will make better decisions about content, organization, and style.

Case: Belmont Industries (continued)

To some extent, your position as assistant to the president defines the image you wish to convey: others expect you to play that role. But knowing your boss as you do, you do not want to appear overconfident, smug, or closed minded. You decide that the image you want to project is that of the objective and fair-minded researcher, not blind to potential problems but open to innovation.

> In addition to openness, you want to appear sensitive to the changes and temporary inconveniences that the implementation of word processing could bring to Belmont Industries. You must convey your genuine appreciation for the problems your secondary readers will face.
>
> Along with sensitivity, you want to appear competent and knowledgeable. You want your reader to realize that you have researched the subject meticulously, reasoned logically, and communicated ideas effectively.

Planning to Meet Your Deadline

Most writing assignments come equipped with a deadline. On the job, however, you may be told at 10:00 A.M. to have a written report on the boss's desk before you leave, which may be as late as 10:00 P.M. Such requirements are not uncommon, and although you cannot anticipate every deadline, you can develop a procedure suitable for a three-*week* or a three-*hour* deadline.

Proportion is the key. You can allot a proportionate amount of time to each of the four steps in the problem-solving process: defining, analyzing, decision making/drafting, and editing. The shorter the time available, the less time you can allow for each step, but however condensed, you must include each step so that you will produce the best document possible.

Part of defining any writing problem is planning to meet the deadline. Therefore the more complex the assignment, the more detailed your planning has to be.

Suppose it is now March 15, and a formal report is due in your business communication class on April 22, a not uncommon experience for most students. Let's draw up a detailed plan for meeting that deadline.

You must begin by being realistic about the time you can spend on the report. There is no point in making idealistic plans if you have little chance of carrying them out. For example, you could decide to devote "as much time as possible" to your report until it is complete. That vague plan does not take into account, however, the two tests—one in calculus—you have to take over the next two weeks. You decide that you cannot get started on the report much before April 1, which allows three weeks for its completion.

You break the overall larger problem into smaller ones, assigning a realistic block of time and a deadline for each: so many days for defining the problem, so many for analyzing, and so on. On the job, a writing project might involve additional tasks, such as having your report ready for a quick check by your manager, allowing time for typing, duplicating, and mailing.

Making such a schedule enables you to visualize the time you have for each step. It also helps you meet your overall deadline more easily by letting you know at any point how much more work you have to do and how much time it will take. Writers without a schedule often produce what is essentially a rough draft for their deadline. The result can be complaints from their boss or client about the need for editing. Plan your work so that it is the best you can produce in the time available.

Case: Belmont Industries (concluded)

Don Poole expects your report within two weeks, but you do not have two full weeks to prepare. In that period, there will be meetings to attend, phone calls to make and take, and an in-basket full of correspondence to be answered. In the middle of the second week you must attend an exhibition of Belmont products in Denver.

You estimate that you can spend an average of two hours a day on this report for the next two weeks, except for the three days in Denver. That's a total of 14 hours in which to plan, research, dictate, and edit the report. That leaves the last afternoon to have it typed and on Poole's desk. On some of those days, you may be able to devote more than two hours to it, and you can always work evenings and one weekend.

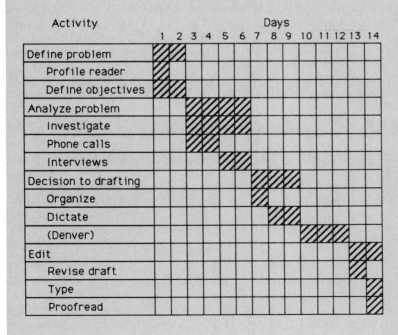

Figure 1.4
Gantt chart. Report to Don Poole.

And so you sketch the chart that appears in figure 1.4. Such a chart is called a Gantt chart, and writers frequently use it as a planning tool. Budgeting your time concludes the first step of solving your writing task—defining the problem.

Summary

The problem-solving technique, including the steps of (1) defining the problem, (2) analyzing the problem, (3) deciding on the best solution and committing yourself, and (4) following up, can be applied to rhetorical problems encountered in the business environment. Applied to writing, the four problem-solving steps can be stated as:

1. Defining the writing problem
2. Analyzing the writing problem
3. Deciding about information, organization, and style and writing a first draft
4. Revising and editing

Chapter 1 explains the first step, defining the writing problem. The two substeps are developing a reader profile and defining your goals. To develop a reader profile, you must answer the following five questions about your reader:

1. *For whom are you writing?* Identify your primary and secondary readers. The primary reader is the person to whom the document is addressed; the secondary reader is anyone else who will probably read the document.
2. *What do you know or can you learn about your reader?* Estimate your reader's capacities and educational background and shape your writing accordingly.
3. *What is your relationship to your reader?* You can be on the same level (lateral communication), on a lower level than your reader (upward communication), or on a higher level (downward communication). A different tone, or attitude toward the subject and your reader, is appropriate to each type of communication. Selecting the right tone and achieving it through such means as word choice, sentence length, and level of diction can mean the difference between a positive and a negative reception by your reader.
4. *What are the reader's likely preconceptions?* Anticipate the reader's probable reaction to your document—positive, neutral, or negative—and select and organize your information accordingly.

5. *What are the reader's needs?* Use language your reader will understand, supply information the reader needs, and provide emotional support if it seems necessary.

The second substep, defining your goals, includes the following steps:

1. Specify the response you desire from your reader. For example, do you want to inform the reader? Do you want to persuade? You must keep your goal in mind to avoid unconsciously drifting from one goal to the other.
2. Define the image you want to project. You can then shape your tone and other elements to convey the impression you wish.
3. Plan to meet your deadline by realistically estimating the time available and apportioning time to each of the four problem-solving steps.

Writing Problems

1. As a zone manager for Beta-Car, a division of National Motors, Inc., you intend to write a letter to local Beta-Car owners who bought their cars three to seven years ago inviting them to a sale of new Beta-Cars. The sale is by invitation only, and you are inviting these people to test-drive a new Beta-Car. There is no obligation to buy a car, and each guest will receive a free gift—either a desk-top digital clock radio valued at $42.95 or a 40-piece socket wrench set valued at $41.39. The guests may stop in at any of four participating area dealerships. They will have a large inventory of cars from which to select, or they may place a factory order for the car of their choice. This sale will take place two weeks before a sale open to the general public. The sale to which you are inviting these potential customers runs on three consecutive days—June 14, 15, and 16, from 10:00 A.M. till 9:00 P.M. Write a memorandum to your instructor defining this rhetorical problem. (For memorandum format, see chapter 5.) You should develop a detailed reader profile and define your goals.
2. You are the manager of Accounts Receivable for Burkhart's, a wholesaler in the office furniture industry. Normally you offer your customers a 15 percent discount if they pay their invoices within 30 days of purchase. Lately several smaller firms you sell to regularly have been exceeding the 30-day limit but deducting the 15 percent from their payment anyway. You can sympathize with their attempt to solve some of their own cash flow problems in this way, but your company is losing profits as a result. Over a year's time, this practice could cause cash-flow problems for your own company. You decide to write a letter to each customer who sends in a payment after the 30-day limit

and still deducts the 15 percent. You want to retain their goodwill and patronage but at the same time make them understand your problem and your need to receive the full payment when the 30-day limit has been passed. Write a memo to your instructor in which you develop a reader profile and define your goals for writing this letter.

3. You are the supervisor of the word processing center at the home office of Minnesota Life and Casualty Company. One of your most capable word processing operators is Lee Obermayer, who has worked in the center for three years. Lee has excellent typing skills, gets along well with all members of the department, follows instructions, and functions smoothly as a team member. Since your assistant has recently left the firm to take over the supervisor's post for another company, you recommend Lee for the job. This recommendation angers Gale Billings, a leading word processing operator with two years' seniority over Lee. Gale also has excellent typing skills, but he does not get along well with people. Gale is quick to point out other workers' shortcomings, but he is overly sensitive to criticism of his own work. You do not feel Gale is ready for management responsibilities; however, you want to maintain morale and goodwill. You intend to write a memorandum to Gale that will restore his self-esteem and morale while making it clear that you expect him to cooperate with Lee. Write a memo to your instructor developing a reader profile and defining your goals in this writing problem.

4. You are a customer service representative for Pollard Stores, a national chain of retail department stores. Benjamin Kabakoff, a long-time customer of Pollard's, has had an unpleasant experience with one of your branch stores. He visited the store three weeks ago and purchased on his charge account a 32-foot extension ladder, which he ordered delivered to his home at 19 Doris Court, Peoria, Illinois 30927. In his absence, a 28-foot ladder was delivered, for which his son, not detecting the mistake, signed the delivery receipt. Kabakoff phoned the store later that day and reported the mix-up. He was told that the error would be corrected. The following day a delivery person brought him the correct ladder and took the wrong-sized ladder, but when Kabakoff received his next monthly statement from Pollard's, he was charged for both ladders. Frustrated, he sent a check for the ladder he had received and a note canceling his charge account. You intend to write a letter apologizing for the mix-up, regaining as much goodwill as possible, and asking Kabakoff to reopen his charge. But you are not permitted to offer Kabakoff any special discounts or gifts. Write a memo to your instructor developing a reader profile and defining your goals in writing the letter.

5. You are the office manager for Niemann Office Supply, a retailer selling everything for the office from furniture to carbon paper. The owner of this small but thriving firm is D. C. Niemann, the founder's son. Niemann is amiable and generous to his employees, for example, giving everyone a 10 percent end-of-year bonus. He is less and less frequently in the office, being occupied with other business interests; he owns a hotel downtown and is part owner of a bowling alley. The business is steadily expanding, and you need to hire another clerk in the office to help with answering the phones, billing, and inventory. Since you don't get much time to converse with Niemann, you intend to put your case for the new clerk in writing. Write a memo to your instructor profiling your reader and defining your goals.

6. As the manager of the Evanston National Bank, you intend to draft a one-page notice to be available in all your branches telling customers about the bank's newest service, the Wage Earner NOW account. It is a checking account that pays interest and combines the customer's savings with checking to add up to a higher monthly balance. The customer must maintain a minimum balance of $1,500, or an average monthly balance of $2,000. If either of these is maintained, checking is free and 6 percent interest is paid on the balance. Interest is compounded daily and paid monthly. If the account falls below the minimum balances, there is a $6 charge for that month along with $.25 for each item posted, for example, deposits, checks, and transfers. Write a memo to your instructor on the project, profiling the reader and defining your goals in this writing problem.

7. You are the assistant manager in the Administrative Services Department of Wagner, Takeyama, and Flanagan, Consultants. Many of the clerks in this department frequently complain about lower back discomfort caused by their chairs. Unfortunately, the chairs are too new to discard and too old to return to the vendor. So far as you know, your boss, Sidney Takeyama, has not yet heard of these complaints and has, on the contrary, mentioned several other pressing budgetary priorities for the department, none of which has anything to do with new chairs. You suspect that the boss will not be enthusiastic about such a request, but it is clearly your job to communicate the feelings of the clerks to your boss, which you intend to do in a memorandum. Write a memo to your instructor defining this writing problem, profiling the reader, and defining your goals.

Extended Application

You may, if you choose, select any one of the previous problems to develop fully over the next three chapters.

CHAPTER 2

Analyzing the Writing Problem

In chapter 1, we worked on defining the business writing problem: specifying audience, creating an image, and clarifying objectives. With these concepts in mind, we can analyze the writing problem further to gain a clearer understanding of this complex rhetorical process. Through analysis, we think about our topic. Then we illustrate that topic in a way that will help us draft a document.

We begin by explaining various types of analyses:

1. Simple outline
2. Interpretive label outline
3. Note card deck
4. Simple-sequence flow chart
5. Complex-sequence flow chart
6. Deductive decision tree
7. Inductive decision tree
8. Row-column matrix

We then show how these formats can assist business writers in meeting their objectives and explain how each example given reflects its writer's definitions of audience and image.

Chapter 2 concludes with a discussion of the recursive nature of analysis and a reminder that successfully completing this problem-solving stage may require you to revise your writing-problem analysis. You will see how to make interpretive notes and journal entries to begin such revisions. Finally, we suggest how you might use those notes and entries to refine your analysis.

For this chapter, the ongoing case will be that of the Jasper Moving and Storage Company, which does local and interstate moving for both household and corporate customers. In addition, the company owns a number of storage facilities throughout the country. Jasper is operating in an industry (interstate moving) that is in flux because of federal deregulation and stiff competition from truck rental companies, which simply rent vehicles and allow customers to do their own moving.

Examples of first drafts that might result from analysis of a writing task range from writing for customers to writing for subordinates, peers, and superiors. They include topics in customer relations, marketing, operations, and other areas of business. Memos, letters, proposals, and formal reports are included. The tasks require writers to project images of themselves as concerned, enthusiastic, conservative, confident, incisive, or a combination of those attributes. All the sample drafts result from the application of the analytic format to a writing problem.

The Simple Outline

An outline depicts logical relationships between a topic and its subtopics. In the type of outlining taught most frequently in our schools, roman numerals indicate the most general, or first-level, topics. Capital letters represent less general, or second-level, issues, each of which elaborates on a first-level element. The **simple outline** indicates lower levels of specificity through the use of arabic numerals, lowercase letters, and use of these numerals and letters in parentheses for more specific items, as in the following format:

        I.
            A.
            B.
                1.
                2.
                    a.
                    b.
                        (1)
                        (2)
                            (a)
                            (b)

II.

    A.

    (et cetera)

The outline is based on three assumptions: (1) that each topic can be further subdivided into two or more subtopics, (2) that each group of subtopics is subordinate only to one topic, and (3) that the sequence of topics in the outline will be followed in the written document. Of course, you may choose to reorder these issues as you revise, but the sequence of the final outline will be pretty much the sequence of the document's first draft.

Let's say that Doris Hollister, a marketing analyst for the moving and storage company, is preparing a report on how the firm should diversify. We can define her writing task in this way:

- *Objective* To prepare a report defining a single problem, identifying specific factors affecting that problem, and suggesting a solution to the problem
- *Audience* Company vice-president for Operations
- *Writer's desired image* Logical, respectful, yet confident

Doris can prepare a simple outline, such as the one in figure 2.1, to help meet her writing objective. She will not specify possible solutions before fully researching the topic. At this stage, she simply labels first- and second-level issues in their logical relationships to one another. She also specifies the order in which these issues might be treated in a rough draft of the report.

Problem: How should a moving and storage company diversify?

  I. Deregulation
    A. Business practices
    B. Competitors
  II. Economy
    A. Housing market
    B. Corporate business
III. Storage facilities
    A. Land
    B. Buildings

Figure 2.1 Simple outline

Problem: How should a moving and storage company diversify?

    I. Deregulation of interstate moving industry
        A. Innovative business practices are now possible.
        B. Competitors will mount campaigns to gain a larger share of the market.
   II. Tough economic times
        A. Poor housing market and high mortgage rates hurt interstate movers.
        B. Corporations no longer can afford to contract with moving and storage companies to move transferred executives and their families.
  III. Underutilized storage facilities
        A. Both business and household goods depots are on prime real estate.
        B. Unused facilities can be sold to increase company's capital for new projects.

Figure 2.2   Interpretive label outline

The Interpretive Label Outline

If Doris already knows more about the issues affecting diversification and has some opinions on them, she may create an **interpretive label outline,** whose contents specify more than bare-bones topics. Instead of just noting "Economy" as a first-level issue, she acknowledges that these are "tough economic times." Figure 2.2 shows Doris's outline with interpretive labels. From this outline, as well as from later stylistic and organizational decisions, the following two paragraphs of Doris's draft might emerge:

Draft

REPORT ON DIVERSIFICATION

Diversification in today's moving and storage industry depends on understanding three factors. First, the industry is not the same as it was before deregulation. Next, ours is a business more affected by swings in the economy than most. Finally, our company's concerns with strengthening our moving operations should not blind us to the potential for growth in the storage business.

Both moving and storage must respond to changes in interstate regulations. Through deregulation, innovative business practices have become possible. We may offer rates based on supply and demand, for example, as well as tie-ins that provide storage discounts to customers. In addition, we can compete for corporate cargoes in such fields as high technology. Whatever we do, we must work quickly. Our competitors are getting a head start on us.

Outlining offers distinct advantages: it is familiar to most of us, and it requires only a pencil and paper. For a business-writing topic with only a few subtopics, each with an apparent relationship to the main topic, outlining can prove a particularly useful analytic tool.

The Note Card Deck

Another frequently taught method for analyzing a writing topic is to use a **note card deck.** These three-by-five-inch or four-by-six-inch cards, with their headings and space for documentation, are actually a variation on outlining.

Let's say that Doris Hollister has a slightly more complex task than preparing a single report on company diversification. Instead, she might need to prepare *two* draft reports on the topic. In one draft, she emphasizes the role of the economy in future diversification. In the other draft, she stresses the part federal deregulation will play. She will ask some coworkers to look at both drafts and let her know which one they think she should give to the vice-president for operations. Her writing task is thus defined as follows:

- *Objective*   To prepare two draft reports, each stating a single problem, identifying specific factors affecting that problem, and suggesting a solution to the problem
- *Audience*   Company vice-president for Operations
- *Writer's desired image*   Logical, respectful, yet confident

In such an instance, a deck of cards such as those depicted in figure 2.3 might prove a useful means for analyzing her writing problem. She can

I. A. ECONOMY--poor housing market and high

mortgage rates hurt movers.

Relocation costs average two times higher

than 1980 averages, five times 1977

averages.

Source: Curtis, C. E. "No Moves Is Bad

News." Forbes 7 June 1980: 158.

I. B. ECONOMY--corporations find personnel

moves too costly. "... The recession has put

a damper on corporations transferring

executives." (p. 93)

Source: "Rough Times for Long Haul

Movers." Dun's Business Report
Sept. 1982: 93-94.

II. A. DEREGULATION--shocks to industry.
Deregulation should promote innovative

business practices among moving/storage

companies.

Source: "HHG Deregulation Should Help

Both Shipper, Carrier." Distribution

Nov. 1980: 20.

Figure 2.3
Six sample note
cards

Figure 2.3
Continued

II. B. DEREGULATION--competitors will mount campaigns for increased market share. Atlas Van Lines has increased its market share of the corporate personnel moving market.

Source: Mitchell, G. "Keep 'em Truckin': Despite Economic Potholes, Atlas Van Lines Is Speeding Along." Barron's 15 Mar. 1982: 44.

III. A. STORAGE FACILITIES--many are unproductive. Bekins had both business and household storage depots that were unproductive and occupying prime real estate.

Source: "Bekins: A Household Moving Leader Highballing into Related Services." Business Week 1 Nov. 1982: 58-59.

III. B. STORAGE FACILITIES--can be sold for cash. Bekins has increased its cash flow available for new ventures by selling some storage facilities.

Source: "Bekins: A Household Moving Leader Highballing into Related Services." Business Week 1 Nov. 1982: 58-59.

rearrange the deck without rewriting information. She can write new issues on blank cards and insert them into the deck without making the mess that would result from rewriting an outline.

Doris could benefit from these advantages by simply arranging the cards in two ways: (1) in the order given in figure 2.3 when she wished to emphasize the economy and (2) in an order that would place cards IIA and IIB before cards IA and IB. From this new sequence of placing deregulation considerations first, Doris could prepare a second draft report. The resulting opening paragraphs of these reports would differ in emphasis:

Draft 1: Economy Stressed

The wide swings in our economy over the past decade have severely affected our company. Federal deregulation and our outmoded storage facilities have also played major roles in affecting profits. Inflation, with its disproportionate rise in mortgage and thus relocation costs, however, wields the greatest influence. Many companies are simply unwilling to spend the money now necessary for an executive transfer. We must first address these economic factors as we decide how to diversify our operations.

Draft 2: Deregulation Stressed

Deregulation of the interstate moving industry has been a traumatic event for every interstate carrier. When combined with the unpredictable economy and our company's outmoded storage operations, deregulation challenges our ability to increase profits. This change in Interstate Commerce Commission rules also offers an opportunity for improving those profits in spite of the economy and our storage problems. We must therefore diversify into new operations.

For obtaining two or more drafts from one analysis, the card deck can prove efficient. It does have its drawbacks—the need for space to display all cards at once to get an overview, and the possibility of losing cards from the deck. Card decks do, however, offer a flexibility that outlines do not. You just can't shuffle an outline.

The Simple-Sequence Flow Chart

Sometimes the goal of a writing task is to specify a series of consecutive steps for your reader to follow. For example, Carl Kuuri, the moving and storage company's director of customer relations, may decide to write a memo explaining consecutive steps the company should take to improve services for household customers. The director hopes that improved service will increase the volume of household moving business.

- *Objective* To prepare a memo proposing a series of steps in chronological sequence
- *Audience* Vice-president of Operations
- *Writer's desired image* Informed, clear, straightforward

Figure 2.4 shows a **simple-sequence flow chart.** It identifies the writing problem in its subtitle and breaks that problem into five consecutive steps from left to right. When there is no more room at the right side of the page, the chart continues at the left-hand column, directly below the first step.

As with all the analytic systems presented, the simple-sequence flow chart can be revised; but in its final form, the chart will determine the sequence of ideas in your rough draft. Thus, if figure 2.4 represents the final version of the analysis of the customer service memo, the director of customer relations might begin a draft in this way:

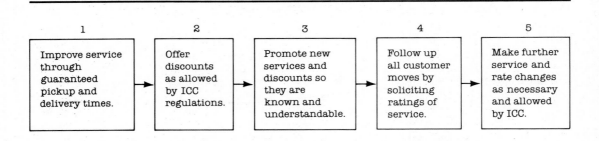

Figure 2.4 Simple-sequence flow chart. Memo specifying steps a company should take to improve its household customer service and moving volume.

Draft

Date: March 19, 1986

To: Jill Cass-Logan, Vice-President, Operations

From Carl Kuuri, Director of Customer Relations

Subject: Steps for Improving Household Customer Service and Volume of Household Moving Business

After studying results of our household customer moving survey, the Customer Relations Department recommends the following five steps for improving our service and thereby increasing the volume of our household moving operation:

1. We must increase our on-time pickup and delivery of goods. Lateness was the number-one problem specified by household customers. No matter what else we do, if we cannot make good on our dates, then we will lose old and new customers as word gets around and we get a poor service rating in Interstate Commerce Commission publications.

2. Once we have an on-time service record of which we can be proud, we need to become more competitive in our rates. ICC deregulation allows us to give special discounts. I know we are planning such discounts for our corporate clients, but let's not forget our household customers! Good household service improves our corporate business, and vice versa.

3. Once improved rates and service are in place, let's promote and explain them. Our household customer survey and the logged calls of our department point to frequent customer confusion about rates and services. Our contracts specify rates and services in "legalese" very foggy to our household clients. Perhaps we need a packet of information to accompany the contract or to be provided by our sales agents to customers.

4. Having made these changes, we should continue to monitor customer satisfaction. The current survey notes consumer complaints as well as praise (for our drivers' courtesy and care with household possessions, for example).

5. Above all, let us continue to be flexible. We must make changes as indicated from customer feedback. With improved customer satisfaction we can increase household volume. Without the knowledge and willingness to act on customer problems, we can only lose out to more aggressive competitors.

The simple-sequence flow chart works well when applied to a writing problem that requires starting from a point in time and progressing through later points. Because Kuuri's memo describes a series of steps for the company to follow, none of which requires returning to earlier steps, the simple-sequence flow chart suffices. It allows a writer to think about the problem chronologically and to write in a simple, chronological sequence.

The Complex-Sequence Flow Chart

Frequently, procedures that occur over time require a reader to go back to earlier steps in order to meet unexpected contingencies within the sequence. Knowing that our topic involves starting at step A and going to a later step Z is still crucial to analyzing the rhetorical task. Now we need a way to show that somewhere between the beginning and end of the procedure we may have to return to an earlier step and redo it.

The **complex-sequence flow chart** offers this medium. Our customer relations director might wish to develop a letter to corporate customers giving them procedures to follow prior to and on the day of a local move. Figure 2.5 analyzes this writing task.

The first step, providing instructions to inventory all equipment to be moved, starts out in the same way as a simple-sequence chart. In this complex sequence, however, two lines, rather than one, flow from the first step. The right line indicates that the corporate client has chosen a lower-priced moving service providing only pickup, delivery, and uncrating. The left line indicates the client has selected a premium moving service that includes crating, pickup, delivery, uncrating, and placement. This branching, indicating that a letter will have to make clear the options available to customers, is one feature differentiating the complex- from the simple-sequence flow chart.

More branching occurs along both the selected and full-service lines. These branches show what will happen if the customer requires additional services at the time of delivery. This branching feature lets the customer relations director think about how to write a first draft. The draft begins on page 48.

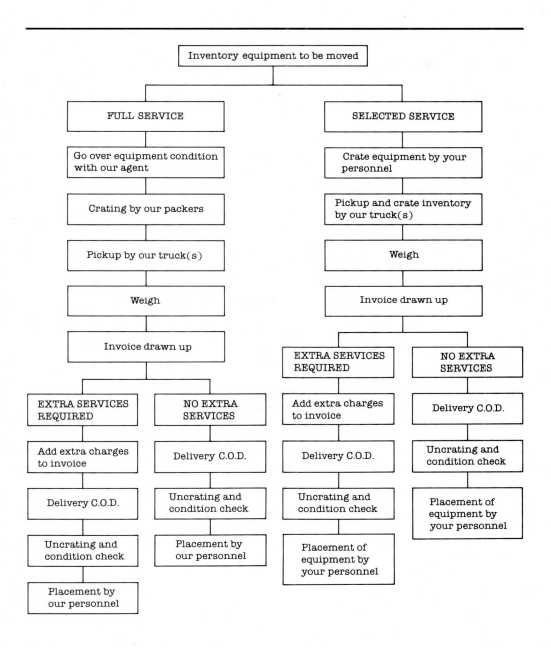

Figure 2.5   Complex-sequence flow chart. Letter to business customers specifying procedures for moving business equipment: day of a local move.

Draft

March 21, 1986

Dear Customer:

As the day of your local move approaches, we would like to remind you of procedures for that shipment. The steps vary depending upon whether you have chosen our "selected service" or "full service."

For a selected-service move, the procedure is as follows:

1. Before the day of the move, prepare a written inventory of all items to be transported.
2. Before the day of the move, your personnel should have crated all equipment. Please check to see that items are securely packed, with appropriate padding to cushion fragile equipment against any shocks.
3. On the morning of the move, our delivery personnel will pick up all crates, inventory them, and load them onto our truck(s). Although condition of crate contents in a selected-service move is the customer's responsibility, we take responsibility for any damage the crates sustain while in transit. Accordingly, our driver(s) will note any external damage to the crates as they are inventoried.
4. From there, the movers will go directly to our terminal scales to weigh the shipment. You will receive both a gross weight (the truck plus your shipment) and a tare weight (the weight of your shipment alone).
5. After weighing, we will process an invoice that will itemize all charges up to the time of local delivery. You will be informed by telephone of the amount due upon delivery.
6. Upon delivery, our driver will present the invoice for C.O.D. payment (cash or certified check) before goods are unloaded.

NOTE: If at the time of delivery you request additional services (for example, hauling crates upstairs by our personnel), the driver is authorized to add those services and charges to the invoice, payable at the time of delivery.

7. You and our personnel will then check crates for damage other than that specified in the pickup inventory (step 3). You may make claims for crate damage at this time. Our personnel will uncrate equipment.
8. Your personnel may then place uncrated equipment in its new location.

For a full-service move, the procedure is as follows:

1. Before the day of the move, prepare a written inventory of all items to be transported.
2. On the day of the move, our agent will meet with you to go over and note in writing the condition of each item to be shipped.

3. Our professionally trained packers will crate all equipment in our shock-resistant cartons.
4. Our delivery personnel will pick up all crates, inventory them, and load them onto our truck(s).
5. From there, the movers will go directly to our terminal scales to weigh the shipment. You will be provided with both a gross weight (the truck plus your shipment) and a tare weight (your shipment alone).
6. After weighing, we will process an invoice, which will itemize all charges up to the time of local delivery. We will inform you by phone of the amount due on delivery.
7. Upon delivery, our driver will present the invoice for C.O.D. payment (cash or certified check) before goods are unloaded.

NOTE: If at the time of delivery you request additional services not specified in the full-service move contract (for example, placement of equipment already at the destination), the driver is authorized to add those services and charges to the invoice. Payment for these additional services will also be due at the time of delivery.

8. You and our personnel will then check crates for damage. Our personnel will then uncrate equipment and note any damage. You may make claims for damage at this time.
9. Our personnel will place all crate contents according to your instructions. Please provide written instructions as to where you wish each piece of equipment to go, as our full-service move includes only one placement per item.

This letter should clarify the basic procedures followed on our local business moves. If you have questions, please contact us. We intend to make yours an efficient, successful move.

Sincerely yours,

J. M. Kuuri
Director, Customer Relations

By analyzing the writing problem with a complex-sequence flow chart, Kuuri is able to visualize the two-part arrangement with separate steps for selected-service and full-service moves. Kuuri also discovers the need to highlight the additional charges that occur if a customer wants service

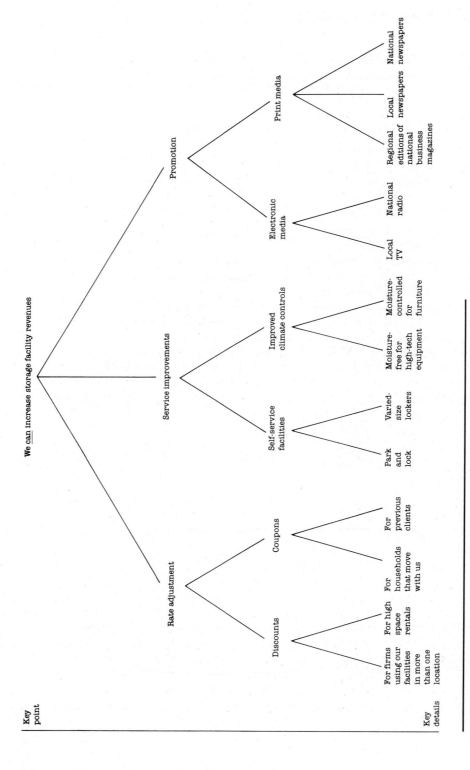

Figure 2.6   Deductive decision tree. Written proposal on how to increase storage facility revenues.

beyond that specified in the invoice. As in the simple-sequence flow chart, chronology is important. In this case, however, the branching features of the complex flow chart acknowledge the fact that a writer may have to depart from strict chronology to accommodate special circumstances.

The Deductive Decision Tree

Sometimes you must state a position and compose a document that supports it. The logical process by which you discover facts supporting that position is deduction. The **deductive decision tree** can help you to visualize how those facts support your position.

A **decision tree** is a depiction of topics and subtopics. It resembles a tree visually because the lines that show relationships between the main topic and subtopics look like tree branches. The process of creating those branches helps the writer to see relationships between items at higher and lower levels of generality as well as among issues at the same level of generality.

When the tree trunk starts at the top of the page and its branches spread downward through more and more specific levels, we call the decision tree **deductive.** Figure 2.6 depicts a deductive decision tree that grows from the need of Danielle Jackson, Jasper Moving's storage services manager, to develop a proposal showing that the company can increase storage revenues and suggesting ways to do so. The storage services manager has already defined the writing task as follows:

- *Objective*   To prepare a report stating a main argument and supporting the argument with increasingly specific levels of detail
- *Audience*   Vice-presidents of Operations, Finance, and Marketing
- *Writer's desired image*   Conservative, yet enthusiastic

Note that the key point, "We *can* increase storage facility revenues," appears at the top of the tree. Lines radiate downward from the main argument to subordinate-level issues. In turn, lines radiate from those issues to even more specific items, and so on. You can prepare the deductive decision tree the same way you do an outline. In thinking about ways to increase revenues, Jackson might have decided upon "rate adjustment" as a key operation. She would then think about ways to develop such adjustments, for example, "discounts" and "coupons," at the next level of specificity.

Working downward from "discounts," Jackson would then consider "firms using our [storage] facilities in more than one location" and customers with "high space rentals" as specific recipients of the discounts.

Then she would return to the more general "coupon" issue and repeat the process of finding more specific examples of clients ("households that move with us" and "previous clients") who might receive coupons.

Next, Jackson would return to the level just beneath the key point and repeat the same process of finding specific examples to support more general ones. Done this way, the order of decision-tree analysis matches that of outline development:

I. Rate adjustment
    A. Discounts
        1. Multiple-location customers
        2. High-volume customers
    B. Coupons
        1. For people who move with the company
        2. For previous customers of storage service
II. Service improvements
    A. Self-service facilities
        1. Park and lock
        2. Varied-size lockers
    B. Improved climate-control system
        1. Moisture-free for high-technology equipment
        2. Moisture-controlled for furniture
III. Promotion
    A. Electronic media
        1. Local television
        2. National radio
    B. Print media
        1. Regional ads in national business magazines
        2. Local newspapers
        3. National newspapers

The decision tree, however, offers what the outline cannot, an immediate view of relationships among issues at the same levels of specificity.

Moreover, the deductive decision tree offers the manager the option of building in a way different from the construction of an outline. Jackson can develop one whole branch independently before going on to develop other branches. Perhaps Danielle has been able to identify issues—"rate adjustment," "service improvements," and "promotion"—that are just below the main-issue level. She is still having difficulty finding details to support the first of these subissues, "rate adjustment." With the decision tree, Jackson is free to tackle the issue of service improvements first, developing her analysis into more specific issues ("self-service facilities" and "improved climate controls") before returning to other subtopics. In short, the deductive decision tree lets the analyst explore any facet of a problem in any desired order, since all issues eventually support the key point.

Following this analysis, the service manager's draft proposal might begin with these paragraphs:

Draft

Proposal For Increasing Storage Revenues

We can increase our storage revenues without adding new facilities. To do so, we need to act in three areas:

1. Rate adjustment will allow us to succeed in a highly competitive industry.
2. Service improvements can offer us both new and repeat business.
3. Active promotion of our storage service can help us target and reach previously uninformed consumers.

Rate adjustment should be our first priority. To compete in a saturated market with established moving and storage firms as well as with truck rental and self-service storage companies, we must offer discounts. To increase revenues throughout our storage system, we could give discounts for corporations that contract for service in more than one of our locations. These discounts might be in the form of a sliding scale in which companies using two of our locations would get 10 percent off; three locations, 15 percent; and four or more locations, 20 percent off their total bills. We could also offer discounts for high square footage rentals.

We could do the same for households that move with us. We might give such coupons to customers who have used our storage services within the past year as one inducement to continue their use of our facilities. The key benefit for us would be to increase the volume of our storage business. We would then work to retain the coupon holders as full-paying customers.

However, to retain any customers, with or without coupons, we have to improve our service record. With the sharp increase of self-storage businesses in recent years, . . .

The deductive decision tree has guided this writer in drafting a proposal that not only follows a preanalyzed sequence but also suggests ways to employ transitional words and phrases. For example, Jackson used the word *however* as a link between the last sentence of the third paragraph and the first sentence of the last paragraph. In chapter 4, we demonstrate ways to "edit in" transitional words and phrases. Nevertheless, using an analytic device such as the decision tree can help you see early in the writing process transitions that will make your document more coherent.

The Inductive Decision Tree

Sometimes you confront seemingly unrelated data from which you must develop a coherent piece of writing. The logical process by which you discover how those facts group together to support an argument is induction. The **inductive decision tree** can help you visualize how those facts logically lead to your position. An inductive tree looks like a deductive tree, but upside down. To create an inductive tree, you list specific data across the top of a page. When you find data that, viewed together, suggest a more general topic, you place the data next to each other and draw lines from the specific to the general. Figure 2.7 shows an inductive decision tree resulting from Walter Seiko's analysis of a writing problem. Seiko, a Jasper marketing employee, has the task of writing a form letter urging potential customers to use Jasper's interstate moving service.

What you see in figure 2.7 is a finished inductive decision tree growing from the following problem definition:

- *Objective*   To prepare a letter offering specific details leading to increasingly general arguments for taking an action
- *Audience*   Households likely to move within a short time
- *Writer's desired image*   Sincere, reassuring, competent, concerned

In the finished inductive decision tree, adjacent key details have lines leading neatly to more general issues. Creating this finished tree was not a simple task. Seiko had a particularly difficult time figuring out which key details should go next to each other. He did know certain facts of interest to customers:

- A 24-hour hotline is available for consumers to get information about their move.
- Shipment arrival dates are guaranteed.
- Tax adjustments and deductions are available on interstate moves.
- Moves are tracked by computer.

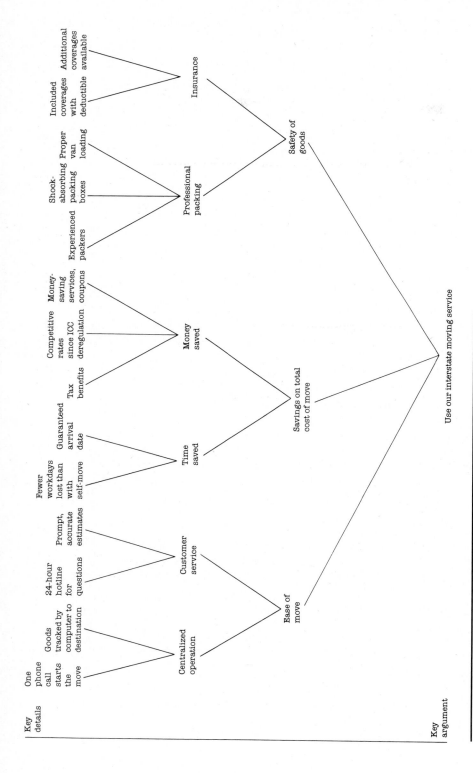

Figure 2.7 Inductive decision tree. Form letter to potential customers on why they should use our commercial interstate moving service.

- The company employs experienced packers.

- Jasper offers special, shock-absorbing boxes at nominal cost.

- It takes just one telephone call to the mover to get everything in motion.

- Moving service saves workdays normally lost when people move themselves.

- Basic insurance coverages are included.

- The company agents offer prompt, accurate estimates.

- Rates are competitive since the Interstate Commerce Commission's deregulation of the industry.

- Drivers load vans properly to minimize the danger of breakage.

- Additional insurance coverage is available.

- Jasper offers money-saving coupons for destination or in-transit services, such as storage of goods not wanted upon arrival.

Seiko tried several ways to group these facts. His first attempts were not successful. Guaranteed arrival dates seemed to have little in common with tax advantages. Needing only one telephone call to get the move started and providing supplemental insurance coverages were real, but apparently unrelated, benefits. After discarding several unfinished inductive decision trees, Seiko finally developed the one in figure 2.7.

Note how the tree allowed Walter to combine two or more facts across a horizontal line and then to use arrowed lines to point to common generalities suggested by those facts. For example, "one phone call to start the move" and "goods tracked by computer" are both features of the "centralized operation" offered by the company. Likewise, the "24-hour hotline" and "prompt, accurate estimates" are facts that suggest that Jasper's "customer service" is outstanding.

The grouping of second-level items—"centralized operation," "customer service," "time saved," "money saved," "professional packing," and "insurance"—suggests higher levels of generality. For example, time and money savings combine to suggest that Jasper can offer "savings on the total cost of the move." All facts at all levels of the tree ultimately point to the key argument that the marketing employee was able to synthesize for potential customers: "Use our interstate moving service for the best possible move."

The first four paragraphs of Seiko's draft form letter follow. Whereas the first paragraph of the draft developed from the deductive decision tree above began with a general statement, this draft opens with a specific detail:

Draft

April 24, 1986

Dear Friend:

We want you to know that a smooth move with Jasper Moving and Storage is only a phone call away. Our toll-free number, 800-555-4141, will put you in immediate touch with your closest system agent.

This call-handling system is the same kind of centralized service we will provide to track your move by computer every mile from pickup to destination.

Of course, computers are only as good as the people behind them. Our 24-hour hotline for questions about your move and the reasonable estimates you'll receive from our agents are only two of the customer services that make us a recognized industry leader.

Centralized operation and customer service--put them together and you get the easiest move possible. But there are many more reasons to consider Jasper for your next move.

Our efficient system assures you of a speedy move, one that will ...

After completing your inductive decision tree and your inductively sequenced document, you may discover that you prefer a *de*ductively arranged document. To accomplish this, simply read the tree from bottom to top as you draft. If Seiko wanted to make such a change, he would start his letter with the key argument found at the bottom of figure 2.7.

Draft

April 24, 1986

Dear Friend:

For the best possible move, just call Jasper! With so many moving services available, why should you select us? Let me give you a few of the many reasons a Jasper move can save you time, money, and aggravation.

Have you ever wondered in advance of the van's arrival how much your move would cost? Our national computer network will ...

Note how Seiko turned his inductive decision tree into a flexible tool for trying out two types of drafts, one following the tree from top to bottom, presenting details first and key issues later, the other following the tree from bottom to top, announcing key issues first and then supporting them with details.

With both inductive and deductive decision trees, your analysis yields general statements and specific facts or issues, all of which you can depict in relation to each other. The result is a clear picture of the hierarchy of relationships that you have discovered.

The Row-Column Matrix

Decision trees illustrate issues on the same horizontal line having the *same* level of generality or the *same* level of importance. When you need to analyze a rhetorical problem presenting *unequal* influence or specificity among issues on the same horizontal line, a **row-column matrix** can depict this new factor of unequal weighting.

The origin of the concept of matrix (in its archaic form, a matrix was a breeding animal) survives in the figurative sense of a breeder of ideas. Because it lets a problem solver display issues having three or more dimensions on a two-dimensional sheet of paper, the matrix is used in many disciplines. Writing is one of them.

Figure 2.8 applies a row-column matrix to analysis of a short report in which a Jasper accounting executive, Harriet Greene, will discuss possible results of a poor economy and federal deregulation on the moving and storage industry. Greene wants to identify results as primary (having greater impact on the industry) or secondary (having less impact). She has defined her problem as follows:

- *Objective* To prepare a short report predicting effects of unequal impact resulting from two causes
- *Audience* Executive vice-president
- *Writer's desired image* Informal, knowledgeable, open to further communication on the topic

The matrix enables Greene to display complex interrelationships in a simple format. Some of the items and their relationships may be summarized (1) between the poor economy and self-moving, (2) between the poor economy and executive moves, (3) between self-moving and executive moves, and (4) among the poor economy, self-moving, and executive moves. The visual simplicity of the format helps Greene draft this informal report to Jasper's executive vice-president, Chris Flower:

Figure 2.8
Row-column
matrix

Effects of Poor Economy and Deregulation on Jasper Moving and Storage Company

Cause	Primary Result	Secondary Result
Poor economy	More people will rent trucks and move themselves.	Fewer corporations will contract for executive moves.
Deregulation	We will have more opportunities for innovative business practices.	We expect our competitors to use new tactics.

Draft

Date: May 2, 1986

To: Chris Flower

From: Harriet Greene

Subject: Key Economic and Regulatory Issues

Here's a quick overview of issues facing the moving and storage industry in today's poor economy and unregulated state. First of all, our market research tells us that more people than ever are renting trucks and moving themselves. This is the biggest threat to our household moves that I can see. A less pressing problem, but one with serious ramifications should the trend continue, is that a slightly lower percentage of corporations are contracting for executive moves than in previous years. Accounting Department projections suggest that both trends will decrease revenues for at least three quarters.

Next, deregulation poses both challenges and opportunities for our industry as a whole and our company in particular. We can engage in innovative practices that were not permitted under strict regulation. However, we must realize, but <u>not</u> be immobilized by, the fact that our competitors know this as well. They have been employing innovative tactics to gain a share of the market for the past two years.

These are what I see as crucial issues facing the industry. If you'd like to, I'll be happy to discuss specific economic effects of these issues with you.

The row-column matrix worked well for the straightforward task of preparing a short report with two causes, each resulting in two effects of unequal importance. Let's take a look at a more complicated task. The vice-president for marketing, Sandy Frye, wants to prepare a report on two company goals, increasing its share of the interstate moving industry and increasing its storage business. To accomplish these aims, the marketing vice-president sees two means, each of which has two possible results. Frye can define the writing problem as follows:

- *Objective*   To prepare a report showing possible consequences of using two means to reach each of two goals
- *Audience*   Marketing staff, vice-presidents of Operations and Finance, executive vice-president, and president
- *Writer's desired image*   Knowledgeable, insightful, incisive

Figure 2.9 shows a row-column display of this problem. By using the matrix format to analyze the writing problem, Frye is able to draft this first paragraph:

Draft

This report discusses ways of attaining company goals to increase our share of the interstate moving and storage markets. It begins by suggesting two ways to increase our share of the moving market and predicts possible results of each of these approaches. The report then offers two means for increasing our share of the storage market and predicts their possible results. It concludes with a recommendation for immediate actions.

Figure 2.9
Complex
row-column matrix

Options for Achieving Moving and Storage Company Goals

Goal	Means	Most Likely Result	Less Likely Result
Increase interstate market share	Offer discount rates	Larger volume but lower profit margin	Price war with lower profit margin and lower volume
	Decentralize offices in high-volume regions	Increase in corporate business	Weaker coordination between management and staff
Increase storage business	Offer discount rates	Larger volume but lower profit margin	Price war with lower profit margin and lower volume
	Open new facilities	Larger volume and higher debt to finance new construction	Underutilized real estate generating no income

The row-column matrix allows the marketing vice-president to see the highly complex writing problem clearly, to decide upon the sequence in which the first draft of the report will appear, and to outline that sequence in the first paragraph of the draft report.

Do not be afraid to construct a row-column matrix analysis when you have a complex business-writing problem to solve. Trying to display three or more dimensions of a problem on a sheet of paper may seem difficult at first. But being able to see how parts of a complex writing problem are related to one another *before* you draft a document will make your work more efficient. By adapting the examples we present in figure 2.8 and 2.9 to your own complex writing problems, you will be able to make informed choices about arranging your ideas as you draft.

Some Reassurances and Cautions about Analysis of Business Writing Problems

You need to keep in mind that the writing problem and the business problem are sometimes interrelated. When they become as involved as those presented in row-column matrices, understanding one is frequently necessary to understanding the other. Our experience in teaching writing has shown us that a confused writer produces confused and disorganized work. Conversely, when the writer clearly understands the subject and the rhetorical considerations governing its development, the result is usually a clearly organized, coherent document.

While we wish to reassure you that these analytic devices are indeed techniques for analyzing writing, we also want to add a few words of caution. These flow charts, decision trees, and matrices may lull you into thinking you've simplified the writing problem rather than clarified it.

This hope of simplifying the problem may encourage you to force relationships that don't exist. For example, you might refer to Figure 2.9 and note that "larger volume" was a possible result of offering discount rates both to increase the moving market share and to increase the storage market share. If you were to conclude from this that offering discount rates would necessarily result in larger volume in both moving *and* storage, you would be incorrect, since a price war with resulting lower storage volume might be the actual result of applying discounts. In short, there is no substitute for rigorous thought in developing and applying any of these analytic techniques.

The Recursive Nature of Analysis

Just as you revise a rough draft so that it becomes more and more the document you wish it to be, so you can revise a problem analysis until it provides you with the clearest possible understanding. This is the recursive nature of writing. You proceed through part of the process; then you return to an earlier step so that you can advance further. You hope that your returns to earlier steps are brief compared to the first time you went through them, but sometimes it proves difficult to get back to the more advanced point you left.

Two writing techniques can greatly assist this revision of an analysis and keep it from becoming a dead end that takes up more time than necessary. By providing additional detail and interpretation of that detail, interpretive note taking and journal keeping help you decide which issues in a decision tree are more general than others, or which items in a row-column matrix should be depicted as more influential than others.

Figure 2.10
Interpretive notes

Observation of Northwestern Storage Facilities

Fact	Interpretive Note
Northwestern storage facilities are operating at only 38 percent of capacity.	I wonder whether that is in line with our northwestern competitors' rates.
Customer Relations Department reports an increase of 18 percent in the number of complaints involving our northwestern storage facilities this year.	Could this be a result of poor physical plant, personnel, chance increase, or other factors, such as weather?
There have been two minor fires at northwestern storage facilities within the last five years.	How are our insurance rates for these facilities affecting our profits in the northwestern district?

Interpretive
Note Taking

In **interpretive note taking,** in addition to jotting down facts and observations, you also record thoughts and questions about what you have observed. Continuing with our moving and storage example, a Jasper financial analyst, Richard Brun, working on a report analyzing problems in the company's northwestern storage business, might produce interpretive notes such as those in figure 2.10. As the figure shows, interpretive notes preserve your reactions to facts, reactions that might prove useful in initiating action. If you don't record your reactions, you might dismiss them at the time or forget them.

With interpretive notes in hand, Brun can return to the initial analysis and make revisions. Perhaps the first analysis involved a deductive decision tree suggesting how to organize a draft discussing why the Jasper Moving and Storage Company's northwestern storage district revenues have fallen. This first tree, however, neglected to include the fact of recent fires at two facilities. By including a branch in the decision tree to note the fires, and by continuing this branch to reveal statistics about skyrocketing insurance rates, Brun can prepare a draft that now includes a crucial issue that helps to explain revenue loss. In this case, the factual note about the fires provides the key data. But it is the interpretive note that leads the writer to record the fact that insurance rates provide the vital cause-and-effect connection between the fires and lost revenues.

Journal Keeping

Another technique for improving subsequent analysis of a writing problem is **journal keeping.** This is not a diary of personal experiences. Rather, it is a chronicle of observations related to a problem, along with ideas that occur to the writer for problem analysis. Note how it has been used in figure 2.11 to keep a record of events, initiatives, and reactions to the moving and storage case. This sample journal page specifies the time Brun noted each development or idea.

Note that the 1:00 P.M. notation specifies the task (to develop a list) as well as at least some of the items on that list. The report writer's original deductive decision tree had neglected to include a branch for accounts payable and receivable. Items e and f on the journal page in figure 2.11 alert the financial analyst to the need to include these factors in a decision tree that serves as the basis for the draft of the northwestern district storage report.

The crucial advantage to the journal is that you can keep it during a workday in which you may not spend time working on a particular writing project. The journal offers a way of jotting down observations without taking big blocks of time. Five minutes of effort an hour can yield insights critical in revising problem analyses.

Return to the
Earlier Analysis

Now we can illustrate how interpretive notes and journal keeping help a writer to prepare a fuller analysis of a writing task. Figure 2.12 shows new items, underlined, that have been added to the deductive decision tree.

Journals and interpretive notes are quick ways to increase the information available for revising problem analyses. Sometimes you may have to do more extensive research. In that case, we refer you to such techniques as direct observation, interviewing, questionnaires, library research, and computer databases, which we detail in chapter 8.

Reflecting on the
Analysis

For now, let us hope that journal keeping or interpretive note taking has been sufficient, or that the initial analysis proves satisfactory. Once you have completed an in-depth analysis of the writing problem, leave it alone for a few days if deadlines permit. This time enables your subconscious to work on a problem, and from such reflection you may gain new perspectives.[1]

It is now time to revise your problem definition as needed. For example, you may remember that Carl Kuuri, the director of customer relations, defined his writing task leading to the simple-sequence flow chart in figure 2.4 in this way before making the flow chart:

[1]For a detailed discussion of the effect of the subconscious on writing, see James Britton et al., *The Development of Writing Abilities (11–18)* (London: Macmillan Education, 1975).

January 8, 1986

9 A.M.   Received quarterly earnings report; moving profits up 12%; storage profits down 18%

10 A.M.   Meeting of executive board on quarterly report; decision to look into ways of increasing storage revenues

11 A.M.   Assigned personnel to inspect storage sites for up-to-date reports on physical plant

1 P.M.   Need to develop list of priorities for evaluating storage situation:

   a. physical plant conditions
   b. total storage capacity
   c. % of capacity in use
   d. current rates per square foot
   e. accounts receivable
   f. accounts payable
   g. other pertinent statistics
   h. real estate market for our holdings
   i. real estate holding equities

Figure 2.11   Sample journal page with time referents

Before Analysis

- *Objective*   To prepare a memo proposing a series of steps in chronological sequence
- *Audience*   Vice-president of Operations
- *Writer's desired image*   Informed, clear, straightforward

A series of interpretive notes helped Kuuri realize that the audience should include the vice-president of marketing because the marketing department promotes any service changes requiring discounts. Knowing that the vice-president of marketing responds positively to executive enthusiasm for a project, Kuuri also revises the "writer's desired image" to stress this point. Thus, a revised writing problem definition emerges:

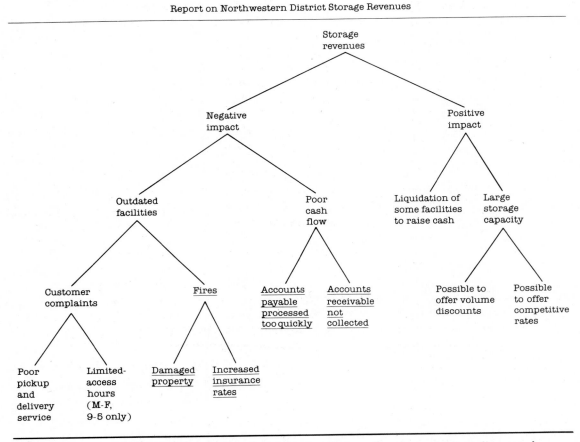

Report on Northwestern District Storage Revenues

Figure 2.12   Revised deductive decision tree based on additions discovered through interpretive note taking and journal keeping

After Analysis

- *Objective*   To prepare a memo proposing a series of steps in chronological sequence
- *Audience*   Vice-presidents of Operations and Marketing
- *Writer's desired image*   Informed, clear, straightforward, enthusiastic about topic

These changes shape decisions about drafting, such as those explained in chapter 3. The final document will be much different from what it would have been before analysis. For example, Kuuri's report originally ended this way: "Without the knowledge and ability to act on customer problems, we can only lose out to more aggressive competitors." It might now close by expressing confidence in the company's ability to meet the challenge of improving customer service: "Jasper will become the most customer-oriented moving and storage company there is. We will promise household customers the best and deliver on that promise as we deliver their shipments."

Summary

Analyzing the writing problem is the second problem-solving step. Analysis allows you to depict the problem in a way that will help you draft your document. Your analysis can be structured in a number of ways: outlines, note card decks, flow charts, decision trees, and matrices.

In a simple outline you list topics and subtopics in the order you will treat them in the rough draft. The interpretive label outline allows you to state your opinions and comments on the topics and subtopics. Note card decks allow you to rearrange information quickly and add new data easily.

Simple-sequence flow charts can help with a writing problem that requires specifying a series of steps for readers to follow. Complex-sequence flow charts let you build contingencies into a set of prescribed steps.

Deductive decision trees help you visualize how facts support a position you will take in your document. Inductive decision trees show how a group of seemingly dissimilar facts may support a key argument in your writing. Row-column matrices assist in the analysis of multidimensional topics when the dimensions may not be equally important.

Analysis, like the entire writing process, is recursive. You may need to return to an earlier step to redefine a writing problem or to change your original analysis. Two techniques that are helpful in refining the original analysis are interpretive note taking, in which you jot down thoughts and questions in addition to facts and observations, and journal keeping, in which you note events, queries, and suggestions even while you are busy with other projects.

With a clear definition of the writing problem and a complete, accurate analysis of its contents, you are ready for the third phase in the problem-solving process: making decisions that lead to a first draft of your document.

Writing Problems

1. A savings bank wants to send a short form letter to its depositors. The letter will describe the benefits of a new money market account the bank is offering (guaranteed higher interest than passbook, fully insured, free checking privileges, dividends declared monthly, dividends credited day of deposit to day of withdrawal, the same friendly service for which the bank is known for money market depositors, Saturday and weekday evening banking hours, drive-up window, free gifts to depositors). The definition of the writing problem is as follows:

   - *Objective*   To prepare a short letter specifying a single action that might be taken by the reader and noting positive consequences of that action
   - *Audience*   All depositors of a small-town savings bank
   - *Writer's desired image*   Friendly, reassuring, factual

   Given this definition, prepare an outline analyzing the writing problem.

2. An appliance retailer has overstocked a particular model of television. The retailer is putting the TV on sale and also wants to mail to customers a one-page, two- or three-paragraph flier describing the TV. However, the retailer is uncertain whether the flier should begin by emphasizing the television's many "luxury" features or its manufacturer's record for reliability. Some features of the television are color, high-fidelity sound, pushbutton channel selection, built-in digital clock, capacity for 100 cable channels, attractive walnut cabinet, automatic fine tuning, six-month warranty, and respected manufacturer. The definition of the writing problem is as follows:

   - *Objective*   To prepare two drafts of two- or three-paragraph fliers, each stating a single argument and identifying factors supporting that argument
   - *Audience*   Customers in a local television and appliance store
   - *Writer's desired image*   Enthusiastic

   Given this definition, prepare a deck of six to eight note cards modeled on those shown in figure 2.3 analyzing this problem.

3. The owner of a local antique shop must make weekly trips by pickup truck to view and purchase items for the shop. As the owner's accountant, you need to write a letter specifying the order in which the owner should write down each item of expense associated with

each trip. Having a specified order in which to record expenses will make tax preparation more efficient. In no particular order, the travel expense categories the owner should use are tolls, meals, miscellaneous expenses, date of return from trip, reason for trip, hotel expenses, date of departure on trip, gasoline, vehicle mileage, vehicle repair costs, name and location of hotel, name and location of restaurant, name of destination, and location of owner's antique shop. The definition of the writing problem is as follows:

- *Objective*   To prepare a letter specifying a series of steps in chronological order

- *Audience*   Owner of a local antique shop

- *Writer's desired image*   Clear, cordial

Given this definition, prepare a simple- or complex-sequence flow chart analyzing this writing problem.

4. A major food processor has a research facility to which it invites consumers to taste-test products currently under development. You have been assigned to prepare a memo specifying the steps the consumer testing department will follow when conducting taste tests. In no particular order, the department must send thank-you notes to community organizations that bring busloads of members to serve as taste testers, ask participating consumers to complete questionnaires about their food-shopping routines, give a "sample pack" of your company's products to each participating consumer, meet with consumers in an auditorium to introduce them to the taste-testing procedure, assign groups of five consumers each to staff members who take them to testing rooms, ask each consumer to fill out a questionnaire about any food-related allergies he or she might have and ask each one to sign a release saying that the company is not responsible for any illness resulting from the taste test, bring the consumers who have taken the taste tests to an exit from which they can leave or wait for the rest of their group to finish the taste test, and give the taste tests in cubicled testing areas. The definition of this writing problem is as follows:

- *Objective*   To prepare a memo proposing a series of steps in chronological order

- *Audience*   Staff members of your company's consumer testing department

- *Writer's desired image*   Clear, forthright

Prepare a simple- or complex-sequence flow chart analyzing this writing problem.

5. A candy company has been successful at making one product, a plain, milk chocolate bar. You have been assigned to write a proposal for expanding the company's line of products. You think that several items, including a chocolate bar with cashews, a bar with marshmallow and pecans, and a bar with almonds and raisins, would be successful. Your reasons include the company's prior experience; the popularity of marshmallow, nuts, and raisins; the need to compete with companies offering such products; the need to increase company revenues; predictions for an overall increase in national chocolate consumption; the interest expressed by supermarket chains in new products from your company; the current availability of a nearby candy plant that your company could buy to increase production; and medical research showing that raisins and nuts are excellent health foods. The definition of this writing problem is as follows:

- *Objective*   To prepare a report stating a main argument and supporting the argument with increasingly specific levels of detail
- *Audience*   Vice-president of Marketing
- *Writer's desired image*   Authoritative and enthusiastic

Prepare a deductive decision tree analyzing this writing problem.

6. A company has been experiencing difficulties with its travel arrangements for executives and other personnel. These difficulties include incorrect ticketing of airline passengers, hotels not honoring reservations, rental cars not available at airports, incomprehensible company credit-card travel charges, excessively high restaurant bills, missed planes, travel on multistop flights when nonstops were available, customs document mix-ups for international travel, exorbitant foreign hotel rates, exorbitant charges for telephone calls from foreign hotels to the company headquarters, and a host of other difficulties. You have been assigned to study these difficulties and suggest a solution or solutions (for example, creating a company travel department to handle all travel matters, contracting with a travel consultant to handle all company travel matters, making company department heads responsible for all travel arrangements in their departments, creating a company code of travel regulations describing procedures and allowable expenses). The definition of this writing problem is as follows:

- *Objective*   To write a report offering specific details moving toward increasingly general arguments for taking an action
- *Audience*   Vice-president of Finance
- *Writer's desired image*   Authoritative, logical

Prepare an inductive decision tree analyzing this problem.

7. You manage a chain of three photocopying shops. The owner has asked you to prepare a report explaining what new equipment the chain will need in the coming year and why the shops will need the equipment. In your report, you will need to take into account the following factors: (1) the location of each shop (one in an industrial park, one in a shopping mall, one in a downtown business district); (2) the general business climate at each location (when nearby businesses are doing well, they need more photocopying); (3) the types of new equipment available (very complex, very expensive machines that can copy in color, reduce or enlarge size, collate, and perform other functions versus less expensive machines that are more appropriate for consumer copying—for example, student papers and multiple copies of single pages). The definition of the writing problem is as follows:

- *Objective* To prepare a report showing interrelationships among three factors and to suggest an action or actions based on those interrelationships

- *Audience* Your employer, the owner of a printing shop chain

- *Writer's desired image* Reasoned, clear, conservative

Prepare a row-column matrix analyzing this problem.

Extended Application

Take a business writing problem you defined at the end of chapter 1. Depending on that problem's stated objective, prepare a writing problem analysis using one of the formats presented in this chapter. Then prepare a series of interpretive notes that help you think in a new way about your analysis. Finally, revise your analysis in the light of what you learned through your interpretive note taking.

CHAPTER 3

From Decision Making to Drafting

he first two chapters explained how to define and analyze a writing problem. When you have specified an objective, identified an audience, selected an image, and performed an analysis, you are ready to make additional decisions.

You need to make two kinds of decisions before drafting a document: (1) choosing information and (2) deciding upon a main point. This chapter shows how to make such decisions. It also details how to get started and keep going with your draft — the first version of a document.

The ongoing example for this chapter is a national hotel and motel chain called WYORCA, Inc. This company began with single hotels in Wyoming, Oregon, and California resort areas. Over the years, it has become a large corporation that owns restaurants as well as hotels and motels. WYORCA also owns and manages extensive real estate holdings. By presenting several corporation employees as they make writing decisions and draft documents, this chapter shows you how to get your ideas onto paper and ready for editing.

Why Make Decisions before Drafting?

By defining and analyzing your writing problems, you clarify your under-standing of an audience's needs and you develop effective organizational strategies for your topic. Deciding on the information to include and the main idea to emphasize in your draft serves as a bridge between your thinking and the physical act of writing. The result is a combination of mental preparedness and written material that makes drafting more efficient.

Ask yourself four questions about the information you plan to include in your first draft:

1. Do you have all the information necessary to begin drafting?
2. Is there any information you should *not* include in your draft?
3. Is the information you have sufficiently detailed to meet the expecta-tions of your audience and to accomplish your writing objective?
4. Are all the details you plan to include accurate?

Decisions about
Information

If you can answer "yes" to all four of these questions, and if the information you plan to include in your draft is at hand (for example, in a letter, memo, report, journal, or notes) or in your mind, then you have two options. You can prepare yourself to draft by either updating your problem analysis to include the information or simply keeping information nearby for inclusion in your draft as you need it. But should you need to do extensive research for a longer, formal report, we suggest that you follow the procedures specified in chapter 10, "Formal Reports."

To see how a WYORCA employee answers questions about information, let us follow the company's vice-president for accounting, Dawn Campbell, as she prepares to draft a memo. Campbell needs to report on WYORCA's restaurant performance compared to the corporation's other revenue pro-ducers—hotels, motels, real estate, and miscellaneous holdings. Campbell defines her writing problem this way:

- *Objective* To prepare a memo comparing restaurants' revenue and operating profit and loss performances with those of WYORCA's hotels, motels, real estate, and miscellaneous holdings

- *Audience* WYORCA's top management (president, executive vice-president; vice-presidents for marketing, operations, and personnel; division heads for hotels, motels, restaurants, and real properties)

- *Writer's desired image* Analytical, impartial

Figure 3.1 shows the inductive decision tree Campbell develops to analyze her writing problem. Based on data for the most recent year, Campbell regards restaurant operations as a definite drain on WYORCA's profits.

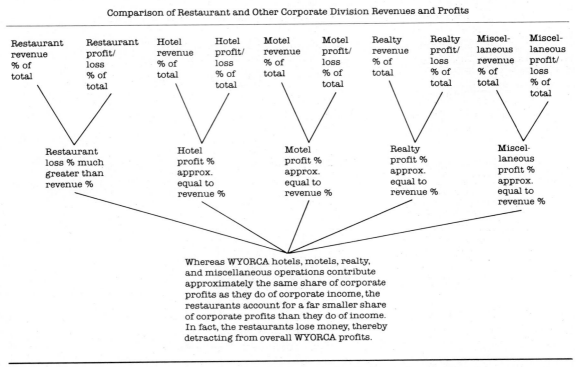

Figure 3.1   Inductive decision tree before information decisions

Her main recommendation will be that the corporation study the restaurant operations in depth and consider taking action to prevent continued losses.

With her initial analysis complete and with one year's revenue and profit and loss data at hand, Campbell asks herself questions about information. If she is not satisfied with her own answers, then she can take action to get the information she needs.

■ *Question 1*   "Do I have *enough information* at hand to be able to assert that the restaurants have been a continuing drain on profits?"

Answer to Question 1   "Not really. I need revenue/profit/loss data from a number of years before the most recent one to show that the restaurant losses have been consistent."

Action Taken   Campbell asks her secretary to get revenue/profit/loss summaries for each of the four previous years.

■ *Question 2*   "With all this new information, is there any data I should *not* include in my draft?"

Answer to Question 2   "Yes. WYORCA bought its restaurants only three years ago. Thus, the revenue/profit/loss summaries for the two earliest years do not contain subcategories for restaurants and don't seem to be meaningful for tracing restaurant performance."

Action taken   Campbell sets aside the summaries for the two earliest years (she does not throw them away; she may need them later in preparation of the memo). She now has summaries for the most recent year as well as for the two previous years.

▪ _Question 3_   "Do my three years of revenue/profit/loss summaries offer the level of detail I need to present the restaurant situation as clearly as possible?"

Answer to Question 3   "No. WYORCA owns two restaurant chains, one offering only 'fast food' service, the other offering 'full menu, waiter and waitress service.' To present the situation clearly, I will need a breakdown of restaurant revenue, profit and loss by chain."

Action Taken   Campbell asks her secretary to get computer printouts of the desired information.

▪ _Question 4_   "Is all my information accurate?"

Answer to Question 4   "Yes. I can rely on my accounting staff for accurate information."

Having answered her own questions about the sufficiency, specificity, and accuracy of her information, Campbell decides that she now has the data required to begin drafting. At this point, Campbell has two options. She can return to her inductive decision tree and expand it to include details that she will use in the draft. Or she can simply keep the revenue, profit and loss summaries handy for reference as she writes.

Campbell chooses to expand her decision tree. To do so, she builds new "branches" above the top line of the tree. Figure 3.2 shows a segment of her expanded tree. With her _additional_ information now integrated into the decision tree, Campbell can draft this memo:

Draft

Date: January 15, 1986

To: Claire Simons, President; Dale Stone, Executive Vice-President; Sally
   Sears, Vice-President for Marketing; Ken Cantrell, Vice-President for
   Operations; Gerry Gardner, Vice-President for Personnel; Gene Harper,
   Division Head for Real Properties; Hector Uribe, Division Head for
   Restaurants

From: Dawn Campbell, Vice-President for Accounting

Subject: Restaurant Division Revenue/Profit/Loss Position

At the executive vice-president's direction, I have prepared this memo integrating our most recent data into our ongoing discussion of restaurant operations.

Data are now available from the final quarter of last year. Revenue, profit and loss figures for the quarter are consistent with those for the rest of the year. Figures for the entire year are consistent with those for the past three years.

Over those years, the portion of revenue generated by each of WYORCA's divisions has remained fairly constant, averaging as follows: hotels (37 percent); motels (33 percent); real properties (16 percent); restaurants (12 percent); miscellaneous holdings (2 percent).

During that same period, the portion of WYORCA's total profit and loss attributable to each division has also remained fairly constant, averaging as follows: hotels (38 percent); motels (38 percent); real properties (22 percent); restaurants (-3 percent); miscellaneous holdings (5 percent).

In the three years since WYORCA purchased its fast food and full-service restaurant chains, the division has posted an average loss of 3 percent per year. Average loss broken down by chain has also been 3 percent for fast food and 3 percent for full service.

As we have all agreed during the past year, WYORCA must study its restaurant operations. Otherwise this business that accounts for less than one-eighth of our revenues will continue to place a strain on our primary hotel and motel operations to make up for continued losses.

Should we go ahead and make a formal study of restaurant operations, the Accounting Department will, of course, be prepared to provide any needed financial data. We can also project financial consequences of such actions as restaurant divestiture, restaurant leasing, or capital infusion.

You will receive a complete set of fourth quarter, previous year, and previous three-year revenue, profit and loss tables before 5:00 P.M. today.

Decisions about Main Ideas

Being able to put the main idea of your document into words will help you to keep focused on your objective as you draft. Sometimes your analysis will state your main idea explicitly, as was the case with Campbell's memo on

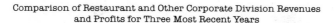

Comparison of Restaurant and Other Corporate Division Revenues
and Profits for Three Most Recent Years

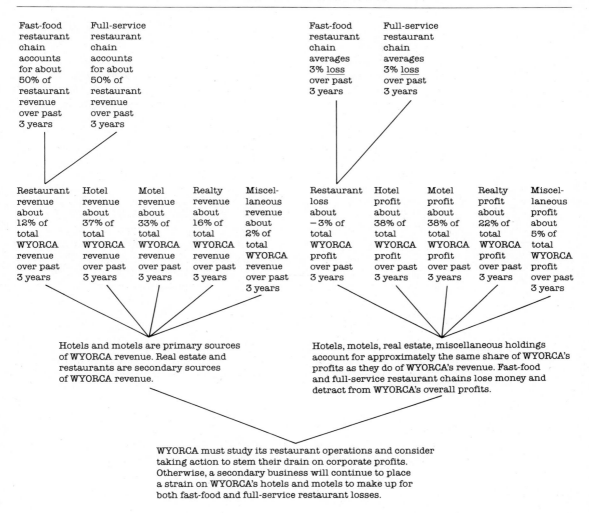

Figure 3.2   Inductive decision tree revised and expanded after information decisions

WYORCA's restaurant revenues and losses. The trunk of Campbell's inductive decision tree *was* her main point (see figure 3.2).

At other times, you will need to look at both your analysis and your information to discover a central idea. Let us look at an instance where this review is necessary.

Samuel Tate, who coordinates WYORCA's training program for new hotel registration-desk personnel, must prepare a memo specifying the steps trainees should take when greeting a guest. Figure 3.3 shows the flow chart that Tate prepares to analyze the problem involved in writing the memo. Although the chart gives a specific set of steps that trainees should follow, it does not state any central idea that Tate should emphasize in the memo.

In addition to the flow chart, Tate has the following information about WYORCA hotel check-in procedures:

- New front-desk personnel have received more than their share of guest complaints.

- Check-in lines have developed as new front-desk personnel have tried to solve the problems created by guests without reservations.

- Hotels have lost money when guests say they will pay with cash or a traveler's check and then leave without doing so. In most of these cases, new front-desk personnel have not required a deposit from these guests.

By studying this information in combination with the flow chart analysis, Tate formulates this main point: *Front-desk trainees require a clear set of check-in procedures to decrease the chance of guest complaints, reservations confusion, and losses due to unpaid room bills.* With this main point, the information given above, and the flow chart at hand, Tate is able to begin to draft his memo:

Draft

Date: March 8, 1986

To: Front-Desk Trainees

From: Samuel Tate, Training Coordinator

Subject: Guest Check-In Procedures

Front-desk trainees require a specific, written set of procedures to follow for guest check-in. Please memorize these procedures <u>and</u> include a copy in the

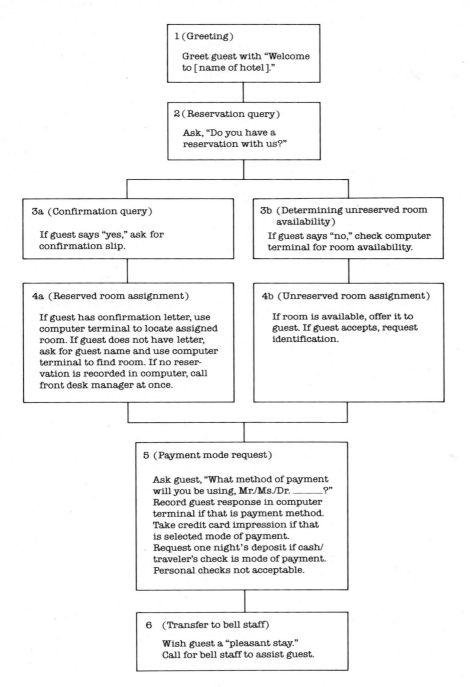

1 (Greeting)

Greet guest with "Welcome to [name of hotel]."

2 (Reservation query)

Ask, "Do you have a reservation with us?"

3a (Confirmation query)

If guest says "yes," ask for confirmation slip.

3b (Determining unreserved room availability)

If guest says "no," check computer terminal for room availability.

4a (Reserved room assignment)

If guest has confirmation letter, use computer terminal to locate assigned room. If guest does not have letter, ask for guest name and use computer terminal to find room. If no reservation is recorded in computer, call front desk manager at once.

4b (Unreserved room assignment)

If room is available, offer it to guest. If guest accepts, request identification.

5 (Payment mode request)

Ask guest, "What method of payment will you be using, Mr./Ms./Dr. _____?" Record guest response in computer terminal if that is payment method. Take credit card impression if that is selected mode of payment. Request one night's deposit if cash/traveler's check is mode of payment. Personal checks not acceptable.

6 (Transfer to bell staff)

Wish guest a "pleasant stay." Call for bell staff to assist guest.

Figure 3.3 Memo flow chart: Main idea not specified

trainee binder that you will be required to keep with you throughout your probationary period. By learning these steps, you will be able to minimize guest complaints, reservations confusion, and nonpayment of room charges.

1. Greet every guest in this way: "Welcome . . ."

Note how Tate integrates his flow chart analysis and available information to start a draft that will, when revised and edited, give his subordinates clear, step-by-step directions.

Drafting

Drafting is the act of writing a preliminary version of your document. You can prepare one, two, three, or more drafts before producing the final document. In this chapter, however, we treat preparation of your *first* draft—a piece of writing that you can later improve through revision and editing. Throughout our discussion of drafting, we will follow Jean Soo, an engineer employed by WYORCA. Soo's task is to prepare a memo highlighting key similarities and differences among three sites WYORCA is considering for a new hotel.

Materials Needed
for Drafting

In addition to the actual tools, paper, pen, pencil, typewriter (or word processor), needed to make the ideas inside your mind visible, you will require several items for efficient drafting. Here are the four materials Jean Soo will keep close as she works on her memo:

1. Problem Definition

    - *Objective*   To prepare a memo highlighting key similarities and differences among three potential hotel sites
    - *Audience*   Pat Cummins, vice-president for corporate development
    - *Writer's desired image*   Logical, *non*technical

2. Analysis

INTERPRETIVE LABEL OUTLINE

I. Downtown site
    A. Demolition of current structure will take from two to four months.
    B. Available site will require high-rise construction.

      C. Adjacent space has multiple, possible uses:
         1. Parking garage
         2. Shopping arcade
         3. Health club
      D. Municipal convention facilities would be nearby.
      E. Transportation features include:
         1. 25 minutes from airport--limousine and taxi service available
         2. 20 minutes from northern suburban industrial area--taxi service available
         3. Located within downtown business/commercial area

  II. Northern suburban site
      A. Land is not presently developed--no demolition costs.
      B. Amount of acreage available offers architectural options:
         1. High rise
         2. Low rise
         3. Combination high-rise and townhouse suites
      C. Shopping mall is nearby.
      D. No indoor parking is needed.
      E. Hotel would have to include private convention facilities.
      F. Transportation features include:
         1. 40 minutes to airport--taxi and courtesy van services
         2. 15 minutes to downtown--taxi service available
         3. Located within northern suburban industrial area--taxi service available

 III. Southern suburban site
      A. Land is not presently developed--no demolition costs.
      B. Amount of acreage available offers architectural options:
         1. High rise
         2. Low rise
         3. Combination high-rise and townhouse suites
      C. Adjacent land is available for development of shopping mall.
      D. No indoor parking would be needed.
      E. Hotel would have to include private convention facilities.
      F. Transportation features include:
         1. 10 minutes to airport--taxi and courtesy van services
         2. 15 minutes to downtown--taxi service available
         3. 30 minutes to northern suburban industrial areas--taxi service available

3. Additional Information (in form of interpretive notes)

Fact	*Interpretive note*
Downtown area has new department and specialty stores.	These might remove need for shopping arcade but increase value of parking garage.

Northern suburban site is located within 30 minutes of popular parks and family attractions.	Combination of hotel and motel units would be feasible given available acreage.
Southern suburban site has river frontage.	Flood protection is excellent; marina facilities would be feasible.

4. Main Idea Statement

Each site offers its own benefits and range of planning options.

When to Draft

It is fortunate that Soo is this well prepared because the best time to begin drafting is right now—immediately after decision making. At this point, she is thinking about the topic logically. Having just returned from a last look at the sites where she made her interpretive notes, Soo wants to get her observations down on paper while they are still fresh in her mind. She will want to pause later before revising her memo, but for now, she wishes to get started before she loses her momentum.

How Long to Keep Going

After you get started on your draft, how long you keep at it will depend mainly on the length of the document. If it is short, try to write the entire first version without stopping. If it is long, try to work in stretches of about 45 minutes to one hour. Then, pause for a cup of coffee, a drink of water, or a few minutes of stretching. This work schedule allows you to get a large number of ideas down but should not prove so tiring that your drafting efficiency decreases sharply.

Take a break *after* introducing a new idea, because this idea may occur in the first sentence of a new paragraph or in the first paragraph of a new section of the document. When you go back to work, the new idea will get you writing more efficiently and fluently. In the case of Soo's memo, she might finish her discussion of the second hotel site and write the first sentence of her discussion of the third hotel site before taking a break:

Draft

Because of its location near the northern industrial area, the suburban site's main appeal would be to the business traveler. The proximity of popular parks and family attractions could lure a second clientele, adults with children on weekend and summertime vacations. Serving both types of customers would present WYORCA with special architectural and engineering challenges.

THE SOUTHERN SUBURBAN SITE

In many respects the benefits and design options of the southern suburban site are similar to those of the northern suburban site. For instance, . . .

When Soo resumes drafting after her break, she can reread what she has written. That rereading allows her to recapture her train of thought. With the first sentence of the "southern suburban site" section already written, she can begin immediately without having to stop and recreate the logical connection between the two sections.

All the best advice about when to draft and how long to continue is not very useful unless you can write your first sentence. Because the object of so much business writing is the transmission of information from writer to audience within a particular business context, stating the background for your writing is often the best way to begin. You may recall that this is how Dawn Campbell began her memo about WYORCA's restaurant division: "At the executive vice-president's direction, I have prepared this memo integrating our most recent data into our ongoing discussion of restaurant operations."

Getting Started

For documents that transmit information to audiences willing to accept a more direct approach, simply getting to the main point may be the most efficient way to begin. The first sentence of Samuel Tate's memo to trainees about guest check-in procedures opens: "Front-desk trainees require a specific, written set of procedures to follow for guest check-in."

Soo decides to begin her memo by reminding her audience, the vice-president for corporate development, of the document's origins: "On July 5, you requested a memo highlighting key elements of the complete site feasibility study."

To continue your first paragraph beyond its opening sentence, you can take one of several tacks:

Writing Introductions

1. Use the opening paragraph to preview the rest of your document. To do this, Soo might follow up her first sentence in this way:

    On July 5, you requested a memo highlighting key elements of the complete site feasibility study. This memo examines engineering, architectural, and operational factors affecting site selection. The first of these factors is the need for demolition of existing structures. The second element is the type of construction required. A third aspect is adjacent space. The memo then deals with the need for hotel convention facilities. A look at available ground transportation concludes discussion of each of the three sites.

2. Provide additional background to the document in your opening paragraph. If Soo chooses this approach, she might continue her draft like this:

On July 5, you requested a memo highlighting key elements of the complete site feasibility study. The evaluation team completed its study on July 10, 1986. After reading the technical report and meeting with team members individually as well as collectively, I have prepared this summary.

3. Go directly from your opening sentence to the substance of your document. If Soo wished to address site evaluation details immediately, she might choose this option:

On July 5, you requested a memo highlighting key elements of the complete site feasibility study. The first of these elements concerns needed demolition work at the downtown site. An office building constructed in 1922 now stands where the hotel would rise. Because of the old building's sturdy construction and its downtown location, demolition and lot clearance could take from two to four months. At that point, construction workers could begin laying a foundation for the new hotel.

Keeping Going

Now that you have gotten started, you can take several steps to keep yourself drafting. First, consult your writing problem analysis. This analysis will remind you of the order in which to present your ideas. If you have additional information to include in your draft, you may find it useful to mark *where* in your document's main section that information should go.

Soo does this by marking where she will add her interpretive notes as she follows her outline:

Where to Include Interpretive Notes in Draft

Fact	*Interpretive Note*
1. Downtown area has new department and specialty stores.	These might remove need for shopping arcade but increase value of parking garage.

Include interpretive note 1 after outline section I.C.2. ("Downtown site; adjacent space has multiple possible uses; shopping arcade").

2. Northern suburban site is located within 30 minutes of popular parks and family attractions.	Combination of hotel and motel units would be feasible given available acreage.

Include interpretive note 2 after outline section II.F.3. ("Northern suburban site; transportation features include; located within northern suburban industrial area—taxi service available").

3. Southern suburban site   Flood protection is
   has river frontage.   excellent; marina facilities
                                would be feasible.

Include interpretive note 3 after outline section III.C. ("Southern suburban site; adjacent land is available for development of shopping mall").

To ensure you are sticking to your topic, consult your problem definition and main point statement from time to time. A good time for this self-monitoring is between paragraphs in a short document. For longer drafts, double-check between subtopics.

Note when Soo refers back to her problem definition and main topic statement:

- *First time:* between outline items I.E.3. ("Downtown site; transportation features include; located within downtown business/commercial area") and II. ("Northern suburban site")

- *Second time:* between outline items II.F.3. ("Northern suburban site; transportation features include; located within northern suburban industrial area—taxi service available") and III. ("Southern suburban site")

By defining and analyzing your problem, checking your information, and writing your opening paragraph, you will have gone most of the way toward insuring coherence in your draft. With organization guided by your analysis and fleshed out through whatever information you have at hand, the coherence of the draft should emerge naturally. But you can do something else to enhance that coherence. By using transitional words and phrases to connect sentences and paragraphs, you can clarify the logical relationships among your ideas, thereby creating a more fluent document.

Chapter 4 shows how to "edit in" transitions to clarify the logic of a completed draft. Before that, during drafting, we have found it helpful to use transitional words and phrases to help keep a draft going smoothly. Some of these words and phrases show connections dealing with *time*:

afterward	later
as long as	meanwhile
as soon as	next
at last	now
at that time	previously
before	since

first (second, third)	then
formerly	until
in the meantime	when
	whenever

Some transitions show connections dealing with *locations*:

above	further
at	here
behind	inside
below	nearby
beside	over
elsewhere	there
everywhere	underneath
farther	where
	wherever

Some transitions show a variety of logical relationships, such as *cause/effect, comparison/contrast, illustration,* and *elaboration:*

all in all	moreover
also	nevertheless
as a result	of course
because	on the contrary
consequently	on the other hand
finally	otherwise
for example	overall
for instance	still
however	therefore
in addition	thus
indeed	too
	yet

By adding judicious use of these transitional words and phrases to all her other problem-solving efforts, Soo creates a draft of the site evaluation memo. She then pauses before writing her concluding paragraph(s). Figure 3.4 shows this draft. You will see that Soo has chosen to use the introduction that reminds the vice-president for corporate development of the context in which she is drafting her memo. Soo's transitional words are underscored.

Draft

Date: July 17, 1986

To: Pat Cummins, Vice-President for Corporate Planning

From: Jean Soo, Site Evaluation Engineer

Subject: Highlights of Site-Evaluation Team Feasibility Study

On July 5, you requested a memo highlighting key elements of the complete site feasibility study. The evaluation team completed its study on July 10, 1986. <u>After</u> reading the technical report and meeting with team members individually as well as collectively, I have prepared this summary.

The downtown site poses a problem not presented by the two other locations. Demolition of the structure presently on the site will take from two to four months. The combination of the old building's sturdy construction and the business district location will make demolition a painstaking process. Crews will have to be especially careful when they use wrecking balls and explosives.

Once the site is clear, hotel construction can begin. <u>As you know</u>, our architects have rendered three versions of the new building. All of these are of multistory design, as necessitated by the downtown location and space constraints. One design depicts a pentagonally shaped building constructed around an open courtyard. A <u>second</u> rendering shows a rectangular, glassed-in tower. A <u>third</u> version presents a circular tower connected to shopping areas, a parking garage, and other public facilities by above-ground walkways.

According to the evaluation team, this third, circular design combines engineering, design, and operational features in a way that would allow for maximum public access to the hotel while insuring guest privacy. With this third design, we can make a number of possible uses of space adjacent to the hotel. This space could be used for needed services to supplement existing shopping areas. <u>For example</u>, WYORCA could lease space for hair styling, ticket agency, and sundries shops to be located in hotel-owned

1

Figure 3.4   Introduction and body of a draft memo. Highlights of a hotel site feasibility study.

Figure 3.4
Continued

space on the above-ground walkways. We could ask our architects to add a second walkway to the parking garage. By designating one walkway and one garage level for hotel guests and the other walkway and level for transient parking, we could greatly facilitate check-in and check-out. <u>Indeed</u>, the combination of hotel-leased service shops, already existing above-ground shopping, and ground-level department and specialty stores may well cause us to request a redesigned, larger garage facility from our architects.

<u>In addition</u>, the circular design would allow for a low-rise, separate health club. A walkway from the lowest hotel guest floor would serve those staying with us; a street-level entrance would serve local health club members.

The site-evaluation team agrees that having the municipal convention facility within walking distance of the hotel is a major benefit of the downtown location. With prospects bright for greatly increased convention center bookings, WYORCA could be certain of steady room occupancy all year round.

<u>Of course</u>, the downtown location would provide guest transportation options competitive with those of other center city hotels. Scheduled limousine service and on-call taxis can make trips to the airport in 25 minutes. Taxi service would <u>also</u> be readily available to the northern suburban industrial area, approximately 20 minutes away, depending upon the particular company a guest needed to visit. <u>Because</u> downtown commercial establishments would be within walking distance of the hotel, many guests would choose this way to reach their destinations. <u>However</u>, for guests wishing such services and especially during inclement weather, business district taxis and public buses are plentiful.

<u>In short</u>, the team believes that the downtown location offers the benefits and constraints typical of center city sites. WYORCA's experience in building and operating such hotels in other urban areas nationwide will certainly be applicable here.

<u>In contrast</u> to the downtown site, the land on which we hold an option to build a northern suburban hotel is presently

2

Figure 3.4
Continued

undeveloped. Our architects assert (and the engineers on our in-house site evaluation team agree) that construction can begin as soon as we choose a contractor's bid. All needed sewer, gas, electric, and water lines are in place adjacent to the property. As you mentioned to me when we spoke on July 13, our attorneys have received the local township's promise to make any necessary improvements an immediate priority should we select the northern site.

Having 300 acres of land makes for virtually limitless building design options. The preliminary architectural renderings show how each design takes a different approach. One shows a rather traditional concrete and glass facade. A second depicts a sprawling low-rise design. The third, which the team found most logical for the site, combines a high-rise structure with a cluster of low-rise, townhouse suites. The team felt that this design combination was particularly in keeping with the northern site's location at the edge of an industrial suburb bordering a semirural, recreational area.

A major shopping mall is located within a five-minute drive of the northern site. If the hotel offered courtesy van service to and from the mall, WYORCA could limit its need to provide in-house shopping facilities.

With so much land available, no indoor parking is required. Nevertheless, some team members felt that we should ask our architects to provide a parking lot design that would simplify later construction of a multistory parking garage. With prospects for the northern suburb's long-term development certain, the team foresees a time when land might be at a premium and parking lot expansion not feasible--particularly if the hotel expands.

It goes without saying that the design of needed convention facilities would depend upon which building plan WYORCA would select. The high-rise plan takes a traditional approach to convention facility location (mezzanine-level ballrooms and larger function rooms; below-ground-level smaller meeting rooms). The low-rise design places convention facilities in a

3

Figure 3.4
Continued

separate building connected to the hotel by a covered walkway. Once again, the team was impressed by the use of convention space in the combined high-rise/townhouse design. By centralizing ballrooms and large function rooms in the main building and designating several of the connecting townhouses for smaller meeting rooms, we could accommodate both large and small conventions simultaneously while providing a sense of exclusivity for both.

Transportation features are typical of suburban industrial area locations--with one key drawback. Because the airport is located south of the city, a one-way trip by courtesy van or taxi would take approximately 40 minutes. On the other hand, the site's location in the heart of a vast array of major plants would make the hotel very popular with business people who do not have to fly into the city. Again, for those without automobiles, taxi service would be available to local industries and to the center city (approximately 15 minutes).

A reexamination of the northern suburban location reveals that it is ideally situated for quick access to family recreation and amusement areas north of the city. This fact suggests a possible further alteration to the high-rise/townhouse design. An area of one-story units might provide greater flexibility to the hotel complex and enable it to maintain high occupancy through traditionally slack summer and weekend periods.

Like the northern suburban location, the southern suburban site is not presently developed. Thus, there would be no demolition costs for the project.

The same amount of acreage (300) as the northern site makes the same design options available. Once again, the evaluation team favors the high-rise/townhouse suite plan.

Unlike the northern suburban location, the southern location has no nearby shopping mall. WYORCA might consider developing its own mall or leasing part of its acreage for such development. Another difference is that the southern location fronts the river.

4

Figure 3.4
Continued

Flood protection from a state-built floodwall is excellent. Its riverside location would make a marina attached to the hotel highly desirable and entirely feasible. Certainly such a facility would offer an attraction no other area hotel could match.

The site team endorses the same design alteration as in the northern location to make the parking lot convertible to a multilevel garage. Furthermore, the team finds the mixed convention facilities (ballrooms and large function rooms in the high-rise, smaller meeting rooms in the townhouses) to be appropriate for this location as well.

Transportation availability is as follows: taxi and courtesy van services to the airport (10 minutes); taxi service to downtown (15 minutes); taxi service to northern suburban industrial area (30 minutes). In future years, the southern suburbs will see greatly increasing industrial activity, making this location more attractive.

5

Closing the Draft   The first sentence of your *last* paragraph can be as important as the opening sentence of your entire document. It is the first sentence of the last paragraph that leads your audience toward a sense of closure. There are several ways in which this sentence can preview how you will end your draft. Soo experiments with each one before finally deciding:

1. A summary of what the body of the document has said: "This memo has highlighted similarities and differences among WYORCA's three possible sites for a new hotel."
2. A restatement of the writer's main point: "As you can see, each site offers its own benefits and range of planning options."
3. A closing call for action by the audience or an offer of action on the audience's behalf by the writer: "As you know, the evaluation team will be anxious to know of the executive board's final site decision; of course, we are prepared to offer any additional assistance you might require before that time."

Soo combines elements of her restatement and offer of assistance within her closing paragraph:

Draft

As you can see, each site offers its own benefits and range of planning options. The downtown site would give us a central location in a new market. The northern suburban location situates us ideally to serve a largely untapped clientele of businesspeople who must travel to one of the region's largest industrial areas. The southern suburban location would emphatically make us the full-service hotel closest to one of the nation's major airports. In addition, both the suburban sites offer almost total design flexibility for expansion in rapidly growing areas. The evaluation team eagerly awaits the executive board's final site selection; we stand ready to offer any additional assistance you might desire before that time.

Without a sense of closure such as that offered to WYORCA's vice-president by Soo's last paragraph, you will almost certainly leave your audience up in the air. By providing your audience with this closure, you will satisfy readers that you have said everything you wanted to say about the topic. Moreover, you will have stressed that *you* understand the significance of what you have written.

When she finishes the last sentence of her draft, Soo correctly quits work on her summary for the day. Even if you are working on a very short document or if you are under a tight deadline, try to take at least 15 minutes off between drafting and polishing your work before sending it. If you can take a longer break, so much the better. The next chapter, "Revising and Editing," shows how this time off from the writing problem can help you complete your document more effectively.

Summary

Before drafting, make certain you have all the information you need, and no more than you need. Review the information you intend to use to be sure that it is sufficiently detailed and accurate.

Start drafting as soon as possible after you have decided that your information is sufficient. Draft the entire document if it is short, but take regular breaks during drafting of longer documents.

Decide whether to start the draft of your document with the background of its writing or a direct statement of the business at hand. Use your opening paragraph to preview the document, provide additional background to its development, or state its substance. Consult your writing problem analysis to help you decide how to continue your draft. Use transitional words and phrases to keep your writing flowing and coherent. Make certain that the conclusion of your draft provides your reader with a sense of closure. When you finish drafting, take a break before revising your document.

Writing Problems

1. You are an accountant for a small chain of variety stores. As of June 30 of the current year, your employer, Sandy Webster, finds herself with a cash surplus of $100,000. She has asked you for your advice on whether to (1) invest the $100,000 in a taxable security or (2) use the $100,000 to buy additional inventory for her stores. You have defined the writing problem:

   - *Objective*   To prepare a memo to your employer in which you specify the benefits and drawbacks of two ways to spend $100,000
   - *Audience*   Sandy Webster, owner of a small chain of variety stores
   - *Writer's desired image*   Conservative and thoughtful

After defining the writing problem, you completed this short, interpretive label outline:

I.   Webster finds herself with $100,000 cash surplus as of June 30 of the current year.
II. Webster specifies two ways she will consider using the cash:
     A. Purchase of taxable securities
     B. Purchase of new inventory
III. Before purchase, Webster should consider possible outcomes of each purchase:
     A. Tax consequences
        1. Securities
        2. Inventory
     B. Earnings projections
        1. Securities
        2. Inventory
     C. Additional expenses
        1. Securities
        2. Inventory
IV. On balance, Webster should buy the securities.

After investigation, you collected the following information about the two possible investments:

- Interest from the securities is fully taxable as income.
- The amount of inventory still unsold as of January 1 of next year is subject to a state business property tax.
- The securities pay a flat 10 percent interest a year, thereby yielding $10,000 in interest annually.
- Sales projections suggest that Webster could sell approximately 50 percent of the new inventory by January 1 of next year.
- If she does sell 50 percent of the inventory by January 1 of next year, Webster can expect to net $10,000 from the sales.
- Webster will have to pay a brokerage fee of approximately $500 if she wishes to sell the securities.
- Providing warehouse space and distribution of the new inventory to chain outlets would cost approximately $500.
- If Webster postpones the securities purchase six months, the interest rate will likely stay about the same—10 percent.
- If Webster postpones the inventory purchase six months, its cost will likely rise about 1 percent ($1,000).

Given this problem definition and short interpretive outline, do the following:

  a. Select which of the above pieces of information to <u>include</u> in your memo to Webster.
  b. In one sentence, state the main point of your memo.
  c. Draft your memo to Webster.

2. You work in the marketing research department of the DMR Coffee Company. DMR makes two brands of instant coffee: Zip, a regular blend, and Unlax, a decaffeinated blend. DMR now wants to make a decaffeinated version of Zip (Zip Decaffeinated). Your market research has provided you with the following information:

   ▪ Of people who drink Zip, 88 percent will not drink Zip Decaffeinated.

   ▪ Of people who drink Zip, 79 percent will not drink Unlax.

   ▪ Of people who drink Unlax, 77 percent will not drink Zip.

   ▪ Of people who drink Unlax, 81 percent will not drink Zip Decaffeinated (the name makes them nervous).

   ▪ Of people who drink neither Zip nor Unlax, 75 percent *might* try Zip Decaffeinated (it sounds as if it will taste good but not jangle their nerves).

   ▪ Most (65 percent) of the supermarket chains that carry Zip and Unlax will give you additional shelf space to market Zip Decaffeinated on a trial basis.

   ▪ Your biggest competitor, REX Foods, Inc., has just marketed a decaffeinated version of their best-selling instant. Many supermarket chains have already given it shelf space.

   You will need to write a memo to your immediate superior stating your findings and recommending or not recommending introducing Zip Decaffeinated to the market. You define the writing problem:

   ▪ *Objective*   To prepare a memo specifying market research findings

   ▪ *Audience*   Dan Landreaux, director of Marketing

   ▪ *Writer's desired image*   Logical and enthusiastic

   Given this problem definition and information:
   a. Use a decision tree to analyze the writing problem.
   b. Decide whether or not to include in your draft the percentages given for each piece of information.
   c. Write the main point of your memo.
   d. Draft the memo to Landreaux.

3. You are an executive for a new local radio station. The station has just received the results of a listener survey. The results specify the kind of

programming that potential listeners would prefer: rock music, easy-listening music, all news, miscellaneous musical programming, miscellaneous nonmusical programming. In a memo to the station's owner, report on survey results and propose that the station should play "light" rock music in order to appeal to both listeners who enjoy rock music and those who enjoy easy-listening music. You define the writing problem:

- *Objective* To prepare a memo specifying results of a listener survey and my recommendation for programming
- *Audience* The station owner
- *Writer's desired image* Informed and convincing

You analyze the writing problem through the following inductive decision tree:

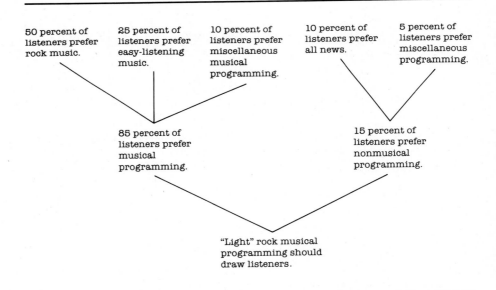

4. You own a local flower shop and are about to hire your first employee. This employee will assist you when you are present and will run the shop one day a week so you can have a day off. After you have trained your assistant, you want to leave this employee with a note specifying procedures to follow for opening the shop on days you are not on the premises. You define the problem:

- *Objective* To prepare a note specifying procedures for an assistant to follow when the owner of the flower shop is not present

• *Audience*   A new employee

• *Writer's desired image*   Matter-of-fact

You analyze the writing problem through the following simple-sequence flow chart:

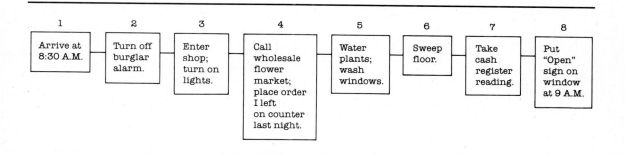

Given this problem definition and flow chart:

a. Decide whether you need to delete any of the information in the flow chart as being unnecessary for your employee to run the shop efficiently.

b. Write the main point you will make in your note to your assistant.

c. Write a draft of the note.

5. As director of security for UKN Industries, you must write a memo informing employees of changes in security procedures. The body of the memo will give the employees the following directions:

• Use magnetic cards to open doors to your authorized work area.

• Wear an identification badge with current photograph at all times.

• Lock all office doors when leaving work.

• Use magnetic cards when you leave your building after work.

• Sign in or out with security attendant when entering building anytime between 6 P.M. and 7 A.M., Monday through Saturday or anytime on Sunday.

You define the writing problem:

• *Objective*   To prepare a memo specifying new security procedures

• *Audience*   All employees of UKN Industries

• *Writer's desired image*   Courteous and firm

Given this problem definition and the body of your memo, draft an introductory paragraph for your memo.

6. You work in the data processing department of a gas and electric utility company. After the company received approval for a rate increase from the state public service commission, you reprogrammed your billing system to reflect the change. You need to inform your customer service agents of details in the billing change, a task for which you prepare the following problem definition:

- *Objective*   To write a memo specifying changes in gas and electric rates and billing information
- *Audience*   Company customer service agents
- *Writer's desired image*   logical

Here is the draft introduction and body of your short memo. Draft its concluding paragraph.

Draft

Date: September 27, 1986

To: Customer Service Agents

From: [Your name], Data Processing Department

Subject: Billing Changes

The newly approved rate and billing system is now in place. This means that when you call up a customer's billing information on your video display terminal, you will see several new categories of information as well as most of the data previously displayed. However, we have eliminated two categories of customer data.

New data categories are as follows: customer kilowatt electric usage for each of the preceding 12 months, and customer cubic-foot gas consumption for each of the preceding 12 months.

Data categories that will no longer appear on your screen are: the date the customer first connected to our service, and service calls made to the customer's address over the last 12 months. This information is available on your video display terminals. However, you will have to request it specifically by keyboarding the following: customer account number followed by either FIRST CONNECT or SERVICE CALLS, depending on which information you need.

7. One of your first assignments as a sales representative for the Outland Auto Accessories Company is to attend a trade show. You will be tending a booth at the show. The booth displays a variety of Outland products. To supplement the display, you have to write a flier high-lighting the advantages of several new Outland products. You hope that buyers for retail stores will pick up these fliers and remember your new products when it comes time to place orders, or when an Outland sales representative calls on the retailer. You define the writing problem:

- *Objective* To prepare a one-page flier highlighting the advantages of three new auto accessories

- *Audience* Retail store buyers attending an auto accessories trade show

- *Writer's desired image* highly enthusiastic

The new products you will be promoting are:

- A mock-velvet steering wheel cover that adjusts to fit any size wheel; the top half of the cover is reinforced so that the material will not wear down through constant contact with the driver's hands; the cover wholesales for $3 each, with a suggested list price of $6 each.

- A stain-resistant, wear-resistant, carpeted auto floor mat that comes in a wide variety of flashy designs (checkerboards, antique cars, racehorses, monograms); the floor mats wholesale for $8 each for compact car sizes ($18 suggested retail), and $16 each for full car sizes ($36 suggested retail).

- Kits for customized hood ornaments that let a car owner create his or her own design; the ornament kit wholesales for $10 a unit, with a suggested retail price of $20 a unit. Given this problem definition and information about the new products, draft your flier.

8. You are a quality control engineer for a company that manufactures hand tools for the do-it-yourselfer. You have discovered that the dies from which your company manufactures its one-half-inch drill bits have been wearing out earlier and earlier. The present dies are good for 5,000 fewer drill bits than the previous dies, which were good for 5,000 fewer bits than their predecessors, and so on. You need to bring the fact of this decreasing performance to the attention of your company's general manager, so she or he can take action to correct this problem. Here is your writing problem definition:

- *Objective* To prepare a memo reporting on the declining quality of dies your company uses to manufacture drill bits

- *Audience* The company general manager

- *Writer's desired image* Respectful and to the point

Given this writing problem definition, it is your job to:

a. Write one sentence stating the main idea of your memo.
b. Draft your entire memo.
c. Underline all transitional words and phrases you have used to insure your memo's coherence.

Extended Application

Take the writing problem that you began in chapter 1 and analyzed after chapter 2. Now take your problem through the decision-making and drafting process. You will need to decide whether you have enough information to start drafting, and whether it is sufficiently detailed. Be certain to double-check your information's accuracy as well. Develop a one-sentence statement of your main point. Then prepare a complete first draft of your document.

CHAPTER 4

Revising and Editing

*T*his chapter introduces the last of the problem-solving steps—revising and editing. So far, we have considered how to define and analyze a writing problem and have examined how the kind of information we assemble and the main points we make combine to shape a rough draft. Throughout this discussion, we have noted that it is often necessary to return to earlier problem-solving steps to complete later ones.

During the revising and editing phases, you will make changes in your rough draft. **Revising** involves large-scale changes in your information and its placement. **Editing** is the smaller-scale changes that polish your revised draft for its intended audience. Editing changes include alterations not only to sentences and words but also to the physical appearance and packaging of your document.

In this chapter, our ongoing example will be that of a regional business machine retailer, The Business Machine Store. This company has five stores in two cities. Of these, one is in each of the cities' downtowns, two are in malls, and one is located in a suburban industrial park. The stores sell a wide range of items, including typewriters, calculators, photocopiers, paper shredders, ditto machines, and other paraphernalia for handling the paperwork of a business.

Preparing to Revise

The literal definition of *revise*, "to see again," describes accurately the first thing you need to do with your rough draft. *Reexamining* what you have written makes you realize how rough—even coarse—a first draft may be. You are returning to the rough draft to look at it through the reader's eyes. You want to know whether you have implemented the decisions you made before drafting, and if so, how well those decisions turned out.

Between completing the draft and returning to it, you may have time to clear your mind and then to question certain assumptions influencing the draft. Must the report be five paragraphs long? Should the memo to a superior be deferential in tone? Do you really want to use technical vocabulary in the progress report you are submitting to a client? For one reason or another, you may indeed find it necessary to do these things. Some time away from the draft, however, lets you reexamine your assumptions and make certain that they are things you *must* do rather than things you *think* you should.

Besides giving you a chance to question assumptions, a little time away from a rough draft can provide an opportunity for the incubation of new ideas. These ideas may take the form of details or examples that will improve the finished work.

At other times, a break between drafting and editing simply gives you a chance to reduce the mental and physical fatigue that accompanies the hard work of preparing a rough draft. With a refreshed perspective, you may be able to notice errors or words you wish to change that your tired eyes might have overlooked.

Whether you have the luxury of time off between the draft and revision or have to plow right on to meet a deadline, you must review some of that draft before starting its revision. First, you make a quick mental return to earlier steps to fix in your mind the audience, subject, and purpose of your work. Then, you are ready to start revising.

Asking Large-Scale Questions about the Draft

Start by asking large-scale questions about the draft—its specificity, main point, and arrangement:

1. Have you included the amount of detail required by your audience?
2. Have you stated your main point at a place in the draft where it will create the desired impact?
3. Does the overall progression of the document meet the needs of your audience?

Through answering these questions, you can double-check work you have already done and then make needed changes systematically.

As you begin to revise, you want to know whether your draft provides your audience with the amount and specificity of information you decided upon before drafting. For instance, does this letter drafted by The Business Machine Store's director of marketing to previous customers—most of whom are administrative assistants or purchasing agents for local companies—give its audience details that will be of interest to them in purchasing a copier?

Meeting Audience
Needs for Detail

Draft

November 5, 1986

Dear Valued Customer:

Because of your patronage in the past, we wanted you to be the first to know about the Morton 1900, the advanced copier now in stock at all five of our locations.

This device contains the latest in integrated circuitry. The glass on which originals are placed is of a special kind produced just for the 1900. Output bins are of industrial strength alloys.

Morton's testing program has proven the 1900 to work at temperatures of 150 degrees Fahrenheit and -25 degrees as well. This ruggedness is due, in part, to the insulation protecting the microchips that direct the machine's functions.

We're sure you'll agree that the Morton 1900 is a breakthrough in photocopying technology. Come in and see it in action at any of our locations.

Once again, our thanks for your continued confidence in The Business Machine Store.

Yours truly,

S. L. Vines
Director of Marketing

mj

It's hard to fault Vines for the tone of this letter. It is courteous and concise. Unfortunately, it does not provide much useful information for someone who wants to buy a photocopier. Although a person like Vines, who has seen hundreds of photocopiers come to market, might be intrigued by new advances in metallurgy and stress tests, it is unlikely that these facts will mean much to the people who need photocopiers every day or to those who may use them occasionally. To provide the detail his audience needs, Vines might reformulate the draft letter, retaining the cordial tone while introducing facts that will heighten customer interest:

Draft

November 7, 1986

Dear Customer:

We wanted you to be the first to know about the Morton 1900, the advanced photocopier now in stock at all five of our locations.

The Morton offers many features found only in copiers costing twice as much:

1. Automatic collating
2. Multicolor reproduction
3. Reduction and expansion of copies from originals
4. Automatic paper loading
5. Automatic paper size selection
6. Distortion-free copying of bound documents
7. "Set and forget" computer controls
8. Low maintenance costs

The 1900 has undergone some of the most extensive and grueling testing ever performed on a photocopier. In addition, it has met the rigid criteria of The Business Machine Store's purchasing staff for affordability, reliability, and ease of operation.

Our sales staff is ready to demonstrate the 1900 at your convenience, and our service staff has just completed a training course at the Morton headquarters.

We think you will find the 1900 an exciting addition to our photocopier line. Why not stop in this week to see it in action?

Once again, our thanks for your continued confidence in The Business Machine Store.

Yours truly,

S. L. Vines
Director of Marketing

mj

Vines's revised letter will more clearly meet the needs of his audience. He has stressed information of special interest to administrative assistants and purchasing agents, thereby increasing the chance that they will consider the Morton 1900 from The Business Machine Store when they plan to buy or price photocopiers.

Quite a different writing problem faces Charlene Culver, the store's customer service representative. She must confront the anger of a dissatisfied customer who has bought a calculator from The Business Machine Store. In a draft letter, she specifies the name of the service manager at each location:

Draft

August 28, 1986

Mr. Andrew Gray
66 Bogart Avenue
Ft. Thomas, KY 41075

Dear Mr. Gray:

We are sorry that you are having problems with a calculator purchased from our Industrial Park outlet.

Please bring your calculator to any of our five stores during business hours (9:00 A.M. to 5:00 P.M. Monday-Wednesday, 9:00 A.M. to 9:00 P.M. Thursday and Friday, 9:00 A.M. to 6:00 P.M. on Saturdays). At our Northern Mall location, ask for Steve; at the Southern Mall store, Ann; at the Industrial

Park store, Andy; at the downtown Centreville site, Carolyn; at the downtown Saylorton store, Jim.

Any of these service people will be pleased to correct any problem while you wait or loan you a calculator at no cost if additional service or parts are required.

Once again, our apologies for any inconvenience. We want you to know that The Business Machine Store stands behind every product it sells.

Yours truly,

Charlene Culver
Customer Service Representative

Reexamining her draft, Culver realizes that Gray is not going to be at all interested in the names of the service people. This annoyed customer wants only to know how to get the calculator repaired and some assurance that The Business Machine Store does care about its reputation. Consequently, Culver simplifies her letter in this revision:

Draft

August 28, 1986

Mr. Andrew Gray
66 Bogart Avenue
Ft. Thomas, KY 41075

Dear Mr. Gray:

We are sorry that you are having problems with a calculator purchased from our Industrial Park outlet.

Please bring your calculator to any of our five stores during business hours (9:00 A.M. to 5:00 P.M. Monday through Wednesday, 9:00 A.M. to 9:00 P.M. Thursday and Friday, 9:00 A.M. to 6:00 P.M. on Saturdays). Simply ask for the service manager.

Any of these managers will be pleased to correct any problem while you wait or loan you a calculator at no cost if additional service or parts are required.

We want you to know that The Business Machine Store stands behind every product it sells.

Yours truly,

Charlene Culver
Customer Service Representative

mz

Through her elimination of each service manager's name, Culver insures that her final document communicates *only* those things it needs to. When he receives the letter, Gray will know *what* to do (bring in the calculator), *where* to do it (at any of the five stores), *when* to do it (specified business hours), and *how* the repair will be accomplished (as quickly as possible and with another calculator loaned to Gray if necessary).

One of the decisions you make before drafting helps you to identify your document's main point. After writing, you double-check a draft to make certain that you have placed that main point where it will have its desired impact on your audience. To show how placing the same key idea at various places in a document can change the effect the document has on a reader, look at four versions of an introductory paragraph from a letter to a potential customer describing a new office intercom system:

Getting to the Point at the Right Time

1. *Immediate introduction of main point, creating a sense of urgency:*

   It's time you considered our new Plaza intercom systems. We can set you up with a complete five-station system, including main station, wall units, and FM-stereo tuner/speakers for use when voice communication is not desired. The price will be $2300 complete.

2. *Main point introduced after introductory sentence, creating a sense of limited cordiality:*

   We have appreciated your business in recent years. Here is a new intercom system that we feel will meet your company's needs at a reasonable price. This is a five-station system with main station, wall units, and FM-stereo tuner/speakers for times when voice communication is not desired. The price is $2300 complete.

3. *Main point introduced at end of opening paragraph, creating an openly cordial impression:*

> We have appreciated your business over the past several years. In particular, we hope that you are still as satisfied with the products received from The Business Machine Store as you were at the time of their purchase. We wished to notify you, as a preferred customer, about a new intercom system that we feel will meet your company's needs at a reasonable price.

4. *Main point not introduced during the opening paragraph, creating a relaxed impression:*

> We have appreciated your business over the past several years. In particular, we hope you are as happy with products received from The Business Machine Store now as you were at the time of purchase. It's always a pleasure to visit with you. Our sales and service staff receive such cordial treatment from your personnel. We're always on the lookout for something that might interest you.

Even this last version *might* be an appropriate opening paragraph for a company with whose representative The Business Machine Store's salesperson is on a very friendly basis.

By taking the time to look back to your audience definition and desired writer's image, you can make certain that what you finally emphasize in your document helps you attain your writing objective.

Overall Document Progression and Audience Needs

Chapter 3 discussed using your writing problem analysis to shape the progression of ideas as you draft. Now it is time to double-check that the existing order of ideas is still your desired arrangement. For example, in arranging information about an electronic typewriter, The Business Machine Store's general manager employs a particular order in her memo to the salespeople who will be demonstrating the machine to the public:

Draft

Date: October 19, 1986

To: All Salespeople

From: Janet Klein, General Manager

Subject: Crest 20 Electronic Typewriter

When you introduce the Crest 20 to customers, deal with its features in the order that will impress them most: speed, display, memory, price, and technical specifications.

Most customers will be considering the purchase of an electronic typewriter because of its speed. The Crest 20 prints at a rate of 20 characters a second. This speed makes it possible to print a single-spaced, one-page business letter in approximately three minutes.

The Crest 20 has an 18-character display. This feature lets a typist make corrections in words even before they can be stored in the machine's memory.

The Crest 20's standard memory is 8,000 characters--enough for any single typed page. Optional expansion cartridges allow the customer to increase this memory to 64,000 characters. In addition, the typewriter comes with a port that allows for connection of a disk drive to add unlimited storage on flexible diskettes.

At $579, the Crest 20 is highly competitive with similar electronic typewriters. Indeed, it retails for $200 less than any other comparable machine we sell.

Remember to give customers who appear interested in the Crest 20's technical specifications the one-page flier provided to us by the manufacturer. Refer all technical questions you cannot answer to your branch's service manager.

ml

As you can see, Klein's memo to salespeople moves from what the general manager thinks will be the most important topics to customers to the least important:

1. Speed of the typewriter
2. Display
3. Memory
4. Price
5. Technical specifications

Klein varies this order for a different audience. Even though she presents the same information in her memo to branch service managers that she does in her memo to salespeople, her reordering of that information shows her sensitivity to the needs of a different audience:

Draft

Date: October 19, 1986

To: Branch Service Managers

From: Janet Klein, General Manager

Subject: Crest 20 Electronic Typewriter

Now that the Crest 20s have arrived at all our branches, please take some time to acquaint yourself with this new machine.

Be certain to examine the technical manuals supplied by the manufacturer. I have instructed salespeople to refer all technical questions they cannot answer to you.

Pay particularly close attention to manual sections dealing with memory, display, and printing speed. I will mention general features briefly here so that you can see where the Crest 20 fits into our product line. This data should also alert you to the types of questions you may expect from customers.

The Crest 20's standard memory is 8,000 characters. Optional expansion cartridges allow the customer to increase this memory to 64,000 characters. In addition, the typewriter comes with a port that allows for connection of a disk drive to add unlimited storage on flexible diskettes. The Crest 20 also has a standard 18-character display and prints 20 characters a second.

We will be selling the Crest 20 for $579. At this price, we expect a high sales volume. If you feel you need more information than the manufacturer's manuals provide, please let me know immediately.

mz

In the memo to service managers, Klein uses the same categories in writing to salespeople, but she rearranges them in this order:

1. Technical specifications
2. Memory
3. Display
4. Speed of the typewriter
5. Price

In so doing, she emphasizes the importance of technical specifications for her audience and shows how the remaining categories relate to the service managers' role in marketing the new typewriter. By taking the time to double-check the organizational decisions that she made before writing a draft, Klein uses her revising time efficiently to reach two audiences with the same information.

Making Large-Scale Revisions

We have discussed the sorts of revision questions to ask about the rough draft. We have also provided examples of how business writers might answer those questions in specific situations. Now, let us suggest some techniques that can help you make revisions efficiently.

When we speak of **cutting and pasting**, we mean an actual restructuring of a document using scissors and tape. Suppose you had drafted the following three-paragraph summary of reasons for trading in an electric typewriter for an electronic typewriter and were going to use it as part of a letter to former customers:

Cutting and Pasting

Draft

Electronic typewriters allow you to store documents in a memory device for repeated use. Imagine! No more retyping of that form letter you send to clients every six months. No more wasted effort as you laboriously type address labels from a list. What's more, corrections are as simple as touching a button.

Are you or your secretaries sick and tired of typing the same letters and mailing labels over and over and over? Do you grit your teeth and "do it all over again" when you discover a typo that requires changing a whole line? Or do you get out the correction fluid, knowing all the while that using it may be easier than retyping the entire page but the results will hardly project the professional image you want?

The answers to your dilemmas are here, now, at The Business Machine Store. We have a complete line of competitively priced electronic typewriters for every size operation, with all the features you want most, and from all prominent manufacturers. What's more, our trained, courteous sales personnel will be happy to take the time to show you and your staff how to operate these reliable, efficient machines. In no time, you will be producing error-free documents and reproducing those letters and other texts you use frequently--all as easy as inserting a piece of paper and pushing a button. Call The Business Machine Store today or just stop by. Remember, we value your patronage. Our satisfied customers are our best advertising.

You look at the draft and realize that the second paragraph with its questions about the needs that an electronic typewriter can meet would actually work best as the first of the three paragraphs. Conversely, the information provided in the first paragraph would answer those same questions very nicely. The simple solution is for you to take your scissors, cut out the second paragraph, and tape it above the first paragraph. The resulting paragraph arrangement would be:

Draft

Are you or your secretaries sick and tired of typing the same letters and address labels over and over and over? Do you grit your teeth and "do it all over again" when you discover a typo that requires changing a whole line? Or do you get out the correction fluid, knowing all the while that using it may be easier than retyping the entire page, but the results will hardly project the professional image you want?

Electronic typewriters allow you to store documents in a memory device for repeated use. Imagine! No more retyping of that form letter you send to clients every six months. No more wasted effort as you laboriously type address labels from a list. What's more, corrections are as simple as touching a button.

The answers to your dilemmas are here, now, at The Business Machine Store. We have a complete line of competitively priced electronic typewriters for every size operation, with all the features you want most, and from all prominent manufacturers. What's more, our trained, courteous sales personnel will be happy to take the time to show you and your staff how to operate these reliable, efficient machines. In no time, you will be producing error-free documents and reproducing those letters and other texts you use frequently--all as easy as inserting a piece of paper and pushing a button. Call The Business Machine Store today or just stop by. Remember, we value your patronage. Our satisfied customers are our best advertising.

Don't be afraid to get out the scissors! The end product may be much the better for it.

Inserting Information

If you follow the problem-solving steps recommended in this text, you will more often than not find yourself doing most of your revisions by restructuring your draft and cutting out excess material. There are times, however, when it is necessary to *add* data to clarify meaning. Often, the key to finding parts of a document that need more information is to note words that are vague, for example, *great, much, really, things*. Use of such words may indicate that you need additional specific information to insert into the document. In this way, you provide your reader with more useful data than by simply stating "there's really great stuff in this document."

The following draft memo from the company president to branch-store managers requires specific data to make it the forceful document it should be:

Draft

Date: November 21, 1986

To: Branch Managers

From: Arlene Johnson, President

Subject: Strategy Meeting of November 20, 1986

Having reflected upon yesterday's strategy meeting, I am pleased that we accomplished much. It was great to know that you are as pleased as I about adding to our inventory a line of cordless telephones designed specifically for office use.

I am also pleased that there was so much support for shifting sales staff from our downtown locations to our mall locations during the upcoming holiday season. This shift will enable us to reach customers who will be seeking the sort of things we sell for home use.

Our agenda for next week's meeting is really packed with many things. Be prepared for a lengthy meeting.

The revised memo concentrates on inserting specific information where vague words originally appeared:

Draft

Date: November 21, 1986

To: Branch Managers

From: Arlene Johnson, President

Subject: Strategy Meeting of November 20, 1986

Having reflected upon yesterday's strategy meeting, I am pleased that we accomplished both the objectives listed on our agenda.

The consensus in favor of adding a line of cordless telephones to our inventory indicates to me that the branches and central administration of our company agree on product diversification.

I am also pleased that there was unanimous support for shifting one salesperson from each of our downtown locations to each of our mall locations during the upcoming holiday season. Doing so will enable us to reach consumers seeking items traditionally associated with office use (photocopiers, calculators, electronic typewriters) as gifts for home use.

Our agenda for next week's meeting contains three items:

1. Plans for taking end-of-year inventory
2. Discussion of sales promotions for February
3. Consideration of personnel deployment so service managers can attend much-needed training seminars on cordless telephones and on new electronic typewriter models we will be introducing in April

Be prepared for a lengthy meeting. We will begin promptly at 2 P.M., next Tuesday, November 27.

The revisions above add specificity by adding details at points containing a single, vague word.

Sometimes, however, as you reflect upon your work, you discover the need to add more than a single sentence. When you add one or more paragraphs, take care to merge the new information smoothly with the original content. This merging requires the use of such devices as (1) transitional words (for example, *furthermore, also, moreover*) and (2) transitional phrases (for example, *in addition, on the contrary, as a result*). Should the previous memo require an additional paragraph reminding branch managers to be particularly solicitous of customers during the holiday season, you might insert it in this way:

Original paragraph

I am also pleased that there was unanimous support for shifting one salesperson from each of our downtown locations to each of our mall locations during the upcoming holiday season. Doing so will enable us to reach consumers seeking items traditionally associated with office use (photocopiers, calculators, electronic typewriters) as gifts for home use.

Newly inserted paragraph immediately following original

On the subject of the holiday season, let me ask you to remind your branch personnel to be particularly solicitous of customer needs. The holidays can be times of stress for all of us, and our customers require our particular attention and courtesy during this time.

The "glue" binding the new paragraph to the previous one is the phrases *on the subject* and *of the holiday season*. Through revision this memo has become more detailed due to the added paragraphs as well as the added words, phrases, and sentences within the memo's original paragraphs.

Creating a Fresh Copy

If you are making revisions using a typewriter, pen, and/or pencil, there comes a time when the revised draft becomes a mess. With cutting, pasting, crossing out, and inserting, the draft may become so messy that it is impossible to read and get a proper sense of its overall impact. At this point, a newly written or typed copy can assist you in taking either a last look at the document before preparation of a final copy or deciding on further revisions. Figure 4.1 shows the "worked over" draft of a brief sales proposal. Compare the messy draft in figure 4.1 with the freshly typed copy in figure 4.2. Can you sense the difference in understanding between this final copy and the messy draft preceding it?

Concluding Large-Scale Revisions

When does large-scale revision stop and editing begin? When you are satisfied with the quality of what you have said and when the logistics of deadlines, expenses, and the relative importance of the writing task indicate, it is time to start polishing the draft into its final form. This polishing occurs during **editing**. As with every phase of rhetorical problem solving, you may need to return to a previous step—in this case large-scale revision—even during the final editing procedure. Once the editing phase begins, however, you now focus on the specific aspects of writing that will tell the reader, "This is a well-crafted document."

December 1, 1986

Mr. Tom Eichel
Purchasing Manager
James Media Associates
511 Elm Street
Covington, Kentucky 41011

Dear Mr. Eichel:

~~Thanks so much~~ *Thank you* for the opportunity to demonstrate our line

of electronic typewriters to you and your staff. We are pleased to

be able to make you this proposal for your purchase of 25 ~~of the~~

Crest 15's, our best-selling office model. With the price ~~we quote~~ *quoted below,*

you will be able to save ~~a great deal~~ *23 percent* off ~~both~~ list price and *7 percent off* the

nearest written quotation you showed us, ~~from any of our~~

~~competitors.~~

Once again, ~~be assured~~ *rest* ~~Remember, as well~~, that The Business Machine Store is ready

to service everything we sell and that your office is strategically
within ~~fifteen~~ *15 minutes of our industrial park and*
located ~~to two of our branches.~~ *Southern Mall branches. Our service managers at all our branches are specially trained to work on Crest 15's and we carry a complete inventory of replacement parts.*

The ~~aggregate~~ *combined* price for all ~~twenty-five~~ *25* machines would be

$22,400, plus state sales tax. This includes the machines, dust

---

Figure 4.1   Draft with handwritten large-scale revisions. Brief sales proposal.

covers, six-month warranty, and installation. We also are offering

you a full parts and service contract for all the machines at the

price of $2,000 for one year, beginning on the day after the

Either the cash basis or the 12-month credit arrangement (1 percent per month interest charges) we discussed at our meeting yesterday

original warranty expires and renewable on a yearly basis. ~~discussed at our meeting yesterday~~

insert A

we agreed,

As ~~per our agreement,~~ I will meet with you at your office on *would be acceptable.*

Thursday, December 6, at 10:30 A.M.

We look forward to adding you to our family of satisfied

corporate customers. *If there is any additional information I can provide between now and next Thursday, please contact me.*

Yours truly,

Kevin DiFillipo
Sales Representative

ps

THE BUSINESS MACHINE STORE
1000 Southern Avenue
Florence, Kentucky 41042

December 1, 1986

Mr. Tom Eichel
Purchasing Manager
James Media Associates
511 Elm Street
Covington, Kentucky 41011

Dear Mr. Eichel:

Thank you for the opportunity to demonstrate our line of electronic typewriters to you and your staff. We are pleased to be able to make you this proposal for your purchase of 25 Crest 15's, our best-selling office model. With the price quoted below, you will be able to save 23 percent off list price and 7 percent off the nearest written quotation you showed us.

The combined price for all 25 machines would be $22,400, plus state sales tax. This figure includes the machines, dust covers, six-month warranty, and installation. We also are offering you a full parts and service contract for all the machines at the price of $2,000 for one year, beginning on the day after the original warranty expires and renewable on a yearly basis. Either the cash payment basis or the 12-month credit arrangement (1 percent per month interest charges) we discussed at our meeting yesterday would be acceptable.

Once again, rest assured that The Business Machine Store is ready to service everything we sell and that your office is strategically located within 15 minutes of both our industrial park and Southern Mall branches. The service managers at all our branches are specially trained to work on Crest 15's, and we carry a complete inventory of replacement parts.

Figure 4.2   Freshly typed draft. Brief sales proposal.

As we agreed, I will meet with you at your office on Thursday, December 6, at 10:30 A.M.

We look forward to adding you to our family of satisfied corporate customers. If there is any additional information I can provide between now and next Thursday, please contact me.

Yours truly,

Kevin DiFillipo

Kevin DiFillipo
Sales Representative

ps

Smaller-Scale Editing Changes—Asking Questions about Particular Parts of a Document

There are certain questions that you should ask yourself as you work from a revised draft toward a finished document.

Does the Introductory Material Provide Appropriate Amenities?

Different cultures place different values on "getting to the point." In northern European societies, for example, stating one's business immediately is viewed in a positive light. In Latin American cultures, on the other hand, beginning a meeting with a discussion of crucial business matters may be viewed as overanxious or even rude. In the United States and Canada, a fine balance exists between making pleasantries and "getting down to business."

The same sense of timing applies to written documents. We will discuss ways of beginning specific business writing formats in the chapters on memos, letters, proposals, feasibility studies, and formal reports. Before we get to those chapters, it is useful to consider how readers react to various ways of beginning a piece of writing. For example, will a business client respond more positively to a letter in which the first two sentences are "I hope you're digging out of those 12 inches of snow you folks had Tuesday. As we discussed during our meeting, the plans for your campaign will be ready on January 29"? Or will the client prefer "Your campaign will be ready on January 29. The art department assures me that all materials will be completed by that date"?

Will your coworker in a distant branch office appreciate and be more receptive to a memo that begins by asking after her family's health? Might your superior in the office down the hall find the same sort of inquiry coming before your memo's substance to be an overfamiliar, time-wasting way to start a document? Are your relations with the reader sufficiently cordial so that you may use his or her first name? Or should you use Mr. or Ms.? A proper balance of respect and courtesy will make the reader more amenable to what you have to say.

Are Logical Connections between Ideas Present yet Unobtrusive?

In the discussion of drafting in chapter 3, we spoke about the importance of arranging ideas logically. We showed how including transitional words and phrases in your draft can make your organization of ideas apparent to your audience.

The editing stage is a time to *look back* at your draft to see whether you have arranged your ideas logically and reinforced your arrangement by using transitions. You may find that looking first at transitional words and then at transitional phrases speeds your editing. When we speak of transitional words, we are thinking of adverbs, such as:

Word	*Sample Logical Purpose*
accordingly	reinforces logical relationships
besides	shows additive relationship
consequently	underscores causal connection
finally	announces the last in a series of items or ideas
furthermore	reinforces previous data with new data
however	subordinates the importance of previous data
indeed	reinforces the accuracy or importance of previous data
likewise	shows parallel relationship
moreover	adds to previously stated data
nevertheless	subordinates the importance of previous data
therefore	shows causal relationship between previous and new data

Demonstrative pronouns may also be noted, such as *this, that, these,* and *those.* Such pronouns may function as adjectives in sentences to reinforce references to previously stated data—for example, "The Ultra Paper Shredder destroys documents quickly and quietly. *This* shredder is state-of-the-art technology applied to a business setting."

Transitional phrases include such phrases as the following:

Phrase	*Sample Logical Function*
as a result	shows a causal relationship between new and previously stated information
for example, for instance	signal a specific detail to support a previously stated generalization
in conclusion	signals the introduction of a closing paragraph or sentence
in the first place	indicates the beginning of a series of logical arguments
in the meantime	shows an event contemporary with one previously stated

What relationship do these words and phrases have to editing? They can be added during the editing phase to help strengthen the logic of a draft. For example, take the text of a memo on inventory at The Business Machine Store's branches:

Draft

Date: January 20, 1986

To: Branch Managers

From: Janet Klein, General Manager

Subject: Inventory

Based on recent sales figures and projections, our mall branches should be considering increased inventory of lower-priced goods. Good quality machines for personal use are one possibility. A large selection of brands would be appropriate.

At the downtown and industrial park locations, we should stock larger, top-of-the-line items. Carry only two or three major brand names. Think about housing all our repair services at these locations.

With a few additions, the writer can tighten the logic of the memo:

Draft

Date: January 20, 1986

To: Branch Managers

From: Janet Klein, General Manager

Subject: Inventory

Based on recent sales figures and projections, our mall stores should be considering increased inventory of lower-priced goods. <u>This</u> new inventory might take the form of good quality merchandise priced for personal users. <u>Moreover</u>, we should offer a large selection of brands as appropriate.

<u>On the other hand</u>, at the downtown and industrial park locations, we should stock only top-of-the-line items. <u>This</u> restriction will mean carrying only two or three major brand names. <u>Before our next managers' meeting</u>, think about housing all our repair services at these locations.

mz

The five additions to this memo accomplish the following:

1. *This* (in the first paragraph) emphasizes the message about increased inventory and connects it with the need to consider personal users of business equipment.
2. *Moreover* shows that information is pertinent and will add to details specified in the previous sentence.
3. *On the other hand* shows readers that the general manager wants branch managers to think of inventory as a contrast of strategies between mall stores and downtown or industrial park branches.
4. *This* (in the second paragraph) emphasizes the message about limiting inventory and connects it with the need to consider the preferences of business users for several major brands.
5. *Before our next managers' meeting* sets a time limit to the thinking that the branch managers should be doing about this topic.

The result of editing in connecting words and phrases is more cohesive writing. The memo writer in this case has emphasized crucial relationships among ideas in the document. Thus the reader not only receives data but is prompted to think about that data in ways favored by the writer.

Wordiness and unnecessary repetition of ideas make reading more difficult, so cross out unnecessary words. Sometimes you can replace phrases with single words:

Are Individual
Sentences Concise?

Instead of	*Use*
at this point in time	now
by and large	mainly
by virtue of the fact that	since.
for all intents and purposes	essentially
for the reason that	because
in a great many instances	often
in the event that	if
in the final analysis	finally
on account of the fact that	because

Sometimes the phrases can be deleted altogether, and the remaining words will communicate meaning clearly. Once in a while you may decide to leave some phrases in because they add just the right touch of emphasis to a document. The following draft of a complaint letter from the service department manager and president of The Business Machine Store to a supplier benefits from eliminating, changing, and even leaving in certain phrases:

Draft

November 12, 1986

Ms. J. M. Snider, Business Relations
AZC Photocopier Corporation
1234 Industrial Drive
Cow Neck, NY 11050

Dear Ms. Snider:

By virtue of the fact that our service department has received 12 complaints in the last month about your AZC 1500 copier, which we retail through our stores, I am writing to underscore the complaints of our customers and to ask satisfaction in the form of an improved product, replacement of defective merchandise, and free on-site parts and repair by your corporate personnel for copiers bought through our stores.

Until such time as you see fit to comply with these requests, we will be forced to recommend that our customers not purchase AZC products because of the 1500's problems with jammed paper feeds, overheating, and erratic warning light operation.

In the event that you cannot satisfy us or our customers between now and December 15, 1986, we will be forced to discontinue our line of AZC products.

In the final analysis, we do not wish to sever our relationship with your company. However, we are unable to continue to offer our customers anything less than the best possible office equipment we can stock.

Yours truly,

James Rivera, Service Manager
Arlene Johnson, President

By considering whether to replace certain phrases with single words or to leave them as they are, it is possible to create a more efficient, businesslike letter:

Draft

November 13, 1986

Ms. J. M. Snider, Business Relations
AZC Photocopier Corporation
1234 Industrial Drive
Cow Neck, NY 11050

Dear Ms. Snider:

Because our service department has received 12 complaints in the last month about your AZC 1500 copier, which we retail, I am writing to underscore the complaints of our customers. We wish you to provide satisfaction in the form of an improved product, replacement of defective merchandise, and free on-site parts and repair for copiers bought through our stores.

Until you meet these requirements, we will recommend that our customers not purchase AZC products because of the 1500's problems with jammed paper feeds, overheating, and erratic warning light operation.

If you cannot satisfy us or our customers between now and December 15, 1986, we will be forced to discontinue our line of AZC products.

We do not wish to sever our relationship with your company. However, we are unable to continue to offer our customers anything less than the best possible office equipment we can stock.

Yours truly,

James Rivera, Service Manager
Arlene Johnson, President

rl

Be concise, but do not sacrifice clarity for brevity. You may compose only short sentences, not realizing that conciseness also requires that writing be clear. Sometimes very short sentences may not be clear, for example, "It didn't." Such sentences require at least a few more words to communicate a complete idea, for example, "The calculator didn't work properly."

Other sentences may be too long and require cutting, for example, "The calculator, a programmable model, never did work properly from the first day it was purchased." Pare such sentences by deleting excess words; the revised sentence reads, "The programmable calculator never worked properly."

Is Subordination Used to Vary Sentence Length?

Just as being concise is necessary for focusing your reader's attention on only the information you want to communicate, varying the length of your sentences is helpful in maintaining reader interest and the momentum from one idea to another.

If you are particularly concerned about being concise, you may also tend to compose many consecutive short sentences. Such sentences may seem choppy to your reader. To combine several short sentences into a single, more fluent one, choose one of your short sentences as your base. Then use subordinate elements—for example, relative pronouns (*who, which, that*) or subordinating conjunctions (*although, as, because, since, when*)—to connect the information in your other short sentences to your base sentence:

Choppy:	The training seminar is for day-shift personnel. It will be on Thursday. It will be repeated for late-shift personnel on Saturday.
Better:	The training seminar *that is* for day-shift personnel on Thursday will be repeated for late-shift personnel on Saturday.
Choppy:	We advertised on television. Television advertisement increased our sales 15 percent. This is very good news for our cash flow.
Better:	Because of our television advertising, sales have shown a 15 percent increase, which is very good news for our cash flow.

Remember that the goal of subordination is to *vary* the length of your sentences. If you use too many consecutively subordinated sentences, you may have to "decombine" some long sentences to achieve variety. Don't be afraid to keep editing your writing until you are satisfied that it flows as smoothly as possible.

Is There Parallelism within Sentences?

When two or more elements in a sentence have the same grammatical form and function, they are parallel. Parallel sentence elements can help you to inform and persuade your reader. They help to *inform* because your reader can understand logical relationships between elements in a sentence more easily when those elements are parallel. They help to *persuade* because parallel elements create a regular rhythm in a sentence that assists in reinforcing an argument or point of view. Conversely, elements that are not parallel may confuse your readers by interrupting the smooth rhythm of their reading or forcing them to search for logical connections between ideas that should be evident or implicit.

Here are three pairs of sentences. In each pair, one sentence exhibits parallel structure, the other, nonparallel structure:

- *Parallel:* "Remote pagers, cordless phones, and portable calculators typify today's mobile executive." Each of the subjects in this compound subject consists of a noun modified by a single adjective.

- *Nonparallel:* "Remote pagers, cordless phones, and carrying other light-weight equipment typify today's mobile executive." The first two subjects in this compound subject are nouns modified by single adjectives, but the third subject is a gerund phrase.

- *Parallel*: "We want to know if a product will appeal to the public and if it will comply with federal regulations." The objects of the infinitive *to know* are both subordinate clauses.

- *Nonparallel:* "We want to know if a product will appeal to the public and about compliance with federal regulations." The first object of the infinitive is a subordinate clause, but the second is a prepositional phrase.

- *Parallel:* "We decided to (1) review all the pertinent information about faxing, (2) compare various models of fax machines, and (3) lease one for a year." Numerical coordinators, (1), (2), and (3) join infinitive phrases.

- *Nonparallel:* "We decided to (1) review all the pertinent information about faxing, (2) compare various models of fax machines, and to (3) lease one for a year." The repeated infinitive marker *to* breaks the sentence's rhythm because *to* was not also repeated before the numerical coordinator (2).

By making small-scale editing changes that turn disconcerting nonparallel structures into smoother parallel ones, you can improve your chances of meeting your writing objective—to inform or to persuade a reader.

In chapter 1, we discussed suiting wording to your reader and noted that you may want to use comparatively simple wording for less educated readers but more technical or complex vocabulary for intelligent, educated readers. However, if you string together too many long words into "gobbledygook," even your most educated readers will become confused. What's

Is Wording Free of Gobbledygook?

worse, they may come to dislike you because of what they see as a self-important tone in your writing. The result will be that you fail to inform *and* fail to persuade.

Small-scale editing is the time to make certain you have not used long words where shorter ones will do. Check these places where gobbledygook *may* lurk:

- *Very long words (of four or more syllables).* Do you really need to write "We must replace our *antiquated* adding machines with desk-top calculators"? Or will "We must replace our *old* adding machines with desk-top calculators" make your point without making you seem stuffy to the supervisor you are trying to convince to buy the calculators?

- *Words that sound learned or scholarly.* Writing "Please *eschew* expensive hotels on your next sales trip" may waste your salespersons' time by sending them to a dictionary to figure out that you mean salespeople should stay in less expensive hotels. In addition to confusing your readers, inappropriately used scholarly words may cost you readers' goodwill. Who likes a writer who tries to make himself or herself sound better than the reader?

- *Technical jargon used out of proper context.* Writing to your subordinates "Let's *interface* tomorrow at 3:00 P.M. in the conference room" will not only create the undesirable impression that you think you're a "slick, high-tech operator" but will also suggest to your subordinates that you don't know much about computers (since only computers and related machines can *be* "interfaced" so that they can share information). Once again, write what you mean ("Let's *meet* tomorrow . . ."), not what you think sounds modern.

- *Confusing noun compounds.* A store selling business machines is not an "automation-technology emporium." A discount is not a "price-reduction opportunity." A salary is not a "period compensation disbursement." Your reader will know that you are trying to make your subject and yourself seem important. You and your subject will both fail to impress the reader. Instead, your reader will consider you stuffy and your topic confusing, boring, or both.

- *Nouns that have become verbs by addition of the suffix* -ize. There are almost always simpler ways to say such words. Compare, for instance, these two sentences from a memo proposing a method of faster typewriter repair:

  1. "I can *conceptualize* a way to speed up our typewriter repair service without sacrificing quality. If we *prioritize* our work from the most complicated to the least complicated repair jobs, we can *finalize* work more quickly."

  2. "I *know* a way to speed up our typewriter repair service without sacrificing quality. If we *order* our work from the most complicated to

the least complicated repair jobs, we can *finish* more quickly." The simpler verbs *know, order,* and *finish* communicate more clearly that the writer has a specific method, not a vague, pompous sounding concept, for speeding up service.

Changing unnecessarily long words, inappropriately used scholarly terms, out-of-context technical jargon, confusing noun compounds, and unclear *-ize* verbs to their "plain English" equivalents does require you to spend some time looking carefully at individual words you have drafted. However, the confusion you save your readers and the goodwill you save yourself make this editing effort worthwhile.

As you edit your draft to make certain its words communicate information clearly, also check to see if your words convey your intended attitudes accurately and productively. For instance, when you refer to your salespeople as "sales representatives," you show that you think of them positively as professional business people who carry the image, goods, and services of your company to the public. But when you call your competitor's sales force "hucksters," you show that you think of them negatively as pushy, disreputable people who would do anything to close a sale.

Does Your Wording Show Concern for the Power of Connotation?

The attitudes your words convey are their **connotations**. Not only can the connotations of your words reveal your attitudes about your subject but they can also arouse emotions in your readers. Doing so may be useful when you are writing to persuade but may get in the way of your attempts to inform. Consider, for example, these three sentences:

- *Positive connotation: Prestigious* business machine stores mark up merchandise 200 percent over wholesale cost.

- *Negative connotation: Ripoff* business machine stores mark up merchandise 200 percent over wholesale cost.

- *Neutral connotation: Some* business machine stores mark up merchandise 200 percent over wholesale cost.

Even though these sentences differ by only one word, each conveys a completely different attitude about the same kind of store. Whereas a retailer might be flattered to have his or her store called "prestigious," the same retailer will probably be angry to be thought of as the proprietor of a "ripoff." When you are trying to *inform* your reader, use a word with more neutral connotations. *Some* doesn't tell how you feel about the stores in question; it simply states the fact that there is more than one store that has a 200 percent markup. Even when you are trying to *persuade* your reader, consider the potential effect of connotation before you use a word.

Here is a short list of pairs of words that might be choices for editing your draft:

More Positive Connotation	*More Negative Connotation*
tax shelter	tax-avoidance scheme
tough competitor	ruthless competitor
union official	union boss
established firm	long-running operation
past due account	deadbeat

Using the words on the left would communicate a more positive attitude about your subject than using the words on the right. For instance, you believe a person with a "past due account" will eventually pay the bill, but you know a "deadbeat" will try to escape payment.

When you use words with strong connotations, either positive or negative, you will arouse your reader more than if you use neutral vocabulary. If you do choose strongly connotative words, be certain to use them judiciously. Even the most positive or negative words can lose their power when overused. When in doubt, stay with a neutral word.

Does Wording Follow Guidelines for Nonsexist Language?

Business people show increasing sensitivity to language that reinforces biases about sex roles. Editing is a time to make certain that you employ **nonsexist** wording. Two particular dilemmas face business writers in their efforts to avoid sexist language: the use of singular pronouns to refer to a person in a particular job or professional category, and the use of words with sexist connotations.

Use of Singular Pronouns   While revising a draft, you might find yourself reading a sentence such as, "When an engineer arrives at a job site, he should use interpretive note taking to analyze the situation." Reference to *engineer* as *he* reinforces the stereotype that engineers *are* men. To avoid such stereotyping, you would have several options:

- *The use of two singular pronouns:* "When an engineer arrives at the job site, *he or she* should use interpretive note taking to analyze the situation." This technique *is* effective. Its critics point out that the double pronoun creates awkward, hard-to-process sentences. However, *he or she, she or he, she/he,* and *he/she* alert readers that you *are* sensitive to the power of language in shaping thought and *are* willing to write so as to eliminate bias.

- *A switch to plural antecedents:* "When engineers arrive at the job site, *they* should use interpretive note taking to analyze the situation." This switch is appropriate when the plural does not change the meaning of the sentence. Thus, if you mean "any engineer," switching to the plural is acceptable. When you mean the arrival of *one* engineer, then saying *engineers* will not do.

■ *A change of wording to avoid the dilemma entirely:* "An engineer arriving at the job site should use interpretive note taking to analyze the situation." You may work out pronoun reference problems in this way sometimes, but not always. The key is to use whichever technique will create a nonsexist document without changing your meaning.

Use of Words with Sexist Connotations   Certain words carry connotations that imply exclusion or are demeaning to people in business settings because of their sex. Correction simply means changing such usages to their gender-neutral alternatives:

Instead of	*Use*
salesman	salesperson
manpower	personnel
lady accountant	accountant
female lawyer	lawyer
woman executive	executive
office girls	secretaries, administrative assistants, or other job titles

Editing is a chance to double-check the accuracy of your wording. For example, have you selected the correct one of a confusing word pair, as in *effect* or *affect, principle* or *principal, stationary* or *stationery?*

Are Wording and Sentence Structure Accurate?

Editing also means examining a document to make certain it follows certain conventions of English usage. We will simply point out items that frequently need checking, leaving examples for the Handbook at the end of the book and detailed explanations for a usage textbook.

Editing Checklist for Grammatical Conventions

Question	*Frequent Problems*
Are all sentences actual sentences?	Run-ons and fragments
Are noun and pronoun cases correct?	Pronoun case and number
Are verbs used correctly?	Agreement and verb tense
Are adjectives used accurately?	Comparative and superlative
Are adverbs used properly?	Modification of verbs, adjectives, adverbs
Are punctuation marks used properly?	Paired marks—parentheses, brackets, quotation marks; comma splices

Are capitals used properly?   Proper nouns, state name
                                         abbreviations, personal titles

Is spelling accurate?   Words of which you
                                         are uncertain

Document Preparation

Once the revised draft has been checked for grammatical conventions, you have reached the point where you can prepare the final version of the document. The revision and editing process may have taken you days, hours, or even just a few minutes. Because the problem-solving approach is flexible, you can speed up or slow down the operations detailed previously to meet the needs of particular document length and the pressures of deadlines.

At the point of document preparation, you can make more choices.

What Sorts of Materials Should You Use?

Company letterhead stationery is usually appropriate for outgoing letters. Interoffice memo forms are correct for correspondence within the company. Multicopy forms are sometimes used to speed messages to several readers. In every instance, the paper stock, if you have a choice, should be the best quality possible, preferably bond, and definitely not erasable stock, which smudges very easily.

Typefaces should be consistent (all pica or all elite, all 10 characters per inch or all 12 characters per inch, all uppercase and lowercase fonts, very rarely all capital letters or script fonts). Carbon typewriter ribbons, as opposed to fabric ones, produce crisp, professional-looking copy. The following correction systems are listed in order from most to least acceptable:

- Electronic text editing systems
- Lift-off tapes that remove single characters
- Liquid correction fluid
- Correction sheets that cover up single characters

If handwriting is necessary—for example, in an interoffice memo—it should be neat, with consistently formed letters. In all cases, make certain that handwriting is absolutely necessary. If you are in doubt, type!

What Physical Traits Should the Finished Text Possess?

Margins should be ample all around the edge of a document (at least one inch at top, bottom, left, and right sides). If a report requires binding, allow at least an additional half-inch on the left or top margin, depending on where the binding will go.

Spacing and centering conventions vary depending on the kind of writing. In general, however, double-space between lines in reports; single-space in letters and memos with double spaces between paragraphs. Center and capitalize main headings. Allow three spaces above and below these main headings.

Number pages consecutively, but do not place the number 1 on the first page. Keep the location of the page number consistent, whether at the top center, top right, or bottom center of the page.

The first and most crucial thing to do is to proofread the document. To avoid overlooking any errors, we recommend the following procedure. First, read the document from beginning to end to make certain it makes sense, that there are no words missing, that there are no unwanted repetitions of words, and that you have picked up spelling or typing errors. Second, read the document word by word from the end of the text to the beginning. This back-to-front reading lets you focus on the spelling of individual words. The meaning of the document cannot distract or lull you into thinking that what is actually incorrect is right. Reading backward helps you to pick up typographical errors that appear much like correctly spelled words. If the document is exceptionally important, let a trusted colleague check what you have written. Someone who is unfamiliar with the text will catch errors that you may miss.

What Should You Do When the Document Is Completed?

Finally, give that important document your own last look. Remember, every document is the writer's responsibility—even if it was ghostwritten! Follow the document as far as possible to its drop-off point. If it is going out of the company, double-check the address and the spelling of the recipient's name, company, street, and city. Also check the street number and zip code. Use the nine-digit zip code where applicable. This new system allows the postal service to use optical character scanners that can speed the delivery of your document.

Make certain that envelopes contain return addresses and that you follow your company's proper mailing procedure. Know both your drop points and your company's procedures for overnight mail service when you need fast delivery.

Follow up to make certain your reader has received the document, where such follow-up is appropriate and will not be seen as pushy. Sending documents "return receipt requested" lets your recipient know you think what you have written is important and assures you that a crucial document has arrived safely. If no answer comes to your letter or report, a letter or telephone call requesting verification of receipt is acceptable in most cases.

Adjusting Editing to Deadlines and Document Length

The length of a document and the time available between its drafting and transmittal will affect the way you edit. For example, longer documents will require attention to each of the large- and small-scale editing tasks discussed in this chapter. With practice, however, you can handle different tasks at once. There is no particular reason that you cannot cross out and insert new material, for instance, during a single rereading of a report. One reading may also be enough to note the adequacy of introductory, connecting, and concluding material as well as to check for sentence variety and nonsexist language.

Drafts of short documents, such as brief letters, may require only brief readings and revision before they reach the final copy preparation stage. Usually, a deadline will dictate how much time you can spend on editing. If there is no time for anything else, *at least* be sure you are saying what you mean to say and that your message follows acceptable usage, wording, spelling, and punctuation.

The key to speeding up the editing process is practice. The more you edit what you write now, the more efficient you will become at polishing your writing in the future.

Summary

This chapter discussed revising and editing. Begin revision by asking large-scale questions about your draft. Does your document include the amount and kind of detail needed by your audience? Is your main point positioned where it will make the impact you desire? Does the overall progression of your document meet your reader's needs?

If you are *not* satisfied with the answers to these questions, cut and paste your draft or insert information as needed. After you make a fresh copy of your revised draft, you are ready to make smaller-scale editing changes.

During editing, make certain that the introductory material in your draft provides appropriate amenities. Check to see that logical connections between ideas are present yet unobtrusive.

Make individual sentences concise. Then vary the length of your sentences by using subordination. Double-check your sentences for parallelism. Eliminate gobbledygook and make certain that your remaining words convey the connotations you desire. After insuring that your draft follows guidelines for nonsexist language, double-check the accuracy of your wording and sentence structure.

Before you prepare your document for transmittal, choose the writing materials and typeface you will need. Plan the margins, spacing, and other physical aspects of your document. When the document is complete, proofread it carefully and see to it that it reaches your audience.

Adjust your editing to your deadline and the length of your document. As you practice editing, you will become more efficient at completing this last phase of rhetorical problem solving.

Writing Problems

1. A real estate broker has drafted the following memo to summarize a recent sales meeting and to announce plans for the next meeting. Revise the memo by cutting, pasting, crossing out, or inserting:

Draft

Date: May 15, 1986

To: Sales Staff

From: M. L. Martinez, Broker

Subject: Sales Meeting of May 13, 1986

After we agreed to focus attention on condominium sales, we proceeded to a discussion of rentals at the Southern Mall.

By virtue of the fact that we accomplished all business on our agenda, we will not need to meet again until Monday, May 27, at 10:00 A.M.

By the way, our newly listed residential properties were detailed at the opening of the meeting. The number and desirability of these properties portends a profitable summer of sales.

By and large, we can look forward to a busy season. This reminds me that we noted our extended summer office hours, 8:00 A.M. to 8:00 P.M., seven days a week, at the beginning of the meeting.

2. The manager of an office supply store needs a photograph and measurements for new models of file cabinets manufactured by each of two companies whose products the store sells:

   ▪ Security File, Inc., which manufactures the "Guardian" three-drawer cabinet, has a history of responding slowly or not at all to retailer queries. The manager of the office supply store does not know anyone personally at Security File.

   ▪ Armor Cabinet, Inc., which manufactures the "Sentry" two-drawer cabinet, has a history of responding quickly and fully to retailer queries. The office supply store's manager is on a first-name basis with Edith Chung, Armor Cabinet's regional sales representative.

   Write the two letters, one each to Security File and Armor Cabinet, requesting the desired information. Suit the content and wording to what you know about the companies' past histories of responding to inquiries. *Optional:* You may work on this application with a classmate, each of you writing one of the letters.

3. The introduction of the following draft-report contains accurate data. Revise it by adding words, phrases, and/or clauses that clarify logical relationships among details:

Draft

TRAVEL EXPENDITURE SUMMARY

The amount spent on travel in October is up 10 percent over September's expenditures. The amount spent on local travel is up 4 percent. National travel is up 1 percent. International travel expenses increased 43 percent. Total October travel expenses were $55,000 for all travel in October. The total for September travel was $50,000. The biggest jump was in international travel. This was $14,300 in October. It was $10,000 in September. The increase is the greatest in that category in our company's history. The jump was expected. The jump is mostly attributable to the October meeting in Montreal. Expenses were paid for our legal counsel to attend this meeting. Expenditures are detailed in the tables. All figures are rounded off to the nearest hundred dollars. Next month's travel summary will include graphic representation of expenditures. Graphs will give us a clearer picture of how we allocate travel money. We will make decisions about future travel expenditures.

---

4. L. K. Weaver manages a new local health spa. Below is a draft of Weaver's form letter to residents of the town in which the spa is located. Help Weaver by editing the letter so the underlined sentences contain more nearly parallel structures. Also, change any wording that may have negative connotations for people who feel defensive about their physical condition. Next, edit any sentences you think contain gobbledygook. Finally, prepare a fresh copy of the letter.

Draft

                                                        January 8, 1986

Dear Neighbor:

Now that the holidays are over, it's time to lose all your disgusting fat! We don't promise miracles at the AJAX Health Center, but working hard can be expected to take off the pounds and inches you've accumulated since Thanksgiving.

We will put you on a biomedically, physiologically revivifying exercise regimen. We will also start you on a well-balanced diet including each of the four main food groups: (1) vegetables/fruits, (2) grains, (3) the dairy, and (4) flesh from the fish/fowl/meat group.

Stop by to tour our new facility. If your body needs a major demolition and rebuilding job, we think AJAX is the place for you.

Best of health,

L. K. Weaver
Manager

5. K. M. Swenson, a customer relations manager for a tire company, has to write a letter to a customer who has complained that a tire purchased from the company is worn out after only six months of use. Swenson drafts the letter below. All of its facts are correct; however, he can use your help editing the letter. In particular, you should change words with strong negative connotations to more neutral vocabulary that communicates the company's views on the customer's complaint firmly yet politely.

Draft

April 7, 1986

Mr. Alan Cranshaw
36 Garfield Way
Newtown, OH 45244

Dear Mr. Cranshaw:

Your letter complaining about the bias-belted tire you bought from us last November is way off base. First of all, the tire is guaranteed for 10,000 miles which you have already exceeded since its purchase. Secondly, you refused to have the wheel balanced at the time of tire purchase, so what do you expect? Finally, our service representative found that the tire was changed from the car for which you originally purchased it to a much heavier vehicle.

Don't you know that this increased stress will cause quick tread wear and invalidate your guarantee, to boot? All of this is to say nothing of the fact that your wheels are out of alignment, causing uneven tire wear.

We do our best at B-Z Tire to satisfy our customers, but it becomes difficult to do so in response to inappropriate requests for free service and merchandise.

Yours truly,

K. M. Swenson
Customer Service Manager

---

6. The following draft of a letter needs revision for sentence structure, spelling, punctuation, and usage. It also requires some editing to avoid sexist language. Edit, type, and proofread the letter. *Optional:* Trade your typed letter with a classmate and proofread each other's letters.

Draft

May 20, 1986

Mr. Byron Jamison
1 E. 53rd Street
New York, NY 10022

Dear Mr. Jamison

Thank you for you're recent purchase of office suite furniture from Working furniture Inc. As specialists in office furniture for lawyers, we know that an attorny wants furniture that reflects the dignity of his profession, yet is both comfortable and desireable. You and your partners appreciating the colonial style suit we have provided. It is our award-winning design, the style is timeless.

Be assured that we will service all of your new furniture. Should you have additional need for furniture accessories, please call on us.

Yours truly,

Shawna Pearlman, President

---

7. As the finance manager of a farm implement dealership, you routinely write memos to salespeople. These memos detail financing arrangements for farmers who wish to purchase equipment. Below is your draft memo about a tractor purchase. Edit the draft by correcting errors in usage, spelling, and punctuation. Then type a final copy for transmittal to the salesperson. *Optional:* Trade your typed memo with a classmate and then proofread each other's memos.

Draft

Date: December 4, 1986

To: Stacy Kearney, Sales

From: [Your name], Finance Manager

Subject: Tractor Financing for M. A. Sato

Here is financing information on M. A. Satos' purchase of a Merit Tractor.

The base price $24,000. Sales taxes $1,200 for a gross price of $25,200.

Trade in allowed for Satos' old tractor $4,000 making net price of $21,200.

Since Sato makes a cash downpayment of $5,000. The balance to finance is sixteen thousand, two hundred dollars.

Loan will be handled by our agency with a flat interest rate of 10% this makes for a total interest charge opf $1,620.

The total loan amount is 17,820. The period over which paying back is 5 years (sixty months) of monthly payments at $297 <u>per</u> month.

Satos' loan will be colatoralized by the customer's Merit Combine current value of $20,000--depreciating at 9% per year.

The 10% interest rate offer is good for contracts signed on or before December 11, 1986. After that date, a new rate <u>may</u> be charged.

---

8. You are a customer service representative for a shoe company. An unhappy customer has just telephoned you to complain about shoes manufactured by your company. You define the writing problem in this way:

   - *Objective*   To prepare a letter responding to customer complaints about my company's product
   - *Audience*   An irate consumer
   - *Writer's desired image*   Concerned and apologetic

During the customer's phone call, you jotted down the following information about his complaints:

- Shoe soles have started to separate from rest of shoe.
- After customer walked in rain, shoe leather started to discolor.
- Shoe pinches customer at his instep.
- Shoes purchased one month ago at a discount department store.
- Store gave your name and phone number to the customer.

Given this problem definition and list of pertinent information, you will need to:

a. Write a draft of a letter responding to the customer's call and offering to refund him the full cost of his shoes. In your draft, include your main point, the offer of a refund, a list of steps the customer should take in the future to preserve the shoes, and a one-sentence amenity expressing regret over the customer's problem.

b. Revise and edit the draft as necessary. As you do so, pay particular attention to the positioning of your main point and how the overall progression of your document meets the needs of your audience and supports your desired writer's image. Also check to see if you have connected your ideas logically. Check for conciseness of individual sentences. Also examine your sentences for parallel structure. Make sure your wording avoids gobbledygook and shows a concern for connotations that might further anger an already irate customer. Finally, examine your draft letter for wording and sentence structure.

c. Incorporate all needed revision and editing changes into a final draft of your letter.

Extended Application

After chapter 1, you selected a writing problem and prepared a reader profile of that problem. Following chapter 2, you analyzed that problem. After chapter 3, you developed a rough draft of the problem. Now take your draft through the editing process. Make the sorts of large- and small-scale revisions explained in chapter 4. Then prepare a finished version of your document for transmittal.

PART 2

Communicating in Business

*P*art 1 examined the four steps of rhetorical problem solving: defining the writing problem, analyzing the writing problem, decision making and drafting, and revising and editing. Part 2 applies that four-step technique to the forms of writing most used in business. This part of the text also discusses research methods, the use of graphs and illustrations, and oral presentation.

Chapter 5, "Memos and Short Reports: Writing to Insiders," examines the three major strategies of memos and reports: first, writing to inform (the progress and status report); second, writing to persuade (the recommendation and justification report and the "bad news" memo); and third, writing to direct (the policy statement, procedure, job description, and performance appraisal).

Chapter 6, "Letters: Writing to Outsiders," describes the qualities of good letters, their strategies, and the most common business letters, such as the sales letter, the credit letter, and the collection letter.

Chapter 7, "Getting a Job: The Process," details the job search process, covering such topics as the job market, targeting and researching companies, writing cover letters and resumes, and preparing for as well as participating in the interview.

Chapter 8, "Research," explains library research, interviewing, and opinion sampling as standard means of acquiring information. Chapter 9, "Using Graphs and Illustrations," describes such charts as the pie, bar, column, line, flow, organization, and Gantt.

Chapter 10, "Formal Reports," examines the process of developing a formal report, from pre-writing to documentation. Chapter 11, "Feasibility Reports and Proposals," offers advice on these two planning tools. Chapter 12, "Oral Presentations," shows how some oral presentations, such as the sales talk, share enough in common with writing that the problem-solving technique may be usefully applied to their development.

CHAPTER 5

Memos and Short Reports:
Writing to Insiders

n the job, the terms *memo* and *short report* are often used interchangeably and are not to be distinguished from each other but
from *letters*. The first two are usually written to those inside the
firm, and letters to those outside.

The following list suggests the kinds of reports used in business today:

Accident report	Periodic report
Activity report	Project report
Analytical report	Proposal report
Audit report	Recommendation report
Credit report	Staff report
Feasibility report	Status report
Financial report	Trip report
Justification report	Trouble report

Because types of reports often overlap in function, only about half of this
list will be discussed in detail. For example, you can barely distinguish the

activity from the status report, or the audit from the analytical report. So in our discussion these varied memos and reports are categorized according to their overall purpose as (1) writing to *inform*, (2) writing to *persuade*, and (3) writing to *direct*.

Internal Writing Classified by Purpose

Informing, persuading, and directing are not mutually exclusive. To persuade, for example, you must often inform; and to direct, you must usually explain in detail what you want your reader to do. Still, each kind of business document does have a distinct emphasis that may be used as a basis for classification.

Writing to Inform

Writing to inform includes the **progress** and the **status report**, both of which may be described as *upward* communication addressed to a superior about one's on-the-job activities. They differ only in that the status report focuses on principal activities over a period of time, and the progress report focuses on a particular project. If the progress report could sum itself up, it would say, "Here's how work is going on the XYZ project." Taking a longer view, the status report says, "Here are the significant jobs I've been doing over the past quarter."

Both reports save time, essentially because they eliminate the need for more lengthy conferences. They also serve to document an employee's or a department's activities and may be consulted when desired.

The Progress Report   The progress report reviews a specific project and is addressed to a superior who has ultimate responsibility for the project. It is usually written by the project leader at regular intervals—weekly, monthly, or quarterly.

In the rest of the chapter, the discussion of and advice on writing each kind of document (including the progress report) are presented in two parts: an outline or plan specifically designed for the particular form under discussion, and the problem-solving steps as developed in part 1 of this text. In this chapter these steps are applied to the writing task and are shortened to the following terms: *define, analyze, draft,* and *revise and edit.* Thus each kind of report will be followed by a particular document plan and general problem-solving steps. The application of both should help you develop effective and satisfying reports.

Document Plan

Overview   The author briefly summarizes the project's progress, remaining tasks, and probable completion date.

Statement of Work Completed The author describes the completed tasks, that is, a general rather than detailed statement about what has been accomplished to date on the particular project.

Statement of Work in Progress The author describes the tasks begun, indicating, if possible, when each is expected to be completed. If any of these tasks has presented problems, the author discusses feasible solutions.

Statement of Work to Begin The author estimates the beginning dates and probable duration of each task, including solutions to anticipated problems.

Conclusion and Forecast The author states whether the project is ahead of schedule, on schedule, or behind schedule. The author then forecasts the completion date of the project.

To write an effective progress report, you can apply the problem-solving steps of defining the problem, analyzing the problem, writing a draft, and revising and editing.

Problem-Solving Steps

Define A progress report is addressed to your immediate superior, who may pass it up the chain of command. If so, you will need to write in language that upper management will understand, possibly keeping technical vocabulary to a minimum. If, however, you know your reader, then you can better judge the level of technical vocabulary to use.

Your readers like concise reports, so extensive treatments of problems and detailed plans should appear as an appendix or attachment.

Analyze The schema given previously will cover most contingencies of the progress report. It is flexible and can be adapted. For example, if you have encountered no problems in carrying the project forward, the middle of your report may be brief, as is the case in figure 5.1. Thus the entire report can take up only a few paragraphs. On the other hand, complex problems will tend to make the report longer and more detailed.

Draft Because your purpose is to inform, write your report succinctly and objectively. Its style will thus be more clipped and precise than reports intended to persuade or build goodwill, and the reader will appreciate your getting straight to the point with a minimum of words. The sample progress report in figure 5.1 illustrates this point.

Revise and Edit Be concise. Have you included more detail than your reader needs? Your reader wants to know what's finished, what's in progress, and what's yet to be done in your project. If you answer these three questions at the level of detail your reader should have, you have written an effective report. Delete unnecessary words.

Because your reader wants to know who does what, use the active voice in the progress report. For example, if you're expecting Chris Lazelle to furnish some documentation by April 2, use Chris Lazelle's name and specific verbs. You may use the passive voice to cover for subordinates—for example, "Unfortunately, the operation documentation cannot be completed on schedule."

*A*mory Systems, Inc.

Date: February 28, 1986

To: Meredith Fraser
        Vice-President, Finance

From: D. W. Cohen
          Director, Corporate Information Systems

Subject: Installation of RAM Software for Order Processing,
              Inventory Control, Billing, and Accounting Control

We have completed two major tasks on this project--the analysis of all
functional requirements and the design of a system to meet them.

We have also begun the following tasks: defining the hardware
requirements (for terminals, printers, lines, modems, etc.); writing
the user and operation documentation; and coding modules and unit
testing.

We expect to complete the hardware installation, code/testing, and
user and operation documentation by April 2. We will complete the
user training program by July 2. By that date we should also have
finished user testing/acceptance. Thus we should reach the overall
conversion stage by that date.

We have hit no snags in the project and are on schedule. You should
receive my next report on April 15.

jo

Figure 5.1   Progress report

The Status Report   The status report focuses on an individual's or a department's activities. Department heads may submit regular status reports on the activities in their departments. Thus a status report is usually broader in scope than a progress report because the progress report is limited to one project, whereas the status report reviews and brings up to date the major projects in a department. Some writers use the terms *status report* and *progress report* interchangeably. We won't quibble about terms as long as the writer of the report knows what the reader expects.

The status report cannot be organized exactly like the progress report, but there are some guidelines you can follow. It is important to group the material into "chunks" that the reader will perceive as units. A good status report should not merely be a list of activities; it should select the key activities and present them in some order. For example, the author may move from the most important to the least important activity or divide tasks into completed, ongoing, and planned activities. Or the author may group activities into problems and solutions. He or she may report on routine and nonroutine activities or report in a chronological order.

Generally the status report will focus on the more significant accomplishments and problems of a project. For example, it will stress measurable productivity in the department, supplying figures to back up claims. An increase in sales volume, a decline in absenteeism, or faster turnaround time are items that would appear in a status report. See figure 5.2 for an example of a status report.

Problem-Solving Steps

Define   Normally you will be writing for your boss, so you will know his or her preconceptions and your relationship. While your audience's needs will shape your report generally, strive for succinctness and a businesslike tone. You want to project the image of the competent, able manager. While highlighting your accomplishments, however, also try to project the image of the reliable reporter—realistic about problems and solutions. A status report that is glibly optimistic will not impress the reader.

Analyze   As noted, your organizational options are broad, but you must decide on a plan that effectively presents your material. Ask yourself how you want your boss to see your report, what conclusion you want him or her to draw from it. Your answers to those questions will indicate the kind of organization you want. For example, if there have been problems in your department in the period covered by the report, you may want the manager to conclude, "Sure, there have been some problems, but they are being addressed, and there has been progress." Such an analysis might lead to a "problems solved" and "problems being solved" organization.

Note the structure of the status report in figure 5.2. The headings reveal the chronological order: Step 1, Step 2, Step 3. In a status report, you must tailor the structure to the material.

CHANDLER CORPORATION

Date: August 15, 1986

To: Merle Herzog
    Executive Vice-President

From: Alexis Dubose
      Director, Corporate Information Systems

Subject: Status Report on the Office Automation Project for the
         Industry-Government Relations Staff

Summary of Activities

Having met with representatives of all sections of the Industry-
Government Relations Staff, I determined the needs for and interest in
word processing in each staff section. I then got a ranking of these
needs. Based on this information, I selected the Gemini 8900 Office
System to implement word processing in the Industry-Government
Relations Staff.

Background

In March, you recall, I was directed to review the information needs of
the Industry-Government Relations Staff (IGR) and select a word
processing system to handle them. The intent was to propose a
system which, while meeting individual section needs, would also
meet the needs of the entire IGR staff.

Word processing, as you have indicated, is simply the first phase of
office automation for IGR. The goal of this first phase is to integrate
word processing into the daily operations of the staff and provide a
means of electronically communicating documents between IGR
sections and other staffs.

Step 1: Determining Needs for and Interest in Word Processing

In an attempt to enhance the positive impact of word processing
within IGR, I met with representatives from all staff sections to
determine what their potential word processing use would be. Thus I
would be able to place equipment in those sections with a high volume

Figure 5.2 Status report

of typing, position papers, testimony, memos, and reports. Also, I could factor into the decision the degree of interest in word processing within the section.

Step 2: Determining Priorities for Word Processing

The representatives from the staff sections then helped to rank their needs. The primary need was for strong word processing capabilities in the form of text editing and text manipulation. Following that, the priorities for the first phase were

1. Interstaff communications
2. Intrastaff communications
3. Printing capabilities (including automatic envelope handling)
4. Data processing interface

Additional considerations were cost, vendor support, and the vendor's ability to bring advanced technology to the market consistently.

Step 3: Selecting a Word Processing System

We selected the Gemini 8900 Office System after a review of the capabilities of the Aries, Pisces, and Capricorn systems. The 8900 clearly meets the first phase needs of the IGR staff. It also has the long-range backing of Gemini Systems, providing for continued development to meet future staff needs, and the system is cost competitive.

The 8900 is a shared logic system. It has a central processing unit with intelligence and a large number of semi-intelligent terminals cabled to it. Thus all data is stored in the central processor, with access to individual data achieved by passwords. The 8900 provides security, maintaining individual privacy through the use of these passwords and individually determined file names.

The 8900 has demonstrated its effectiveness in locations throughout the corporation, including the ROA Staff, Legal Staff, and Purchasing Division. Due to the increasing number of installations within Chandler Corporation, Gemini will be giving us a 15 percent volume discount.

od

2

Draft   Having decided upon an organization, determine the desirable degree of specificity. How much detail is enough and how much is too much? Use details sparingly. Your reader can always call for a more detailed explanation, but he or she cannot conveniently ask for a less detailed report. Notice the fourth paragraph in figure 5.2 ("In an attempt to enhance the positive impact . . ."). It could have been more detailed, but it tells the reader just enough and no more.

As with the progress report, use the active voice to underscore the role of individuals; use the passive voice when you want to deemphasize their activities. The style should be crisp and direct. The purpose is to inform, and you are the reporter, not the advocate. Note the tone of figure 5.2. It uses *I* several times, yet it sounds relaxed, confident, and professional.

Revise and Edit   Note also the underlined headings in figure 5.2. This device is effective because activities in a status report may require more extensive classification. Notice also the numbered list on the second page, another useful device. You can vary sentence structure for interest in a status report more than is usually desirable in a progress report (such as the one in figure 5.1). The direct, objective style of the progress report would not be appropriate to the status report, which allows its author freedom to comment as well as to report. Your style may also be slightly more personal in the status report.

Writing to
Persuade

Persuasion includes three short report forms: (1) the recommendation report, (2) the justification report, and (3) the bad news memo.

Many of you remember the essentials of persuasion from speech or composition class. The persuader must be logical, supply credible evidence for assertions, and be perceived as unbiased and fair-minded. That is true, but we're going to stress another side of persuasion, that of identification with the needs and objectives of the person to be persuaded.

To persuade, you must first determine a person's specific needs and objectives. Then you must create in that person's mind a credible link between fulfilling those needs and attaining those objectives and your goals. For example, assume that you want to convince your employer to buy dictation equipment for the office. If you can connect the purchase of the dictation system with greater productivity, an objective of the employer, your chances of succeeding increase. If your employer prizes professionalism and you can connect dictation equipment with it, your chances are better yet.

In writing inside the company, persuasion is more subtle. There's usually little hard sell, as in a line like, "Say Marge, all the leading agencies have dictation equipment!" Rather, you identify your goal with one of the reader's goals. Let's look at some specific forms of persuasion.

The Recommendation Report   As its name implies, the central element in the **recommendation report** is the recommendation it offers. The report structure is like a pyramid, with the recommendation being the topmost stone, supported by every stone beneath it.

Normally this kind of report describes a business problem, explores various possible solutions, and presents a solution in the form of a recommendation. The author has usually solved the business problem before beginning to write the report, so the purpose of the report is to present the solution to the business problem in the most convincing light.

Document Plan

Summary   The author summarizes the business problem and the recommended solution, often citing key reasons for the recommendation.

The Problem   The author describes the business problem and any limitations, for example, "How do we do X without doing Y?"

Relevant Information   The author describes the results of any investigation into the problem: data, figures, interviews, and sampling.

Analysis   The author interprets the information gathered and draws conclusions about what will and what will not contribute to solving the business problem.

Recommended Solution   The author describes the steps or action required to solve the business problem.

The recommendation usually appears both at the beginning in summary form and at the end as the logical conclusion of the discussion. Placing it at the beginning helps the busy decision maker who wants to get the essence of the report quickly. If the reader questions the recommendation, he or she can then read the rest of the report, which should prove that the recommendation is justified.

Problem-Solving Steps

Define   Keep in mind that we're speaking of the *writing* problem, not the business problem. We're talking about a report that recommends a solution already arrived at. This distinction can be seen in figure 5.3. There the business problem is how to offer employees some typing support without hurting the cost-effective image of the department. The writing problem is how to win the support of the reader for the recommended solution.

The recommendation report will usually be addressed to the manager of your department or office, so you will know your reader. But you must be aware of any preconceptions your reader might have. Preconceptions become exceptionally important in the recommendation report, because you must persuade the reader that your recommendation is justified. The goal of the report is to get your reader to think, "Yes, I agree with your analysis and your recommendation."

argus corporation

Date: June 30, 1986

To: Hilary Fitzpatrick
     Vice-President

From: Lauren Tschudi
       Director, Administrative Services

Subject: Recommendation on Support for Personal Typing

<u>Summary</u>

Typing personal work for employees presents the Word Processing
Center with a dilemma. If we do too much of it, we appear less
cost-effective to management; if we do too little of it, we appear
miserly to our users. I recommend that we continue to type some
kinds of personal work as long as it does not infringe on more
important tasks.

<u>The Problem</u>

First, how much, if any, personal typing should the Word Processing
Center do for employees? Second, if the center is to do some personal
typing, should it do all kinds or only certain kinds?

<u>Background</u>

Since 1976, when word processing began in the Finance Department,
we have unofficially followed the practice of supporting most personal
typing requests when our workload has permitted. For example, we
have generally typed the personal work that has some relation to
business, such as speeches, seminar outlines, and membership lists
for professional organizations. We have also typed civic and
church-related personal work. However, we have generally refused to
type such personal work as resumes and term papers for relatives.

From the user's point of view, our current practice is not entirely
satisfactory, since sometimes we accept personal work and sometimes
we refuse--depending on our own workload. From our point of view,
the current practice is satisfactory except when our refusal
antagonizes the person refused.

Figure 5.3   Recommendation report

Discussion

There are three reasons why we have accepted some kinds of personal work. First, since personal typing support was available before word processing, we would create some ill will by eliminating it. Second, we have tried to use this support as a means of promoting goodwill for the Word Processing Center. And third, we realize that our refusal to support this kind of work would only perpetuate the boss-secretary relationship word processing seeks to supplant.

While there are no published guidelines for typing personal work, there are three alternative viewpoints on the subject:

1. No personal typing should be done on company time since the company has no obligation to support personal work.

2. Some personal typing should be done on company time, as the workload permits, because this is an employee benefit provided voluntarily by the company. (This viewpoint corresponds to our current practice.)

3. Certain kinds of personal typing should be done on company time and even in overtime, because the company has an obligation to provide typing support for certain kinds of personal work.

Thus personal typing presents a dilemma. On the one hand, I would like to keep our cost figures low, but not at the expense of appearing miserly to our users. On the other hand, I would like to continue to offer this support when we can, but not at the expense of appearing overly generous with our time and resources in the view of management.

Recommendation

I recommend that you allow us to continue our current practice as long as personal typing support does not lead to the use of overtime or the hiring of additional staff. If you approve this recommendation, I will report to you periodically on the volume and kinds of personal work we support.

ob

2

Ask yourself how the reader may view your recommendation. If favorably, you can keep evidence to essentials. If neutrally, you had better increase the evidence. If negatively, you had better do two things: (1) give ample evidence for your recommendation and (2) omit the summary at the beginning and make your recommendation last, giving the reader time to digest the facts before facing the recommendation.

Also, it is important to define the image you wish to project. If the recommendation is good news to your reader, your tone can be poised and positive. If it is bad news, your tone should be objective and neutral.

Analyze   First, you must investigate the business problem thoroughly; second, you must analyze the information you collect, drawing conclusions from it; and third, you must make a recommendation that follows logically from the first two steps. The tools of analysis discussed in chapter 2, for example, note card decks and decision trees, will help you analyze the business problem.

We suggest that you follow the organization plan given previously. You will probably need to adapt it to your situation, however. For example, if several feasible solutions to the business problem emerge, you may wish to develop criteria to distinguish the best solution and apply the criteria to each solution, reaching your recommendation by a process of elimination. Doing so would mean expanding the analysis section of the special outline for recommendation reports, perhaps even creating a special unit and heading for each alternative solution. (See figure 11.3 for an example.) But before you expand the report, ask whether your reader expects and needs the expanded version.

Draft   As indicated, the level of specific detail in the report will depend on your reader's attitude, as you estimate it, and your decision to include alternative solutions.

Conciseness remains a stylistic goal. Note that our sample recommendation report (figure 5.3), while including all the components of our plan, is still concise.

Revise and Edit   Review the report with an eye to seeing that your original decisions about the image and tone you wish to project have been achieved. If you are doubtful, ask an associate to read the report as the intended reader, and ask his or her opinion about image and tone.

Make sure that the report is no longer than it needs to be to achieve your goals. You do not want to overdo the details. Remember: When in doubt, leave it out. (Or put it in an appendix.)

The Justification Report   Similar to the recommendation report is the **justification report**. It is written for a superior justifying the purchase of some equipment, such as a photocopier, computer, or dictation system. The justification report is a kind of persuasive writing because the author must convince the reader that the purchase—usually substantial—is justified and that the equipment requested is both well suited to the job and cost-effective. This kind of report is only mentioned now because it is better treated as a proposal, which we discuss in a separate chapter. See figure 11.2 for an example of a justification report.

The Bad News Memo   Sometimes in business we must convey a negative message to a coworker. We may have to refuse a request, take a position on an issue that may antagonize a colleague, or insist on one of our rights. Sometimes it may be easier and better to do so face to face, but there are times when we will want to communicate in writing. A memo serves as a record of what we actually think and have stated. It also allows the other person a chance to "cool off" before responding.

Every business person at times faces the problem of writing a negative message, sometimes under considerable emotional pressure. But a memo written hastily and in anger will antagonize a reader and lead to undesirable results. If you wait until you are composed and use the strategy of the **bad news memo**, you can diminish the negative effect of the message.

But we need to qualify the term *bad news memo*. The purpose of this kind of memo is to convey the negative message while retaining the goodwill of the reader. Thus the strategy that we will shortly explain is for use only when you decide that goodwill must and can be preserved.

Bad news usually implies disapproval. Though you cannot eliminate the *actual* refusal or the disagreement, you can diminish or even eliminate the *sense* of disapproval. The strategy is to convey, along with the negative content, some positive sense of approval. For example, if your employee asks you for a larger raise than you think justified, in refusing the request you may be able to salvage goodwill by some compliment about the person's work. Do not, however, so compliment the employee that you encourage a sense of injustice ("If I'm so valuable, why don't I get the raise I want?"). But you can make the person feel justly appreciated.

Document Plan

Opening   The author establishes common ground by affirming shared values or goals, by admitting some specific valid point in the other's position, or by demonstrating sympathy for the other's point of view, for example, by restating it in other terms, thereby showing understanding.

Reason(s) for Negative Position   The author creates an impression of being compelled by logic and facts to hold this position or take this action.

The Negative Position   The author states the bad news briefly yet clearly, for example, "While I understand your position, I feel constrained to . . ."

The Positive Element   If possible, the author may offer a satisfactory alternative to a conflict. The writer of the memo may recognize the recipient's motives as praiseworthy, may compliment the reader in some credible way, or may offer to discuss the problem or just to listen to the complaint. It is important to note that offers of an alternative and further discussion are suggested only if the author *really* can offer an alternative or *wishes* to discuss the matter further. If that is not the case, such offers may raise false hopes of agreement and thus do still more damage.

Problem-Solving Steps

Define   In most such cases you will be writing to someone on your level or to a subordinate—either lateral or downward communication. Ask yourself what you have in common with the recipient of your letter that will help establish a sense of mutual interest or shared values or objectives. Notice how the writer in the sample bad news memo in figure 5.4 does so, emphasizing the shared objective of better communication and cooperation.

The problem, of course, is to achieve two conflicting objectives—to retain the other's goodwill without sacrificing your own position. Achieving both may be impossible in practice, but even demonstrating that you *want* to keep this person's goodwill may help you keep it.

Analyze   Have you looked at this problem from the other's point of view? You need not agree, but you must show sympathy for the other person's viewpoint. Role play. If your positions were reversed, how would you feel? What would be your main concerns? If you can understand some of the reader's misgivings, you may be able to establish some common ground.

Will any point you intend to make unnecessarily lessen the other's self-esteem? You'll seldom persuade someone if you insult him or her.

Draft   Do not write more than you have to. Do not go into great detail to point up the errors in the other person's position. Doing so will only prove that he or she is somehow at fault, not that you are right.

Be careful about your tone. Often it's not so much the disagreement that offends as it is the sarcastic tone, the slightly perceptible sneer behind the words. A second reader (usually a friend) can detect this tone in a document better than you can.

Revise and Edit   Delete any unnecessarily harsh or negative statement, phrase, or word. Is your tone accusatory? How can you make it firm and still conciliatory? Do your reasons for the negative position sound valid? If one of them sounds specious, cross it out. Does the positive gesture you make at the end sound sincere or artificial? "I have always admired you and hope we can still be friends" sounds phony. In figure 5.4 the author ends on a positive note without sounding timid.

 Rifkin Industries

Date: September 25, 1986

To: Fran Conner
        Director, Building and Maintenance

From: Evelyn McGhee
          Manager, Claims Administration

Subject: Moving to 7th Floor

Fran, I hope that, after reading this message, you will agree that you and I need to communicate more effectively if we are to move my department to the 7th floor smoothly and efficiently.

You recall that we met with our colleagues on August 2 and set December 1 as the target date for our move. We have, as I stated then, the chance to get a $2,300 trade-in on a microprocessor if we can make a final decision on this move.

On several occasions since then you told me that I would have cost figures from the movers very shortly and that your assistant would very shortly begin the floor plan. Neither has reached me as of this writing.

I am sure that you understand the importance of this move to my department and want it to go off without a hitch, just as I do. But I need to receive feedback from you when a deadline cannot be met.

Can we meet early next week to work out a mutually acceptable solution to this problem? My secretary will be glad to set up a conference.

ds

Figure 5.4   Bad news memo

Writing to direct refers to six varieties of short reports: (1) the policy statement or directive, (2) the procedure, (3) the job description, (4) the performance appraisal, (5) the warning, and (6) the commendation.

As you move through your career, your responsibilities will increase, as will the number of people under your direction. Thus, writing clear directions to your subordinates will become increasingly important. The more effectively you write for your subordinates, the more effective you will be as a manager. As an executive, if you can write clear, courteous directives, you will probably obtain greater cooperation. Conversely, if your directives are unclear or discourteous, the cooperation you achieve will be limited, and you may have to spend time clarifying your intentions, building morale, or both.

To prepare you to write well for your subordinates, we will discuss the most common types of downward writing and offer suggestions on how to write each kind.

The Policy Statement or Directive   The **policy statement** generally originates with top management as a statement of company goals and philosophy. It sets guidelines without specifying the ways in which those guidelines are to be carried out. In practice, policy statements, directives, and statements of guidelines cover a broad range of topics, including such subjects as accounting practices, advertising, inventory, cash flow, sick leaves, absenteeism, promotion, vacations, holidays, jury duty, pension plans, overtime, and performance appraisals. Policy statements, directives, and guidelines are the written "rules" of the company.

As such, they save managers time. With new employees joining a company every day, imagine all the time managers would spend answering the same questions if policy statements weren't available. Policy statements serve as a means of coordinating employee behavior toward achieving company goals. Furthermore, having standard guidelines governing such practices as performance appraisal and absenteeism fosters a sense of fairness among employees. Most companies collect all policy statements into a manual known variously as the administrative manual, employee handbook, policy and procedures manual, staff manual, or personnel manual. It is usually bound in such a way that updating is easy, for policy and procedure statements are revised periodically.

Now let's distinguish between a policy and a procedure. Briefly, **policy** determines what an employee should do in certain circumstances. For example, the policy statement in figure 5.5 explains what the employee should do when renting a car. The **procedure** statement explains how to do something. Policy presumes more than one procedure and specifies the desired procedure.

In drafting a policy statement you must remember that it can never cover every case. If it covers *most* cases, it is probably a good one.

Libra Corporation

CORPORATE POLICY   (Domestic)

Approved by: Effective Date:

Issue No.:   Page: Policy No.:

Subject: Automobile Rentals for Corporate Travel

As a Libra employee engaged in company business, you may rent a car only when more economical means of transportation--an airport limousine, for example--are not available. In determining that a rented car is the most economical means, consider the distance being driven and the length of your stay at the destination, since a daily rental rate is charged whether or not you drive the car every day. In renting a car, please follow these guidelines.

1. Use a compact or subcompact car whenever possible.

2. Show the rental agency your corporate identification and/or your company discount card or sticker to qualify for any discount in effect. (Discount cards or stickers are available from Corporate Purchasing.)

3. Go with the rental agency that offers the best rate. The larger companies have toll-free numbers for rate information. Since some rental outlets have a limited supply of compact cars, ask whether reservations are guaranteed and, if not, whether they will provide the next larger size car at no additional charge.

4. Use the XYZ Charge Card to pay for car rentals. In the absence of an XYZ Card, use a personal credit card. Do not bill the car directly to the Libra Corporation Accounting Departments. Pay the expense directly and submit the receipt for reimbursement.

5. Do not pay for additional insurance because the Corporation insurance policy already covers you for injury and damages.

6. Rent the car in your name and the company name.

7. To ensure reimbursement, you must submit gas and oil receipts when these are not included in the rental rate.

Figure 5.5   Policy statement

Problem-Solving Steps

Define The policy statement is exceptional in business writing because you have a wider audience than usual—all members of a department, a division, or even the company. Since your reader profile becomes more generalized, the question of your reader's vocabulary, education, and intelligence becomes more important but less certain.

Tone is equally important. The nature of the policy statement can lead the writer, even unconsciously, to assume an authoritarian and possibly condescending tone. Later we'll offer some suggestions for achieving a tone and style that are sufficiently formal without being pompous.

Analyze In writing guidelines to cover a broad spectrum of cases, we try to cover all the possibilities. The guidelines thus become longer and more complex as we anticipate additional contingencies. And the longer and more complex guidelines become, the greater the chance for readers to become weary and confused. Therefore, if you want people to follow your guidelines, keep them simple and short.

Next, organize your statement. Most policy statements move from the most important to the least important point. The policy statement in figure 5.5 begins with the most general ideas, for example, employees should rent cars only when the car is the most economical means of transportation available. Then it moves to more specific ideas, such as the fact that employees should rent compact cars whenever possible. It then moves to the most specific ideas in that it explains how to pay for the car rental and gain reimbursement.

Draft Especially in writing guidelines, address the reader directly. Use the second person *you* or the imperative mood: *rent* a car, *choose* a compact. Use the active voice: it will create a sense of immediacy with your reader and prevent you from sounding pompous. The policy statement in figure 5.5 addresses the reader directly without sounding too casual.

Revise and Edit Review your statement to see whether you have left out anything important, such as a reason for some important point. If employees know the reason for a policy, they are more apt to cooperate.

Have one or more of the addressees read the policy statement and tell you in their own words what they think it says. Compare their version with the message you intended.

Check whether the document is too long or complex. Is the language simple enough to be understood by the intended readers? Consider itemizing with a numbered list, as shown in figure 5.5. Breaking the policy into discernible units of thought will make it more intelligible.

If the policy has legal ramifications, consider having an attorney read it to make suggestions for revision. Performance appraisal policies, for example, can be subject to legal action if they violate an employee's rights.

The Procedure   Procedures are the means by which policy is carried out. Both policy statements and procedures are often collected into one manual, but some companies prefer to separate the two into a policy manual and a procedures manual.

A **procedure** explains how a task is to be carried out, specifying who does what, when, how, and where. But it is not to be confused with a **job description**, which specifies the tasks of a person in a particular job. While a job description covers the activities of only one person, a procedure may cover those of the several persons or departments involved in the task. For example, closing a sale may involve the sales representative, sales manager, and credit manager.

Procedures can be written for any of the activities carried on by the firm, but white-collar workers are the most common users of procedure manuals. Departments of accounting, data processing, sales, and administrative services often generate procedure manuals. Step-by-step instructions help these people carry out company policies.

Procedures are often written by the head of the department in which the activity described takes place; so, as a department head, you may write the procedures used in your department. We will offer general suggestions on how to write an effective procedure, but since policy and procedure manuals differ in format from company to company, you will want to follow the format used in your company or division. Figure 5.6 shows a sample procedure that uses the commonly practiced **playscript format**. This format is especially useful for describing procedures involving the activities of more than one person or department.

Document Plan

1. The playscript format introduces the procedure, giving its purpose and rationale.
2. It divides the specifics of the procedure into two columns. The column on the left lists the person or department responsible for performing the step; the column on the right lists the steps to be performed. These columns are often labeled *Agent* and *Responsibility.*
3. It breaks down the actions of the procedure into specific steps that are numbered.

Problem-Solving Steps

Define   How will your readers use this procedure you have written? Some procedures are designed to train newcomers in a task; some are used as reference materials for experienced workers to check when they are doubtful about a certain step in the procedure. If you are writing for the newcomer, your instructions will be much more detailed than if you are writing for the experienced worker.

EQUIPMENT REQUISITION PROCEDURE

This bulletin outlines the required procedure for requisitioning office machines and equipment for use throughout the Company.

Because it may take several weeks to obtain the items you request, advance planning and early requisition will ensure timely delivery.

To process your requests efficiently, fill out the Equipment Requisition Form (ERF). This form will: (1) supply the appropriate departments complete information on your needs, (2) obtain the required authorizations, (3) record the transaction, and (4) inform you of approval and expected delivery date.

The information you give will enable the Planning Division to evaluate your needs and to provide you with proper equipment. The agents and their responsibilities are listed below.

AGENTS	RESPONSIBILITIES
Requesting Department	1. Evaluate need for equipment. Request analysis from Equipment Consultant, if necessary.
Supervisors/ Managers	2. Complete Equipment Requisition Form (ERF). Give specific reasons for request.
	3. Obtain signed authorization from your equipment coordinator. Keep Requester's Copy. Send Original and Disposition Copies to Planning Division.
Planning Division	4. Receive ERF. Verify need for the equipment.
	5. Identify/verify proper brand and model necessary to meet the need.
Planning Systems Department	6. Check inventory to see if equipment is on hand and, if so, where available.
Equipment Consultant Section	7. If available, and need is only temporary, assign as loaned equipment. Complete Transfer of Equipment Form (TEF).

Figure 5.6   Procedure

8. Obtain three competitive bids from suppliers.

9. Select supplier, determining specific description of equipment, price, and expected delivery date.

10. Determine best means to acquire (buy, rent, or lease). Verify with Internal Audit Department, as required.

11. Obtain executive approval, as required.

12. Complete Purchase Authorization Form (PAF).

13. Send PAF to Purchasing Division, Purchasing Clerical Department.

Purchasing Division

Purchasing Clerical Department

14. Process the PAF.

15. Send Vendor Copy of Purchase Order to Planning Division, Planning Systems Department, Equipment Consultant Section.

Planning Division

Planning Systems Department

Equipment Consultant Section

16. Compare Purchase Order and ERF. Correct any mistakes in the Purchase Order.

17. Send disposition copy of the ERF to the requester.

18. Copy the Purchase Order, sending the original copy to the vendor.

19. Set up required follow-up evaluation on delivery and installation.

20. File copies of PAF and ERF chronologically by subject in Order File.

2

What level of language should you use? Are you assuming a familiarity with concepts or practices that your reader may not have? Or are you perhaps using an overly sophisticated vocabulary? Will drawings or photographs help your reader to understand your directions?

Above all, don't leave any steps out of the procedure, even substeps. The omission of an essential step is the downfall of the procedure writer, yet it is so easy, especially when explaining a process a writer has performed often. For example, in teaching someone how to drive, so many things one takes for granted about steering, accelerating, braking, and cornering will be new to the student. One quickly learns not to assume too much.

Analyze   A good way to make sure you are not omitting a step from the procedure is to take notes as you actually perform the procedure or as you watch someone else perform it. You will then directly experience the steps and be less likely to omit the most familiar ones. If you are not personally familiar with the procedure, interview a person who often performs it. You may wish to tape-record the interview as a form of note taking.

A note card deck is an effective way to analyze a procedure problem—using one card for each step. Doing so allows plenty of flexibility to add steps or substeps as you become aware of them.

The organization of the procedure will naturally be chronological—the order in which you actually do the steps when you perform the task.

Draft   The most important aspect of writing procedures is the level of detail, especially if you're writing for a newcomer to the task. Researching the steps as we suggested above will help.

When you write, imagine yourself speaking directly to the reader and use action words. Notice how each step in figure 5.6 begins with an action word: *evaluate, complete, obtain*. Make sure you specify who is to carry out each action—the playscript format is especially useful for such specification.

As you write, do not rename things or people. To do so can confuse the reader. If you start out by referring to a given person as the *supervisor*, don't call that person the *boss* later on. If you start out by referring to the *project*, don't call it the *job* later on. Variety in word choice is good, but clarity is more important.

Finally, refer to people not by their proper names but by their job titles: that way you won't have to revise the procedure when somebody leaves a job in the department.

Revise and Edit   To check the draft for any omitted steps, ask at least one employee involved in the procedure to read it. Or test the procedure on a newcomer to the task—see whether he or she can perform, or at least understand, the task using the written procedure as a guide. Such a test will reveal any unclear passages. If neither of these tests is feasible, perform the task yourself following only your written procedure. This may uncover any snag.

Check the text for overly technical language and unnecessary repetitions. Last, edit the procedure to insure that similar steps in the process are expressed in grammatically parallel form. For example, note how the procedure in figure 5.6 introduces each step with parallel commands: *evaluate, complete, obtain, receive*. (If you're not sure about the meaning of parallelism, consult the term in the handbook at the end of the book.)

The Job Description   A **job description** is a statement of the duties, accountabilities, and required skills associated with a specific job. Some companies operate with no job descriptions, but most large companies have them for most positions. Figure 5.7 is a sample job description.

The job description has many uses. It helps the company recruiter to match the right candidate with the job and helps the job candidate decide on the suitability of the job. It lets the new employee know what the company expects of him or her, and describes such behavior as levels of decision making. It helps management to set a salary range for a specific job based on the duties, decision-making authority, and training and skills required. It helps settle disputes over the qualifications required for a specific job and deals with questions about equal pay for equal work.

Another important use of the job description is in the performance appraisal. Managers often use the job description to develop standards by which to measure the employee's performance. This appraisal can result in raises, promotions, and even terminations.

Document Plan

Job Identification   This section includes the job title, the job code number, the grade level, the department, the location of the job, the pay, the date the description was written, and the signatures of the author and the department head. It also may specify whether the job is full-time or part-time.

Summary   Here you state the basic job function in a few sentences.

Job Duties and Accountabilities   This part describes the job responsibilities along with the major goals.

Reporting Relationships   Here you describe reporting (who reports to this position, and to whom does this position report?). It also describes the decision-making authority connected with the position and the jobholder's contacts with others in and out of the organization.

Job Specifications   The education, experience, special training, skills, qualities, or licensing required for this position are described in this section.

HERITAGE INSURANCE COMPANY

Job Description

Job Title: Claim Reviewer   Job Number: 972

Department: Claims   Division: Claims Administration

Group: Service--0782

Reports To (Job Title): Section Head, Claim Reviewers

JOB SUMMARY

Maintains records on disabilities by setting up control cards on new disabilities and updating the cards for renewed and discontinued disabilities; audits quick claims; codes A&S claims and handles system input/output for the Division. These duties involve personal contact with employees at the clerical level in the Division and in other departments (Actuarial, Central Records, Medical, Treasury, and Data Input).

DUTIES AND RESPONSIBILITIES

1. Batches claim payments to be sent to Treasury several times each day by gathering A&S claims in lots of 20 and preparing an adding machine tape of the total amount payable for each lot and coding a batch control sheet so that accurate disbursement and accounting are accomplished for the claims. Audits approximately 550 such claims per week.

2. Prepares and updates Disability Control Cards by creating new cards, manually updating the cards each time a disability is renewed, and removing the cards when the disability ends to maintain current records. Handles approximately 1,000 renewal disabilities per month.

Figure 5.7   Job description

3. Records information on A&S claims by answering phone calls from our District Offices and recording the claim information to be used by the Examiners to make claim payments. Handles approximately 130 such phone calls per week.

4. Updates systems information from an A&S claim by coding data to both the Weekly Premium and Ordinary Systems at the time of claim payment. (Information to be used for statistical studies.) Codes approximately 200 claims daily.

5. Batches input abstracts to be sent to keypunch several times each day by gathering individual abstracts into lots of 25 and coding a batch control sheet so that control is maintained in data sent to Data Input for computer processing.

6. Sorts computer output alphabetically and by clerk code number and distributes to Groups I and II and to Service Group. Does this promptly each morning.

JOB SPECIFICATIONS

1. Basic mathematics skills (addition, subtraction, etc.).

2. Ability to do a variety of clerical tasks.

3. Ability to file both alphabetically and numerically.

4. Ability to communicate orally and to write legibly.

Chris Wagner   11/13/86

Job Description Writer   Date

Pat Stanhope   11/19/86

Director or Manager   Date

Problem-Solving Steps

Define   The audience for a job description can be diverse, as the uses of the job description suggest. The employee will use it to understand the job and management's expectations. Management may use it to develop standards of performance. In case of an appeal over an alleged injustice, outsiders, such as attorneys, may read it to determine its fairness and compliance with equal opportunity and other employment laws. The outsiders will be interested mainly in how this job compares with other jobs: does the salary range correspond to that of jobs requiring comparable duties, skills, and education, for example? Therefore you may wish to consult other company job descriptions on this level as a part of your research.

In specifying duties for the position, it is good to distinguish between the employee's overall duties and responsibilities and his or her daily tasks. A good job description states the duties and accountabilities—levels of productivity, for instance—but not necessarily such daily routines as arriving at work at 9:00 A.M.

Analyze   To help you research the duties and responsibilities of the position, consider involving the employee in writing the job description, since normally he or she knows the job best. Ask the employee to keep an informal log of activities for some days or weeks.

In researching the duties and accountabilities of the job, try for objective, measurable statements that can be used to develop performance standards. Notice how figure 5.7 specifies, wherever possible, the number and the time frame for each duty, for example, "Audits approximately 550 such claims a week." Try to avoid vague, catchall phrases like "and other duties as specified by management." Such phrases can be easily misinterpreted, both by management and by counsel.

Draft   The key here is not to omit important skills because you assume them. For example, in the Job Specifications section in figure 5.7, the author explicitly lists the ability to write legibly, a critical skill in the job described.

Try to specify duties in terms of numbers wherever possible. Note, for example, how the author of the job description cited in figure 5.7 specifies such requirements as coding 200 claims daily and auditing 550 claims weekly. Also, write in terms the employee can understand. If, for instance, you are writing a description for a technical position, you will probably use some technical terminology. But remember the other possible readers, such as department heads and attorneys, and try to keep the description as untechnical as the needs of the job allow.

Revise and Edit   At this point you might ask the employee in the job to review the description to see whether it is complete and clear. You might test it as well on a manager or member of the company legal staff, if that is feasible.

Review the description to be sure that you have specified duties and not mere tasks. Have you made them measurable wherever possible? Would an outside reader of similar experience and in a position similar to your own tend to agree that the expectations are reasonable?

The Performance Appraisal   Most companies have adopted the practice of regularly reviewing the performance of their employees—annually, semiannually, or even quarterly. Many larger companies arrange training sessions to give managers practice in **performance appraisal**.

Performance appraisal practices vary widely among companies, and it is not our purpose to advocate a specific method. Rather, we will cover the purposes of performance appraisal, the process, and the kinds of writing involved.

Performance appraisal has several purposes. It should let the employee know what management expects of him or her. It can also give the employee a chance to help formulate the standards and performance objectives involved in the appraisal. It should give the employee a sense of what he or she is doing well and where improvement is needed. It should help the superior to assess the quality of the employee's work and to determine training needs. It can also help the superior in making recommendations about salary, promotion, and assignments. Finally, it can give management a better insight into the employee's potential and desire for promotion.

Generally, the process of performance appraisal involves the employee and his or her immediate superior, although someone else, such as a personnel officer, may conduct the appraisal. These two will normally hold at least one conference and may meet several times to complete the appraisal. Usually, the appraisal process involves at least three operations. First, the standards used to measure performance must be developed, possibly jointly by the superior and the employee. Second, those standards must be applied to the employee's performance for a specific period—a year, six months, or a quarter. Third, goals and objectives must be developed for performance in the next period.

Depending on company practice, there can be either little or a fair amount of writing in performance appraisal. Some companies recommend that the superior involve the employee in developing the job description, standards, and objectives for the next period, all of which are to be written down, with both parties agreeing to them and receiving a copy. As a practical matter, though, we cannot offer suggestions on all these subjects. Rather, we will concentrate on writing the performance appraisal, which largely includes these other tasks. The document does not preclude interviews with the employee, however.

Figure 5.8 shows a sample of a written performance appraisal. Many companies use forms similar to the one shown in the figure, with the manager filling in the appropriate information. However, we will not specify a plan for this form because practice is too varied.

HERITAGE INSURANCE COMPANY

EMPLOYEE PERFORMANCE EVALUATION

Last Name	First Name	Job Number	Title	Job Code
Witkowsky,	Gale	972	Claim Reviewer	05941

Group	Period Evaluated
Service--0782	1/5/85--1/5/86

Type of Increase

X̲ Merit   __Promotion   __Merit and Promotion

Effective Date of Increase 1/6/86

Weekly Increase Recommended $30.00

I. Performance

Quality of Work	Quantity of Work	Human Relations	Progress
A (B) C D E	A (B) C D E	(A) B C D E	A (B) C D E

Where is employee's performance most proficient?

Gale's work is usually superior. She is methodical and careful to perform each task correctly. There is seldom an error in the 500 or so A&S claims she audits weekly. In fact, I have used her to train a new employee in auditing these claims.

She is accurate in updating the Disability Control Cards. She is courteous and effective in communicating with our District Offices and recording claim information given over the phone. She is accurate in coding A&S claim data to the Weekly Premium and Ordinary Systems. Also, she is accurate in filing computer output.

In human relations, Gale is superior. She cooperates with management and fellow employees, voluntarily helping others learn, and she has made suggestions that have improved work flow. She assisted in the rewriting of a part of the department's procedures manual.

Since her last review, Gale has increased the volume of her work in auditing A&S claims—from 400 to approximately 500 per week.

Figure 5.8   Performance appraisal

Where does employee's performance need improvement?

Gale needs to improve in productivity. Her processing of 500 A&S claims per week still falls below the norm of 550. She especially needs to become more productive in handling Disability Control Cards. The norm there is approximately 1,000 per month. Over the past year, Gale has averaged no more than 825 per month. Gale must become more familiar with Disability Control Card procedures.

List performance objectives for next evaluation period.

1. Gale will spend a morning working with me in order to become more familiar with Disability Control Card procedures and raise her monthly output of 825 to 1,000 cards.

2. Gale will raise her auditing of A&S claims from 500 to 550 per week.

Overall Performance Rating (circle one).

A--Outstanding. Consistently exceeds job requirements. Performance results stand out.
B--Excellent. Consistently meets job requirements and very often exceeds them.
Ⓒ-Good. Consistently meets job requirements.
D--Acceptable. Meets most job requirements but requires some special attention.
E--Unsatisfactory. Critically below job requirements. Immediate action required.

II. Attendance And Punctuality

Is attendance and/or punctuality a problem to the extent that this increase is reduced or deferred?
No.

Expected date of next performance evaluation 1/5/87

Signature of Rater   **Date**
Verna Lenahan   1/10/86

Signature of Employee   **Date**
Gale Witkowski   1/10/86

The form in the figure identifies the employee and the position. It specifies the period of evaluation and the date of the next evaluation and any raise or promotion recommended. It asks the superior to identify the good points in the employee's performance, any improvement needed, and performance objectives for the next evaluation period. It requires an overall performance rating. This particular form requires an evaluation of the employee's attendance and punctuality. Last, it requires both the superior and the employee to sign the form.

Problem-Solving Steps

Define   Here we are defining the rhetorical problem, not any problem experienced with the employee. Obviously, the employee, the primary reader, will be pleased by the positive points and at least a little displeased by the negative ones. Nonetheless, you must state the negative points clearly if you expect improvement. You do the employee a disservice by glossing over a need for improvement; besides, almost every appraisal is going to contain some bad news.

The key to stating the bad news acceptably is to define carefully for yourself the image you wish to project. The image of the objective evaluator with the employee's best interests at heart would seem an effective one to project. It becomes even more important that you create the image of an impartial evaluator when you consider that the appraisal may be read by others, such as a representative of the company human resources department, a representative of the union, or even the employee's attorney. Answering the questions supplied in the next section will contribute to creating such an image. Also, be careful about tone—a touch of sarcasm can cut deeply and can be taken as evidence of bias.

Analyze   You must answer these questions. First, what is the employee doing well? It is important to show appreciation of positive performance. Second, what is the employee doing less than well? And, more important, what corrective steps should the employee take? Is there anything you or the company can do to help the employee improve performance? Third, what performance objectives should the employee strive for in the next evaluation period? These should be specified in terms of quantity and time frames as far as possible, for example, three more sales closed every week or two more audits a month.

Since performance appraisal is an ongoing process, one way to be ready to answer these questions is to keep an informal log about your subordinates. In this log, you may make regular entries that document both the employee's successes and failures by recording a brief description of each incident, the date, and the location. You may also record a summary of any conversation you have with the employee about performance, with its date and location. Such a log is useful when you want to justify raises, promotions, and disciplinary action. This log is your private record and need not be shown to the employee or anyone else.

The organization of the performance appraisal will probably be determined by the design of the company evaluation form.

Draft   As you discuss mistakes and successes, try to keep a balanced perspective. Avoid the tendency to overstress single, uncharacteristic incidents in employee performance. Although the employee might have mishandled one particular job, he or she may have a decent record overall. Likewise, a single notable success does not make for an outstanding record.

Stick to objective facts, such as "Vern has exceeded last year's quota by 20 percent," rather than generalizing about attitudes and personalities: "Vern is a pleasure to work with." The latter statement is a subjective judgment. Also, avoid hearsay: "Merle says that Vern is discourteous to customers."

Revise and Edit   First, read the document from the point of view of the employee. Ask yourself what message the reader will get from it. Is it the message you want to send? Ask yourself, "If I were in this job and had this record and received this appraisal, would I consider it just? Would I know what to do specifically to improve my performance? Would I understand the performance objectives and consider them attainable?"

Read the document from the point of view of a third party—the human resources person, the union representative, or the attorney. Does it sound fair-minded, objective, and supported by solid evidence? Would the performance objectives seem reasonable?

Avoid such sarcastic words or phrases as "Pat *claims* to suffer from severe hay fever" or "It would seem that Pat is never wrong." Above all, look for any evidence of bias, either of antagonism or favoritism.

The Warning   Sometimes a manager must give a written **warning** to an employee to correct a problem in work or work-related behavior. This warning is not always given at performance appraisal time because the manager may feel that the problem cannot wait. But since the written warning normally becomes a permanent part of the employee's personnel file, it is normally given only for a serious infraction of company policy or procedure, for example, insubordination, habitual tardiness, sexual harassment, rudeness to customers, or other disruptive behavior.

Document Plan

Salutation   Address the memo to the employee by name, not to Personnel or File.

The Problem   Describe the details of time, place, and circumstances of the infraction or performance failure.

Effect of the Problem   Explain the implications of this problem for the company—the reason(s) why the company objects to this behavior.

The Record   Mention any prior occurrence of the problem, including date(s). Summarize any prior communication with the employee regarding the problem.

Required Action   State the steps the employee must take to correct the problem and specify time frames for those steps.

Results of Inaction   Specify the action management will take if the employee fails to comply.

Review Date   Name the date on which management will review the employee's progress toward correcting the problem.

Problem-Solving Steps

Define   (Again, we are defining the rhetorical, not the employee, problem.) Such a warning must be bad news to the employee, but one can do little to change that fact. The purpose of such a memo is normally to get the employee to correct the problem, and, if he or she does not, to document management's efforts to correct the problem in case the employee appeals a decision or takes legal action. The employee receives a copy, and a copy becomes part of the permanent record.

Differences in objectives between the written warning and the bad news memo have been explained earlier in the chapter. In the bad news memo, there are two equal goals—conveying the negative message and maintaining goodwill. Although writing a warning memo does not preclude an attempt to preserve goodwill, the main purpose is to correct the problem or provide a basis for disciplinary action, which can include even termination of employment.

Secondary readers could include upper management, a hearing officer, and the employee's attorney. The memo should be written so that a fair-minded outsider can see what the problem is, what you expect the employee to do about it, and what you will do if the employee does not correct the problem.

What kind of image do you wish to project to your reader? What response do you want from your reader? Only you can answer these questions, but it is a good idea to answer them before you begin writing.

Analyze   First, as a manager, you would consult the company policy and procedures manual to see whether it specifies any guidelines for writing the warning memo. That done, it is time for research. We have already suggested that a manager involved with performance appraisals keep an informal, confidential log on subordinates. Such a log is an invaluable source in writing a warning memo, because it could contain, among other things, a detailed record of the occurrences of any problem and summaries of conversations about it.

Draft   The memo should be specific and complete enough so that an objective outsider will agree that you have acted fairly. But do not include as "evidence" hearsay or opinion, statements like "I am told by reliable sources that Dale. . . ." Avoid lines such as "Dale's supervisor feels that. . . ." Stick to facts. Note the warning memo in figure 5.9. In it the author deals strictly in fact—the departmental averages versus those of Dale Hendershot.

The *warning* tends to sound formal and condescending. Despite the seriousness of such documents, your tone can be firm without sounding smug. Note the firm yet relaxed tone of the warning memo in figure 5.9. It achieves this effect by using the personal pronouns *you* and *I*, the active voice, and short sentences. Note that the author achieves a human touch in the last paragraph by offering help, but without undercutting the seriousness of the message.

Revise and Edit

Review the memo for fairness. Be sure it does not select negative facts to support a bias. Do any passages sound sarcastic? You may wish to ask your superior to serve as your editor, but be careful of showing the memo to coworkers—you may be violating the employee's right to privacy.

The Commendation   In contrast to the warning, the **commendation memo** has a multiple purpose. It recognizes some significant accomplishment of a subordinate or colleague, and it usually becomes part of that person's permanent personnel file. Therefore it influences performance appraisal and may build morale in its receiver and foster goodwill for its author. Figure 5.10 shows a sample commendation memo.

We will suggest no special organizational pattern for the commendation memo, nor does the problem-solving approach apply well in this case, but we offer two suggestions. First, the writer should specify in some detail the reasons for the commendation. Note the detail in figure 5.10, especially paragraph two.

Second, the praise should be credible. Avoid such excessive praise as "You're the best public relations director this firm has ever had!" That might be true, but it could be hard to justify. Note the compliment in the last paragraph of figure 5.10—a little understated perhaps, but sincere.

Memo and Short Report Format

As they overlap in content, the memo and the short report overlap in format, but some reports have special forms. For example, job descriptions and performance appraisals follow a prescribed format and even use a printed form. The precise form will vary from company to company. Therefore company practice will determine format for such reports.

HERITAGE INSURANCE COMPANY

Date: October 4, 1986

To: Dale Hendershot

From: Sidney Del Vecchio

Subject: Written Warning

Over the past year, Dale, it appears that your productivity as a Claim Reviewer has declined critically.

Consider your averages for the last year. A Claim Reviewer is expected to audit approximately 550 A&S claims per week; you have averaged 350 per week. A Claim Reviewer is expected to handle approximately 1,000 renewal disabilities per month; you have handled an average of 600 per month. A Claim Reviewer is expected to take approximately 130 calls weekly from District Offices; you have taken an average of 65 calls weekly.

Other Claim Reviewers in the Section have complained to me about having to do extra work because you are not meeting your quotas. If this problem continues, morale will decline.

We discussed your decreased productivity in the last two quarterly review conferences in my office on 7/4/86 and 4/3/86. On both occasions you assured me that temporary personal problems were the root cause of the difficulty but that your output would soon improve. That improvement has not taken place.

Dale, within three months you must bring your quotas up to departmental averages (550 A&S claims weekly, 1,000 renewal disabilities monthly, and 130 phone calls weekly from District Offices). If you do not, your association with Heritage Insurance will end.

I will review your progress with you on 12/4/86. I hope by that time that you will have brought your quotas up to departmental averages. If I can help you to do so, please let me know.

Figure 5.9   Warning memo

Rondex Corporation

Date: January 5, 1986

To: Vern Marco

From: Gwyn Chafin

Subject: San Diego Bankers' Meeting

Vern, just a note to thank you formally for the outstanding job you did for us in preparation for the meeting of our bankers in San Diego last week.

The meeting was an unparalleled success. Many of the bankers commented favorably on the quality of the presentations and the forthright manner in which their questions were handled. The tour of the plant and the banquet afterward also drew many compliments-- and those activities provided a valuable opportunity for the guests to get to know Rondex management on a more personal basis.

When things get a little hectic--around the eleventh hour--it's a pleasure to work with a real professional.

fw

cc: Sam Eggers

Figure 5.10   Commendation

For memos and short reports written in memo form, the format is fairly standard, allowing for minor variations. The company will have a printed form for its interoffice memos. This form will usually include at the top of the page the company name and the words *date, to, from,* and *subject,* along with spaces for typing in the date, the name of receiver, the name of sender, and a phrase indicating the subject of the memo. Figure 5.1 supplies a typical example.

Normally, memos are single-spaced, but double-spacing is acceptable either when the memo is short (say, under 200 words) or when readers might wish to write longhand notations between the lines. It is a good idea to use ample margins for your memos (at least one inch on both sides) so that readers may also make marginal notations.

Leaving ample space for margins helps you to make effective use of "white space," which refers to the portions of the page not occupied by typed words. Short paragraphs of about three to five sentences make your memo visually neat and attractive. Headings break up the blocks of text on the page and therefore also make good use of white space. For an example of a memo that uses margins, paragraph length, and headings to enhance its appearance, see figure 11.2.

A final convention of the memo is the indication in the bottom left corner of

1. The identity of the typist, given by lowercase initials (see figure 5.10)
2. The copy distribution, if any, indicated by the letters *cc*: and the name(s) of anybody receiving a copy (see figure 5.10)
3. Any enclosure, indicated by the typing of the word *enclosure* or *attachment* immediately below the initials of the typist or copy distribution

There are finer points regarding the typing of memos, but they concern the typist more so than the writer. If you must type your own memos, most bookstores and libraries provide reference works on the format of letters and memos.

Summary

The most common documents written by business people are memos and short reports. The two forms are closely related since many short reports are written in memo form, and both may be categorized according to their dominant purposes of informing, persuading, or directing.

Writing to inform includes progress and status reports. The progress report is an update on a specific project, usually written by a subordinate for a superior. It presents an overview of all work on the project, describes the work completed, work in progress, and work not yet begun, and ends with a forecast about the completion of the project. A status report is an update on the significant activities of an individual or department and is normally written for a superior.

Writing to persuade includes the recommendation report, the justification report, and the bad news memo. In persuasion, one should associate recommendations with the goals and needs of the reader. The organization of the recommendation report depends on one's estimate of the reader's reaction to the recommendation. But generally it contains a summary, a statement of the problem, an analysis of the problem, and a recommendation. The justification report is a recommendation report that supports the purchase of a piece of equipment or a service. We treat it in chapter 11, "Feasibility Reports and Proposals."

The bad news memo has two equal goals, to state a negative position and to retain the goodwill of the reader. To achieve these goals, the writer opens the memo by establishing common ground, gives the reasons behind the negative position, states the position, and concludes with a positive, supportive statement.

Writing to direct covers the policy statement or directive, the procedure, the job description, the performance appraisal, the warning memo, and the commendation memo.

The policy statement or directive will become more important as a career advances. It is a statement of guidelines covering particular situations. Most policy statements begin with the most important point and progress to the least important point.

The procedure is a statement of the method by which policy is to be carried out in concrete situations. The playscript format is often used for organizing and writing procedures.

Most companies regularly require performance appraisals of their employees. The three phases of most performance appraisals are explained: establishing standards by which to judge performance, applying them to performance, and setting performance objectives for the next appraisal period.

The warning should not be confused with the bad news memo because its purpose is different. The author of the warning tries to correct poor performance. The warning documents management's dissatisfaction and willingness to work with the employee, describes in measurable terms the improvement that must occur, and specifies the action that will be taken if the problem is not corrected.

The commendation is basically a morale builder in which the writer praises either a colleague or a subordinate for a job well done.

This chapter includes an outline and problem-solving techniques for creating these various kinds of contemporary business documents.

Writing Problems

1. As the assistant manager of Employee Communications, one of your responsibilities is to edit the company newspaper, the *LinCorp News*. Because this is your first year in the job, your boss, Leigh Neltner, has asked for a written progress report. You have the following information to report:

   - The deadline for submission of manuscripts was January 4. You were able to send the copy to the typesetter on January 16, receiving the last copy back from the typesetter on January 19.

   - You sent the captions, headlines, and layouts to the keyliner on January 23; keylining was done between January 24 and 26. Today is January 27.

   - The boards are due in to you today, and corrections are to be completed by January 30.

   - Camera and stripping work is to be finished by January 31, and the proofs are due back to you by February 1.

   - You are to give your go-ahead to print on February 2. Plate making should be finished February 3; printing will take place on February 6 and 7; the printed copy will go to the bindery on February 8 and thence to the post office on February 10.

   - The project is on schedule.

   Write a progress report to your immediate supervisor in memo form.

2. You are the manager of Systems II, reporting to Meredith Gualdoni, second vice-president and director of the Systems Department. You are writing a status report on a word processing pilot study, authorized by Gualdoni several weeks previously, to be conducted in your division. The program will begin on August 10.

   Over a period of one month most of the writing done in the division will be sent in longhand form to the Word Processing Center for typing. Exceptions will include overtime authorization sheets, vacation slips, and similar materials. Your division will keep logs on the turnaround time and the accuracy of the work received from the center. If the results are satisfactory, your division will be trained in phone dictation and begin sending in your typing by that method. This phase should last approximately two weeks. If the results of this phase are satisfactory, you plan to extend the process to other Systems Department divisions one at a time, using the same method. You and your people will be working closely with the center to solve any problems and monitor the results. You will report back to Gualdoni at the end of each phase.

   Write the status report in memo form.

3. As manager of Systems II, you have completed the pilot study described in problem 2 and are now prepared to recommend that word processing become a permanent and major part of your division. The following is a description of the experience on which the recommendation is based:

   Word processing alleviates routine typing, such as progress reports, draft copies, and certain correspondence. Secretaries are thus freed to help with more important tasks, such as the preparation of statistical reports and the maintenance of departmental records. Word processing cuts down on storage space because the document is stored on an electronic medium, which also simplifies the editing of rough drafts so that corrections can be made without retyping the entire draft.

   The Word Processing Center has a Confidential Typing Section, in which access to material is limited to a few specialists cleared for security.

   Normal turnaround time is three hours, but a rush job can be done more quickly. Typing errors are fewer than in documents typed by personal secretaries, due in part to the proofreading capabilities of the word processor. Word processing is available before and after normal working hours because of the phone-in capacity of the system. Portable dictation units are available for out of town use.

   Write the recommendation report to Meredith Gualdoni.

4. Formerly the company sales manager, you are the recently promoted vice-president of Marketing. One of your first responsibilities is to select the new sales manager from the present sales staff. The two contenders are former colleagues with whom you have been on cordial terms, and you want to keep it that way. But only one can be promoted, and you must write a memo conveying the bad news of no promotion to the other, Pat Wittkamp.

   For the past two quarters Pat has topped the department in sales, making more sales calls than anyone else in the department, early and late. But selling is not managing, and your judgment tells you that Pat will not succeed as a manager.

   Pat is quickly bored by meetings and shows it. Pat seldom attends departmental sales meetings, preferring to be briefed privately. Pat seems happiest—and most effective—working "solo" with a client. Pat does not write well. Pat has no academic background in management. Without going into details, you feel that the other candidate has the qualities that lead to success as a manager.

   Write a memo that will convey the bad news and minimize the negative reaction. Be careful not to adopt a back-slapping tone; if your letter is to be successful, it must be sincere.

5. Since you are the director of Administrative Services, the Word Processing Center is one of your responsibilities. The center has a Confidential Typing Section, in which sensitive documents are typed. Only confidential correspondence secretaries are permitted in this restricted area. But yesterday, the section head reported to you that there have been encroachments on this restricted area by other center personnel and occasionally by persons from outside the center. The section head feels that confidentiality has not been compromised yet, but it could be if the present practice continues.

   You have decided that an employee of the center who enters the confidential section without your explicit permission will be reprimanded and placed on probation. If an employee from outside the center enters the confidential section, you will notify the intruder's superior of the incident.

   Any business with the confidential correspondence secretaries should be conducted at the counter in the entrance. Only if people observe this policy can they and others feel free to send sensitive documents to the center for typing.

   Write a policy statement to be placed in the company policy and procedures manual. Follow the format indicated in figure 5.5.

6. Select a procedure from one of your courses that involves several steps. Here are a few examples:

   Preparing an income statement
   Performance appraisal process
   Collective bargaining
   Writing a formal report
   Systems design
   Market research
   The sales process
   Production control procedure
   A data processing procedure
   A word processing procedure

   Write a procedure for the process addressed to someone who has general knowledge of the field but is not familiar with the particular procedure.

7. Write a job description for the position of Administrative Specialist I. This person works in the Field Administration Department and reports to the district administrative manager. The job is located at the Easton, Maryland, branch office. The job code number is 387-42.

   This person must have at least three years of related office experience. An associate's degree in business is required, and the applicant must have good math skills and know general office procedures.

This employee would perform some accounting and payroll functions; prepare location accounting reports, government reports, and personal property and sales tax reports; prepare and process internal charge vouchers for income disbursements and the general ledger; manage the local petty cash fund for the branch office, balancing the register, auditing expense statements, making travel advances, and maintaining a record of outstanding travel balances; assist in reconciling balance sheet accounts and sales revenue statements; process employment documents and weekly payroll and expense statements; maintain personnel files; distribute group benefits information and handle United Fund, savings bond, and union dues deductions; serve as the local credit union representative; audit and process equipment and software orders and billings; and maintain order files.

The prospective employee will work for the district administrative manager but will receive direction from an administrative specialist II or financial specialist.

8. You are the district administrative manager to whom the Administrative Specialist I (of problem 7) reports. This person's name is Robin Petrou, and it is time for Robin's semiannual performance review. Following are your observations about Robin's performance for the last six months. (You may decide not to include all these observations.)

Robin prepares timely and accurate location accounting reports, government reports, and personal property and sales tax reports. Robin is efficient in preparing and processing internal charge vouchers for income disbursements and the general ledger. Robin does not always handle the local petty cash fund for the branch office satisfactorily. (There is no question of Robin's honesty.) Robin is often slow to audit expense statements and hesitant to bring audit problems to your attention, as you have clearly directed. You worry that some sales representatives may be improperly reimbursed.

Robin is always diligent and helpful in reconciling balance sheet accounts and sales revenue statements. Robin is efficient and punctual in processing employment documents and handling all personnel benefit and union transactions. Robin seems to have a good working relationship with the administrative specialist II and the financial specialist, both of whom sometimes function as Robin's immediate supervisor. Robin seems to get along well with everyone in the office.

Robin is generally punctual, but three or four times a week Robin takes longer than the 15 minutes allowed for coffee breaks. While you do not feel that these excessively long breaks interfere with Robin's overall efficiency, you feel that Robin's behavior sets the wrong example to other employees.

Write a performance appraisal for Robin, following the format given in figure 5.8.

9. You are the office manager for a small wholesale supplier of heavy equipment parts. Part of your job is to supervise the five customer service representatives who take orders from customers calling in from all parts of the company. One of these reps is Merle Grooms, who has been with the company for nine years.

   Merle is a devoted employee, never late and almost never missing a day of work. However, in recent months Merle has become increasingly rude to customers over the phone. You have personally received three telephone calls from customers complaining about Merle's rudeness, and you can confirm these complaints personally. If this behavior continues, you feel the company may lose accounts. Merle is also setting a poor example for less experienced service reps.

   You have initiated discussions about Merle's rudeness with him on three occasions, the first in Merle's last performance appraisal, the second three months ago, and the third two weeks ago. Merle admitted the "impoliteness" and promised to correct this tendency. But yesterday you overheard a telephone conversation in which Merle used profanity to a customer. You have decided to give Merle a formal warning. Write the memo.

10. You are the director of corporate communications for a medium-sized manufacturing firm. Chris Ostrowski of your department has served as this year's project leader in charge of researching, writing, and editing the company's annual report. Chris was also responsible for the design and layout of the published report. This project entailed many hours of work, many of them at night and on weekends as the deadline drew near. Chris headed the annual report working committee, conducting its meetings, assigning individual tasks, and coordinating the work of several committee members. Chris also coordinated the contributions to the project from within and outside the company.

   Despite internal committee disagreements, budgetary limitations, and deadlines, Chris showed remarkable staying power. You have sent the president a copy of the published report and received in turn compliments on its appearance, content, and the image the report projects of the company and its management. Write a commendation memo to Chris.

CHAPTER 6

Business Letters: Writing to Outsiders

*T*he last chapter discussed memos and short reports, the principal ways people write to those *inside* their company. Now we take up the business letter, the principal way people write to those *outside* their company. Apart from slightly different formats, no major differences exist between letters and memos, so the same problem-solving approach will help you solve both writing problems.

Business letters vary more than memos and short reports, and to save time, many companies have developed **form letters**, sometimes called **guide letters**, to deal with recurring circumstances. For example, when a shareholder writes to ask a common question, the person answering the letter can simply dictate the shareholder's name and address and the number of the guide letter. The one responsible for answering the request then receives an individualized letter from the word processing department to sign. Memos and short reports usually have distinctive content that does not lend itself to such a form response.

Of course, not all business communication can be reduced to form letters. Still, it is important for you to be able to write a good form letter and to recognize a good one when you see it.

This chapter will cover five qualities *all* business letters must have regardless of industry—namely, clarity, courtesy, sensitivity, positive wording, and naturalness. We will then discuss two important organizational plans that will help you organize most business letters effectively—the direct and the indirect plans. Also, the chapter will describe common business letter types, such as the sales, credit, claim, and adjustment letters. Finally, business letter parts and formats will be treated.

Qualities to Stress in All Business Letters

Clarity, courtesy, sensitivity, positive wording, and naturalness are important in all communications but especially in letters. For example, if a memo is not clear, its receiver can easily dial your extension and ask what you had in mind. A customer can't always do that. Or if your memo is lacking in courtesy, you may still get, reluctantly, the cooperation you want, but a discourteous letter will usually go straight to the wastebasket. Let's look at these qualities separately.

Clarity

Although achieving clarity is always one of the goals you specify in the first part of the problem-solving approach, in the business letter it takes on a special import because you are almost always writing for the "lay" reader. Writing for a lay audience means using relatively short, familiar rather than technical terms. It means using relatively short sentences, usually between 15 and 20 words a sentence. And it means using relatively short paragraphs, an average of five to seven lines to a paragraph.

But clarity is not always a matter of short words, sentences, and paragraphs. It has much to do with adopting the reader's viewpoint—organizing your material in the way easiest for the reader to grasp rather than in the way easiest for you to write. You can always "test" a letter's clarity by having a lay reader examine it and paraphrase the message. Comparing that version of your message with the one you intended to send may lead you to revise the document.

Courtesy

Most business letters are "customer relations" correspondence because you are often dealing with present or potential customers. Fostering goodwill is therefore always an important objective; you must strive to make the reader feel respected and valued. Doing so is not a matter of any elaborate ritual; it's a matter of treating people with respect. When you deal with the bank teller, you appreciate a smile and a pleasant "How are you today?" With letters it is the same way. Saying "please" and "thank you" are signals to the reader that you value him or her.

Figure 6.1 is an example of a courteous business letter. The first courtesy the writer can show the addressee is to spell his or her name correctly. Notice also that the writer opens the letter by expressing appreciation for the reader's suggestion. The writer closes the letter with another expression of gratitude and an offer to be of further assistance. Although declining to take the reader's suggestion, the writer conveys a sense of valuing the reader, the essence of courtesy. Figures 6.3 and 6.4 likewise close courteously. Note that most of the customer relations letters in this chapter open by thoughtfully thanking the reader for writing in the first place.

In addition to courtesy, you must be sensitive to the reader's emotional needs. Whereas courtesy emphasizes outward expressions—thanking or asking politely—sensitivity focuses on appreciation of the reader's viewpoint. This appreciation doesn't necessarily mean agreeing with the reader. The customer is not always right: if the customer were always right, who would pay those monthly utility bills, or any bills for that matter? It would be more appropriate to say, "The customer is always right about *something*."

Sensitivity

In other words, you must establish some common ground with your reader. You may not be able to comply with the reader's wishes, but communication will be easier if you meet the reader's need for understanding. The writer of the letter in figure 6.1, though declining the reader's request, still creates a climate sympathetic to the reader. The two middle paragraphs focus on needs of the reader (to forecast and budget, to get timely service, and to keep prices low). The author of the letter in figure 6.6 focuses throughout on the reader's need to keep the life insurance policy in force. In figure 6.11 the writer does not accuse the company of making a mistake but suggests that either its service or billing department is "unaware" that her company has a service contract.

Often in business, it's not so much *what* is said that offends but *how* it's said. Sensitivity to the reader's ego can salvage goodwill even in negative situations.

People respond favorably to positive connotations more often than to negative ones. Most people prefer to describe their height as "almost six feet tall" rather than as "only five feet ten." Which of the following statements sounds better to the smoker: "No smoking" or "Thank you for not smoking"? Which statement sounds better to the customer: "We cannot deliver your purchase until after the first of the month" or "We will deliver your purchase immediately after the first of the month"? Most people prefer the positive version.

Positive Wording

In business letters you try to state matters in their most positive light but not to distort facts. Distorting the truth can be a grave error because the reader will usually sense the underlying manipulation. To help you apply this principle of positive wording, several paired statements follow. Each

C A P S T O N E   S E R V I C E   C E N T E R
128 Winding Way Drive Juneau, AK 99804

March 19, 1986

Mr. Carl Burger, Director
Administrative Services
Dooley Enterprises
Ketchikan, AK 99905

Dear Mr. Burger:

Thank you for your letter expressing concern over our request for
advance payment of maintenance premiums and suggesting that
monthly payments would be more acceptable. Because we are eager to
serve our customers more effectively, we appreciate their suggestions.

The reasons behind our request for advance annual payment are
essentially two. First, doing so allows you, the customer, to make the
necessary adjustments to your forecasts and budgets. Second, doing so
provides us with the lead time necessary to schedule your service
needs more accurately.

On the other hand, billing you on a monthly basis, you'll agree, would
result in higher administrative costs that could well result in higher
rates. Annual payment therefore ensures you of efficient service at
very competitive rates.

Thanks again for your thoughts on this matter. If I can be of further
assistance, please call or write.

Sincerely,

Merle Carnes

Merle Carnes
Customer Service Representative

dj

Figure 6.1   Letter showing courtesy and sensitivity (policy justification letter)

says essentially the same thing, but one statement relates the message in a negative manner and the other uses positive language.

Negative: We cannot accept this alternative.
Positive: Let's adopt another alternative.

Negative: We are not communicating well.
Positive: We need to communicate more effectively.

Negative: Your company has consistently failed to meet deadlines.
Positive: Your company must hereafter meet deadlines.

Negative: Brand X is not as good as Brand Y.
Positive: Brand Y excels Brand X.

Negative: Don't forget that . . .
Positive: Remember that . . .

Negative: The office furnishings are old-fashioned.
Positive: The office needs to be refurnished.

Negative: It's no bother.
Positive: It's a pleasure.

Negative: They make many billing errors.
Positive: They need greater accuracy in billing.

Negative: Merle complained about their . . .
Positive: Merle suggested that they improve . . .

Negative: We cannot ship the order until January 5.
Positive: We will ship the order by January 5.

Negative: We are losing sight of key objectives.
Positive: Let's concentrate on key objectives.

Negative: We have run out of . . .
Positive: Demand for . . . has exceeded the supply.

Negative: We cannot extend credit terms.
Positive: We will serve you on a C.O.D. basis.

Negative: I do not doubt that . . .
Positive: I am confident that . . .

Negative: This model should not malfunction.
Positive: This model should function smoothly.

From time to time, negative ideas must be a part of business letters. For example, sometimes you must insist that your firm will fill an order to a customer only on a C.O.D. basis because the customer has not paid for the previous order. But even here, choose the positive version of the statement. For example, you might write that you will be "happy to process the order promptly, C.O.D." and assure the customer that credit will be reinstated as soon as you receive payment for the previous order.

Naturalness

Sometimes it is hard to be natural, especially with strangers. But strive to write the way you speak when you are speaking to someone you respect and whose good opinion you value. Doing so will lessen the tendency to mimic old-fashioned business letter style, which is characterized by heavy use of the passive voice, third person pronouns, and formulaic expressions. The old-fashioned business writer is "in receipt of" your letter, "trusts this letter finds you well," "advises" rather than "informs" you, asks that you "enclosed please find," and ends by "thanking you in advance." Figure 6.2 shows the same letter depicted in figure 6.1 but expressed in an old-fashioned business letter style. We have exaggerated the tendency a little, but contrast the two letters and you'll easily see which is easier to read and more attuned to the reader as a person.

Two Organizational Plans for Business Letters

A letter can follow various organizational plans, for example, the order of importance, chronological order, cause and effect, and step-by-step process. But there are two plans you will find especially helpful in letter writing, the *direct* and the *indirect*.

The Direct Plan

As the phrase suggests, the **direct plan** delivers the main point of the message in the first paragraph. Use this plan generally when you expect the reader to react either favorably or at least neutrally to your message.

When you have good news, tell your reader right away: if you are awarding a contract, announcing a decision to hire, or agreeing to a request. Figure 6.3 is such a letter. The writer *first* informs the reader that she has been selected for an interview, then goes on to explain the details—for example, the kind of program she will be considered for, the timing, and the location of the interview. For obvious reasons, this plan is often called the "good news" strategy.

The direct plan also works well when the news or main point of the message is neutral. For example, a letter to a friend in another company requesting a copy of a speech given by that company's president or an announcement of the time and location of a meeting are neutral messages that would be well conveyed by the direct plan.

C A P S T O N E   S E R V I C E   C E N T E R
128 Winding Way Drive   Juneau, AK 99804

March 19, 1986

Mr. Carl Burger, Director
Administrative Services
Dooley Enterprises
Ketchikan, AK 99905

Dear Mr. Burger:

This is to acknowledge that the writer is in receipt of your letter
expressing concern as per his request for advance payment of
maintenance premiums and your suggestion that monthly payments
would be more acceptable. Be assured that as the writer is eager to
serve his customers as per the most effective way, he appreciates
their suggestions.

Accordingly, be advised that the reasons as per his request for
advance annual payment of maintenance premiums are essentially
two. First, allow the writer to point out that doing so allows the
customer to make the necessary adjustments to his or her forecasts
and budgets. Secondly, permit the writer to say that doing so provides
the writer with the lead time necessary to schedule the customer's
service needs more accurately.

Be advised, on the other hand, that billing the customer on a monthly
basis would result in higher administrative costs that could well
result in higher rates. Annual payment therefore ensures the
customer of efficient service at very competitive rates.

As per your thoughts on this matter, allow the writer to state that
your suggestion is at hand and appreciated. But the writer regrets to
inform you that he cannot gratify your wishes as per acting in
accordance with your suggestion.

Notwithstanding, avail yourself of the opportunity to write or call the
writer any time to advise of future suggestions. Thanking you in
advance, the writer remains,

Very truly yours,

Merle Carnes

Merle Carnes
Customer Service Representative

dj

Figure 6.2   Old-fashioned style

CRANLEY BUSINESS SYSTEMS, INC.
5001 N. Broadway Avenue
Davenport, IA 52814

July 14, 1986

Ms. Ramona Jorge
24 Fielding Terrace
Burlington, IA 52602

Dear Ms. Jorge:

Thank you for your application letter and resume. Yes, we do have
on-the-job training programs, and yes, we would like to interview you
for our field engineering training program.

Cranley Business Systems is always eager to recruit new talent in field
engineering. Our training programs for qualified persons often lead to
lifetime careers in the preventive and remedial maintenance of our
systems. I would welcome the opportunity to discuss this particular
program at some length with you and ask you to write me regarding a
time when it would be convenient to come to our Vanora facility for
an interview. I am enclosing a brochure which will acquaint you with
the essentials of the training program.

Because we realize that you are approaching an important crossroad,
we want you to make the best possible decision. Again, thanks for
writing us, and I look forward to meeting you.

Sincerely,

Shelley Morrison

Shelley Morrison, Director
Executive Recruiting

lc
Enclosure
c.c.: Jan Regalbuto, Engineering

Figure 6.3   The direct plan

When you estimate that your reader's reaction to the main point of your message will be negative, lead off with the reasons or supporting evidence for the main point, saving the negatives until late in the letter. Such "bad news" includes announcing a price increase, refusing a claim, turning down a bid, rejecting an applicant, refusing a request, or denying credit. Because this plan calls for presenting reasons first and deferring the real message, it is called the **indirect plan**, or sometimes the "bad news" strategy.

The Indirect Plan

The rationale for using this plan is that hearing bad news gradually rather than abruptly is less shocking to the recipient. Figure 6.4 uses the indirect plan to minimize the reader's alienation. The main point of the letter—that the service call is not covered by the service agreement—is delayed until the last third of the letter. Delaying the bad news will not always put the reader into a more receptive frame of mind. When you start off with the reasons supporting a negative decision, the reader may sense the coming bad news and skim the rest of the letter until he or she finds it expressed. The strategy still helps, however, because the fact that you *tried* to soften the blow shows that you care about your reader's feelings, and that alone might foster goodwill.

We do not suggest that you use the indirect plan every time your message is negative. Use it when your reader profile indicates that it will be the best method of organizing your material. For example, in breaking bad news to a friend, the direct plan may be better if you feel the friend probably wants to know the truth immediately. Only you can judge which plan to use.

Some Common Business Letter Types

Some common business letters are the inquiry, the response to an inquiry, the sales letter, the credit letter, the collection letter series, the claim letter, the adjustment letter, the policy justification letter, and the goodwill letter.

One of the most commonly written business letters is the **inquiry**, in which the writer requests information about a product or service offered by the reader's company. The writer may ask for a price list or promotional materials, may inquire about discounts or about forthcoming sales. Or the writer may inquire about company policy or practice. A customer may want to know whether the company has plans to upgrade present products and services or to enter a new market. Someone may want to know whether the company is hiring in a particular field or whether it sends out speakers to civic groups, and if so, what kinds of presentations are available.

The Inquiry

Dalton Business Machines, Inc.
4500 Ammon Drive
Oklahoma City, OK 73114

August 19, 1986

Ms. Lorine Zelinski, Manager
Dexter & Signa
897 Garey Street
Houston, TX 77232

Dear Ms. Zelinski:

Thank you for your letter expressing concern over being billed for the replacement of the "year" wheel on your Dalton Cash Register. I can understand your feeling that such a service should be covered under the maintenance agreement.

As you know, the maintenance agreement states that the "year" wheel will be replaced only when it wears out due to normal use. But this wheel can also "wear out" because it has been advanced the maximum number of times so that it no longer is engraved with the current year. A new wheel must then be installed. In this case the installation is not due to normal use, and so the maintenance agreement does not cover it.

I appreciate the opportunity to explain our position in this case; and if I can be of further assistance, please contact me.

Sincerely,

Jan Dirksen

Jan Dirksen
Customer Service Representative

rt

Figure 6.4   The indirect plan (letter refusing an adjustment)

Document Plan

1. Give a clear statement of the desired information together with a concise explanation of the reason(s) for the inquiry. You might open with a question, such as, "Does your firm have a service center within 200 miles of Fargo, North Dakota?" Be precise. Do you want a price list or a demonstration of equipment or both?
2. Elaborate on your request if necessary. Ask specific questions.
3. Appeal to the reader's self-interest, especially when inconvenience without obvious benefit is involved.
4. If you need the information by a certain time, say so, but don't make it sound as though you're giving the reader a deadline.
5. If you are requesting sensitive information, assure the reader you will keep it confidential.
6. Thank the reader for his or her attention, but do not thank the reader "in advance" for responding to your inquiry, because you do not want to sound presumptuous.

Problem-Solving Steps

Define   Before the writing, specify information you want, whether a price list or a demonstration, for example. Specify the reason for the inquiry if you think the reader is interested, and then consider how fully you need to explain it. If the reason is self-evident, you may only need to say, "I am considering the purchase of several memory typewriters for our Springfield branch office." On the other hand, if you are requesting information about a company procedure, you may have to justify fully the request.

If you are requesting information not easily provided, consider what form your appeal will take. Can you appeal to the reader's self-interest or sense of professional courtesy?

Analyze   The direct plan is normally best for the inquiry. To organize the inquiry, we suggest that you follow the approach outlined previously, but you may need to adapt it. For example, if the information requested is not sensitive, you will not need to promise confidentiality. If it is fairly involved, however, consider using a format that will make the response easier for the reader, for example, a numbered list of questions.

Draft   Keep the letter brief, supplying only the detail that you feel the reader will need to act favorably upon your request.

The tone of the letter should be friendly and respectful because you are making a request. Even if there are built-in reasons for the reader's compliance, such as the possibility of making a sale or building goodwill, you want the reader to think of you as courteous and sensitive to his or her needs.

Revise and Edit   Put yourself in the place of the reader. Would this person know what you want and why you want it? Are your questions necessary, clear, and sufficiently elaborated? If you have specified a date beyond which the information will no longer be useful, have you avoided sounding as though you are giving the reader a deadline? Is your tone throughout businesslike but courteous? If not, revise. Figure 6.5 shows an effective inquiry letter.

The Response to an Inquiry

In responding to an inquiry, your primary goal is to supply the information the reader has requested, and sometimes this means writing a short, courteous letter enclosing materials the reader has at least implicitly requested. But in practice, informing often leads to *advising*, especially where decisions are involved. And remember, responding *promptly* to an inquiry promotes goodwill.

Document Plan

1. Answer the reader's question directly, if possible in a single summary sentence.
2. Elaborate on the answer, responding to any questions the reader has asked in the order he or she has asked them. Anticipate questions the reader may have regarding your answer and respond to them, too.
3. Offer help or suggestions growing out of your answer to the reader's inquiry, for example, an offer to demonstrate a product or a tactful offer of advice.
4. Close with a statement that promotes friendliness and goodwill.

Problem-Solving Steps

Define   Define your goal in responding to the inquiry. Do you want only to give information or do you also want to offer advice, even to persuade the reader? Note the example of the response letter given in figure 6.6, in which a policyholder, Mr. Robert Chung, has written to his insurance company inquiring whether he can cash in his insurance policy and, if so, for how much. In responding, the author, Gale Vitale, has two goals—to answer the question affirmatively but also to convince the policyholder that a better alternative exists, namely, to take out a loan on the policy.

In writing to inform, you must first decide how much information your reader needs. The letter in figure 6.6, for example, gives the reader, Mr. Chung, just enough information on which to base a decision. The author includes no unnecessary information, such as citing a case similar to Mr. Chung's. However, the letter includes a fair amount of reasoning, showing Chung the advantage of borrowing on rather than surrendering the policy.

Finnegan Realty, Inc.
2387 Winding Way
Clarkesville, OK 74003

January 25, 1986

Sales Manager
K & W Office Supplies Company
12 N. Eling Street
Barcelona, OK 74004

Dear Sales Manager:

I am interested in purchasing five filing cabinets for my new office. I
need a description of the models you carry together with a price list. If
you have a current catalog, I would appreciate a copy, since I will be
purchasing office supplies from time to time.

All five of these cabinets should contain five drawers. Two of the five
cabinets should be legal size; three of them should be letter size. All
five should have thumb latches and locks.

What colors do your cabinets feature? I especially wish to avoid the
drab iron gray color.

I would appreciate having this information within 10 days or two
weeks. I shall appreciate any assistance you are able to provide me
and look forward to doing business with you.

Gratefully,

Hilary Finnegan

(Ms.) Hilary Finnegan
President

et

Figure 6.5   Inquiry (full block style)

SCORPIO LIFE & CASUALTY COMPANY
1200 Franklin Boulevard
Alexandria, VA 22307

February 11, 1986

Mr. Robert Chung
112 Channing Place
Tacoma, WA 98407

Subject: Policy # 5923561

Dear Mr. Chung:

Yes, of course you may cash in your insurance policy at any time you
see fit. The present cash surrender value of your policy is $1,739.82,
which includes the accumulated dividends. Naturally, if you surrender
the policy, you would be paid only that amount, and the policy would
have no further value.

On the other hand, since the death benefit of the policy is $10,110.28,
it would be to your advantage to keep the policy. As we grow older, the
cost of insurance increases; thus you would have to pay more in the
future for the same protection you now enjoy under your current
policy.

Let me suggest an alternative plan. Your policy contains a loan
provision which will allow you to borrow against its cash value. You
could borrow up to $1,723.46. You would pay 6 percent interest and
you could repay the loan in amounts of $10 or more whenever
convenient. And, by taking a loan (instead of surrendering the policy),
you retain the insurance coverage.

I have enclosed a loan application. But if you decide to surrender the
policy, simply complete the reverse side of the application and return
it along with the policy in the envelope provided.

Figure 6.6   Response to an inquiry

Mr. Robert Chung   2   February 11, 1986

However, I hope that you will consider the financial advantages--and
greater security--involved with taking out a loan and keeping
the policy in effect. Please call or write me if you have further
questions.

Sincerely,

Gale Vitale

Gale Vitale, Supervisor
Policy Service Division

et
Enclosure

Second, you must define how you want your reader to react to this information. The writer of the Chung letter is careful not to preempt Chung's right to make up his own mind. The writer therefore explains the procedure for surrendering the policy if that is Chung's decision, projecting an image of the knowledgeable professional who is interested in Chung's welfare.

Analyze   Often when you are responding to an inquiry, you already have the necessary facts or they are readily available, so the need for research is minimal. Generally, the direct plan, explained previously, is the best way to organize the response.

Draft   Choosing the right style will not be difficult if you follow the advice we have given previously about clarity and naturalness. The letter in figure 6.6 uses such a style from the first sentence: "Yes, of course you may cash in your policy at any time you see fit." The author addresses the reader directly in the sentence "Let me suggest an alternative plan." Generally, the sentences are short and conversational.

Revise and Edit   Place yourself in the position of the reader—will this person get your message from this letter? Will your points be clear? If you are advising, have you explained the reasons behind your advice sufficiently well to persuade the reader? Do you sound patronizing? Does the letter sound courteous? Is there a negative statement anywhere that you can rephrase in more positive terms without distorting the truth?

The Sales Letter

Most of us think of **sales letters** as the smooth, word processed letters we get in the mail that sell subscriptions, insurance, or credit cards. But ordinary business people write sales letters in which they attempt to sell customers on their product or service. Figure 6.7 is such a letter, written by a sales representative for dictation equipment to the office manager of a law firm interested in dictation equipment.

Whether or not the sales letter is the first contact with the prospective buyer, it can serve as a transition to further contact, leading to the closing of the sale. It is an economical means of contacting new prospects and keeping in touch with existing accounts, for example, informing them of sales, discounts, or new products. A sales letter can accompany a catalogue sent to an industrial account or a private consumer.

Document Plan

1. Gain the reader's attention by evoking a problem the reader is experiencing or by stressing an unfulfilled need of the reader.
2. Assure the reader that you have the solution to that problem or the answer to that unfulfilled need.
3. Supply evidence to support your claim, for example, facts, figures, or expert testimony.

Libra Dictation Systems
321 S. Platt Avenue
Chicago, Illinois 60625

September 25, 1986

Ms. Joyce O'Shaugnessy, Office Manager
Dunne, Esposito, and Jasper, Attorneys at Law
204 Hollis Lane
Chicago, Illinois 60604

Dear Ms. O'Shaugnessy:

Thank you for the opportunity to introduce you to the benefits of a
Libra Dictation System. If you will also allow me to demonstrate this
system to you and members of your staff, I can show you why it is the
most advanced system on the market today.

Libra's new Model 3540 is the ultimate state-of-the-art system on the
market with its exclusive features of insertion, holding, and
Messenger, which are not available on any other system today. The
enclosed brochure will elaborate further on these features and other
benefits of the system.

The new Libra 3540 clearly excels its competition in its superior
sound quality, ability to handle priority documents, phone-in capacity,
telephone conversation recording capacity, and electronic indexing.
This last feature of the Libra 3540 saves considerable secretarial time.

In addition, our excellent service support guarantees a 24-hour
turnaround on service for the unit, a feature a busy office manager
will appreciate, I'm sure. However, there are other benefits to the
system which I cannot cover in a brief letter. That is why I would ask
a 30-minute demonstration period at the convenience of yourself and
your people.

The sheet I am enclosing will demonstrate part of the cost savings on
the trade-in value of your present dictation system.

Ms. O'Shaughnessy, I will call you on Thursday morning to request a
time frame for my presentation.

Sincerely,

Lesley Wittgenstein

Lesley Wittgenstein
Sales Representative

mo
Enclosures

Figure 6.7   Sales letter (block style)

4. Ask the reader to make some commitment to the product or service, for example, a phone call or a mailing. Reemphasize your ability to supply the benefit the reader desires.

Problem-Solving Steps

Define   Defining the goal of a sales letter is easy—to sell your product or service. The reader profile is thus very important. You must specify at least in general the following: the need you intend to satisfy or the problem you intend to solve; the person's educational background; and, in the case of a consumer, the person's social status and lifestyle. You must also anticipate his or her likely preconceptions about your product or service. For example, is the reader likely to be somewhat skeptical about your product, thinking, "Another sales pitch for an employee insurance program?" If so, you must counteract that preconception by demonstrating the uniqueness of your plan.

Analyze   First, target the real decision maker, for example, a buyer or purchasing agent, an executive, or the consumer. If no marketing study has already been done, get to know your reader. Or research the company or industry you wish to sell to in trade and business journals and newspapers or through the grapevine. Research their problems, for example, high turnover, production shutdowns, low productivity, or financial losses. The sales letter in figure 6.7 points out features of the dictation system that would particularly appeal to an office manager.

Second, know your product thoroughly. Make a list of its desirable features. Here you may need some advice from your technical people. For an organizational plan, we suggest that you follow the document plan outlined previously, adapted to your special circumstances.

Draft   Decide which specific need or problem of the reader you will focus on, and which desirable features of your product or service seem most likely to meet that need or solve that problem. Doing so will give you the material for the first two parts of the letter, the attention getter and the claim. Then develop the third part, supporting evidence. You may cite results of laboratory or field tests, case histories, or the testimony of satisfied customers, and you may even offer a money-back guarantee. Anticipate and answer questions the reader may have about the product or service.

Choose the style best suited to sell the product or service to *this* reader. If you are writing to a purchasing agent or buyer, your style will be more restrained but still enthusiastic. The author of the letter in figure 6.7 strikes such a note of restrained enthusiasm. If you are writing to the general public, your style may need to be more forceful to get the message across.

Revise and Edit   Reread the letter to judge whether you have made a convincing case for your claim. Is the tone right—enthusiastic without sounding phony? Are there negative phrases you can change to positive ones? Are the sentences varied and the paragraphs not too long?

As a consumer, you are probably familiar with the fundamentals of credit transactions. You may have bought a car, house, boat, or appliance on credit. Businesses operate much the same way, in applying for credit from other companies and in extending credit to their customers. Most firms use the telephone, standard forms, and computers to process credit applications, but letters can still be written for two reasons: granting credit and refusing it.

The Letter Granting Credit   The letter **granting credit** is a "good news" message that uses the direct plan of organization. It is more than an announcement that credit terms are available, however. It is also an opportunity to explain those terms and thus preclude later misunderstandings, especially late payments. Such letters also give you another chance to "sell" the customer on the wisdom of doing business with your firm.

Document Plan

1. State the favorable credit decision.
2. Describe the terms of credit. Specify the date of payment, any discounts for early payment, and penalties for late payment.
3. End the letter with a goodwill statement. Assure the customer that he or she has made the right choice in deciding to do business with your firm. Express gratitude and the desire to serve.

See figure 6.8 for a letter granting credit.

Problem-Solving Steps

Define   Your goal is first to explain the favorable credit decision and second to increase the customer's interest in your product or service and confidence in your firm. You want to create an image of the confident professional who is eager to serve.

Analyze   You will already have the credit terms before you; they will normally be the standard terms offered to such a customer. The direct plan is normally better for this letter, and the list suggested previously should enable you to plan the draft of the letter.

Draft   The letter should be brief, but it should also project an image of a person welcoming a new customer. The tone should be friendly, and the emphasis should be on the relationship that is developing between your reader and your company—one hopes a satisfying, long-lasting associaton.

Revise and Edit   The first point to check is clarity; have you made the terms of credit clear? Then check for the tone of the letter. Have you used positive wording as much as possible? Above all, does the letter convey the impression that your firm welcomes this customer's business and looks forward to giving years of satisfying service?

THE

AQUARIUS

FURNITURE COMPANY
542 ASTARTE COURT·
ROUSEVILLE, N.D. 58712
·1-800-701-256-8700·

April 19, 1986

Ms. Lesley Dillon
Director of Purchasing
The Savoy House
980 De Witt Place
Balbo, UT 84605

Dear Ms. Dillon:

It is a pleasure to extend credit terms to the Savoy House for the purchase of 60 Kirst Windsor Back Rockers (K-280576) at $369.99 each.

As agreed in our phone conversation of April 15, we will be expecting payment of $23,087.38 (taxes included) within 60 days. If you pay that total within 10 days of receiving the invoice, we grant a 5 percent discount, reducing your total invoice to $21,933.01.

We know that your guests will find in the Kirst Windsor Back Rocker a touch of colonial elegance added to their rooms. And we know that you will find them amazingly durable, retaining for many years their hard cherry finish. And as years pass, these chairs continue to appreciate in value, becoming collectors' pieces.

The chairs will be shipped one week from today via Bowie Express, Inc., reaching the Savoy House on May 1. Please call me if they do not arrive on that date.

It is always a pleasure to serve you and the Savoy House, Ms. Dillon.

Sincerely,

Meredith G. Solvig

Meredith G. Solvig
Credit Manager

pt

Figure 6.8   Letter granting credit

The Letter Refusing Credit   When you must convey a negative credit decision, you face the challenge of explaining the refusal while keeping the reader's patronage on a cash basis. Moreover, the reader's financial circumstances could change so that your firm may at some future date allow credit purchases. So you must maintain the customer's goodwill and interest in your product or service in your letter.

Document Plan

1. Open the letter by thanking the customer for applying for credit, complimenting his or her interest in your product or service.
2. Give the reasons for the decision, followed by a tactfully worded refusal. Do not suggest that the customer is untrustworthy or irresponsible.
3. Move immediately to focus on the alternative of a C.O.D. purchase, stressing the attractive points of your product or service. You may, if circumstances warrant, suggest that credit is possible in the future, once difficulties are removed.
4. Close the letter with a goodwill statement stressing your eagerness to serve the customer and your hope that a long-standing and satisfying business relationship will develop. Figure 6.9 shows a letter refusing credit.

Problem-Solving Steps

Define   Your goals here are to refuse the application for credit while keeping the reader's goodwill and persuading him or her to pay cash. If the application is refused because of a poor credit rating, the reader will doubtless know of the rating, so you must be sensitive about his or her feelings. The tone of your letter must not impute any moral untrustworthiness to the reader; it should be as positive as possible, focusing on the benefits of your product or service to the reader and on your eagerness to serve.

Analyze   You will probably already have all the information necessary to write the letter, for example, a report on the customer from a credit bureau, letters from other companies that have dealt with the customer on a credit basis, or both. We recommend the indirect plan for this letter as specified previously in the document plan.

Draft   Tone is critical! Courtesy, sensitivity, and positive wording are especially valuable in refusing a customer's request for credit. The reasons for the refusal must be handled skillfully: they should be stated objectively and without value judgments. For example, do not write, "Your firm is considered a poor credit risk because you either do not pay your bills or pay them too slowly." Phrase the idea tactfully: "According to reports we have received, your firm is often behind in its payments to creditors." Above all,

THE

A Q U A R I U S
F U R N I T U R E   C O M P A N Y
5 4 2   A S T A R T E   C O U R T ·
R O U S E V I L L E,   N . D .   5 8 7 1 2
· 1 - 8 0 0 - 7 0 1 - 2 5 6 - 8 7 0 0 ·

April 19, 1986

Ms. Lesley Dillon, Director of Purchasing
The Savoy House
980 De Witt Place
Balbo, UT 84605

Dear Ms. Dillon:

We are delighted that you are interested in purchasing 60 Kirst
Windsor Back Rockers (K-280576) at $369.99 each. Remodeling time
can be hectic, but I'm sure that your efforts will be more than
compensated by the increased patronage the Savoy House will enjoy
as a result.

In your letter of April 10, you mention the subject of credit. Normally,
we would be happy to discuss a payment plan with you, but a review
of our records of your last purchase indicates that the payment was
90 days overdue when received.

We appreciate your patronage, Ms. Dillon, but as a business
professional, you can appreciate our cash flow problems when we
have to carry an account for that period of time. This time, we will
gladly ship your order on a C.O.D. basis. Moreover, for a cash
purchase, we grant a 5 percent discount, which will reduce your total
invoice to $21,933.01 (taxes included). After this purchase, possibly
future transactions can be worked out on a credit basis agreeable to
us both.

We know that you will be happy with your Windsor Back Rockers. In
addition to the comfort these chairs provide, we know that your
guests will find in the Kirst Windsor Back Rocker a touch of colonial
elegance added to their rooms. And we know that you will find them

Figure 6.9   Letter refusing credit

amazingly durable, retaining for many years their hard cherry finish. And as years pass, these chairs continue to appreciate in value, becoming collectors' pieces.

If you call us at our toll-free number, the chairs will be shipped within one week via Bowie Express, Inc., reaching the Savoy House within two weeks of your phone call. We look forward to serving you and the Savoy House, Ms. Dillon. If I can answer any questions please call me.

Sincerely,

Meredith G. Solvig

Meredith G. Solvig
Credit Manager

pt

respect the right to confidentiality of any firms that have shared credit information with you. Neither statement quoted above identifies a specific firm.

Revise and Edit   Ask yourself whether you would like to receive this letter if you were in the reader's position. Edit out any condescension to the reader, such as: "We may extend credit to you at some time in the future, should your credit rating improve." Instead write: "We look forward to extending credit to you in the future as soon as circumstances will permit."

Make certain that the emphasis of the letter is on the product or service you offer, not on the refusal. If you have devoted more space to the reasons for the refusal than to your product or service and your willingness to serve, you may wish to edit the letter accordingly.

The Collection Letter Series

When a company that has extended credit to a client does not receive a payment for delivery of a product or service, it waits a certain time and initiates its process of debt collection. The process and its timing vary, but most companies mail out computerized statements, some marked "Past Due" when that point is passed. The company may telephone the business or individual regarding the past due account. If phone calls do not work and if the debt is large enough, the company may send the customers a series of letters called a **collection series.** If the statements, phone calls, and collection series have no effect, the company may hand over the account to a collection agency or to an attorney.

The collection series of letters is more applicable to collection of a debt from a company than from an individual. When an individual refuses to pay a relatively moderate debt from a retail chain store, probably no collection series will be sent, due to the expense involved. But the larger the debt, the more likely one will be used. Thus the collection series is part of an overall process, and we do not imply that it will succeed in every case. Our intent is merely to offer advice on how to create an effective series.

The collection series includes several letters sent out at planned intervals to the client. As soon as the client responds, the letters stop. If the client does not respond, the letters become progressively more forceful. Figure 6.10 shows a collection series.

Figure 6.10
Collection series

IRVIN OFFICE PRODUCTS, INC.
1226 SUFFOLK BOULEVARD
BILLINGS, MT. 59004

July 25, 1986

First Letter

Ms. Donna Burgess, General Manager
Marley Office Supply Company
2578 Amity Road
Billings, MT 59004

Dear Ms. Burgess:

Thank you again for your order of 5/14/86 for 25 Munro Visible Card Files (No. 942-760) at $452.50 each, which we gladly shipped on 5/21/86. However, although two reminder notices have been sent, we have not as yet received your payment of $11,878.35.

We trust that we have filled the order correctly and that the Card Files have arrived in good condition. Please let us know if there is any problem with the order. If not, we look forward to receiving the payment in the mail at your earliest convenience. If you have already mailed it, thank you, and we look forward to serving you in the future.

Sincerely,

August 10, 1986

Second Letter

Dear Ms. Burgess:

We have sent you two reminder notices and one personal letter concerning your outstanding balance of $11,878.35. We refer, of course, to the order of 25 Munro Visible Card Files, which we shipped to you on 5/21/86.

We are puzzled at not hearing from you. We assume that the shipment reached you in good condition and that you have received our correspondence. Since you would have contacted us by this time if the problem were on our end, we assume that you must be experiencing some problem with payment. Every business has a cash flow problem from time to time, but usually it is only temporary. If conditions are such that you cannot immediately send us a check, then let us hear from you. I'm confident that we can work things out.

I look forward to your call.

Sincerely,

Third Letter

August 25, 1986

Dear Ms. Burgess:

Now I really am perplexed. After two reminder notices and two personal letters, I have had no response from you concerning your account, which has been overdue since last June 21.

As a businesswoman, Ms. Burgess, you can appreciate our position. We cannot maintain high standards of service and reasonable prices if we are forced to carry large accounts receivables such as yours, for $11,878.35 for the 25 Munro Visible Card Files. To serve our customers best, we must collect on our accounts, as you must on yours.

Therefore, I feel compelled to insist that if you cannot mail us a check for the full amount, you contact me by phone or letter as soon as possible. I am sure that we can solve this problem together.

Please let me hear from you as soon as possible!

Sincerely,

Fourth Letter

September 9, 1986

Dear Ms. Burgess:

Another two weeks have passed without my hearing from you. We have tried in every way to be understanding and patient up to this point. We cannot continue to do so and meet our own obligations to our suppliers.

This time, Ms. Burgess, I must absolutely insist that you contact me by phone or by letter within five (5) working days. If at the end of that time I have not received either your check for $11,878.35 or a letter or phone call from you, you will compel me to assign your account to our collection agency. I don't want to do that, Ms. Burgess; so please call, write, or send us your check.

Sincerely,

September 16, 1986

Dear Ms. Burgess:

I am offering you a last--and final--opportunity to work out the problem of your account--$11,878.35 for 25 Munro Visible Card Files--past due since last June 21.

As I have repeatedly stated, if you are not able to pay us the full amount, at least call me to set up an appointment in which we can discuss a payment plan. If you do not call me at (912) 421-6734 within 48 hours of receiving this letter by registered mail, I shall have to hand over your account to our collection agency. Spare us both the unpleasantness of seeing your credit rating tarnished.

Please call--within 48 hours!

Sincerely,

Think of the collection series as a unit and write it as such. No two letters in the series should be alike: each should display more determination than the preceding one. Despite their differences, the letters in the series have the following common elements.

Document Plan

1. Each letter specifies the amount of the debt, the product or service provided, and/or the invoice number. Doing so precludes any mistake about which debt is to be collected.
2. Each letter summarizes the creditor's attempts to collect the debt, for example, citing past due notices.
3. The letter may appeal to the reader's sense of fairness or desire to protect a credit rating and/or standing in the community.
4. Each letter calls for some action from the debtor, for example, payment or at least a phone call. This call for action may be couched in positive terms that stress the ongoing relationship between the reader and the writer's company.

Not every letter needs to contain all these elements or to treat them in this order.

Finally, the series can be individually written or it may be made up of word processed form letters. Since even a series made up of form letters has

to be written by somebody, we will deal with the process as an individually
written series, one that could be made into a form letter series if required.

Problem-Solving Steps

Define   The series has the two goals of collecting the money and maintaining goodwill. The assumption in most collection processes is that the
customer *will* pay and that the company will do business with this customer
again. Companies cannot afford the luxury of doing business only with
preferred customers. Besides, some good customers are simply slow to pay;
their business cycle does not allow them to pay when they would like, or
they experience a temporary cash flow problem that subjects them to the
collection process. Therefore the assumption is that you are dealing with a
respectable customer who will pay the bill. As a writer, you must guard
against any implied cynicism about the customer's honesty. Whatever your
private opinions, for the record you must be polite but firm. If you are
discourteous or sarcastic, you stand less chance of gaining your goals—
prompt payment and continued patronage.

Therefore courtesy and sensitivity are important in a collection series,
but they must be balanced with a clear determination to be paid. The series
in figure 6.10 maintains this balance. The first letter asks whether there was
any problem with the way in which the order was filled, requesting payment
if there was not. The second letter assumes that the order was correctly
filled, concluding that perhaps the firm is experiencing a temporary "problem with payment" but asking it at least to make contact. The third letter
expresses disbelief at not hearing from the firm and "insists" on being
contacted to "solve this problem together." The fourth letter escalates to a
demand that unless the firm is heard from within five working days, the
account will be handed over to a collection agency. The fifth letter narrows
the response time allowed to 48 hours.

Analyze   Research in this area is not normally difficult, because you will
generally have ample information about the customer's past payment record. You should also ascertain whether the order was correctly filled—a
phone call to the customer will verify your records. Sometimes the credit
manager of your company can suggest or negotiate a payment plan for the
customer. If this is possible, the collection series can refer to it as an
inducement for the customer to make contact.

You may consider the benefits to the customer deriving from payment:
protecting credit ratings, preserving standing in the business community,
securing future deliveries, taking advantage of discounts, and avoiding
service charges. You can focus on one or two of these benefits and emphasize them in the collection series.

Draft   Write the series as a unit so that you will achieve continuity and a sense of escalating urgency. In each letter, specify the total amount owed and exactly what action you expect from the customer, for example, a telephone call within 48 hours. The rest of the letter can appeal to the benefits of paying the debt, but each letter of the series should be short. The five letters in figure 6.10 are each only two or three paragraphs long.

Revise and Edit   Reread the series, asking yourself this question: "If I owed this amount of money and received this collection series, how would I react?" Delete any passages that may express sarcasm or cynicism about the reader's motives.

Reread to determine whether you have achieved a balanced tone—polite but firm. Do the letters sound too easygoing or harsh? Or are the early letters all politeness and the later ones all firmness? In the series in figure 6.10, even the last two letters, both of which state an ultimatum, have a polite tone: "I don't want to do that, Ms. Burgess, so please call, write, or send us your check." And "Spare us both the unpleasantness of seeing your credit rating tarnished. Please call . . ." These statements imply that the writer still believes the problem can be solved amicably and is concerned for the reader's welfare.

After a sale has been made and the invoice collected, there can still be differences between buyer and seller. When the buyer feels that the goods or services are in some way defective, he or she makes a **claim**. For example, when there is a billing error, a delivery mix-up, or a slip-up in service, the customer usually phones the company to straighten out the matter. But some people prefer to make their claim in letter form because it provides a record of the transaction if the claim is not settled to their satisfaction.

The Claim Letter

As a claimant, it is important that you deal with your own emotions before writing the letter if you find that you are angry over the claim. You have paid for something that you either did not receive or received in a condition you did not expect. You may have a right to be angry, but don't abuse the adjuster who handles your claim since this person probably had nothing to do with the mistake. Even though the adjuster is probably used to handling angry claimants, venting your anger on him or her will seldom expedite your claim. Figure 6.11 shows a well-written claim letter.

Document Plan

1. Identify the product or service that is the subject of your claim, for example, by such items as invoice number, price, model number, or date of purchase.
2. Describe the difficulty you are experiencing with the product or service. You may also describe any inconvenience or loss of money you have suffered as a result.

897 Garey Street Houston, TX 77232

August 11, 1986

Customer Service Department
Dalton Business Machines, Inc.
4500 Ammon Drive
Oklahoma City, OK 73114

Dear Sir or Madam:

One of our Dalton Cash Registers recently needed service, and so,
having a Dalton maintenance agreement, I called your Service
Department, which promptly sent a technician to our store to correct
the problem.

However, about ten days later I received an invoice billing me for both
the part--a "year" wheel--and the labor. I am enclosing a copy of the
invoice. It occurred to me that possibly either your Service
Department or Billing Department was not made aware of our
maintenance agreement, which covers both the cost of labor and
parts.

I am sure that this little misunderstanding can be cleared up very
quickly. I look forward to hearing from you.

Sincerely,

Lorine Zelinski

(Ms.) Lorine Zelinski
Manager

yd
Enclosure

Figure 6.11   Claim letter

3. End by specifying what you believe should be done to correct the difficulty if you know what that is; otherwise, conclude by expressing confidence that the company will investigate the difficulty and take the proper steps to correct it.

Problem-Solving Steps

Define   First, decide what you want: a total or partial refund or a correction of the product or service. Second, enlist the goodwill of the adjuster, because this person may be able to do more for you than you would expect. Remember that he or she probably handles many such cases and possibly expects anger from customers. Breaking the mold by being gracious or sympathetic may disarm the person.

Analyze   Research the malfunction or the service problem. For example, question knowledgeable employees involved with the operation on your end and take notes on the business problem. Generally, the indirect plan will work well in this situation.

Draft   Be sure to give enough background on the claim that the adjuster will understand your letter. Describe what is wrong and, if you know, what you feel should be done to correct the problem.

Be fair and objective in describing the business problem and what you want done. Give the adjuster's company credit for what it has done *right*. For example, in figure 6.11 the writer acknowledges that the other company "promptly" responded to the service call and corrected the malfunction. Also, do not imply that the company is irresponsible. The writer of the letter in figure 6.11 suggests that the company may simply be unaware of the service contract—that's better than accusing them of not honoring it.

Keep the tone as positive as possible for the circumstances; for example, the letter in figure 6.11 ends with the author expressing confidence that "this little misunderstanding can be cleared up very quickly." Above all, *avoid any hint of sarcasm*; it will only alienate the reader.

Revise and Edit   Put yourself in the place of the adjuster and read your letter. Does it make you want to help its author? Does it sound courteous? Is it clear and complete enough to enable you to process the claim?

When *you* must deal with a claimant who is dissatisfied with your product or service, you must control any tendency to be rude to the claimant who shows little consideration for you. An angry claimant will only be made angrier by a discourteous response.

Two Kinds of Adjustment Letters

The easiest kind of **adjustment letter** to write is the one that grants the adjustment the claimant is seeking. The one that refuses the claim or grants only part of it is more challenging.

The Letter Granting an Adjustment   At times you will grant a totally satisfactory adjustment to the claimant. In effect, you concede that he or she is right and announce your intention to correct the difficulty. The following list suggests an effective way to write this kind of letter.

Document Plan

1. Open with a gracious apology to the claimant for any inconvenience or loss incurred.
2. Assure him or her that you intend to rectify the problem, specifying in detail how you will do so.
3. Include a passage that resells the product or service if feasible.
4. Thank the claimant for bringing the matter to your attention and close by expressing your firm's desire to serve him or her in the future. (See figure 6.12 for a letter granting an adjustment.)

Problem-Solving Steps

Define   Although the customer will no doubt be pleased to learn that his or her claim will be favorably settled, your goal is to restore any faith in your product or service that may have been lost. You can do so by projecting an image of fair-mindedness and willingness to be of service.

Analyze   Before answering the claimant's letter, be sure that you have thoroughly understood the complaint, since nothing will exasperate the claimant more than realizing from your letter that you did not pay sufficient attention.

Draft   Be concise. Consider your goal of restoring confidence. But do not go overboard with apologizing; one apology at the beginning should suffice. Most of the letter should focus on your explanation of what you plan to do for the claimant and why your product or service is still a good buy.

Revise and Edit   Place yourself in the claimant's position as you review your draft. Does it sound as though this writer understands your particular problem? Does the writer seem genuinely interested in correcting your problem? Or does the whole thing sound routine, as if a yawning adjuster were saying, "Bring it in and we'll have a 'looksee' at it"?

Edit for positive wording. Revise negative statements such as, "We regret having caused you all this trouble." Instead, write, "We apologize for the experience you've had with our delivery service, and we look forward to serving you better in the future."

The Letter Refusing an Adjustment   Writing a letter granting an adjustment is relatively simple compared to writing a letter **refusing an adjustment**. If your investigation of the facts leads to the conclusion that the claim is unjustified or justified only in part and the decision is not to satisfy the claim, you must write what is essentially a "bad news" letter.

THE

A Q U A R I U S

FURNITURE COMPANY

5 4 2   A S T A R T E   C O U R T ·

R O U S E V I L L E ,   N . D .   5 8 7 1 2

· 1 - 8 0 0 - 7 0 1 - 2 5 6 - 8 7 0 0 ·

May 12, 1986

Ms. Lesley Dillon
Director of Purchasing
The Savoy House
980 De Witt Place
Balbo, UT 84605

Dear Ms. Dillon:

Please accept our apology for the error in the shipment of the Kirst Windsor Back Rockers! You did indeed order 60 chairs, but you received only 58.

We are shipping the two missing rockers via Bowie Express, and they should reach the Savoy House no later than May 17. If they have not arrived by that date, please call me immediately.

By this time, I'm sure you have had time to inspect the rockers that arrived on time. I'm sure that you have also noted the beauty of the cherry wood together with the understated satin finish on the chairs. I have one of these chairs in my own living room and can attest to its comfort and durability.

Thank you for bringing this matter to my attention so promptly. We look forward to serving you and the Savoy House again in the future.

Sincerely,

Meredith G. Solvig

Meredith G. Solvig
Credit Manager

pt

Figure 6.12 Letter granting an adjustment

Document Plan

1. Open by thanking the claimant for bringing the concern to your attention. Show that you understand and sympathize with the reader but not to the extent of seeming to accept responsibility for it.
2. Move on to the reasons why the claim cannot be granted or can be granted only in part.
3. Tactfully state the decision not to grant the claim or to grant it only in part.
4. End with a goodwill statement, stressing future dealings with and service to the claimant (see figure 6.4).

Problem-Solving Steps

Define   Your main goal is for the claimant to agree that the decision is fair and reasonable. The secondary goal follows from that: to retain the claimant's goodwill and patronage. The image you project will therefore be important because you want the claimant to see you as fair-minded and reasonable. Also, you want the claimant to see you as someone who appreciates his or her position even though it is impossible to grant all the claimant's wishes.

Analyze   You will already be familiar with company practices, so you will know what you can offer the customer and what you cannot offer. You will probably use the indirect plan. The adjustment letter in figure 6.4 applies this plan. The opening paragraph thanks the claimant for "expressing concern" and displays sensitivity to the claimant's viewpoint, saying, "I can quite understand. . . ." The middle paragraph gives the reason the claim cannot be honored and concludes with the bad news—the service contract does not cover the claim. The writer closes by thanking the claimant for "the opportunity to explain our position." The result is a gracious refusal, which is better than an ungracious one.

Draft   Keep the letter fairly brief, not much longer than the letter in figure 6.4. The real issue is to decide how specific to be in giving the reasons for the refusal of the claim. Only you can judge how detailed your explanation should be, but if possible, do not resort to stock phrases like *not our practice* or *company policy.* Such cliches explain nothing. *Show* how the company policy or practice is reasonable.

If you are writing for a lay reader, do not use technical terms in your explanation. The claimant who receives a letter that he or she cannot understand is apt to wonder whether the jargon curtain is being drawn to conceal an unfair decision.

Above all, do not use phrases that suggest cynicism about the claimant's honesty or competence, for example:

I do not understand how . . .

You seem to be under the impression that . . .

If, as you allege, . . .

Your assertion that . . .

Do I understand you to say that . . .

When you claim that . . .

Give the claimant credit for honesty and basic intelligence.

Revise and Edit   Assume the role of the claimant in reading your letter. Would you understand the reasons given for the decision? Would you find them convincing? Would you tend to say, "While I am disappointed that I was refused, I can understand their position"?

Go over the letter for negative statements that can be expressed in more positive terms. Look for opportunities to be courteous, for example, saying "thank you" and "please." Does the letter show sensitivity to the claimant's circumstances? Pay special attention to the closing—it is easy in writing a refusal letter to end on a hollow note: "Although we were unable to grant your claim of $5,000, we look forward to serving you again in the future."

The Policy Justification Letter

Sometimes, although no claim is involved, a customer will write to question the firm's decision or policy. A new price increase, service charge, payment policy, or zone charge can elicit such a letter from a customer. Sometimes members of the general public will write to the company questioning a decision, such as moving a facility out of state, or a practice, such as an advertising campaign.

Although the company may not change the decision or policy, goodwill is at stake, and most companies feel that such a letter deserves a personal response. Figure 6.1 shows a **policy justification letter** responding to a customer protesting a new advance payment plan adopted by a company.

Document Plan

1. Thank the reader for writing to express his or her concern over the policy or decision. (But don't talk down to the reader: "We're always glad to hear from you folks out there.") Or show that you sympathize with the reader's goals or values if not with his or her methods of achieving them.

2. Give the reasons for the policy or decision. If possible, relate them to benefits to the customer, for example, lower prices, greater convenience, or more efficient service.

3. Conclude, perhaps only by implication, that the policy or decision must be adhered to.

4. End by stressing some positive benefit to the customer, preferably one flowing from the policy or decision. Offer to be of further assistance.

Problem-Solving Steps

Define You already know the important preconceptions of your reader from the letter or telephone call. For example, you will know that the reader disapproves of the decision or policy and the reasons for this disapproval. If you could succeed totally, your goal would be to have the reader endorse the decision or policy. Practically, you should probably be content with getting the reader to admit the reasonableness of the decision or policy. Equally important, you want the reader to continue to think well of your company. Therefore you want to project an image of a fair-minded, reasonable individual who is sensitive to the reader's point of view.

Analyze The letter will probably lend itself to the indirect plan outlined previously because you're going to disagree with the reader, but graciously, rationally, and courteously.

The main question in this kind of letter will center on the amount of information and reasoning the reader requires to conclude that the company position is reasonable. You should limit yourself to about one page of material. The letter in figure 6.1, for example, states only three reasons for the company position—convenience for the reader, more efficient service, and lower rates. Notice, by the way, how all three reasons for the decision are addressed directly to the reader.

Draft If possible, open with a paragraph that establishes common ground with your reader, such as the opening paragraph of figure 6.1. The author thanks the reader for the suggestion, adding that the company welcomes any idea for improving services. Thus the author and the reader are agreed on the goal to constantly improve services.

Move to the reasons for the policy decision, tying them, if possible, to the reader's benefit, as does the author of figure 6.1. Finally, conclude positively by thanking the reader for concern, patience, or just for writing.

Revise and Edit Reread the letter from the reader's viewpoint. Does it sound convincing and sincere? If not, the problem will often lie in the reasons for the policy. If they sound unconvincing, go back to the analytical stage and devise better reasons.

Have you shown sensitivity to the reader's point of view, even though you may not share it? Can you point to any specific passages that show this sensitivity? Is the letter courteous? The letter in figure 6.1 opens and closes by thanking the reader.

The Goodwill Letter Companies sometimes receive letters that seem unusual and even a little bizarre. For example, one famous top executive reports receiving a letter from a person seeking advice on the proper cathartic to take. But since even eccentrics are potential customers, many business writers find themselves answering such letters. For example, the letter in figure 6.13 responds to a customer's request about front-window vents—no longer part of this company's car.

Many companies regard answers to these letters as a chance to build goodwill and to advertise their products. Notice that the writer of the **goodwill letter** in figure 6.13 uses the opportunity to explain how well designed and fuel efficient the company's present cars are. The letter becomes a sales letter, because not only does it stress the company's product but it subtly flatters the reader, implying, "See, we care about your opinions—that's why we take the time to write to you." The person who receives the letter in figure 6.13 will probably be more apt to buy from this company.

Document Plan

1. Thank the reader for writing. Show sensitivity to the reader's point of view by taking his or her question seriously.
2. Answer the question.
3. Focus the reader's attention on your product or service, mentioning something new about it; reinforce his or her good feelings about your company.
4. Offer to assist the reader in the future.

Problem-Solving Steps

Define   You want to make the writer feel good about your company, and thus you must be convincing that the company values his or her concerns and patronage. As noted, the fact that you are writing this letter will help accomplish this goal. Second, you want to highlight your company's products.

Analyze   As with the sales letter, you have to know your products thoroughly to sell them effectively. In the goodwill letter, the point is to connect the customer's interests with your product, which will not normally be difficult since the customer is writing you about some company matter. For example, in figure 6.13 the writer uses the subject of front-window vents as a transition to talking about the air conditioning and good mileage of the company's present cars.

Because the goodwill message is usually short, you do not need to include a great deal of specific information. The reader is usually content with summary statements, such as in the letter in figure 6.13. Also, the organizational plan of a goodwill message is often the direct plan because reader reaction is presumed to be positive, there being little or no negative content to the message.

CHANDLER CORPORATION
1 CHANDLER PLAZA · DETROIT, MI 48123

December 24, 1986

Mr. Ermin Ward
10290 Thalia Drive
Harrisburg, PA 17107

Dear Mr. Ward:

Thank you for your letter asking about front-window vents in Chandler cars. I'm afraid that vents have gone the way of running boards and tail fins. The fans and air conditioning installed in most Chandler cars provide sufficient air flow without vents in the front windows--although some of our models have vents in the rear windows.

We used to make cars with front window vents, but now we think our cars are much better without them. As you probably know, driving with the windows open can use more gasoline than running the air conditioning with the windows closed--an important consideration, you'll agree.

The answer to your second question is yes, we do want you to buy one of our cars. As in the days of front-window vents, Chandler cars are still your best buy--that hasn't changed.

And thanks again for writing.

Sincerely,

Meredith Cohen

Meredith Cohen
Manager, Editorial Services

ew

Figure 6.13   Goodwill letter (semiblock style)

Draft   Because of the positive content, you can easily slip into a patronizing tone. For example, it would be easy to begin the letter in figure 6.13 with the line "Surely you realize that front-window vents have gone the way of running boards and tail fins." Such a line would make the reader feel out of touch. Instead, the writer in figure 6.13 gently "breaks the news" to the reader that the vents are gone forever.

And because the goodwill letter is usually short, be careful not to sound breezy, as if the letter were considered a sop to somebody in the outback— the "Let-us-hear-from-you-any-time!" tone. Being breezy is another way of patronizing the reader.

Revise and Edit   Read the letter from the viewpoint of the reader. What image of the writer and the company does it project? Does that image match the one you wish to convey? Can you point to specific passages in the letter that show sensitivity to the reader?

Business Letter Parts and Formats

The parts and the format of the business letter go together, because format is the way the parts are arranged on the page, and both are considerably standardized. This chapter covers only the essential parts of the business letter and five formats because most business people have access to some secretarial services, though few have private secretaries.

Figure 6.14 displays the essential business letter parts in the following list. The numbers on the list correspond to the numbers in parentheses in the figure.

Business Letter Parts

1. *Letterhead*: gives the name and address of the author's company.
2. *Date*: gives the date on which the letter was written.
3. *Inside address*: gives the name, usually the title, and the address (including zip code) of the recipient of the letter.
4. *Salutation*: addresses the recipient by name if possible.
5. *Body of the letter*: contains the text of the letter.
6. *Complimentary closing*: precedes the personal signature of the author.
7. *Author's identification*: gives the author's name and position.
8. *Transcriber's initials*: identifies the person who typed the letter.
9. *Enclosure notation*: indicates that a separate document has been enclosed.
10. *Copy distribution*: indicates the name(s) of anyone receiving a copy of the letter.

Sometimes the inside address and salutation can create problems when you do not know the recipient's name. You may discover the person's name by

CRANLEY BUSINESS SYSTEMS, INC.
5001 N. Broadway Avenue
Davenport, IA 52814

Letterhead (1)

Date (2)

July 14, 1986

Inside address (3)

Ms. Ramona Jorge
24 Fielding Terrace
Burlington, IA 52602

Salutation (4)

Dear Ms. Jorge:

Body (5)

Thank you for your application letter and resume. Yes, we do have on-the-job training programs, and yes, we would like to interview you for our field engineering training program.

Cranley Business Systems is always eager to recruit new talent in field engineering. Our training programs for qualified persons often lead to lifetime careers in the preventive and remedial maintenance of our systems. I would welcome the opportunity to discuss this particular program at some length with you and ask you to write me regarding a time when it would be convenient to come to our Vanora facility for an interview. I am enclosing a brochure which will acquaint you with the essentials of the training program.

Because we realize that you are approaching an important crossroad, we want you to make the best possible decision. Again, thanks for writing us, and I look forward to meeting you.

Complimentary
closing (6)

Sincerely,

Shelley Morrison

Author's
identification (7)

Shelley Morrison
Executive Recruiting

Transcriber's initials (8)

lc

Enclosure notation (9)

Enclosure

Copy distribution (10)

c.c.: Jan Regalbuto, Engineering

Figure 6.14   Parts of a business letter

calling the company switchboard and asking for it, along with the correct spelling. If you cannot learn the name, you will have to address him or her by position, for example, sales manager or credit manager.

Handling the salutation when you do not know the person's name requires tact. One option is to use the position, for example, "Dear Credit Manager." Another option is to use "Dear Sir or Madam" or "Ladies and Gentlemen." A third option is to use the name of the department, for example, "Dear Service Department." Above all, do not assume you know the gender of the recipient by addressing him or her as "Dear Sir" or "Gentlemen." If the officer in question is a woman, she may not appreciate your assumption about gender. Whichever option you use, we suggest that you avoid the awkwardly impersonal "To Whom It May Concern."

There is also the question as to how to address a woman whose name is known but whose preference in regard to *Ms.*, *Miss*, and *Mrs.* is not. If you have a letter from her, check the author's identification, because some women indicate their preference there: (Ms.) Aileen N. Fitzgerald, Credit Manager. You might also call the writer's secretary to determine her preference.

Finally, in the inside address (and on the envelope), use the modern, postal abbreviations for the state:

AK	Alaska	MN	Minnesota
AL	Alabama	MO	Missouri
AR	Arkansas	MS	Mississippi
AZ	Arizona	MT	Montana
CA	California	NC	North Carolina
CO	Colorado	ND	North Dakota
CT	Connecticut	NE	Nebraska
DC	District of Columbia	NH	New Hampshire
DE	Delaware	NJ	New Jersey
FL	Florida	NM	New Mexico
GA	Georgia	NV	Nevada
HI	Hawaii	NY	New York
IA	Iowa	OH	Ohio
ID	Idaho	OK	Oklahoma
IL	Illinois	OR	Oregon
IN	Indiana	PA	Pennsylvania
KS	Kansas	PR	Puerto Rico
KY	Kentucky	RI	Rhode Island
LA	Louisiana	SC	South Carolina
MA	Massachusetts	SD	South Dakota
MD	Maryland	TN	Tennessee
ME	Maine	TX	Texas
MI	Michigan	UT	Utah

VA	Virginia	WI	Wisconsin
VI	Virgin Islands	WV	West Virginia
VT	Vermont	WY	Wyoming
WA	Washington		

Major Business Letter Formats

The five most common business letter formats are (1) full block style, (2) block style, (3) semiblock style, (4) simplified style, and (5) personal style. We will cover the distinguishing features of each.

The Full Block Style All the letter parts are typed even with the left margin, with no indentations except such as would result from tables or lists included in the body of the letter. Figure 6.5 exemplifies the full block style.

The Block Style All letter parts are typed even with the left margin except for the date line, complimentary closing, and author's identification. These three parts are typed even with an imaginary vertical line bisecting the page. See figure 6.7.

The Semiblock Style This style follows the block style in all particulars except one: it indents the first line of each paragraph five spaces, as in figure 6.13.

The Simplified Style This style aligns all the letter parts with the left margin, but it omits the salutation and complimentary closing. However, it adds a subject line (typed in capital letters). It also puts the name and position of the author on the same line at the bottom of the letter. The name and the position are separated by a dash and are typed in capital letters. See figure 6.15.

Personal Style This style is used by private individuals for their business correspondence; hence, no letterhead appears at the top of the page. Instead, the address of the author and the date are typed at the top of the page, even with an imaginary vertical line bisecting the page. In all other respects, the personal style follows the semiblock style, as in figure 7.5.

None of these letter styles is preferable to the others. The block style (number 2) is the most popular, but many companies are starting to use the full block style (number 1) because it is easier and faster to type since there are no indentations. The simplified style (number 4) is a relative newcomer that you will see only occasionally. The personal style (number 5) is normally used by private individuals rather than employees of companies, although it can be used when the author does not wish to use company letterhead.

CRANLEY BUSINESS SYSTEMS, INC.
5001 N. Broadway Avenue
Davenport, IA 52814

July 14, 1986

Ms. Ramona Jorge
24 Fielding Terrace
Burlington, IA 52602

AN INVITATION TO COME FOR AN INTERVIEW

Thank you, Ms. Jorge, for your application letter and resume. Yes, we
do have on-the-job training programs, and yes, we would like to
interview you for our field engineering training program.

Cranley Business Systems is always eager to recruit new talent in
field engineering. Our training programs for qualified persons often
lead to lifetime careers in the preventive and remedial maintenance of
our systems. I would welcome the opportunity to discuss this
particular program at some length with you and ask you to write me
regarding a time when it would be convenient to come to our Vanora
facility for an interview. I am enclosing a brochure which will
acquaint you with the essentials of the training program.

Because we realize that you are approaching an important crossroad,
we want you to make the best possible decision. Again, thanks for
writing us, and I look forward to meeting you.

Shelley Morrison

SHELLEY MORRISON--DIRECTOR, EXECUTIVE RECRUITING

lc
Enclosure
c.c.: Jan Regalbuto, Engineering

Figure 6.15   Simplified letter style

A final consideration is the envelope. The envelope displays the return address in the upper left corner—usually printed for the company. The name and address of the recipient of the letter are typed in approximately the center of the envelope, as shown in figure 6.16. Be sure to use the zip code and modern state abbreviations for both the return address and the address of the recipient.

Summary

Whereas the memo and short report are used for communicating inside the company, the business letter is used for communicating outside the company. There is a greater variety of business letters than there is of memos and short reports, and business letter writing tends to be specialized by industry. Therefore we concentrate on explaining the basic qualities and strategies of business letter writing, which we then apply to some common business letter types.

Five qualities are especially important in writing business letters, many of which go to actual or potential customers:

1. Clarity, which is especially important in writing to readers outside the company
2. Courtesy
3. Sensitivity, the habit of putting yourself in the reader's place and seeing the issue from his or her viewpoint
4. Positive wording, the habit of expressing ideas in their most favorable terms without distorting them
5. Naturalness, which brings the qualities of good conversation to the business letter

Two organizational plans are useful in business letter writing. The direct plan applies when the essence of the message will be either good or neutral news to the reader. The indirect plan applies when you have bad news for the reader. The chapter describes some common business letter types, suggests an approach for each of them, and applies the problem-solving steps to each.

In the inquiry, the writer usually seeks information about a product or service. In the response to the inquiry, the writer supplies requested information and sometimes advises the reader. In the sales letter, the writer connects a product or service to the unfulfilled needs or unsolved problems of the reader.

Two kinds of credit letters are covered. In the letter granting credit, the writer announces the favorable credit decision and promotes the product or service. In the letter refusing credit, the writer deemphasizes an unfavorable credit decision while persuading the reader to buy on a cash basis.

CRANLEY BUSINESS SYSTEMS, INC.
5001 N. Broadway Avenue
Davenport, IA 52814

    Ms. Ramona Jorge
    24 Fielding Terrace
    Burlington, IA 52602

Figure 6.16
Letter envelope

In the claim letter, the writer explains a problem with a product or service and specifies what is to be done to correct the difficulty. The adjustment letter is a response to a claim letter. There are two kinds: the letter granting the adjustment, in which the writer announces the decision to settle the claim favorably and diminishes any loss of confidence in the product or service, and the letter refusing the adjustment, in which the writer deemphasizes the decision not to satisfy the reader's claim and attempts to persuade the reader that the decision is reasonable.

In the policy justification letter, the writer attempts to persuade the reader that a company policy or decision is justifiable. In the goodwill letter, the writer responds sympathetically to a reader's unusual question and uses the opportunity to promote the company's products or services.

Finally, the parts of the business letter and five business letter formats are described and illustrated. These formats are the full block style, block style, semiblock style, simplified style, and personal style.

Writing Problems

1. Below is the text of a letter explaining to a customer why the company has found it necessary to cancel the customer's maintenance plan. Revise the letter for greater courtesy, sensitivity, positiveness, and naturalness.

Draft

Dear ___ ___ ___:

This letter acknowledges receipt of your recent letter expressing your dissatisfaction over our termination of your Maintenance Plan. We desire to answer your complaint by advising you of the reasons behind our decision.

First, surely you must be aware that parts for your antiquated model are indeed hard to come by. Your case is by no means unique. We, like other manufacturers, are constantly faced with a shortage of parts for these outmoded machines. In many cases, the parts are simply no longer available. That is true in your case. We therefore have no choice but to cancel the Maintenance Plan. You have to realize that we cannot continue a Maintenance Plan when we have no way of fulfilling the terms.

We regret this action, but we have no choice. Notwithstanding, we look forward in the future to serving you on a time and material basis. Also, if you would be interested in purchasing up-to-date equipment at a reasonable price, do not hesitate to call or write us.

If I can be of further service, feel free to contact me. I remain,

Very respectfully yours,

2. You are the director of the computer center at St. Athanasius College, a small private school enrolling 950 students. The computing needs of the college have been increasing steadily, and the dean, Sister Marcella, has decided to (1) upgrade both the hardware and software capacities of the center and (2) increase its staffing as necessary. She has appointed you to chair the committee that will recommend an accounting firm to serve as consultant for these changes. You have decided to send the same letter to five firms. In it you will describe in general terms the computing tasks of the college: registration of students, billing for tuition and board, posting grades, class scheduling, payroll and benefits for faculty and staff, alumni mailings, support for faculty and institutional research, and budget and investment analysis. Presently the computer center employs, besides yourself, two programmers and one full-time secretary. You have one Topaz-5400 computer, a high-speed Delphi printer, and a Dixon dot matrix printer. You will want the account-

ing firm to do a complete study of your needs in hardware, software, and staffing. The recommendations must be realistic in terms of the college's budgetary requirements, and they must be presented in final report form to the dean by June 30. It is now January 5. Write the inquiry letter. You will not supply the names of the five addressees.

3. You are the assistant controller for Consolidated Utilities of Salem, Oregon. The head of the commercial division has informed you that there has been a computer error by which a higher rate on water bills has been assessed the Salem Mini-Dome, a local sports and pop concert center. The higher rate has been assessed for the last 18 months, resulting in an overcharge totaling $6,359. Consolidated will refund the money plus interest; you will personally see to it that the correct amount is billed in the future. The management of the Mini-Dome is, as far as you know, unaware of the billing mistake. Write a letter explaining the situation to Robin Padgett, general manager of the Salem Mini-Dome. Explain what happened and what you propose to do about it. Try at the same time to maintain the goodwill and trust of the Mini-Dome management. The street address of the Mini-Dome is 789 Creighton Avenue, Salem, OR 97308. The street address of Consolidated Utilities is 825 Edison Boulevard, Salem, OR 97310.

4. You are Jean Parchman, the assistant general manager of Acres of Bargains, a medium-sized retail outlet located in Filmore, South Dakota, a small town of 8,500 persons. The printer you use for billing has malfunctioned; you call the toll-free number of the service department of Bentley Business Systems, located 358 miles away in downtown Wolf Point, Montana. They respond by sending a service technician who arrives the following day, diagnoses the problem, corrects the malfunction, and soon has your monthly statements churning out again. Having a service contract with Bentley, you are surprised to note that an extra charge has been added to your monthly payment, a zone charge of $400. You call Bentley to inquire why a zone charge has been assessed; the service manager informs you that your store's location has been classified as *remote*. The extra charge covers the expense of sending the service technician on a remote service call. You check the service contract, which confirms that provision and the existence of such a classification. Still, you do not feel that the charge is equitable; at least you're going to try to have it voided. Write a letter explaining your claim to Marion Fakori, the general sales manager at Bentley. The street address is 9087 Rudell Place, Wolf Point, MT 59901. The street address of Acres of Bargains is 508 Woodbine Avenue, Filmore, SD 57503.

5. You are the general sales manager of Bentley Business Systems, and you receive the claim letter written by Jean Parchman in the preceding problem. You sympathize with Parchman for having the extra charge for each service call added to the cost of the service contract, but here is the situation. Prior to implementing the zone charge policy, Bentley maintenance customers located more than 50 miles from service centers were charged 15 percent over the basic rate. The new policy provides for rates based on the distance from the nearest service center. It is costly to provide service to remote locations. The present zone charge policy allows Bentley to recoup the money its service people spend on travel; it also puts the burden of payment on those who use this service. Otherwise, rates for all customers, near and far, would go up. Write a letter to Parchman, refusing the claim but doing as much as you can to maintain the goodwill of the Acres of Bargains management. The street addresses are in the previous problem.

6. You are the supervisor of investor communications for a manufacturing firm. One of your shareholders has recently written to the company asking about a feature called *dividend reinvestment*, a plan offered by your company. It has two features: automatic reinvesting of dividends and optional cash contributions. Either way, the shareholder is able to acquire additional shares of your company's common stock without paying brokerage commissions and service charges. But the plan is designed only for "shareholders of record" and not for "street name" shareholders. The company assumes that this particular shareholder's broker must be holding the shares in the street name, because the company cannot find the shareholder's name in its records. Write a letter responding to the inquiry, informing the shareholder of the outline of the plan and the situation. You are enclosing a prospectus describing the plan and a green booklet that includes a sign-up form if the shareholder is interested. The shareholder is Leigh Spilka of 42 Apple Orchard Lane, Baton Rouge, LA 70803. Your company is Phoenix Industries, 8867 Lenahan Drive, Honolulu, HI 96813.

7. You are the sales manager for Ernest Orzali Company, a supplier of business and school equipment. You are mailing copies of your new catalogue to businesses in a three-state area, and this year you have decided to write a sales letter to introduce the catalogue. The same letter will be sent with each catalogue. The readers will probably include owner-operators and managers of small businesses or their secretaries. Your company handles art supplies, audiovisual equipment, office furniture and supplies, duplicating products, instructional materials, and paper products. This year's catalogue features

an expanded offering in office furniture. To stimulate sales in this area, you are offering a 15 percent discount on any purchase of office furniture totaling $1,500 or more. You wish to highlight the bargains in executive desks, high-back executive swivel chairs, conference room furniture, reception room furniture, secretarial units (desk and chair), microprocessor stations, bookcases, display cases, and utility tables. You feel that in price and quality you are offering exceptional buys this year. The catalogue has an index at the end—easily accessible because its pages are blue. At the end of the catalogue there is also a map showing directions to the company, which is located at 58 Dorchester Avenue, St. Louis, MO 63113. An order form is also at the end of the book, but orders may be placed by a toll-free telephone call to (800) 587-9800. No delivery charge is expected if delivery is made by one of your trucks. Write the letter.

8. You are the credit manager of Montoya and Associates, specialists in commercial landscaping. You have been contacted by George Barnwell, president of Barnwell & Collins, Construction Engineers. He wants their building at the new Latonia Terrace Mall landscaped. Your boss, Lana Montoya, has submitted a bid on the job for $6,750, including all shrubs, trees, materials, and taxes. In a telephone call, Barnwell has indicated that he expects credit for 30 days. (In spite of the warranty, he probably wants to be sure the job is done right.) You call the credit bureau and learn that his credit rating is excellent, so you decide to go ahead with the transaction. Barnwell will receive credit for 30 days. He will receive a 3 percent discount if he pays his bill within 10 days of receiving it. If he does not pay his bill in 30 days, a service charge of 5 percent will be added to the total. Write the letter granting credit to Barnwell. His firm's address is 547 Latonia Terrace, Mojave, CA 93502. The address of Montoya and Associates is 890 Pisces Street, Fresno, CA 93601.

9. All details of the preceding problem apply to this problem, with the exception of the following. The credit bureau reports that Barnwell & Collins is slow to pay at best. For example, the company that carpeted the present downtown offices two years ago still has not received payment. The janitorial service that cleans the office also reports difficulties in collecting its fees. Based on this report, you decide you had better be paid in advance. Write a letter to Barnwell refusing to grant credit, but attempt to persuade him to place the order anyway.

10. You are the credit manager of Montoya and Associates, described in the previous two problems. Two months have passed since Barnwell placed his order and your firm landscaped the new office of Barnwell & Collins. You received full payment previously. But in this

morning's mail you receive a letter from George Barnwell, stating a claim. It seems that all three of the holly trees have died or almost died. Since the warranty calls for replacement of any tree or shrub that dies within one year, Barnwell asks that these three trees be replaced at no charge as soon as possible. You wonder whether the trees were properly watered, but because you want to keep Barnwell's goodwill, you decide to replace the trees at no charge. Write him a letter granting the adjustment.

11. You are the treasurer of Corporate Training Associates, Inc., a small consulting firm specializing in customer relations management. One of your responsibilities is to collect on past due accounts, such as that of B. G. Dexter and Company. It is now June 7. Last January your firm conducted a three-day seminar in customer service skills for 18 customer service representatives from B. G. Dexter and Company. One consultant conducted three full days of instructional workshops on January 5, 6, and 7. According to a written agreement, B. G. Dexter was to pay $2,840 for the seminar. Computerized statements were mailed to B. G. Dexter on January 12, February 9, and March 9. Thus far you have received no response. Write a collection series of three letters to the executive vice-president of B. G. Dexter, Hilary Dornacher, persuading the company to pay and retaining as much of their goodwill as possible. You are hoping that they will pay and that you will conduct future seminars for them. Assume that B. G. Dexter does not respond in any way to the first two letters of the series. The dates for the three letters will be April 9, May 24, and June 7. In the last letter, you may invoke the possibility of legal action to collect the debt if you believe it is necessary. The address of B. G. Dexter is 755 Western Avenue, Salem, OR 97304. The address of Corporate Training Associates is Suite 901, The Saint Paul Building, St. Paul, MN 55112.

12. You are the assistant to the executive vice-president of First National Bank of Finley, Connecticut. Your manager often has you answer routine inquiries and comments. One customer, Dale Holloway, who has had both a savings and a checking account with your bank for nine years, has written to make two suggestions. First, Holloway suggests that the bank install a Fund-Card window at the branch Holloway patronizes, the Beryl Valley Branch. Fund-Card is a computerized system that allows for withdrawals, deposits, and certain other transactions 24 hours a day. Recognizing that the bank may not be able to follow up on this suggestion, Holloway suggests an alternative, namely, extending banking hours at this branch to Saturday morning. Either alternative would mean considerable convenience to customers who work during the day and cannot use the

opportunity offered by the Friday evening banking hours (till 8:00 P.M.). Actually, the bank does have plans to install a Fund-Card window at the Beryl Valley Branch, but not for at least 18 months. As to the second alternative—Saturday banking hours—the bank cannot do that because there is not a large enough population base in the Beryl Valley area to justify the expense. Write the letter to Holloway, stating the facts of the case but also making Holloway feel valued and respected as a customer. Holloway lives at 24 Verna Lane, Beryl Valley, CT 06703. The street address of the bank is 750 Hamilton Avenue, Finley, CT 06704.

13. You are a public accountant who does the bookkeeping and annual federal and state income tax statements for a number of small businesses. You have not increased your professional fees for two years, but you now feel that an increase is warranted. You must meet your own personnel and office expenses and make a profit. You have decided on an across-the-board increase of 10 percent, considering that the last increase was three years ago. Rather than letting your clients learn of the increase through their invoices, you have decided to include a letter announcing the increase. The same letter will be sent to all your clients. Consider whether your letter should specify the percentage of increase (since the invoice will reveal that, anyway). You want your clients to feel that the increase is reasonable and justified. Write the letter. Your street address is Suite 236, The Garfield Building, 806 Michigan Avenue, Camden, NJ 08115.

CHAPTER 7

Getting a Job: The Process

inding the right job is much like finding someone to share your life: making a good choice can determine the course of your life. The same principle underlies both situations—you have to persuade someone else that you are the person best qualified to fill the position. As the race is not always to the swift, the job offer is not always to the best-qualified applicant. The job offer goes to the individual who *persuades* the decision maker that he or she is the right person.

Being well qualified for a job is important; if a job requires a degree in engineering, someone with a degree in economics is no doubt wasting time to apply. But among those with an engineering degree, who gets the job? One might have the highest grade point average, another the most experience, still another the best communication skills. The decision maker must choose, and where alternatives exist, persuasion becomes crucial. Our approach to the process of getting a job therefore assumes that the process is primarily one of selling a product—yourself.

We also assume that you have already decided on the kind of job you want, and therefore we will not patronize you with advice about the kind of job you should be seeking. That decision made, you could use some help in finding the position you are looking for.

Most generally, you should regard the process of arriving at suitable job offers as a single communication problem involving writing, speaking, and listening skills. For example, writing an effective resume and cover letter is only half the battle: you must succeed in the interview to get a job offer. But if you do not write an effective resume and cover letter, you will probably never *get* an interview.

The overall process of getting job offers is divided into the following six steps:

- Identify and research your target companies, developing a file of companies to contact. Research these companies, creating a company profile for each, and tailor all communications to this profile.

- Develop a persuasive resume. Stress results, skills, and accomplishments. Customize the resume to the kind of job you are seeking.

- Write persuasive cover letters. Show how you can meet the needs of *this* employer.

- Prepare to interview. Prepare to answer interviewer questions and to ask questions of your own.

- Meet the interview challenge. Master the role of interviewee, projecting predefined qualities.

- Write persuasive follow-up letters. Follow up on leads from the interview, tying your qualifications even more closely to the company's needs.

The Process of Getting Job Offers: Six Steps

Your ultimate hope is to receive several attractive job offers, from which you will be able to choose the one best suited to your professional and personal ambitions. How long that will take no one can say, but professional recruiters say that it takes one week of full-time job hunting for every $1,000 of annual salary desired. That's an approximation; people have landed fine jobs in a few days or weeks of searching. But often the process takes months, especially if the job searcher does not accept the first offer, so we suggest that you begin the process early in your final year of college.

You know in general the kind of job you are seeking and the kind of companies that offer it. Right now you could probably name at least five firms you are planning to contact about job openings. But most job seekers need a much larger pool of job leads to get just one or two attractive offers. We suggest that you develop a card file of many job leads and that you research those companies well enough that you can shape your self-marketing to fit their needs.

Step 1: Identify and Research Your Target Companies

Identify Target Companies   A target company is any firm that offers the kind of job, rewards, and potential for advancement you are looking for. How many companies you identify will vary with your circumstances. For example, if you're looking for the right job in any of the 50 states, you may target 100 or more companies. If you're looking for the right job in Atlanta, your list of target companies might be from 20 to 40. Err on the side of too many rather than too few.

Use a file of large index cards for your notes on target companies. Index cards can be added and discarded readily, so they are the best way of keeping an up-to-date file. On each card, write the company's name, address, telephone number, and anything you can learn about that company and the people who will decide whether or not you are hired.

How do you find job leads? Most people would think of the classified section of the local newspaper as the first place to start. Newspapers can be good sources of job leads, but they are by no means the only place to look because the majority of job openings are never advertised.

Look beyond the local newspaper. Check the classified sections of the metropolitan dailies around the country, which are available in your university library—*The Los Angeles Times, The Chicago Tribune, The New York Times, The Wall Street Journal, The San Francisco Examiner, The Atlanta Constitution, The Louisville Courier-Journal,* and *The Washington Post,* to name a few.

People you know can also provide job leads. Parents, relatives, neighbors, friends, sorority sisters, fraternity brothers, teachers, secretaries, barbers, clergy, alumnae/alumni, and members of social, civic, and religious groups may know about jobs in your field. Ask them.

Place your name with respected employment agencies. They know of many job openings that will not appear in any newspaper. Do not overlook the local office of the state human resources bureau.

Check the trade journals in your field. They may list jobs available or describe expanding firms that may be hiring. Consider joining professional organizations, such as the American Management Association, the American Marketing Association, the National Association of Accountants, the Administrative Management Society, or the American Society for Personnel Administration, to name a few. Organizations are good sources of job leads, especially if you attend their national or regional meetings. Some of these groups have computerized resume services, by which resumes of job searchers are matched up with openings in companies around the country.

Finally, the university library and the local public library will have directories of companies. The reference librarian will help you locate directories that contain descriptions of each company and the names and addresses of its officers. Write to the company and ask about job opportunities in your field. You will usually receive a response.

From your personal and professional contacts and your own research, develop a file of companies and send to each a copy of your resume and a cover letter.

Research Your Target Companies   Researching the companies to which you plan to write will serve you well. For one thing, you can save time because you will not negotiate with companies that are inappropriate. But research will serve two other functions as well. First, you will have to research any company that interviews you—at your interview the company expects you to know something about its products, size, growth pattern, and facilities. But more important, your research will enable you to construct a collective reader profile of the kind of company for which you are writing your resume and cover letter. Since the resume is primarily persuasive, selling you, it must be directed to the needs of its audience, which research will reveal.

Research the company's product lines, sales patterns, facilities, location, personnel, organization, reputation, philosophy, financial history, subsidiaries, growth potential, personnel policies, compensation, and benefits. Does the company seem to be growing, standing still, or declining? Find out about its ownership and about any problems it faces; learn its strengths and weaknesses. For example, what does it do to meet consumer demand and to insure customer satisfaction? You may not have the time to investigate each of these points, but reading about the firm and talking to knowledgeable people about it will give you a sense of its corporate identity.

To research a firm, start in the college library or public library, both of which will often have copies of the company's annual report going back several years. If libraries do not have the report, you can write to the firm's public relations office or treasurer. Study the reports of the last three to five years, remembering that they are public relations documents designed to create a favorable image. Also available from public relations are company newspapers and newsletters, which can add to your knowledge.

In the library, check such sources as the following:

- *The Career Guide: Dun's Employment Opportunities Directory* (Dun's Marketing Services)
- *Million Dollar Directory Series* (Dun & Bradstreet)
- *Million Dollar Directory: Top 50,000 Companies* (Dun & Bradstreet)
- *Moody's Complete Corporate Index* (Moody's Investors Service)
- *Predicasts F & S Index of Corporate Change: A Definitive Guide to Corporate Organizational Developments* (Predicasts, Inc.)
- *Predicasts F & S Index: United States Annual Edition* (Predicasts, Inc.)
- *Standard & Poor's Register of Corporations, Directors and Executives* (Standard & Poor's Corporation)
- *Thomas Register of American Manufacturers and Thomas Register Catalog File* (Thomas Publishing Company)
- *The Value Line Investment Survey* (Arnold Bernhard)

Also check the indexes of *The Wall Street Journal* and *The New York Times, The Business Periodicals Index,* and trade publications in the field of your interest.

Gradually, you will begin to develop a sense of whether or not you will fit into this firm, and if so, how. Note the problems faced by the firm or the industry. As you communicate with the firm, you will want to suggest ways in which you can contribute to solving its problems. You should not make exaggerated claims to solving major problems, but you will want to show some understanding of and interest in them.

Step 2: Develop a Persuasive Resume

Now that you have a good idea of what your readers are like, develop a resume aimed at persuading them that they need you. That means combing your background and experience, looking for the skills that this company needs. An effective resume is not merely an outline of your education and job experience; it creates an image of yourself—and that image must appeal to the managers who make the hiring decision. Use the problem-solving approach to developing your resume:

1. Define the resume problem.
2. Analyze your skills, experience, and background.
3. Decide on a resume format and develop a draft.
4. Edit and reproduce the resume.

Define the Resume Problem   To define the resume problem, profile your reader and define your goals. Many people will read your resume, so you will have to focus on a general reader rather than on a specific person. In general, two kinds of managers will read your resume, recruiters and line managers. We can identify three kinds of recruiters: (1) the professional company recruiter who visits university campuses to interview candidates and to screen them for further on-site interviews at the home office; (2) the professional recruiter who works for an employment agency or executive search firm retained by the company to help it fill a certain position; (3) the company personnel officer, who does essentially the same thing as the other two. The second general kind of resume reader is the line manager who will actually make the decision to hire you. This manager usually heads up the department in which you may work.

Thus you will have to write for two readers. The recruiter will be more of the generalist, probably more interested in the generalist in you, whether you fit the type this firm usually hires. Also, the recruiter may read as many as 200 resumes and cover letters in a single day. In the initial screening stages, the recruiter will probably give no more than an average of 20 to 30 seconds to each resume. Therefore you must make the most attractive features of your resume stand out easily to a reader who is skimming rather than reading slowly. The line manager reads fewer resumes and will read more as a specialist, anticipating how well you would fit into his or her department and what kind of contribution you would make.

Now you must define your goal in developing a resume. While your long-range goal is to get several attractive job offers, your short-range goal in mailing out a resume and a cover letter is to persuade the reader that you deserve an interview. Normally your resume and cover letter exclusively determine this decision, because they are the only criteria the reader has to judge your suitability for an interview. How critical these two pieces of writing become in that context!

They must project the kind of image the reader is looking for, as far as you can determine that image. Ultimately, there is no way to know for sure what a company representative is looking for, but it is possible to predict the qualities that most employers will find attractive and to project as many of those qualities as possible.

You surely want to stress professional qualifications—experience, education, and background—that equip you for the job. That sounds obvious, but "the job" may not be so easy to specify. Indeed, the one point in the resume about which the experts give conflicting advice is how specifically to define the job objective. Some say *not* to define any job objective on the resume. Others say to define it but broadly so that it does not limit you to one exclusive job. Still others say to define your objective specifically, for example, a position as systems analyst.

The difference of opinion is understandable. If you define your job objective too narrowly, you exclude yourself from consideration for all other jobs. If, on the other hand, you define your job objective broadly as, for example, a position in marketing, you give the reader little to go on and run the risk of appearing indecisive and vague about your career. In fact, most of us could qualify for more than one position: the same person could be qualified for a position in public relations or as a corporate trainer, for instance.

One answer to the problem is multiple resumes. If you want to be considered for more than one position, develop a separate resume for each. In the previous example, the job candidate would have one resume stressing public relations qualifications and another stressing training qualifications. It is not unusual for candidates to develop three or four resumes. Shape any resume you develop as specifically as possible to the kind of job you are seeking.

But whatever the job, your resume should stress achievements more than education and experience. After all, education and experience do not guarantee performance. Results and achievements suggest the kind of performance of which you are capable. For example, you might have chaired a committee to get out the vote for student government elections. Stress that as a result of your drive and tenacity, voter turnout was up 25 percent over the previous year. Business managers like quantifiable results, so whenever possible, use numbers.

Here is a list of qualifications and skills managers like to see in a candidate:

Ability to complete a project
Energy and willingness to work hard
Motivation; ability to work without close supervision
Communication skills
Enthusiasm
Cooperation; ability to get along with others
Integrity and reliability
Leadership skills
Loyalty; the desire to be a team player
Organizational ability and planning skills
Professional commitment

While the company representative doesn't expect one candidate to have all these qualities to a preeminent degree, he or she will be alert to detect them. Therefore, throughout the entire job search process, resume included, try to project these traits. You must be subtle: the candidate who merely affirms that he or she is loyal, enthusiastic, reliable, and hardworking may be making empty assertions. Point out aspects of your record that imply these desirable traits. For example, you can suggest reliability by indicating that you have not missed a day's work in 18 months. If you were elected senior class vice-president, you demonstrate leadership and the ability to get along with people. Regularly attending meetings of a professional organization suggests professional commitment.

A final point on goals. There is the temptation to misrepresent one's qualifications on the resume. One may theorize that since items on resumes often go unchecked, one is generally safe in making claims that are substantially untrue. Furthermore, proponents of this practice argue that since "everybody does it," those who tell the truth about themselves will appear bland in contrast with those who are making impressive but untrue claims.

While we will not offer ethical advice, we challenge the belief that qualifications listed on resumes go largely unchecked. References, for example, are checked! And if your resume is found to contain misrepresentation, you will have thereby excluded yourself from consideration, so the price of detection is steep. We suggest that you make no statement that you cannot substantiate but that you tell the truth in its most favorable light. Also, you are not obliged to volunteer anything unfavorable about yourself. For example, a salesperson who has been fired for failing to meet the sales quota set by management does not have to (and should not) volunteer that information.

Last, business managers generally agree that a one-page resume is desirable for most candidates. A two-page resume is acceptable, but mainly for persons with plenty of job-related experience. A three-page resume would be acceptable only for the most unusual case—for example, a top executive who has had varied and extensive experience. For most of us, however, considering that our resumes may at first be read in 20 or 30 seconds, a one-page resume will do.

Analyze Your Skills, Experience, and Background   Analyze your experiences and background to get the raw material from which you will construct the mosaic of your resume, the image of yourself you wish to project. Take plenty of time for this stage of the resume, doing it in three or four sittings. Develop another card file, placing one item about yourself on each separate card. What kinds of items should you list? You have to develop a feel for resume items. While some facts obviously belong—for instance, your anticipated degree—others may also reflect important traits or skills. For example, if you got one of the two A's in Professor Kramer's statistics class of 60 students, that fact implies something about the kind of person you are.

Start by tracking down your accomplishments. Think beyond the kinds of achievements that are reported in the newspaper to the things you have done that make you proud of yourself. For example, maybe you learned about computer programming or word processing. Perhaps you maintained a 3.0 grade point average in four college courses while taking care of a family and holding a job. Not everything you put on a card will go into your resume, so when in doubt, list it on your cards. Later you can decide whether an item will be meaningful to a company representative. Also, items that may not seem important themselves may fit into a pattern later.

During this analytical part of the resume, you will be gathering facts to gain a new perspective on yourself. Mediocre resumes sometimes result because people do not take the time to discover what is unique about themselves. You may feel that there is little that is special about yourself, but the overall pattern of your life will be yours alone. For example, you may create through the mosaic of your resume the image of a well-rounded person who gets along well with others—the kind of person the job calls for. Answering the following questions about yourself can start you thinking along the right lines.

A Professional and Personal Inventory

1. What are your strengths as an employee? How have you demonstrated these strengths?
2. What achievements have made you feel good about yourself?
3. What three positive words or phrases would you use to describe yourself? What actions have demonstrated these traits?
4. Name some activities in which you have achieved quantifiable results, for example, an increase in the number of people participating in some activity or an increase in items sold.

5. Name some activities you have coordinated, for example, programs, events, or speakers.

6. In a job, have you ever been awarded a high performance rating? If so, why?

7. Point up instances in your experience that show your ability to carry a project through to its completion.

8. What actions of yours show that you are a hard worker and a self-starter?

9. What actions demonstrate that you have good oral and written communication skills?

10. What actions show that you get along well with peers? That you are a team player?

11. What actions show that you are dependable and reliable?

12. What actions show your leadership ability?

13. What actions show your organizational and planning skills?

14. How have you demonstrated professional commitment?

15. What professional organizations do you belong to? Which meetings have you attended?

16. Has anyone such as a boss or a teacher ever taken an individual interest in you? What qualities seemed to attract this interest?

17. Have you ever received a certificate of any kind? Even a certificate of perfect attendance?

18. What compliments have you received from people who were not relatives or close friends? What did they notice about you?

19. Have you ever taught anybody anything? If so, what? Have you ever supervised others? If so, what did you supervise?

20. Have you ever won a contest, for example, the best essay in your sophomore class? The most tickets sold?

21. Were you valedictorian or salutatorian? A member of the student council? An athlete? A cheerleader? A performer in a play?

22. Did you work on the school newspaper? In what capacity?

23. Have you ever given a speech? To whom?

24. Have you ever held an office in a club? What were your duties?

25. What is your most attractive trait?

26. What have you done that shows that you are ambitious?

27. What committees have you served on?

28. Did you ever run a meeting?

29. What kind of volunteer work have you done?

30. Have you written anything that has appeared in print?

31. Are you good in mathematics or statistics?

32. How would you state your job objective in one sentence?

33. Do you speak any foreign languages? Do you have a reading knowledge of any?

34. Do you have any special licenses (not driver's) or certificates?

35. What are your hobbies or leisure-time activities?
36. Does either your grade point average or your class standing reflect favorably upon you?
37. What is your college major? Do you have any minors? Or do you have any course groupings that virtually amount to a minor, for example, five courses in mathematics or six courses in psychology?
38. Have you been on the honor roll or dean's list? Are you graduating *cum laude*?
39. If you served in the military, what was your last rank and what were your responsibilities?
40. Do you have any experience with computers?
41. Do you presently have a job (either full- or part-time)? What are your duties and responsibilities? Do you have any supervisory or decision-making experience in this job? What accomplishments have you achieved in this job? What have you done that someone else might not have done as well?
42. Have you ever been promoted? Have you received any pay raises or rewards for meritorious service?
43. Have you ever received a scholarship or financial aid based on ability?

By answering these questions and writing your answers on cards, you have probably accumulated much information about yourself. Not every detail will go into your resume, but even the facts that you do not use may help you answer questions about yourself in the interview stage. Developing a resume, writing cover letters, and preparing for interviews is a process of self-discovery, giving you a more accurate sense of your own worth.

Now that you have completed the inventory phase, let's suggest ways in which to evaluate and organize the notes you have collected. While resume formats vary, there is general agreement about the building blocks. These basic components of the resume follow.

Education   List your education from present to past. Start with your latest degree, diploma, or degree work and work backward. For example, if you expect a bachelor's degree at the end of this semester, list that first. If you also gained an associate's degree a year ago, list that after your bachelor's degree. List the dates of each degree, even the date you expect to receive the degree. For example, "B.S. in psychology expected June 1987" (see figure 7.2). Listing your high school education is optional, since the further you get from high school, the less relevant that education becomes. Another point about listing high school experience is that generally you should avoid any reference to religious affiliation, and attendance at a religious school can suggest such affiliation. The point is to prevent even unconscious discrimination on the reader's part. While you need not name your high school, you can list any honors or relevant experiences gained there.

List majors, minors, and any group of courses that would be relevant to the kind of job you are applying for. Class rank or grade point average should be listed if either reflects well on you. A grade point average of 3.0 or above is a plus; one of 2.3 is not. If your grade point average in your major field is good, list it.

Do not list the courses you have taken in college, even those taken in your major field. Once you mention your major field, the reader will know most of the courses, since they are fairly standard. An exception might be the situation of the person who has very little else to report. Even that writer should list only the courses most relevant to the job sought.

Work Experience   As with education, start with your most recent job and work back to previous ones. Include part-time and summer jobs. Give the job title (and the company name and city) and specify the duties and responsibilities. Also specify any accomplishments connected with the job (see figure 7.2 for an example). Give the dates (months and years) for your employment in each job. If you have worked for one company for several years, name your positions, with the dates, duties, and responsibilities of each. If you have left a company, do not give the reason.

In describing your employment history, do not be content merely to list the job titles and the companies that have been a part of your career—they tell little about you, because job titles have different meanings in different companies. Stress your responsibilities more than job titles. And concentrate on significant responsibilities: don't clutter your resume with minutiae, for example, you answered the telephone and were responsible for locking up.

Above all, **stress anything that implies quality performance, such as promotions, commendations, and awards.** Stress accomplishments in which you exceeded a quota, increased sales or productivity, did more than was expected, or did something more efficiently than others. For instance, if you sold 10 percent more magazines than other magazine salespersons in your territory, mention that. If you collected more past due accounts than others, mention that. Or if you did something with fewer errors than others, mention that. Do not misrepresent or grossly exaggerate, but emphasize results.

Job Objective Statement   As indicated, this part is optional. If your job objective is fairly specific, include a job objective statement such as you find in figures 7.1, 7.2, and 7.4. Developing one or two alternate resumes—each with a different job objective, as in figures 7.1 and 7.4—may solve the problem. Or you may choose to omit the job objective statement, as in figure 7.3. When you omit the objective, you should state the job you desire as specifically as possible in the cover letter accompanying the resume. For example, "I am applying for an entry level position as a systems analyst."

Personal Information   List your address and telephone number. It is critical that prospective employers be able to contact you to set up an interview.

Most potential employers will call you during business hours, so along with your home phone, you might list the telephone number of a trusted associate who will relay a message to you. If you are employed, do not give your business telephone, because if your present employer realizes that you are looking for another job, he or she may let you go.

Many people list their birth date, marital status, number of children, height and weight, and health status ("excellent") on the resume. Legally, no employer has a right to ask about any of these items, so some people do not include this information. An older person, for example, may not wish to give his or her age. A person who is overweight may decide not to include his or her height and weight, but the individual who is tall and thin may wish to give both. Unless a specific employer requests a photograph, do not include one; it is an outmoded practice.

You may include additional personal data that create a sense of your character and personality. These could be hobbies, sports, and leisure activities. Be judicious in listing such details, however; a few suggest that you are a well-rounded person, but too many may suggest a preoccupation with social life.

Miscellaneous Information   List items that reflect favorably upon you as a student and an employee. Here is a partial list of such items:

Scholarships
Honors and awards
Licenses and certificates
Committees served on
Offices held
Publications
Military service
Memberships in professional organizations
Percent of college expenses earned
Foreign languages
Computer experience
Volunteer work

References   Ask three or four people for permission to list them as references, if you are sure they will write a good letter on your behalf. Always get permission in advance because those you list without it may resentfully write a less favorable letter. When asking someone to serve as a reference, say, "Could you give me a strong recommendation for this position?" That phrasing offers the person who does not wish to serve as your reference a way out. You do not want unenthusiastic references.

Select your references judiciously. Friends, relatives, neighbors, and clergy are not normally good choices. Could you imagine your pastor or rabbi saying unkind things about you? Choose people who know you professionally—college professors, supervisors (present and past), and business associates who occupy management positions. For example, if you have been a clerk in a retail store, a fellow clerk will not make as good a reference as the store manager.

Do not list your references; instead, use a phrase ("references gladly furnished on request") that indicates willingness to supply them at the proper time, usually in the interview. There is a good reason for protecting your references until you learn that the firm is seriously interested in you. A reference that appears on a resume can be contacted easily. Thus if you send out 30 to 50 resumes, your references may be contacted repeatedly and give you a progressively less enthusiastic recommendation simply because they are tired of the phone calls or of writing letters.

A few final remarks. As you omit references to religion, omit any references to race or political affiliation. Also, if you are employed, do not indicate on your resume either your present salary or the salary you expect to be paid. For many jobs the salary range is standard; and where the salary is negotiable, the late interview stage is the time to discuss it. For now, you are trying to get the employer interested enough in your qualifications to interview you.

Decide on a Resume Format and Develop a Draft   Having completed your analysis you are ready to select the resume format that best suits your job objectives and qualifications. The following three formats will be the most useful: the chronological (inexperienced) format, the chronological (experienced) format, and the skills format.

The Chronological (Inexperienced) Format   The most commonly used format is the **reverse chronological format**, in which you list your experience and education in reverse chronological order (see the resume in figure 7.1). Note that under the two major headings (Education and Work Experience) the resume lists the most recent items first and works backward. For example, college is treated before high school; the most recent job (sales representative) is treated before the earlier job (sales clerk). The reverse chronological order is strictly followed only with work experience and education. For example, under a heading such as Memberships, there is no need to follow chronological order. More important memberships should precede less important ones.

The distinctive feature of the **chronological (inexperienced) format** is that it emphasizes education (by placing it first) and is therefore best suited to job candidates with little or no work experience. Since recruiters often just scan resumes, you must put your most impressive features first, where the reader will most likely see them. In figure 7.1, the candidate obviously feels that the Education material deserves more attention than the Work Experience information.

The Chronological (Experienced) Format   Many candidates have valuable work experience in two, three, or more jobs, and they will want to highlight

LYNN J. ORTEGA
1359 Observatory Road
Cincinnati, OH 45213
(513) 281-6642

JOB OBJECTIVE:

Entry level position as Marketing Representative.

EDUCATION:

B.S. Degree expected June 1985 from University of Cincinnati, Cincinnati, OH. Major in Marketing; minors in Speech Communication and Psychology.

Quality Point Average of 3.4 overall; 3.7 in Speech Communication coursework. "A" in Business Writing course.

Elected to Marketing Department Chairperson's Student Advisory Committee. Polled student opinion, representing student viewpoint to chairperson; explained departmental policies and procedures to students.

In high school, served as editor of the yearbook, responsibile for writing and editing copy, deciding layout, coordinating activities of four associate editors, scheduling and chairing meetings of editorial staff. Member of the debating team, winning second place in state regional debating competition. Graduated 16th out of class of 358.

WORK EXPERIENCE:

Sales Representative (part-time). Telemarketing Associates, Cincinnati, OH (telephone subscription sales). July 1975 to September 1981. District sales leader for two years. Marketed wide variety of magazine subscriptions; recruited and trained team of four salespersons.

Sales Clerk (part-time). Casual Footwear, Montgomery, OH. August 1979 to September 1981. Duties included customer service, inventory, display work, operating and closing out of cash register. Handled some receiving and interstore shipping; trained my replacement.

MEMBERSHIPS:

American Marketing Association
Society for the Advancement of Management
Speech Club

ACTIVITIES:

Jogging, scuba diving, attending Cincinnati Symphony Orchestra performances, Friends of WGUC (Public Radio).

PERSONAL:

Height 5'8"; weight 123 lbs.; age 30. Willing to relocate.

REFERENCES:

Available on request.

Figure 7.1   Resume: Chronological (inexperienced)

their work experience over their education. Our second resume format—
the **chronological (experienced) resume**, shown in figure 7.2—does that.
Even though the job candidate, Mark G. Upson, has an impressive education, he judges his work experience to be even more significant. Using the
chronological (experienced) format, he highlights his work experience by
placing it before his education. As in any chronological order, in both the
Experience and the Education sections, the candidate begins with the most
recent item and works backward.

   The Skills Format   The **skills format** is for people who wish to highlight
neither education nor work experience but certain skills they have acquired. As figure 7.3 shows, this format places a list of skills at the top of the
page, shifting education and employment history to the bottom. The skills
listed will vary, but each skill listed is supported by concrete evidence. For
example, the skill of communicating is evidenced in part by an A in a
business writing course. Other evidence follows; a list of skills, by themselves, would be unconvincing.

   To use the skills resume effectively, you must have a reasonably clear
idea of the kind of job you will be applying for so you can focus on the
appropriate skills. For instance, if you are applying for a position in
accounting, you would stress not only your accounting skills but also that
you are detail-oriented, self-starting, and able to work long hours. For a
position in advertising, you would stress your creativity, communication
skills, and competitiveness.

   The skills format is similar to another format, the functional, which you
may encounter occasionally. In the **functional resume**, the list of skills is
replaced by a list of functions—jobs held and a brief description of the
duties of each job. The list of jobs might include the following: account
executive, sales manager, and public relations specialist. Often the functional resume does not give the names of the companies for which the
candidate worked or the dates of employment in each job. Since the functional resume stresses the jobs over other items, it can be useful to candidates who have had many jobs or to those with gaps in their employment
history that they wish to deemphasize. For example, a person may have
taken time off to travel or write.

   You may be tempted to use the functional resume, but we advise against
it. Savvy employers recognize that the functional resume can cover gaps or
problems in the candidate's background; they may wonder whether the
applicant using the functional resume has something to hide. This kind of
resume is sometimes said to be a desirable option for homemakers who
have been out of the workplace for a long time. Such candidates, however,
can easily adapt one of the two chronological formats to their needs by
inserting a brief statement to the effect that certain years were devoted to
child rearing.

MARK G. UPSON
253 Pinehurst Drive
Columbus, OH 43204
(614) 786-5113

JOB OBJECTIVE:
Company Treasurer.

EXPERIENCE:
Treasurer/Controller, Brennan Insurance Agency, Columbus,
OH, November 1977 to the present. Supervise and control all accounting
functions, including cash management, monthly and annual financial
statements, annual budget coordination and preparation, and special
project analysis such as acquisitions. Additional responsibilities include
personnel, office management, and supervision of the Word Processing
Department.

Assistant Divisional Controller, Gilchrist Tool & Die, Inc., Columbus, OH,
July 1974 to November 1977. Supervised the local accounting department;
developed a perpetual inventory system; created internal control reviews;
directed conversion from a manual to an automated accounting system;
and coordinated the preparation and analysis of five monthly financial
statements.

Staff Accountant, Esco Industries, Columbus, OH, June 1973 to July 1974.
Prepared state income, sales, and use tax returns, monthly consolidated
statements, audits of plant inventories, account analysis, and full general
ledger.

EDUCATION:
M.B.A., Ohio State University, Columbus, OH, June 1985. GPA of 3.8.

B.S., Accounting, University of Kentucky, Lexington, KY, June 1973.
Ranked 15th in a class of over 500, finishing with GPA of 3.9. Elected to
Beta Alpha Psi, (honory accounting society) and Beta Gamma Sigma
(honorary business society). Appointed marshal at graduation with
Magna Cum Laude distinction.

C.P.A. License received in Ohio in May 1974.

INTERESTS:
Tennis, swimming, camping, chess, and Civil War history.

PERSONAL:
35 years old; 5'10" tall; weight 142 lbs.; single. Willing to relocate.

REFERENCES:
Available on request.

Figure 7.2   Resume: Chronological (experienced)

LYNN J. ORTEGA
1359 Observatory Road
Cincinnati, OH 45213
(513) 281-6642

SKILLS:

Planning:

Devised and implemented program for training sales personnel in retail store. Scheduled meetings; planned agendas. Planned and met series of deadlines involved in publishing yearbook.

Communicating:

"A" in Business Writing course. G.P.A. of 3.7 in Speech Minor. College Speech Club; high school debating team, winning second place in state debating competition.

Supervising:

Edited high school yearbook, supervising and coordinating efforts of four associate editors; scheduled and chaired meetings. Society for the Advancement of Management.

Selling:

Sales Representative for telephone subscription service. District sales leader for two years. Gained valuable experience in dealing with claims of dissatisfied customers. American Marketing Association.

Recruiting and Training:

Recruited, screened, and trained telephone sales personnel. Marketing Department search committee to screen and interview candidates for faculty position. Practice with interviewing job candidates included in Business Writing course.

Counseling:

Performance appraisal workshop included in Management course. Counseled students on departmental policies and procedures as member of Marketing Department Chairperson's Student Advisory Committee.

EDUCATION:

B.S. Degree expected June 1985 from University of Cincinnati, Cincinnati, OH. Major in Marketing. Minors in Speech Communication and Psychology. Quality Point Average of 3.4.

EMPLOYMENT HISTORY:

Sales Representative (part-time). Telemarketing Associates, Cincinnati, OH. July 1975 to September 1981.

Sales Clerk (part-time). Casual Footwear, Montgomery, OH. August 1979 to September 1981.

PERSONAL:

Height 5'8"; weight 123 lbs.; age 30. Willing to relocate.

REFERENCES:

Available on request.

Figure 7.3   Skills resume

Note that the skills resume depicted in figure 7.3 shows the candidate's employment history toward the bottom of the page. Positions, company names, and dates of employment are specified, thus removing doubts the recruiter might have about the candidate's record.

Creating Alternate Resumes You will recall the discussion of the problem of specifying a job objective. The job candidate may want to apply for more than one kind of job, so specifying only one job objective could narrow the options. Multiple resumes were advised as one solution to the problem. To demonstrate how a candidate might do multiple resumes, consider the fictitious job candidate Lynn J. Ortega. Using essentially the same data, three distinct resumes for Lynn J. Ortega have been created.

functional

Figure 7.1 depicts the resume Ortega might use to apply for a position as a marketing representative. It accentuates skills, education, and experiences in Ortega's background relevant to marketing, such as:

Bachelor of science degree in marketing

Communication skills (speaking and writing)

Sales experience (two part-time jobs)

Membership in the American Marketing Association

Figure 7.4 shows the resume Ortega might use to apply for a position in personnel administration. The information is the same as for the marketing representative resume, but this one highlights details in Ortega's background that are relevant to personnel administration.

A minor in psychology

"Personnel-related" experience in coursework

Recruiting, screening, and training experience

Experience with keeping records

Dealing with the public (customers)

Speech club membership

Figure 7.3 shows the skills resume that Ortega might use to apply for a position requiring many of the skills listed (planning, communicating, supervising, selling, recruiting and training, and counseling). Such a position might be as a public relations specialist or as a corporate trainer. The cover letter accompanying this resume would state specifically the kind of job Ortega is seeking.

Creating alternate resumes is not difficult once you have analyzed your background. It's just a matter of reorganizing the materials to point toward a slightly different career, since people usually do not become interested in *totally* dissimilar careers. The four Ortega resumes (marketing representative, personnel administrator, public relations specialist, and corporate trainer) detail the same general skills and experience. Since Ortega possesses those skills, developing the alternate resumes would not be difficult.

LYNN J. ORTEGA
1359 Observatory Road
Cincinnati, OH 45213
(513) 281-6642

JOB OBJECTIVE:
  Entry level position in Personnel Administration.

EDUCATION:
  B.S. Degree expected June 1985 from University of Cincinnati, Cincinnati,
  OH. Major in Marketing, Minors in Psychology and Speech
  Communication. Quality Point Average of 3.4 overall; 3.6 in Psychology
  Minor. "A" in Business Writing.

  Personnel-related experience gained in coursework: Management course
  included practice in performance appraisal interviewing; Business
  Writing included practice in interviewing job candidates.

  As member of Marketing Department Chairperson's Student Advisory
  Committee, acted as go-between for chairperson and students; counseled
  students on departmental policies and procedures. Appointed to
  departmental search committee to screen and interview candidates for
  faculty position.

  In high school, served as editor of the yearbook, coordinating activities of
  four associate editors--scheduling and chairing meetings; responsible for
  writing copy and for deciding layout. Member of the debating team,
  winning second place in state regional debating competition. Graduated
  16th out of class of 358.

WORK EXPERIENCE:
  Sales Representative (part-time). Telemarketing Associates, Cincinnati,
  OH (telephone subscription sales). July 1975 to September 1981.
  Recruited, screened, and trained telephone sales personnel. Maintained
  records for this group. District sales leader for two years.

  Sales Clerk (part-time). Casual Footwear, Montgomery, OH. August 1979
  to September 1981. Duties included customer relations, inventory, display
  work. Gained valuable experience in dealing with dissatisfied customers.
  Designed and implemented training program for my replacement.

MEMBERSHIPS:
  Speech Club, Society for the Advancement of Management, and American
  Marketing Association.

PERSONAL:
  Height 5'8"; weight 123 lbs.; age 30. Willing to relocate.

REFERENCES:
  Available on request.

Figure 7.4 Alternate resume

Creating the First Draft   Having examined the most practical resume formats, you are ready to select the one that best suits your needs. Then you can consider the notes you made on your skills, experience, and background and begin the draft of your resume.

Your first step will be to survey your note cards and decide upon tentative headings. Such a list might include the following:

Job objective statement (if desired)

Education

Work experience

Personal information

Miscellaneous information

References (an offer to furnish them)

Tailor your list of headings to your own desired profile. Everyone will use some of these, for example, Education and Personal Information. But you may need to create a heading or two to highlight special aspects of your profile. For instance, if you have received two or more special awards or honors, you may wish to create a heading entitled Awards and Honors. The need for special headings will assert itself as you review your note cards.

Next, begin drafting the individual sections. Gradually the major components of your resume will fall into place. At this point, do not worry about length, polished phrases, or format. Try instead for a flowing continuity, placing emphasis on your major accomplishments by devoting the most space to them. Now you are ready for editing.

Edit and Reproduce the Resume   Allow for a time lapse of at least a day between your drafting and your editing stage. Then reread your draft critically. What sounded like a catchy phrase on Monday may sound contrived on Wednesday. Do you still like the emphasis you have given your various accomplishments? If you were the recruiter, what kind of an image would you have of the resume's author? Are there any chronological gaps? Have you described your work experience clearly?

When you are satisfied with the larger issues, edit for conciseness. Conciseness becomes more important in a resume than in a memo because you're limited to one page. Go over your resume line by line, deleting the unnecessary words and phrases. The resume uses a telegraphic style, which omits the first person pronoun as the subject of the sentence. For example, instead of writing "I researched market conditions," you would write "Researched market conditions." Doing so avoids the constant repetition of the pronoun *I*. Do not refer to yourself in the third person on your resume; it sounds artificial.

Next edit for tone. Tone in a resume results largely from choice of words, especially verbs and descriptive adjectives. Here we would like to introduce lists of verbs and adjectives that are likely to create a positive tone:

Action Verbs

accelerated	edited	organized
accomplished	effected	performed
adapted	eliminated	pinpointed
administered	established	planned
advised	evaluated	programmed
analyzed	expanded	promoted
arranged	expedited	proposed
clarified	facilitated	recruited
communicated	forecasted	reduced
compiled	formulated	reinforced
completed	generated	reorganized
computed	guided	reviewed
conceived	implemented	revised
conducted	improved	scheduled
controlled	increased	simplified
coordinated	initiated	solved
counseled	integrated	streamlined
created	launched	stengthened
delegated	led	structured
demonstrated	maintained	supervised
designed	managed	surpassed
developed	mastered	systematized
directed	motivated	

Positive Adjectives

active	disciplined	organized
adaptable	discriminating	perceptive
aggressive	economical	persuasive
alert	effective	positive
ambitious	efficient	practical
accurate	energetic	precise
analytical	entrepreneurial	productive
astute	enthusiastic	proficient
careful	fair	professional
competitive	forceful	proven
comprehensive	imaginative	reliable
constructive	keen	resourceful
courteous	logical	sophisticated
creative	loyal	systematic
decisive	methodical	thorough
dependable	orderly	vigorous
detailed		

We are *not* suggesting that you use these words indiscriminately: they are not a list of buzzwords that will automatically impress the recruiter. Indeed, indiscriminate use of these words might have just the opposite effect. But if you can introduce some of them into your resume, its tone will become more action-oriented, confident, and positive. See especially figure 7.3 for a resume that uses these words effectively.

Finally, edit for format, which is especially important in the resume. Before the recruiter reads a line of your resume, he or she receives an impression from its format—and you want that impression to be favorable. At your typewriter you may wish to experiment with different formats. Basically, you have four tools to work with: headings, underlining and capitalizing, indenting, and white space. Skillfully used, these tools can give your resume the neat, professional appearance attractive to recruiters.

Notice that the sample resumes we have shown display their headings prominently, with each heading capitalized and underlined. To make the heading stand out more dramatically, the material under it is indented from the left margin. Note that figure 7.2 goes a step further, creating subheadings (for example, Treasurer/Controller) under the major headings. Figure 7.3 uses a variation, capitalization and boldface for the headings and underlining for the subheadings (Planning, Communicating, Supervising, and so on). Making your headings stand out enables the recruiter to pick out the most important data quickly.

Using white space effectively is also important. If the resume looks crowded on the page, it may convey an impression of bulk weight, which is intimidating to the reader. But since it is desirable to condense your material to one page while omitting nothing that could help you, the need for white space cannot take precedence over the need for adequate detail. The sample resumes in this chapter provide examples of effective use of white space without sacrificing content. See especially figures 7.2 and 7.3.

When you have developed your final draft, have it edited by a professional. You do not want any errors in style, grammar, spelling, or punctuation, because a recruiter will discard your resume for any such errors. We are not suggesting that you take your resume to a professional resume service. Quite the contrary, for recruiters can easily spot the professionally prepared resume, and they may wonder about the candidate who must resort to a professional to prepare his or her resume. Inquire at the English department of your university or college about professors or others who do private consulting and editing of employment correspondence. Their services will be worth the investment.

You are now ready to have the resume typed and reproduced. Generally, we advise against typing the final copy yourself. But if you are a good typist and have access to a good electric typewriter or word processor, do it yourself. Be sure to use a fresh typewriter ribbon and clean typewriter keys. Otherwise, seek out the services of a good secretary who does typing on the side. The secretary will type your draft with a professionalism that enhances the final positive impression of your resume.

The resume should be typed on good bond paper, and the resume, cover letter, and envelope paper should match. Use white or off-white, avoiding such colors as yellow, blue, and pink.

Now reproduce the resume, for you will presumably be sending out many of them. One option is to photocopy the original; many photocopy machines produce good copies on bond paper. Another option is to have the resume printed. Either one is satisfactory, but most experts advise having your resume neatly typed and photocopied, thus avoiding the impression of sending out large numbers of them. Do not reproduce your finished resume on a ditto or mimeograph machine. Send out a product that is absolutely neat and professional looking.

Step 3: Write Persuasive Cover Letters

To write a persuasive cover letter, you must understand the difference between the cover letter (sometimes called a letter of application) and the resume. The resume summarizes your qualifications for a particular kind of job and is designed for several companies that employ people in this kind of job. The cover letter is an attempt to persuade a *particular* company that you can fill their job well. Taken together, the resume and cover letter have the purpose of getting you an interview with the officer of the company who is most able to further your cause.

So the cover letter must emphasize the match between you and the company. It is a mistake to write the cover letter as a brief summary of the resume—a needless repetition. Instead, write the cover letter as an answer to the question "Why should *we* hire you?" Focus on the needs of the company.

For those needs, refer to the research you have done on the company or to their ad announcing the position. What problems are they experiencing that you can help solve? What qualities do you think they are looking for in a candidate for such a position? Go over your resume and your experience, looking for connections between their requirements and your qualifications. For example, if you are applying for the job of assistant marketing manager, you must be a good communicator. Look for evidence in your background proving that you *are* a good communicator; if the job calls for a self-starter, look for evidence that you *are* a self-starter.

To whom in the company should you address your cover letter? If you are answering an advertisement, the company will supply a person's name, a position, or a post office box number to which you should send the letter. But if you are not answering an ad, you may write directly to the personnel manager of the company, to the officer to whom you would report if hired, or directly to the president of the company.

The last option may require some explanation since presidents seldom hire entry level personnel. The rationale is that the president or the president's office will probably route your letter to the person in charge of the department in which you would work, and this manager may believe that the president has forwarded your cover letter and resume, so he or she might pay more attention to your application. But this technique is not unknown to presidents and recruiters, so some of its effectiveness has probably already been diminished.

We recommend that you find out the name and position of the officer to whom you would report if hired. Earlier in the chapter we suggested sources for names of company officials. If that doesn't work, telephone the switchboard of the company and ask for the officer's name and address. Be sure to get the correct spelling of the name.

By the way, if someone has referred you to this officer, be sure to state that fact early in your letter, for example, "Ms. Roth suggested that I write to you." The cover letter in figure 7.5 opens with this approach. It is the cover letter written by Lynn Ortega to accompany the resume in figure 7.4 to apply for an entry level position in personnel administration. Note how the letter connects Ortega's experience to the requirements of the potential employer, Edward Cho.

If you cannot identify the individual to whom you would report, identify the personnel manager and write to him or her.

In addition to gaining you an interview, a cover letter has a less obvious but equally important function—it shows how well you write. So let's go over some specifics about the content of the cover letter. First, do not use a trite opening, for example, "I read about your need for an assistant marketing manager in *The Wheeling Gazette*." Since the company will not find your study of the want ads relevant, get to the point: "I wish to apply for the position of assistant marketing manager" or "When you have read this letter and the enclosed resume, I believe you will agree that I can make a valuable contribution to your department as assistant marketing manager." If you can think of a more interesting opening that still sounds genuine, use it. But do not use the opener "Having read the job description for assistant marketing manager, I am amazed at the similarities between the job specifications and my credentials." That line too has become trite.

Devote the body of your letter to showing how your qualifications meet the needs of the company. If you are answering an ad, specify the major qualifications mentioned and be sure to address each one, preferably in the order given in the ad. Doing so shows the employer that you are attentive to company needs. If your qualifications do not precisely match the job description, explain how you are still qualified for the position. If you can make credible suggestions about costs and productivity, do so.

Do not volunteer information about your past history or your salary expectations. If you are answering an ad that specifically requests either of these, respond with a range figure, for example, "the low twenties." But be sure that the range you quote corresponds to market conditions unless you

1359 Observatory Road
Cincinnati, OH 45213
May 19, 1985

Mr. Edward Cho
Personnel Administrator
Omicron Corporation
Norwood, OH 45214

Dear Mr. Cho:

Mr. Michael Soluski, an analyst in the traffic department of your firm, informs me that your assistant, Ms. Emily Landman, has resigned her position. I believe that my skills, work experience, and education will enable me to serve you well as your assistant.

As you know so well, Omicron is automating more of its manufacturing functions through the use of robotics, and many workers are being displaced. I understand that it is your responsibility to determine which of these workers are retrainable and to develop training programs for them. While I do not pretend to have the answer to this industry-wide problem, I feel that I could contribute to the solution.

For example, I have experience at training homemakers in telephone subscription sales. I have served on a search committee for a new faculty member, and my class work has given me practice in appraisal and employment interviewing. My experience as a clerk in a retail store has given me a background in dealing with the public, especially with the claims of dissatisfied customers, which should serve me well in dealing with hourly employees. Moreover, my psychology minor has given me valuable insights into the mind of the displaced worker.

My strong background in speaking and writing will equip me for the communication tasks so vital in Personnel Administration. Please see the attached resume for further details.

As Omicron confronts the challenges of a fast-paced and evolving technology, it will need people who enjoy meeting a challenge, who are not afraid of change. I hope to play a significant role in meeting the challenges of Omicron's future.

Please call or have your secretary call me at 281-6642 to arrange a convenient time for an interview.

Sincerely,

Lynn J. Ortega

Lynn J. Ortega

Enclosure

Figure 7.5   Resume cover letter

are extremely well qualified for the position. Respond to other legitimate informational requests stated in the ad, such as willingness to travel or geographical preference.

Conclude by tactfully requesting an interview. Do not sound presumptuous: "I shall telephone early next week to schedule an interview." Rather, you might say, "Please phone me to arrange a convenient time for an interview." And be sure to include your telephone number in the last paragraph for easy reference. The cover letter may become separated from the resume, so both documents should contain your telephone number (including the area code). Remember to keep the cover letter to one page.

A final word about tone. As we said, you are selling yourself to a potential employer. You must not oversell, thus appearing too sure of yourself. Avoid such statements as "I have an outstanding record." Let the recruiter conclude that it is true. Confine yourself to credibly positive statements as exemplified in the letter in figure 7.5. You should sound poised but not arrogant, enthusiastic but not gushy. Figure 7.5 balances these tones.

One last tip. A duplicated cover letter indicates a superficial interest in the company. Making sure that each cover letter is typed for the particular company means more work, but it is work worth doing.

If several weeks pass with no response to a cover letter and resume sent to a company, don't become apprehensive. The possible reasons for the delay are many, ranging from a backlog of paperwork to your having been selected as a finalist. In fact, a quick response is often negative: "We presently have no openings for which you are qualified but will keep your application on file." Assume nothing, because you don't know. Instead, consider your options: you may continue to wait, telephone, or write.

If you decide to either telephone or write, each has its advantages. Phoning the officer is more immediate, but you may not get through to the person for several reasons. And if you do reach the officer, he or she may not be willing or able to tell you much. If you write, you will almost certainly get through to the officer. Writing also offers further documentation of your eagerness for the position.

If you decide to write a resume follow-up letter, limit it to three or four paragraphs. Your goal is to show your continuing interest in the position and to get this person to contact you. Assume that the person has received your resume and cover letter; avoid such glib openers as, "I assume the mails have not delivered my materials." In no way suggest that the reader is negligent for not answering your inquiry—you won't succeed if you make the reader feel guilty.

Open the letter by reintroducing yourself and stressing continuing enthusiasm for the job. Follow with a brief summary of your qualifications, but do not copy the approach of your cover letter, since the person has probably already read that material. Close by asking for an interview.

Include your telephone number beneath your signature. Figure 7.6 shows a resume follow-up letter. If you decide to telephone rather than write, follow the same strategy stressing your continuing interest, qualifications, and desire for an interview.

We do not encourage a second resume follow-up letter, since a third inquiry will probably succeed no better than the first two. Devote your time to better prospects.

Step 4: Prepare to Interview

Having mailed out several cover letters and resumes, having waited and hoped, you will one day receive the letter or telephone call asking you to visit a firm for an interview. Or the interview may take place on campus. It may even take place through teleconferencing. Wherever the location and whatever the method, more than anything else the interview determines whether or not you get the job, so you must prepare well for it.

It will help if you understand the interview process. Though this process varies with each firm and recruiter—whether a professional, a personnel manager, the manager to whom you would report, or possibly the head of a small company—the interviewer has three objectives: (1) to assess how well you could be expected to perform in this job, (2) to assess how satisfied you would be in this job, and (3) to create a positive image of the company in your mind.

A company will spend thousands of dollars training a new employee, especially in the early years. If that employee resigns after two or three years, that training and money are largely lost. Thus it is important that the recruiter assess accurately how well you would perform and how satisfied you would be in the position. And whether the company hires you or not, it wants your goodwill. Because a major corporation interviews thousands of candidates each year, it cannot afford to alienate the thousands—all potential customers—it doesn't hire.

The average interview will last about half an hour. The recruiter will spend part of that time describing the company and the job. The recruiter will also question you about your qualifications and background. Finally, he or she will probably allow time for you to ask questions about the position, company practices, and your future with the company. These topics will not necessarily appear in every interview, nor will every interview follow that order. Be prepared for a relatively informal, give-and-take conversation.

Between notification of the interview and the interview itself, review the research you have done on the company. Do not just read the last annual report of the company—recruiters assume everyone will be familiar with such material and will not necessarily be impressed by your knowledge of it. Go back to the sources suggested earlier in the chapter for more information. Write to the company's public relations department asking for as much pertinent literature as they can conveniently send you. Do not hesitate to identify yourself as a candidate for a position with the company.

1359 Observatory Road
Cincinnati, OH 45213
June 27, 1985

Mr. Edward Cho
Personnel Administrator
Omicron Corporation
Norwood, OH 45214

Dear Mr. Cho:

A few weeks ago I wrote to you asking to be considered for the position of your assistant. Since I have not had the pleasure of hearing from you as yet, I assume that I am still being considered for the position. Allow me to underscore my interest in the job and my desire for an interview.

With my degree in marketing, with minors in psychology and speech communication, with my committee-level experience, and with my four years of practical sales experience, I know I can serve you well.

If you have not received the letter and resume I sent, please let me know so that I may send you a copy of each. I am eager to meet with you at your convenience to discuss this challenging opportunity.

Sincerely,

Lynn J. Ortega

Lynn J. Ortega

281-6642

Figure 7.6   Resume follow-up letter

Being well informed about the company will not only add to your self-confidence as you anticipate the interview but will send a signal to the recruiter that you are genuinely interested in this company.

The next step is to prepare to answer the interviewer's questions and to ask some of your own. The recruiter will not necessarily be favorably impressed if you merely respond to questions; he or she may take that as a sign of passivity. Following is a list of questions sometimes asked in interviews. Not every recruiter asks all of these questions, but the list provides a representative sample that will enable most people to be prepared.

Questions Recruiters May Ask

1. What is your idea of success?
2. What motivates you?
3. What are some of your past accomplishments?
4. How do you function under pressure?
5. What are your main strengths and weaknesses?
6. What has been your most valuable experience?
7. What do you see yourself doing in our company in five years?
8. What words or phrases describe you best?
9. Which is more important to you, money or status?
10. What contribution could you make to our company?
11. How aggressive / ambitious / assertive are you?
12. How long would you plan to stay in this job?
13. What is the best idea you've had in college?
14. Describe extracurricular activities you participated in during college. Which did you enjoy most?
15. Why does this job interest you?
16. What is the toughest challenge you have met so far?
17. Do you think you can make it to the top? Why or why not?
18. What goals would you pursue in our company?
19. How much of your college expenses did you earn?
20. How do you feel about working overtime?
21. What college courses did you like best and why?
22. What do you know about our company?
23. What did you like and dislike about your last job?
24. Will you go where the company sends you?
25. How did you become interested in our company?
26. What do you want in a job?
27. How do you spend your spare time? Do you have a hobby?
28. How would you describe your personality?
29. Can you accept criticism?

Some of these questions probe for information directly related to job performance, such as your attitude toward overtime work; others probe for personal traits, such as your ability to accept criticism. Prepare answers to most of these questions, remembering two guidelines. First, never volunteer negative information about yourself. For example, if you are sensitive to criticism, do not say so. If that question is asked, translate your sensitivity to criticism into positive terms: "I don't enjoy being criticized, of course, but usually I can learn from it." To make your point convincingly, you might then give an example from your background in which you learned from criticism.

Second, recall the list of desirable traits most employers seek in candidates; reflect on the traits required for success in the job you are seeking. Make a list of qualities you wish to persuade the recruiter that you possess. For each quality, develop one or two examples from your experience that demonstrate that quality. For example, if you are seeking an entry level position in an accounting firm and you wish to stress your willingness to work long hours, you might mention that while carrying a full load of courses during your senior year in college you also worked 40 hours a week at a retail outlet.

Remember that your overall strategy in the interview is artfully to persuade the recruiter that you are well suited to the job and the company. Therefore you must not appear to sidestep any of the questions: vague responses or failure to answer questions can count against you. Use every opportunity in answering questions to construct the image of a person undoubtedly qualified for the job and good for the company.

Take the question that asks you to describe your main weaknesses. One job candidate might answer this question by claiming to be unaware of any weaknesses, thereby appearing conceited. Other candidates might volunteer negative information about themselves, for example, difficulty in getting to work on time. A better approach would be to admit to a character trait that implies a potential flaw but that actually reveals something favorable about you from the company's viewpoint. For example, you might say, "I'm a bit of a workaholic, I'm afraid," or "I sometimes take on more work than I should, but that's because I enjoy the challenge of seeing several projects through to completion."

Asking intelligent questions shows that you are perceptive and savvy. Consider asking some of the questions on the following list. You may not ask all of them, but do not sit in the interview and merely let yourself be interrogated. By asking questions, you should show yourself to be an assertive self-starter.

Questions You Might Ask

1. How much latitude for decision making goes with this position?
2. What are the duties and responsibilities of this job?
3. Where is the job located?
4. What qualifications should a person have to succeed in this job?

5. What would the higher position be after this job?
6. How much travel does the job involve?
7. What is the main priority for someone in this position?
8. Will advanced training or education be important for this job?
9. To whom would I report in this job? Who would report to me?
10. Is relocation normally considered part of the job?
11. What criteria will be used to evaluate performance in this job?
12. Does the company provide management development assistance in any form?
13. Does the company normally promote from within?
14. How does the company feel about new ideas?
15. What new products has the company developed in recent years?
16. Does the company plan any expansion in the next few years?

Avoid asking the following questions. You may be curious about them, but it is best to let the recruiter bring them up. You want to market yourself as being more interested in performing the job well than in gaining the rewards the job offers.

Questions Not *to Ask the Recruiter*

1. What will my salary be?
2. When do I get a vacation and how long will it be?
3. When may I expect a raise?
4. Will the company object if I go to law or graduate school?

The suggestion that you resist asking the last question about law or graduate school requires an explanation. Especially in your early years, your employer expects you to devote much energy to your job. Attending law or graduate school might absorb energy that would otherwise be available for your work. Indeed, mentioning your plans to attend law school may, in some fields, signal an unwillingness to continue long in that field. For example, if you are applying for a position in sales and plan to go to law school, the recruiter might conclude that you will leave your sales job after graduation. There are exceptions. If the advanced degree will enhance your work for this company, do not hesitate to ask about it. For example, if you're applying for a position as a claims adjuster in an insurance company and want to go to law school, go ahead and ask about it.

Let's consider some less obvious preparations for the interview. If the interview site is a company located in an unfamiliar area of your town, make a dry run before the interview. Driving to the interview site beforehand will insure that on the assigned day you arrive punctually.

Plan your attire. Conservative suits are preferable. Consider buying a new outfit for your interviews—it will add to your self-confidence, a worthwhile investment. Also wear a good pair of shoes and, if you carry a briefcase, be sure it is attractive. Women should be conservative in their choice of hairstyles, accessories, and jewelry. Men with beards should have them neatly trimmed. Perfume, cologne, or aftershave lotion should be used sparingly.

One last suggestion about appearance. Being noticeably overweight can hurt your chances in an interview. Although no valid connection exists between weight and job performance, overweight people are stereotyped unfavorably. Therefore, if you look overweight, you might consult your physician about what you could do to improve your appearance.

Possibly, you and a job-seeking classmate might get together to conduct mock interviews with each other, alternating roles from interviewer to candidate, leading to a discussion of each other's performance as a job candidate. The practice should add to your self-confidence in the real interview.

The dress rehearsal is past; it's time for the performance. Think of the interview as a performance, because that's what it is. Expect to be somewhat nervous: keyed-up nerves are a sign that you want to succeed. Taking a deep breath every few minutes will help calm you. Also, consider that the recruiter expects you to be a little nervous; he or she interviews nervous people for a living.

Step 5: Meet the Interview Challenge

To build your confidence, review your qualifications for the job. Consider your education, experience, and the reliability of your character. Consider the preparations you have made for this interview—your research into the company, your resume and cover letter, and your familiarity with interviews. Consider your communication skills. Recall that you look your best. Think of yourself as the best person for the job.

Arrive at the interview location with time to spare, about 10 minutes early. Do not arrive half an hour early because it will make you appear too eager. Ask anyone who accompanies you to remain outside. If the location is an office, be polite to the secretary; recruiters may ask their secretary for an evaluation of your preinterview behavior.

Observe impeccable manners before and during the interview. Do not chew gum. Even if you are invited to do so, do not smoke. Do not call the recruiter sir or ma'am; use Mr. or Ms. unless you are asked to use the first name. In either case, get the name right even if you have to ask for it the second time. If her name is Terri, don't call her Jerri. If the recruiter offers to shake hands, do so with a firm but not crushing handshake. (You may consider a firm handshake unimportant, but some recruiters attach significance to it.)

Don't look at your watch or at the wall clock. Don't fidget. Don't tell jokes, and avoid any possibly offensive humor. Try not to interrupt the recruiter, and do not ask to use the telephone.

During the interview, projecting enthusiasm is important. You can overdo it, but you can appear enthusiastic without going overboard. For example, use body language to convey a positive attitude. Don't sit on the edge of your chair, but lean slightly forward to suggest attentiveness. Nod and smile occasionally to indicate understanding and agreement. Maintain frequent eye contact with the recruiter—as much as 50 percent of the time. No one feels comfortable with a person who stares at a picture on the wall while supposedly talking to him or her.

Much of the interview's content will depend on the recruiter. But if you have researched the company adequately and thought out answers to the interview questions given earlier, you are well prepared. Nonetheless, note these few suggestions.

Demonstrate interest in the work you would be doing for the company. In addition to asking the questions already suggested about your job, try to find out as much as possible about your daily duties. This knowledge will help you to decide whether you really want this job.

Employers value dependability. At one or two points in the interview, tactfully allude to your dependability and cite an example that demonstrates this important trait.

Another desirable quality in an employee is ambition. You can create the impression that you are ambitious by asking the recruiter about the company's promotion policies. You can explain briefly how far along you expect to be in the company in 5 and 10 years.

Do not bring up salary and benefits. If the interview goes well, the recruiter will mention this subject. Interviews often proceed in two stages: an initial screening interview, which often takes place on campus—the kind we have been describing—often followed by a second interview at a company facility, in which the candidate meets his or her future department head and probably some coworkers. At this second interview there will be time to discuss salary, benefits, and perks. If you're genuinely concerned about whether the company will offer a competitive salary figure, you might ask about the range for this job description.

If you have had significant job experience and the recruiter asks why you left a particular job, never criticize a former employer. It's bad form to do so; besides, the recruiter will perhaps wonder how you will speak of his or her company when you leave it. Rather than saying you left a job because you were underpaid or there was little chance for promotion, simply say that you felt the need for greater professional growth and challenge.

At the end of the interview, thank the recruiter for the chance to discuss the job and express confidence in your ability to meet the challenge the position offers. Also, ask what the next steps in the process will be. Will someone call or write you, and if so, who will that be?

Step 6: Write Persuasive Interview Follow-up Letters

During the week following your interview, write a follow-up letter to the recruiter. It enables you to reinforce important features in your qualifications for the job, and it allows you to make important points you did not emphasize in the interview. The follow-up letter also demonstrates your enthusiasm for the position and the company.

Since you no doubt learned much in the interview about the job you are seeking, you now have a clearer idea of the duties, problems, and challenges of the position. Therefore you are now able to argue more convincingly that you are the best person for the job. As soon as possible after the interview, make notes about it. Write down (1) the duties described, (2) the problems you would face in this job, and (3) the qualities needed for success in this position.

These notes will help you to write a good follow-up letter. In the letter, show that you understand the major problems you will face in this job and how your background and experience will help you to solve those problems. Figure 7.7 shows the follow-up letter Lynn Ortega would write after the interview for the position of assistant personnel administrator. The letter carefully ties Ortega's work experience and educational background to the needs of the position.

The letter closes by expressing confidence in the author's ability to serve the corporation well. Also, Ortega's telephone number appears under the signature.

After writing the follow-up letter, wait a few weeks. If you have heard nothing by that time, you could try a telephone call asking whether the recruiter received your follow-up letter and expressing continuing interest in the job. But don't be obnoxious. It is the company's turn to act. Devote your time to applying for other positions and preparing for other interviews. You will find a good job sooner or later, because you are going about it in the right way.

When you get that good job, write a thank-you note to your references, telling them briefly about your new job. They will appreciate knowing the positive outcome. Besides, you may need them as references again in the future.

Summary

Getting a job requires you to practice the art of persuasion on your own behalf: you are the product that you sell to a company representative as the best qualified candidate for the job. This persuasive process involves the separate tasks of researching the job market; analyzing your own skills and abilities; writing resumes (probably more than one), cover letters, and follow-up letters; and interviewing.

This persuasion process can be broken down into six steps. First, identify and research your target companies, the number depending on your professional and personal preferences but ranging from 25 to 100 companies. Find out as much as you can about each one's industry, problems, policies, philosophy, management, and reputation. Develop a profile of each company that will guide you as you write to them and interview with them.

1359 Observatory Road
Cincinnati, OH 45213
May 30, 1985

Mr. Edward Cho
Personnel Administrator
Omicron Corporation
Norwood, OH 45214

Dear Mr. Cho:

I surely enjoyed our visit last Tuesday. The tour of the Omicron facility at Norwood was exciting, and the luncheon was excellent.

Now that I have a better idea of the duties of the Assistant Personnel Administrator, I feel even more confident that I can make a vital contribution to your office. Maintaining personnel records will tie in well with my background. When I coordinated a team of telephone subscription personnel, I was responsible for keeping records of all their activities, from the number of clients contacted to the responses of the clients. My curriculum has included a course in Information Systems, which will help me to understand the computerized record system at Omicron.

Researching trends in Personnel Administration and reporting on these to you will be more efficient and easy because of my coursework in Business Communication, which emphasized research and short written reports.

I look upon these and the other tasks you described as a challenge--and I enjoy challenges. I hope you will allow me the opportunity to prove my value to Omicron and to you.

I look forward to hearing from you soon.

Sincerely,

Lynn J. Ortega

Lynn J. Ortega

281-6642

Figure 7.7   Interview follow-up letter

Second, develop a persuasive resume. Identify your goals and consult your reader profile—know the kind of person who will read and evaluate your resume. Spend considerable time accumulating note cards on your accomplishments, skills, experiences, and qualifications. Become familiar with the various formats of the resume so that you can select the one best suited to market your own profile. After drafting your resume, edit it scrupulously. Choose the appropriate medium for reproducing your resume.

Third, write persuasive cover letters to the targeted firms, stressing what you can do for the company rather than what the company can do for you. If necessary, write a resume follow-up letter. Fourth, prepare to interview. Learn the purpose and steps in most employment interviews, along with the kinds of questions recruiters may ask. Prepare to answer those questions. Find out how to dress for the interview and prepare your clothes. Fifth, meet the interview challenge, showing enthusiasm, answering the questions, and conducting yourself with poise. Sixth, follow up on the interview with a letter and, if necessary, one or two telephone calls.

Writing Problems

1. Pick an entry level position in a company that you would like to work for after graduation, one for which you would be reasonably well qualified. Using the techniques suggested in this chapter, research the company and the job as far as possible. In a memorandum to your instructor, describe what you have been able to learn about the company, its management, products, facilities, policies, financial position, and reputation. Describe the job, detailing the responsibilities involved, the measure of decision making allowed, problems anticipated, possible means of dealing with those problems, and the qualities needed for success in this position.

2. Consult several trade journals in the field you plan to enter upon graduation. From these select an ad describing a position for which you would be reasonably well qualified upon graduation. Or consult the classified sections of several metropolitan newspapers and select such an ad. Perform the same process called for in problem 1, writing the same kind of memo to your instructor.

3. Develop your own persuasive resume, completing the four steps as explained in this chapter:
   a. Define the problem.
   b. Analyze your skills, experience, and background.
   c. Decide on a resume format and develop a draft.
   d. Edit and reproduce the resume.

The resume should state a job objective, an entry level position in the field of your choice. Make up your final activities between now and graduation, for example, your final grade point average. But do not invent improbable achievements. You need not have the resume professionally typed.

4. Having completed problem 3, produce an alternate resume aimed at a job objective in a related field. For example, you might move from sales to advertising or from accounting to data processing. You will be able to use all the analytical notes you made for your first resume. Essentially, you will use the same data but give it a different emphasis, aimed at your different job objective.

5. Write a persuasive cover letter to accompany the resume you developed for problem 3 or 4. Address the letter to a company recruiter or the person to whom you would report if hired. (You may invent a person for the latter case, but the person's job and responsibilities should correspond to those of a real individual in such a position.)

6. To develop interviewing skills, pair up with another member of the class preferably someone majoring in the same or a related field, with similar job aspirations. Together choose a company to research and write a job description for a realistic position that each of you could fill. Each of you will then submit to the other your resume and a cover letter addressing the other as the officer to whom you would report if hired. Then hold two mock interviews for the position in which each one role plays as the company officer and as the job candidate. After the "interviews," write a memorandum to each other (with a copy to the instructor) detailing how each performed as a job candidate— citing both strengths and weaknesses. Each will also write an interview follow-up letter as the job candidate (sending a copy to the instructor).

7. Identify someone in business presently filling the kind of position you imagine for yourself after graduation. The person should be located in your city, because you're going to write asking for a half-hour interview in which the two of you will discuss the position he or she now occupies. You will discuss its duties and responsibilities, challenges and problems, but make it clear that you do not intend to discuss confidential company matters. After the interview, write a memorandum to your instructor summarizing the main points to emerge from the discussion and a thank-you note to the person interviewed.

8. Develop a persuasive resume and cover letter for Dale Sachs, based on the information that follows. You need not use all the information given, so decide what to use and how to use it. Decide what format will best suit Dale's resume.

Avid chess player

Cumulative G.P.A. of 3.2

Management major

21 years old, married, no dependents

Member, Erie State Glee Club, for three years

B.S. degree expected this June, Erie State University, Erie, Ohio

Brown belt in karate

Two-years' part-time work at fast-food restaurant

Financed 50 percent of college expenses

Grade of C in business writing course

Height: six feet, two inches

Plans to attend law school

Delivery person part-time for pizzeria for two years

Member of Delta Alpha Sigma

Played lead role in senior class play in high school

Member, Society for the Advancement of Management (SAM)

SAM program committee member during junior year

Lifeguard at Fort Scott country club, four summers

Cumulative G.P.A. of 3.5 in management major courses

Delta Alpha Sigma membership committee chairperson, sophomore
  year

Minor in sociology

Captain, high school swim team

Address: 52 Ross Avenue, Erie, OH 45208

Phone number: (503) 241-4587

The cover letter to accompany the resume should be addressed to
Jean Beloit, Employee Relations Manager, Hennessy Stores, 901
Orchard Lake Road, Grand Rapids, MI 49505. Hennessy's is a chain
of retail outlet stores in three states. Their newspaper ad indicates an
opening at the assistant store manager level. Previous retail management experience is desirable but not required. A college degree in
management is desired. The factors listed as required are: good
decision-making and communication skills, the ability to plan and
organize, leadership ability, and willingness to work weekends and to
relocate. Hennessy's will provide a six-week training program. Applicants are asked to submit a resume including work history and salary
requirements. No salary range is indicated, but Dale knows from an
acquaintance that the range for the job is the low twenties.

CHAPTER 8

Research

hapters 1 through 7 described a systematic method of solving writing problems in business and offered concrete problems designed to allow you to practice the varied forms of writing used in business today. We have occasionally suggested that tapping your own investigative powers and the expertise of others might help you improve your business writing.

This chapter explains how to investigate and to make use of others' expertise. The term **research** refers to the systematic study that takes you beyond your present knowledge of a topic. Such effort may be necessary to uncover the information required to complete a writing task, even beyond what you can find by using such tools as the interpretive notes and journal entries described in chapter 2.

For this chapter, the ongoing case will be the EZ-Life Company. EZ-Life, which manufactures women's sportswear, has a main office and factory in New York City and sales offices in Chicago, Los Angeles, Houston, Tokyo, and Paris.

We begin by discussing the following research tools:

1. Direct observation
2. Questionnaire

3. Interviews
4. Experiments
5. Secondary sources

We then show how employees of EZ-Life use these tools to complete writing tasks, including memos, letters, proposals, feasibility studies, formal reports, and even oral presentations, all forms we present in this book.

We also explain how EZ-Life employees apply these research tools at different phases of the writing problem-solving sequence: to obtain information necessary for defining an audience, to gather examples of how other writers have analyzed a similar writing problem, to collect data influencing decisions about preparing a document draft, to add to or correct key information during revising and editing. This chapter details the tools you can use to conduct the research necessary for the solution of writing problems in business.

Direct Observation

By systematically observing a situation, you can create a convincing document. Systematic, **direct observation**, as opposed to informal observation, requires you to specify your purpose for gathering information. In addition, it may mean that you must use statistics, often as simple as counts of objects that you personally observe.

Let's see how direct observation might improve writing at EZ-Life. The company's policy on duplication of important documents of 10 pages or more is to send them to the Information Services Department for pickup by a local printing service. Sylvia Martinez directs EZ-Life's Information Services Department. The company's general manager, Herb Levy, has asked Martinez to compare sending out long documents to renting a high-speed copying machine. With a six-week deadline in which to complete her study, Martinez decides to keep track of the number of copies made by the outside printing service for EZ-Life, the cost per page of those copies, and the time it takes the service to pick up and return work. Her observations will cover a four-week period, after which she will prepare a memo to Levy in which she will report her conclusions and make a recommendation.

At the end of each week, Martinez tallies her observations. Figure 8.1 shows her four-week totals. She concludes: (1) the company sends out a roughly equal amount of copying each week; (2) the currently used printing service does a first-rate job of copying and collating documents; (3) the amount of time from pickup to delivery is consistent.

Now Martinez contrasts her findings with the projected cost, quality, and efficiency of renting a copy machine. By inquiring with several vendors, she finds a reputable firm that will rent a high-speed machine for a flat five cents a copy with a minimum of 10,000 copies for a four-week period. Based on EZ-Life's pay scale, she estimates that it will cost the firm $250 a week (including benefits and social security) to hire a clerk to run the machine and collate documents. She projects costs for paper, toner, developer, and electricity for the machine at $25 a week. With these figures, Martinez calculates the cost for each copy for the same 9,052 copies required during the observation period as $.172 a copy.

With her research completed, Martinez can begin drafting her memo to Levy. She defines her writing problem as follows:

- *Objective*   To prepare a memo reporting results of research on company copying service policy
- *Audience*   A superior, the general manager of EZ-Life (the general manager is interested in conclusions and recommendations, not the details of the direct observation or all of its resulting statistics)
- *Writer's desired image*   Logical, respectful, convincing

Figure 8.1
Direct observation

Week-by-Week Data on Printing Service Cost and Efficiency

Week	Dates	Copies/ Cost per Copy	Quality (Clarity, Collating)	Average Turnaround
1	4/2-8	2303/6.6 cents	Excellent	1 day
2	4/9-15	2115/6.6 cents	Excellent	1 day
3	4/16-22	2405/6.6 cents	Excellent	1 day
4	4/23-29	2229/6.6 cents	Excellent	1 day
Total	---	9052/6.6 cents	Excellent	1 day

She next prepares a row-column matrix, shown in figure 8.2, to assist her analysis of the writing problem. From her matrix, Martinez drafts this memo to Levy:

Figure 8.2
Row-column
matrix from direct
observation

Comparison of Outside Printing Service with Copier Rental

Factor	Outside Service	Copier Rental	Conclusion
Cost	6.6 cents/copy	17.2 cents/copy	Outside less expensive
Quality	Excellent	Unknown	Outside with proven record
Efficiency	1 day service	Variable (from immediate to 1 day based on backlog)	Rental can be faster in a pinch

Draft

Date: May 8, 1986

To: Herb Levy, General Manager

From: Sylvia Martinez, Director of Information Services

Subject: Copying Policy

I have finished comparing cost, efficiency, and product quality of our present copying service with that offered by a rental machine. My findings are as follows:

1. Cost per copy of our current service is $.066. Projected cost for rental machine copies for the least expensive but still reputable copier is $.172 a copy. This price includes rental copy fees, clerical help, copier supplies, and utilities. Projecting our present outside copying needs over a 52-week period, we would save approximately $13,000 a year if we retained our current service.

2. Copy and collating quality proved to be uniformly excellent over the four weeks studied. Pages were clear and crisp. Documents were collated accurately and securely. Rental machine copy quality would be dependent on the particular machine leased, although the vendor promises prompt maintenance and replacement if necessary. Collating quality would depend upon the work of the newly employed clerk.

3. Turnaround time for documents sent to our service is 24 hours. The service provides two pickup times, 1:00 P.M. for documents written that morning, and 5:00 P.M. for documents produced that afternoon. Documents picked up the previous day at 1:00 P.M. are delivered the next business day at 1:00 P.M., and those picked up at 5:00 P.M. the previous day are delivered the next business day at 5:00 P.M. A rental machine would offer turnaround time ranging from immediate delivery to one day, depending on the backlog of work. In a pinch, the copy clerk could make copies immediately, thereby pushing back the completion of other work.

I recommend that we stay with our present service for copying crucial, long documents. The outside service is much less expensive and its product quality is excellent. When important documents need immediate copying, we can send someone from our office to the printing center for their "while-you-wait" premium service. This system would insure duplicating only those documents urgent enough to warrant releasing personnel from routine duties.

Please let me know whether you have any questions about these findings and recommendations.

Martinez's direct observation of the duplicating system allowed her to gather evidence for a convincing memo. Once she had obtained the necessary data, she was able to apply the problem-solving steps detailed in part 1 to her primary task, producing a memo for her superior.

Questionnaires

Martinez was able to carry out research necessary to solving a writing problem by systematic and direct observation. Sometimes we must go beyond our own observations because our understanding may be biased or the writing problem involves a topic that covers a wider geographical area than we can personally observe. Sometimes we want to know what a number of other people think about a subject.

One way to poll these people is through a questionnaire, a list of queries asking for opinions or information on a particular topic. In business writing, three types of questionnaires can be especially helpful in obtaining the viewpoints or data needed to prepare a document: forced-choice questionnaires, ranked-order questionnaires, and scaled questionnaires.

Let's see how EZ-Life's trade show coordinator, John Carr, might employ each of these questionnaires. Carr's task is to prepare a one-page flier for distribution at an upcoming trade show. The flier will highlight features of EZ-Life's autumn sportswear line. Buyers for retail stores should be able to pick up the flier and see at a glance features that will entice them to stay for EZ-Life's fashion show at the trade show or to visit the company's showroom.

Carr knows what the fall season line contains. He also knows that the company's sales force has a much better sense of which of the line's features will appeal to buyers. Carr decides to garner the salespersons' opinions of what to include in the flier by sending them a questionnaire. Before making his final decision, Carr drafts three questionnaires, one of each kind noted previously.

Forced-choice questionnaires require respondents to make a decision between or among options. This decision may simply take the form of yes or no answers to questions, as in figure 8.3. From this forced-choice instrument, Carr can gain a sense of the sales force's views on what will appeal to the buyers.

Forced-Choice
Questionnaires

Here is a list of 10 key features of the autumn line of sportswear we will be displaying at the Trade Show. Please circle whether you think buyers will consider each feature <u>important</u> or <u>unimportant</u> in making their decisions to consider our offerings, see our fashion show, and/or visit our factory showroom. We will use your answers to help prepare the flier to be distributed at our display booth.

Feature

Tailored style	Important	Unimportant
Puffed sleeves	Important	Unimportant
Plaids	Important	Unimportant
Pleated skirts	Important	Unimportant
Earth tones	Important	Unimportant
No-iron fabrics	Important	Unimportant
Solid colors	Important	Unimportant
Coordinated skirts/blouses	Important	Unimportant
Stripes	Important	Unimportant
All sizes available	Important	Unimportant

Figure 8.3 Sample forced-choice questionnaire. Importance of sportswear features to retail buyers.

Ranked-Order
Questionnaires

Ranked-order questionnaires ask respondents to place a set of items into some order, for example, from best to worst or from most to least important. Figure 8.4 shows the ranked-order questionnaire Carr drafts for the trade show flier. Through the ranked-order questionnaire, Carr learns which features the sales force thinks are most important to buyers. But the questionnaire doesn't specify that the highest ranked items are necessarily important or that the lowest ranked are necessarily unimportant.

Here is a list of 10 key features of the autumn line of sportswear we will be displaying at the Trade Show. Please rank them in order of what you think their importance will be to buyers in making their decisions to consider our offerings, see our fashion show, and/or visit our factory showroom. Specify your rankings from 1 (most important) to 10 (least important) on the line provided next to each feature. We will use your answers to help prepare the flier we will distribute at our display booth.

Feature

_____Tailored style   _____No-iron fabrics
_____Puffed sleeves   _____Solid colors
_____Plaids   _____Coordinated skirts/blouses
_____Pleated skirts   _____Stripes
_____Earth tones   _____All sizes available

Figure 8.4 Sample ranked-order questionnaire. Importance of sportswear features to retail buyers.

Scaled
Questionnaires

Scaled questionnaires offer respondents the chance to express opinions in degrees about a topic, for example, *how much* they agree with a statement, *how important* something is, *how good or bad* an idea may be. Figure 8.5 shows Carr's draft of a scaled questionnaire. From this questionnaire, Carr will be able to get a fine tuning on the degree of importance the sales force attaches to each of the autumn line's features.

Carr selects the scaled questionnaire, mails it to the company's 40 salespersons, receives answers, and by averaging the responses to each question, determines that the salespeople feel this way about the features: the earth tone colors, no-iron fabrics, coordinated skirts and blouses, and tailored styling are very important; the wide range of sizes and plaids/solids/stripes available are somewhat important; and the availability of puffed sleeve blouses and pleated skirts are relatively unimportant to buyers.

With this information in hand, Carr drafts a document based on the following problem definition:

▪ *Objective* To prepare a flier highlighting sportswear features of importance to retail buyers

- *Audience* Buyers from large retail chains and large individual stores all over North America
- *Writer's desired image* Enthusiastic and direct

Here is a list of 10 key features of the autumn line of sportswear we will be displaying at the Trade Show. By circling the appropriate response, please specify how important you think each feature will be to buyers in making their decisions to consider our offerings, see our fashion show, and/or visit our factory showroom. We will use your answers to help prepare the flier we will distribute at our display booth.

Figure 8.5
Sample scaled questionnaire. Importance of sportswear features to retail buyers.

Feature

Tailored style

| very important | somewhat important | no opinion | somewhat unimportant | very unimportant |

Puffed sleeves

| very important | somewhat important | no opinion | somewhat unimportant | very unimportant |

Plaids

| very important | somewhat important | no opinion | somewhat unimportant | very unimportant |

Pleated skirts

| very important | somewhat important | no opinion | somewhat unimportant | very unimportant |

Earth tones

| very important | somewhat important | no opinion | somewhat unimportant | very unimportant |

No-iron fabrics

| very important | somewhat important | no opinion | somewhat unimportant | very unimportant |

Solid colors

| very important | somewhat important | no opinion | somewhat unimportant | very unimportant |

Coordinated skirts/blouses

| very important | somewhat important | no opinion | somewhat unimportant | very unimportant |

Figure 8.5
Continued

Stripes

| very important | somewhat important | no opinion | somewhat unimportant | very unimportant |

All sizes available

| very important | somewhat important | no opinion | somewhat unimportant | very unimportant |

Draft

<u>Fall Line Features</u>

We are proud to present our autumn line of women's sportswear. Our blouses, skirts, shirts, scarves, socks, and other fine apparel have all the features needed for high retail sales this autumn:

--THE MOST POPULAR EARTH TONES

--NO-IRON FABRICS

--A FULL LINE OF COORDINATED SKIRTS AND BLOUSES

--THE TAILORED LOOK THAT WILL BE "IN" THIS FALL

All of our items are available in a wide range of plaids, stripes, and solids. We are ready to manufacture and ship any order in a full range of sizes from junior petite to misses for July delivery.

WANT TO KNOW MORE? STOP BY THE CONVENTION CENTER'S KNICKERBOCKER ROOM ANY DAY OF THE TRADE SHOW FOR OUR DAILY 3:00 P.M. SHOWINGS. OR VISIT US AT OUR FACTORY SHOWROOM AT 688 SEVENTH AVENUE (12TH FLOOR).

Note that Carr's questionnaire supplied the information he needed to draft his flier. By obtaining the views of those who know his audience of buyers best, Carr was able to highlight those features buyers would think important, include but downplay those features buyers might think less vital, and omit those they would consider unimportant.

1. Before designing questions, make certain you know the objective of your questionnaire and decide how you will score it.
2. If possible, pilot test your questionnaire by trying it out on a small group of respondents who are similar to those you will be querying. This will give you a chance to correct problems in the questionnaire before you actually administer it.
3. Leave space on the questionnaire for respondents' comments. Respondents may be able to give you some useful information that none of your questions address. Or respondents may make suggestions for improving the questionnaire itself.
4. Make certain that directions for completing the questionnaire are clear.
5. Keep the questionnaire as short as possible for gathering the necessary information.

In addition to the preceding suggestions, if you must mail questionnaires (as opposed to administering them to people who are physically present), you will increase the number of responses and increase their quality by:

- Providing a brief cover letter that explains how the information will be used and that thanks respondents for their time and expertise
- Specifying a deadline for return of the questionnaires
- Including with the questionnaire a self-addressed, stamped envelope
- Sending polite follow-up letters to those who have not returned responses by the deadline date

The higher the rate of return on a questionnaire, the more valid will be your picture of the views of those queried and the more likely you will be to get the information you need to write your document. Perhaps the most important way to predict whether a questionnaire will be returned is to ascertain how important it is for the respondent to complete and mail it. Because Carr's salespeople depend on appealing to the trade show buyers, he knows he will collect enough information to prepare an effective flier.

Interviews

Carr finds the questionnaire a useful way to acquire specific information from a large number of people. Antoinette Small of EZ-Life's accounting department has a somewhat different task. She wants to obtain some detailed information as quickly as possible from three people. Small is in charge of EZ-Life's accounts receivable. She wants to get expert information on the sequence of letters to send retailers who have overdue accounts with EZ-Life.

Provided with the names of three debt-collection consultants by the director of accounting, Small decides to **interview** each of these experts. In chapter 7, we suggested techniques for responding to an interview in which you are being considered for a job. Although such an interview does give you a chance to learn something about the company considering you for employment, it is primarily a chance for an employer to find out about *your* qualifications and attitudes. Small's interview is different in the sense that its aim is to get from the interviewee information that will help complete a document.

The interview will enable Small to ask questions directly of each consultant. In today's business world, an interview may well take place over the telephone or by electronic mail instead of face to face, yet it still provides immediate responses to the interviewer's questions. The interviewer can thus follow up on the basic questions to obtain clarification or elaboration of responses. Even with this possibility for ad lib queries, carefully prepared questions are crucial to the success of an interview. In preparation for her interviews, Small develops the following questions:

1. How long should we wait before sending a letter with our overdue notice to a delinquent account?
2. What should the tone of this first letter be?
3. At what intervals should we send subsequent letters?
4. What should their tone be?
5. At what point should we threaten specific action by EZ-Life?

She will telephone each of the consultants. A phone call is certainly a more efficient and economical way to ask a short series of questions than a face-to-face visit. Let's listen in on part of Small's conversation with one of the consultants, Charles Anderson:

SECRETARY: Anderson Accounting Consultants, Good morning.

S(MALL):   This is Antoinette Small. May I speak with Mr. Anderson?

SECRETARY: Yes, of course. He's expecting your call.

A(NDERSON):   Hello, Ms. Small. I'm pleased to hear from you. Your accounting director said you'd be in touch about your policy for sequencing your overdue letters.

S: That's right. I've got a few questions. Why don't we start with those? May I tape our conversation? If that's O.K., you'll hear that beep required by the phone company every 15 seconds.

A: That's fine.

S: We were wondering how long to wait before sending out our first letter on an overdue account. Our present policy is to send it out 30 days after the final payment date.

A: By present standards that's a bit long to wait. Since in your industry you know your buyers pretty well, you'll be the best judge of how individual accounts will react. Still, when you consider that those overdue payments restrict your cash flow and cost you interest that your company could be earning, 15 days would seem quite a reasonable period to wait.

S: Our current first-notice letter is rather straightforward. We simply say, "Your account is now overdue. Please remit the balance of blank dollars promptly." Do you think this is an appropriate tone for a first overdue notice?

A: No. As important as it is to collect your accounts due in a timely manner, it is even more important that you not offend those accounts if you can avoid it. One effective approach to collecting accounts from small creditors such as the local clothing shops that make up a large part of your business is to enclose a copy of the statement with a personal note to your contact in the buyer's accounts payable department. If you can get that person's name, it often works well to send a note with a friendly tone—something like, "Dear Ann—Our records show that we haven't yet received payment for the shipment you accepted on May 19. If you haven't already sent payment, we are enclosing a duplicate invoice for your convenience. Thank you very much for your attention to this inquiry. We appreciate your continued business. Yours truly, et cetera." The key is to treat your small account as if it were a consumer account. Try to make your contact person feel a sense of responsibility for payment while at the same time reminding her that you value their patronage and cordial business relations.

S: You said that this works for small retailers. What about our large chain store accounts?

A: Now, that's a different matter. Many of them would be offended by such familiarity. Here we recommend the more traditionally businesslike tone you already use. . . .

We'll leave the interview at this point. Notice that Small asked her first two prepared questions and then asked an ad lib question about the tone of a letter to a larger retail chain. The interview allowed her immediate feedback to her questions and the chance to probe that feedback for the specific information she was seeking. After speaking with each of the consultants and recording those conversations with the interviewees' permissions, she arrived at a consensus of the consultants' opinions by listening to the tapes. Alternatively, she might have taken notes during the conversation. Having the tape recorder going, however, allowed Small to concentrate on the substance of the interview and provided her with an exact record of what was said and in what context.

From the interviews, Small finds that the three consultants essentially agree on the following points:

1. Overdue notice letters should be sent every 15 days, starting 15 days after the final payment date.
2. The tone of the letters should not be threatening until the final notice before the account is turned over to a collection agency or to the company's attorneys.
3. The tone of the letters should progress from neutral or even cordial in the first letter to urgent in the last letter.

With her interviews and their analysis completed, Small can draft her memo using this problem definition:

- *Objective*   To prepare a memo from information gathered through telephone interviews on the subject of overdue notice letters
- *Audience*   Director of Accounting
- *Writer's desired image*   Logical, respectful

Draft

Date: May 22, 1986

To: Ed Finch, Director of Accounting

From: Antoinette Small

Subject: Recommendations on Sequencing Past Due Letters

I have completed interviews with each of the consultants you asked me to contact. Based on my analysis of their responses to questions about sequencing of past due letters, here are my recommendations:

1. Our first letter should go out to overdue accounts 15 business days after the last payment date specified on the invoice.

2. For our large accounts, the first letter should be a neutral statement reminding them that payment is due and enclosing a copy of the original invoice.

3. For our smaller accounts, the first letter should be a cordial note asking them to remit payment if they have not already done so.

4. If the first letter does not bring payment, the second letter should go out 15 business days after the first letter.

5. For all accounts, the tone of the second letter should be polite but firm: "According to our records, your account is now 30 days overdue. Please remit payment."

6. If the second letter does not bring payment, the third letter should go out 15 business days after the second letter.

7. For all accounts, the tone of the third letter should be firm: "Your account is now 45 days overdue. Remit payment immediately."

8. If the third letter does not bring payment, the fourth letter should go out 15 business days after the third letter.

9. For all accounts, the tone of the fourth letter should be formal. The fourth letter should specify action to be taken (turning account over to a collection agency for small accounts, turning it over to an attorney for a larger account) if the account is not settled within 15 days--for example, "Your account is now 60 days past due. If payment is not received within 15 days, we will be forced to turn your account over to our collection agency." Note that we begin using a passive construction to create a sense of increased distance between us and the delinquent account.

10. If the fourth letter does not bring payment, the specified action should be taken after 15 business days. At the same time, a fifth letter should go out. This letter should inform the delinquent customer or client that action has been taken.

11. The tone of the fifth letter should be matter-of-fact--for example, "Your account is now 75 days past due. The matter has been turned over to our collection agency."

As you can see, the consensus of the consultants is that we should speed up our overdue notice process and sequence our letters so they progress from cordial or neutral to urgent. In addition, I have incorporated Charles Anderson's specific recommendation that we differentiate our first overdue notices for large and small accounts.

I am now ready to prepare drafts of all necessary form letters to be used as overdue reminders in a revised collection letter series. Please let me know if there is any additional information I might provide as you consider these recommendations.

Direct observation, questionnaires, and interviews require that the business writer view a situation or ask others to view a situation as it is. Martinez observed EZ-Life's current photocopying procedures. Carr asked for salespersons' views on the preferences of buyers as they understood them. Small queried her consultants on the merit of EZ-Life's overdue notice policy.

Experiment

At times you want to know what will happen if you change an element of a situation, and you may need the results of such an **experiment** to complete a business writing task. Such experiments are similar to those in science, in which you begin with a hypothesis or informed guess about the effect of a change in a situation. You then take steps to prove or disprove your guess. For gaining information about how to solve business writing problems, these experiments usually take one of two forms:

- Simply making a change and seeing how it works out—for example, using red ink to highlight important ideas in interoffice memos for a period of time, then asking for coworkers' reactions to the procedure, and finally deciding whether to continue using the two-color scheme or go back to typing all memos in black ink only.

- Making change(s) in one portion of an operation while retaining current procedure in another portion. For example, you might have half a small company's executives try phoning in their dictation to a central word processing center while the other half continues to dictate via cassettes for transcription by a secretary in their own department. Then you compare results for cost, turnaround time, and accuracy.

Our example of an EZ-Life employee's experiment is of the second kind—simultaneous comparison of new and old procedures. In the company's New York headquarters, Vanessa Parker edits the in-house newsletter for EZ-Life. This weekly publication reports on company news, presents simplified production and sales data, and carries a message from a different department head each week to inform employees about what goes on in other departments. Parker's office has routinely finished editing the newsletter on Thursday mornings and then sent the copy to the company's word processing center. After receiving the document, Parker's office has proofread, corrected, made stencils from the originals, collated, and placed newsletters into addressed envelopes for personnel in both the domestic and international sales offices. When the newsletters arrive at their destinations, a mailroom worker distributes them.

At 9:00 A.M. on Friday, Parker's office sends the newsletters to the mailroom, which processes them for an 11:00 A.M. mail pickup. The newsletters are sent airmail to Los Angeles, Houston, Chicago, Tokyo, and Paris. Personnel in the New York office receive their copies through interoffice mail.

EZ-Life's director of information services, Sylvia Martinez, worries that by the time the sales offices receive the newsletter, its information is no longer fresh. As Parker's superior, Martinez has asked her to study alternative ways of getting the newsletter to the sales offices and to prepare a memo reporting findings and recommendations for its distribution.

Parker decides to experiment with three ways of delivering the newsletter to domestic and international sales offices. For four weeks, she will send three copies of each newsletter to each sales office employee, one by each method: (1) all newsletters for each office packed into a single envelope and sent airmail (the present system); (2) all newsletters for each office packed into a single envelope and sent by overnight express service (an experimental system); (3) one copy of each issue of the newsletter sent electronically over telephone lines using a facsimile reproduction system (*fax*) that allows a secretary in each office to take an exact copy of the newsletter and duplicate enough copies for employees in that office (an experimental system).

During the four weeks, Parker will keep careful records of the speed and cost of each delivery system. This procedure is an experiment because Parker changes the current procedures and then observes the effects of this change. Figure 8.6 shows Parker's chart of results after the four-week period. She specifies mailing methods down the left column. The middle and right columns show the average delivery time, the slowest delivery time during the four weeks, and the cost per newsletter of each type of delivery to the United States and overseas offices. From her experiment with several methods of mailing the newsletters, Parker is able to draft her memo using the following problem definition:

- *Objective*   To draft a memo incorporating information gathered from an experiment on ways of mailing newsletters to branch offices
- *Audience*   Sylvia Martinez, Director of Information Services
- *Writer's desired image*   Factual, logical, respectful of reader's right to make decisions based on data presented in the memo

---

Draft

Date: July 14, 1986

To: Sylvia Martinez, Director of Information Services

From: Vanessa Parker, Newsletter Editor

Subject: Newsletter Delivery--Domestic and International Sales Offices

I have finished comparing delivery time and costs for three ways of mailing our newsletter to our sales offices. The attached chart [Authors' Note: This is the same as figure 8.6] shows results of this four-week experiment.

Based on those results, I recommend that we use an electronic mail fax system for our United States offices. The cost for reaching all of our 44 personnel in our U.S. branch offices by fax is only $1.32 a week more than by airmail.

The difference in costs between airmail and fax to our Tokyo and Paris offices is much greater than for our domestic branches. It would cost $20.10 a week more to switch to fax. I leave it to your judgment as to whether the benefits of the overseas offices receiving the newsletter immediately outweigh the fact that it would cost $1045.20 a year more to implement.

Thank you for your support during this experiment. I hope the results prove useful in making your decisions about newsletter distribution.

Figure 8.6
Experimental
results

Three Systems for Mailing a Newsletter

DELIVERY SYSTEM

	U.S. Delivery			International Delivery		
	Average	Slowest	Cost/ Newsletter	Average	Slowest	Cost/ Newsletter
Airmail	2 days	5 days	$0.27	6 days	9 days	$0.60
Overnight express	1 day	1 day	$1.18	3 days	4 days	$7.80
Electronic mail (fax)	Immediate		$0.30	Immediate		$2.61

Note: Cost per newsletter figures were computed by dividing the total cost of delivery for each system to all domestic or international offices by the number of personnel (44 U.S.A., 10 international) who receive a newsletter. Fax newsletters were sent during prime business hours in receiving countries at prime overseas telephone rates. Overnight express rates were based on two-pound envelopes sent to each of our domestic offices and one-pound envelopes sent to each of our international offices.

By trying out several newsletter distribution procedures, Parker was able to determine how three different mailing procedures would work. She based her recommendations on the reasonable belief that the changes she observed over the four weeks would remain constant in the future.

Experimentation can be a valuable way to test new ideas to gain information for preparing a document. But one should be cautious about using experiments to solve business problems:

1. Since by definition an experiment requires changing procedures, *be certain you have a superior's approval before starting any such study.*

2. Because any recommendations growing from an experiment assume that observed effects will be essentially the same if the same changes are made again, *be sure the change you make is a valid, "real-world" test.* In the newsletter distribution example, this test would mean keeping the number of pages of the newsletter the same for each of the mailing options. If Parker had added extra pages to the newsletters shipped airmail, their weight might have increased the mailing cost. This higher cost would have biased the experiment because (a) the newsletter is always the same number of pages long for each recipient, and (b) the methods with which she contrasted airmail would have had the unfair advantage of lesser weight.

3. Even though you may attain a pleasing result from an experiment, *be cautious about applying your conclusions too broadly.* For example, Parker and Martinez may be happy to know that electronic mail service will cut domestic newsletter distribution time, but if they tried using electronic mail for *all* domestic correspondence, the result would be too costly for correspondents without access to terminals.

Secondary Sources

You conduct or commission research involving direct observation, questionnaires, interviews, and experiments. Because these methods create original data, we call them **primary sources** of information. **Secondary sources** are those that you can tap to find information that others have discovered.

Not too long ago, this section would have been simply titled "Library Resources," for that is where most such information would have been found. With the development of computerized data bases, however, you may be able to obtain much of this data without leaving your desk if you have access to a computer or terminal. We do not intend to downgrade the importance of libraries and librarians in the least. No one is better prepared to assist you in finding the material you require than a reference librarian. Indeed, the modern reference librarian is well qualified both to use and advise you on using computer-based data banks.

Because there are thousands of secondary sources of information, this review of sources is limited to presenting six categories particularly useful to business writers: indexes, compendia, trade publications, government publications, academic sources, and computerized searches. For each of these categories, two kinds of examples are offered: first, a few sources used frequently in business, and second, other sources of particular interest that will illustrate how EZ-Life employees use secondary sources for writing.

Don't be puzzled if you see overlapping among the categories we present. For instance, you can find references to certain trade publications in some indexes. And computerized searches can yield bibliographies that cite references from every other category. This overlapping is necessary to insure that by using the suggested categories, you will achieve efficient coverage of available sources. True, you *might* find the same statistics cited in a trade publication that you find in a government document. But, then again, you might not. If you must have those statistics to write an effective document, then you would much rather take the chance of seeing them twice than not at all. Whether your search for secondary sources begins with a visit to a corporate, public, university, or other library or starts when you turn on your computer, certain sources should help you get the information you need.

Indexes

Each of the following six sources cites recent articles in a wide range of business publications:

- *Business Periodicals Index* provides a comprehensive reference to articles in all areas of business.

- *Predicasts F & S Index United States* cites articles on business operations in the United States; it contains a special section referencing articles on specific companies arranged alphabetically by the firm's name.

- *Predicasts F & S Index International* cites articles on business operations outside the United States.

- *Management Contents* lists documents on a variety of business topics, with special emphasis on management.

- *Business Index* offers a mechanized, microform general business index, which allows fast searching for recent citations.

- *Business Education Index* cites business education articles, research studies, and textbooks on a wide range of business topics.

To see how you might use one of these indexes, you can follow EZ-Life's sales director, Mike Schiller, as he prepares a form letter. Schiller's letter will go to buyers from higher-priced, "upscale" stores that have purchased sportswear from EZ-Life in the past.

Schiller wants to announce EZ-Life's move into high-quality activewear, particularly leotards, sweatshirts, leg warmers, and exercise shorts. It will be no secret to the buyers that activewear has become increasingly profitable in the sportswear business. Schiller, though, wishes to emphasize that exercise clothes in particular have increased in popularity.

To find evidence to support this claim, he turns to the *Business Periodicals Index*. Looking up *Sportswear* in the most recent edition of the index, Schiller finds listings situated alphabetically between *Sports promoters* and *Sportswriters*. Figure 8.7 displays what he sees. After looking through the sportswear listings, Schiller records the *Advertising Age* citation as promising. He also checks the cross-reference to *Department stores—Sportswear departments* to see whether that section contains any other useful references. It does not. If Schiller wishes additional, older citations, he can check back issues of the index. He decides to read the *Advertising Age* article first to see whether it suffices. It does.

Schiller uses this problem definition to draft the form letter:

- *Objective*   To prepare a letter announcing the availability of a new line of women's apparel
- *Audience*   Buyers for stores offering higher-priced sportswear
- *Writer's desired image*   Enthusiastic, informed, but with a hint of snobbishness

---

SPORTS PROMOTERS

Behind the scenes of a major sports promotion [Hagler-Duran championship fight] Ed Publ Fourth Estate 116:14–15 D 24 '83

SPORTSWEAR

See Also
Bathing Suits
Department stores—Sportswear departments
Activewear finds comfortable niche [survey] graph il Chain Store Age Gen Merch Ed 59:32 + D '83
Designer bodywear falling flat? il Chain Store Age Gen Merch Ed 59:56 + N '83
Hot workout phenomenon explodes on fashion front il Advert Age 54:3 + N 21 '83
It's a surfing Safari in active looks. Chain Store Age Gen Merch Ed 59 sec2:21 0 '83

SPORTSWRITERS

Blacks in sportswriting. D. Hunt. Ed Publ Fourth Estate 116:44 S 3 '83

Figure 8.7   Entries from the *Business Periodicals Index*. References to sportswear to support a form letter to buyers. (Source: *Business Periodicals Index* copyright © 1984 by The H. W. Wilson Company. Material reproduced by permission of the publisher.)

Note that the form letter salutation and inside address contain generic labels. EZ-Life's word processing department will replace those labels with specific buyers' names and addresses.

Draft

May 15, 1986

Mr./Ms. Buyer
Store Name
Street Address
City, State Zip

Dear [First Name]:

   As frequent retailers of EZ-Life's various sportswear lines, we wanted to give you advance notice of our newest offerings for your fashion-conscious customers. In response to growing consumer interest in becoming fit and looking stylish while doing so, EZ-Life is proud to announce its line of upscale exercisewear.

   The new line will include leotards, leg warmers, exercise shorts, and matching tops. These will come in all the popular colors and sizes (as well as special petite sizes).

   As you know, consumer interest in all activewear, but particularly in exercisewear, has skyrocketed in recent years. More importantly, it has remained at this high level for long enough that we can characterize it as a true change in preference rather than a fad.

   If you saw the recent Advertising Age article about exercisewear's "explosive" impact on the fashion industry, you know the sales potential for this merchandise. Our sales staff will be happy to arrange an appointment to show you our line, which we believe has just what it takes to tap that potential for your sophisticated customers. Of course, we also welcome your in-person visits to EZ-Life's showroom.

   Thank you again for your continued confidence in our sportswear. We think you will be as excited as we are about our new offerings.

Cordially,

Mike Schiller
Director of Sales

Looking at a recent index helped Schiller find the article that lent an air of authority to his form letter. For their timeliness and rapid access to citations, business indexes can prove similarly invaluable places to look first for information on a wide range of topics.

Whereas indexes give bibliographic references to documents containing information, compendia present the information itself. Each compendium discussed here presents concise information arranged according to varied criteria.

Compendia

Encyclopedias   Sources of specialized information can be extremely useful in providing background knowledge on a problem. *The Encyclopedia of Management*,[1] for example, offers descriptions of such terms as *executive traits, personnel testing,* and *security.* In addition, it furnishes a bibliography of printed sources for all entries.

Another helpful compendium is the *Encyclopedia of Associations.*[2] This multivolume reference gives names, acronyms, addresses, telephone numbers, names of chief officials, number of members, affiliations, name changes, publications, and additional information for business and other organizations. EZ-Life employees might use this guide to find data about the National Knitwear and Sportswear Association, the National Outerwear and Sportswear Association, the American Apparel Manufacturers Association, and the New York Skirt and Sportswear Association.

Dictionaries   These texts offer explanations of commonly used terms and important information in a particular field. For instance, *The Dictionary of Administration and Supervision*[3] explains such abbreviations as FAA (Foreman's Association of America). It also describes such business-related laws as the Ramspeck Act, a 1940 ruling putting many federal positions under Civil Service regulations. It even defines slang terms, such as *scuttlebutt,* meaning "rumor."

---

[1] Carl Heyel, ed., *The Encyclopedia of Management*, 3d ed. (New York: Van Nostrand Reinhold, 1982).

[2] Denise S. Akey, ed., *Encyclopedia of Associations*, 18th ed. in 5 vols. (Detroit: Gale Research, 1984).

[3] Ivan S. Banki, *The Dictionary of Administration and Supervision* (Los Angeles: Systems Research, 1971).

As its title suggests, *Words of Wall Street: 2000 Investment Terms Defined*[4] details terminology from the securities industry and provides examples and illustrations to support the definitions.

Handbooks   These are generally "how-to" guides that explain basic procedures for operating in a particular situation. For example, the *AMA Management Handbook*[5] reveals a wealth of techniques and responsibilities for managers. Another, the *Handbook of International Business*,[6] details topics in international business environment, trade, finance, law, marketing, and management. It also provides an appendix with additional sources of information on international business.

Directories   These volumes provide names, addresses, and other pertinent information about people, institutions, and businesses in a particular field. Typical is the *Directory of Business and Financial Services*,[7] which has such entries as the *Laser Report*, a service that gives information on advances and uses of laser technology. This directory also cites the *Penny Stock Reporter*, a service describing trends and offering tips on low-priced stocks. A more familiar service, *Standard and Poor's NY Stock Exchange Reports* is also listed, as is *Trends in the Hotel & Motel Business*.

A valuable directory for information about larger companies is Dunn & Bradstreet's *Million Dollar Directory Series*.[8] This is a four-volume document listing approximately 160,000 companies. Each listing includes such data about the company as its address, telephone number, line of business, subsidiaries, bank, legal counsel, state of incorporation, number of employees, annual sales, and top executives' titles.

---

[4]Allan H. Pessin and Joseph A. Ross, *Words of Wall Street: 2000 Investment Terms Defined* (Homewood, IL: Dow Jones-Irwin, 1983).

[5]William K. Fallon, ed., *AMA Management Handbook*, 2d ed. (New York: American Management Associations, 1983).

[6]Ingo Walter, ed., *Handbook of International Business* (New York: Wiley, 1982).

[7]Mary M. Grant and Norma Cote, eds., *Directory of Business and Financial Services*, 7th ed. (New York: Special Libraries Association, 1976).

[8]*Million Dollar Directory Series*, 4 vols. (Parsippany, NJ: Dunn & Bradstreet, 1985).

You can even consult a *Directory of Directories, 1983,*[9] which lists general business directories by state, country, and region. In addition, this volume specifies directories by industries and business lines. The supplementary title and subject indexes make this an easy-to-use, comprehensive reference.

Almanacs   These are compendia on particular topics stressing developments during a particular year. *The 1981 Dow Jones-Irwin Business and Investment Almanac,*[10] for instance, reviews business events for that year on a day-by-day basis. It also provides business and economic data for those 12 months in graphic and tabular forms. Other sections of this work include international trade information.

The *Almanac of Business and Industrial Financial Ratios*[11] can be extremely useful when you have to write a document comparing a particular company to an industry as a whole. An EZ-Life accountant might employ this almanac to compare the company's capital allocation, net worth, overhead, and use of sales revenues with industry standards based on data from 8,269 women's and children's clothing enterprises.

Yearbooks   These are similar to almanacs in that they focus on a particular year. In the case of the *1977–1979 Pick's Currency Yearbook,*[12] three years are covered. This volume provides information for that time on 112 international currencies—their circulation, exchange rates, black market statuses, and other pertinent data. It also gives gold prices in 37 international trade centers.

The International Monetary Fund publishes another useful yearbook, the *Government Finance Statistics Yearbook,*[13] which offers a broad range of data on international government finance. The 1983 book yields information on such diverse topics as Greece's export duties, Paraguay's excise taxes, and Zaire's social security funds.

---

[9]James M. Ethridge, *Directory of Directories, 1983* (Detroit: Gale Research, 1983).

[10]Sumner N. Levine, ed., *The 1981 Dow Jones-Irwin Business and Investment Almanac* (Homewood, IL: Dow Jones-Irwin, 1981).

[11]Leo Troy, ed., *Almanac of Business and Industrial Financial Ratios*, 1983 ed. (Englewood Cliffs, NJ: Prentice-Hall, 1983).

[12]Franz Pick, *1977–1979 Pick's Currency Yearbook* (New York: Pick Publishing, 1981).

[13]*Government Finance Statistics Yearbook* (Washington, DC: International Monetary Fund, 1983).

Atlases Many of us know atlases best as books of maps of various world regions or as collections of interstate highway maps. By presenting maps in a business context, atlases can also provide geographic, demographic, and economic information that is useful for business writing. The *Hammond Sales Planning Atlas*[14] displays maps and offers such explanatory information as populations, zip codes, Metropolitan Statistical Area data, highway mileage, and air distances. Another business atlas, the *United States Zip Code Atlas*,[15] shows county boundaries, lists all towns with a population over 1,000, and details state census data.

Literature Reviews These compendia can direct us to business-related, book-length publications. *The Wall Street Review of Books* reviews such publications on a quarterly basis. The summer 1982 issue, for example, reviewed Andre Gunder Frank's *Reflections on the World Economic Crisis*[16] and Robert L. Veninga and James P. Spradley's *The Work/Stress Connection: How to Cope with Job Burnout.*[17]

How can compendia help EZ-Life employees improve their writing? A collaborative writing team consisting of the director of marketing (Leah Chou), the director of accounting (Ed Finch), and the general manager (Herb Levy) is preparing a short report on industry trends as they affect the company. When they finish the report, Chou, Finch, and Levy will distribute it to supervisory personnel throughout EZ-Life.

The collaborators have now reached the point where they are editing the document and want to do two things: double-check their use of technical vocabulary and add specific data to sections of the report that seem a bit vague. To find this information, they split the task, and each one turns to an appropriate compendium: a dictionary, a collection of industry surveys, and a periodical collection of demographic statistics. Here is a section of the report requiring such secondary sources during the editing stage:

---

[14]*Hammond Sales Planning Atlas* (Maplewood, NJ: Hammond, 1983).

[15]*United States Zip Code Atlas* (Maspeth, NY: American Map Corporation, 1983).

[16]Andre Gunder Frank, *Reflections on the World Economic Crisis* (New York: Monthly Review Press, 1981); reviewed by Ashok Bhargava, *The Wall Street Review of Books* 10 (Summer 1982):224–28.

[17]Robert L. Veninga and James P. Spradley, *The Work/Stress Connection: How to Cope with Job Burnout* (Boston: Little, Brown, 1981); reviewed by Dennis D. Murphy, *The Wall Street Review of Books* 10 (Summer 1982): 244–48.

. . . the general growth of the apparel industry. With trends pointing
to particularly strong gains in the sportswear segment of the
industry, we want to reexamine our need for skilled sales personnel. One
location requiring special attention will be Houston. That metropolitan
area's rapid growth has been typical of other urban and suburban centers in
the Southwest. We know that competition for salespeople with apparel
industry experience is keen in the region. Because of this, we should start
looking into ways we can tap qualified workers with special needs and
preferences.

We might want to consider hiring former salespeople who cannot or do
not wish to work full-time. Perhaps we can consider some sort of "flextime"
arrangement in which two salespeople share full hours, client lists, and
commissions. These are clearly departures from our past policies, and
admittedly, there are problems we need to work out before trying such
innovations. . . .

In looking at this segment of the report, the writers saw the need to change
or check several things:

- To support the general statement about the growth of the sportswear
  business with some authoritative documentation, one of the team members looked at *Standard & Poor's Industry Surveys* for January 1984.
  There she found an entry on "Apparel Markets." A specific section of
  the entry dealt with sportswear, calling it "one of (the) leading growth
  areas in the apparel business."[18]

---

[18]"Apparel Markets," *Standard & Poor's Industry Surveys,* January 1984,
pp. T88–T92.

- To offer statistical evidence of the Houston area's population spurt, a second team member checked *Sales and Marketing Management* for its 1983 and 1973 "Survey of Buying Power" issues. From these, he found that while EZ-Life's other domestic locations (New York, Los Angeles, and Chicago) had remained first, second, or third in metropolitan area population rankings, between 1972 and 1982, Houston had jumped from thirteenth to eighth place.[19]

- To double-check that they were using the term *flextime* correctly, a third team member consulted the *Dictionary of Business and Management.* Under *flextime,* he found: "*flextime*: a system that allows employees to choose their own starting and finishing times within a broad range of available hours. Workers still have to work their regular number of hours."[20]

As you can see, *flextime* was *not* the term the collaborators wanted to use. By going back to the draft, a team member found some hints about where to look in the dictionary to discover the correct word. After trying *shared time, flexyear,* and *time sharing,* this collaborator found *job sharing* and its definition: "*job sharing:* a scheduling innovation that permits two or more employees to do the same job by working different hours, days, or even weeks. The total hours worked by job sharers are usually equivalent to the hours worked by one full-time worker."[21]

Having consulted these reference works, the collaborators could revise their report according to this problem definition:

- *Objective*   To prepare a short report on the influence of apparel industry trends upon a sportswear company

- *Audience*   All supervisory personnel in the company (generally subordinate to writing team members)

- *Writers' desired image*   Optimistic and informed

The next draft of the report contained this segment:

---

[19]"1973 Survey of Buying Power," *Sales Management,* 23 July 1973, p. B-10.
   "Survey Highlight: Top 25 Metropolitan Markets: Atlanta Up, Dallas Down," *Sales and Marketing Management,* 25 July 1983, p. A-14.

[20]Jerry M. Rosenberg, *Dictionary of Business and Management,* 2d ed. (New York: John Wiley, 1983), p. 207. Copyright © 1983 by John Wiley & Sons, Inc. Reprinted by permission of John Wiley & Sons, Inc.

[21]Rosenberg, *Dictionary of Business and Management,* p. 274. Copyright © 1983 by John Wiley & Sons, Inc. Reprinted by permission of John Wiley & Sons, Inc.

... the general growth of the apparel industry. With industry analyses such as <u>Standard & Poor's Industry Surveys</u> for January of 1984 pointing to sportswear as "one of (the) leading growth areas in the apparel business" (p.T89), we want to reexamine our need for skilled sales personnel.

One location requiring special attention is Houston. That metropolitan area's 10-year spurt from thirteenth place to eighth in population in <u>Sales & Marketing Management's</u> "Survey of Buying Power" is typical of other urban and suburban centers in the Southwest. We know that competition for salespeople with apparel industry experience is keen in the region. Because of this, we should start looking into ways we can tap qualified workers with special needs and preferences.

We might consider hiring former salespeople who cannot or do not wish to work full-time. Perhaps we can develop some sort of job-sharing arrangement in which two salespeople share full hours, client lists, and commissions. These are clearly departures from our past policies, and admittedly, there are problems we need to work out before trying such innovations. . . .

By looking into compendia, the writing team members were able to locate the data they needed. Because they tend to be published in book-length format, compendia have citations in library card catalogues. If you have difficulty locating a compendium of information to meet your needs, consult your reference librarian. In our EZ-Life case, we saw that using concise collections of related facts speeded up the collaborators' search for information. The variety of compendia allowed them to get just the facts they wanted, to add clarity to their writing, and to insure accuracy in their report.

Trade Publications

For current information on particular industries, trade publications are highly useful. There are thousands of such publications. Some are published daily (*Motion Picture Daily, The Oil Daily Publication, Consumer Electronics Daily, Broadcast Daily*), and others come out weekly (*Floor Covering Weekly,*

Publishers Weekly, Fur Age Weekly). Still others are published every other week (*Public Utilities Fortnightly*), monthly (*United States Banker, Minority Business Newsletter, Industrial Marketing*), bimonthly (*Canadian Journal of Public Health*), quarterly (*Electronic Perspective*), or at other intervals (*Bell Telephone Magazine* has five issues per year). Whatever their publication schedule, trade periodicals can provide a wealth of highly specialized information with which to understand a writing problem more clearly.

The apparel industry has a wide array of trade publications. Albert Corso of the EZ-Life marketing department makes use of several. The director of marketing has assigned Corso the task of writing her a memo highlighting marketing trends in sportswear. To get information on those trends, Corso will look first at some indexes, but he will also consult recent issues of the trade publications themselves in case the indexes do not cite some short articles containing highly specialized information.

From his search through the indexes and such apparel trade publications as *Apparel World, Knitting Times, Textile World, Apparel Merchandising, Women's Wear Daily,* and *Chain Store Age—General Merchandise Edition*, Corso discovers three articles that fit his needs exactly:

- "Junior Consumers Seek Satisfaction" from the May 1984 issue of *Apparel Merchandising.* The article's main point is that retailers are emphasizing style and quality in their advertising and are downplaying special promotions.

- "Monograms Give 'Animals' a Run for Their Money" from the November 1983 issue of *Chain Store Age—General Merchandise Edition.* The article's main point is that many retailers are offering monograms on more items of clothing than sweaters.

- "Stores' Europe Trip Ends in a Ready-to-Spend Mode" from the *Women's Wear Daily* issue of March 30, 1984. The article's main point is that retail store buyers are finding European sportswear more marketable than in the past.

Figure 8.8 shows how Corso takes the details supporting these main points and uses an inductive decision tree to analyze the task of writing the memo growing from the following problem definition:

- *Objective*   To prepare a memo highlighting industry marketing trends
- *Audience*   Director of marketing
- *Writer's desired image*   Logical, concise

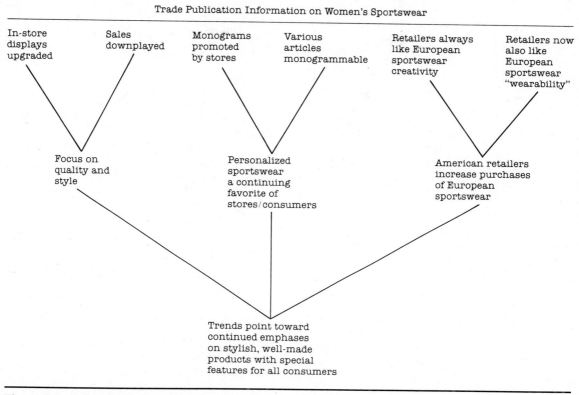

Trade Publication Information on Women's Sportswear

Figure 8.8   Inductive decision tree for marketing trend memo

Draft

Date: June 1, 1986

To: Leah Chou, Director of Marketing

From: Albert Corso, Marketing Department

Subject: Marketing Trend Highlights

My reading of industry marketing trends makes me think that sportswear marketing will continue to emphasize quality. If consumers are certain that the products they are buying are wearable and durable, they will then want to embellish them with special features. Let me illustrate with examples from three trade publications.

Apparel Merchandising reports that junior consumers are responding to marketing that emphasizes quality and style. Consequently, retailers are emphasizing in-store displays and fashion shows, while deemphasizing newspaper ad promotions. Image and look, not sales, are what motivate today's junior shopper.

Chain Store Age--General Merchandise Edition details the continued popularity of monogramming. Stores are running promotions not only on monogrammed sweaters but also on such unlikely garments as lingerie. The popularity of monogramming is symptomatic of consumer interest in special features such as embroidery, expensive cuff buttons, and decorative belt loops.

Women's Wear Daily tells how impressed American retailers have been with European sportswear recently. In addition to the usual creative flair that characterizes European fashion, U.S. buyers have begun to find continental sportswear commercially attractive. The article specifies that some American retailers will increase their European purchases from 15 to 30 percent this year.

What does all this mean for EZ-Life's marketing efforts? I think we face some clear challenges. On the one hand, we must continue to promote our traditional strength--our high-quality product. On the other hand, we must compete with Europe on their strong point--originality of style--just as they have competed on ours (durability and commercial appeal). We must continue to let retailers know that our clothes offer customers (particularly the juniors, who will be our target consumers for years to come) not only basic quality but also the special features giving sportswear a personal touch. In short, we must be many things to many types of customer, but always a leader in product quality to all our buyers.

Note that the trade publications gave Corso information of special interest to sportswear manufacturers. There is scarcely a business or industry for which a specialized trade periodical cannot do the same.

Government Documents

The United States government publishes books, pamphlets, catalogues, and other sorts of documents on almost every conceivable subject. For example, you can get a booklet on *Managing Consumer Complaints*. You can find a book on *Starting and Managing a Small Service Business*. You can obtain a "Checklist for Going into Business." The government publishes statistics on every industry and advice on labor negotiations. It offers a free handbook for women who wish to establish their own businesses. Whatever your area of business interest, there is a reasonable chance that the federal government has a pertinent document. That's the good news.

The bad news is that finding such information can be difficult. According to the federal pamphlet *Depository Libraries: Your Source for Government Information*, the government puts out more than 25,000 *new* publications a year. Although there is a *Monthly Catalog of Government Publications*, finding just what you need can be a time-consuming, frustrating effort. Here are some shortcuts:

1. Locate one of the more than 1,370 Federal Depository Libraries. These libraries receive selected government titles on a regular basis. In addition, 50 regional depository libraries across the country receive *every* unclassified federal publication. Your local or university librarian can help you find the nearest depository library; once you get there, the depository library's government documents specialist can assist you in locating the publications you want.

2. If one is in your area, contact one of the more than 20 U.S. government bookstores. These stores stock the most popular federal titles and can order any other one for you. Also, the *GPO Sales Reference File* lists every Government Printing Office title for sale. Consult your librarian for the location of this file.

3. Call the closest Federal Information Center. They are in more than 70 metropolitan centers. The center's staff members will answer your questions, direct you to someone who can, or specify a helpful government publication.

State governments also publish documents. From them you can obtain statistical and other reports. Many states have clearinghouses through which you may order materials or which you may visit to use publications. Consult your local reference librarian for details about your particular state.

You can see how government documents provide information for writing as you follow EZ-Life's marketing director, Leah Chou. She will need to consult government documents as she prepares a memo to her corporate peers—the director of accounting and the general manager. Chou has long thought that EZ-Life should expand its international operations beyond the small sales offices now operating in Paris and Tokyo.

She goes in search of evidence to support the feeling that she has gotten from her recent overseas trips that the time is now right for EZ-Life to act. Chou begins by calling a Federal Information Center. She asks whether someone can direct her to publications giving market information for the apparel industries of Japan and Australia. The center directs her to the local office of the Department of Commerce, which tells her about the *Country Market Survey—Apparel—Japan* (1980) and the *Country Market Survey—Apparel—Australia* (1980). These publications are part of a series of pamphlets providing statistics and recommendations for various businesses considering overseas expansion.

Now Chou calls a nearby depository library and asks if it has those titles. It does. By reading one of the surveys, Chou learns that Japan is a "prime prospect for exports of U.S. apparel" (p. 1). From the survey of Australia, she finds that whereas that nation offers possibilities for gaining a part of the clothing market, apparel makers there will have to compete with high-cost, high-style goods from Europe at one end of the price spectrum and with low- to medium-cost goods from the Far East at the other end (pp. 1, 17). Chou prepares her problem definition, and then drafts her memo:

- *Objective*   To prepare a memo suggesting that an apparel company plan expansion of sales in one country and start of sales in another
- *Audience*   Two managerial peers (director of accounting, general manager)
- *Writer's desired image*   Cordial, informed, somewhat informal

---

Draft

Date: November 11, 1986

To: Ed Finch, Herb Levy

From: Leah Chou

Subject: Overseas Market Expansion

Here's some information I've found that may be helpful if we decide to recommend expanding our international sales force. The Department of Commerce's Country Market Survey--Apparel--Japan views that country as a "prime prospect for exports of U.S. apparel" and presents plenty of data to support that claim. Coupled with our steady sales growth out of the Tokyo office, this federal survey could give us the leverage we need to make a convincing argument to our president and board of directors. At the least, I think we would want to propose the increased Japanese sales force about which we talked at Wednesday's meeting.

An additional possibility to keep in mind is the opening of a new sales office in Melbourne or Sydney. The Department of Commerce apparel market survey for Australia suggests possibilities for apparel exports to that country. The survey cautions about top-of-the-line competition from Europe and low-to-medium-price competition from the Far East. But we know all that already. Could EZ-Life sportswear fill a niche between Europe and Far Eastern exports? Just something to think about.

I'll bring copies of these Commerce pamphlets to our meeting on Monday. If you would like to see them before then, let me know.

Chou needed supporting information on a topic (international commerce) about which she thought the federal government might publish documents. She had a plan for locating such documents: calling a Federal Information Center to identify titles and then calling a depository library to locate the documents themselves. Finally, she found a way to integrate the information she discovered so that it underscored her memo's point of view and call for action.

Once in a while, you may need information contained in university graduate students' dissertations or university faculty members' conference papers. You would not begin an information search with such academic-based literature. But if you had a specialized need, you might find one of the following resources helpful:

Academic-Based
Literature

- *Dissertation Abstracts International* indexes dissertations on business topics in its monthly volumes, including specific sections for business administration, economics (general, agricultural, commerce-business, finance, history, theory), management, and marketing. The abstracts come in two volumes, A (The Humanities and Social Sciences) and B (The Sciences and Engineering). Volume A references the business disciplines. However, information for special business writing needs, particularly in technology, will often appear in volume B.

  All of the dissertations are indexed annually under *key words*, the terms that are most likely to connect searchers with useful information. Thus, if you are searching for data on *labor relations*, you might look that term up in the key word index and find dissertations with that term in their titles. You could then go directly to the abstracts for a brief synopsis of each dissertation.

- The *Directory of Published Proceedings*[22] can alert you to organizations that might have published information presented at such conferences as the American Marketing Association's 1980 Chicago convention, "Marketing in the 1980s: Changes and Challenges," or the Industrial Management Society's 1979 Arlington Heights (Illinois) meeting, "Teaming Up for Profits."

- Professional associations such as the American Management Associations (AMA) can offer another source of book-length works on a topic. Upon request, the AMA will send you a catalogue of their books on a wide range of management-related topics.

Margaret Greenbaum, president of EZ-Life, has just the sort of specialized task that sends her to academic literature. As a public service, she will be

---

[22]Directory of Published Proceedings, Series SSH, 13, no. 4 (October 1980): 20, 23.

making an oral presentation to a management class at a local community college. She will be speaking about what it was like for her to become a top-level executive at a time when very few women did so.

Because her talk will draw mostly upon her personal experience, Greenbaum wants to find some research material that either supports or contradicts her belief that today's executive women view themselves differently than those of an earlier generation. She wishes to use that data as part of a written introduction to the less formal part of her presentation.

Greenbaum sends an administrative assistant to a public library a few blocks from the EZ-Life office. With the help of the reference librarian there, the administrative assistant locates, photocopies, and gives to Greenbaum an abstract of Deana Ruth Katz's Ph.D. dissertation, "Changing Values of Women Towards Work: Will Tomorrow's Young Female Managers Differ from their Older Counterparts?" Katz surveyed women managers in the Philadelphia area as well as undergraduate business administration students. She compared her findings for each group and discovered, among other things, that the traditional work ethic and values intrinsically related to work (for example, job satisfaction) motivated the managers. The students, on the other hand, tended to value extrinsic rewards (for example, salary and prestige) more highly. Katz concluded that maturity and on-the-job experience might operate to change the women's views as they progressed in the business world.

Greenbaum worked with this problem definition:

- *Objective*   To prepare an oral presentation on the experiences of a woman who became an upper-echelon executive when such advancement was rare
- *Audience*   Community college management students
- *Presenter's desired image*   Informed, concerned

Using what she had learned from the abstract of Katz's dissertation, Greenbaum could begin her presentation in this way:

I am delighted to be here today. One question that I am often asked by future managers such as yourselves is, "Why did you persist in the face of the obstacles against advancement of women towards upper management positions?" At the beginning of my career, I must admit that the lures of high pay and prestige motivated me most of all. Nowadays, however, other things excite me about management: the satisfaction of expanding our markets, the pleasure of directing a team of skilled apparel industry professionals, and the excitement just before a new line of sportswear debuts.

From reading an abstract of a study by Deana Ruth Katz, I have learned

that my change in motivations makes me similar to many of my

management contemporaries. As I take a few minutes to trace my

experiences in the fashion industry, you might think about your own

motivations for entering management and how those motivations can lead

you in various ways during your careers. . . .

Greenbaum had a specialized need for research on a specific aspect of
business. In her case, academic-based literature gave her the sort of scholarly information she needed to solve a writing problem.

Numerous sources, including some discussed previously, are available
through computer searches. Most of these searches work similarly. The
searcher (often a reference librarian) consults a data bank in the requested
subject area and keyboards terms that may describe helpful documents.
The computer then scans its files for entries indexed by the selected terms.
For instance, an accountant who needs information on cash flow and debt
collection in the hardware business might ask the librarian to look for
information in the following ways:

Computer
Searches

Cash flow with debt collection with hardware business. This will find citations
about debt collection *and* cash flow in the hardware business.

Cash flow with hardware business. This will find citations about cash flow
in the hardware business.

Debt collection with hardware business. This will find citations about debt
collection in the hardware business.

Depending on the data bank used, the accountant might receive a computer printout listing articles and reports or other documents, abstracted
documents, or even complete documents.

A few data banks that librarians use to search for business documents
include:

- *Management Contents:* the same index referred to earlier in the chapter,
  but accessed by computer rather than by looking in bound volumes

- *Predicasts Terminal System:* again, a computerized version of hard copy
  indexes

- *ABI/INFORM:* a general business data bank

Individuals who have access to terminals hooked into these systems can, of course, use the data banks themselves. In addition, some data banks are specially designed for personal computer users at the office or in their homes. Dow Jones News/Retrieval service offers subscribers such sources as summaries of stories from *The Wall Street Journal,* current stock market quotations, coverage of business and political news from Japan, and corporate financial information. Another data bank, CompuServe, offers access to newspapers, stock market data, corporate information, Associated Press news stories, and many other sources. A valuable aid to writers who are considering using data banks is the *Omni Online Database Directory.*[23] This directory lists and describes over 1,000 data banks.

It is important to remember that many of these data banks are themselves businesses that charge fees for finding and printing information. Your company may already subscribe to a service or your library might have an arrangement by which it can obtain data for users free or at reduced cost. To find out about these possibilities, consult your reference librarian.

Devon Crews, a data processor for EZ-Life, does just that in her search for information about the role of computers in the apparel industry. When the general manager, Herb Levy, asks her to prepare a memo citing several examples of successful computer use in the apparel industry, Crews asks her librarian to search for articles under the descriptors *clothing industry and computers.* The librarian searches the ABI/INFORM data base and finds references and abstracts for three such articles:

- "Apparel Manufacturing: Improving Distribution to Retailers/Expediting Shipping and Billing/The Turning Point" from the May/June 1983 issue of *Viewpoint*
- "Control for Apparel Manufacturers" from the July/August 1981 issue of *Viewpoint*
- "DDP Collars Shirt Makers' Inventory Woes" from the March 13, 1978, issue of *Computerworld*

Figure 8.9 reproduces one of these three citations/abstracts as it appears on the printout.

With her abstracts handy, Crews drafts a memo based on the following problem definition:

- *Objective*   To prepare a short memo citing several instances of successful computer use by an apparel company
- *Audience*   General manager
- *Writer's desired image*   Straightforward, factual

---

[23]Mike Edelhart and Owen Davies, *Omni Online Database Directory* (New York: Macmillan, 1983).

```
83021173
Apparel Manufacturing: Improving Distribution to Retail-
ers/Expediting Shipping and Billing/The Turning Point
   Anonymous
   Viewpoint v11n3 PP: 7-13 May/Jun 1983 ISSN: 0091-5017 JRNL
   CODE: VIE
   DOC TYPE: Journal Paper     LANGUAGE: English LENGTH:  7
   Pages
   AVAILABILITY: IBM Corp., P.O. Box 2068, Atlanta, GA 30301
   Jonathan Logan Inc., a $400 million women's apparel cor-
poration, uses 2 IBM 4341 computers from International
Business Machines Corp. in its Secaucus, New Jersey, office
to handle financial applications. The new system has helped
the company speed up shipments and improve customer ser-
vice, especially in the fastest growing division, Etienne
Aigner. The system's major benefit is that it allowed for
growth without any cost increase in controlling that
growth. Servicing accounts has become much faster at Cupid
Foundations, an undergarment manufacturer, since the in-
stallation of an IBM System/34 at the firm's New York head-
quarters. Model 5251 display stations are also used. Two
order entry methods are used at the company--one for Sears
Roebuck and one for the other accounts. The company used a
card system prior to installing the System/34 in August
1981. At Talbott Knitting Mills (Reading, Pennsylvania),
the IBM System/38 was an important factor in turning around
the women's sportswear company's profitability. The company
runs its Apparel Business System (ABS) on the System/38,
allowing it to track orders daily and spot any trends. User
flexibility is one of the most important advantages of the
system according to Bert Shlensky, president of Talbott.
```

Figure 8.9 Sample abstract from a computer-based document search. Successful computer applications in the apparel industry. (Source: Reprinted by permission of Data Courier Inc., 620 South Fifth Street, Louisville, KY 40202.)

Draft

Date: July 11, 1986

To: Herb Levy, General Manager

From: Devon Crews, Data Processing

Subject: Computer Applications in Apparel Industry

My data search yielded three examples of apparel concerns that are improving operations through computer use. These are Jonathan Logan, Inc., which uses computers to speed shipment and improve customer service; Dolfin Corp., which gets help with its sales analyses, accounts receivable, and manufacturing control; and the Enro Shirt Co., which employs its computers for sales order entry, inventory updates, and shipping.

I have citations and abstracts for each of the articles from which this information came. I'll be happy to send them to you by interoffice mail if you'd like.

Suggestions for Using Research Tools

We close with suggestions for getting the most out of the research tools just discussed. Keep in mind that research is an aid to writing, not an end in itself. If you are not careful, you might find that you enjoy the research process so much and discover so much about a topic that you forget your problem definition. Your report will then wander from its objective or contain an unmanageable amount of information. To counteract this tendency, remember that readers want pertinent, not extraneous, information.

Perhaps you will encounter the opposite problem: not enough information. If you are having difficulty finding what you need from one research technique or from a particular secondary source, try another. Finally, don't be afraid to ask for help. We have intentionally repeated our urgings to consult reference librarians. Along with such professionals as government documents specialists and instructors of business writing, librarians can provide much assistance—if you ask them nicely.

Summary

Several research techniques can provide you with the necessary information to complete a document. Through direct observation, you can collect data systematically. From a questionnaire, you can gain facts and opinions from a group of people. Through interviews, you can probe individuals for information. During an experiment, you can alter one aspect of a situation to see what effect your change will have.

Sometimes you will need to find out what others have written on a topic. To obtain such information, consult secondary sources. Indexes will help you find articles in business publications. Compendia will give you concise information on various business topics. Trade publications will provide you with articles on particular industries. Federal and state government documents will present you with information on a wide range of topics. Academic-based literature will provide you with specialized, scholarly research data. Computer searches will offer you citations, abstracts, and documents on many business subjects.

Writing Problems

1. You work for the Sandel Toy Company as a market analyst. Sandel is considering manufacturing a new doll, and you have been asked to get firsthand information about children's preferences. You need answers to several questions: Do children prefer fabric or plastic dolls? Dolls with baby clothes or grown-up clothes? Period costumes or modern costumes? Dolls that do things (walk, talk, close their eyes) or dolls that don't move in any way? You may prepare and administer a questionnaire to a few children or set up an interview with several youngsters to get some data. Be certain to make your questions understandable to children. In addition to administering a questionnaire or conducting interviews, you may read secondary references found through an index and/or in trade publications. From these secondary sources, find out toy industry trends. Use what you find out to prepare an inductive decision tree as described in chapter 2. Use the decision tree to develop a draft of a memo advocating a new doll. Your audience for the proposal is Sandel's vice-president for marketing.

2. You work in the accounting department of a municipal bus line in a large city. A member of the bus line's public relations department has just sent you a prepared statement that she will read at a public hearing on raising fares. In essence, the statement says that fares should be raised from $.50 to $.75 to meet rising costs. Your department is concerned that this fare increase will result in decreased

revenues because so many riders will start using private cars rather than pay the new fare. Investigate what occurs when a transit system raises fares. Then prepare a revised statement advocating one of the following positions: increasing fares by $.25; increasing fares, but only by $.10; not increasing fares. Because you are in the accounting department, you are in a position to know whether the bus line can survive with the smaller fare boost or with no fare increase at all. Remember that the audience for your revised statement is a public that may not be very happy with your company no matter what it does.

3. A local bakery has hired you as a consultant. The bakery is considering producing two types of brownies, one very chewy, one more cakelike. You are to conduct an experiment in which you ask about 10 people to taste-test each type of brownie and state a preference for one or the other. Buy or bake the two types of brownies, then conduct the preference test. As you record the testers' preferences, take interpretive notes (as described in chapter 2) on their reactions. From your notes and your experimental results, write a letter stating your findings to the bakery's owner.

4. As the marketing director for a local car rental agency with two offices (one downtown, one at the airport), you have been asked to prepare a memo to the company's president. Your memo should report on what types of locations car rental companies favor. Record your findings on a deck of note cards (as described in chapter 2) and use the cards to prepare your memo.

5. You are the general manager of a local restaurant chain. Your company runs five medium- to high-priced restaurants, each with a distinctive cuisine and atmosphere: a seafood restaurant; a steakhouse; a French restaurant; an Italian restaurant; a dinner theater. Your task is to find three area businesses listed in the *Million Dollar Directory Series*. Then prepare a writing problem definition for a letter you will draft to the president of each company. You wish to advise her or him of the advantage to her or his company of opening up a charge account with your chain. Some of those advantages are direct billing, itemized invoices, varied cuisine and atmosphere for entertaining clients, assurance of personalized reception by the maître d'hôtel, and special discounts for corporate customers. Be sure your problem definition includes a statement of objective, audience, and writer's desired image.

6. As an accountant for Q & K Condominium Corporation, you have been asked to prepare a memo to the vice-president of finance. In it, you comment on your company's practice of counting as current income mortgage notes your firm holds on condominiums it has helped to finance for buyers. The mortgages are to be paid over 30

years, so the actual revenue will be realized only over a period of time. Find out how other companies would treat such long-term notes for accounting purposes. Use that information to revise the draft of your memo, which now reads:

Date: [Month, day, year]

To: Vice-President, Finance

From: [Your name], Accounting Department

Subject: Should We Treat Long-term Notes as Current Income?

Based upon my knowledge of appropriate accounting practice, we should treat only monies actually received as current income.

---

7. As a marketing director of an agency that contracts with companies to supply temporary office help, you are preparing a form letter to personnel directors in particular industries. To find industries that are growing so that you can target your letter to likely customers, consult appropriate secondary sources. Once you have a list of five such industries, prepare a writing problem definition in which you specify the writing objective, audience, and desired image. Then write the form letter to personnel directors in one of the targeted industries.

8. In this exercise, you will need to work together with two classmates as a member of a three-person, collaborative writing team. The team works for a large corporation that makes electrical appliances. Each team member has been asked to choose a different foreign nation and research the potential for marketing *consumer* electronic appliances there. When each member has the necessary information, prepare collaboratively a memo to your company's marketing director for consumer electronics. In the memo, detail what you have discovered about each country studied and make your recommendations about expanding into each nation.

Extended Application

Take the topic of the writing problem on which you have been working since the extended application in chapter 1. First, search for articles on your topic in a current annual index. Then, if it is feasible, search the same topic for the same year via a computer database. Write a memo to your immediate superior in which you report observed differences between manual and computer searching (for example: Which search technique yielded more references? Which provided more recent citations? Which offered more references actually pertinent to your topic? Which specified citations from more types of documents? Which cost more?). If you cannot have a computer search done, then contrast findings for two different indexes, for example, the *Business Periodicals Index* and the *Business Index*.

CHAPTER 9

Using Graphs and Illustrations

W e use the word *graph* to mean the presentation of information or ideas visually. We will be using the terms *chart* and *graph* interchangeably. The charts discussed in this chapter will be the pie, bar, column, line, flow, organization, and Gantt charts. Other kinds of charts are also used in business, but only those most often employed will be covered. The chapter also discusses illustrations, such as maps, drawings, and photographs, and looks at developments in computer graphics. Finally, we offer suggestions on how to blend graphs into your text.

The use of graphs in business is growing steadily. Every week it seems the computer generates more information and data, thus prompting many to label our era the Information Age. The more information, the more need for ways to display it. If you have taken courses in information systems, you are aware of the immense capacity we now have to store and retrieve data. To get some idea of the range and quantity of data available, spend a little time browsing through the government documents department of your university library—you may be amazed at the amount and diversity of the information contained there.

Business draws on this vast source of data and creates many data bases of its own. Graphs enable us to present data intelligibly: a graph is worth a thousand printouts. Examine the three column charts in figure 9.1, which depict changes occurring in farming in past years, to see for yourself. The three charts show changes in farming more dramatically than any set of tables could. You see the pattern quickly: the farm population and the numbers of farms have decreased markedly but seem to be stabilizing in 1980 and 1981, the last two years shown. Conversely, the average farm size has increased markedly, but it too seems to have stabilized in those years. We will not clutter your vision with the tables that accompany these charts, but given a choice, most people prefer charts over lists of numbers arranged in tables.

A list of some of the ways in which business uses graphs follows:

Analyzing trends in a market

Analyzing market demographics

Forecasting sales

Comparing actual and anticipated sales

Reporting sources of income

Reporting budgetary allocations

Projecting personnel needs

Monitoring productivity levels

Comparing profits and sales

Analyzing production statistics

Analyzing inventory records

Displaying accounting records

Preparing financial models

Planning investments

Monitoring stock performance

Producing Graphs

You can generate graphs in a number of ways to assist in decision making or in selling a decision to others. If you work for a large company, you may be able to call on its graphic artists to turn out graphic presentations, or you may have access to personal computers with graphics capacities. But if you have neither of these options, you can still draw your own graphs.

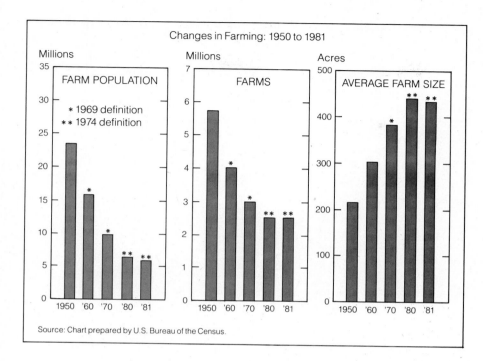

Figure 9.1
Charts convey data quickly

But wait a minute, you protest; you can't draw a straight line, so how can you produce presentable graphs? The answer is that you *can* produce graphs with a little help. With the purchase of three or four inexpensive tools, you can produce attractive charts. In our classroom experience, we have found that anyone can, but you must have the right tools.

The four tools you will need appear in figure 9.2. You need a 90-degree triangle, a decimal ruler, a geometric compass, and a protractor. Most college bookstores and discount stores carry all four of them, and at a moderate price. Notice that we did not mention graph paper. You may work with graph paper if you prefer, but that will prove unnecessary if you follow our guidelines.

We want you to draw your own charts for two reasons. First, drawing several kinds of charts is the best way to gain an understanding of those charts. You will learn by doing them yourself. Second, you can enhance many of your research reports by adding graphs. Imagine what a report reinforced with hand-drawn graphs implies about the sophistication and commitment of its author!

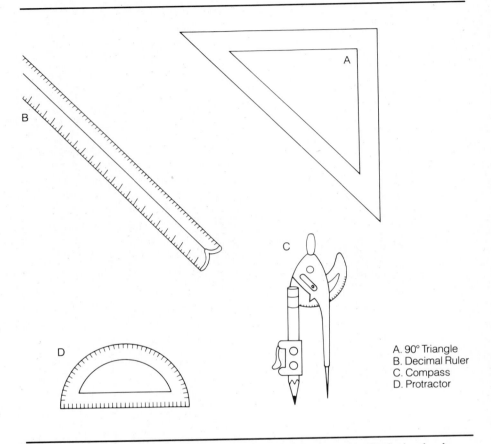

A. 90° Triangle
B. Decimal Ruler
C. Compass
D. Protractor

Figure 9.2   Tools for drawing graphs: (A) 90-degree triangle, (B) decimal ruler, (C) compass, (D) protractor

The Graphs Most Commonly Used in Business Today

We will deal with the following popular graphs:

Pie chart

Bar chart; column chart

Line chart

Flow chart

Organization chart

Gantt chart

What It Is   The **pie chart** is a graph drawn in the form of a circle that
represents some totality. The circle is divided into labeled parts, each of
which represents a certain part of the totality. Figure 9.3 shows a common
use of the pie chart, depicting the composition of federal spending at
five-year intervals. Pie charts are often used in small groups to show the
development of trends over a period of time. Notice that each of the pies is
labeled—1970, 1975, and so on. Within each pie the segments are labeled
with percentages. For example, in the 1970 pie, the segments are labeled—
moving clockwise from the top—as 13 percent, 7 percent, 8 percent, and so
forth. A key at the bottom of the chart identifies each segment of the pie.
The 40 percent stands for the amount spent on national defense, the 13
percent for the amount spent on the "all other" category, the 7 percent for
the amount spent on interest. Note the title of the figure, The Composition
of Federal Spending, and please note the source (at the bottom); *Budget of
the United States Government, Fiscal Year, 1983.*

When to Use It   Since a pie chart depicts whole-to-part relationships, use it
when you are explaining the breakdown of larger amounts into smaller
ones. For example, a pie chart could show the racial makeup of your work
force, the sources of income of your firm, or the firm's budget for the
coming fiscal year. By using more than one pie chart, you can depict the
development of your component parts over a period of years. For instance,
take the four pie charts in figure 9.3, which depict the changes in federal
spending over a 15-year period. You can see how national defense spending
decreases considerably in the first 5 years, stays relatively stable in the next
5 years, but begins to increase in the last 5 years indicated.

 The pie chart can depict either percentages or absolute amounts (or
both). The spending in figure 9.3 could have been represented not as
percents but as dollars. The pie chart can have a dramatic effect if one of
the parts significantly exceeds the others. In figure 9.3, note the relative
dominance of the category payments for individuals. It attracts your attention, doesn't it? However, the pie chart becomes less effective as the number of parts in the whole unit becomes greater. Our example in figure 9.3
has five sections. But what if federal spending broke down into 15 major
categories in the years under consideration? Because a pie chart with 15
sections would lose some effectiveness, you might consider a different kind
of chart, possibly a bar chart.

 For special emphasis, you can separate one section of the chart from the
rest of the pie. In figure 9.4, for example, the real estate segment is
emphasized by being "exploded" from the pie. This kind of graph is known
as an **exploded pie chart.**

How to Make It   As we take up drawing the pie chart, let's make an
important point about drawing *any* graph. You must keep your graph

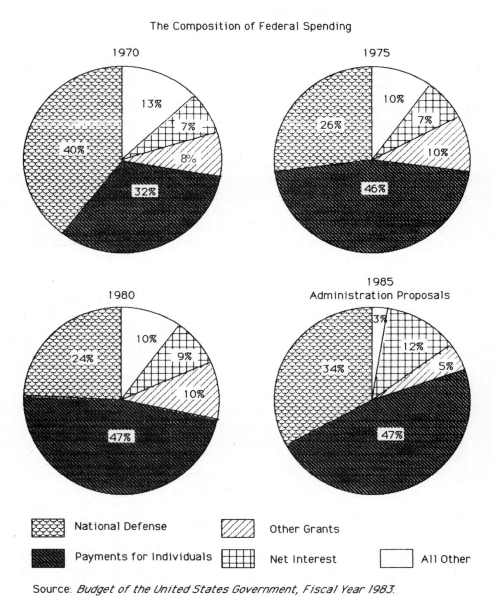

The Composition of Federal Spending

Figure 9.3   Four pie charts

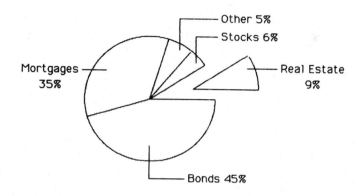

Investments of Temcorp

Figure 9.4
Exploded pie chart

relatively simple if you want people to understand it. We have all seen complicated graphs that looked so impressive and technical that we were intimidated by them. Don't intimidate your reader by making graphs too complicated.

So, having decided that the pie chart is the most suitable format for your data, you must then decide on the right size for the circle. There are no rigid rules in this business, so a sense of proportion will be your guide. Most single pie charts do not occupy a whole page; at most they take up one-half or one-third of the page. Make the chart large enough that you can label each section of the pie, if only from the outside. Note that the chart in figure 9.5 has three sections that are too small for inside labeling, so the labels appear outside the pie.

Having decided on the size of the circle, you will divide your circle into parts. To do this, you will use one of the tools you have purchased—the protractor (pictured in figure 9.2). If your amount figures are in absolute numbers, use a calculator to change them to percents. You do not have to display them in percents, but it will be easier to use percentages to draw the chart.

It is simple to translate the percent figures of your pie chart into degree figures measurable on your protractor. As you know, the circle has 360 degrees, and 1 percent of 360 degrees is 3.6. So multiplying any percent figure by 3.6 translates that figure into a degree figure that, with your protractor, you can mark off on your circle. For example, 15 percent translates into 54 degrees. So if one of your pie segments is 15 percent, use

Distribution of FY 80 Receipts by Type of Claim

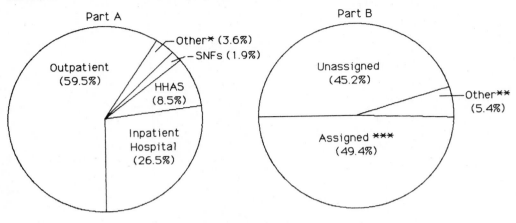

Source: *Deptartment of Health and Human Services, 1980.*

Figure 9.5   Pie chart with outside labels

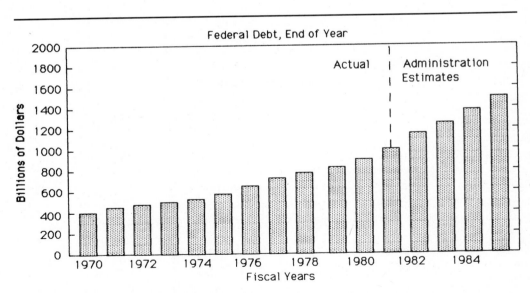

Source: *Budget of the United States Government, Fiscal Year, 1983.*

Figure 9.6   Column chart

your protractor to mark off 54 degrees on your circle. Repeat this process until you have marked off all your pie segments on the circle.

To add distinctiveness to each section of the pie, you can shade the various sections, color them, or use different patterns of lines, as shown in figure 9.3. If you have colored, shaded, or lined your pie sections and have not otherwise labeled the parts, be sure to add a key at the bottom of the chart, as shown in figure 9.3.

You also should add a title and figure number to every chart, either at the top or at the bottom of the chart (it doesn't matter which—just be consistent). If you are borrowing the chart from a source, you also add a source line, as shown in figure 9.3. When a source line occupies the bottom of the chart, you may place the figure number and title at the top, even though you have placed the other figure numbers and titles at the bottom of the chart.

What They Are The bar and the column charts are treated together because they are so similar. Both use sets of bars placed in parallel form within a rectangle, or *grid*, as it is often called. The obvious difference between the bar and the column chart is the direction of the bars on the page. When the bars run across the page, we call it a **bar chart**; when they run up and down the page, we call it a **column chart.** Because of the considerable variety among bar and column charts, only the most common forms are discussed here, but all of them use bars running up and down or across the page within a rectangle or grid. Note the column chart pictured in figure 9.6. Figure 9.7 is a bar chart showing how much of the world's minerals are produced in the United States in one year.

The Bar Chart and the Column Chart

Sometimes both kinds of charts use groups of bars, so we speak of **grouped bar charts** and **grouped column charts.** Figure 9.8 shows two grouped column charts. Note the use of the key in the upper right corner, showing the meaning of the different columns: purchases, depreciation, and net investment. The reader of the chart can see how these three variables (purchases, depreciation, and net investment) have changed over the three years shown—both in current dollars and in constant 1972 dollars.

Another variation is the chart in which each of the bars or columns represents a 100 percent total. Take figure 9.9, for instance. Each of the seven parallel bars represents 100 percent, and within each bar different shading indicates the distribution. The scale at the bottom of the chart underscores the 100 percent.

In figure 9.10 the columns also represent 100 percent each. The chart also indicates the total number of graduates for each of the years shown. Within each column, different shading indicates the percentages of degrees awarded in the various disciplines. Again, note the key to the meaning of each kind of shading (arts and sciences, engineering, and so on).

Figure 9.7
Bar chart

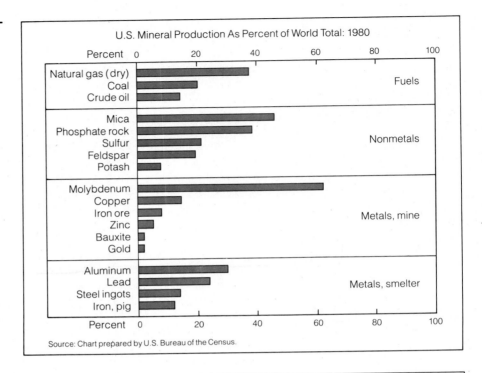

U.S. Mineral Production As Percent of World Total: 1980

Source: Chart prepared by U.S. Bureau of the Census.

Figure 9.8
Grouped column
charts

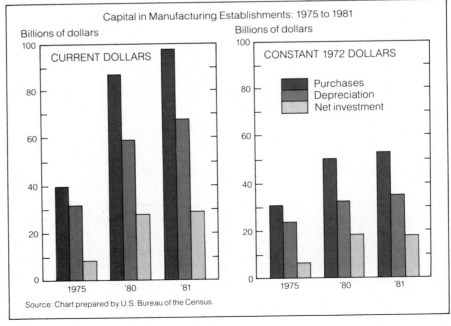

Capital in Manufacturing Establishments: 1975 to 1981

Source: Chart prepared by U.S. Bureau of the Census.

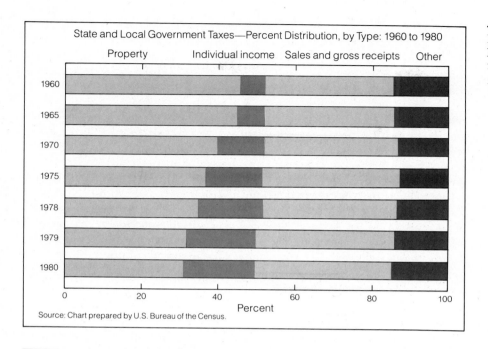

Figure 9.9
Bar chart with bars representing 100 percent

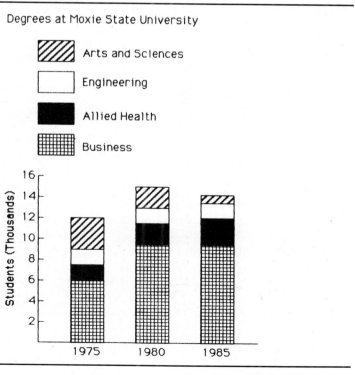

Figure 9.10
Column chart with columns representing 100 percent

Sometimes a single bar or column is used as a 100 percent bar or column chart, as in figure 9.11. Note the similarity of the 100 percent bar or column chart to the pie chart. Each depicts a whole-to-part relationship, the whole constituting a 100 percent total. Such is the flexibility of bar and column charts.

When to Use Them   While pie charts are effective for depicting whole-to-part relationships, particularly in terms of percents, bar and column charts are especially adapted for showing amounts in percents or absolute numbers. Although the pie chart and the 100 percent bar chart do much the same thing in depicting the whole-to-part relationship, other bar and column charts can do more than that. Figure 9.10 is an example. Three pie charts could show the proportions of college degrees awarded in the four fields mentioned for each of the three years cited. But the pie charts could not also show the overall number of degrees awarded each year and the trends that might emerge over the years in terms of total number of degrees awarded. In sum, the bar and column charts are able to reveal more dimensions than the pie chart.

Figure 9.11
100 percent
bar chart

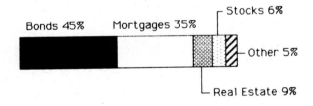

Temcorp Investments

How to Make Them   Though it is almost impossible to advise you on how to make *every* kind of bar or column chart, we can present guidelines for most kinds of these charts. They are all made up of different sizes of rectangles. For this job, you will need only your decimal ruler and your 90-degree triangle.

Let's assume that you have already decided to depict your data in the form of a column chart. Everything we say about the column chart will apply to the bar chart, except for the direction of the bars.

First you have to decide on the size of the grid or rectangle that frames the columns. Column charts don't usually take up a whole page. Half a page should be plenty of room, and some column charts may take up only a third of the page. Just make the chart large enough to show its components clearly and simply. How many columns are you allowed to have? There are no set rules: you may have as few as 2, but exceeding 10 might create a cluttered chart, especially if the chart is not to cover an entire page. Common sense and proportion are your guides. Remember, see the chart as your reader will see it. Always ask yourself this question: "Will this chart strike my reader as intimidating and difficult to understand?" If so, consider using the line chart, which will be explained in a few pages.

Since this is a column chart, in which the vertical scale measures variable amounts, you should establish the unit of measurement for that scale. That means finding the most suitable scale on your decimal ruler and using it to measure off your vertical column. There are six scales on the ruler from which to choose. The first scale divides the inch into 10 parts, the second into 20, the third into 30, and so on. Choose the scale that allows you to measure your columns accurately and to keep the rectangle within the limits you have allowed yourself. Consider your tallest column: the top of the vertical scale should be a little taller than the tallest column. Mark off your units of measure on the vertical scale. These marks are usually called *ticks*.

Keep the scale numbers as simple as possible. If the numbers are large, say in millions, use only the first two digits of the numbers and label them at the side as millions (as in figure 9.13). Also note that you do not have to number each tick (see figure 9.14).

Now you are ready to complete the remaining three sides of your grid. Your 90-degree triangle will help you to draw the rectangle perfectly square. As figure 9.12 shows, lining up either of the two shorter edges of this tool with the vertical scale will let you draw a perfect line at a 90-degree angle every time. Complete the remaining three sides of your rectangle, as figure 9.12 indicates.

Next, you draw in the columns, using the same decimal ruler scale to proportion each column correctly. Be sure to draw each column to the same width and at the same distance from its neighbors. If one of the columns is considerably taller than the others, break it and indicate the break also in the rectangle, as shown in figure 9.13.

Consider shading your columns with patterns or coloring them with pencils or pens to give them emphasis. If you want to do an even better job, you can buy special rolls of colored tape for the columns at a local art store.

Next, label the columns at the bottom, as shown in figure 9.13. You can either print or type all your numbers and labels (typing is usually neater). Give a figure number and a title to the chart, as shown. If you have been especially ambitious and have divided your columns into 100 percent blocks with different percentage parts, as does figure 9.10, be sure to add a key indicating the meaning of the different shading.

Figure 9.12
Drawing the grid

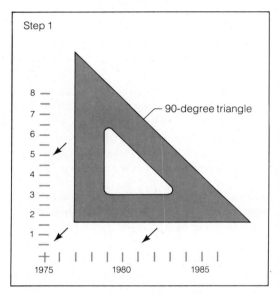

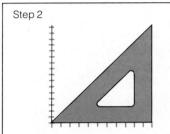

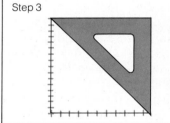

Figure 9.13
Column chart with
broken column

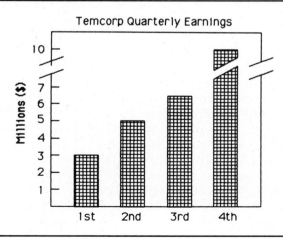

What It Is   A few pages back we mentioned that you might need too many columns to represent your data in the form of a column chart and might therefore wish to use a line chart. For a moment, imagine a column chart with 20 columns. On seeing this chart, your eye would automatically begin to pay less attention to individual columns and more attention to the overall *trend* of the columns. A **line chart** stresses not individual numbers but the overall trend of the numbers.

Figure 9.14 exhibits a simple line chart showing the federal debt as a percentage of the gross national product. The chart shows that this percentage has remained relatively stable over the years shown, and the chart projects that the percentage should remain relatively stable in the last years shown (1981–1985).

A line chart can depict movement or trends because essentially it depicts a relationship of two variables, one of which is a measurement of time—for example, months, quarters, years. This measurement is the independent variable and is always plotted on the horizontal scale. This variable changes at a fixed rate; for example, the interval in figure 9.14 is two years—1970, 1972, 1974, 1976, and so on.

The dependent variable, on the other hand, is always an amount—for example, percentages, dollars, tons—and it is always plotted on the vertical scale. This variable changes at an irregular rate, sometimes rising, sometimes falling—for example, 39, 38, 36, 37, 39. Figure 9.15 shows the location of such independent and dependent variables on the grid of a line chart.

You can imagine the line of the graph as being made up of an infinite number of dots, each dot representing the coordination of a given amount with a given point in time. Read altogether as a continuous line, the dots show the trend of the amounts over a period of time.

So far we've touched on the essential components of a line graph:

1. At least one line
2. A vertical scale measuring amounts (the dependent variable)
3. A horizontal scale measuring the time periods (the independent variable)

But we can add other lines representing other items and hence compare the items represented by the lines. Figure 9.16 becomes a study in these relationships. The surfaces between each of the four lines on the chart have been shaded for greater emphasis. (That's why we call this particular kind of line chart a **surface chart.**) Take a moment to examine it.

Note that national defense, while rising at a fairly constant rate, begins to accelerate around 1979, while payments for individuals follows roughly the same course as national defense. Not so with net interest, which starts a gradual swell around 1976. And look at the category described as all others: as the other three items continue to grow, the chart projects a decline in this category. Thus a line chart with several lines encourages a more sophisticated analysis than the other kinds of charts.

Like bar and column charts, the line chart can depict negative as well as positive values. It does so by extending the vertical scale below zero and letting the line or lines follow a downward path. Figure 9.17 illustrates this feature.

Figure 9.14
Line graph

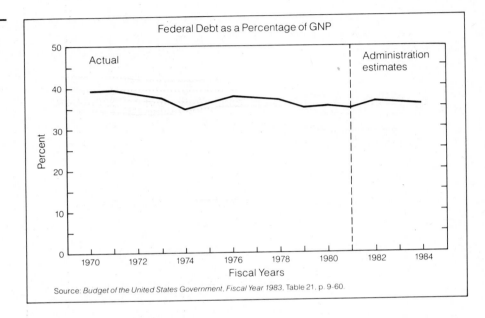

Source: *Budget of the United States Government, Fiscal Year 1983*, Table 21, p. 9-60.

Figure 9.15
Line chart makeup

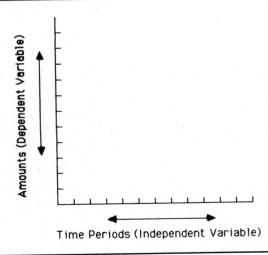

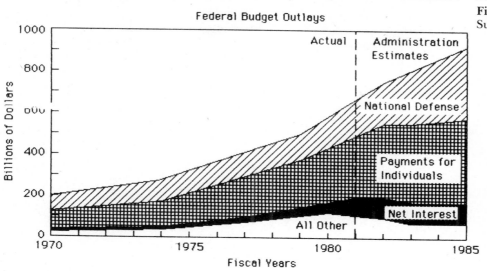

Figure 9.16
Surface chart

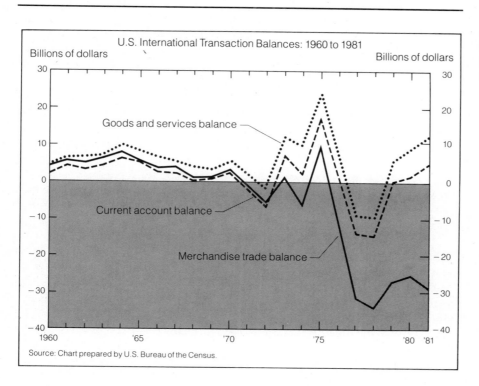

Figure 9.17
Line chart depicting
negative values

When to Use It   Explaining what a line chart is tells much about its use. To see the different uses of the line chart, consult figure 9.16, Federal Budget Outlays. Not only does the line chart show trends in variables over periods of time but it also enables you to make projections based on these trends. Notice that the section at the right side of the chart extends the actual trends into administration estimates about those trends in the future.

Also, this kind of chart enables you to compare or contrast the behavior of the different variables plotted, allowing you to see correlations and deviations quickly. For example, it is easy to infer a correlation between the rise in spending for national defense, payments for individuals, and net interest and the corresponding drop in spending in other categories. Finally, the line chart enables you to see the part-to-whole relationship because the line at the top of the shaded parts of the chart is the total of all the parts. Thus you can see the overall dramatic rise in federal budget outlays for the years shown.

How to Make It   To make a line chart, you need your decimal ruler and your 90-degree triangle. The critical question is what size to make the grid or rectangle. That depends in part on the complexity of the chart: how many lines will be on the chart? Again, there is no set rule here: some charts effectively use nine lines. But consider your reader's immediate reaction to a chart containing seven to nine lines. Will the reader be overwhelmed? Another factor is the pattern of the various lines. If the lines are jagged and irregular, several might make the chart difficult to comprehend. We suggest that you limit the number of lines to four or five. If there are more variables than that, perhaps you should make two charts.

The number of lines will affect the size of the chart. A chart with one line may require only one-third of the page, while a chart with five lines could require half, two-thirds, or even the whole page. You will have to be the judge, but a preliminary sketch should enable you to determine approximately the proper size of your rectangle.

Another factor affecting the size of your chart is the *range* of the lines to be drawn. The highest and lowest numbers will indicate approximately the number of units of measure needed on the vertical scale. Your grid must be large enough to accommodate the range of your variables.

Say you decide tentatively on a rectangle four inches high. Select on your decimal ruler the scale that best coincides with the number of units you will require on that vertical scale, and mark them off as tick marks. Then, with your 90-degree triangle, draw the two horizontal lines of your rectangle. Now determine the decimal ruler scale that best coincides with the number of units you will require on the horizontal scale. This number will be determined by the number of weeks, months, or years that you wish to show. Mark off the tick marks. Then draw the fourth line of the rectangle— your second vertical—and mark off the units in tick marks on it.

Now begin to draw your lines on the rectangle. First, draw them in pencil, lightly, and go over them later. Soon you will see the overall impression your chart creates. A well-proportioned rectangle should be just large enough for the various lines to run their courses. If all your lines are bunched up in a small part of the rectangle, you need to reduce the size of the rectangle, possibly by a break in its vertical sides. Figure 9.18 shows two line charts depicting the same numerical data. The one on the left has a grid that is too large for it: the line occupies only the top half of the chart. The chart on the right "breaks" the grid, reducing it to the size required by the line.

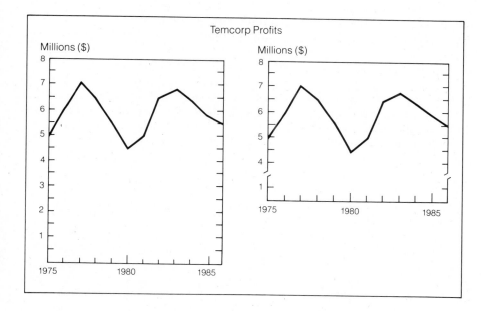

Figure 9.18
Chart showing break in the vertical scale (on right)

One more point about proportioning the grid. Changing the size of the rectangle can change the *impression* the chart conveys. For example, making the chart wider can smooth out the lines, while making it taller can accentuate the fluctuation of the lines. In figure 9.19, the same data is drawn both ways.

As pointed out earlier, there is no precise formula for determining the proportions of the chart. But be sure to avoid distorting your chart intentionally, since readers familiar with charts will spot distortion quickly and perhaps lose confidence in the presentation. Consider the following guideline: draw every chart as if the numerical data upon which it is based were to appear in a table on the same page. Thus the reader would be able to compare the *apparent* relationships depicted in the chart with the *actual* numerical relationships, spotting any discrepancy. For example, the reader would notice if the numbers did not rise as sharply as the line. This guideline will keep your charts "honest."

Drawing the rest of the chart poses no real problem. If you have not already done so, you can now write in the numbers on the vertical scale. You should round them off and reduce the number of zeros by labeling the column as billions or millions. The vertical scale normally begins at zero, but it may be broken to keep the proportion reasonable, as described earlier. Each scale has a label, of course, as the examples of line charts indicate. You may type the labels or print them neatly.

You can pen in the lines in two ways. If you're doing a surface chart like figure 9.16, first shade the different surfaces. Second, pen in each line, making the top one the thickest. Finally, print or type in the label for each surface.

On the other hand, you may not wish to make a surface chart perhaps because your lines crisscross. In this case, you distinguish the lines by different patterns, as in figure 9.20. Or you may use different colors of ink to differentiate the lines. In either case, include a key that explains each line, or label each line on the chart.

Figure 9.19
Charts distorting data

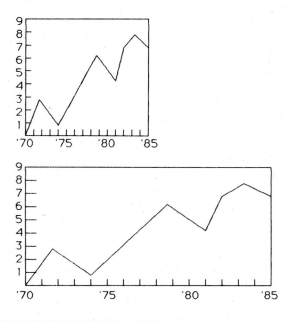

At the top or bottom of your graph, print or type a figure number and a title. In the text immediately before your chart, you may wish to include the table of data from which the chart is drawn. Doing so allows the reader to compare the chart and the data on which it is based to see that it does not distort the data.

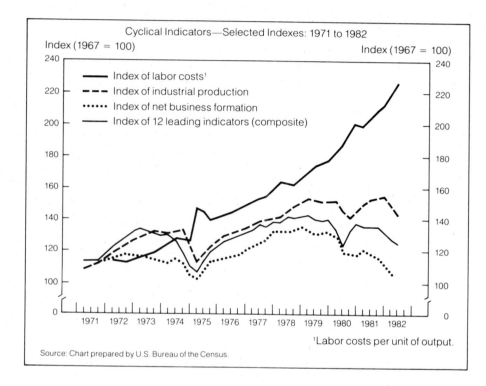

Cyclical Indicators—Selected Indexes: 1971 to 1982

Index (1967 = 100)

— Index of labor costs[1]
- - - Index of industrial production
••••• Index of net business formation
— Index of 12 leading indicators (composite)

[1]Labor costs per unit of output.

Source: Chart prepared by U.S. Bureau of the Census.

Figure 9.20
Chart with key in upper left corner

What It Is   The **flow chart** is a graphic description of the steps in a process. Often the flow chart will use symbolic shapes to convey the different kinds of steps. Figure 9.21 describes the most common ones.

The flow chart in figure 9.22 depicts the problem-solving approach to writing, using standard flow chart symbols. The arrows connecting the flow chart symbols establish the order of the steps. For instance, the reader profile precedes the definition of goals. The dashed lines indicate that some actions depicted are recursive. Specifically, the decision step at the lower left side of the chart is a time to return to the earlier reader profile and the definition of goals.

The Flow Chart

Figure 9.21
Some flow chart
symbols. (Source:
American National
Standards
Institute.)

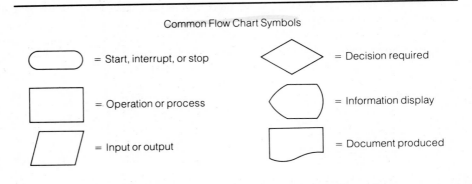

Common Flow Chart Symbols

= Start, interrupt, or stop

= Operation or process

= Input or output

= Decision required

= Information display

= Document produced

Figure 9.22
Flow chart. The
problem-solving
approach to
writing.

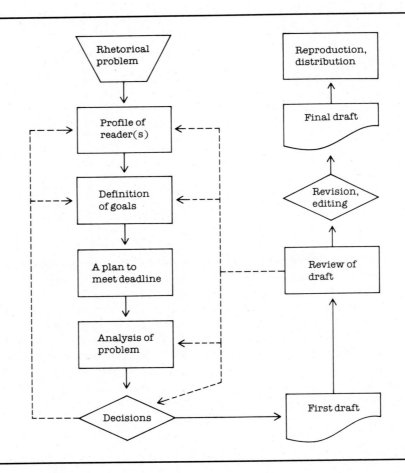

When to Use It   When you want to explain a fairly complicated process, you may use a flow chart, but you would not indicate every substep in the process. The flow chart is particularly useful in training sessions and in proposal writing to show the various stages in the process you propose to implement. It gives the reader an overall survey of the process before you start to explain its specific steps. It's like reading a road map before starting on a long drive.

How to Make It   The main concern, again, is proportion. Flow charts, unlike most other charts, often occupy the entire page. The chart must be large enough to accommodate the flow chart symbols so that their labels will be clearly legible. You may position the chart on the page as in figure 9.22 or as in figure 9.24. The position in figure 9.22 is generally favored because the reader does not have to rotate the document in order to read the chart. However, not all charts will fit into that format.

Drawing the rectangles is simple with your 90-degree triangle and decimal ruler. You may use different-sized rectangles, but keep the ones on the same level of importance the same size. For example, in figure 9.22, notice how the four identical rectangles in the left-hand column indicate that these four steps are of equal importance. Drawing the other shapes may present more of a challenge, but most art stores and college bookstores carry templates that allow you to draw these shapes quickly and accurately.

Type in the labels. If you type them on scrap paper before you draw the chart, you'll get a good idea of how large to make each shape. Don't forget to label your chart at the top or bottom, depending on the position of other chart labels in your text.

What It Is   The **organization chart** is a graphic description of reporting relationships within an organization. It uses lines to show which person reports to whom, as in figure 9.23. For example, in the service division, the controller reports to the vice-president of planning and controls. In these charts, solid lines indicate line or direct authority relationships; dashed lines indicate staff or advisory positions. Sometimes the names of the officers are given just below their positions.

Note that not all the boxes are the same size and shape. For example, the three boxes in the middle of the chart containing the titles of the vice-presidents of the division are larger than the boxes on the lowest level. Sometimes the size of boxes will indicate the importance of the position.

The Organization Chart

When to Use It   Use the organization chart in instructing people who are unfamiliar with the chain of command—new employees, potential customers, or representatives of government. Anyone who needs to learn quickly who handles what responsibilities in the organization may appreciate an organization chart. Should a department within an organization need to be reorganized, such a chart would make immediately clear the proposed reorganizaton.

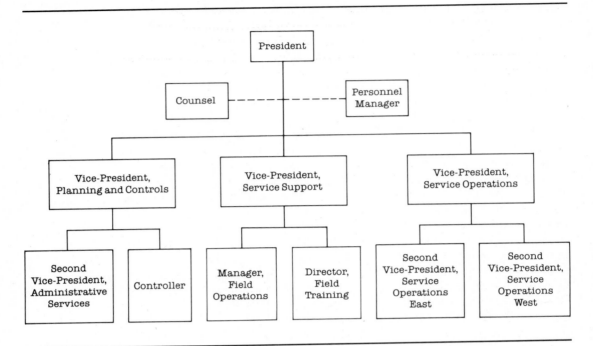

Figure 9.23   Organization chart. Service Division, XYZ Corporation.

How to Make It   As with the flow chart, the position on the page of figure 9.23 is favored because the reader need not rotate the document to read the chart. A preliminary sketch will indicate whether your chart will fit without being turned. If the chart will fit, a preliminary sketch can also give you an idea of how much space on the page the chart will cover—one-third, one-half, or more. Like the flow chart, the organization chart often occupies the entire page to allow for greater legibility of the phrases in the boxes.

You need to decide how large the boxes containing the position titles will be. Their size depends on the size of the chart: the larger the chart, the larger the boxes, and vice versa. Each box must be large enough to contain the position title and the name of the officer if the name is to appear. Your decimal ruler will help you to draw their sizes consistently, and your 90-degree triangle will help you to draw each of the right angles perfectly.

Draw the bottom line of boxes first, because that line will normally be the broadest, and drawing it first will insure that your chart will fit on the width of the page. If you begin by drawing the uppermost box, you may find that the bottom row of boxes is too broad for the page and you may have to start over.

You may wind up with more officers than available boxes. You might solve this problem by deleting the lowest level of boxes from the chart. Or you may need to make additional charts showing the organization of some departments separately. Don't feel that you have to show every existing job on the chart, but don't leave out important managers or key staff personnel. Remember the purpose of the chart, to give your audience a survey of the structure of your organization.

Not all organization charts can be constructed in the pyramid form shown in figure 9.23, because the particular organizational structure may not lend itself to that form. Consider the chart in figure 9.24. At the far left of the chart, the stack of nine boxes catches the eye. Indeed, this particular structure seems to have shaped the rest of the chart: the two main job clusters in the middle of the chart are likewise arranged vertically. Notice also the use of different-sized boxes—three distinct shapes in all. Finally, consider how many people work for the Department of Energy and how few of their jobs are listed on this chart. Be selective in designing an organization chart.

What It Is   The **Gantt chart,** named for its originator, Henry L. Gantt (1861–1919), is essentially a planning tool. Managers can use it to coordinate the scheduling involved in a complex project. It breaks the project down into its various tasks and by means of a kind of bar chart shows the time each task will require. Thus managers and everyone else involved in the project can tell from looking at it (1) the amount of time required for the project and each of its various tasks and (2) the progress made up to any given point. Figure 9.25 is a Gantt chart showing the schedule you might create for a paper to be written for a business communication class.

The Gantt Chart

When to Use It   You may use the Gantt chart to plan any project with several phases. If you are responsible for coordinating the activities of a group of people over a period of time, think of the Gantt chart. When you're developing a new program, sales campaign, fund-raising effort, proposal, or feasibility study, consider using a Gantt chart.

How to Make It   To make it, you need a decimal ruler and a 90-degree triangle. As always, proportioning the grid is critical. It must be large enough to accommodate your list of tasks in the left column. Pick out the scale on your decimal ruler that allows sufficient space for each task description. As with other charts, you may have to experiment on scrap paper to get the right proportions.

Choose the scale for your units of time (days, weeks, months). Do not choose a scale so small that these units will appear crowded, so that the double-digit numbers (11, 12, 13) become hard to separate. At the top of the chart write in the unit of time.

In the column at the left, print or type the task descriptions. You may use both general and specific descriptions: note in figure 9.25 that the more

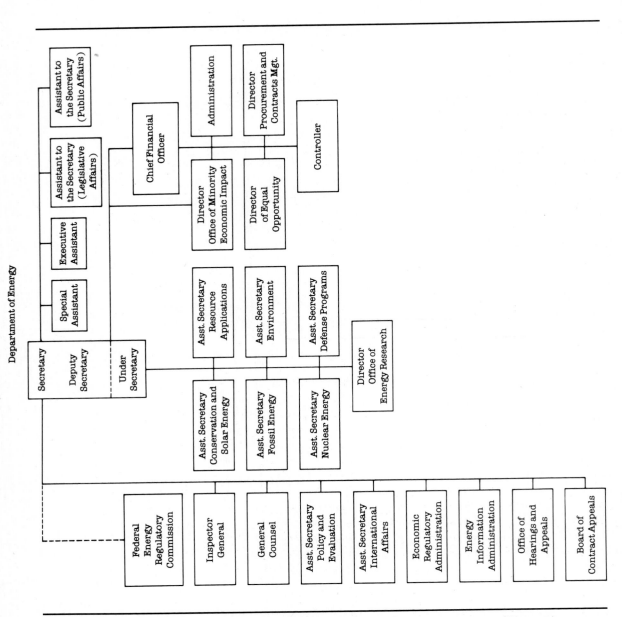

Figure 9.24 Organization chart with unusual structure. (Source: U.S. Department of Energy.)

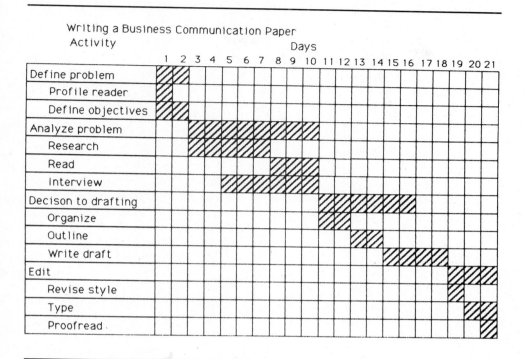

Figure 9.25 Gantt chart

specific tasks are indented from the left margin. Be sure to list each task in chronological order. Some tasks may overlap partially, but the Gantt chart can show that. Next draw in the bars to show the time limits for each task. You might use a felt-tip pen for this job, but we suggest that you use a pattern of diagonal lines, as in figure 9.25. Doing so will later enable you to superimpose another form of shading to show the daily progress in each category. Thus you gain the two advantages of the Gantt chart—depicting overall planning and providing daily progress reports.

Other Useful Graphic Aids

Maps can help you in many ways, especially when your firm plans expansion. When you are trying to discover the best location for a new branch of a bank, a shopping center, plant, warehouse, food store, gas station, or fast-food restaurant, you must have maps of the area. In marketing your product, maps can be a necessity: for establishing sales districts, determining access to markets, and planning direct-mail campaigns.

Consider this example. An automobile manufacturer may use maps to determine the best location of its dealerships. The computer plots a map showing all owners of its cars in a certain locale. The map also shows the locations of its area dealers, along with those of competing dealerships. Managers are then able to determine whether a new dealership would be useful and, if so, where to locate it.

Almost any map can be generated by computer if your firm has the right hardware. But you may have to locate maps on your own, using some detective work. If you're looking for local and regional maps, you might begin with your state's department of highways or department of transportation, which may have a local office near you. There will be a nominal charge for the map. If the map is too large to use in your report, photocopying can reduce its size to 8½ by 11 inches. (Just be sure that when you reduce the map size you do not make the copy too small to read.) Public libraries are also sources of maps. Check the government documents section of your university or public library.

Drawings and Photographs

The thought of using drawings may seem impractical, but you may one day work for a company with an art department or one that sends work out to commercial art firms. For this reason, we urge you to start becoming aware of the advantages of illustrations in explaining your ideas. For example, if you are explaining the tools that are most useful for drawing graphs, the illustrations of the four tools shown in figure 9.2 will make your task easier. (If you don't believe that, try to explain in words alone what a decimal ruler is and what it looks like to someone who has never seen one.)

If drawings are presently out of your reach, however, photographs may not be because many students are amateur photographers. If you are explaining a piece of equipment, for example, a photograph could make your job much easier. Of course, you should not add drawings or photographs to a report just to adorn it, but when illustrations form an integral part of a report, they reflect well on the author.

The Evolving Technology of Computer Graphics

Engineers and scientists have been using computer graphics for a long time, but business people have held back until recent years. Now, however, computer graphics have arrived on the business scene for two basic reasons. The cost of the equipment, the *hardware*, has been falling consistently; as a result many more business programs, the *software*, have been written. Visit a computer store and look at their software or notice the many ads in business periodicals promoting software programs. The programs range from letter writing to accounting to graphics.

Computers produce pie, bar, column, line, organization, and scatter charts, along with maps. With the right equipment, you can produce these charts in color. Also, the computer produces them much more rapidly than they could be produced manually.

A cycle has been developing. The computer produces massive amounts of numerical data. This in turn creates a need for easier ways to assimilate the data. Managers find it increasingly difficult to keep up with this print-out glut, but now the graphics capacities of the computer have to some extent solved this problem. The graphs make the printout data more comprehensible so that they have become an important support in decision making.

We do not imply that you will necessarily work for a firm that relies heavily on computer graphics. That depends on the size, needs, and other variables present in your organization. But in any event, you should know about this evolving technology. For example, imagine a bank with many branches. How does its management monitor the performance of its branch managers? Management could study computer printouts on the performance of each manager, but comparisons would be time-consuming. Using computers, however, management can generate from its data-base for the branches charts comparing the performance of the branch managers.

Or take the case of a retail chain store with branches throughout the country. Planning is critical for such a company since no two of its regional markets are alike, and some vary widely. Using computer graphics, the chain's management can generate from their sales database charts that show how each product line is performing in each of its districts.

The selection of devices from which to choose has grown rapidly, and we will not attempt to catalogue all of them. Essentially, computer graphics depend on a terminal into which you type your commands. You insert a diskette containing a software program into the disk drive unit of the computer. You use the keyboard to interact with the computer—to tell it what kind of graph you want and to make adjustments in the dimensions of the graph designated.

Computer Graphics Hardware

The computer is connected to a plotter, which prints out your graph. Plotters come in many different forms and produce a wide variety of graphic illustrations. Graphics output devices can produce charts on paper, on acetate for transparencies (for use with overhead projectors), and on 35-mm slides, in black and white or in color.

You do not have to be a programmer to use contemporary software for computer graphics, since English language commands deliver the instructions to the computer. These software programs are available even for

Computer Graphics Software

personal computers. Consider some of the things this software can do for you. If you wish to depict numerical data in the form of a pie chart, you have only to load the appropriate software into the computer terminal and give it the appropriate commands. The computer offers you a list of options, asking the kind of chart you wish to create, for example. Having selected the pie chart, you type in your data. The computer allows you to determine the size of the pie and to explode a segment of the pie if you wish. It may also offer you a choice of colors for the pie segments. You will have to type in the figure number and the chart title. You next type the command for the computer to send the chart to the plotter to be printed, either on paper or acetate (for overhead transparencies). Some computers allow you to produce your chart on 35-mm slides as well. This entire process takes a few minutes.

In constructing a bar or column chart, the software allows you to determine the proportions of the chart, to establish the scale measurement, and to choose the shading or colors of the bars or columns. The same kind of options come with software for the line chart.

Here we add a qualification. We do not want to create the impression that you can, without any training, sit down at a graphics terminal and turn out graphs in minutes. The process presumes some familiarity with both the terminal and the software. You will need some hours of training and practice before you master the system, but the time spent will be a good investment in your future productivity.

Four Suggestions for Integrating Graphs with Text

However graphs are generated, you must integrate them smoothly into your text. Graphs and illustrations can never be an end in themselves—they must support your writing. To use that support, here are four suggestions:

1. *In your text, point out the significant features of your graph.* Do not expect your reader to interpret the graph: tell him or her the significance of the graph. For example, assume that you are using the line graph in figure 9.26. You might point out that the expenses of farm production have risen at a constant rate during the years shown. The gross income from farming, however, while rising over the same period of years, shows periods of leveling off. Consequently, the net income from farming, while also rising, fluctuates regularly.

2. *Physically place the graph as near to the text discussion as possible.* Do not force the reader to page back and forth between the graph and its discussion in the text. For the same reason, resist the temptation to

place all your graphs in an appendix. Imagine the difficulty you might have had understanding this chapter if all the figures had appeared in an appendix.

3. *Give each graph, map, or photograph a title and a figure number and refer to it by figure number (rather than page number) in your discussion.* Doing so will avoid the problem of estimating the page number on which the graph will eventually appear. And always double-check to see that text references to illustrations agree with numbers on the figures. If you have taken the data for the graph from an outside source, indicate that fact in a source line at the bottom of the graph. For example, figure 9.26 has a source line indicating that the chart originated with the U.S. Bureau of the Census.

4. *If you are drawing your own graphs, draw them to scale on scrap paper before typing the report.* Thus, as you type, you can leave enough space for the graph. You can draw in the graph later. Or some people prefer to tape the graph into the space allotted and photocopy the page.

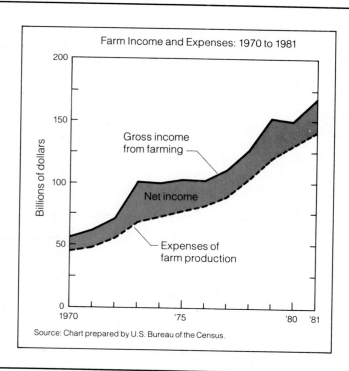

Figure 9.26
Explain your graph

Summary

The use of graphs in business is expanding because of (1) the growing amount of data businesses must deal with, (2) recent developments in computer graphics, (3) decreasing costs of computer hardware, and (4) a growing variety of graphics software packages.

Although charts may be generated by computer, you are asked to learn to draw your own charts in this chapter to give you a greater familiarity with their function. To make charts you need four inexpensive tools—a 90-degree triangle, a decimal ruler, a geometric compass, and a protractor.

The charts discussed in this chapter are the most commonly used charts in business today. The pie chart is a graph drawn in the shape of a circle that represents a totality. It depicts part-to-whole relationships. The bar and column charts use parallel bars to depict the relative sizes of amounts. The line chart plots at least one line against both a horizontal and a vertical scale, each of which measures a variable (a series of numbers). The line chart depicts trends over a period of time. The flow chart is a graphic description of the steps in a single process. The organization chart is a graphic description of the reporting relationships in an organization. It is useful to those unfamiliar with working relationships within the organization. The Gantt chart is a graphic representation of the scheduling involved in a complex project, showing the timing and overlapping of tasks and making it possible to chart the progress of the project. It is useful to coordinate a project in which several individuals or departments are involved. Other illustrations, such as maps, drawings, and photographs, can also make information easier to grasp quickly.

The use of computer graphics is also increasing as personal computers become more common in the office. Contemporary software packages allow you to produce a pie, bar, column, or line chart in minutes, provided you know how to use the computer and the software.

Your graphics will be most effective if you follow four suggestions on integrating them into the text of a document. First, point out the significant features of your graph in your text. Second, place the graph as close to its text discussion as possible. Third, give each graph or illustration a figure number and a title and refer to it by figure number in your text. Fourth, when drawing a graph, draw it to scale on scrap paper before typing your report.

Writing Problems

1. One set of numerical data can often be graphed in more than one form; for example, the same data may be graphed as either a pie or a bar chart. You must choose the form of graph that will best display the aspect of the data you consider most important, such as trends, relative amounts, or fluctuation. Below are several tables, each of which can be graphed in at least one of the following forms: pie chart, bar or column chart, or line chart. Most of these tables can be graphed in more than one form. First, in a memo to your instructor, write a brief explanation of the ways in which each table might be graphed. Second, draw two of the graphs. Do not draw both graphs in the same form; that is, if you draw a column chart, don't draw a bar chart as your second chart. Having drawn your two charts, include in your memo an analysis of each one, pointing out to your reader what aspects each form tends to stress. Usually, you will have to plot decimal numbers, but here you may round off numbers. For example, 16.4 can be rounded to 16.5 and 19.8 to 20. Finally, don't hesitate to use color or shading in your charts.

Table 1
Exports of Selected States, 1980
($ billions)

	Manufactures	Agriculture	Total
California	16.5	3.3	19.8
Illinois	10.2	0.7	10.9
Indiana	4.7	3.5	8.2
Michigan	8.8	1.3	10.1
New Jersey	4.4	0.2	4.6
New York	9.2	3.0	12.2
Ohio	10.4	0.2	10.6
Pennsylvania	7.6	0.7	8.3
Texas	10.5	1.7	12.2
Washington	8.7	0.6	9.3

Source: U.S. Department of Commerce.

Table 2
Export Share of GNP for Selected Countries
1960–1980
(percent)

	1960	1971	1980
United States	4.1	4.4	8.5
Japan	7.7	9.8	12.2
Federal Republic of Germany	15.8	18.4	21.8
South Korea	.8	9.6	30.4
Netherlands	35.7	37.1	37.9

Source: International Monetary Fund, International Financial Statistics.

Table 3
U.S. Direct Investment Flows Abroad
(in millions of dollars)

Year	Developed Countries	Developing Countries
1970	5,161	1,565
1971	5,131	1,527
1972	5,110	1,555
1973	10,154	630
1974	10,681	3,506
1975	7,800	6,440
1976	9,606	3,025
1977	9,816	2,487
1978	11,110	5,784
1979	17,438	6,941
1980	18,873	8,597
1981	8,762	2,832

Source: U.S. Department of Commerce.

Table 4
EC Self-Sufficiency in Selected Commodities
(in percentage of self-sufficiency)

Year	Wheat	Sugar	Poultry	Beef & Veal
1968	96	82	100	93
1969	88	90	101	90
1970	86	81	192	92
1971	98	99	103	93
1972	97	94	101	87
1973	103	90	104	87
1974	111	79	102	103
1975	100	115	101	102
1976	102	100	105	100
1977	97	126	106	97
1978	118	123	105	95
1979	113	131	104	100
1980	126	129	109	104
1981	123	128	111	103

Source: U.S. Department of Agriculture.

Table 5
Direct Investment Position
($ billions)

Year	U.S. Direct Investment Abroad	Foreign Direct Investment in United States
1972	90	14
1973	101	21
1974	110	25
1975	124	28
1976	137	31
1977	146	35
1978	163	42
1979	187	54
1980	215	54
1981	227	90

Source: U.S. Department of Commerce.

2. You are the assistant to the executive vice-president of a national accounting firm, O'Flaherty & Steinberg. Your boss has assigned you the task of writing a section of a proposal report that will be submitted to Woodrow Wilson University, which intends to upgrade its data processing capabilities. Your section of the proposal report will be entitled "An Overview of the Entire Project" and will consist of a flow chart and a one- to two-page textual description of the process described in the flow chart.

   Here is the information you will need to complete your assignment. The university has established a computer services policy committee to make decisions about the upgrading of its data processing capabilities. Your firm will advise this committee about hardware, software, and computer center staffing and organization. Your firm will make a study of university requirements and then draw up a five-year plan for computer use at the university. The activities of your firm would include the following eight steps:

   - There would be an organizational meeting with the computer services policy committee to review goals and methods.
   - Your firm would review existing university reports on computer hardware, software, and requirements.
   - Your firm would interview the computer center staff and key university administrators regarding needs in hardware, software, staffing, academic computing, and word processing.
   - Your firm would review and document the present computing system in use at the university.
   - Your firm would review all operating reports used by the various university offices.
   - Your firm would review all existing controls designed to insure accurate and timely transactions.
   - Your firm would interview all department heads to determine how they use the reports they obtain from the system.
   - Your firm would analyze all its findings from the first seven steps and present a written report making recommendations for the following five years. These recommendations would cover decisions regarding purchases of hardware and software, computing, and computer center staffing and organization.

   Construct the flow chart and write the section of the proposal report.

3. Your position is the same as in the preceding problem. Your assignment is to prepare another section of the proposal report described above, this to be entitled "The Project Timetable." The report will consist of a one- to two-page description of the timetable outlined

below, including a Gantt chart to illustrate the timetable. The steps are exactly as described in the preceding problem. The dates for each of these eight steps occur within the same calendar year.

- There would be an organizational meeting with the computer services policy committee on January 5 to review goals and methods.
- Between January 6 and January 14 your firm would review existing university reports on computer hardware, software, and requirements.
- Between January 15 and 20 your firm would interview the computer center staff and key university administrators regarding needs in hardware, software, staffing, academic computing, and word processing.
- Between January 15 and January 29 your firm would review and document the present computing system in use at the university.
- During the same period (January 15 to 29) your firm would review all operating reports used by the various university offices.
- Between January 30 and February 10 your firm would review all existing controls designed to insure accurate and timely transactions.
- During the same period (January 30 to February 10) your firm would interview all department heads to determine how they use the reports they obtain from the system.
- Between February 10 and March 1 your firm would analyze all its findings from the first seven steps and on March 1 present a written report making recommendations for the following five years. These recommendations would cover decisions about purchases of hardware and software, computing, and computer center staffing and organization. Construct the Gantt chart and write your section of the proposal report.

4. Design a flow chart for a process with which you are familiar. If you already have a job—full- or part-time—you might consider depicting a process that takes place in your department, for example, the process by which orders are filled or the training process through which new employees pass. Or you might consider depicting a process at school, such as registration, getting someone elected to student government, or applying for entrance into law or graduate school. Submit along with your flow chart a memo to your instructor providing a narrative description of the process, alluding at different points to the flow chart.

5. You work in the headquarters office of a trade association, The National Association of Office Equipment Retailers (NAOER). Part of your job is to present briefings on the operations, structure, and history of the association to new headquarters personnel. Design an organization chart that depicts the reporting relationships of the NAOER and write a one-page description of the organizational structure your chart describes. In your text refer at different points to the chart. The company is headed by the president. Two staff positions report directly to the president: the assistant to the president and the general counsel. All other officers occupy line positions. There are three vice-presidents, all of equal authority. Three officers of equal rank report to the vice-president of development: the managers of conferences, public relations, and membership services, respectively. Three officers of equal rank report to the vice-president of communications: a managing editor, a production manager, and an advertising director. The following officers of equal rank report to the vice-president of administrative services: the managers of administrative services, accounting, word processing, and data services, respectively.

6. Review several business periodicals, collecting several examples of various kinds of charts. In a memo to your instructor, write an analysis of each chart. Point up any unique features of the chart— good or bad. Where feasible, also mention alternative forms that might have been used to graph the same data and explain the advantages and limitations of each form. Submit photocopies of the charts along with your memo.

CHAPTER 10

Formal Reports

 his chapter offers techniques presented in the actual order you would follow for preparing a formal report. Note how these techniques cluster so that they form a problem-solving sequence:

Defining the Problem

1. Receiving your assignment
2. Gathering sources of information
3. Selecting sources for use in preparing your report

Analyzing the Problem

4. Creating a note card file
5. Developing a formal outline

From Decision Making to Drafting

6. Finding your focal idea
7. Drafting your introduction, report body, and conclusion

Revising and Editing

8. Making large-scale revisions
9. Making small-scale editing changes
10. Preparing a new copy of the introduction, body and conclusion
11. Adding support material (headings, abstract/executive summary, bibliography, tables, figures, appendixes, list of tables and figures, table of contents, and title page)
12. Proofreading
13. Transmitting the report

Do any of these 13 operations sound familiar? We certainly hope that *some* of them do! The problem-solving approach you have learned and applied so far is the same one you will use to prepare formal reports.

As you go through this chapter, you will see (1) more steps used to complete the report than are required for other writing forms and (2) a stricter sequence for those steps. In short, the nature of the writing process you follow will be similar, but the way you implement that process will be more complex and less flexible. By following the specified procedures in the suggested order, you can insure that your formal report will contain the elements necessary to communicate extended and complex information.

For this chapter, the ongoing example will be Joymar Savings and Loan. Joymar is a small bank with three suburban branches. It employs 43 workers, for whom it provides a group health plan covering hospital costs. We will explain more about the health plan as we introduce the techniques of formal report writing.

Receiving Your Assignment

In the business world superiors usually assign reports to their subordinates. Because so many reports are assigned, you will rarely, if ever, need to think up a report topic "from scratch." Either you will receive a specific assignment (for example, "Prepare a report detailing steps to improve our company's market position") or you will get a more general request ("Report on what you think are important trends in our industry so that we can plan marketing strategy"). Whether the assignment is explicit or general, the first thing to do is to *stop* and *think* about what you have been asked to do. Then, prepare a preliminary definition of your writing problem, as explained in chapter 1.

Preparing such a definition is just what Adam Daniels, Joymar's personnel director, does after receiving an open-ended report assignment. The bank president, Joan Kenmore, has asked Daniels to prepare a formal

report "discussing health insurance issues" that would be of interest to a
bank such as Joymar. Kenmore will share the report with Joymar's vice-
president, as well as with each of the three branch managers. Together with
Daniels, these executives will decide which benefit(s) to add to the present
health insurance plan. Daniels already has the results of a questionnaire
asking bank employees to rank in order of preference benefits they would
like added to their health plan.

With his questionnaire results as background, Daniels can jot down a
preliminary definition of the writing problem:

- *Objective*   To prepare a formal report pointing out major issues in
  employee health insurance. Issues selected for the report should appeal
  to a savings and loan institution that wishes to work with its employees
  to make needed changes in employee benefits.

- *Audience*   Two superiors (president and vice-president); three peers
  (three branch managers). All five have limited knowledge of the field of
  group health insurance.

- *Writer's desired image*   Informed (about insurance field), pertinent (to
  bank's situation), conservative (about making recommendations), sensitive (to employees' desires).

Gathering Sources of Information

With a preliminary definition in mind, Daniels begins searching for information to shape his report. Because of his need for a wide range of
current, specialized information, Daniels wants to supplement his questionnaire results with secondary source data. He will also interview a member of
the local insurance trade association to get information on employee health
insurance trends in the region. Note, however, that other formal reports
may require information from other sources—direct observation or experiments, for instance. To find the information he needs, Daniels follows this
sequence of activities to make his work as efficient as possible.

He Consults an Expert for Sources of Information on a Topic   For current
data on his topic, Daniels turns to a reference librarian at a local university
library. The librarian suggests that Daniels first check recent issues of
indexes listing articles on business topics and then consult the subject heading "insurance, health," in the card catalogue for book-length sources. (For
more information on business indexes and their use, please see chapter 8,
"Research.")

He Makes a List of Potentially Useful Bibliographic Sources   As he looks
through the indexes and card catalogue, Daniels finds titles that might be

pertinent to his report. Each time he finds a promising title, he jots down bibliographic information on an index card. In addition, Daniels specifies the library call letters/numbers for books so that he can find the sources themselves later.

He Follows a Consistent Bibliographic Style   In making his jottings, Daniels follows a consistent bibliographic style. By being consistent now, he will save time when he makes a list of references for the final report. At that point, Daniels will be able to transfer citations for the sources he actually uses from his original list to alphabetical order in a bibliography that will follow the text of his report.

To be consistent, Daniels decides to follow the bibliographic style recommended by the Modern Language Association (MLA). He might also have selected the style recommended by the American Psychological Association (APA) or by the University of Chicago. All of these style manuals require Daniels to use a shortened form of reference in the text of the document. Such a system is more efficient than one using numbered footnotes for each citation because it provides information without breaking a reader's train of thought.

Here are sample bibliographic entries for most sources you will use for formal reports. These entries are modeled on the form specified by the second edition of the *MLA Handbook for Writers of Research Papers*.[1] Once Daniels finds sources that may give him information, he will follow the format of the examples below in preparing a deck of bibliography cards for his report.

Signed article in a journal that numbers pages continuously throughout an annual volume:

> Fishburn, Peter C. "Foundations of Risk Measurement. I. Risk as Probable Loss." <u>Management Science</u> 30 (1984): 396-406.

Note: 30 is the volume number; 396–406 are page numbers.

Signed article in a journal that numbers pages in each issue from the beginning:

> Sheth, Jagdish. "Emerging Trends for the Retailing Industry." <u>Journal of Retailing</u> 59.3 (1983): 6-18.

Note: 59 is the volume number; 3 is the issue number.

---

[1]Joseph Gibaldi and Walter S. Achtert, *MLA Handbook for Writers of Research Papers*, 2d ed. (New York: Modern Language Association, 1984).

Signed article in a monthly magazine:

Hargrave, Sarah. "The Executive Alternative." Working Woman Feb.
1984: 94-96.

Note: Abbreviate all month names except for May, June, and July.

Unsigned article in a weekly magazine:

"Plans for a Big British Merger." Business Week 28 May 1984: 42.

Note: The day of the month comes before the name of the month.

Unsigned article in a newspaper:

"Greek Consumer Prices Up." The Wall Street Journal 25 May 1984,
sec. 2:32.

Note: If a newspaper is published in sections, give section numbers (Sec. 2)
before page numbers (32).

Book by one author:

Tivey, Leonard J. The Politics of the Firm. New York: St. Martin's, 1978.

Note: Use a shortened form of the publisher's full name (St. Martin's Press).

Book by two or three authors:

Louderback, Joseph G., III, and Geraldine F. Dominiak. Managerial
Accounting. Belmont: Wadsworth, 1975.

Notes: Only the first author's name is reversed. The second edition of the
MLA Handbook does not require state abbreviations following names of
American cities of publication.

Book by more than three authors:

Farish, Roger F., et al. Calculator Analysis for Business and Finance.
New York: McGraw-Hill, 1978.

Note: Et al. means "and others."

Book with institutional or corporate author:

American Institute of Certified Public Accountants. Taxation of the
Formation and Combination of Business Enterprises. New York:
AICPA, 1979.

Book with editor(s):

Brigham, Eugene F., and Ramon E. Johnson, eds. Issues in Managerial
Finance. Hinsdale: Dryden, 1976.

Book in edition other than first:

Wert, James E., and Glenn V. Henderson, Jr. <u>Financing Business Firms</u>. 6th ed. Homewood: R. D. Irwin, 1979.

Multivolume book:

Gallup, George H. <u>The Gallup Poll: Public Opinion 1972-1977</u>. 2 vols. Wilmington: Scholarly Resources, 1978.

Book in a series:

Gluck, Samuel E., ed. <u>Moral Values in Management Textbooks</u>. Series 14 of the Hofstra University Yearbook of Business. Hempstead: Hofstra University, 1979.

Selection from an edited anthology:

Kingshott, A. L. "Financial Forecasting." <u>The Role of Forecasting in Corporate Planning</u>. Ed. David Ashton and Leslie Simister. London: Staples Press, 1970.

Published conference proceedings:

<u>Proceedings: International Industrial Diamond Conference</u>. Chicago, 20-22 Oct. 1969. Moorestown: Diamond Association of America, 1970.

Note: Chicago was the site of the conference; Moorestown is the place of publication.

Government document:

United States. Small Business Administration. <u>Government Paperwork and Small Business: Problems and Solutions, Paperwork Measurement and Reduction Program</u>. Washington: GPO, 1979.

Unsigned reference work article:

"Gas Processing." <u>International Petroleum Encyclopedia</u>. 1980 ed.

Unpublished dissertation or thesis:

Myers, Mildred Sochatoff. "Written Communication at the Managerial and Professional/Technical Levels: A Case Study." Diss. Carnegie-Mellon U., 1981.

Interview:

Smith, Sharon. Personal Interview. 1 June 1984.

Personal letter:

Rivera, Inez. Personal Letter. 23 Oct. 1980.

Lecture notes:

Franco, Wayne. "Financial Forecasting." Lecture delivered to the Business Club, Fort Thomas, KY, 11 Sept. 1983.

Television show:

VanCaspel, Venita. "Financial Planning." Money Talk Marathon, Financial News Network. 28 May 1984.

After looking through several years' worth of indexes as well as the card catalogue at his library, Daniels compiles a deck of fourteen bibliography cards. Here are the first six cards from his deck:

"The Insurers' Big Push for Home Health Care."

Business Week 28 May 1984: 128 + .

Card 1

Note: The plus sign indicates that an article has discontinuous pagination. This article begins on page 128 and then skips to page 130.

Card 2

"Driving Down the Costs of an Aging America."

Business Week 26 Mar. 1984: 58-60.

Card 3

Norris, Eileen. "Insurers Rewrite Their Old

Marketing Policies." Advertising Age 26 Sept.

1983: M20-M21.

Card 4

Callet, David P., and Patricia A. Casey. "Health-

Care Plan Changes for the Older Employee:

The Employer as Primary Provider."

Employment Relations Today 10 (1983):

235-40.

Card 5

Cain, Carol. "Health Insurers Start Covering Liver

Procedures." Business Insurance 15 Aug.

1983: 1 +.

Card 6

Library of Congress Call Letters: HG 9383. H4x

Health Insurance Association of America. Health

and Health Insurance: The Public's View.

Washington: HIAA, Summer, 1982.

He Arranges Bibliography Cards in the Order Most Efficient for Finding the Actual Sources   After preparing his bibliography cards, Daniels separates cards with book titles from those with periodical titles. He uses his library's book location system (interlibrary loan, if necessary) to find the books he needs. Daniels then arranges periodical cards alphabetically by the periodical title from which they came. Bibliography cards from the same periodical are arranged with the most recent citation first. This arrangement will allow Daniels to request all the older issues of a periodical he needs at the same time should these issues be on microfilm or in closed stacks. By following this procedure, Daniels now has the six sample cards shown previously in this order: 6, 3, 5, 1, 2, 4.

Selecting Sources for Use in Preparing Your Report

In formal report writing, once you have your reference card deck in order, it is time to find and skim the sources listed on those cards. Notice the word *skim*, not *read*. A quick run through the document, checking its opening paragraphs, headings, illustrations, tables, closing paragraphs, and table of contents and index if it is a book can indicate whether the work is likely to be useful to your writing. If so, you should make a brief statement, called an *annotation,* about its contents at the bottom of the bibliography card. If skimming shows that the document seems to offer little that will help you, you can simply put the bibliography card aside. (Don't throw the card away. As you write your report, you *may* find that the document that once seemed irrelevant to your needs has become more closely related to your topic.)

Note how Daniels goes about selecting sources for his report. After skimming all 14 of the sources he found in the indexes, Daniels puts aside 2 cards—"Driving Down the Costs of an Aging America," because its contents are too general for his report, and an article entitled "Chrysler Hopes to Trim Health Costs 10%," because it focuses on procedures followed in a corporation that is much larger than Joymar Savings and Loan. Here are four samples of Daniels's annotations on the remaining cards:

Norris, Eileen. "Insurers Rewrite Their Old

Marketing Policies." Advertising Age

26 Sept. 1983: M20-M21.

(details recent changes in how health

insurance companies market their services)

Cain, Carol. "Health Insurers Start Covering Liver

Procedures." Business Insurance

15 Aug. 1983: 1 +.

(reports on added coverage for liver and

other types of organ transplants)

Jacobs, Bruce A. " 'Takin' Care' of High Medical

Costs." Industry Week 25 July 1983: 79.

(shows how one company enlisted employee

assistance in cutting health care costs)

Health Insurance Association of America.

Health and Health Insurance: The

Public's View. Washington: HIAA, Summer

1982.

(surveys Americans on various aspects

of the health insurance industry)

Having identified 12 of his original 14 sources as potentially useful, and having annotated their cards, Daniels is ready to read the sources. Because of the annotations, he has the option of either reading them now or returning to consult them later on, certain that he knows where to find the documents and what each is about.

Creating a Note Card File

While preparing a formal report, you should record important ideas, quotations, and data on index cards. Creating and arranging a note card deck are first steps in analyzing the writing problem. Here are several guidelines for preparing note cards and note card decks:

1. Write the author's name (or, if no author is specified, an abbreviated version of the title) on each note card.
2. If you have more than one source by the same author, write *both* the author's name *and* an abbreviated version of the title on each note card.
3. Write only one idea, quotation, or statistic on each note card; this limitation makes it easier to reorder information later.
4. Write on the note card the page number(s) from which you got the idea, quotation, or statistic; having the page number allows you to refer to the correct place in the source of your information.
5. If you copy a quotation that goes from the end of one source page to the start of the next page, specify where the page breaks the quotation. This enables you to select only a portion of the quotation for use in your report without having to go back to the source to see whether your excerpt comes from one page or both.
6. After completing the note card, place a heading at the top of that card to identify its subject—for example, General Information, Carriers Change Focus, Survey Sample.

Daniels follows these guidelines as he prepares a note card file. Figure 10.1 shows the annotated bibliography card and three note cards that Daniels prepares on Callet and Casey's article, "Health-Care Plan Changes for the Older Employee: The Employer as Primary Provider."

After reading his 12 sources, Daniels has a deck of 25 note cards. To these he adds note cards with material from his interview with Candace Williams of the local insurance trade association. He now reviews the cards to see whether they group themselves into topics in health insurance. After this review, the following headings emerge in his mind:

Callet, David P., and Patricia A. Casey.

"Health-Care Plan Changes for the Older

Employee: The Employer as Primary

Provider." Employment Relations Today,

10 (1983): 235-40.

(details employer responsibilities for

offering health plans to older employees)

Figure 10.1   Note cards from an annotated bibliography card. Article on health care and the older employee.

Annotated bibliography card

Callet and Casey 1

Summary

Discusses an aspect of the Tax Equity and Fiscal

Responsibility Act of 1982--primary health care

for employees 65-69 years of age.   (p. 235)

Note card 1

Callet and Casey 2

Equal Treatment

"Employers must provide health insurance

coverage to older workers 'under the same

conditions' as those under sixty-five. [PAGE

BREAK] Thus, if the health plan provided

to younger employees covers their spouses,

older employees' spouses must also be covered."

                    (pp. 237-38)

Note card 2

Note card 3

> Callet and Casey 3
>
> Key Rule
>
> Employers can't offer "supplemental" plans to Medicare. They must offer primary coverage.
>
> (p. 240)

Figure 10.1   Continued

General Information about Health Insurance
Public Awareness of Health Insurance Coverage
Coverage of New Procedures
Recent Laws Concerning Health Insurance
Employee Role in Managing Health Costs
Home Care Benefits
Dental Benefits
Outpatient Benefits
Psychological Benefits

He next arranges the cards so that they are grouped according to the headings. For the first three of these headings, the order of the cards becomes:

General Information about Health Insurance
    Jacobs 1, General Information
    Norris 1, Health Insurance Market
    Norris 2, Why Industry Interest in Marketing?
    Norris 3, Carriers Change Focus

Public Awareness of Health Insurance Coverage
>   Marquis 2, Factors Affecting Awareness
>   Marquis 3, Survey Conclusions
>   Marquis 4, Survey Recommendations
>   Marquis 5, Survey Sample

Coverage of New Procedures
>   Cain 1, Added Coverages
>   Cain 2, Liver Transplants

With the note card deck in this order, the main subdivisions of Daniels's report begin to emerge on paper. The first step in his problem analysis is therefore complete.

Developing a Formal Outline

In writing a report, you might think it unnecessary to prepare an outline *after* compiling an organized note card deck. The outline, however, allows you to refine your note card analysis in two ways:

1. It allows you to visualize how each topic relates to a previously mentioned topic or subtopic. Making these connections between topics can help you improve your report's coherence.
2. The outline shows where there are gaps in your information so that you can *go back to the earlier information-gathering step* and find details needed to make your report more convincing. The possibility that you may have to return to an earlier step to advance to a later one recalls our discussion in chapter 2 about the recursive nature of the problem-solving process.

For his health insurance report, Daniels uses an interpretive label outline to make his analysis specific enough to allow him to start drafting the report itself. Figure 10.2 shows his outline. Note that Daniels has included references to his note cards within the outline. When he drafts the report, he will know just where to look for specific items. He will also have quick access to his bibliographic information so that he can put references into his documents.

As an additional aid, Daniels puts *Joymar questionnaire* in parentheses whenever information on the outline comes from the bank's polling of its employees' preference for additional health insurance benefits. The parentheses let Daniels know when to cite the questionnaire in his report.

TRENDS IN HEALTH CARE INSURANCE

I. General information shows the industry growing and
changing.
   A. $287 billion U.S. health care expenditure (Jacobs 1)
   B. Annual growth 15 percent (Jacobs 1)
   C. Market for health insurance companies competitive
      1. Many large corporations funding own plans
         (Norris 2)
      2. Carriers competing over small companies
         (Norris 3)
   D. Changing technology forcing carrier flexibility
      (Norris 1)
II. Insurers are now covering innovative procedures.
   A. Heart transplants often covered (Cain 1)
   B. Liver transplants added recently (Cain 1)
      1. Liver transplants requiring six weeks in hospital
         (Cain 2)
      2. Liver transplants costing $70,000-$100,000
         (Cain 2)
III. Psychological benefits are being decreased by some
carriers.
   A. Lower priorities for employees (Joymar
      questionnaire)
   B. Private psychiatric hospitals increasing marketing
      efforts to counteract trend (Gordon 1)
IV. Dental insurance is being added by some companies.
   A. High priority for employees after hospital benefits
      (Joymar questionnaire)
   B. Data on dental coverage supporting its popularity
      1. In 1981, about 86 million Americans with dental
         coverage (HIAA Sourcebook 1)
      2. Forty-six percent of employees in HIAA survey
         with dental coverage (HIAA Sourcebook 2)
      3. Sixty percent of employees in HIAA survey with
         dental coverage also with orthodonture benefits
         (HIAA Sourcebook 2)
      4. In our region, 62 percent of employees with dental
         coverage (Williams interview 1)
      5. Eighty-eight percent of our region's employees
         covered by dental insurance also with
         orthodonture benefits (Williams interview 2)

Figure 10.2 Interpretive label outline for a formal report. Trends in health
care insurance.

Figure 10.2
Continued

   V. Outpatient benefits are good for both employer and
     employee.
     A. Survey showing more employee understanding of
       in-hospital than of outpatient services covered
       (Marquis 1)
     B. Outpatient costs generally less than hospital stays
      *1. No room costs
      2. Fewer nonmedical service staff needed
  VI. Home care benefits are a logical outgrowth of outpatient
     successes.
     A. Fifty-three percent of companies in survey with home
       care benefits (Insurers' Big Push 1)
      1. For example, nursing care
      2. For example, physical therapy
     B. Home care with typical savings of five days of hospital
       bills per situation (Insurers' Big Push 2)
     C. Doctors supportive of home care benefits as long as
       doctors order it (Insurers' Big Push 3)
      1. Doctors approving of psychological benefits
      2. Doctors approving of home atmosphere
 VII. Whatever benefits are offered, recent laws will have an
     effect on a company's health insurance plan.
     A. Tax Equity and Fiscal Responsibility Act of 1982
       affecting employers of older (65-69) workers (Callet
       and Casey 1)
      1. Requires equal treatment (Callet and Casey 2)
      2. Requires "primary" coverage for older workers
        (Callet and Casey 3)
     B. Bill H.R. 3021 covering benefit extensions to laid-off
       workers (Tarnoff 1)
      1. Ninety-day extension
      2. Same proportional employer/employee
        contribution
      3. Spouses and family members of workers eligible
     C. Pregnancy benefits required for male employees' wives
       (Oliver 1)
VIII. Employees can play a vital role in managing rising costs.
     A. Employees knowing that taking good care of
       themselves can cut health costs (Health and Health
       Insurance 1)
     B. Employees being consulted about priorities (Jacobs 2;
       Joymar questionnaire)
     C. Employees being educated to control own health costs
       (Levine 1)

Figure 10.2
Continued

IX. Companies ultimately need to increase employee
awareness of health insurance factors.
   A. Survey of 3,218 families (Marquis 5)
      1. Plan complexity effect on consumer understanding
         (Marquis 2)
      2. Consumers' misunderstanding of benefit details
         (Marquis 3)
      3. Survey recommendations (Marquis 4)
         a. Simplified benefit structures
         b. Consumer education
   B. Explaining Joymar questionnaire results to our
      employees (Joymar questionnaire)
      1. Our employees' priorities
      2. What implementing those priorities will cost
         a. Comparative cost
         b. Picking and choosing new benefits

Finally, Daniels puts an asterisk next to any outline subdivision for which he would like to find additional information. In figure 10.2, this asterisk appears next to the outline subdivision V.B.1. Daniels would like to find data that underscore his view that saving hospital room costs is a valuable benefit of outpatient care.

Daniels finds such data in the Health Insurance Association of America's *Sourcebook*. He makes up a new note card, HIAA Sourcebook 3, on which he records the fact that in 1980, 1981, and 1982, the cost for a hospital room for urban consumers increased over 43 percent, a pace far outstripping the increases in other medical costs. On the same card, Daniels specifies that he found this data on page 57 of the HIAA *Sourcebook*.

Daniels then revises section V. of his outline to look like this:

V. Outpatient benefits are good for both employer and employee.
   A. Survey showing more employee understanding of in-hospital than of outpatient services covered (Marquis 1)
   B. Outpatient costs generally less than hospital stays
      1. No room costs
         a. Room cost increase of over 43 percent during period 1980-82 (HIAA Sourcebook 3)
         b. Room costs outstrip physicians' fees, prescription items, and other medical costs during same period (HIAA Sourcebook 3)
      2. Fewer nonmedical service staff needed

Finding Your Focal Idea

Once you have revised your outline and have your note card deck handy, it is time to make some choices. The first decision involves stating a focal idea for the report. To do this, review your problem definition's objective. Then examine your outline. Can any specific statements in the outline be synthesized into a single, more general main point? If there are no such statements in the outline, can you write your own main point? Is that point compatible with your objective?

Daniels develops his focal idea by looking first at his outline's roman numeral I ("General information shows the industry growing and changing") and then merging that key point with those in roman numerals VIII ("Employees can play a vital role in managing rising costs") and IX ("Companies ultimately need to increase employee awareness of health insurance factors"). The resulting focal statement becomes: *With today's health insurance industry growing and changing, encouraging employees to take an active interest in the company health plan can help Joymar manage costs and meet employee needs.* With this statement as a reference point, Daniels will be able to double-check the pertinence of his data as he drafts the report.

Drafting

With your problem definition, data analysis, and focal idea complete, you can begin drafting the report. By following Daniels as he prepares his first draft, you will see how he uses his preliminary work to create each section of the draft.

Drafting Your
Introduction

Daniels considers two options for writing the introduction to the formal report from among those mentioned in chapter 3. He may look at all the main topics in his outline and use an introduction to "announce" them. Or he may take his roman numeral I topic and use the material about that topic to detail his first paragraph.

Because the heading "General information shows the industry growing and changing" leads logically to the later roman numeral topics, he selects the health care industry's dynamism as the controlling idea of his introduction.

Draft

Introduction

By expending $287 billion a year on health care, Americans have made medical insurance into a major industry (Jacobs, 1983). With annual national health care costs increasing at a rate of 15 percent, insurers can only see their business growing (Jacobs).

As they grow, health insurance companies must also change. Alarmed at skyrocketing premiums, many large corporations are starting to fund their own plans, forcing insurers to compete more vigorously for the business of smaller companies (Norris, 1983). In addition, rapidly changing technologies are forcing major rethinking of what is possible in medicine as opposed to what is affordable (Norris).

In addition to working from the beginning of his outline, Daniels has done the following things in his draft introduction:

1. *Changed to triple spacing.* By leaving additional space between lines of his draft, Daniels gives himself ample room to handwrite in changes when he revises the draft.
2. *Written two paragraphs.* The data under roman numeral I of the outline split logically into two subtopics, industry growth and industry change. Because Daniels saw both growth and change as necessary components of the general concept of industry dynamism, he dealt with each subtopic in its own paragraph. To tie the paragraphs together logically, he used the dependent clause "As they grow."
3. *Enclosed references in parentheses.* By including references in the rough draft, Daniels avoids having to hunt down which reference goes with what sentence in a revised draft and thus saves time later.

We suggest using a shortened author and date reference system for business sources:

For references with an author given, use the author's last name and the year of publication:

(Author, Year of Publication)

Examples:

(Tivey, 1978)
(Sippl and Dahl, 1979)
(Farish et al., 1978)

When no author is given, use the first item in the bibliographic entry as the first item in parentheses:

Examples:

(American Institute of Certified Public Accountants, 1979)
("Gas Processing," 1980)

When it is necessary to use more than one source by the same author, the year will generally identify the specific reference:

Example:

(James, 1983) or (James, 1984)

When there is more than one source by the same author published in the same year, a lowercase letter after the date distinguishes the references:

Example:

> (Roberts, 1984a) or (Roberts, 1984b)

Note: When the need for lowercase letters arises, marking those letters at the end of the corresponding bibliography card will identify which source yielded which data.

Example:

> Roberts, Paul Craig. "The Current Wisdom on the Trade Deficit is Dead Wrong." <u>Business Week</u> 26 Mar. 1984: 21. (a)
> Roberts, Paul Craig. "Hard Evidence That Dispels Myths about the Deficit." <u>Business Week</u> 21 May 1984: 22. (b)

Citations to sources appear in parentheses in the text as follows: If a sentence mentions neither author nor year, the reference appears at a natural pause in the sentence as soon as possible after the idea or data drawn from the source:

Examples:

> Insurers are adding pancreas transplants to covered services (Cain, 1983).
> One insurance survey (Marquis, 1983) questioned American families.

If the sentence mentions the author but not the year of publication, only the year appears in parentheses immediately following the author's name:

Example:

> Marquis (1983) surveyed 3,218 American families about their health insurance benefits.

If the sentence mentions the year but not the author, the author (or first bibliographic item if no author is given) appears in parentheses immediately following the year:

Example:

> Results of a survey of American families' health insurance benefits were published in 1983 (Marquis).

If the sentence mentions *both* the author *and* the year of publication, no parenthetical reference is necessary:

Example:

> In a 1983 article, M. Susan Marquis reports on a survey of American families' health insurance benefits.

When a reference is a direct quotation, page number(s) of the source from which the quotation was drawn appear immediately after the year of publication:

Example (short quotation):

> In a national poll, 69 percent of the 1,500 Americans questioned agreed that "encouraging people to take better care of themselves will significantly reduce health care costs" (Health Insurance Association of America, 1982, p. 16).

Example (quotation of four or more lines, indented, blocked, and not set off by quotation marks):

> Every year the Health Insurance Association of America publishes a sourcebook of Health Insurance Data. Each edition
>> provides the latest available data on major forms of health insurance: hospital, surgical, physician's expense, major medical, disability and dental insurance. Also included is information on medical care costs, morbidity and health manpower in the United States. The data have been compiled from reports of insurance companies and other health insurance plans, government agencies and hospital and medical associations. (Public Relations Division, 1982/83, p. 3)

When more than one source supports a particular statement, references to all those sources appear within the same parentheses; a semicolon separates citations. Citations normally appear in chronological order, but when two or more references have the same publication date, they are arranged alphabetically by authors' surnames:

Example:

> Several researchers have surveyed the health insurance field (Health Insurance Association of America, 1982/83; Marquis, 1983; "Insurers' Big Push for Home Health Care," 1984).

Later references to an already cited work need not repeat the year of publication (unless the year is necessary to distinguish between two works by the same author or between works by authors with the same last name):

Example:

> The cost of employee benefits has escalated rapidly this decade (Jason, 1984). Now hundreds of employers report the need to cut back on many plans (Jason).

If the drafted introduction concludes with a logical lead-in to topics handled in the bulk of the outline, then drafting the main body of the formal report can begin immediately. Otherwise, it may be necessary to construct

Drafting the Body of Your Report

your own lead-in using the transitional devices discussed in chapter 3.

Daniels's last sentence in his introduction presents the idea of new health care technologies. He is thus able to use a simple transitional device such as referring back to previous information with a demonstrative adjective (*these*). (*Note:* This draft contains wording, spelling, and other errors that Daniels will correct through small-scale editing.)

Draft

<u>Body of Formal Report</u>

These technologies are causing insurance companies to change their benefit packages. For example, many carriers now offer heart transplant benefits (Cain, 1983). An even more recent development, liver transplant survery, has also been added by some companies (Cain). These new procedures are hardly small items. A typical liver transplant requires six weeks of hospital care and costs from $70,000 to $100,000 (Cain).

At the same time that carriers are adding new procedures, some employers are dropping other benefits in an attempt to control premium costs. Hard hit among these coverages is psychological or psychiatric care. Private psychiatric hospitals have launched a marketing campaign to counteract this trend (Gordon, 1983). The magazine ad campaign depicts harried, troubled executives who have regained mental well-being and productivity through access to psychological or psychiatric care (Gordon). However, our own in-house questionnaire results (see table 1) support industry findings that such benefits are lower priorities for employers than others.

For Joymar Savings and Loan employees, it is clear that a dental plan would be the most welcome addition to our present coverages. Available data on dental insurance support its popularity. As of 1981, approximately 86 million Americans held dental coverage of one sort or another (HIAA, 1982/83). A Health Insurance Association of America survey suggests that 46 percent of the of American workers have dental coverage and that 60 percent of those possess orthodonture benefits (HIAA, 1982/83). According to Candace Williams of our local insurance association, our regional figures are even higher (62 percent of employees with dental coverage, 88 percent of those with orthodonture). The orthodonture benefit was adjudged a particularly desirable part of overall dental coverage by our own employees.

What other coverages are popular? Another type of coverage being widely promoted by insurance companies and their clients alike is outpatient service. In her article for the Health Care Financing Review (1983), M. Susan Marquis reported that employees generally understand such services less well than they do the more typically covered in-hospital costs. However, if we keep in mind that in-hospital costs have grown at a far faster rate than all other aspects of medical coverage in recent years[1], we can understand why employers favor outpatient care when feasible. At the very

least such care saves on room costs. In addition, it requires considerably

fewer nonmedical service staff to deliver.

One logical outgrowth of the popularity of outpatient coverage is the

recent push for increased home care benefits. In home care, even the

overhead associated with outpatient services in a hospital or medical center

can be reduced or eliminated. Benefits consultants have found that about 53

percent of the companies they have surveyed now have home care coverage

("Insurers' Big Push, 1984). Among the covered services are home nursing

care and physical therapy. According to Kathleen M. Daley of Connecticut

General Life Insurance Company, "We estimate that you save five days of

hospital bills for each home care situation" ("Insurers' Big Push," 1984,

p. 128). Physicians echo employers and insurers' enthusiasm. As long as

they are in control of ordering use of home care and as long as such use is

appropriate to a case, doctors believe that home care has particular

psychological benefits for the patient who can be treated in the familiar

surroundings of the home ("Insurers' Big Push").

Whether Joymar Savings and Loan offers its employees transplant,

dental, psychological or psychiatric, outpatient, home care, and/or other

types of benefits, it will have to consider the impact of recent legislation upon whatever decisions it makes. One law, the Tax Equity and Fiscal

Responsibility Act of 1982, has particular impact on employees aged 65

through 69. In particular, this act requires that employers provide such

employees treatment equal to that offered younger workers in the form of

"primary"[2] health insurance coverage (Callet and Casey, 1983).

A second law, Bill H.R. 3021, deals with benefits extended to laid-off

workers. H.R. 3021 specifies that all benefits offered employees must be

offered to laid-off personnel for a period of 90 days after termination

(Tarnoff, 1983). Furthermore, employers must contribute the same

proporation of the employee's former salary to the cost of the benefits as they

did when the worker was employed (Tarnoff). Yet another provision of H.R.

3021 mandates that laid-off workers' spouses and family members continue

to be eligible for the same benefits as when the wage earner was employed

(Tarnoff).

Another ruling to keep in mind is the 1978 emendation of the 1964 Civil

Rights Act, Title VII. By the 1978 ruling, pregnancy benefits must be given to

male employees' wives if spouses are typically covered under other

provisions of a company health plan (Oliver, 1983).

With all this recent legislation, with costs skyrocketing, and with options

increasing, it is important to engage employees in management of health care policies, costs, and choices. A first step, which we have already taken at Joymar, is to consult employees about their health coverage priorities (Jacobs). Educating workers about the realities of today's health care should accompany such consultation. Some information is generally known. For example, surveys show that some principles of health care, such as knowledge that taking care of oneself can cut health costs, is generally acknowledged among employees (HIAA, 1982).

However, other facts are less understood. Marquis's survey of 3,218 American families revealed that many consumers do not understand the finer points of their coverages. In essence, employee understanding of a plan varies inversely with that plan's complexity (Marquis). What is needed, says Marquis, is a two-pronged attack: simplification of benefit structures and intensified consumer education.

Because we already know what Joymar's employees favor by way of added benefits, consumer education would mean explaining to our personnel such factors as the comparative costs of various coverages or ways to modify existing benefits to accommodate new ones. Simplification of the benefit structure is a responsibility of management. We can certainly request that our present carrier simplify policy language. We can also ask that our insurer make company personnel available to answer employee questions.

Explanatory footnotes:

1. The United States Department of Labor's Bureau of Labor Statistics reports that whereas "hospital room" costs went up 43.6 percent during the period 1980-82, the increase for "all medical care items" was only 33.3 percent (HIAA, 1982/83, p. 57).

2. "Primary" health coverage denotes the main or first-line source of insurance, as opposed to "supplementary" insurance, which would cover the difference between Medicare payments and actual billed medical costs. Needless to say, primary insurance premiums are far higher than supplementary premiums.

As Daniels drafts the body of the formal report, he does the following:

1. *Uses explanatory footnotes when appropriate.* Even though the documentation styles we recommend dispense with footnotes for citing references and direct quotations, these systems still offer the option of using explanatory footnotes. Such notes communicate material that is potentially interesting to a reader but not so closely related to the report topic that it can appear in the document text without disrupting a reader's train of thought. Daniels uses explanatory footnotes to accomplish two purposes—namely, providing detailed statistics tangential to the report and defining a technical term (*primary coverage*) with which the bank executives might not be familiar.

   Daniels directs his audience's attention to explanatory footnotes by placing a raised (superscript) arabic number after the word, phrase, or sentence to receive further discussion in his footnote. He numbers the footnotes consecutively throughout his report.

2. *Refers to supporting tables, figures, and illustrations.* Drafting is the time to direct readers to any materials that will clarify their understanding of the report. As with parenthetical references, specifying those tables

during drafting can save time later. For information on constructing tables and other graphic aids, see chapter 9.

3. *Supplies logical transitions.* If the outline is serving its purpose—providing main ideas for topic sentences and supporting details—then you can concentrate on making those sentences connect smoothly. In Daniels's draft, making such connections means using the strategies discussed in chapter 4 (for example, demonstrative pronouns and transitional words and phrases).

Drafting Your Conclusion

We offer no special advice for drafting the conclusion of a formal report. Rather, we refer you to the discussion in chapter 3. As with every other business writing form, the conclusion is a chance to underscore your objective. Take advantage of this opportunity by summarizing what you have already written, explaining how the report body meets your objective, or making a call for action, whichever is appropriate to your document.

Here is Daniels's drafted conclusion. As you examine it, keep in mind that his objective is to prepare a report about health insurance trends of interest to a savings and loan association that wishes to work with its employees to make needed changes in benefits.

Draft

Conclusion

To explain the pros, cons, and costs of various benefits to employees, the committee considering coverage changes must first understand them clearly themselves. Three actions can prove especially helpful to the committee. The first is to call in a representative from the present carrier to explain current coverage in detail. The second is to request literature from our present carrier as well as from various other carriers about the benefit additions found desirable by our personnel. Finally, we should interview representatives of insurance companies whose promotional literature seems to offer the clear benefit structures including the particular coverages

preferred by Joymar's employees. Through consultation with insurance

professionals and our employees and among ourselves, we should be able to

obtain a desirable policy at a manageable cost.

Making Large-Scale Revisions

The fact that formal reports often rely heavily on ideas and data garnered from printed sources adds a particular caution to large-scale revision. Whereas changing the way we state a particular idea in a letter, memo, or informal report may simply require us to rethink what we want to say and then write that thought down, revising a formal report idea may mean we have changed *someone else's* thoughts. Fortunately, if we have specified our parenthetical references during drafting, as we revise we can distinguish our ideas from those we have taken from others.

Figure 10.3 shows Daniels's large-scale revisions of the first seven paragraphs of his draft report. Note that he makes different types of large-scale revisions. For instance, in paragraph 2, he increases the accuracy of his details by specifying that insurers are competing not only for small but also for medium-sized companies' business. He adds, then discards all of paragraph 4 because debate over the morality of live organ transplants and artificial organ implants departs from the report problem definition. In paragraph 7, he eliminates an extraneous detail. Daniels also double-checks to make certain each of his paragraphs gets to its main point clearly and at the right time. For instance, he deletes the first sentence of paragraph 7 so that his main point begins the paragraph. By double-checking his draft against this outline, Daniels is satisfied with his report's organization and chooses to make no revisions to the document's overall arrangement.

Introduction

PARAGRAPH [1]

By expending $287 billion a year on health care, Americans

have made medical insurance into a major industry (Jacobs, 1983).

With annual national health care costs increasing at a rate of 15

percent, insurers can only see their business growing (Jacobs).

[2]

As they grow, health insurance companies must also

change. Alarmed at skyrocketing premiums, many large

corporations are starting to fund their own plans, forcing

insurers to compete more vigorously for the business of smaller *and medium-sized*

companies (Norris, 1983). In addition, rapidly changing

technologies are forcing major rethinking of what is possible in

medicine as opposed to what is affordable (Norris).

Body of Formal Report

[3]

These technologies are causing insurance companies to

change their benefit packages. For example, many carriers now

offer heart transplant benefits (Cain, 1983). An even more recent

Figure 10.3 Large-scale revisions of a formal report draft. Health insurance industry trends.

Figure 10.3
Continued

development, liver transplant survery, has also been added by

some companies (Cain). These new procedures are ~~hardly small~~ *extremely expensive*

items. A typical liver transplant requires six weeks of hospital

care and costs from $70,000 to $100,000 (Cain).

~~We have only to look at current controversies over the~~   **[4]**

~~morality of organ transplants to see how touchy a subject this is.~~

~~Now that artificial organ implants have joined live organ~~

~~transplants as well-publicized procedures, the arguments rage~~

~~even more fiercely.~~

At the same time that carriers are adding new procedures,   **[5]**

some employers are dropping other benefits in an attempt to

control premium costs. Hard hit among these coverages is

psychological or psychiatric care. Private psychiatric hospitals

have launched a marketing campaign to counteract this trend

(Gordon, 1983). The magazine ad campaign depicts ^*formerly* harried,

troubled executives who have regained mental well-being and

productivity through access to psychological or psychiatric care

(Gordon). However, our own in-house questionnaire results (see

Figure 10.3
Continued

table 1) support industry findings that such benefits are lower

priorities for employe*e*s than others.

[6]

    For Joymar Savings and Loan employees, it is clear that a

dental plan would be the most welcome addition to our present

coverages. Available data on dental insurance support its

popularity. As of 1981, approximately 86 million Americans held

dental coverage of one sort or another (HIAA, 1982/83). A Health

Insurance Association of America survey suggests that 46 percent

of the of American workers have dental coverage and that 60

percent of those possess orthodonture benefits (HIAA, 1982/83).

According to Candace Williams of our local insurance association,

our regional figures are even higher (62 percent of employees

with dental coverage, 88 percent of those with orthodonture). The

orthodonture benefit was adjudged a particularly desirable part of

overall dental coverage by our own employees.

[7]

    ~~What other coverages are popular? Another type of~~ *Insurance companies*
and their clients alike are promoting outpatient
~~coverage being widely promoted by insurance companies and~~
service widely.
~~their clients alike is outpatient service.~~ In her article for the

Figure 10.3
Continued

Health Care Financing Review (1983), M. Susan Marquis

reported that employees generally understand such services less

well than they do the more typically covered in-hospital costs.

However, if we keep in mind that in-hospital costs have grown at

a far faster rate than all other aspects of medical coverage in

recent years[1], we can understand why employers favor outpatient

care ~~when feasible~~. At the very least such care saves on room

costs. In addition, it requires considerably fewer nonmedical

service staff to deliver.

Making Small-Scale Editing Changes

You need to check parenthetical references, footnotes, and tables as well as the text of the report to make necessary changes in sentence structure, wording, and mechanics. Because formal reports often contain many proper names and statistics, you need to check back to your bibliography and note cards if you think you might have misspelled a name or incorrectly typed a set of numbers.

Figure 10.4 shows Daniels's small-scale editing changes to the remaining first six paragraphs of his draft. Note that Daniels deletes words in paragraph 4 to ensure conciseness. Also, in paragraph 4, Daniels adds a phrase with a demonstrative pronoun ("In spite of *these* efforts") to increase his report's coherence. In paragraph 5, Daniels deletes unintended extra words; later in the report, he makes such mechanical changes as correcting misspellings and adding needed punctuation marks. In paragraph 6, Daniels places the explanatory footnote number after the comma to conform with MLA style. You can note all of Daniels's mechanical changes by contrasting the first draft of his report as it appears in the text of this chapter with the final version of his report as shown in figure 10.5.

Introduction

By expending $287 billion a year on health care, Americans

have made medical insurance into a major industry (Jacobs,

1983). With annual national health care costs increasing at a rate

of 15 percent, insurers can only see their business growing (Jacobs).

As they grow, health insurance companies must also change.

Alarmed at skyrocketing premiums, many large corporations are

starting to fund their own plans, forcing insurers to compete

more vigorously for the business of small and medium-sized

companies (Norris, 1983). In addition, rapidly changing

technologies are forcing major rethinking of what is possible in

medicine as opposed to what is affordable (Norris).

Body of Formal Report

These technologies are causing insurance companies to

change their benefit packages. For example, many carriers now

offer heart transplant benefits (Cain, 1983). An even more recent

development, liver transplant surgery, has also been added by

some companies (Cain). All of these new procedures are extremely

PARAGRAPH [1]

[2]

[3]

Figure 10.4   Small-scale editing changes in a formal report draft.
Health insurance industry trends.

Figure 10.4
Continued

expensive items. A typical liver transplant requires six weeks of

hospital care and costs from $70,000 to $100,000 (Cain).

At the same time that carriers are adding new procedures,

[4]   some employers are dropping other benefits in an attempt to

control premium costs. Hard hit among these coverages is

psychological or psychiatric care. Private psychiatric hospitals

have launched a marketing campaign to counteract this trend

(Gordon, 1983). The magazine ad campaign depicts formerly

harried, troubled executives who have regained mental well-being

and productivity through ~~access to~~ psychological or psychiatric

In spite of these efforts,
care (Gordon). ~~However~~, our own in-house questionnaire results
             ∧

(see table 1) support industry findings that psychiatric benefits

are lower priorities for employees than others.

For Joymar Savings and Loan employees, it is clear that a

[5]   dental plan would be the most welcome addition to our present

coverages. Available data on dental insurance support its popularity.

As of 1981, approximately 86 million Americans held dental

coverage of one sort or another (HIAA, 1982/83). A Health

Figure 10.4
Continued

Insurance Association of America survey suggests that 46 percent ~~of the~~ of American workers have dental coverage and that 60 percent of those possess orthodonture benefits (HIAA, 1982/83). According to Candace Williams of our local insurance association, our regional figures are even higher (62 percent of employees with dental coverage, 88 percent of those with orthodonture). The orthodonture benefit was adjudged a particularly desirable part of overall dental coverage by our own employees.

Insurance companies and their clients alike are promoting outpatient service widely. In her article for the <u>Health Care Financing Review</u> (1983), M. Susan Marquis reported that employees generally understand such services less well than they do the more typically covered in-hospital costs. However, if we keep in mind that in-hospital costs have grown at a ~~far~~ *much* faster rate than all other aspects of medical coverage in recent years, we can understand why employers favor outpatient care. At the very least such care saves on room costs. In addition, it requires considerably fewer nonmedical service staff to deliver.

[6]

Preparing a New Copy

Because he has made so many deletions, insertions, and other changes, Daniels finds it helpful to prepare a fresh copy of the report. With this revised draft complete, he is ready to add necessary supporting materials.

Adding Supporting Materials

We now come to the part of formal report preparation concerned with supplementing the report text. Headings, abstracts, bibliographies, appendixes, page numbers, lists of tables and figures, and title pages all help readers of formal reports find the information they want and understand it better once they find it.

Headings

Headings are the labels that identify major segments of a report. These labels help a reader in several ways. They (1) announce major new topics within the report; (2) break up the text into apparent subdivisions; (3) show logical relationships among topics; and (4) highlight the writer's view of the relative importance of topics. To get these benefits from headings, you should decide which headings are your most general ("first level"), next most general ("second level"), and so on. Then you should follow a consistent format for displaying them.

Heading Level	Used For	Typing Conventions
FIRST	REPORT TITLE	ALL CAPITALS; CENTERED ON TITLE PAGE
Second	Introduction, Conclusion, Main Topics	Upper and Lowercase; Centered on Page; Underlined
Third	Subtopics within Body of Report	Upper and Lowercase; Centered; Triple Space Above/Below; Not Underlined
Fourth	Sub-subtopics	Upper and Lowercase; Triple Space Above; Flush with Left Margin; Underlined

There are lower-level headings, but they are so specific that they are more appropriate for books than for formal reports. Because Daniels's document is relatively short as formal reports go, his headings reach only to the second level:

TRENDS IN EMPLOYEE HEALTH INSURANCE

Introduction

New Medical Technologies

Psychiatric/Psychological Coverage

Dental Benefits

Outpatient Provisions

Home Care Plans

Recent Legislation

Employees' Role in Health Care Plans

Management Responsibilities

Conclusion

Had Daniels's report been longer, he might have used lower-level headings in this way:

TRENDS IN EMPLOYEE HEALTH INSURANCE

Introduction

New Medical Technologies

Heart Transplants

Liver Transplants

Pancreas Transplants

Psychiatric/Psychological Coverage

Daniels draws his headings from his outline. Each heading, other than the introduction and conclusion, contains the essential information communicated by a roman numeral label from the outline. Thus the second heading, New Medical Technologies, comes from roman numeral II ("Insurers are now covering innovative procedures"); the third heading, Psychiatric/Psychological Coverage, comes from roman numeral III ("Psychological benefits are being decreased by some carriers"), and so on.

Alternatively, Daniels might have used the roman numeral labels themselves as a way of summarizing each section of the report. The choice to extract headings from an outline or to use the outline labels as they are depends on your objective and desired image. In general, the headings extracted from the outline are effective in reports whose key objective is to inform readers. The complete outline label with its additional information may serve as a forceful way to emphasize major points in a report whose objective is to persuade readers.

Abstracts

An abstract distills the material in a formal report. Generally shorter than 150 words, the abstract lets your reader grasp the report's essence quickly. You should state the most important points in your report as concisely as possible and in the order in which they appear in the report. A busy executive reading the abstract can then decide whether to read the entire report immediately or put it aside for later examination. Indeed, some writers refer to abstracts as *executive summaries*.

Abstracts appear immediately before the first page of the formal report text. Here is Daniels's abstract of the health insurance report. He has prepared it *after* revising the report so that it reflects what is actually in the final document.

Draft

Abstract

Employee health insurance is a growing, changing industry. Carriers are offering new medical technologies in benefit packages but withdrawing other more familiar coverages. Dental benefits are very popular with employees, while employers and insurance companies are pushing outpatient and in-home care. Recent legislation forces employers to rethink aspects of employee health plans. Getting the best plan for the money will now mean getting employees involved in cost control and requiring management to take on added policy-making responsibilities.

Daniels's abstract of approximately 85 words states the gist of his report. His readers will have to look at the document itself for details.

A bibliography (sometimes known as a *reference list*) tells readers where they can obtain further information on sources cited in the report. You create this bibliography by going through the revised report from beginning to end. Each time you come to a reference, take the corresponding bibliography card and put it aside. After looking through the entire report, you should have a stack of bibliography cards—one for each work cited.

Next, arrange the bibliography cards in alphabetical order by the last name of a source's author. If there are works by authors with the same surname, the first names serve as alphabetizers. For multiple works by the same author, alphabetize by title. When no author is given, the first item on each bibliography card (for example, the title) is the alphabetizing element.

Take the alphabetized card deck and copy its information, double-spacing between lines and indenting the second and subsequent lines of each entry.

Daniels's bibliography appears in figure 10.5 immediately after the last page of the report text. Although this final list cites all sources quoted or paraphrased in the report, it does not contain all of the sources recorded on his annotated bibliography cards assembled when he was selecting information. In writing the report, he finds no need to include material from Hermine Zagat Levine's article, "Can Skyrocketing Employee Healthcare Costs Be Contained?" Daniels thus exercises selectivity throughout the problem-solving process.

When you wish to include all the numerical data from your direct observation, questionnaires, or experiments, use a table. Tables let you take such statistics out of the report text, where they would be confusing, and place them immediately after the text. Daniels's table in figure 10.5 shows clearly the results of the Joymar questionnaire. The title of the table gives the origin of the statistics. The table's subtitles state clearly what information they subsume. Daniels arranges the table's rows logically by the alphabetical order of the benefits; he arranges the columns in order of descending employee preference for each listed benefit.

Note that Daniels uses a parenthetical comment ("See table 1") to refer his readers to the questionnaire results. By looking at the table, readers will quickly learn that the dental benefit is the overwhelming first preference of Joymar employees, a fact which Daniels hopes to underscore. When you wish to include supporting graphs, charts, and other illustrations with your report, identify them as figures. Refer your reader by number to an appropriate figure (for instance, "See figure 1 for a pie graph showing distribution of our company's health insurance expenses by type of benefit"). For a detailed discussion of such figures, see chapter 9, "Using Graphs and Illustrations."

Bibliography

Tables and Figures

Appendix

Appendixes contain extra material that will be useful to your reader but that does not belong in the text of the report. For instance, the appendix might include copies of related correspondence, lists of individuals in a group referred to collectively in the report, or reproductions of documents used to gather data for the report. Each appendix receives a title so that your reader can find its location and topic by looking at the report's table of contents. Many of the items that might go into an appendix are lengthy. Before appending them, ask yourself whether these items will be so useful to your reader that their benefits justify the time they will take to read.

In his health care insurance report, Daniels places the questionnaire used to discover employee benefit preferences in an appendix. This appendix appears immediately after the bibliography in figure 10.5.

Pagination

Number formal reports with arabic numbers starting with the first page of the text. Place numbers at the bottom center or top right corner of each page except page 1, which receives no number. Number all material *after* the title page and *before* the first page of the report text with lowercase roman numerals (i, ii, iii, iv, v . . .).

List of Tables and Figures

Make a list of all tables and/or figures in the report in the order they appear. Specify the word *figure* or *table*, the number, and the title:

LIST OF FIGURES AND TABLES

Because Adam Daniels's report has only one table, his list will be short. That list appears in figure 10.5 immediately before the abstract.

Table of Contents

The table of contents comes immediately before the list of tables and figures if there is one. Otherwise it precedes the abstract. The locations of the list of tables/figures, abstract, all headings, bibliography, and appendixes should be shown in the table of contents. See figure 10.5 for the health care report's table of contents.

Place the title page in front of all other material. Center the title of the report (in all capital letters) halfway down the page. Ten lines below the report title, place the name(s) of the author(s) of the report (centered, upper and lowercase). On the following line, place the title(s) of the author(s) (centered, upper and lowercase). On the next line, place the name of the company (centered, upper and lowercase). See figure 10.5 for Daniels's title page.

Title Page

Proofreading

Proofreading a formal report, like revising it, can be tricky because of its statistics, bibliography, and other specialized supporting materials. Take your time and double-check your tables and bibliography. Follow all of our proofreading advice from chapter 4 as well. Figure 10.5 shows Daniels's complete formal report after proofreading.

TRENDS IN EMPLOYEE HEALTH CARE

Adam Daniels
Personnel Director
Joymar Savings and Loan Association

Figure 10.5 Complete formal report

Figure 10.5
Continued

TABLE OF CONTENTS

i

Figure 10.5
Continued

LIST OF TABLES AND FIGURES

ii

Figure 10.5
Continued

ABSTRACT

Employee health insurance is a growing, changing industry. Carriers are offering new medical technologies in benefit packages but withdrawing other, more familiar coverages. Dental benefits are very popular with employees, while employers and insurance companies are pushing outpatient and in-home care. Recent legislation forces employers to rethink aspects of employee health plans. Getting the best plan for the money will now mean getting employees involved in cost control and requiring management to take on added policy-making responsibilities.

iii

Figure 10.5
Continued

<u>Introduction</u>

By expending $287 billion a year on health care, Americans have made medical insurance into a major industry (Jacobs, 1983). With annual national health care costs increasing at a rate of 15 percent, insurers can only see their business growing (Jacobs).

As they grow, health insurance companies must also change. Alarmed at skyrocketing premiums, many large corporations are starting to fund their own plans, forcing insurers to compete more vigorously for the business of small and medium-sized companies (Norris, 1983). In addition, rapidly changing technologies are forcing major rethinking of what is possible in medicine as opposed to what is affordable (Norris).

<u>New Medical Technologies</u>

These technologies are causing insurance companies to change their benefit packages. For example, many carriers now offer heart transplant benefits (Cain, 1983). An even

Figure 10.5
Continued

more recent development, liver transplant surgery, has also been added by some companies (Cain). All of these new procedures are extremely expensive items. A typical liver transplant requires six weeks of hospital care and costs from $70,000 to $100,000 (Cain).

Psychiatric/Psychological Coverage

At the same time that carriers are adding new procedures, some employers are dropping other benefits in an attempt to control premium costs. Hard hit among these coverages is psychological or psychiatric care. Private psychiatric hospitals have launched a marketing campaign to counteract this trend (Gordon, 1983). The magazine ad campaign depicts formerly harried, troubled executives who have regained mental well-being and productivity through psychological or psychiatric care (Gordon). In spite of these efforts, our in-house questionnaire results (see table 1) support industry findings that psychiatric benefits are lower priorities for employees than others.

2

Figure 10.5
Continued

<u>Dental Benefits</u>

For Joymar Savings and Loan employees, it is clear

that a dental plan would be the most welcome addition to

our present coverages. Available data on dental insurance

support its popularity. As of 1981, approximately 86

million Americans held dental coverage of one sort or

another (HIAA, 1982/83). A Health Insurance Association

of America survey suggests that 46 percent of American

workers have dental coverage and that 60 percent of those

possess orthodonture benefits (HIAA, 1982/83). According

to Candace Williams of our local insurance association, our

regional figures are even higher (62 percent of employees

with dental coverage, 88 percent of those with

orthodonture). The orthodonture benefit was adjudged a

particularly desirable part of overall dental coverage by our

own employees.

<u>Outpatient Provisions</u>

Insurance companies and their clients alike are

promoting outpatient service widely. In her article for the

3

Figure 10.5
Continued

Health Care Financing Review (1983), M. Susan Marquis

reported that employees generally understand such

services less well than they do the more typically covered

in-hospital costs. However, if we keep in mind that

in-hospital costs have grown at a much faster rate than all

other aspects of medical coverage in recent years,[1] we can

understand why employers favor outpatient care. At the

very least such care saves on room costs. In addition, it

requires considerably fewer nonmedical service staff to

deliver.

Home Care Plans

One logical outgrowth of outpatient coverage's

popularity is the recent push for increased home care

benefits. Through home care, even the overhead associated

with outpatient services can be reduced or eliminated.

Benefits consultants have found that about 53 percent of

the companies they have surveyed now have home care

coverage ("Insurers' Big Push," 1984). Among the services

covered are home nursing care and physical therapy.

According to Kathleen M. Daley of Connecticut General Life

4

Figure 10.5
Continued

Insurance Company, "We estimate that you save five days of hospital bills for each home care situation" ("Insurers' Big Push," 1984, p. 128). Physicians echo employers' and insurers' enthusiasm. Doctors believe that treating patients in familiar surroundings has particular psychological benefits ("Insurers' Big Push").

Recent Legislation

Whether Joymar Savings and Loan offers its employees transplant, dental, psychological/psychiatric, outpatient, home care, and/or other types of benefits, it will have to consider the impact of recent legislation upon its decisions. One law, the Tax Equity and Fiscal Responsibility Act of 1982, has particular impact on employees aged 65 through 69. This act requires that employers provide older employees treatment equal to that offered younger workers in the form of "primary"[2] health insurance coverage (Callet and Casey, 1983).

A second law, Bill H.R. 3021, deals with benefits extended to laid-off workers. H.R. 3021 specifies that all

5

Figure 10.5
Continued

benefits offered employees must also be offered to laid-off

personnel for a period of 90 days after termination

(Tarnoff, 1983). Furthermore, employers must contribute

the same proportion of the employee's former salary to the

cost of the benefits as they did when the worker was

employed (Tarnoff). Yet another provision of H.R. 3021

mandates that laid-off workers' spouses and family

members continue to be eligible for the same benefits

(Tarnoff).

Another ruling to keep in mind is the 1978 emendation

of the 1964 Civil Rights Act, Title VII. By the 1978 ruling,

employers must give pregnancy benefits to male employees'

wives if spouses are typically covered under other

provisions of a company health plan (Oliver, 1983).

Employees' Role in Health Care Plans

With all this recent legislation, with costs

skyrocketing, and with options increasing, it is important

to engage employees in managing health care policies,

costs, and choices. A first step, which we have already

6

Figure 10.5
Continued

taken at Joymar, is to consult employees about their health

coverage priorities (Jacobs). Educating workers about the

realities of today's health care should accompany such

involvement. Surveys show that employees already

understand some principles of health care (for example,

that taking care of oneself can cut health costs) (HIAA, 1982).

However, workers understand other facts less well.

Marquis's survey of 3,218 American families revealed that

many consumers do not understand the finer points of

their coverages. The more complex the plan, the less people

understand it (Marquis). What is needed, says Marquis, is a

two-pronged attack: simplification of benefit structures and

intensified consumer education.

Management Responsibilities

Because we already know what Joymar's employees

favor by way of added benefits, consumer education would

mean explaining to our personnel such factors as the

comparative costs of various coverages or ways to modify

existing benefits to accommodate new ones. Management

7

Figure 10.5
Continued

must simplify the benefit structure. We can certainly request that our present carrier clarify policy language. We can also ask that our insurer make company personnel available to answer employee questions.

Conclusion

To explain the pros, cons, and costs of various coverages to employees, Joymar's benefits committee must themselves understand those coverages. Three committee actions can prove especially helpful. The first is to call in a representative from the present carrier to explain current coverage in detail. The second is to request literature from our present company as well as from various other carriers about the benefit additions our personnel want. The third is to interview representatives of insurance companies whose promotional literature seems to offer clear benefit structures. Through consultation with insurance professionals and our employees and among ourselves, we should be able to obtain a desirable policy at a manageable cost.

8

Figure 10.5
Continued

Explanatory footnotes:

1. The United States Department of Labor's Bureau of Labor Statistics reports that whereas "hospital room" costs went up 43.6 percent during the period 1980-82, the increase for "all medical care items" was only 33.3 percent (HIAA, 1982/83, p. 57).

2. "Primary" health coverage denotes the main source of insurance as opposed to "supplementary" insurance that covers the difference between Medicare payments and actually billed medical costs. Needless to say, primary insurance premiums are far higher than supplementary.

9

Figure 10.5
Continued

Table 1
Results of Employee Benefits
Preference Questionnaire

Possible Benefit Additions or Upgrades	Number of Employees Indicating Each Rank of Preference						
	1st	2nd	3rd	4th	5th	6th	7th
Dental (excluding orthodonture)	38	1	2	0	0	0	2
Home care	0	3	17	21	2	0	0
Maternity	0	0	2	16	15	3	7
Orthodonture	2	29	0	2	1	0	9
Outpatient	2	8	21	3	9	0	0
Psychological/ psychiatric	1	2	0	0	2	16	22
Transplant	0	0	1	1	14	24	3

10

Figure 10.5
Continued

BIBLIOGRAPHY

Cain, Carol. "Health Insurers Start Covering Liver Procedures." <u>Business Insurance</u> 15 Aug. 1983: 1 +.

Callet, David P., and Patricia A. Casey. "Health-Care Plan Changes for the Older Employee: The Employer as Primary Provider." <u>Employment Relations Today</u> 10 (1983): 235-40.

Gordon, Richard L. "Dental or Mental? Ads Sell Psych Hospital Insurance." <u>Business Marketing</u> 68.8 (1983): 11 +.

Health Insurance Association of America. <u>Health and Health Insurance: The Public's View</u>. Washington: HIAA, Summer 1982.

"The Insurers' Big Push for Home Health Care." <u>Business Week</u> 28 May 1984: 128 +.

Jacobs, Bruce A. " 'Takin' Care' of High Medical Costs." <u>Industry Week</u> 25 July 1983: 79.

Marquis, M. Susan. "Consumers' Knowledge about Their Health Care Insurance." <u>Health Care Financing Review</u> 5.1 (1983): 65-80.

Norris, Eileen. "Insurers Rewrite Their Old Marketing Policies." <u>Advertising Age</u> 26 Sept. 1983: M20-M21.

Oliver, Anthony T., Jr. "Pregnancy Benefits." <u>Personnel Journal</u> 62 (1983): 616 +.

Public Relations Division of the Health Insurance Association of America. <u>Sourcebook of Health Insurance Data, 1982-1983</u>. 24th ed. Washington: HIAA, 1982/83.

Tarnoff, Stephen. "Layoff Legislation Could Sting Small Employers." <u>Business Insurance</u> 11 July 1983: 3 +.

Williams, Candace. Personal Interview. 17 July 1986.

11

Figure 10.5
Continued

APPENDIX

EMPLOYEE BENEFITS PREFERENCE QUESTIONNAIRE

TO: All Joymar Personnel

FROM: Adam Daniels, Director of Personnel

DATE: January 8, 1986

SUBJECT: Employee Health Insurance

In a few weeks, executive and branch management will be
considering additions to and improvements in our present
employee health care insurance. We would appreciate your
assistance in determining employee preferences. Please rank the
following seven types of additions or improvements from 1 (most
preferred) to 7 (least preferred). Place your rankings in the
spaces next to each addition or improvement. Please return your
completed preference forms to me by January 15, 1986.

Type of Addition/Improvement   Your Ranking

Dental (excluding orthodonture)   _____
Home care   _____
Maternity   _____
Orthodonture   _____
Outpatient services   _____
Psychiatric/psychological   _____
Transplant surgery   _____

12

Memo or Letter of Transmittal

Be certain to send a memo or letter to your primary reader, letting him or her know you have enclosed your formal report. This **transmittal** document should:

1. Name the person requesting that you write the report.
2. Note the report's subject and purpose.
3. Specify major findings or recommendations.
4. Express appreciation for assistance you received in preparing the report.

Figure 10.6 shows Daniels's memo of transmittal to Joymar's president.

Summary

Writing an effective formal report means following a sequence of problem-solving steps. After receiving your report assignment, gather potentially useful sources of information. Then select those sources that actually provide you with the data you need.

Next, create a note card file from which you develop a formal outline. After finding a focal idea for your report, draft an introduction, body, and conclusion.

Make needed large-scale revisions and small-scale editing changes. Then prepare a fresh copy of your report's text. Now add supporting materials in this order: (1) headings, (2) abstract, (3) bibliography, (4) table(s) (optional), (5) figure(s) (optional), (6) appendix(es) (optional), (7) pagination, (8) list of tables and figures (if necessary), (9) table of contents, (10) title page.

Finally, proofread your document and transmit the report with an accompanying memo or letter.

Writing Problems

1. A financial officer of a small company is preparing a report on the climate for entrepreneurial ventures. The references found by the accountant are jumbled, sometimes incomplete, and sometimes full of information not needed for an annotated bibliography card. Given the following information, prepare annotated bibliography cards for at least five of the following sources. To make your cards, you will have to find the original sources and supply any missing bibliographic

Date: July 31, 1986

To: Joan Kenmore

From: Adam Daniels

Subject: Health Care Report

At your request, I have written the enclosed report, "Trends in Employee Health Care." My major recommendations are that we (1) interview a representative from our insurance carrier about our present coverage, (2) obtain literature from various carriers about desirable health insurance benefits, and (3) interview representatives from insurance companies whose plans might be better than our current one.

I wish to express my appreciation to two individuals, Candace Williams, of our local insurance trade association, for providing me with information about our region's employee health insurance trends, and Denise Long, of the state university library, for suggesting sources of current data on the topic.

I hope you find this report useful in preparing for our meeting next Wednesday.

Figure 10.6   Memorandum of transmittal. Employee health care report.

data. You may also have to delete some bibliographic information that is not supposed to appear on the annotated cards. Finally, you will have to reorder each card into Modern Language Association, American Psychological Association, or University of Chicago bibliographic style.

- Source 1: an article from *Money* (April 1983), vol. 12 of the magazine. The article begins on page 111 and is entitled "Backing New Ventures."
- Source 2: "Here Comes the 'Intrapreneur.'" This piece appears in *Business Week* in its July 18, 1983, issue. It begins on page 188.
- Source 3: Victoria Corbett has written an article for *The Accountant*. Her article is entitled "Where to Go for Venture Capital in 1984" and appears on pages 5–6 in the May 17, 1984, issue of this biweekly.
- Source 4: *Forbes* from December 19, 1983 (volume 132), contains R. Phalon's article "University as Venture Capitalist." It appears on pages 82–92.
- Source 5: Lynn Asinoff wrote "Rapidly Growing Venture Capital Fairs Evolve into a Potent Force in the Industry" for *The Wall Street Journal*. It appears in the April 10, 1984, issue on page 31.
- Source 6: M. D. Stewart's "Venture Capital and the American Dream" is from *Inc.* magazine, vol. 5, July 1983. It begins on page 116.
- Source 7: *The CPA Journal* (volume 53) includes the article "Funding a New Business with Venture Capital" on pages 74–75 of its August 1983 issue.
- Source 8: *Fortune* contains the article "Venture Capitalists' Private Bets" in vol. 109, number 9 (April 30, 1984), pp. 139–140, 44, 46. This piece is by Tom Alexander.

2. Top executives of the Cereng Corporation, manufacturer of industrial ceramics, want to begin thinking about opening up a factory and selling their products in Japan. As one part of their preliminary investigations, Cereng management has requested that a team of management and marketing specialists collaborate on a report on the climate for foreign business in Japan. Here are five annotated bibliography cards prepared by a member of the project team:

Card 1

"Exporters Brace for the Shock of a

Strengthening Yen." <u>Business Week</u> 9 Jan.

1984: 42.

(describes how changes in international

monetary rates may affect the U.S.-Japan

balance of trade)

Card 2

"A Kodak Camera Made in Japan." <u>Newsweek</u>

16 Jan. 1984: 66.

(explains how a major U.S. corporation

teamed with a Japanese corporation to

produce and market an item)

Card 3

Lohr, Steve. "Japan's Wary Financial Revolution."

<u>The New York Times</u> 22 Apr. 1984, sec. 3: 1 + .

(details how Japan is gradually opening its

financial markets to foreigners)

Card 4

> Smith, Lee. "Japan Hustles for Foreign
>
>   Investment." <u>Fortune</u> 28 May 1984: 152 + .
>
>
> (reports that foreign companies looking
>
> for business opportunities in Japan
>
> receive a warm welcome and practical
>
> assistance)

Card 5

> "World Business." <u>U.S. News & World Report</u>
>
>   12 Mar. 1984: 45-46.
>
>
> (A section of this regular feature reports
>
> that Japanese markets are good for
>
> engineering plastics, fine ceramics, carbon
>
> fibers, silicon, and optical fibers.)

Your task is to assist the writing team by finding and preparing note cards on at least three of these five sources.

3. You work in the accounting department of Freetime Manufacturing, a privately owned maker of patio furniture. Freetime has expanded greatly in recent years, requiring company executives to travel extensively by car and airplane. The expansion has also meant hiring new salespeople, who visit retailers trying to get them to stock Freetime products.

    For the first time, your company will need a fleet of approximately 40 automobiles to meet executives' and salespersons' needs. The question before the president and general manager of Freetime is whether to purchase or lease the new fleet.

You have already completed a problem definition, bibliography cards, note cards, and an outline for a formal report on key issues related to leasing as opposed to purchasing of company fleets. These items appear below:

- *Objective*   To prepare a formal report on key issues affecting a company's decision to lease or to purchase a fleet of automobiles
- *Audience*   The company president and general manager
- *Writer's desired image*   Knowledgeable, objective, respectful

---

Blyskal, Jeff. "The Car Leasing Dream."

    Forbes 14 Mar. 1983: 176.

    (discusses banks' roles in car leasing)

Annotated bibliography card 1

Blyskal 1

Popularity of Leasing

    ". . . as auto prices have continued to climb, the number of cars leased has more than doubled since 1971."

            (p. 176)

Note card

Note card

> Blyskal 2
>
> Leasing Advantages
>
> 1. No down payment
> 2. Lower monthly charges
> 3. Business tax deductions
>
> (p. 176)

Note card

> Blyskal 3
>
> Banks and Leasing
>
>   Presently, many banks buy cars and lease them to customers. This lets banks compete with dealerships for leasing business.
>
> (p. 176)

Note card

> Blyskal 4
>
> An Advantage of Purchasing a Car
>
>   Purchase is ultimately less expensive unless the purchaser can obtain substantial tax benefits through leasing.
>
> (p. 176)

"Discounting Leaves Fleet Sales in Chaos."

Business Week 31 Aug. 1981. 54+.

(describes how in times of generally weak
auto sales, fleet purchasers get large
discounts from automakers)

Annotated bibliography
card 2

Discounting 1

Specific Discounts

On 1982 models, Ford, Chrysler and
American Motors gave $200 to $600 per car.
Ford gave an extra $100 off with factory air
conditioning. Ford and General Motors
guaranteed interest rates depending on the
contracted loan's repayment period.   (p.56)

Note card

Discounting 2

Unclear Which Cars Best

All U.S.-made cars have improved fuel
economy, but in 1982 none had been in use long
enough to provide information on fleet durability
and performance.

(p. 56)

Note card

Annotated bibliography card 3

Gawronski, Francis J. "Fleet-Car Service Life Is

29 Months." Automotive News

19 Mar. 1984: E-4.

(presents statistical data on industry car

fleet use)

Note card

Gawronski 1

Fleet-Car Average Life

Companies keep fleet cars for over 29

months and slightly over 56,000 miles, according

to survey by National Association of Fleet

Administrators.

(p. E-4)

Note card

Gawronski 2

Leased versus Company Owned

Leased vehicles held for shorter time and

driven fewer miles than company-owned

vehicles.

(p. E-4)

Gawronski 3

How to Get Rid of Fleet Cars (Leased or Owned)

Sell them:

1. to employees

2. at auto auctions

3. to auto wholesalers

(p. E-4)

Note card

Gawronski 4

Ownership versus Leasing Popularity among

Commercial Firms

    About equal (53,000+ owned; 51,000+

leased); this breakdown is based on survey

information from 178 United States commercial

firm fleet administrators.

(p. E-4)

Note card

Lapham, Edward. "Lessors Trying Out New

    Finance Ideas to Boost Business."

    Automotive News 28 June 1982: 1+.

(describes creative financing plans for car

leasing)

Annotated bibliography card 4

Note card

> Lapham 1
>
> Alternative Financing Plans
>
>   In one plan, General Motors Acceptance Corporation (rather than a local, small dealership) holds title to the vehicle. This helps cut lease finance rates while giving the small dealership its lease profit "up front."
>
> (p. 1)

Note card

> Lapham 2
>
> Alternative Financing Plans
>
>   In one plan, a customer puts deposit into a financial institution. The interest on the deposit covers the monthly cost of the lease.
>
> (p. 1)

Note card

> Lapham 3
>
> Popularity of Alternative Financing Plans
>
>   Alternative financing plans have been successful in getting people to lease cars in the northeastern United States. However, they have not been as popular in a midwestern test area (Cincinnati, Ohio).
>
> (p. 38)

"One Auto Sector Is Alive and Well: Car Leasing."

Industry Week 20 Sept. 1982: 16.

(shows why investment benefits of leasing

are increasing its popularity)

Annotated bibliography card 5

One Auto Sector 1

Investment Benefits of Leasing

Leasing lets the customer put assets into

higher return investments rather than tying up

those assets in a down payment on a car that will

depreciate in value.

(p. 16)

Note card

One Auto Sector 2

Popularity of Leasing

When auto financing becomes increasingly

difficult to obtain, leasing becomes a popular

alternative.

(p. 16)

Note card

Note card

> One Auto Sector 3
>
> Popularity of Leasing Will Continue
>
> "...automakers will do less financing of car sales to concentrate on what they're supposed to do best--manufacturing."
>
> (p. 16)

OUTLINE

I. Introduction
    A. Why Freetime needs a car fleet
    B. The options
        1. Leasing
        2. Purchasing
II. Data on American companies' car fleets
    A. Statistics (Gawronski 4)
    B. Vehicle life
        1. All fleet vehicles (Gawronski 1)
        2. Leased as opposed to company owned (Gawronski 2)
III. Leasing's rise in popularity
    A. With rising car prices (Blyskal 1)
    B. With increasing difficulty of financing (One Auto Sector 2)
IV. Why leasing's popularity will continue (One Auto Sector 3)
V. Financing considerations
    A. Where to lease (Blyskal 3)
    B. How to finance (Lapham 3)
        1. Customer deposit (Lapham 2)
        2. General Motors Acceptance Corporation (Lapham 1)
    C. Discounts (Discounting 1)
    D. Current finance information for Freetime's location
        1. Lease costs (use lease rates found in automobile advertising section of your local newspaper)
        2. Lease finance rates (use information found in automobile advertising section of your local newspaper)

   VI. Miscellaneous problems confronting fleet administrators
       considering whether to lease or purchase cars
       A. Determining which cars are best for the fleet (Discounting 2)
       B. Figuring out what to do with cars after a certain period of time
          1. If leased,
             a. Return to lessor
             b. Purchase from lessor and sell:
                (1) to employees (Gawronski 3)
                (2) at auction (Gawronski 3)
                (3) to wholesaler (Gawronski 3)
          2. If company owned, sell:
             a. to employees (Gawronski 3)
             b. at auction (Gawronski 3)
             c. to wholesaler (Gawronski 3)
  VII. Advantages of each approach
       A. Leasing (Blyskal 2; One Auto Sector 1)
       B. Purchasing (Blyskal 4; see your local newspaper automobile
          advertising section to make comparisons between the total
          cost of leasing and the total cost of purchasing, disregarding
          any tax benefits for either option)
    V. Conclusion

Your task is to prepare the introduction, body, and conclusion of this
brief formal report. In addition to the information provided in the
problem definition, cards, and outline, you should consult the automobile advertising section of your local newspaper for information on
current auto purchase and leasing rates in your area. Assume that the
Freetime Company is in your locale.

4. The Xtrol Pharmaceutical Company is considering equipping each of
   its traveling salespeople with portable personal computers. The director of data processing has prepared a short formal report outlining
   the various types of portable computers available. The report does
   not mention brand names (except in the titles of referenced articles)
   but rather presents basic information on the topic to provide a starting point for the vice-president for operations to begin looking at
   specific makes and models. After completing the report, the director
   has assigned you the task of preparing all supporting material. Here
   are the annotated bibliography cards for the report and the text itself:

Card 1

Shapiro, Ezra. "The HP 110: A Light and Powerful

Portable." <u>Byte</u> June 1984: 111+.

(reports on Hewlett-Packard's portable

computer's capabilities and uses)

Card 2

Hedberg, Augustin. "Get Ready for the Lovable

Luggables." <u>Money</u> May 1983: 154+.

(describes competitive portable computers

on the market)

Card 3

"How Compaq's Portable Leaped Ahead of the

Pack." <u>Business Week</u> 15 Aug. 1983: 89-90.

(shows how a computer company made a

top-selling portable)

Card 4

"The Industry Heavies Move into Lightweights."

Business Week 7 May 1984: 146-147.

(summarizes major computer

manufacturers' competition for portable

market)

Card 5

Aaron, Peter. "Portable, Transportable or

Ergonomic Backache." The Portable

Companion Apr.-May 1983: 32-33.

(praises advantages of portable computers)

Report Text:

Over the past two years, Xtrol has developed many new products and increased its share of the pharmaceutical market. Our sales force now covers more territory and closes more sales than ever before. This additional business has overloaded our sales force with paperwork. As the vice-president for operations has noted, it is time to provide our traveling salespeople with portable computers to keep track of product offerings, orders, and customer data.

Although portable computers are a clear answer to our problem, we must decide which type of portable will best suit our sales staff's needs. There are presently scores of portables on the market. They come in different sizes with different capabilities. This report discusses three types of portable computers. It examines each type's ability to interact with other data communicating equipment. Finally, it summarizes each type's advantages and disadvantages.

The "sewing machines" are the heaviest group of portable computers. They range in weight from approximately 26 to 30 pounds ("Industry Heavies," 1984) and come in carrying cases resembling those housing portable sewing machines. Typically, these machines come with a keyboard, a built-in video display, and one or two disk drives. They allow a user to store from 40 to over 100 double-spaced, typewritten pages (or the equivalent) on a single disk.

Some models come "bundled" with word processing, accounting, database, and/or other software. Other models require purchasers to buy needed software. Prices range from $1,300 to $3,000, depending on the brand and model selected ("Industry Heavies," 1984).

Lighter and smaller than sewing machine portables, "candy boxes" fold up into or can fit into briefcases. Typically weighing from 7 to 11 pounds, the candy boxes may offer battery-powered operation, a disk drive, tape cassette storage, and video display. Prices range from $1,300 to $6,000, depending upon brand, model, and special features desired ("Industry Heavies," 1984).

Analysts agree that this segment of the portable computer market is growing explosively ("How Compaq's," 1983; Shapiro, 1984). As more and more models appear, deciding among competing machines will become increasingly difficult.

Lightest and smallest of the three categories of currently available portables are the approximately 4-pound "notebooks" ("Industry Heavies," 1984). Offering battery power, built-in software, and a small video display, these portables fit neatly under a user's arm. Prices range from $500 up, usually depending on the amount of data memory built into or added onto the computer.

As with candy-box-sized models, the notebook portables are proliferating. According to Augustin Hedberg (1983), the computer industry "will continue to bring forth a generation of lighter, tighter, and more self-contained portables" (p. 158). What this development will mean for prices is hard to predict. Supply will certainly increase. However, so will demand as more and more business people discover applications for light, small computers.

One consideration for Xtrol's sales force is a portable computer's ability to link with various data communication devices. For example, a computer-telephone modem connection lets salespeople send orders to our main office instantly at the end of each day. A modem would also let our sales managers send printed meeting schedule changes, names and addresses of potential new customers, and other current data to our people on the road.

Would-be customers of portables have expressed concerns about modem and computer compatibility. Some manufacturers have answered those concerns by building a modem right into the machine.

With other portables, the user needs to purchase a modem (usually very small, but still separate from the computer). All our salespeople equipped with a portable computer will also need a modem.

A printer that transfers data from the computer to paper is another device that might be important to many salespeople. Our representatives who have large territories with small populations might find it particularly useful to have printed copies of new product offerings, special promotions, or limited-time discounts to send ahead to customers whom they will not be visiting for several weeks. These salespeople stay out on the road for much longer stretches than our personnel in more populous regions and cannot always get back to their regional offices in time to reach customers with messages before their next sales call.

Some portables of each type have built-in printers as standard or optional. Almost all portables have ports through which they connect to lightweight printers. The built-in printers are usually of the dot matrix variety. By making various arrangements of dots on paper, these machines' printheads create letters, numbers, and in many cases, graphs and charts.

The third important data communication component is a video display. These displays range from very small 4-line, LCD displays (the type found on most digital watches) to full-size 25-line, cathode ray tube (CRT) displays just like those on desk-top models.

Our salespeople may desire the CRT if they wish to show clients graphs, charts, or other data directly on the screen. Business Week ("Industry Heavies," 1984) reports that "a 25-line LCD, for example, cannot match the clarity of a CRT" (p. 147). For instance, people looking at the computer screen from an angle can usually see CRT displays more easily than LCD displays. This fact would be crucial if a client were looking over the shoulder of a salesperson sitting at the keyboard giving a demonstration. If this sort of demonstration were not needed, then LCD displays, which take up less room and weigh less, would be perfectly acceptable.

Table 1 summarizes the desirability of these data communication features for various types of salespersons. The choices Xtrol can make are many. We can either purchase one model portable for all of our sales force or we can assign certain types of computers to salespeople with certain needs. We can even ask our sales staff itself what their preferences are. Whichever system we choose, it is important to know that all portable computers are not alike.

Table 1
Sales Force and Data Communications Media
for Portable Computers

Medium	Salesperson Needing This Medium
Modem	All
Printer	Staff with large, sparsely populated sales territories
CRT Display	Salespersons giving demonstrations on the computer
LCD Display	Salespersons concerned with size/weight of computer

Your task is to prepare the following supporting materials:
a. All necessary headings (including a title for the report)
b. Abstract
c. Table of contents
d. List of tables
e. Bibliography
f. Title page
g. Draft of a transmittal memo from the director of data processing to the vice-president for operations

5. As a manager in a local cable television company that will start broadcasting within a year, it is your responsibility to prepare a short formal report on the types of specialized program that your system might offer the public. As starting points, you have two sources: a survey of people in the viewing area you will serve and a list of 11 articles discussing various aspects of specialized cable programming.

The survey tells you that television owners in your service area ranked their specialized programming preferences in this order from most to least preferred:

Feature motion pictures

Sports programming

News and weather

Children's programming

Rock music

Country and western music

Business information

Public access (local groups can produce their own shows)

Adult programming

Arts programming

From searching indexes, you have the following bibliographical information about the 11 articles:

- *Time* on March 7, 1983, contained an article on page 69 entitled "Too Few Takers."
- W. Taaffe's "Getting Down to Business" appeared on page 93 of the January 24, 1983, issue of *Sports Illustrated.*
- Ed Levine's "TV Rocks with Music" begins on page 42 of the May 8, 1983, issue of *The New York Times Magazine.*
- *Business Week* of May 2, 1983, contains the article "A Fierce Face-Off Over Television Sports." It appears on pages 107–9.
- *Time* on October 24, 1983, contained an article on page 70 entitled "Sole Survivor."
- "Cable TV's Promise: You're Going to See More of Everything" is an article on page 51 of the February 13, 1984, *U.S. News & World Report.*
- *Business Week* of February 22, 1982, contains the article "Cable Programming Catches Up with Demand." It begins on page 130.
- *U.S. News & World Report* contained the article, "People's TV Is Here—On Cable Systems." It appeared on page 84 of the May 10, 1982, issue and was written by R. A. Taylor.
- *U.S. News & World Report* contained the article "Music Video—TV's Newest Wrinkle." It appeared on page 72 of the February 27, 1984, issue and was written by Gail Bronson.
- M. Christopher's "Hefner Pushing Hard for Playboy Channel" can be found in *Advertising Age*, May 16, 1983, page 52.
- *The Economist* contained the article "Tying Up Films on Cable" in its July 30, 1983, issue on page 73.

Prepare the formal report, including all necessary supporting materials and a transmittal memo to the general manager of the cable system.

6. The director of marketing for a cosmetics company has assigned you the task of preparing a formal report on recent approaches to marketing cosmetics. Here are 10 sources found by searching indexes. They contain the information you need to complete a formal report on the topic. Using as many of the following sources as you can find, prepare your report:

- P. Sloan's article in the November 29, 1982, issue of *Advertising Age* starts on page 32. It is entitled "Cosmetics Marketers Mull a New Look."

- Another article by P. Sloan appears in the March 7, 1983, issue of *Advertising Age*. It is entitled "Cosmetics Marketers Promise Face-Lifts" and begins on page 12.

- A special report on "Toiletries and Beauty Aids Marketing" was carried in the February 7, 1983, issue of *Advertising Age*, section 2, pages M9 through M41.

- "Time to Make a Move" is an article by A. Bernstein for the February 14, 1983, issue of *Forbes*. It appears on page 90.

- "Cosmetics Makers Explore Underdeveloped Black Market" by C. DeAngelis is in the December 1981 issue of *Product Marketing*. It starts on page 1.

- "In-Store Clinics Are an Effective Way to Increase Skin Care Sales" by G. Lebowitz is in the May 1981 issue of *Product Marketing*. It appears on page 4.

- *Forbes* carried H. Rudnitsky and J. Bamford's article "Vanity, Thy Name is Profit" in its May 25, 1981, issue on pages 47–48.

- "Still Trying to Regain a Healthy Glow" is the title of a January 9, 1984, *Business Week* article that appears on page 83.

- M. Borghese's article "Marketing to Special Groups" appeared in the October 1982 issue of *Working Woman* on page 140.

- Jane Ogle's *New York Times Magazine* piece entitled "The Boom in No-Frills Cosmetics" was in the February 8, 1981, issue on page 76.

Be certain to include all necessary supporting materials in your short formal report on practices in cosmetics marketing.

7. The executive vice-president of your manufacturing company has assigned you (the director of personnel) to prepare a formal report on other companies' employee vacation policies. Here is a list of 10 bibliographical sources found by searching indexes. You will need material from the sources to write your report. Using as many of the following sources as you can find, prepare your report.

- "Vacation Breaks," by D. Sammons, appears in the February 1984 issue of *Inc.* It begins on page 128.

- "Braving the Wilds to Survive in the Office," by R. K. Rein, appears in the July 1983 issue of *Money*. It begins on page 75.

- Marilyn Wellemeyer's article "The Purposeful Vacation" is included in the February 20, 1984, issue of *Fortune*.

- The June 1980 issue of *Management Today* contains N. Willatt's article "The Flexilife Future." It starts on page 80.

- The May/June 1981 issue of *Personnel* contains the article "Raises vs. Longer Vacations: Employees Choose." The piece appears on pages 44–45.

- *Industry Week* contains the article "Weekend Vacations—Thank Goodness It's Thursday?" It appears in the August 24, 1981, issue on pages 91–92.

- H. Z. Levine's article "Time-off-with-Pay Practices" appears in the September/October 1981 issue of *Personnel* on pages 4–12.

- S. J. Cooper's article "Upgrade Vacation Policies to Keep Employees Contented" is contained in the May 1983 issue of *Merchandising*. It appears on pages 96–97.

- *Forbes* contains E. Fingleton's article "Give Us a Break" in its August 2, 1982, issue on page 67.

- E. Elliot and W. Susco's article "Don't Expect Vacation and Sick Pay" appears in the May 1981 issue of *Working Woman* on page 16.

Be certain to include all necessary supporting materials in your formal report.

Extended Application

Take the topic of the writing problem on which you have been working since chapter 1. Using whatever sources you wish, prepare a formal report on recent developments in this aspect of business. Look back at the chapter on research if you need more information about the topic. Be sure to include all necessary supporting materials in your finished report. Then submit it, with a letter of transmittal, to your instructor.

CHAPTER 11

Feasibility Reports and Proposals

easibility reports and proposals both deal with similar issues, and each considers a project, service, or product from the perspectives of cost analysis, assumptions, scope, methodology, and risk. Each presents and interprets data and information, considers alternatives, and suggests one or more recommendations to a decision maker. Because these two distinct kinds of report do have much in common, people sometimes use the terms interchangeably. Although related, they are distinct forms, however.

The **feasibility report** advises the decision maker on *whether* to go ahead with a certain project. Essentially it answers the question: "Should we undertake this project?" The decision maker usually commissions a feasibility report. For example, if a hospital were considering adding a cardiac care unit, it would probably commission either an in-house committee or a consulting firm to study the possibility and make a recommendation. The report would analyze the pros and cons of the decision; the authors would function as impartial judges, recommending the best alternative for the hospital.

The **proposal**, on the other hand, advises or persuades the decision maker on a specific *agenda* for implementing a decision. It identifies a need and presents a specific program for meeting that need. It may originate within or outside the company. For example, inside a company, the training division might propose a new training program for data-entry specialists. Outside the company, a consulting firm might propose a program for upgrading the company's computing center. A proposal's author is not an impartial judge but the convinced advocate of an agenda.

Suppose, for example, a university wonders whether it should upgrade its computing capacity. A *feasibility* report would recommend either yes or no after studying the university's present facilities and projected requirements. The university would then want to know *how* to implement this recommendation and so would solicit *proposals* from several consulting firms. The university would study the resulting competitive bids and award the contract to the company with the best proposal.

The Feasibility Report: Advising the Decision Maker

The feasibility report is an expert's recommendation about a particular business venture made by an employee or an outside consultant chosen and hired by a decision maker. For example, a firm contemplating the expansion of its word processing operation into new departments might select the manager of its word processing unit to do a feasibility report recommending for or against the expansion. If the recommendation is *for* expansion, management might also expect the report to recommend the necessary equipment, software, and staffing, thus leading to a specific proposal.

A feasibility report might be commissioned by the following, which gives some idea of its varied uses:

1. A firm contemplating a new data processing operation or word processing
2. A firm contemplating a new product or service or expansion of an established product line or service
3. A person or group contemplating the establishment of a new business
4. A firm planning to open a new branch office or some other new facility
5. A person or group considering a large capital investment, for example, the purchase of a company or real estate
6. A hospital considering expansion in buildings or services

<table>
<tr><td>

Elements of the
Feasibility Report

</td><td>

A feasibility report is classified as either internal or external, depending on whether it is written inside or outside the organization. The internal report is usually called the *in-house feasibility report*, while the external report is usually called the *independent feasibility report*. Both kinds are composed of the same ingredients:

</td></tr>
</table>

- *Letter of transmittal.* States that the report is enclosed. It usually summarizes the recommendations and conclusions of the report and may offer to answer questions as needed.

- *Warranty or certification.* Normally attached only to reports written by an outside consultant. This brief, signed statement declares that the author has no conflict of interest regarding the project covered in the report.

- *Title page.* Gives the report title, the name of the company or person to whom it is directed, the name and company of the author, and the date of submission.

- *Table of contents.* Only for reports of 10 pages or more.

- *List of figures.* Used only if there are figures.

- *Executive summary.* Contains the recommendation of the report and should also summarize the main points from the demand, market, management, and financial sections of the report.

- *Recommendations and conclusions.* Recommends for or against the venture, predicting the most likely result of the action.

- *Assumptions.* States any assumptions made by the author.

- *Scope.* States what will be treated and what will not be treated, specifying any limitations to the study.

- *The business history and future.* Describes how well this industry has fared in the past and anticipates its future performance.

- *Demand.* Assesses demand for the product or service. It may estimate the number of clients and discuss their socioeconomic traits.

- *Market.* Discusses the product or service, considering such factors as pricing structure, production cost, competition, marketing strategy, and risks involved.

- *Management.* Describes the corporate structure of the organization considering the venture. It may also describe the qualifications, responsibilities, and compensation of key officers and production and operations.

- *Financial information.* Supplies balance sheets, an income statement, information on loan conditions, and cash-flow information. It may estimate sales, operating expenses, and taxes. It will probably predict the return on investment over a period of years.

- *Appendixes.* May include such items as product descriptions, maps, land appraisals, building estimates, and sampling techniques.

No single plan can cover the varieties of feasibility reports. For example, the report dealing with the establishment of a shopping center will differ from one dealing with the installation of word processing. The shopping center report would contain sections on traffic patterns, demographics, services, and zoning; the word processing report would contain sections comparing the costs between a word processing system and the existing system. In every report the previous outline must be adapted to suit the purpose of the author.

Figure 11.1 shows part of a feasibility report. Even the opening pages of this report summarize the entire report. Note that the table of contents in figure 11.1 lists the main headings, which essentially, though not rigidly, correspond to the plan given previously.

The feasibility report can be written by one or more authors. A word processing feasibility report, done in-house, for example, may involve people from many levels of the company: executives, supervisors, secretaries, and clerks. In such a case, there will normally be a project leader who has overall responsibility for planning, writing, and editing the report. But whether 2 or 20 write it, the problem-solving approach applies.

Writing a
Feasibility Report

Problem-Solving Steps

Define   Who will read your report? The only audience for an in-house report may be your immediate supervisor. But the larger the investment in commissioning the report, and the larger the investment the report recommends, the more readers, including upper management, it will have.

In doing an independent report for a company that hires you for that purpose, you can also have a variety of readers beyond those who commission the report. Since the report is often used by an entrepreneur to persuade an investor that a venture is worth backing, underwriters, financial rating agencies, and bankers may read it.

Because you are presumably more knowledgeable on the topic of the report than your reader, your main objective is to advise the decision maker whether the project should be carried out. Ideally the reader is looking for a thorough study of the facts and an unbiased recommendation. In practice, some authors are expected merely to make a concrete case for a project already decided upon. Other authors find themselves somewhere between these two extremes.

We do not offer ethical advice: you are no doubt the best judge of what your course of action should and can be in your work. We simply suggest that, at the outset of the project, you base your decisions on a careful analysis of your reader's attitude.

Finally, you will be the expert writing for less expert readers, so don't get too technical for your audience. The technical material that cannot be reduced to lay terminology can be placed in the appendixes.

Stevens and Sherwood, the authors of the report described in figure 11.1, have defined their writing problem as follows: their readers are the officers of a university who must decide whether the university should establish an M.B.A. program with a concentration in health care administration, and the reader profile assumes a group familiar with the background and resources of the university, predisposed to expansion but wary of expanding too rapidly. The authors' goal is to assure the university administrators that the benefits of the new program will justify the expense of implementing it.

Analyze   Answers to the following questions can provide an analysis of a particular project, which, in turn, will enable you to organize your report more effectively:

1. What evidence can you cite for the demand for this product or service?
2. Who will be the most likely clients for it?
3. How many clients are there?
4. What is their socioeconomic status?
5. What assumptions does your report make about the product or service, market conditions, or the management of the company?
6. Does the scope of the report *exclude* anything a reader might expect to see covered? If so, why?
7. What is the cost breakdown of producing this product or service?
8. Is the pricing structure right for market conditions?
9. How is this product or service superior to competing products or services?
10. Do you anticipate any potential competition not yet in the marketplace?
11. What kind of marketing strategy has been developed?
12. What risks does this venture involve?
13. Do the key personnel have the expertise and experience required for it?
14. What kinds of equipment/facilities are needed for it?
15. What federal, state, and local taxes do you estimate?
16. What licenses or certifications are required to produce this product or service?
17. What has been the financial track record of this organization in the past?
18. What sales do you estimate for this product?
19. What return on investment do you predict over the next three to five years?
20. What is the status of any loan studied or recommended?
21. What is the history of this product or service and its industry?
22. What sort of future do you anticipate for this product or service and its industry?

In their report (figure 11.1), Stevens and Sherwood have answered most of the questions just listed, as their summary indicates. They have not, of course, answered the questions on the list that are irrelevant to their subject. For example, in their study of the education of health care administrators, they regarded questions concerning pricing, potential competition, and the status of the loan inapplicable.

Draft   The plan just described suggests a logical order for a feasibility report. But while the _finished_ report begins with the executive summary, it is best to write that part and the letter of transmittal last, because then you will have a better sense of the completed report.

Most feasibility reports are structured alike and include the same building blocks—recommendations and demand, market, management, and financial analyses—but these blocks may be _arranged_ differently, depending on the purpose of the report. When you are structuring your report, we suggest that you remember that there is an element of persuasion in the feasibility report—the author makes a recommendation and must therefore provide convincing support that the recommendation is valid. Thus, whether your basic recommendation is positive or negative, we suggest that you lead with your strongest support. For example, if demand is the strongest support, lead off with it, followed by your next strongest, perhaps lack of significant competition.

Stevens and Sherwood opt for the organization revealed by their table of contents, shown in figure 11.1. The executive summary reveals further details of their organization. They demonstrate the flexibility of the feasibility report structure by placing their strengths and weaknesses section in the middle of the report—because they feel that the strengths far outweigh the weaknesses. In their objectives section, they specify the enrollments expected (demand analysis). They conclude with a strategy summary linking this program to the "medical and healing mission of the university," a factor important to the administrators who will read the report. They relegate the curriculum outline and the degree-plan sheet to the appendixes because these would be of little interest to the administrators.

Revise and Edit   Edit with an eye toward eliminating unnecessary technical language, wordiness, and inconsistent style (when different authors have written sections). Stevens and Sherwood have introduced an effective device at the editing stage—using capital letters to set off major conclusions of the report. Although this technique is not common, it allows the reader to grasp the conclusions of the report quickly.

If possible, have an outsider read your draft to judge whether it adequately supports its recommendation. And finally, see that the report is attractively bound.

FEASIBILITY STUDY
HEALTH CARE ADMINISTRATION PROGRAM
School of Business
Fairfield University
Fairfield, U.S.A.

Prepared by

Robert E. Stevens, Ph.D.
Philip K. Sherwood, Ed. D.

STEVENS-SHERWOOD AND ASSOCIATES
2140 South 78th E Avenue
Tulsa, Oklahoma

Figure 11.1   Feasibility report. (Source: Published by Prentice-Hall, Inc.,
Englewood Cliffs, NJ 07632. From the book *How to Prepare a Feasibility Study* by
Robert E. Stevens and Philip K. Sherwood. © 1982 by Prentice-Hall, Inc.)

Figure 11.1
Continued

TABLE OF CONTENTS

1

Figure 11.1
Continued

CERTIFICATION

We hereby certify that we have no interest, present or contemplated, in the proposed Fairfield University Care Program and that to the best of our knowledge and belief, the statements and information contained in this report are correct--subject to the limitations herein set forth.

Robert E. Stevens, Ph.D.
_____
Robert E. Stevens, Ph.D.

Philip K. Sherwood, Ed.D.
_____
Philip K. Sherwood, Ed.D.

Figure 11.1
Continued

EXECUTIVE SUMMARY

Purpose

The purpose of the Master's of Business Administration concentration in Health Care Administration (HCA) is to produce competent administrators for management in the rapidly growing health care field. This study recommends the establishment of the HCA program at Fairfield University.

1

Environment

The environment and statistics show that the health care industry is expanding worldwide and that the capital expenditures in the field are increasing dramatically. It is the second largest industry in the country in terms of expenditures and accounts for an estimated 10 percent or more of our GNP. Government and private forecasts are predicting as many as 100,000 new jobs by 1985.

2

Locally, the Fairfield area has five major hospitals and the soon-to-be operational University Hospital. The demand and need for a health care administration program appears to be strong worldwide, in Fairfield, and perhaps most dramatically here at the huge University Medical Complex.

3

*THERE IS SUFFICIENT DEMAND FOR HEALTH CARE ADMINISTRATORS TO WARRANT THE PROPOSED PROJECT.

4

3

Figure 11.1
Continued

Strengths and Weaknesses

An analysis of the strengths and weaknesses indicates that the Fairfield University School of Business is well able to build the new health care program on the strong foundation of its MBA program. Joined with support from the University Medical Complex, Fairfield University has the ingredients for a successful and complete master's program in health care administration.

5

There are some potential weaknesses. The university is young and has had only about 20 years to build its reputation and upgrade the quality of its programs. The medical and dental schools may be completely absorbed in securing accreditation and by the demands of rapid expansion, limiting time for contribution to the health care administration program. Another important consideration is the effect of transfer students from the MBA to the MHCA program to the detriment of the MBA.

6

*THE RESOURCES AT FAIRFIELD UNIVERSITY ARE SUFFICIENT TO WARRANT THE ESTABLISHMENT OF THE PROGRAM.

7

Assumptions

There are enough MBA candidates at Fairfield University interested in health care to justify the program. The demand for administrative people in health care will increase. The insufficiency of internship positions in the University Medical Complex will necessitate affiliation with other health-related institutions.

8

4

Figure 11.1
Continued

*THERE WILL BE A SUFFICIENT SUPPLY OF
STUDENTS FOR THE HCA PROGRAM.   9

Benefit/Cost Analysis

The analysis of costs and benefits reveals a slight
deficit in the first year of operation. However, the
amount is only 2.8 percent of the costs of the program.
Often, nonmonetary benefits far outweigh the small   10
incremental cost involved in establishing the
program. The intangible benefits cause the program to
be favorable.

*THE BENEFIT/COST ANALYSIS JUSTIFIES THE
PROGRAM.   11

Objectives

The objectives for instituting the program are the
graduation of 15 MHCAs in May 1983; enrollment of
10 students in Health Care I (HCI) for fall 1982, 20
students in HCI for spring 1983, and 20 students in
HCII for fall 1983; establishment of 5+ internships
for summer 1983; sending Dr. Jones to health care   12
marketing conference; helping Dr. Capelli get HCII
ready for summer; preparing Dr. Jones to teach HCIII
in spring 1983; and the recruitment of faculty for
HCIV in spring 1984.

Strategy Summary

The strategy to establish the Health Care
Administration program will be to maximize the
benefits of the strengths outlined in the report and to
minimize and anticipate the effects of the weaknesses.

5

Figure 11.1
Continued

Coverage support from the university publications,   13
seminars, and university public relations will be
pursued. Long-range planning and financing are
outlined in the full report.

    *THE LONG-RANGE BENEFITS OF ESTABLISHING
THE PROGRAM APPEAR EXTREMELY POSITIVE. IN
THE LONG-RANGE VIEW, THE PROGRAM IS   14
PROJECTED TO BREAK EVEN AND PROVIDE
BENEFIT AND SUPPORT TO THE MEDICAL AND
HEALING MISSION OF THE UNIVERSITY.

6

The Proposal: Persuading the Decision Maker

Proposals are more common than feasibility reports and more complicated. We will discuss their various classifications, present two proposal plans, and suggest how to use the problem-solving technique in their composition.

Proposals may be classified as solicited or unsolicited, internal or external, and formal or informal.

Proposal Classifications

Solicited and Unsolicited Proposals   The **solicited proposal** is requested by the company that receives it, usually by publishing a formal request for proposals (RFP) or a statement of work (SOW). This document describes the problem to be solved and any standards the solution must meet. For example, the federal government may want a certain number of jet engines produced according to certain specifications, in certain quantities, and by a certain deadline.

The **unsolicited proposal**, on the other hand, originates with the proposer. For example, a training officer in a company may identify a need for instruction in letter writing for first-line supervisors. The training officer might develop a proposal for a short-term, in-house course in letter writing to be taught by an outside consultant.

Internal and External Proposals   The **internal proposal** is directed to someone else in the company, often the proposer's superior. For example, the proposal for the letter writing course, directed to the vice-president of administrative services, would be internal.

The **external proposal** is directed to another company, organization, or government agency. For example, the proposal to build the jet engines for the U.S. Air Force is an external proposal. As you can imagine, most external proposals are solicited, because a company will not normally invest substantial time and resources in preparing such a proposal unless requested to do so.

Formal and Informal Proposals   Finally, proposals can be classified on the basis of their *complexity*. The term *proposal* can cover a two-page memorandum proposing the hiring of two part-time rate clerks or it can cover a multivolume document proposing to construct an interstate highway system. The experts have different terms to classify proposals, such as the (pure) research proposal, the research and development proposal, the sales proposal, and the systems proposal. We suggest a simpler classification on the basis of the form of the proposal, which divides proposals into two classes: informal proposals, which include memorandum proposals, letter proposals, and short report proposals; and formal proposals.

Informal proposals are usually only a few pages long and may not contain all of the elements explained below in the plan for an informal proposal. For example, a memorandum proposal urging the purchase of a high-performance printer may not contain a description of competing models with an analysis of each because the anticipated reader might not require that material. But the **formal proposal**—whether 20 pages or 500 pages—will contain most of the elements described in the plan for a formal proposal. The more elaborate formal proposals will usually be solicited because of their expensive preparation costs.

Proposal
Organization

Whatever its length, the proposal will usually answer the following questions:

1. What is the problem to be solved?
2. What is the best available solution to this problem and why is it best?
3. What benefits will accompany this solution?
4. How will the solution be implemented?
5. Who will do what and when?
6. What will the solution cost?
7. Why is the proposer qualified to do the job?

In one proposal, each of these questions could require only one or two paragraphs to answer; in another, each could require 75 pages to answer. The length depends on the complexity of the problem to be solved. If the problem is relatively simple—for example, how to publicize an upcoming sales exhibit—the proposal will be simple and short. But if the problem is complex, such as how to convince legislators to pass a major law, the proposal will be complex and long.

To organize proposals, therefore, we recommend two separate plans, one for informal and another for formal proposals. Both plans offer suggestions, not rules. Since every proposal commission is different, not all of the elements described will always be required.

For example, if you are the office manager in a small accounting firm and you propose to buy another photocopier for the accountants at the other end of the hall, you may define the problem simply by stating the objective of the purchase: to save the time secretaries spend running up and down the hall and waiting in line. Moreover, you may be able to assume that your boss knows you will take care of the details of ordering, installation, and service contract. A different manager, on the other hand, may want all the details about a comparison and contrast of competing models, service contract, and warranty.

Plan for an Informal Proposal   We suggest that the informal proposal normally include the following sections in approximately the following order:

- *The summary.* Briefly states the problem, the recommended solution, and the benefits to be realized. It may include a summary of costs.
- *The problem.* Includes a more detailed description of the problem and often establishes criteria for a satisfactory solution.
- *The alternative solutions.* Lists the alternative solutions in descending order of viability. It discusses each alternative in reference to the criteria, showing advantages and disadvantages. The cost for each alternative may be discussed.
- *The recommended solution.* Presents a relatively detailed description of the solution. It will include methodology, tasks and subtasks, and schedules. It will show why this solution best meets the criteria and will stress benefits and expected results. It will also describe the cost of the project, itemizing all expenditures—for example, payments for equipment, personnel, services, supplies, and travel.

Figure 11.2 shows an informal memorandum proposal. Internal and unsolicited, it is a common type, referred to as an *equipment justification.* It contains most of the divisions just stated and follows the recommended order. The recommendation in paragraph 1 is also the summary—it states what is to be bought and the attractive cost savings of the purchase. The problem section defines the problem—a lack of equipment that can keep up with demand, thus implying the main criterion for the solution. Another implied criterion is that the new equipment must be compatible with the present office system. The solution essentially gives the reasons for the new purchase and specifies the total cost, including the amount to be saved by purchasing a used printer.

Figure 11.3 shows another informal proposal. Internal and unsolicited, it justifies the purchase of a service. More complex than the example in figure 11.2, it contains headings, subheadings, numbered lists, and a title page that give it a more structured appearance. But what is significantly different from figure 11.2 is the degree of detail this proposal offers. For example, in the statement of the problem, under background, there is considerable detail in paragraphs 4 and 5. In the alternatives part, paragraphs 9, 10, and 11 analyze each of three alternatives. And under cost advantages, the list is more itemized than in the previous proposal.

Don't worry about the exact dividing line between the informal and the formal proposal: there is a gray area between the two. If someone wishes to classify the proposal in 11.3 as formal, fine. We consider it informal because of its short length and overall lack of complexity, involving as it does merely a contract and services.

On the other hand, the formal proposal we will look at in figure 11.4, while not long, would involve several people working at least part-time over three months. Quite a difference!

Date: January 25, 1986

To: The Systems Committee

From: Merle D. Escobido, Administrative Services

Subject: Proposal to Purchase 2 Printers and 1 Feeder

Recommendation

To enhance the productivity of administrative
services, I recommend the purchase of a Model 5571
line printer, an additional character printer, and a
twin-sheet feeder to be attached to the Triad System   1
in the Word Processing Center. I also recommend the
purchase of a used line printer, which will save us
$7,469.

Problem

With our present equipment, we are scarcely able to
keep up with the increasing volume of printing
required by the company. Currently we have 16
manuals or portions of manuals waiting to be printed.
Indeed, we are holding off the conversion of the
Medical Department because of this bottleneck. At
present we have only one character printer and one   2
dual-head printer. The dual-head printer was
necessary for oversized documents, especially for
statistical reports. We anticipated it handling volumes
equal to a character printer, but it unfortunately
cannot. Thus we are printer-bound. We would like to
put more work on the Triad System, but the printers
cannot cope with it.

1

Figure 11.2   Informal proposal

Figure 11.2
Continued

<u>Solution</u>

I recommend the purchase of another line printer, character printer, and twin-sheet feeder. This equipment would be compatible with our Triad System, and the line printer has over 10 times the speed of a character printer. Some print quality is sacrificed, but that is more than offset by the increased productivity. The line printer would enable us to take the printing of manuals or other large documents and rough drafts off the character printers. The additional character printer would provide flexibility, backup, and room for expansion. While the used line printer is available immediately, the character printer and the twin-sheet feeder can be delivered in three weeks.

3

While the cost of a new line printer is $17,675 plus tax and delivery, we can purchase a two-year-old printer from a local law firm for $10,206 plus delivery. Assuming Triad inspects and accepts it for maintenance, the used printer would fill the need. Monthly maintenance cost for the line printer would be $203.

4

Another character printer will cost $6,060 plus tax and delivery. This printer would be identical to the standard-carriage character printer already attached to the Triad System. Monthly maintenance would be $49.

5

Another twin-sheet feeder will cost $2,060, and this feeder also would be identical to the twin-sheet feeder already installed. Monthly maintenance would be $49.

6

Total cost of the purchase would be $18,326 plus tax and delivery; total monthly maintenance would be $273. Purchasing the used line printer would save us $7,469.

7

2

A Proposal for Computer-Assisted Color Slides

Submitted to

Meredith Schneider
Vice-President, Corporate Commercial

by Lesley Chou
Director, Presentation Services

June 10, 1986

Figure 11.3 Informal proposal

Figure 11.3
Continued

I) Executive Summary

This proposal offers a plan to reduce the cost of
producing color presentation slides while maintaining their
high quality. By contracting with Formax Corporation,
Presentation Services can design and create color slides and   1
eliminate the expense and time associated with typesetting,
camera-ready artwork, film processing, and so on.

Last year Presentation Services produced 12,000 slides.
The Formax 350 System, with one design station, can
produce 3,000 slides per year. While not all our slides will be
produced on this system, the savings will still be substantial.
Using current methods, it costs $112,500 annually to   2
produce 3,000 slides. The Formax System will produce them
for an annual cost of $37,495, resulting in an annual
savings of $75,005.

II) Statement of the Problem

A) Background

For many years the Presentation Services Department
has produced visual aids (slides, transparencies, flip charts,
and poster boards) for management. In the last few years,
most of these visuals have been 35-millimeter slides. The
demand for these color slides is increasing steadily because   3
of their ease of use, quality, and professional appearance.
During the whole of last year, we produced 12,779 original
slides, whereas in the first five months of this year, we have
produced 5,561 slides.

The cost of producing a color slide can range from $10
to several hundred dollars, depending on the type and
complexity of the material. The average cost of a color slide   4
is $37.50. This cost covers three functions:

1

Figure 11.3
Continued

1. Typesettings and artwork ($22 an hour)
2. Litho processing ($10 a slide)
3. Color photography, film processing, and plastic mounting ($5.50 a slide)

The current manual methods of producing a slide involve eight different steps: 5

1. The preliminary rough sketch of the words and/or illustration
2. Typesetting of words and/or numbers
3. Artwork for charts (pie, bar, line, etc.) or illustrations
4. Litho photography (to make a negative)
5. Adding color gels to the negative and photographing at the Slide Magic Camera stand
6. Processing the film in the Photo Lab
7. Cutting and mounting the film in plastic frames
8. Proofing, boxing, and mailing the slides to the client

These steps are expensive, and under current conditions, there is no discount for volume.

B) Objectives

With the increasing demand for slides and the need to cut costs, our main objective is to find a way to provide these slides more economically without sacrificing the   6
professional quality or the timely service our top management has come to expect.

As a secondary requirement, we need the ability to change a portion of a slide without recreating the entire   7
slide and the ability to maintain a catalogue of the slides thus produced.

2

Figure 11.3
Continued

III) <u>Alternatives</u>

     The computer now makes possible a new technology for designing, producing, and later updating color slides. This technology eliminates several costly steps in the production of slides and lowers the cost of producing new ones. There are three alternative ways that we can use this new technology.

8

A) The First Alternative:
Purchase of a Complete Computer Slide
Production System

     Such a system includes design stations (CRTs), a central processing unit (CPU), a high-resolution camera, a film developer, and slide-finishing equipment. The price of the system would range from $300,000 to $500,000, obviously a significant capital expenditure. Over a period of years, the system should begin to pay for itself, but there would be no immediate improvement in cash flow. Therefore this alternative is unattractive.

9

B) The Second Alternative:
Development of an In-House Slide-Making System

     We could buy the various components required to create a slide-making system, which would cost less than the system described as the first alternative. But there are four major drawbacks to this alternative. First, there are high initial costs; second, there is considerable time lost in the startup phase; third, there is the lack of flexibility to adapt to new technology as it develops; and fourth, there is the question of service--if the system malfunctions, which vendor do we call? These four drawbacks cripple this alternative.

10

3

Figure 11.3
Continued

C) The Third Alternative:
An Outside Service Contract for Slide Making

This alternative would allow us to create slides in-house on a terminal in the Presentation Services Department. We would then electronically transmit the finished designs to the vendor, who would process and return the finished slides. We are currently buying this type of computer-generated slide for certain special needs.

11

We like the Formax Corporation package. The Formax 350 Color Slide System offers the design station and supporting equipment--available to be leased. We would be charged on a per-slide basis. The vendor would install the system on a three-month trial basis. During this period, the cost would be $20 per slide; there would be no charge for equipment leasing during the trial period.

12

IV) Recommended Solution

We recommend the third alternative--the contract with the outside vendor--for the following reasons:

13

1. It is less expensive than the current method.
2. It produces high-quality color slides.
3. It provides a single vendor responsible for service calls.
4. Formax provides a library of software for artwork.

Although there are many advantages and dollar savings in this solution, we must point out that there will be a continuing need to make many slides using the current method. There will always be cases in which time is critical, and when a slide is needed in a few hours, the current method is still the fastest.

14

4

Figure
Continue

V) Cost Advantages

We assume a volume of 3,000 slides per year (possibly
more). Using current methods, the annual cost of producing   15
3,000 slides at $37.50 apiece would be:

$112,500

Leasing the Formax 350 Color Slide System, the estimated
annual cost of producing 3,000 slides would be: 16

Paid to Formax:

Terminal	$4,200
Slides (1200 at $16 a slide)	$19,200
(1800 at $6 a slide)	$10,800
Disks (60 at $7 a disk)	$420

Other Expenses:

Communications 3000 slides at 12-½ cents a slide	$375
Mailing or courier delivery	$2,500
Total	$37,495
Total Annual Savings	$75,005

5

Plan for a Formal Proposal   The range of the formal proposal is so broad that no plan can cover all the cases. Some sections in the following plan list will apply to an external formal proposal but not to an internal one. For example, an internal proposal may not require such items as resumes of key personnel, description of facilities and organizational structure, or a statement about the company's financial status. Thus actual finished proposals you encounter in the business world (or even in this text) do not always correspond exactly to theoretical outlines. The overall pattern, however, *does* describe the essential structure of most proposals.

- *Title page.* Gives the proposal title, the name of the company or person to whom the proposal is directed, the name of the proposing company or person, and the date of submission.

- *Letter or memorandum of transmittal.* A letter accompanies the external proposal, a memorandum the internal proposal. Both state the key points of the proposal and identify the next step in the approval process. The letter usually cites the authority of the author to make the offer and describes any time constraints governing the offer. Both offer to supply additional information as desired.

- *Table of contents.* Only for proposals 10 pages or longer.

- *List of figures.* Appears only if the proposal contains figures.

- *Executive summary.* Summarizes the main features from the three major sections below: technical, management, and cost. It cites the distinctive and most attractive features of the proposal, stressing the ways in which it meets the needs of the client.

- *Technical section.* States the problem to be solved and defines the criteria for an effective solution taken from the RFP. It may list alternative solutions and discuss each, applying the criteria to each. It identifies the alternative chosen and gives reasons for the choice, stressing benefits to the client. It may include methods, equipment, facilities, any assumptions, and any exceptions to the requirements stated in the RFP, along with reasons for each exception. It may identify anticipated problems and describe ways of dealing with them. If something is to be produced, it will explain production methods.

- *Management section.* Describes the project plan—including tasks, subtasks, and schedules for completion of each. It may provide for monthly or quarterly progress reports. It describes reporting, authority, and responsibilities of key personnel, especially those of the project manager. It describes the structure of the proposer's company, if necessary. It may describe employee programs, company policies, training necessary, and useful publications. It describes and itemizes what is to be delivered and the service plan, if any. It states the experience and qualifications of the company and the key personnel (in brief resumes). It may include the names and telephone numbers of past clients as references.

■ *Cost section.* Describes the cost breakdown, including such items as equipment, start-up costs, salaries, wages, benefits, accounting, legal and consulting fees, service contracts, supplies, telephone and telex charges, and travel and training expenses. It explains cost estimating methods and may include a cost breakdown for the alternatives not chosen. It may include the terms and conditions and the contract and may describe the financial condition of proposer's company. It will probably estimate return on investment and describe benefits.

■ *Appendix.* If used, will include such information as equipment lists, flow charts, organization charts, detailed technical and financial data, and resumes.

Figure 11.4 shows an external, solicited *formal* proposal. The proposing company is a national certified accounting house. The client is a state university that seeks consulting assistance for the development of its data processing capability over the next five years.

What makes this a formal proposal? For one thing, it uses many of the distinctive devices of the formal proposal—for example, the letter of transmittal; a statement of exceptions (paragraphs 20 to 24); descriptions of the company, the company's experience, and key personnel; and an appendix, not all of which can be shown.

But more important is the depth of detailed analysis. The technical section (paragraphs 10 to 28) occupies the most space and offers considerable detail. In it three paragraphs describe the genesis of the problem and the definition of terms (10 to 12). After the problem is stated (13 to 15), the objectives are defined in detail—in one and a half pages—with two phases and subheadings. The approach subheading (25 to 28) parallels the objectives part, using the same two-phase format. Again, we note the same kind of detailed analysis. In sum, much work will be done by many people over a period of months, and the proposal reflects that significant commitment.

L&K

Lavelle and Kremer, Certified Public Accountants
10290 Mill Road
Columbus, OH 43112

March 5, 1986

Dr. Marion DiLorenzo
Executive Vice-President
Erie State University
Erie, Ohio 45217

Dear Dr. DiLorenzo:

When you have read the enclosed proposal, I feel that you will agree that we at Lavelle and Kremer have an in-depth understanding of the challenges you face as you attempt to update the university's computing capabilities to meet the needs of a more sophisticated university.   1

Please note particularly the detailed analysis of our objectives--divided into two phases. Our approach to achieving these objectives follows the same two-phase, carefully reasoned pattern. Please note as well the provision we have built into the proposal to work closely with the Computer Services Policy Committee. We intend to be most responsive to your needs.   2

I ask you to note the caliber of our project managers. Each of these professionals has not only data processing and business experience but experience with projects very similar to this one at other, comparable universities. In addition, I would point to the national reputation Lavelle and Kremer enjoy for dependability and leadership in consulting in higher education.   3

Figure 11.4   Formal proposal

Figure 11.4
Continued

I am authorized to make you the offer stated in our proposal. It is our practice to make an offer effective for a thirty-day period, after which we reserve the option to review the terms of the offer.

4

If you or your colleagues at the university have any questions about this proposal, I shall be delighted to answer them or to supply the information requested. We at Lavelle and Kremer are eager to begin work on the project as soon as we receive your approval.

5

Sincerely,

Lee Weber
Executive Vice-President

Figure 11.4
Continued

A Proposal to Provide Technical Expertise in
Computer Utilization for Erie State University

Submitted to

Dr. Marion DiLorenzo
Executive Vice-President
Erie State University

by Lavelle and Kremer,
Certified Public Accountants

March 5, 1986

Figure 11.4
Continued

I) <u>Executive Summary</u>

The computing needs of Erie State University have changed significantly since its founding in 1951. Until recently, rapid expansion of the student body and the campus facilities have been the rule. The University Computer Center struggled--successfully--to keep up with this expansion.   6

Recently, however, the expansion has leveled off, and the university now foresees a stability in student numbers. Meanwhile, with the addition of several new university offices, the Computer Center must update its facilities, programs, and staff to meet the more sophisticated needs of administrative computing and academic/instructional computing.   7

To meet this challenge, the university has established the Computer Services Policy Committee. Lavelle and Kremer will provide the expertise this committee needs to make the best decisions in terms of hardware, software, and Computer Center staffing and organization. We will make an exhaustive study of all computing systems now in use at the university, and we will make a thorough study of the emerging requirements. We will then draw up a five-year plan for computer use at the university. We will discuss all our recommendations thoroughly with the committee before submitting our final written report to the university within three months of the authorization of the project.   8

We will complete this project on time for a total maximum cost of $42,500. Should our own expenses be less than estimated, we will gladly refund the difference.   9

1

Figure 11.4
Continued

II) <u>Technical Section</u>

A) Background

Erie State was founded as a college in 1951 and granted university status in 1965. In the past decade, it has grown so rapidly that some 9,000 students are enrolled in its undergraduate, graduate, and professional programs. During that time, undergraduate enrollment alone grew by a compound annual rate of nearly 16 percent.

    10

The university has attempted to manage this dramatic increase in students. Its day-to-day concerns have been mainly to add new facilities, find enough classroom space, hire new faculty, and seek increased funding from the state legislature.

    11

The university purchased a computer and began putting together a data processing system to assist in two areas:

    12

1. <u>Administration</u>. For example, preparing internal and external financial management reports, registering students, and issuing class lists and grades.
2. <u>Academic/Instructional Activities</u>. For example, supporting professors in their research, processing student evaluations of professors, and supplying data on academic programs, e.g., Engineering or Business Administration.

These computer programs grew as needs became more pressing and as university resources expanded. Many of these programs have performed well and in certain areas, such as financial aid, are ahead of programs at comparable schools.

2

Figure 11.4
Continued

B) Statement of the Problem

In spite of the progress in meeting data processing needs, many of these systems were designed several years ago when needs differed considerably from those of today and the next five years. The rapid growth in the student population of the last decade has now stabilized. Moreover, the structure of the university has expanded over the years, adding to the demand for data processing services. For example, the university has added such offices as Budget and Institutional Research. Also it has expanded its academic programs, adding programs in Engineering, Law, and Allied Health.   13

The university must upgrade its computer system to meet more sophisticated demands. It feels that now is the best time for this expansion because of present conditions in the state legislature and the State Board of Regents. Accordingly, the university has created a computer use project under the direction of its executive vice-president, a project director, and a Computer Service Policy Committee. The charge to this committee is to ensure that the university acquires a modern computer system. The committee likewise will establish directions in hardware, software, Computer Center staffing, and other related areas.   14

The first task of the committee is to select a consulting firm to help it to accomplish the objectives described below.   15

C) Objectives

We shall refer to our company's total service package as the engagement. Our overall objectives in this engagement are to help the university assess its present and future computing needs. We have divided the objectives into the two phases described below.   16

3

Figure 11.4
Continued

Phase One Objectives:

In the first phase of the engagement, our
objectives will be the evaluation of: 17

1. The Purchasing Plan. We will evaluate the
    university's present plan to upgrade its
    administrative computing through the
    purchase of a RAM 5240 Computer and to
    upgrade its academic and instructional
    computing through the purchase of a Delta
    1120 Computer.

2. The Computer Center. We will evaluate the
    Computer Center's organization and staffing.
    We will prepare a five-year staffing and
    organization plan to enable the center to deal
    with the upgrades in administrative computing.

3. The Feasibility of Word Processing. We
    will develop recommendations on the
    feasibility of the university using its present
    or one of its new computers to install word
    processing in its academic and instructional
    computing.

Phase Two Objectives:

In the second part of the engagement, our
objectives will be the preparation of: 18

1. A Requirements Definition. We will prepare a
    general requirements definition in each of
    the three application areas of (a) Student
    Information, (b) Payroll and Personnel, and
    (c) Accounting and Budgeting. Each definition
    will include an analysis of the present systems
    as they affect their users.

4

Figure 11.4
Continued

2. <u>Recommendations and Schedules</u>. We will establish priorities and recommendations for a five-year systems development plan either for developing new software packages or for upgrading present ones to meet user requirements in the three application areas noted in 1.

* * * * * * * * * * *

In both phases described above, we will need the full cooperation of the Computer Services Policy Committee. Some of the issues discussed will be sensitive, e.g., staffing, the possible reorganization of   19
the center, and establishing priorities for the future. Therefore, we will present all our recommendations in draft form to the committee for review and decisions.

D) The Two Limitations of the Engagement   20

We define two limitations of our project. First, in cases where the university has already done a study of an issue related to this project, we will simply review the recommendation of the study to determine   21
whether it is the best course for the university to follow. Specifically, we refer to the study recommending the purchase of two new computers.

Second, the first objective of the second phase described above states that we will prepare a general requirements definition for each of three application areas (Student Information, Payroll and Personnel,   22
and Accounting and Budgeting). In doing so, we will be limited to preparing a conceptual design document which:

* Describes the desired features of the application area.

5

Figure 11.4
Continued

* Can be compared and contrasted with existing capabilities.

* Establishes a policy which the Computer Services Policy Committee can use to coordinate improvements.

* Presents and evaluates three options: (a) revising existing software, (b) developing new software, or (c) buying new software.

Then we will examine each of the three application areas (Student Information, etc.) and recommend the best of the three options for each area. We will then draw up a five-year plan for each of the application areas.   23

However, if you decide to purchase new software for any application area, we will not assist either in the selection of the new software or in its implementation. We would have to submit another proposal for those services.   24

E) Approach

Our approach would be simply to accomplish the phase one objectives first and then to accomplish the phase two objectives. Some of the activities regarding the two phases would no doubt overlap, so that phase one would not necessarily be completed before phase two would begin. Logically, however, we would break the tasks down as follows: 25

6

Figure 11.4
Continued

Phase One Activities:

To accomplish the phase one objectives, we would: 26

1. Meet with the Computer Services Policy Committee to review objectives, limitations, and the approach we would follow for both phases.

2. Review all existing reports on computer hardware, academic and instructional computing, and user requirements. We would go back at least three years and examine reports from committees, task forces, and the Computer Center.

3. Interview the center staff and key university administrators regarding needs in hardware, staffing, academic and instructional computing, and word processing.

4. Analyze all these findings and make recommendations. We would discuss our findings and recommendations with the Computer Services Policy Committee before submitting a final version to the university.

Phase Two Activities:

Phase two involves the development of a five-year plan for the university. To accomplish the phase two objectives, we would analyze the university's present systems in the three application areas of Student Information, Payroll and Personnel, and Accounting   27 and Budgeting. We would determine how well these systems record, classify, summarize, and report information. Therefore, for each of the systems we would have to:

7

Figure 11.4
Continued

1. Review and document the status of the system.

2. Examine and document the flow of original data.

3. Review all operating reports used by the various offices in the management of their daily work, e.g., registers and rejected transaction reports.

4. Review existing controls designed to insure accuracy and timeliness of transactions.

5. Interview various department heads who use the system to determine: how they use the reports they get from the system; what kinds of records they maintain to supplement the system; and what decisions they make in planning for, operating, and controlling their departments.

6. Analyze the findings from all these reviews and prepare recommendations involving a five-year plan for implementation. The recommendations and the plan will be submitted first to the Computer Services Policy Committee for review.

The written report which would result from completing the phase two tasks described above would: 28

1. Define the management objectives of the new system.

2. Describe the kind of organization it would be designed to support and analyze the impact the system would have on the university.

8

Figure 11.4
Continued

3. Identify the operations it would perform.

4. Identify its major inputs, outputs, and the estimated volume of each.

5. Identify its interface requirements.

6. Define its benefits, as far as possible in quantitative terms.

III) <u>Management Section</u>

A) Our Experience and Qualifications

Founded in 1949, Lavelle and Kremer offers accounting, auditing, and management consulting services through our 35 offices in the United States. We have long recognized the needs of a variety of specialized industries--higher education among them. To meet these needs, we have established special practice units from which we organize the project teams that meet the needs of these industries.   29

All of the proposed work for Erie State University will be performed by staff from the company's Columbus, Ohio, and Louisville, Kentucky, offices. The wide range of expertise available from these two regional offices minimizes the need to draw personnel from other parts of the country.   30

Lavelle and Kremer has performed the kind of requirements definitions needed by Erie State for other comparable schools, notably Southfield University, Dorchester State University, and St. Athanasius College. Below we describe each engagement and cite references at the school.   31

9

Figure 11.4
Continued

Southfield University:

We assisted Southfield University, with a student
population of 11,500, in improving their accounting   32
system and evaluating their data processing facilities.

In regard to the accounting system, we analyzed
their procedures, practices, and work flows to identify
the performance requirements of the accounting cycle.   33
We recommended improvements in the chart of
accounts and payroll system.

In regard to data processing, we evaluated their
management, organization, and operation controls in
several areas. These included organization and   34
staffing, programs and equipment, documentation
standards and practices, and the internal auditing
involved in data processing.

For a reference, please contact Dr. Shelley Unger,
Vice-President for Business Services, Southfield   35
University, Southfield, Pennsylvania 15802. Telephone
(814) 522-8911.

---

*Authors' note: For brevity's sake, we will delete the part of the
proposal that explains Lavelle and Kremer's work for the two
remaining universities*

B) Engagement Staffing

We plan to staff this engagement with consultants
and managers who have substantial experience in
data processing, management information systems,   36
and higher education.

10

Figure 11.4
Continued

Mr. Lionel Barth will serve as client partner and have general responsibility for the success of the engagement. He has substantial experience in higher education as both a consultant and university administrator. He has served as the associate dean of the College of Business Administration at the University of Beaufort. Since coming to Lavelle and Kremer, he has successfully managed engagements at such institutions as Danby College, St. Benedict College, and Trevor State University.

37

Ms. Leah Rothstein will serve as engagement partner and assist Mr. Barth in areas that require data processing and management information systems expertise, for example, Computer Center organization and staffing. She has developed an automated on-line personnel information system for Dudley University and has managed a study of equipment requirements for the data processing facility of Morrison University.

38

Mr. Roger Delano will serve as engagement manager and supervise the day-to-day activities of the consultants assigned on-site at the university. He has outstanding experience in data processing and management information systems and has assisted in numerous requirements definitions. His specialty lies in the evaluation and selection of data processing hardware and software and in developing data processing department standards.

39

Ms. Audrey Dunn will manage those activities that relate to systems needs and applications in a university environment. She has over nine years of university experience and, as a consultant, has successfully managed several requirements definitions and systems implementations. At Bainbridge University she served as general supervisor of Accounting and director of Budget and Management Studies.

40

11

Figure 11.4
Continued

Resumes of these key individuals are to be found in the appendix of this proposal.   41

C) Timetable of the Engagement

We are prepared to begin working on the engagement within three weeks of authorization to proceed. We expect to complete it within three months of the date of authorization. We will send monthly written progress reports to the executive vice-president of the university.   42

IV) Cost Section

Our fees are based on the time spent on an engagement and the level of professional personnel involved. Based on our experience in similar engagements, we estimate the total of professional fees and expenses to be $42,500. Expenses for travel, typing, and report production make up approximately   43 30 percent of the total. Your expenses will not exceed the amount quoted. If actual fees and expenses are less than our estimate, we will reduce the bill accordingly. We customarily bill on a monthly basis--with our monthly written progress reports.

V) Appendix

Resume of Audrey Dunn

Ms. Dunn is a senior consultant in the Louisville office of Lavelle and Kremer. She has extensive experience in higher education, having held senior staff positions at universities in Indiana and Illinois.

12

Figure 11.4
Continued

Before joining our firm, she served as director of
Budget and Management Studies for Bainbridge
University. At other colleges and universities she has
served as personnel coordinator, general supervisor of
accounting, and academic budget and planning officer.

44

Examples of her professional accomplishments in
university finance and management include:

45

* Directing accounting operations for a
  consolidated student receivable (tuition, fees,
  housing) that provided some 13,000 students
  with several payment plan options and monthly
  billings.

* Implementing a comprehensive financial
  management system that provided for complete
  program accounting and varying levels of
  financial reporting to meet needs of managers at
  all levels.

* Developing an on-line budget preparation
  capability that monitors and provides
  management reports on budget requests against
  resource allocations.

* Implementing an automated long-range
  financial planning model for a community
  college system in Illinois.

Ms. Dunn holds a bachelor's degree in Business
Administration and a master's degree in Public
Administration, with a concentration in
organizational theory and behavior.

46

Authors' note: Other resumes follow in the complete proposal.

13

Proposal Writing
Employees often write proposals independently of a particular commission or directive, and the ability to write effective proposals can advance your career. You might have a brilliant idea for some improvement in your company, but it might remain only a "good idea" unless you can *convince* upper management that it *is* a good idea.

Usually, you first discuss such an idea informally with a superior, who may tell you, "Send me a memo on it." That means a proposal, which can move up through the organization—with your name on it.

On the other hand, most formal, solicited proposals are written by more than one author—by committees or proposal teams consisting of representatives from many areas of the business. The long, multivolume proposal is almost always written by a team in response to an RFP from government or a large company for a deadline established by the client.

The proposal team is headed by a person usually referred to as the proposal manager, proposal director, or project manager, who is responsible for coordinating all activities of the team and for editing the final draft of the proposal. He or she will usually staff the team with representatives from various departments, which will cooperate in developing the proposal and producing the product or service. Representatives could come from communications, sales, production, engineering, and research and development.

The proposal team will meet first to develop an overall strategy, divide up assignments, and establish scheduling for the various phases of the project. Throughout the project the team will meet to report progress, discuss problems, and review drafts of parts of the proposal. It will also normally review the complete final draft.

Since chapter 15 is devoted to collaborative writing, the details of this process will be reserved till then. This chapter concentrates on how to write a proposal, a process that is essentially the same whether one person or a team does it.

Problem-Solving Steps

Define   To define the proposal problem, follow these three suggestions: (1) connect the proposal to client needs, (2) project an image of credibility, and (3) plan a schedule.

Relate the Proposal to Client Needs   The primary objective of any proposal is to persuade the decision maker that the proposed product or service will satisfy an important *need* of that person. The person may have identified the need beforehand for you or you may have discovered the need through experience or research. Either way, proposal writing is preeminently an act of persuasion, so your reader profile should emphasize client need.

If the proposal is solicited, the client will usually state those needs as requirements or specifications in the RFP. If not, you must discover the client's needs. If you are writing an internal proposal to your department head, you may know those needs well. If your internal proposal is targeted for upper management, you must relate it to their needs—the general objectives of the department, division, or company. Whatever the level, identify this person's objectives—increasing productivity or sales, lowering costs, developing new products, enhancing morale, or improving communications or community relations.

If you're writing an external proposal, determine the client's objectives and priorities. Ask yourself what is most important—time, the quality of the product or service, gaining a competitive edge, the company's reliability, its experience and qualifications, service and/or maintenance. Whatever the answers, you must tie the client's wishes to the benefits your proposal promises to deliver.

Consider also the information your client must have to reach a decision. Here it will help to identify primary and secondary audiences. The primary audience may be the executive decision maker; the secondary audience may be subordinates who will judge the technical aspects of the proposal and advise the decision maker. The major parts of the proposal must be clear enough for the decision maker, but the technical parts must satisfy the subordinates. Here's where the appendixes will come in handy—a place for material that the decision maker would not understand or would find too detailed.

In figure 11.4, Lavelle and Kremer devote most of their executive summary, technical section, and statement of the problem sections to describing in detail the computing requirements of their client, Erie State University. This detailed analysis assures the university administrators that their needs are fully appreciated. The approach specifies how the proposers plan to meet those needs; the management section demonstrates that they have the expertise and resources to meet them.

Project an Image of Credibility   An image of credibility becomes extremely important to the proposer. Thus the client must come to regard your claim that this product or service will meet his or her needs as highly credible. One factor that will promote this sense of credibility is the quality of thought evident in the proposal. For example, in figure 11.4, Lavelle and Kremer carefully design their statement of objectives (paragraphs 16 to 19) to parallel the section on approach (paragraphs 25 to 28). The underlying message of such well-designed passages is that the authors have given careful thought to meeting the needs of the client and thus deserve confidence.

Plan a Schedule   In this early stage, make a schedule for the completion of the major phases of the proposal: information gathering, planning, writing, editing, typing, and reproduction. For this purpose you will find a Gantt chart helpful (refer to chapter 9). Lavelle and Kremer specify when they will begin work, report progress, and complete the job.

Analyze   Information gathering will be a major part of this phase of proposal writing. Your research will probably involve discussions with colleagues, reading, meetings, and perhaps interviews with experts. (The techniques of research presented in chapter 8 should be useful.) Here we will focus on how to handle the results of your research. The following list of questions will help to analyze your writing task:

1. What need or needs of the client do you propose to meet?
2. What is your statement of the problem?
3. How much time will you be allowed to complete this project?
4. What criteria must a successful solution meet?
5. In the light of these criteria, what are the alternative solutions to the problem?
6. Which alternative solution meets most of the criteria or the most important criteria?
7. What assumptions does the solution to the client's problem make?
8. Is the solution limited in any way? For what reasons?
9. What methodology will the recommended solution involve?
10. Will special equipment be needed? What kind?
11. Who will have overall responsibility for the project?
12. Who will be involved?
13. What tasks will each of these people perform?
14. Who will report to whom?
15. Will their qualifications to perform the task be obvious or need to be explained in brief resumes?
16. What deadlines must each of these persons meet so that the overall project will be completed on time?
17. How will progress be reported and when?
18. What problems might arise, and how do you propose to deal with them?
19. What benefits can the client anticipate from the completion of the project?
20. From the client's viewpoint, what will be the most attractive features of the proposal?
21. Have you developed a detailed budget for the project?
22. Are there any terms or conditions accompanying the proposal?
23. What form must the client's approval take?

Not every proposal will require answering each of these questions. In some cases, the answers will be obvious. For example, the client's approval (question 23) may take the form of a short memo from your boss giving you the go-ahead.

Lavelle and Kremer answer most of these questions in their proposal. They do not answer the questions dealing with specifying alternative solutions to the problem (4, 5, and 6) because they wish to keep their proposal relatively brief and understandable to a lay audience.

When you have answered those questions that apply to your project, you will be ready to consider a plan or organization for your proposal. Since there is no universally agreed-upon format or plan for the proposal, headings and organization vary. Below is a list of commonly used headings (those often used interchangeably are grouped together):

- Background, History, Statement of the Problem, Introduction
- Objectives, Purpose
- Methodology, Technology, Approach, Program, Service, System Concept, Implementation Strategy
- Specifications
- Project Management, Personnel
- Requirements, Needs, Information Requirement
- Limitations, Constraints, Exceptions, Assumptions, Scope
- Qualifications, Experience, Organization and Planning
- Cost, Cost Analysis, Budget, Cost Savings

You may encounter headings *not* on this list, and you may occasionally have to invent a heading to serve your purpose.

But while headings vary, the proposals themselves are essentially the same. Sticking to the standard headings and organization will enable you to write formal and informal proposals with some ease and professionalism. But keep in mind that you may have to diverge from these suggested patterns and terminology and develop original alternatives to get your particular job done.

Draft   Answering the questions given in the last section should supply you with the notes for writing, while the plans suggested previously should supply an outline. Whatever kind of proposal you are doing, begin writing with the statement of the problem. Although the executive summary comes first in the finished document, it should be written last. A statement of the problem generates a sequence of thought from defining objectives, developing criteria, judging alternative solutions against the criteria, and finally to selecting the best solution to the problem.

The outline below, which Lesley Chou develops for the proposal shown in figure 11.3, follows such a pattern. This pattern lends itself to Chou's purpose of showing upper management the cost savings in the alternative recommended—the service contract. Chou's list of alternatives implies, "See how much alternative solutions could cost you?"

A Proposal for Computer-Assisted Color Slides

   I. Executive summary
  II. Statement of the problem
     A. Background
     B. Objectives
 III. Alternatives
     A. The first alternative: purchase of a complete computer
        slide production system
     B. The second alternative: development of an in-house slide-making
        system
     C. The third alternative: an outside service contract for slide making
  IV. Recommended solution
   V. Cost advantages

Lavelle and Kremer adapt the format to their purpose. As the outline of their proposal indicates, they omit any discussion of alternatives. They already have a great deal of specific information to impart without discussing alternatives not chosen. Since Lavelle and Kremer assume their readers will trust their professional judgment to select the best alternative, they spend their time detailing it:

A Proposal to Provide Technical Expertise in
Computer Utilization for Erie State University

   I. Executive summary
  II. Technical section
     A. Background
     B. Statement of the problem
     C. Objectives
     D. The two limitations of the engagement
     E. Approach
 III. Management section
     A. Our experience and qualifications
     B. Engagement staffing
     C. Timetable of the engagement
  IV. Cost section
   V. Appendix (resumes)

As you write the body of the proposal, from the statement of the problem to the cost section, stress the benefits of the project. For example, in figure 11.3 Chou devotes the last third of the proposal (paragraphs 11 to 16) to describing the advantages in the service contract—in services, quality, and cost. The cost section is even labeled cost advantages.

If your proposal is to have a transmittal letter or memorandum, executive summary, or general introduction, do not write them until you have completed the other elements of your proposal. Because all of these elements deal with the proposal as a whole, you must be able to see it as a whole before you write them. Note the letter of transmittal at the beginning of figure 11.4. Paragraphs 2 and 3 point out the features of the proposal that Lee Weber, the author, thinks will most appeal to the university administration. He mentions the detailed, careful analysis of the objectives of the proposal and the qualifications of Lavelle and Kremer's firm. The executive summary states precisely what Lavelle and Kremer will do and for how much money (paragraphs 8 and 9). The letter or memo, executive summary, and introduction serve to motivate the client to read the rest of the proposal. These sections should convince the client that you understand his or her need, that you know how to meet it, and that you can do so in a timely and cost-effective manner.

Revise and Edit Let some time elapse between writing and editing the draft, at least a day. Review the draft to see whether you have stressed the advantages of the proposal to both your primary reader, the executive, and the secondary readers, the executive's subordinates. You may often find yourself at this point adding such statements as "A less obvious payback of this feature is its connection with . . ." to remind the more specialized subordinates of hidden benefits.

Add transitions and polish language as you would with any document. But pay special attention to using format to stress important features of your proposal, so that even the busiest reader can decide what is interesting about your proposal as he or she skims it. For example, in figure 11.4, Lavelle and Kremer use headings to make information easily accessible: background, objectives, approach, and cost section. The underlined subtitles in paragraph 17 and 18 are easy to skim, as are the numbered lists scattered throughout the proposal.

Another point: the more formal the proposal, the greater the tendency to use "boilerplate," the standard content that can be word processed into any of several documents. For example, you would be using boilerplate if in adding resumes of key personnel, you merely asked each individual for a current resume and added that material as presented to you in the appendix.

Edit all resumes to include only the qualifications and experience relevant to this project. Each proposal should create the impression that it has been customized for this special client. Lavelle and Kremer include only the relevant expertise of their key managers in their engagement staffing section and in the sample resume in the appendix.

At this stage you might wish to ask an associate to read the proposal to judge its appeal and clarity. The reader should not have helped with the proposal and should, as closely as possible, resemble the client in background and orientation. Ask this person especially to look for unnecessary technical language and repetitions.

Finally, if the proposal is long enough to be bound, don't settle for cheap binding. If you have spent weeks and even months preparing it, you want its visual effect to correspond to its substance.

Summary

The feasibility report and the proposal are two similar but distinct forms of business writing, and both contain sections dealing with cost analysis, assumptions, scope, methodology, and risk.

The author of the feasibility report offers a recommendation on whether the decision maker should go ahead with a specific business venture. The author therefore presents both the positive and negative aspects of the decision and must present convincing evidence that the recommendation is justified.

The feasibility report can be internal or external, depending on the relationship of the author to the reader of the report. The author can be a subordinate writing for a superior within the company or an outside consultant engaged by the company to write the report. Feasibility reports are all formal reports, requiring detailed analysis.

There is considerable freedom in structuring the feasibility report. These reports frequently include a letter of transmittal, a title page, a warranty or certification (of no conflict of interest), a title page, a recommendation, a statement of assumptions and scope, a history of the business and a forecast about its future, a demand analysis, a market analysis, financial information about the company involved, and possibly an appendix containing technical material.

The proposal writer aims at persuading the decision maker to accept a product or service. Thus the proposal author is an open advocate.

Proposals can be classified as (1) solicited or unsolicited, depending on whether the company for whom the proposal is written requests it; (2) internal or external, depending on whether the author is an employee of the company; and (3) formal or informal, depending on the degree of detailed analysis included.

Informal proposals contain a summary, a statement of the problem, an examination of alternative solutions to the problem, and a recommendation. Formal proposals have a title page, a letter or memorandum of transmittal, an executive summary, a technical section, a management section, a cost section, and possibly an appendix. But formal and informal proposals can vary in content and form from this general pattern and may be written by individuals or teams. As in the other forms of business writing, we recommend the problem-solving technique for feasibility reports and proposals.

Writing Problems

1. You are a manager in executive and professional recruitment for Sinc-Corp, a large manufacturer of office equipment systems. You are proposing a program to mail a variety of information materials about Sinc-Corp to key faculty members at targeted universities throughout the country. These key faculty members are those most likely to influence future job applicants and decision makers for computer purchases. The information mailed will make these faculty members more aware of Sinc-Corp and its leadership in the industry.

   At least three faculty members will be identified at each of 200 universities. One of the three will coordinate Sinc-Corp's recruitment efforts at that school. You will recruit the campus coordinators, and they will recruit the other two faculty members. You will then assemble a mailing list.

   The motivation for the faculty members to participate in the program will be a three-day seminar acquainting them with Sinc-Corp's operations. The seminar will be held at a resort motel in Phoenix, Arizona. The faculty members will be encouraged to take full advantage of the recreational facilities during their stay—at Sinc-Corp's expense.

   Examples of materials to be mailed are news releases, product brochures, reprints of articles from trade publications, employee publications, and public relations materials. For the first year there will be six mailings. After that, there will be an evaluation of the program, its costs, and staffing to determine the number of mailings for the second year.

   Write the proposal to your department head, Vern Schulte, Sinc-Corp's director of executive and professional recruitment.

2. You manage the policy change division for Guardian Insurance Corporation and you need to increase your staff by one person in the Lapse and Revival section. Previously you have agreed to a complement of five specialists in this section, but, while they are doing a good

job, they cannot keep up with demand. Last year the clerical standards committee indicated that 664 standard hours were needed and that a complement of five people would result in 648 net hours available. The plan was to make up the difference in hours by the use of part-time employees, but it has not worked.

One of the five specialists was on disability for 30 days during the last year and will be on leave beginning February 1. A second specialist has been off sick for two weeks. Morale is becoming a problem. The specialists are carrying more than their share of work, and yet work continues to pile up. If people are promoted out of the section or leave to take other positions, there will be a problem while new people are trained.

Write a proposal requesting the additional specialist to Gale Predmore, vice-president and director, insurance services department.

3. You are a sales representative for Rite-Mike, manufacturer of dictation systems. Your office address is 110 Monroe Street, Sioux Falls, SD 57005. You are writing a sales proposal to Jan Klein, 38 Komiskey Boulevard, Aberdeen, SD 57402.

You are submitting the following information: Klein may purchase two Model XYZ-9s at $595 each. You will take Klein's two Speak-Easy Model 78s on a trade-in basis. On the other hand, Klein may lease the equipment described above on the following terms: 36 months for $59 a month; 48 months for $52 a month; and 60 months for $49 a month. The leasing charges include full service during the lease period.

The model that Klein will purchase or lease offers an insert feature that allows the dictator to insert passages without erasing. Ends of letters and documents and special instructions are indicated by cue tones and light-emitting diodes, allowing the transcriber to determine the length of the piece as well as locate any special instructions or priorities. The unit has a phone-in capacity from telephones anywhere in the world and can record conversations. It has a feature that eliminates background noise from dictation. It can also record a conference in the office.

Write the sales proposal to Klein.

4. You are the general manager of Tours, Ltd., and your address is 58 Weehauken Terrace, Kankakee, IL 60914. You are writing to Hilary Nordman of 815 Greenlawn Drive, Amelia IL 60522. Nordman is the president of the Amelia Senior Citizen Association. You are proposing to coordinate a weekend excursion for the Amelia seniors to take place this summer on one of three possible weekends: Friday, July 20; Friday July 27; or Friday, August 10.

At 10:00 A.M. in front of the Amelia Municipal Building, the seniors will board a Whiteline Bus, which will transport them to the lodge at Betsy Ross State Park, Rossville, Illinois. There will be a stop for lunch (part of the tour) at the Zuider Zee Restaurant in Crawford, Illinois. The seniors will spend two nights at the lodge, with breakfast and dinner included as part of the tour. On Saturday there will be a guided tour of the reconstructed Fort Hiram Butler and luncheon at the fort cafeteria, also included in the tour. On Saturday evening there will be a square dance at the lodge of the state park.

On Sunday, there will be a tour of the Butler Homestead with luncheon at the Butler Inn, also part of the tour. The cost of the tour for each senior will be $205. Tours, Ltd. will make all the arrangements as part of the fee, but a minimum of 30 seniors must sign up for the tour 30 days in advance. The tour will accommodate no more than 75 seniors.

Write the proposal letter to Nordman.

5. As the manager of the word processing center at Mandrake Corporation, you wish to propose a letter writing program to Fran Gomez, manager of the training and employee relations division. Mandrake employees have a wide variety of writing needs. Some rely mainly on form letters for the little writing they do. Others write often to people in the district offices or to customers and their representatives. Still others compose the form letters and write manuals, reports, and technical documentation.

You plan to offer three basic courses: Letter Writing I for beginners; Letter Writing II for more experienced writers; and Letter Writing III for writers with special needs, for example, sales letters, collection letters, and the like. You plan to use one textbook for all three courses (assigning relevant chapters to each group). The text will be *Business Letter Writing* by Dale McGuffey (Blasedale, CA; Full Court Press, 1986), which costs $29.95 a copy.

Each class will meet for one lecture-workshop period each week for a total of eight weeks. The students will be expected to complete eight writing assignments, mainly on their own time. No grades will be given, but there will be an evaluation. Eight weeks after an individual has completed the course, a questionnaire will be sent to his or her manager, requesting an evaluation of the individual's writing performance since taking the course. The reason for this evaluation is that you feel that the person's motivation will be stronger if his or her manager is involved in the process.

Admission to the course will be voluntary, although some individuals may volunteer at the suggestion of their managers.

Write the proposal.

6. Kevin Rinaldi, an acquaintance of yours and a graduating senior majoring in English, has engaged you to do a feasibility report for him. After graduation, he plans to work on his M.B.A. but desires an income from opening a business—a resume service. He plans to assist clients by writing their resume, cover letter, and follow-up letters. He plans to meet clients at either their home or his apartment and intends to do all the work on his word processor and letter-quality printer.

Research reveals the following. He lives in a university town where at least 1500 job seekers graduate annually, so there is demand for his service. Most of the students enrolled at the university have part-time jobs, many of which require a resume and cover letter as part of the job application. Approximately 5 percent of these students take a writing course that includes instruction in resume writing.

Seven businesses are listed in the local telephone directory as offering resume services. Four of these are print shops. You visit each of the four and collect samples of their work. They offer an economical price but only proofreading and layout advice—not advice on how the client may best present his or her skills and attributes. There are three other resume services, which are priced out of the range of most graduating seniors, their fees averaging a $100 minimum for 25 resumes. The client must write his or her cover and follow-up letters. The products of these three firms have a sleek, artificial look that may count against the job applicant.

Rinaldi's costs will include the following. Ribbons for the printer cost $6.95 each; one ribbon will print 80 single-spaced pages. He will have to pay for paper, envelopes, and maintenance of both the computer and the printer. Normally the letter, resume, and follow-up letters will use a total of three pages. The cost will vary with the quality and weight of the paper used, but typically, a box of good bond paper containing 500 sheets costs $8.00. Matching envelopes cost $5.00 for a box of 500. Rinaldi will do all the typing, printing, and delivering. There will be no billing costs since all business will be done on a C.O.D. basis.

The service will include *any* assistance the client needs—for example, proofreading for spelling, punctuation, and grammar. It will also include advice on resume content, format, and style. There will be an hourly consultation fee of $25. There are several means of marketing the service: placing ads in the student newspaper (at $1 per line) or on the campus radio station ($25 per 30-second spot), phoning seniors listed in the student directory, and posting notices on bulletin boards around campus.

It is difficult to estimate the volume of business this venture could generate, but one could make a reasonable estimate. Assuming that ads are placed in the newspaper and on the radio station once a week, as many as 100 accounts could be serviced in the first year. If these clients are happy with the service and tell others about it, there could be as many as 200 clients the second year. You estimate that the number of clients should not go much beyond 200 a year as long as only one person operates the business, since more clients would pose a quality control problem. The business could eventually prove so profitable that Rinaldi might wish to engage in it full-time. Information about tax deductions for equipment, supplies, and travel will not be considered as part of your report. Nor will you estimate the maintenance costs on the computer and printer.

Write the report. Rinaldi's address is 872 West Third Street, Erie, OH 60872.

CHAPTER 12

Oral Presentations

You may occasionally have to give an oral presentation based on a document you have written. Sometimes you will have to distill a lengthy formal report into a 15-minute talk. At other times, you may need to tell a group of superiors about key points in your feasibility study or support your written project proposal with a face-to-face oral presentation. You could even have to follow up a short letter with an oral presentation elaborating on what you have written.

Gary Schaeffer, sales representative for Strong Business Travel, Inc., must give such a follow-up talk. Strong handles all phases of business travel—including reservations, accounting, and emergency travel service—for any firm to which it is under contract. Schaeffer has written a letter to Connie Manguel, vice-president for accounting at I-E Manufacturing. In his letter, Schaeffer specifies the benefits that a travel services contract with Strong can offer to a company such as I-E. In response, Manguel phones Schaeffer and invites him to make a 30-minute presentation highlighting those benefits for I-E's executive board. Schaeffer accepts the invitation and starts preparing for his presentation.

Schaeffer knows that he can use the same problem-solving approach to develop his oral presentation that he uses to write a document. Indeed, some of the steps, such as defining and analyzing a problem, will be very similar for both speaking and writing.

Other problem-solving steps will require adaptation. Predrafting decisions will still center on information and main point, but style choices will now involve such image-shapers as posture and voice quality. The draft phase of most oral presentations will also differ. Since a fully written-out speech will rarely be necessary, drafting will involve preparing note cards from which to give a presentation. Revisions will require practicing the presentation and changing notes so that they help Schaeffer appear well prepared and engaging.

We will see Schaeffer just before he gives his presentation, during its actual delivery, and throughout a question and answer session. Finally, we will see how he follows his presentation with a letter to Connie Manguel.

Defining the Speaking Problem

When Schaeffer receives the invitation to speak to I-E Manufacturing, he uses what he has learned from his phone conversation with Manguel and from research he has done on the company to prepare a problem definition. Note that Schaeffer must consider his desired image as a visible, audible speaker rather than as a writer whose document conveys the image.

- *Objective* To prepare a 30-minute oral presentation highlighting the benefits that I-E Manufacturing will receive by contracting for the services of Strong Business Travel, Inc.

- *Audience* I-E Manufacturing's executive board (president, executive vice-president, five vice-presidents)

- *Speaker's desired image* Energetic, knowledgeable

Analyzing the Speaking Problem

The same analytic formats that work for understanding writing problems will help you envision the oral presentation problem more clearly. Outlines, note card decks, flow charts, decision trees, and matrices all enable you to review your knowledge of a topic and then depict that knowledge to aid you in developing an oral presentation.

Because Schaeffer's objective is to detail a number of Strong Business Travel's advantages and to lead from those benefits to the conclusion that

I-E will do well to contract with Strong, he chooses an inductive decision tree as his analytic tool. Figure 12.1 depicts Schaeffer's application of the inductive decision tree to his oral presentation problem. As you can see, Schaeffer will show how Strong Travel's well-informed staff, high-volume business, and travel-management experience can save I-E Manufacturing time and money. Schaeffer will also describe how contracting with Strong can improve I-E employees' travel experiences and corporate prestige. Constructing the decison tree helps Schaeffer to arrive at this strategy, while the finished tree reminds him of the presentation's overall structure as he refines his talk.

Deciding on Information and Main Points

You should begin by making decisions about your information and main point for your oral presentation just as you would for your written presentation. Schaeffer asks and answers these questions about the information he has on hand for the I-E presentation:

Question Do I have all the information I need to show I-E's executive board why it should contract with Strong?

Answer No. I need to know several more items. To what destinations do I-E employees travel frequently? How much foreign travel do they do? How much did the company spend on employee travel last year? I can get these answers from Connie Manguel, who offered to provide all non-confidential information I might need for my presentation.

Question Do I already have information that I should *not* include in my presentation?

Answer Yes. I have notes on international travel law. Since my presentation time is very limited, I'll dispense with examples of possible travel law pitfalls and simply state that Strong has a staff that can cope with all sorts of foreign travel regulations, such as visas, vaccination certificates, and international driver's licenses.

Question Is my information sufficiently detailed for the presentation?

Answer Yes. However, I would like a bit more background on I-E than I can ask Manguel to provide. I'll take a few minutes at lunch today to stop at the public library and look up I-E in an industrial directory. This directory will give me some additional information, such as whether they have subsidiaries that might have special travel needs or where they are incorporated, so that I can review appropriate state tax regulations pertaining to business travel.

Question Is all my information accurate and up to date?

Answer I think so. Nevertheless, on the day of my presentation, I will

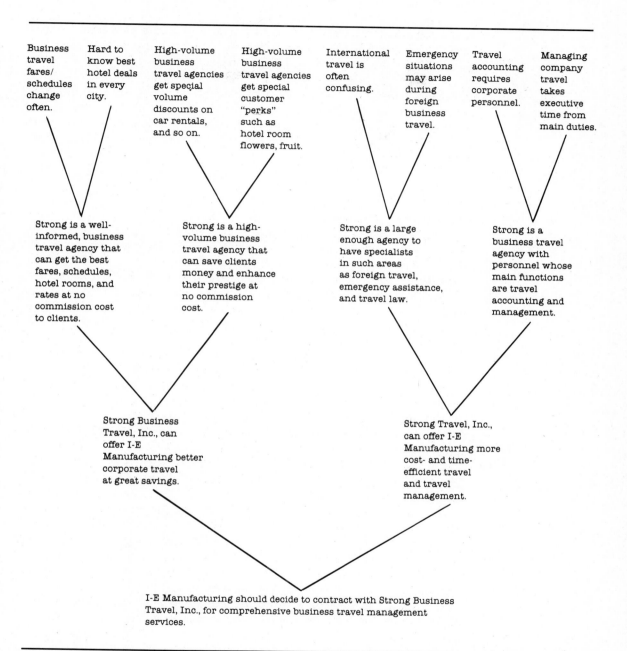

Business travel fares/ schedules change often.

Hard to know best hotel deals in every city.

High-volume business travel agencies get special volume discounts on car rentals, and so on.

High-volume business travel agencies get special customer "perks" such as hotel room flowers, fruit.

International travel is often confusing.

Emergency situations may arise during foreign business travel.

Travel accounting requires corporate personnel.

Managing company travel takes executive time from main duties.

Strong is a well-informed, business travel agency that can get the best fares, schedules, hotel rooms, and rates at no commission cost to clients.

Strong is a high-volume business travel agency that can save clients money and enhance their prestige at no commission cost.

Strong is a large enough agency to have specialists in such areas as foreign travel, emergency assistance, and travel law.

Strong is a business travel agency with personnel whose main functions are travel accounting and management.

Strong Business Travel, Inc., can offer I-E Manufacturing better corporate travel at great savings.

Strong Travel, Inc., can offer I-E Manufacturing more cost- and time-efficient travel and travel management.

I-E Manufacturing should decide to contract with Strong Business Travel, Inc., for comprehensive business travel management services.

Figure 12.1   Analysis of an oral presentation. Inductive decision tree.

double-check our current hotel room and car rental discounts for major destinations. That way I can be certain that I am communicating only the most up-to-date, correct data to the I-E board.

Because Schaeffer has used an inductive decision tree for his analysis and is satisfied with its outcome, his presentation's main idea is the same as the bottom "trunk" line of his decision tree: *I-E Manufacturing should decide to contract with Strong Business Travel, Inc., for comprehensive travel arrangement services.*

Styling Oral Presentations

Your desired image shapes the wording of an oral presentation in much the same way it does your sentence and word choices in a written document. Schaeffer knows that his extensive background in the business travel industry and his careful preparation for the I-E presentation will establish his image as knowledgeable. In addition, he must make sentence and wording choices that help him sharpen what will be the energetic image that will convince the I-E board that Strong will make good on its promise to obtain the best possible travel arrangements for its clients. To this end, Schaeffer jots a note to himself to use forceful, active verb constructions. He also reminds himself to employ first- and second-person pronouns: "*I* assure *you* that *we* at Strong Travel will make *your* traveling employees happy as *we* save I-E Manufacturing money."

Because he will be speaking, Schaeffer considers some image-shapers that are different from those required for writing.

Dress and Grooming

Through his research, Schaeffer learns that I-E Manufacturing is an old-line concern whose employees dress conservatively. Consequently, he will be certain to dress and groom himself so that his appearance will not distract from the message of his presentation. Schaeffer will probably wear a dark suit, solid light-colored shirt, conservative tie, and well-polished shoes. He will make sure his hair has been trimmed and that he otherwise presents the conservative appearance that meets his potential clients' likely expectations.

Had Schaeffer been addressing a different sort of company—for example, a recently founded high-tech firm whose president wears blue jeans and T-shirts to work—he might have modified his dress accordingly, perhaps wearing a sport jacket, dress shirt, and tie. It is unlikely, however, that for even the least formally attired executives, Shaeffer would have worn jeans and T-shirt, since such dress might well trigger even the casually dressed president's suspicions about Strong Travel's abilities to work in such traditional business settings as accounting and international commerce.

When women from Strong Travel make oral presentations, they must make decisions analogous to Schaeffer's. For instance, through research, they must choose whether to wear business suits or slightly more casual attire. Although the most meticulous "dressing for success" can never save a weak presentation from failure, careful attention to dress and grooming can support an effective presentation by helping to focus your audience's attention on what you have to say, not on how you look.

How you present your body in relation to your audience can support or weaken your desired image. In your whole demeanor you want to suggest control, self-confidence, and flexibility, whether standing or sitting. Therefore, you should stand comfortably, with your back straight, weight balanced evenly on your feet. You should appear at ease with your body, in control of its next motion, yet flexible enough to respond as necessary. You should also sit straight but comfortably. This posture will accentuate those times when you wish to lean forward to show you are listening closely or want to swivel right or left to address a listener not seated directly in front of you.

Body Dynamics

What you do with your hands can further support your image of being in control and at ease. We suggest simply keeping your hands at your sides as you speak. When you think it is helpful to make gestures (for example, pointing to a flip chart), do so, but let these gestures be natural, unrehearsed, spur-of-the-moment movements.

Maintain eye contact with your audience. If your presentation is similar to Schaeffer's—for a small group—move your gaze from listener to listener as you speak. The key here is to make the contact neither so short that it seems as if you are uncomfortably "shifty-eyed" nor so long that your listeners feel you are staring at them. It is easier to make eye contact with larger, auditorium-sized audiences. Simply looking at each section of the audience from time to time will create the engaging but not threatening eye contact you desire.

You do not want to wear a silly grin throughout your presentation, but if you feel like smiling, do so. Your facial expression reveals to your audience how you feel about your topic and your listeners. An occasional smile says that you enjoy them both and feel confident enough to show your pleasure.

The room in which you make your presentation controls your physical distance from your listeners and how much you can move around as you talk. Most auditoriums or other large meeting rooms restrict you to a spot at the podium. On the other hand, in smaller conference rooms or boardrooms, you may be able to make slight adjustments in the distance between yourself and your nearest listeners. Being less than four feet away from a speaker makes many Americans feel uncomfortable or even threatened. Therefore, you may have to step back to make your talk if you will be

Presentation Space

standing at the end of a long conference table and listeners are seated immediately adjacent to you, less than four feet away.

The amount of space needed between speaker and listeners to let the nearest audience member feel comfortable varies from culture to culture. When you are making presentations in other countries or to overseas firms located in the United States or Canada, be certain to research cultural conventions. On the question of space, you will find that in some business communities (for example, northern Europe), even four feet may not be enough. In other business settings (for example, Latin America), three feet is sufficient.[1]

In general, stay in one place as you speak. If you move aimlessly around the room, you will make listeners nervous and detract from your presentation's effectiveness. When you do need to take a few steps to draw attention to a chart or flip the pages on a presentation pad, try to speak the words that introduce the reason for your move—for example, "Let me direct your attention to the dry-erase board, where I've listed typical hotel discounts I-E employees might expect in the 10 largest United States cities." Your presentation will be more fluent, increasing its professional appearance.

Vocal Qualities

How you speak can greatly influence your audience's opinion of what you say. To make certain your voice enhances your presentation, keep the following five factors in mind as you prepare your talk.

Volume   Adjust your volume to the room in which you make your presentation. If the room is large, you may need to speak more loudly. If the decor includes sound-deadening carpeting, draperies, or acoustical ceiling tiles, you may need to increase volume. On the other hand, in smaller, noncarpeted areas, you should probably speak more softly since the room will probably amplify your voice.

Because Schaeffer can reasonably believe that the I-E Manufacturing boardroom where he gives his presentation *will* have carpet and heavy draperies, he knows that he will be speaking louder than he normally would. As a result, when he wants the I-E executive board to concentrate especially hard on a point he makes, Schaeffer should be able to focus their attention by speaking more quietly for a few seconds.

Pitch   Pitch describes how high or low you speak. The main suggestion we offer is to vary your pitch when you want to underscore your feelings about a part of your presentation. For instance, Schaeffer might raise his pitch at

---

[1]For a detailed discussion of American and worldwide speaking distance, see Edward T. Hall, *The Silent Language* (Greenwich: Fawcett, 1959).

the end of this sentence: "We can offer you all of these services *at no cost to you.*" By changing the pitch of these last five words, Schaeffer has communicated his enthusiasm for Strong Travel's ability to offer all these services free to clients, a selling point about which he hopes I-E's executive board will be equally excited.

Schaeffer might lower pitch at the close of this sentence: "Suppose it is late at night in a foreign capital and an I-E traveling employee *loses her purse.*" This lower pitch conveys an ominous feeling of impending disaster that only the presence of Strong Travel's 24-hour, foreign-city emergency services can prevent ("Just contact the local Strong Travel agent at the round-the-clock emergency line and you will receive immediate personal assistance").

Speed   Adjust how quickly you speak to the nature of your topic and the needs of your listeners. If you are presenting technical concepts to an audience not very familiar with them, speak more slowly. If your audience is technically expert or if you are communicating nontechnical information, you can speak more quickly.

A good rule is to speak more slowly than you do during a conversation. Remember that during a formal presentation, your audience needs time to understand what you are saying because they cannot ask for clarification during your talk. Even in a presentation where you encourage listeners to "ask me whenever you have a question," most listeners will save their questions for the end of your talk. By speaking slowly enough for them to understand, but not so slowly that you will put them to sleep, you can insure that the post-presentation questions will build upon what you have said rather than force you to rehash facts and figures.

Enunciation   Making certain that you articulate every consonant, vowel, and syllable will also make your speech more intelligible. Your pronouncing clearly each needed sound or group of sounds in a word enables your audience to understand you. Because they will not be frustrated trying to figure out what you meant, they will be able to make sense of those words more easily.

Pronunciation   By checking the pronunciation in a dictionary of any unfamiliar words, you can do yet more to make your presentation effective. While this is important for all words, it is crucial for foreign words.

The travel business requires Schaeffer to be familiar with the correct pronunciations of many foreign proper names. Even English proper nouns (Gloucester's pronunciation, "gläs'tər") can create problems. For his presentation to I-E Manufacturing, Schaeffer checks with his travel agency's international travel specialists to refresh his memory on the pronunciations of such proper nouns as *Schilpol* (Amsterdam's airport), *Okura* (a Tokyo hotel), and *Qantas* (the Australian national airline). To make certain he remembers, he jots down notes with his own pronunciation clues—for example, *Shillpole* for *Schilpol*. In short, Schaeffer has made the decision to pronounce foreign and difficult English words as educated practice dictates. Doing so will show his audience that Strong Travel employees "know their business."

Drafting the Oral Presentation

With information, main idea, and style decisions complete, it is time to start drafting your presentation. Most of your draft will be in note form; a small, but important portion of it should be fully written out. For preparing notes and scripted sections alike, use large (four-by-six-inch) index cards.

A deck of these easily transportable cards will accommodate the amount of information you need for your presentation. In addition, using cards rather than 8½-by-11-inch sheets of paper will suggest to your audience that you are well prepared to speak and flexible enough to move away from your notes.

Introducing the Presentation

Two parts of your presentation—its introduction and conclusion—*should* be written out in advance and memorized. Because the introduction should stir your audience's interest and because it will set the context of the rest of the talk, your having memorized it lets you practice these opening sentences until you can deliver them effectively and with some grace.

An oral business presentation is a cultural as well as a commercial event. That is to say, your audience will expect certain amenities from you before you get down to the main content of your presentation. In the business cultures of the United States and Canada, a one-sentence introductory amenity is appropriate. For a persuasive presentation such as Schaeffer's this opening might be, "I'd like to thank the I-E executive board for this opportunity to show you what Strong Business Travel can offer."

If you find yourself giving a presentation to a company in or from another country, be certain you find out what sorts of opening amenities (and other cultural business behavior) will help your listeners feel at ease. You will find that some business cultures expect lengthier amenities. For instance, Latin American executives may appreciate sincere introductory compliments to their company's city, headquarters, and friendly dealings with your firm and will feel you are overly aggressive if you begin your main topic after only one introductory sentence. Executives from other business cultures, northern European, for instance, may grow impatient with even a single-sentence amenity.

Following your opening sentence, decide on your introductory strategy. You may think it best to jump right into your talk's first key point. This approach is sound if you are sure that your audience will react positively to that first point. Otherwise, you may wish first to summarize what you will be covering in your presentation or provide background information about why you are making the presentation.

Schaeffer decides to take this last approach. Here are the draft index cards he prepares for his introduction. (*Note:* If the cards reproduced here were actually six inches wide, Gary could fit 60 typewritten pica characters/ spaces onto each card line.)

I'd like to thank the I-E executive board for this

opportunity to show you what Strong Business

Travel can offer. Through my talks with Ms.

Manguel, I have come to see many ways in which

we can benefit your employee travel operations.

Card 1:
Draft of Introduction to I-E Manufacturing Presentation

During the next 30 minutes, I would like to show

you eight specific ways in which Strong can

make your employees' travel and your travel

management more productive and less expensive.

Card 2:
Draft Introduction

**Body of the Oral
Presentation**

Preparing the body of your oral presentation requires a different drafting technique from preparing the body of your written documents. Instead of text, you need to prepare note cards. These are crucial to a well-prepared, lively presentation.

Your note cards should list enough information to accomplish your objective but not so much that they undermine the spontaneity of your talk. Once you have written the cards, you should arrange them in the order you will use to give your talk. Your analysis will provide the order for arranging your first-draft cards. As you revise cards, you may wish to rearrange them. For now, let your analysis guide your card arrangement.

On your cards, jot down key words and phrases that will help you remember what you want to discuss at each point in your talk. If you type or word process your cards, use a pica or other large (10 characters per inch) typeface. Double-space your cards for easier reading. Most four-by-six-inch ruled index cards have 15 lines. Thus, you should be able to place up to 8 lines of double-spaced notes on any single card. Whatever format you choose, be certain you can pick up any card you have prepared and read its contents without having to squint or rethink what you put down in the first place.

Number your cards consecutively in pencil, so you can change their order as you revise. Numbering will also be your way of reconstructing the order of your presentation should the card deck become scrambled.

Gary Schaeffer needs to draft just such a note card deck for the body of his presentation. Here are his four cards that immediately follow the introduction on cards 1 and 2. Schaeffer numbers these cards 3, 4, 5, and 6. Note that the order of his cards follows the order of his inductive decision tree (figure 12.1) down each of its branches from left to right.

Card 3: Draft

> Fact of modern business travel:
>
> Fares change often.
>
>   --for example, "super-savers"
>
>   --for example, "business class"
>
>   --for example, "all first class airlines"

Card 4: Draft

Second fact of modern business travel:

Schedules change often.

    --for example, highly competitive routes

      such as New York to Chicago

    --for example, seasonally popular routes

      such as transatlantic

Card 5: Draft

Third fact of modern business travel:

Confusing array of hotel rooms and discounts

here and abroad.

    --for example, corporate discounts at

      international chains

    --for example, special business-travel

      agency client discounts on suites at

      selected independent hotels in major

      commercial areas

Card 6: Draft

Only a well-informed business travel agency

knows all available fares, schedules, hotel

discounts.

Strong is the best-informed agency.

    --full staff of business transportation/

      accommodation experts

    --worldwide computer information network

      updated daily

Concluding the Presentation Draft

Write out the text of your talk's conclusion. A prepared conclusion supports the polished delivery you need to summarize what you have said. It also allows you to tie your main points together and to persuade your listeners to take some action—if that is your presentation's objective.

Here are Schaeffer's note cards containing his draft conclusion. They follow his 2-card introduction and 28-card oral presentation body.

Card 31: Conclusion

> Strong Travel can offer I-E Manufacturing better corporate travel at great savings. We can provide I-E more cost-efficient, time-saving travel management.

Card 32: Conclusion

> For the lowest airline fares, most efficient routing, best hotel accommodations, prestige treatment, travel accounting, and specialized personal service--from New York to Nepal, Los Angeles to Lima, and everywhere else here and abroad--I-E Manufacturing will benefit from Strong's comprehensive travel management contract.

Revising the Presentation Cards

You need to take six actions to revise your note cards for your presentation:

1. Review your cards, inserting delivery cues to yourself about volume, pitch, speed, enunciation, and pronunciation.
2. Practice your presentation. This trial run will let you know whether you need to add new information, delete unnecessary data, or change wording in your introduction and conclusion.
3. Time your practice presentation to make sure it's neither too long nor too short.
4. Create any visual aids you may want to use in your presentation.
5. Ask a trusted colleague to hear your talk and make suggestions for its further improvement.
6. Make yourself a fresh set of presentation note cards incorporating all your revisions.

If there are words or phrases on your cards deserving attention, note how you will treat them. Jot down a clue to remind yourself, for example, how to pronounce difficult words or when to emphasize words.

Inserting Delivery Cues

Let's look at one of Schaeffer's note cards revised for vocal delivery. He uses the following system to cue himself:

Darkened (boldface) words: increase volume (if you are typing, restrike the characters or darken them with a felt-tip pen)

Compressed (smaller) words: decrease volume (if you are typing on a dual-pitch machine, switch to 12 characters per inch; otherwise, hand letter characters smaller than pica type)

Superscripted (raised) words: raise pitch

Subscripted (lowered) words: lower pitch

Underlined words: increase speed

Words separated by slash marks: decrease speed

Words in brackets and all capital letters: pronunciation/enunciation cues

Card 32: Conclusion

For the **lowest** airline fares, **most** efficient

routing, **best** hotel accommodations,/prestige

treatment,/travel accounting,/**and** specialized

personal service--from New York to Nepal

[NEPAHL], Los Angeles to Lima [LEMA], and

everywhere else here and abroad--I-E

Manufacturing will benefit from Strong's
comprehensive
          travel management contract.

Typically you should insert the most vocal cues into your introduction and conclusion cards since they contain the parts of your presentation that you wish to seem most polished. Use vocal cues sparingly throughout the body of your presentation to preserve the spontaneous appeal of your talk while still insuring that important words receive emphasis and correct pronunciation.

Revising for Content and Wording

As you practice your presentation using vocally cued note cards, stop to make necessary data and wording insertions or deletions. Making changes as you practice keeps you from forgetting needed changes. Here is one of Schaeffer's vocally cued note cards before and after content and wording revisions:

Card 5 [with vocal cue]

Third fact of modern business travel:
Confusing array of hotel rooms and discounts
here and abroad.
      --for example, corporate discounts at
        international chains
      --for example, special business-travel
        agency client discounts on suites at
        selected independent hotels in major
        commercial areas

Card 5 [after content and wording revisions]

Third fact of modern business travel:

Confusing array of hotel rooms and discounts here and abroad.

--for example, corporate discounts at chains **throughout the U.S., Canada, and abroad**

--for example, special business-travel agency client discounts on suites at selected independent hotels in major commercial cities such as London, Tokyo, Cairo

In chapter 9, we showed you how graphics can enhance your written documents. This is also true for oral presentations. In addition, because your audience *sees* your talk, you have several ways of displaying graphic aids.

Supporting Your Presentation with Visual Aids

Overhead Transparencies   You can transfer your chart or graph to a sheet of acetate for projection onto a screen. Such overhead transparencies, when they are crisply reproduced versions of large images, such as bar, pie, or line graphs, can help you underscore key points effectively. Overhead transparencies are also effective for highlighting short texts, such as one-page fliers, policy statements, or lists of procedures. Portable overhead projectors weighing less than 20 pounds make it quite simple for speakers such as Schaeffer to create and show transparencies in clients' conference rooms.

35-Millimeter Slides   Photographic slides are particularly effective for displaying graphics in color. Speakers find slides useful for showing photographs and special-effect graphics, such as exploded color pie charts in which a wedge of the pie is highlighted by separation from the rest of the graph. Modern 35-millimeter slide-making equipment allows a speaker to make presentation quality slides directly from graphics displayed on a computer screen. The improved portability and reliability of modern slide projectors have made 35-millimeter slides increasingly popular visual aids to business presentations.

Presentation Easels   You can create effective visual aids by drawing charts, graphs, or key terms on large sheets of paper that are part of a bound pad. When attached to a two-pound, portable easel, these sheets form a *flip chart*, so named because you can flip from page to page to show drawings illustrating different points in a presentation.

Dry-Erase Boards   Dry-erase boards represent a significant improvement over chalkboards for oral presentation. Dry boards, with their porcelain, enamel, ceramic, or specialized plastic surfaces, let you use colored markers to create visuals as you speak. Once you make your point, you can erase your visual so it does not draw attention away from the rest of your talk. Dry-erase boards offer two additional advantages over chalkboards—no sloppy chalk "shadows" after quick erasures and no chalk dust to soil clothing or hands. Portable models that are large enough for conference room presentations weigh from 5 to 10 pounds.

Computer-Produced Handouts   Computer word processing and graphics technology allows you to create single-page charts, graphs, drawings, or fliers to give to each member of your audience. These handouts can be particularly effective because they let your listeners take with them highlights or key data from your presentation, information that may keep your audience thinking positively about what you said long after the presentation. We offer one suggestion about computer-produced handouts: give them out at the end of your presentation. If your listeners receive your handout before or during your presentation, they may look at your handout rather than at you.

Gary Schaeffer decides to use two kinds of visual aids for his presentation to I-E Manufacturing. First, he creates a set of three acetate transparencies. Each depicts a bar graph that he will show on his overhead projector and the screen in I-E's conference room. The graphs compare clients' costs for airfare, hotels, and travel accounting before and after contracting with Schaeffer's company. He makes the actual transparencies by drawing his graphs on bond paper and then placing his drawings in a machine that transfers paper drawings onto acetate transparencies. Figure 12.2 shows Schaeffer's graph depicting clients' average travel accounting costs before and after signing a contract with Strong.

Schaeffer's second visual aid is a one-page handout highlighting the benefits that Strong Business Travel can offer to I-E Manufacturing. Figure 12.3 depicts this highlight sheet.

After creating his bar graph transparency and his word processed handout, Schaeffer returns to his note card deck to jot down cues to himself about when he should show the transparency and when he should distribute the highlight sheet. The following two note cards depict Schaeffer's revisions to include his visual aid display cues, which appear in boldface, uppercase letters enclosed in brackets.

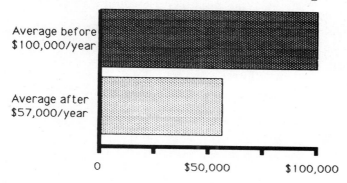

Client business travel accounting costs before and after contracting with Strong

Average before
$100,000/year

Average after
$57,000/year

0          $50,000 $100,000

Figure 12.2
Graphic aid for oral presentation. Business travel accounting costs.

STRONG BUSINESS TRAVEL'S
COMPREHENSIVE SERVICES CONTRACT
OFFERS THESE BENEFITS:

1. LOWEST AIRFARES AVAILABLE AT *NO CLIENT COMMISSION.*
2. BEST HOTEL PRICES WORLDWIDE AT *NO CLIENT COMMISSION.*
3. SPECIAL CLIENT DISCOUNTS ON CAR RENTALS, RESTAURANTS, AND MANY OTHER BUSINESS TRAVEL SERVICES.
4. PRESTIGE CLIENT "PERKS," SUCH AS HOTEL ROOM FLOWERS, THEATER AND SPORTS TICKETS.
5. PERSONNEL TRAINED IN INTERNATIONAL BUSINESS TRAVEL.
6. 24-HOUR EMERGENCY TRAVEL ASSISTANCE *WORLDWIDE.*
7. <u>EFFICIENT, ACCURATE</u> TRAVEL ACCOUNTING SERVICES.
8. EXPERIENCED STAFF MANAGES <u>ALL PHASES</u> OF BUSINESS TRAVEL *FOR YOU.*

INCREASE YOUR BUSINESS POWER
WITH STRONG BUSINESS TRAVEL!

Figure 12.3
Computer-produced oral presentation handout. Business travel services contract benefits.

Card 23 [after inclusion of visual aid display cue]

Two **main** functions for Strong personnel:

--business/travel/**accounting**

--business/travel/**management**

Result for Strong clients--reduced travel

accounting expenses

[SHOW ACCOUNTING EXPENSE

TRANSPARENCY]

Card 32: Conclusion

For the **lowest** airline fares, **most** efficient

routing, **best** hotel accommodations,/prestige

treatment,/travel accounting,/**and** specialized

personal service--from New York to Nepal

[NEPAHL], Los Angeles to Lima [LEMA], and

everywhere else here and abroad--I-E

Manufacturing will benefit from Strong's

comprehensive travel management contract.

[DISTRIBUTE HANDOUT]

**Coworker
Presentation
Critique**

Now that you have added any necessary visual aids to your presentation, ask a coworker to observe your delivery of it. If you can find a colleague whose communication skills you value and who is willing to take the time to listen to your presentation, you can gain valuable ideas for further improving your talk.

To make your coworker's suggestions as productive as possible, provide him or her with two items: your speaking problem definition with its statement of presentation objective, audience, and speaker's desired image, and a critiquing sheet. This sheet is simply a piece of paper on which you have written the following five questions or instructions, leaving space between questions for your listener's responses:

1. In one sentence, write out the presenter's main point.
2. At what point(s) in the presentation does the speaker need to provide more or less detailed information?
3. What words or phrases may not be clear to the speaker's audience?
4. What improvements can you recommend for the speaker's delivery—for example, grooming, dress, volume, pitch, speed, enunciation, pronunciation?
5. What other suggestions can you make for improving the oral presentation—for example, visual aids, introduction, conclusion, order of presentation topics?

Schaeffer has worked out a cooperative critiquing arrangement with another sales representative, Valerie Rusconi. Over the years, Schaeffer and Rusconi have discovered that taking the time to critique one another's presentations has helped them both to close more contract sales. Here is the critiquing sheet that Rusconi gives to Schaeffer after she has listened to his I-E Manufacturing presentation:

COWORKER PRESENTATION CRITIQUE

Critiquer: Valerie Rusconi

Presenter: Gary Schaeffer

Presentation to: I-E Manufacturing

1. In one sentence, write out the presenter's main point.

I-E Manufacturing will obtain ample time and cost benefits by signing a comprehensive travel services contract with Strong Business Travel, Inc.

2. At what point(s) in the presentation does the speaker need to provide more or less detailed information?

a. Tell <u>why</u> international travel can be so confusing (for example, currency restrictions, United States customs regulations on personal goods such as cameras).

b. When you say Strong Business Travel has specialists in foreign travel, emergency travel services, and travel accounting, tell your audience some of these specialists' names; doing so will give your listeners a more personal feeling for our company.

3. What words or phrases may not be clear to the speaker's audience?

Clarify what you mean by the fact that we charge "no client commission" on airfares and hotel reservations (that is, Strong gets its commissions directly from the airlines and hotels receiving our clients' bookings).

4. What improvements can you recommend for the speaker's delivery--for example, grooming, dress, volume, pitch, speed, enunciation, pronunciation?

Your conclusion goes overboard on vocal dynamics. Don't raise the pitch of your voice on the word comprehensive at the end of your talk. A calmer conclusion will reinforce the impression that the benefits Strong will aggressively pursue for I-E are solid.

5. What other suggestions can you make for improving the oral presentation--for example, visual aids, introduction, conclusion, order of presentation topics?

a. Your presentation runs 33 minutes. To save time (and to keep the presentation looking professional as well) have your overhead transparencies already right side up on the shelf of your projector.
b. Reverse the order of your note cards introducing our travel accounting and computerized travel management services. You want to build up to your discussion of travel accounting, since your invitation to make a presentation grows to a great extent from the accounting VP's keen interest in the time and money we can save her operation.

Schaeffer thanks Rusconi for her insightful critique. He then considers each of her suggestions. Gary accepts all of Rusconi's ideas but one—the suggestion that he give the names of some of Strong's foreign travel, travel emergency, and travel accounting specialists. From his background research, Schaeffer knows that all I-E's executive board wants to know is that Strong has the personnel to handle specialized needs.

Making a Fresh Set of Note Cards

Once you have revised your original draft cards, make yourself a fresh set. This is particularly important if you have made extensive changes to your cards that might make it difficult to find the information you need quickly.

Here is Schaeffer's last card (32). We have seen it in its original draft form, after the addition of vocal cues, and after the inclusion of his reminder to himself to distribute the word processed handout. In its final version, you will note that Schaeffer has incorporated Rusconi's suggestion to delete his rise in vocal pitch on the word *comprehensive*. Consequently, this word is no longer superscripted.

Card 32: Conclusion

> For the **lowest** airline fares, **most** efficient routing, **best** hotel accommodations,/prestige treatment,/travel accounting,/**and** specialized personal service--from New York to Nepal [NEPAHL], Los Angeles to Lima [LEMA], and everywhere else here and abroad--I-E Manufacturing will benefit from Strong's comprehensive travel management contract.
> **[DISTRIBUTE HANDOUT]**

Making the Presentation

The time has come for Schaeffer to leave for his presentation. Wearing his dark blue suit and solid maroon tie, he packs his note cards, transparencies, handouts, and portable overhead projector with a spare bulb and three-pronged plug adapter, then drives to I-E Manufacturing.

During the drive, he reviews his problem definition and presentation introduction. Outside the I-E Building, Schaeffer takes a few deep breaths to calm the mild anxieties he experiences even after years of successful presentations. He enters the building and finds the office of the vice-president for accounting 20 minutes before his scheduled presentation. Manguel greets Schaeffer and escorts him to the conference room. In the time before the executive board arrives, Schaeffer sets up and focuses his projector, gets the transparencies right side up on the projector shelf, places his note card deck on the lectern shelf, and adjusts the lectern itself. Schaeffer knows that arriving well ahead of schedule can help prevent last-minute "catastrophes," such as the need to replace a projector bulb when clients are waiting for the presentation to start.

When the board members are seated, Manguel introduces Schaeffer. He thanks her, takes a few seconds to make sure he has his audience's attention, and begins: "I'd like to thank the I-E executive board for this opportunity to show you what Strong Business Travel can offer."

As he talks, Schaeffer adjusts his delivery to his listeners' reactions. If members of I-E's executive board seem to be straining to hear him, he speaks more loudly. On the other hand, if the listeners nearest to him seem to be leaning away from him, he decreases volume to see if that solves the problem. If that does not work, Schaeffer may increase the distance between himself and his closest listeners slightly to see whether that puts them more at ease. He also works to maintain eye contact with his audience.

When he shows his transparencies, Schaeffer asks whether everyone can see them clearly. If not, he adjusts the projector's focus or dims the conference room lights as needed. Throughout the presentation, Schaeffer monitors the general level of attention I-E executives are directing toward him.

After Schaeffer has finished his presentation, distributed his word processed handout sheet, and thanked I-E again for the opportunity to address its executive board, he tells his listeners that he will be happy to answer any questions. In responding to I-E executives' questions, Schaeffer observes the following guidelines.

He listens carefully to each question so that he responds to what was actually asked, not to what he thinks the questioner meant.

Question   What specifically will Strong do to help our employees know customs regulations?

Response   Our international travel specialists will answer any questions about customs regulations by telephone. In addition, we will give each of your employees a list of key customs rules for each country they will be visiting, including regulations for business travelers returning to the United States.

He repeats a long or complex question to make certain he understands it and to make sure the audience has heard it.

Question   Can you explain accounting procedures for handling discounts earned by our employees for frequent plane travel or penalties incurred by our employees for changes in plane reservations booked under special airline promotions?

Response   The request was to explain accounting procedures for handling frequent flier discounts and airline-imposed penalties for changes in special fare reservations. Our accounting system adjusts billing to reflect all such changes on the days they are reported to us by the airlines.

He answers questions accurately; if he does not know the answer to a question, he says so and offers to find out and relay whatever information he can to the questioner.

Question   You quoted a typical corporate single-room rate for a Washington, D.C., hotel near the airport. Do you mean the airport near the city or the one further away?

Response   The rate I gave was for the more distant airport, Dulles. For passengers flying into National, the airport closer to downtown, we look for discount rooms in downtown hotels. I'll be happy to ask our hotel reservations director about downtown Washington hotels we have used recently and discounts we have received. I'll get that information to your secretary as soon as I return to my office this afternoon.

He keeps his composure and remains courteous even if a question seems hostile.

Question   Aren't you promising more than you can really deliver? Who is going to help me if I lose my passport at three in the morning in Manila?

Response   As I mentioned, we have agents on call 24 hours a day in over 50 cities worldwide. Each client employee receives a list of emergency telephone numbers for those cities. Since Manila *is* one of these emergency service cities, you would dial the number and hear a friendly agent suggest that you return to your hotel and get up later that morning to meet him or her in the lobby. From there you would go directly to the United States Embassy to begin the passport replacement process. Of course, we can't be everywhere, but in large cities we can and *do* contract with skilled, reliable agents for this sort of personalized travel emergency service for clients with our comprehensive travel contract.

After answering all of his listeners' queries, Gary asks them to give him a telephone call if they have any additional questions. As soon as he returns to his Strong Travel office, Schaeffer finds out the Washington, D.C., hotel information he has promised to an I-E executive and phones the executive's secretary with that data. Finally, Schaeffer sends this thank-you note to Connie Manguel at I-E Manufacturing.

July 18, 1986

Ms. Connie Manguel
Vice-President, Accounting
I-E Manufacturing, Inc.
State Route 24
Newark, NJ 07101

Dear Ms. Manguel:

Once again, thank you for the chance to talk with your executive board today. We at Strong Business Travel always appreciate the chance to meet with a firm to discuss the benefits of our comprehensive travel programs.

If there is any additional information I might provide, please let me know.

Yours truly,

Gary Schaeffer
Corporate Sales Representative

aj

Schaeffer's *brief* note provides a sincere touch of appreciation for his opportunity to address an audience outside his own company. Use your judgment about whether such a letter is an appropriate follow-up to your presentation. Certainly, it is crucial following a presentation you have made as part of an employment interview. Most often, a similar memo will not be proper after a talk you have given within your own company since you will have been following a superior's orders in preparing the presentation. Our best advice is to judge the situation for yourself. If you think a short follow-up note will provide your audience with just the right sense of closure to your presentation, by all means write it.

Summary

In this chapter, we have explained how you can apply many of the problem-solving techniques you use for writing to preparing an oral presentation. You begin by defining and analyzing your presentation problem much as you would a writing task.

You should then adapt the problem-solving steps of decision making, drafting, and revising to the reality of an in-person audience. In addition to decisions about your information and main point, you need to make choices about your dress, grooming, body dynamics, and relationship to the space in which you make your presentation. You need to control your volume, pitch, speed of delivery, enunciation, and pronunciation.

Write out your presentation's introduction and conclusion beforehand, but use notes to prepare the body of your talk. Revise your presentation cards by writing delivery cues, then make needed content and wording changes. Support your presentation with such visual aids as overhead transparencies, 35-millimeter slides, presentation easels, dry-erase boards, and computer-produced handouts. Have a trusted colleague critique your presentation. Then make a fresh set of note cards.

During your presentation, monitor your audience's response and make delivery adjustments as you talk. After your presentation, answer listeners' questions concisely, accurately, honestly, and courteously. Finally, send a follow-up note to your inviter if such a note seems appropriate.

As you can see, an *effective* oral presentation involves not just the time you spend speaking before an audience but careful planning and practice as well. The problem-solving approach offers a flexible system for making that planning and practice pay off when it comes time to meet your audience.

Problems

1. You work for a local convenience-store chain that is considering building a new market in your town. The chain's owner has asked you to make a presentation to him comparing the advantages of building on two sites. Select two local sites on which you think a convenience store would do well and complete the following:

   a. A problem definition (objective, audience, speaker's desired image) for this oral presentation problem.

   b. A problem analysis applying any of the analytical formats detailed in chapter 2 to any information about your two store sites. This problem analysis would be the base from which you would develop your presentation.

2. Your company has asked you to learn all you can about two cars (car A and car B) it is considering for the company fleet. After completing your study, you are to make an oral presentation to the directors of purchasing, accounting, and operations. You have defined the presentation problem in this way:

   - *Objective*   To prepare an oral presentation detailing car A's advantages over car B as a company fleet car

   - *Audience*   Directors of purchasing, accounting, operations

   - *Speaker's desired image*   Logical, thorough

   Through your research you have discovered the following facts about each car:

   Car A

   - Gets 25 miles per gallon on the highway.
   - Gets 18 miles per gallon on city streets.
   - Has an average on-the-road life of 100,000 miles.
   - Costs $9,800, including automatic transmission, air conditioning, and radio but excluding tax.
   - Comparably equipped three-year-old models have an average resale value of $5,000.
   - Trunk will hold four standard-sized suitcases.
   - Seats five comfortably.
   - Insurance (liability and collision) will cost company $500 per car per year.
   - Car dealership service department rated excellent by five local fleet-owning companies you have contacted.

- Car dealership service department located one mile from your company.

Car B

- Gets 22 miles per gallon on the highway.
- Gets 15 miles per gallon on city streets.
- Has average on-the-road life of 80,000 miles.
- Costs $10,200, including automatic transmission, air conditioning, and radio but excluding tax.
- Comparably equipped three-year-old models have average resale value of $4,000.
- Trunk will hold three standard-sized suitcases.
- Seats five comfortably.
- Insurance (liability and collision) will cost company $600 per car per year.
- Car dealership service department rated only fair by five local fleet-owning companies you have contacted.
- Car dealership service department located seven miles from your company.

Given this information and the problem definition, draft one or more note cards that will introduce your presentation.

3. As a sales representative for an employment agency that supplies temporary workers to business firms, you are preparing for an oral presentation to a local department store chain. Your goal is to convince the store managers to contract with your agency to supply temporary workers during busy seasons and when regular employees are on vacation. You define the presentation problem:

- *Objective* To prepare a presentation convincing a department store's managers to sign a temporary employment services contract
- *Audience* President, vice-president, and four branch managers of a local department store chain
- *Speaker's desired image* Knowledgeable, thorough

You have analyzed your presentation problem through this simple outline:

I. The department store needs replacement personnel.
   A. Busy seasons
   B. Vacation times
   C. Emergencies

   II. Our agency can supply temporary help.
      A. Large group of temporary employees on call
      B. All of our agency's temporary employees with references
      C. All of our agency's temporary employees bonded
  III. Our agency can offer additional benefits to the department store.
      A. Handle all accounting for temporary employees
         1. Wages
         2. Taxes
      B. Offer the department store personnel flexibility
         1. Inform temporary employees whether they will work on a given day
         2. Can supply various types of temporary help on one day's notice
            a. Sales help
            b. Data processing help
            c. Maintenance help
  IV. A year-round temporary employment service contract saves the department store money and time over hiring its own employees.
      A. Projected cash savings of 23 percent
      B. Projected time savings of 500 hours a year for store's main personnel office

Here is the introductory note card for your presentation:

Card 1: Draft Introduction

> Thank you for allowing me to meet with you to
> present the features of our temporary
> employment services plan. During my talk with
> you, I would like to show you (1) how we can
> meet your company's specific needs for
> short-term personnel, (2) what special benefits
> our agency offers clients, and (3) how much time
> and money we can save you this year alone.

Given this problem definition, analysis, and introductory note card, complete this draft by preparing note cards for the body and conclusion of the temporary employment agency oral presentation.

4. You handle accounting for the partners in a local law firm. The firm wants to expand its office space by purchasing land adjoining its

present site and building an addition onto its current building. The firm's partners have asked you to prepare a presentation for them on the advantages of choosing one of these methods of financing a mortgage loan on the new land:

- A fixed-rate loan that would require equal monthly payments over the next 30 years.
- A "floating-rate" loan that would cost less per month for the first year. However, the interest rate would fluctuate each year for the following 29 years, depending on the national rate of inflation.

Here are your note cards for the introduction of your presentation:

Card 1: Draft Introduction

> Let me begin by saying that choosing between a fixed- and floating-rate loan requires the ability to see 30 years into the future. Will interest rates go up, go down, or remain steady? If rates do change, will fluctuations be gradual or sudden? Will one bank raise its floating interest rates more than another?

Card 2: Draft Introduction

> Over the past week, I have consulted with five local banks. During my presentation, I will use both recent economic trends and historic inflation cycles to project the total cost of 30-year fixed- and floating-rate mortgage loans from each bank. As I show you these figures, I ask you to keep in mind that these are projections. Predicting the next week's, let alone the next century's, loan rates is a tricky business indeed.

Your task is to revise these two note cards by adding vocal cues to them. Use the following system for marking your cues: darken words on which you will increase your volume; compress letters of words on which you will decrease your volume; raise letters of words on which you will raise your pitch; lower letters of words on which you will lower your pitch; underline words that you will speak more quickly; separate by slashes words that you will speak more slowly. If your instructor agrees, let your class hear you read your cued introduction.

5. You are regional sales manager for a national condominium construction firm. You will soon have to make a presentation at corporate headquarters. In your talk, you will report on condominium sales projections for the next year in your region. Here are some facts and figures you will need for your presentation:

   - Three years ago, your region sold 3,388 condominium units.
   - Two years ago, your region sold 4,559 condominium units.
   - Last year, your region sold 6,096 condominium units.
   - Next year, you estimate that your region will sell 7,800 condominium units.

   Given this information, prepare a bar or line graph showing past sales and next year's estimated sales. Because you will use this graph as a visual aid to your oral presentation, create the graph on one of these media: an overhead projector transparency, a sheet of paper at least 20 by 25 inches, a dry-erase board at least two feet by two feet. If possible, use colored markers to draw your graph on the transparency, sheet of paper, or dry-erase board. Note: If you need assistance on how to set up your graph, consult the chapter on graphics (chapter 9).

6. A large manufacturing firm is considering relocating in your town. As your town's corporate development representative, you will be giving a presentation to the manufacturing company's top-level executives. The presentation should highlight as many reasons as possible why the firm should relocate in your town.

   Your task is to prepare the complete oral presentation. You will need to produce a set of presentation note cards and at least one visual aid for your presentation. At your instructor's discretion, present a 10-to-15-minute version of your presentation for your class. Optional: Work on this presentation with one or two classmates. If you choose to make a collaborative presentation, divide responsibilities so that each of you gets to speak before your class for approximately 5 minutes.

7. You work for an investment company. A local club has asked you to make a presentation to its members to describe various types of

investments. These should include but not be limited to the following: passbook savings accounts, certificates of deposit, money market accounts, common stocks, preferred stocks, corporate bonds, tax-exempt municipal bonds, and U.S. savings bonds. Here is a problem definition for this presentation:

- *Objective*   To prepare an oral presentation describing various types of investments
- *Audience*   A local club whose members are interested in the topic but *not* knowledgeable about investments
- *Speaker's desired image*   Reassuring, concise

Given this problem definition, your task is to prepare the complete oral presentation. You will need to produce a set of note cards and at least one visual aid for your presentation. At your instructor's discretion, present a 10-to-15-minute version of your presentation for your class. Optional: Work on this presentation with one or two classmates. If you choose to make a collaborative presentation, each team member should have responsibility for presenting information about several types of investments so that each of you gets to speak before the class for approximately 5 minutes.

Extended Application

Take any of the written documents you have prepared on the business topic you have been investigating since chapter 1. Using information you have gathered in preparing those documents, develop a 15-minute oral presentation that accomplishes *one* of the following objectives:

- Describes your topic for an audience that knows very little about it.
- Suggests possible improvements in aspects of the business for which you have been writing documents to an audience familiar with the topic.
- Sells goods or services associated with the business about which you have been writing documents. Assume that your audience knows something about your topic but that it needs to know still more so that it will make the "right" decision and buy your goods or services.

If your instructor agrees, present a 10-to-15-minute version of your presentation to your class.

PART 3

Contemporary Methods in Business Writing

P art 3 of this text details three business writing methods used in many of today's offices. Chapter 13, "Word Processing," examines the role of this technology in modern business writing. In this chapter, you will learn ways to solve rhetorical problems not only more quickly but with more writing options at your disposal.

Chapter 14, "Dictating," discusses the role of dictation in today's office and examines how this business writing method can make you a more efficient writer.

Chapter 15, "Collaborative Writing," presents techniques for working together with superiors, subordinates, and peers to produce an effective document.

Throughout part 3, we show you how to apply the rhetorical problem-solving steps to these modern business writing methods. From the cases and examples we provide, you will discover that rhetorical problem solving is indeed a flexible approach that adapts to the writing needs of today's work place.

CHAPTER 13

Word Processing

*W*alk into today's office and you are likely to find a computerized word processor. This chapter details ways to use modern word processing technology to accomplish two goals: (1) to speed completion of writing tasks created through the problem-solving approach and (2) to make physically possible or economically feasible special technologies not available with a pen, pencil, or manual or electric typewriter. The discussion concludes with a few cautions about word processing that should help you use it judiciously. Through careful use of this technology to *support* your writing efforts, you can enjoy its speed and special features while insuring your finished document's quality.

A **word processor** in this chapter refers to a computer that has the following capabilities: entry of text, usually through a keyboard; retention of entered text in the computer's memory; access to saved text for later revision and editing; and visibility of text on a display screen as it is entered, revised, edited, and printed. **Word processing** refers to the act of using a word processor to perform any of the problem-solving writing operations explained in chapters 1 through 4.

Our ongoing example presents the Hay Watch Company of Chicago. Hay makes a wide range of watches: budget models retailing at less than $100, mid-priced ones ranging from $100 to $250, and deluxe timepieces selling for $250 and up. The company supports its products with a world-wide sales and service network.

Solving Writing Problems Faster through Word Processing

Speed often counts in the preparation of business documents. Completing an important report before the deadline can help impress a superior. Responding promptly to a customer complaint may insure continued business. Writing and sending a detailed project bid on short notice might mean greatly increased revenues. The most quickly produced document, however, can hurt rather than help if it is not also well produced. Careful application of word processing to the problem-solving steps of problem definition and analysis, drafting, large-scale revision, small-scale editing, and manuscript preparation can increase speed while maintaining quality.

With a little preparation, you can use the word processor to store information for your problem definition and analysis. More importantly, the word processor will let you change that information and display your changed version quickly.

Quicker Writing Problem Definition and Analysis through Word Processing

Craig Lindstrom, Hay's director of marketing for Europe, uses a portable, briefcase-sized word processor on his frequent airplane flights. He is starting to work on a formal report that will discuss conditions for Hay's possible entry into the Swedish watch market. Programmed into his word processor, Lindstrom has a form that lists questions whose answers will help him to define the formal report problem:

1. For whom am I writing?
2. What do I know about my reader?
3. What is my relationship to my reader?
4. What are my reader's likely preconceptions?
5. What are my reader's needs?
6. What response do I want from my reader?
7. What image do I wish to project?
8. What is my writing objective?

Whenever Lindstrom thinks of answers to one or more of these questions, he turns on his word processor, displays the questions, keyboards in an answer(s), and saves his work. As the need arises, he changes or adds to his answers. Because he is not working with paper, Lindstrom's first, intermediate, and final answers to the definition questions are neat and ready to use in preparing his analysis.

After working on his definition, Lindstrom now has these answers:

1. For whom am I writing? J. L. Magnus, vice-president, marketing.
2. What do I know about my reader? J. L. is very cautious about entering any new market, particularly one outside the United States. However, J. L. knows that two of our American competitors are also thinking of marketing their watches in Sweden.
3. What is my relationship to my reader? Directly subordinate.
4. What are my reader's likely preconceptions? The Swedish watch market is close to saturation. Therefore, only a very special product will gain a foothold.
5. What are my reader's needs? J. L. needs straightforward information about the Swedish market.
6. What response do I want from my reader? J. L. should feel informed but not pressured to adopt a point of view on expansion into Sweden.
7. What image do I wish to project? Informed, neutral in my views.
8. What is my writing objective? To prepare a report presenting unbiased information about the climate for marketing Hay watches in Sweden.

With his writing problem defined, Lindstrom starts his analysis. This takes the form of a formal, interpretive label outline. Lindstrom draws on three sources of information for his outline: (1) a United States government document on prospects for American businesses in Sweden, (2) Lindstrom's interviews with commerce officials in three Swedish cities, and (3) results of direct observation conducted on Swedish watch retailing practices by Lindstrom's staff.

Lindstrom uses the screen of his word processor as a "scratch pad" for developing his outline. He can add information from each source as he reads it. The first version of the outline that he keyboards into the word processor relies on information from the U.S. government document.

CONDITIONS FOR MARKETING AMERICAN-MADE WATCHES IN SWEDEN

    I. Sweden is a large, sparsely populated nation.
        A. Several major urban areas
            1. Stockholm
            2. Goteborg
            3. Malmo
   II. Swedish consumers are used to high-quality merchandise.
        A. Many "upscale" department stores in cities
        B. Specialty shops in cities and small towns

As he reads through notes from his talks with Swedish commerce officials and his staff's report on its observations, Lindstrom can add, delete, and reorder information on his outline. The word processor quickly reformats the outline, giving Lindstrom this neat, new version:

CONDITIONS FOR MARKETING AMERICAN-MADE WATCHES IN SWEDEN

I. Sweden is a large, sparsely populated nation.
   A. Most of central and northern Sweden rural
   B. Several major urban areas
      1. Stockholm
      2. Goteborg
      3. Malmo
      4. Kristianstad
II. Swedish consumers are used to high-quality merchandise.
   A. Many "upscale" department stores in cities
      1. Carry expensive imported watches
         a. Swiss
         b. Japanese
      2. Display watches very attractively
      3. Offer knowledgeable sales assistance
   B. Specialty shops in cities and small towns
      1. Carry expensive Swiss watches
      2. Display watches very attractively
      3. Offer knowledgeable sales assistance

When the outline is complete, Lindstrom can draft his report. Not only will he have defined and analyzed his problem efficiently but he will have his definition and outline stored in the word processor. He will redisplay some of the outline on one part of his screen while he starts to draft on another part or he will print out a copy of his definition and outline to keep handy as he starts to write.

Writing with a pencil is slow work. This slowness can be frustrating because you can think much more quickly than you can jot down information. As you struggle to record ideas on paper, you lose thoughts that occur to you while you write or which occur to you later. You may actually force yourself to think more slowly in order to keep in step with the pencil. If you switch to a pen, the liquid ink encounters less resistance as it meets the page and writing goes more quickly. If you can type, you can increase the speed of your writing even more. Electric typewriters let you strike keys yet more rapidly. However, even electric typewriters hold you back. You may fear that by working too quickly you will make so many errors that you will need a newly-typed draft before starting revision. Or you may end up typing slowly to avoid mistakes.

Rapid Drafting by Word Processor

Because a word processor lets you make corrections on a video display screen *before* printing a document, the fear of having to retype a draft disappears. If you are a fast typist, you can go as quickly as possible, correcting errors later on. If you are a slower typist, you hunt and peck more quickly, knowing that mistakes will not cause much additional work. Even if you cannot type at all, you can save time. The word processor lets a secretary keyboard handwritten or dictated drafts quickly. The result is faster turnaround time for a fresh copy on which you can then make handwritten revisions for the secretary to enter into the word processor.

Sonia Carter, one of Hay's customer service representatives, is a slow typist when she has to watch for typographical errors. A major part of her job involves writing letters responding to consumer comments and complaints. Hay's policy is that each consumer must receive a personal response. Customer service representatives have to process their own correspondence, but since so many of the letters received require generally similar answers, Carter does know pretty well what she plans to say in response. In addition, she has boilerplate opening sentences and paragraphs stored in the word processor to speed her writing.

Carter has a video display on her desk. This looks very much like a television screen. Beneath the display is a typewriter keyboard, set up in the traditional "QWERTY" format. The whole apparatus, called a **video display terminal (VDT)**, is connected to a powerful computer elsewhere in the office. By typing in her name and a request that the computer let her run the customer complaint program with its boilerplate paragraphs, Carter is able to type a letter and have it appear on her screen.

Here is her rapidly keyboarded draft of a letter to a customer who has had trouble with one of Hay's regional service centers. We have highlighted her typographical errors and placed the boilerplate material within brackets.

August 1, 1986

Candace Cummings
7652 Ocean Avenue (Apt. 2-L)
Long Beach, CA 90801

[Dear] Ms. Cummings:

[Thank you for your letter of] July 28, 1986.

I am sorry that you are not pleased with service from our Southern California Repair Center. Let me respond to each of the concerns you expressed in your letter.

First, Clyde Zahn, **teh** Repair Center manager with whom you dealt, noted that your octagonal watch casing required special ordering of a hinge **form** our central parts depot here in Chicago. This is what accounted for the one-week delay in completion of your repair. Because the octagonal shape is so rare, our regional repair centers may not stock a complete set of every part needed for every model. We apologize for this delay.

Second, the $21.20 charge for the repair is a fee authorized by our main office. This charge breaks down to $5.00 for the replacement hinge, $15.00 for labor (30 minutes at $30 an hour), and $1.20 sales tax. These are standard parts and labor charges **fro** all our repair centers nationwide.

Third,, we are sorry that the casing is still loose after the repair. As you know, we **guarntee** all repairs for 60 days. Just return your watch to the Southern California Repair Center and we will gladly correct the problem. If you prefer, you may return the watch **ot** the repair center for replacement with a new watch of the same model number.

[Hay Watch Company wants to serve its customers well. Letters such as yours enable us to meet our goal of total customer satisfaction.]

[Yours truly,]

Sonia Carter
[Customer Service Representative]

Carter knows from experience that (1) rare watch-casing parts may have to be ordered from the Chicago depot, (2) company policy sets rates for parts and labor, and (3) if a regional repair center manager agrees that a repair was not performed properly on a watch retailing for less than $50, it is company policy to offer a consumer who writes to complain a rerepair or a replacement watch at no cost. She is thus able to write this letter quickly with little or no revision. The only thing that might have caused her to have to retype the entire letter before Hay installed word processing equipment was her tendency to make typographical errors when she keyboarded too quickly.

The Hay word processor stores Carter's letter in its memory. When she asks the computer to redisplay her draft on the screen, she scans the letter to Cummings and finds six typographical errors: letter reversals, missing vowels, repeated punctuation marks. All Carter needs to do is position the word processor's **cursor** (a moving place marker) underneath each word, electronically erase the error, insert the correct spelling or punctuation, then print out the finished letter. The word processor adjusts the document automatically for changes made in spacing by the addition of the letters or the deletion of the second comma. The correction and printing operations take only a few seconds. In the process, Carter has saved herself the approximately 15 minutes it would have taken her to retype a corrected copy.

Faster Large-Scale Revisions

As you saw, Carter had to take a few seconds to edit her draft before printing out the copy she would sign and mail to Cummings. Word processing enables you to make even more complex revisions quickly.

Andy Murawaki supervises a team of quality control engineers for Hay. Unlike Carter, Murawaki has a complete, stand-alone microcomputer that sits on his desk. He uses the computer to make mathematical calculations needed to insure quality control. He employs it to draw pictures of various Hay products so he can show his team enlarged views of potential trouble spots. Murawaki also uses the computer as a word processor on which he writes weekly reports and frequent memoranda. A small, high-speed printer is connected to the computer.

A memorandum this supervisor must prepare often announces the agenda for the quality control team's weekly meeting. This is Murawaki's first draft of one such memo.

Draft

Date: December 11, 1986

To: Quality Control Engineering Team J

From: Andy Murawaki, Team J Supervisor

Subject: Staff Meeting on December 12, 1986

This is a reminder that we meet tomorrow at 10 A.M. in Conference Room 3. During the meeting, we need to discuss a variety of problems that have cropped up in the past few days.

1. There seems to be some disagreement between our team and the Electronics Department over circuit standards in our 1987 digital models. Let us reach a consensus on what we feel are good numbers before next year's production begins. Remember that we will have to negotiate that consensus with Electronics before Operations will approve <u>any</u> production run.

2. This is an old topic. Do we need to make any recommendations on watch-spring tolerances in our manually wound models? With manual models now accounting for only 2 percent of sales, do we wish to take time now to work on tolerances?

3. The sound effects on our novelty, game-playing models have shown some unit-to-unit inconsistency. For instance, the growls of attacking monsters on our H-88 model have come out variously as squawks, purrs, and whines. I may invite Jane Boles, who handles audio effects for Electronics, to sit in with us.

4. With Marketing's push for sales in the upper Midwest, Customer Relations can expect increased complaints on cold-weather failure. I think we may want to toughen conditions on our low-temperature/low-humidity stress tests. To be truthful, we really don't know much about how our products will meet the challenges of the cold, dry weather typical of the region or of the equally typical snow into which our customers will be dropping their watches.

5. Let's keep an eye on calibrations of hour-marking spacings on roman numeral faces. My spot checks have noted problems in the alignment of VIII and IX, leading to a sense of lopsidedness leaning toward the left side of the watch face.

6. New business. With our new, twist-off battery receptacle covers now almost a year old, it's time to touch base with all our field service centers on the durability of the cover threading. I haven't heard of any problems with these, but it can't hurt to stay ahead of possible trouble.

7. We have been experiencing higher than normal unit rejections due to atmospheric contaminants that find their ways into watch casings. Pollution-control standards and procedures will need attention.

As you can see, we have a full slate. Prepare to meet into the evening. We'll order lunch from the commissary. If we do run into the night, we'll have Conti's send up pizzas. But no more extra garlic, OK, Sam?

Murawaki stores the memo draft on a computer disk for retrieval and revision when he has time later that same day. When he sees the draft reappear on the display screen, he has a number of options for large-scale revision.

Automatic Scrolling   Because his memo is longer than the 24 lines of text that fit onto his display screen, Murawaki can ask the computer to display his entire draft one or more lines at a time. This feature allows him to scan what he has written for needed changes as the text **scrolls** up the screen. Whenever he sees a part of the memo he wishes to think about more, he can stop the scrolling and start it up again when he is ready.

Blocking   Once he has scrolled through the document and decided upon some large-scale revisions, Murawaki can use the word processor as an electronic scissors and tape. In the same way he could actually cut out a section of his draft for taping elsewhere in the memo, he can separate part or parts of his draft into **blocks**. Once he creates blocks, Murawaki can move them with the push of a button to another place in the memo. He can also copy a block so that it reappears elsewhere in the document. Murawaki will make use of this feature to designate the entire draft as a block and copy it so he can retain the original draft while he works on revisions. If he wants to remove a part of the draft altogether, Murawaki can mark it as a block and simply delete it from the memo. In short, moving and deleting blocks speeds up what can be done with scissors and tape. Block copying capability adds the power of a photocopy machine to the cutting and pasting operation.

Automatic Reformatting   After Murawaki finishes manipulating blocks so his document contains what he wants in the order he desires, he can push a **reformatting** key or keys. The reformatting feature takes revised text and returns it to the margins and spacing specified before keyboarding of the original draft. The revised document appears on the display screen looking as if it had been freshly typed, not recently subjected to reorderings, copyings, and deletions.

Saving   Murawaki's word processor will, of course, store his revised memo in its memory for further revision or for immediate printout if the quality control supervisor is happy with the new version. In addition, at Murawaki's request, the word processor could also have saved the original draft just in case he did not like the revised memo and wished to go back to the original to start revising again. Every time Murawaki works with his memo, the word processor also saves what is known as a **backup copy**. This extra copy insures that even if he makes a mistake and accidentally erases the document on which he is working, a duplicate will be available.

After scrolling through the memo, Murawaki decides on large-scale revisions:

1. Complete reordering of the agenda items so that they progress from most to least important.
2. Deleting the last three sentences of the memo because they undercut the serious image he wishes to project to the staff on the matter of this week's staff meeting.

Here is how Murawaki uses block manipulations to accomplish these revisions. For purposes of illustration, we have written out Andy's commands in all uppercase letters. In reality, all Murawaki has to do is depress one or two keys at the beginning and end of each text block he wishes to manipulate.

Draft

Date: December 11, 1986

To: Quality Control Engineering Team J

From: Andy Murawaki, Team J Supervisor

Subject: Staff Meeting on December 12, 1986

This is a reminder that we meet tomorrow at 10 A.M. in Conference Room 3. During the meeting, we need to discuss a variety of problems that have cropped up in the past few days.

1. **BLOCK A START** There seems to be some disagreement between our team and the Electronics Department over circuit standards in our 1987 digital models. Let us reach a consensus on what we feel are good numbers before next year's production begins. Remember that we will have to negotiate that consensus with Electronics before Operations will approve any production run. **BLOCK A END; MOVE BLOCK A TO AGENDA ITEM 4.**

2. **BLOCK B START** This is an old topic. Do we need to make any recommendations on watch-spring tolerances in our manually wound models? With manual models now accounting for only 2 percent of sales, do we wish to take time now to work on tolerances? **BLOCK B END; MOVE BLOCK B TO AGENDA ITEM 5.**

3. The sound effects on our novelty, game-playing models have shown some unit-to-unit inconsistency. For instance, the growls of attacking monsters on our H-88 model have come out variously as squawks, purrs, and whines. I may invite Jane Boles, who handles audio effects for Electronics, to sit in with us.

4. **BLOCK C START** With Marketing's push for sales in the upper Midwest, Customer Relations can expect increased complaints on cold-weather failure. I think we may want to toughen conditions on our low-temperature/low-humidity stress tests. To be truthful, we really don't know much about how our products will meet the challenges of the cold, dry weather typical of the region or of the equally typical snow into which our customers will be dropping their watches. **BLOCK C END; MOVE BLOCK C TO AGENDA ITEM 6.**

5. **BLOCK D START** Let's keep an eye on calibrations of hour-marking spacings on roman numeral faces. My spot checks have noted problems in the alignment of VIII and IX, leading to a sense of lopsidedness leaning toward the left side of the watch face. **BLOCK D END; MOVE BLOCK D TO AGENDA ITEM 2.**

6. **BLOCK E START** New business. With our new, twist-off battery receptacle covers now almost a year old, it's time to touch base with all our field service centers on the durability of the cover threading. I haven't heard of any problems with these, but it can't hurt to stay ahead of possible trouble. **BLOCK E END; MOVE BLOCK E TO AGENDA ITEM 7.**

7. **BLOCK F START** We have been experiencing higher than normal unit rejections due to atmospheric contaminants that find their ways into watch casings. Pollution-control standards and procedures will need attention. **BLOCK F END; MOVE BLOCK F TO AGENDA ITEM 1.** As you can see, we have a full slate. Prepare to meet into the evening. **BLOCK G START** We'll order lunch from the commissary. If we do run into the night, we'll have Conti's send up pizzas. But no more extra garlic, OK, Sam? **BLOCK G END; DELETE BLOCK G.**

REFORMAT REVISED MEMO
SAVE REVISED MEMO

Now that his memo contains only the material he wants, reordered as he wishes, Murawaki can print it, make a photocopy for each of his team members, and place it in each of their office mailboxes. By word processing his large-scale revisions, Murawaki finishes drafting, large-scale revision, and document preparation in 15 mintues. These tasks would have taken him some 45 minutes to complete with electric typewriter, scissors, tape, and correcting pencil.

Quicker Small-Scale Editing through Word Processing

Another Hay employee, Fran Dobbs, has found it possible to speed smaller-scale revisions by using the company word processor. Dobbs is a traveling sales representative for Hay Watch. She will soon visit a city served by a chain of department stores with which Hay has done profitable business. She wants to inform the department store's watch and jewelry buyer about the forthcoming visit.

Dobbs is a competent typist who does word processing at a video display terminal in Hay's Chicago office. The terminal connects to a large (mainframe) computer and high-speed printer elsewhere in the building. Dobbs informs the computer when she is satisfied with revision in a document and receives back a printed, ready-for-signature original and carbon copy. Here is her draft letter to the department store buyer:

Draft

March 20, 1986

Ms. Carolyn Delacroix
Savoy Stores
Baton Route, LA 70821

Dear Ms. Delacroix:

I will be spending April visiting our retailers in the Gulf states. My plans call for a visit to Baton Rouge on April 17-18. Could we set up a meeting for one of those two days? I am looking forward to showing you our new models for fall and winter.

Savoy has been such a loyal customer for so many years that I particularly want to be certain we have some time to look at what's new in Hay's high-fashion line. Ask a department store executive anyplace in the nation and he will tell you that this has been a most profitable line.

I will follow up this letter with a phone call during the first week in April. I should be able to rearrange my route that week to accommodate your schedule.

Sincerely,

Fran Dobbs
Sales Representative

The word processor allows Dobbs to make several types of small-scale changes more quickly than she could by handwriting changes onto a draft for later retyping.

Additions   After reading the draft letter, Dobbs wants to add a few sentences and clauses to sound more cordial. Hay has been doing business with Savoy Stores for years, and Dobbs and Delacroix have used each other's first names during their face-to-face meetings. Making these or any other additions simply requires that Dobbs move the video display cursor to the places in the letter where the new material will go. She then types the new sentences. The word processor reformats the rest of the letter automatically so both the original and added material fit together neatly within the original margins.

Deletions   Dobbs can also remove unwanted words, phrases, and sentences from the letter. For example, a rereading of the sentence "Savoy has been such a loyal customer for so many years that I particularly want to be certain we have some time to look at what's new in Hay's high-fashion line" shows Dobbs that deleting *particularly* will create a more fluent sentence. Once again, she moves the cursor, this time to the *p* in *particularly*. Depressing one or two keys causes the word to disappear from the screen and Dobbs's letter to reformat properly.

Deletion and Addition   By combining the word processor's deletion and addition functions, Dobbs can change the wording of the letter. She employs this dual operation for several reasons: to enhance the letter's cordiality by deleting *Ms. Delacroix* in the salutation and *Sincerely* in the closing and then adding *Carolyn* and *Cordially* in their places; to improve sentence conciseness by removing a prepositional phrase at the end of a sentence and adding two adjectives and a conjunction earlier on; to vary wording by deleting *line* the first time it appears in the letter and then adding *collection* instead.

Find and Replace   Another word processing feature allows Dobbs to specify a word or group of words in the letter and move the cursor to that point automatically. Typically, she uses it to double-check the accuracy of addresses, model numbers, and other information requiring keyboarding of numbers. If the cursor moves to the number(s) Dobbs specifies, keyboarding has been correct. If the word processor reports that the desired numbers have not been found, she knows that it is necessary to make one or more corrections.

Dobbs has found another use for the find and replace—as a way to insure the use of nonsexist language. She asks the word processor to find each use of *he, she, him, her, his,* and *hers.* Working with the draft to Delacroix, Dobbs tells the word processor to find the word *he.* In a moment, the screen displays the sentence "Ask a department store executive anyplace in the nation and he will tell you that this has been a most profitable line." Dobbs realizes that the draft suggests only men are department store executives. She then changes the sentence's first object and its referent pronoun to plural. The change results in the sentence "Ask department store executives anyplace in the nation and they will tell you that this has been a most profitable line."

Split Screens   The word processor lets employees divide their display screens so that the top half of the display shows one part or version of a document, while the bottom shows another. This feature lets Dobbs display an original and a revised version of the same sentence simultaneously:

Original version

I am looking forward to showing you our new models for fall and winter.

Revised version

I am looking forward to showing you our new fall and winter models.

With both versions displayed at once, Dobbs can choose the preferred one for retention and formatting within the letter.

Specialized Small-Scale Editing Features   Some word processors offer specialized options. Hay's word processor lets Dobbs check spelling. After redrafting the letter, Dobbs asks the word processor to compare each word in the draft with correctly spelled words in a computerized dictionary. Whenever the word processor encounters a word whose spelling does not match that of a word in the dictionary, it displays that word and the line of the letter in which it appears. Dobbs then has the option of changing the original spelling or letting it remain—for example, if the word were a proper name not in the computerized dictionary.

Through the word processor, Dobbs also has access to a computerized thesaurus that displays a list of synonyms when a writer types in a particular word. Also, a specialized punctuation program assists Dobbs in such operations as making certain that if the revised letter contains paired punctuation marks, such as parentheses, quotation marks, or brackets, both of the paired markings appear. She receives additional help from the word processor on correct placement of hyphens between syllables of words broken at the ends of lines.

Here is Dobbs's letter to Delacroix after small-scale changes:

Revised draft

March 20, 1986

Ms. Carolyn Delacroix
Savoy Stores
Baton Rouge, LA 70821

Dear Carolyn:

I hope you're well and enjoying that beautiful Louisiana springtime. I'll be spending April visiting our retailers in the Gulf states.

My plans call for a visit to Baton Rouge on April 17-18. Could we set up a meeting for one of those two days? I am looking forward to showing you our new fall and winter models.

Savoy has been such a loyal customer for so many years that I want to be certain we have some time to look at what's new in Hay's high-fashion collection. I know you have been pleased with these watches in the past. You are not alone. Ask department store executives anyplace in the nation and they will tell you that this line has been most profitable.

I'll follow up this letter with a phone call during the first week in April. If the 17th or 18th is not possible for you, I should be able to rearrange my route that week to accommodate your schedule.

Cordially,

Fran Dobbs
Sales Representative

Final Document Preparation by Word Processor

Word processing speeds document preparation by automating several formatting tasks. Patsy Dalton, a Hay marketing research specialist, takes advantage of these features as she completes a brief test-marketing proposal.

Dalton cannot type and does not want to learn this skill. Many managers, having discovered how word processors can help them to improve and speed their writing, have taught themselves to keyboard. Various commercially available computerized tutorials as well as corporate and university word processing classes have assisted these managers. However, Dalton still prefers to handwrite her drafts, give them to her secretary, and receive from him freshly word processed copies for further handwritten revisions.

This is a draft of Dalton's memo-report to Hay's vice-president for marketing:

Draft

Date: January 29, 1986

To: J. L. Magnus, Vice-President, Marketing

From: Patsy Dalton, Market Research Specialist

Subject: Sports Watch Test-Marketing Proposal

As you requested in your memo of January 8, I have developed a plan for the test-marketing of our new sports watch line. The plan employs a three-part strategy. Through its application, we should be able to improve one of our regional markets as we learn how best to position the sports watches for year-round sales.

First, let us conduct testing in the upper Midwest region. Our market share in North Dakota, South Dakota, Minnesota, Wisconsin, and upper Michigan has been traditionally low. Test-marketing here presents the opportunity to increase Hay's visibility in the region as we meet the challenge of creating a successful market test.

Selecting a mixture of small, medium, and large cities for testing should give us the range of market data we will need to make final recommendations. Our present retailers in the region give us the outlets we need to test in the following locations: Bismarck and Grand Forks, North Dakota; Pierre and Sioux Falls, South Dakota; Duluth and Minneapolis, Minnesota; Milwaukee and Eau Claire, Wisconsin; Marquette and Sault Ste. Marie, Michigan.

In addition, as a center for year-round recreation, the upper Midwest offers a test of consumer interest for the rugged timepieces that make up the sports watch collection. Certainly, our Hunter, Angler, Slalom, and Aquanaut models have the potential to spark enthusiasm because of their practicality, styling, and competitive pricing.

Second, we should test the entire line at once. Trying out all five models at once will give us the comparative data we need to recommend immediate production, minor changes, or major overhauling before national sales. At the same time, we can offer each model in the choice of casing shape, color, and band styles necessary to gauge whether most interest lies at the upper end of the price range--for example, octagonal, gold-plate casing and band--or the lower end--for instance, round, stainless steel casing, vinyl band.

Testing the entire line may also provide demographic data not obtainable in any other way. We will certainly want to learn whether we appeal more to small-town or big-city shoppers. We also will want to know whether our purchasers are regular customers of our retailers or are shopping there because it is the only local outlet for a Hay sportswatch.

Third, we must move quickly. It will be to our advantage to have the complete line on display in our test retailers' stores by mid-April. This schedule provides time for sales of water sports and fishing models for spring and summer. By running the test through August, we will also get a sense of how our fall hunting and winter sports models will perform. Since fall and winter come early in the upper Midwest, customers are sophisticated in making purchases needed for hunting and skiing.

Testing from April through August also provides us leeway to make necessary recommendations well before the fall and winter holiday season. If we analyze data on a weekly basis, we should be able to project holiday sales in plenty of time to suggest minor product adjustments and sufficient production runs.

To make our schedule work, we must work closely with the Sales Department. By pairing five sales representatives and five marketing staffers, we can create teams to visit each of the five test-marketing states. Each team will meet with representatives of Hay's biggest retail outlet in each of the test cities.

Together, the retailer, sales representative and marketing specialist can discuss in-store displays, market evaluation procedures, and media support. For example, we might support the largest markets (Minneapolis and Milwaukee) with local television, radio, and newspaper advertising. We could offer smaller markets (for instance, Marquette and Pierre) radio and local newspaper spots.

The key to the success of the three-point strategy will be the retailer network we establish. Hay must offer these 10 cooperating outlets all we can in support. Attention from our sales and marketing team as well as media support will be crucial. Perhaps we should go further and support a rebate program. This rebate would enable retailers to increase the sales volume of the test products without endangering their own profit margins. Because of the limited nature of the test, the cost to Hay would be minimal. The twin benefits of increased test-market sales data and retailer goodwill could well justify the expenditure.

Through testing the sports watch line in the upper Midwest, we can explore a relatively unfamiliar territory for Hay. By introducing the entire line at once, we can gain important comparative product data. With a spring and summer testing period, we can insure production runs and distribution of successful models in time for the holiday season. In short, a three-pronged test-marketing strategy offers us benefits that any single testing approach cannot match.

ps

After reading her draft memo, Dalton decides to change some things about its appearance. She can specify these alterations to her secretary, who can process them for her approval within minutes.

Automatic Centering   Dalton's most important decision about the memo is that she no longer wishes it to be a memo. Because the proposal is so important, because it is going to a superior, and because it may well be read by all of Hay's top executives, Dalton decides to change its format to that of a report. This change will require her to specify subtopic headings for each section of the proposal. Her secretary will then have the task of centering each heading on its appropriate line of the revised document. Before Hay installed its word processing system, centering headings required Dalton's secretary to backspace from the center of the page, counting letters as he went. He sometimes misplaced long headings. Misplacement meant either coverup with liquid correction fluid or retyping an entire page, neither a wholly satisfactory result. The word processor's automatic centering feature permits Dalton's secretary to keyboard the heading and press a key that places the heading correctly on center every time.

Margin Changes   Dalton makes another formatting decision, this time to change the listing of test sites appearing in the third paragraph of her original memo. Instead of running the listing in with the rest of the text, she wants her secretary to set off the list 10 spaces from the left margin. This change requires temporarily resetting the left margin, no major effort for either word processor or typewriter. What *is* different, however, is that the word processor will let the secretary reset the margins for indentation and show Dalton the results *before* he creates a printed copy of the report. If Dalton does not like this reformatting, she can simply say so. Her secretary does not waste time retyping the entire document just to accommodate a change on the first page.

Justification   The word processor allows Dalton to request justification of her report's righthand margin. Justification means that every line of her report will end flush with the right margin. Because she wants to give her finished report a symmetrical look, Dalton selects this option rather than the more traditional "ragged" right margin, where lines end at different points, usually within about five spaces of the margin setting.

Vertical Spacing   Changing the single-spacing of Dalton's memo to the double-spacing needed for a report is equally simple on a typewriter and a word processor. At times, however, more refined spacing can prove valuable. For instance, when a letter runs two lines over a single page, it is possible to reset spacing from 6 lines per inch (traditional single-spacing) to 6.1 lines per inch. This hardly noticeable change now allows the letter to fit onto one page. When you need to reproduce the document (as in a form letter or memo going to every worker in a company), being able to fit everything onto one page less can add up to significant savings.

Automatic Page Numbering   The word processor automatically places page numbers on documents. You no longer need to roll paper into the platen and find the same line and space on each page for a number. You can now specify where on the page numbers should appear. You can instruct the word processor to omit the page number 1 from the first page of text and start with 2 on the second. You can order roman numeral page numbering to start anyplace in the document (for example, after the title page of a formal report) and arabic numerals to start when appropriate (for example, with the formal report's introduction). Best of all, page numbers will adjust automatically with each document revision. This readjustment eliminates the need for liquid correction fluid to cover changed numbers or penciled-in numerals on long document drafts. Because Dalton's revised proposal will not contain a title page and executive summary, her secretary will make use of automatic page numbering to omit arabic numeral 1 from the introduction and begin pagination with the number 2 on the second page of the report text.

New Writing Options through Word Processing

The first part of this chapter discussed ways in which word processing speeds completion of writing tasks. This second section details ways word processing makes certain procedures physically possible or economically feasible.

Form Letters and Memos

Word processing allows you to create personalized letters and memos in a fraction of the time it would take to type them individually. You are probably most familiar with the direct mail advertising form letters that promote everything from magazine subscriptions to life insurance. Hay's personnel office, however, has found another use for multiple copies. From that office, Jose Llamas sends annual memos to all Hay employees. These memos specify how much a month will be withheld from an employee's check for pension, company stock options, payroll savings, and the company charity fund.

Understandably, each employee can have a different monthly figure for each of the withholding categories. Before Hay installed its word processing system, personnel secretaries typed each employee's figures on dittoed form memos with spaces left blank for the monthly deduction figures. Besides resulting in amateurish-looking memos, rolling each form into the typewriter and lining up the blanks for proper typing was time-consuming for a company with as many employees as Hay. Now Llamas's secretary merely has to display the list of all Hay employees and their office locations that is already stored in the computer's memory. Next to each name on the list, the secretary types the amount to be withheld each month. Upon completing the statistical typing, the secretary commands the word processor to merge the employee and withholding list with the master memo from Jose Llamas. Figure 13.1 shows the master memo, a segment of the employee and withholding list, and the resulting "merged" memos.

With this technology available, the personnel, accounting, and other Hay departments are able to communicate personalized information within the company. Sales and marketing departments can prepare equally individualized form messages for distribution to retailers outside the company.

Throughout this chapter, ways in which word processing technology assists writers in producing documents have been detailed. Next we explain several options that word processing adds to writers' choices on how to move finished documents to intended audiences.

Word Processing Communication Options

Intracompany Word Processing Networks   Interoffice mail is the traditional way to transmit documents within a company. Hay's word processing system, with its video display terminals linked to a central computer, creates another possibility for employees who must communicate written information quickly. Networks of computers whose operators can communicate with each other can help managers or their secretaries set up meetings by providing immediate responses from all involved, even if they work in widely scattered parts of the company. Such networks also allow writers to send documents to superiors for speedy approval or suggested changes before printing a copy. Interoffice networks allow employees in different parts of the company to write collaboratively by exchanging drafts and comments right on the display screen. Also, employees can obtain information they need to complete a document.

For example, sales representative Fran Dobbs, whom we met earlier in the chapter, is preparing for a sales trip to the South. Dobbs will be promoting Hay's high-fashion watches to retailers. However, before encouraging retailers to buy these watches, Dobbs wants to be certain that Hay has enough inventory to ship orders immediately. Through experience, Dobbs has discovered that nothing sours a manufacturer-retailer relationship faster than inability to ship orders.

Dobbs could telephone Hay's inventory control department and ask the answering clerk to read a list of model numbers and amount of inventory on hand. While the clerk was reading, Fran would be copying down the model numbers and inventory figures by hand. But the list is long, and so Dobbs chooses to send a message to Inventory Control by keyboarding it into the desk-top VDT:

Figure 13.1
Individualized form
memo components.
Personnel
Department
withholding
statements.

Master Memo

FROM: Jose Llamas, Assistant Director of Personnel

TO: _____

SUBJECT: Monthly Withholding for 1986

DATE: December 15, 1986

Personnel records as of December 15, 1986 indicate that your monthly
withholding amounts are as follows:

Pension fund:

Stock options:

Payroll savings:

Company charity fund:

The pension fund withholding represents a fixed percentage of your current
salary. Stock option, payroll savings, and company charity fund withholding
amounts are those you last specified to this office.

IF YOU WISH TO CHANGE THE AMOUNTS WITHHELD FOR NEXT YEAR ON
STOCK OPTIONS, PAYROLL SAVINGS, OR THE CHARITY FUND, PLEASE
INFORM THE PERSONNEL OFFICE NO LATER THAN 5 P.M., DECEMBER 22,
1986.

Segment of employee/withholding list

Employee Name	Department	Pension	Stock	Saving	Charity
Hewlit, L. B.	Assembly	$ 50.00	$ 25.00	$ 25.00	$ 10.00
Hextall, P. J.	Sales	$250.00	$300.00	$ 50.00	$ 50.00
Heyer, D. M.	Accounting	$200.00	$200.00	$ 0.00	$ 50.00

Figure 13.1
Continued

Withholding memo to L. B. Hewlit

FROM: Jose Llamas, Assistant Director of Personnel

TO: L. B. Hewlit, Assembly Department

SUBJECT: Monthly Withholding for 1986

DATE: December 15, 1986

Personnel records as of December 15, 1986 indicate that your monthly withholding amounts are as follows:

Pension fund: $50.00

Stock options: $25.00

Payroll savings: $25.00

Company charity fund: $10.00

The pension fund withholding represents a fixed percentage of your current salary. Stock option, payroll savings, and company charity fund withholding amounts are those you last specified to this office.

IF YOU WISH TO CHANGE THE AMOUNTS WITHHELD FOR NEXT YEAR ON STOCK OPTIONS, PAYROLL SAVINGS, OR THE CHARITY FUND, PLEASE INFORM THE PERSONNEL OFFICE NO LATER THAN 5 P.M., DECEMBER 22, 1986.

Hextall withholding memo

FROM: Jose Llamas, Assistant Director of Personnel

TO: P. J. Hextall, Sales Department

SUBJECT: Monthly Withholding for 1986

DATE: December 15, 1986

Personnel records as of December 15, 1986 indicate that your monthly withholding amounts are as follows:

Figure 13.1   Pension fund; $250.00
Continued

Stock options: $300.00

Payroll savings: $50.00

Company charity fund: $50.00

The pension fund withholding represents a fixed percentage of your current salary. Stock option, payroll savings, and company charity fund withholding amounts are those you last specified to this office.

IF YOU WISH TO CHANGE THE AMOUNTS WITHHELD FOR NEXT YEAR ON STOCK OPTIONS, PAYROLL SAVINGS, OR THE CHARITY FUND, PLEASE INFORM THE PERSONNEL OFFICE NO LATER THAN 5 P.M. DECEMBER 22, 1986.

Heyer withholding memo

FROM: Jose Llamas, Assistant Director of Personnel

TO: D. M. Heyer, Accounting

SUBJECT: Monthly Withholding for 1986

DATE: December 15, 1986

Personnel records as of December 15, 1986 indicate that your monthly withholding amounts are as follows:

Pension fund: $200.00

Stock options: $200.00

Payroll savings: $0.00

Company charity fund: $50.00

The pension fund withholding represents a fixed percentage of your current salary. Stock option, payroll savings, and company charity fund withholding amounts are those you last specified to this office.

IF YOU WISH TO CHANGE THE AMOUNTS WITHHELD FOR NEXT YEAR ON
STOCK OPTIONS, PAYROLL SAVINGS, OR THE CHARITY FUND, PLEASE
INFORM THE PERSONNEL OFFICE NO LATER THAN 5 P.M., DECEMBER 22,
1986.

Figure 13.1
Continued

Date: April 3, 1986

Time: 9:38 A.M. CST

To: Inventory Control

From: Fran Dobbs, Sales

Subject: High-Fashion Line Inventory

PLEASE SEND COMPLETE LIST OF CURRENT INVENTORY ON ALL HIGH-
FASHION MODELS TO VDT #323. THANKS.

The Hay interoffice VDT message network is set up so that a bell rings in
the Inventory Control Department when a message is waiting. The clerk
there reads Dobbs's request and commands the central computer to display
a list of all high-fashion models and inventory and send the display to
Dobbs at VDT #323. Within three minutes, Dobbs is looking at a list of
which this is one segment:

Date: April 3, 1986

Time: 9:41 A.M. CST

To: Fran Dobbs, Sales, VDT #323

From: Inventory Control

Subject: High-Fashion Inventory List

HIGH-FASHION INVENTORY AS OF 4/3/86

MODEL	DESCRIPTION	QUANTITY ON HAND
0939	ROUND/ARABIC/GOLD-PLATE	1,544
0940	ROUND/ARABIC/STAINLESS	2,008
1122	SQUARE/ARABIC/GOLD-PLATE	1,555
1123	SQUARE/ARABIC/STAINLESS	1,989
1208	PENTAGON/ARABIC/GOLD-PLATE	DISCONTINUED
1209	PENTAGON/ARABIC/STAINLESS	DISCONTINUED
1223	ROUND/ROMAN/GOLD-PLATE	1,809
1224	ROUND/ROMAN/STAINLESS	2,289

The list continues for 13 pages. Realizing that copying the entire inventory by hand would take hours, Dobbs commands the word processor to print a copy. The process of scanning the list, requesting a printed copy, and receiving that copy over the sales office printer takes two minutes. Five minutes after writing the note to inventory control, Dobbs has information she might include in letters to retailers to assure them that Hay can ship orders placed during her forthcoming sales trip.

Electronic Mail   The same communication capabilities available for sending documents within a company are available to writers sending letters, memos, and reports to outside readers. For instance, Lowell Sanborn, Hay's purchasing manager, wants to send a message to a supplier of miniature circuit boards necessary for manufacturing game-playing and other novelty watches. The message must (1) reach the supplier immediately and (2) be written so that an exact record exists.

To accomplish this, Sanborn uses the Hay word processor and the commercial electronic mail service to which the company subscribes. This service allows a writer to keyboard a letter or other written communication, specify an addressee, and send the document over telephone lines to a distant word processor. In this case, the supplier has a word processor hooked into the same commercial electronic mail service to which Hay belongs. The shared service lets Sanborn send the important message in figure 13.2. Note that the word processor lets Sanborn recreate the Hay letterhead.

The message reaches DAVON immediately, where Effingham reads it and sends the return confirmation in figure 13.3. Electronic mail has allowed Sanborn to prevent a potentially costly mistake as well as to have a record of the correction request if something does go wrong. Most commercial electronic mail services also offer overnight delivery to addressees *not* subscribing to their service. In such cases, the subscribing company's writer keyboards the document, which is communicated electronically to the mailing services office nearest the addressee. A courier then completes the delivery.

HAY WATCH COMPANY
Cicero Avenue
Chicago, IL 60644

June 28, 1986
1:35 P.M. CDT

Clair Effingham
Shipping Department
DAVON, Inc.
7 Northside Way
Montpelier, VT 05602

Dear Ms. Effingham:

Please note this correction to the order scheduled for shipment to
Hay Watch Company tomorrow (June 29, 1986). The quantities
for items #3499 and #4080 were reversed. The correct quantities
are:

　　　Item #3499--1,500 pieces
　　　Item #4080--1,200 pieces

Thank you for your attention to this correction.

Sincerely,

Lowell Sanborn
Purchasing Manager

Figure 13.2　Electronic mail letter

DAVON, INC.
7 Northside Way
Montpelier, VT 05602

June 29, 1986
2:45 P.M. EDT

Lowell Sanborn
Purchasing Manager
Hay Watch Company
Cicero Avenue
Chicago, IL 60644

Dear Mr. Sanborn:

We have received your message correcting the previous shipping
order. This confirms that the corrected order will be shipped on
June 29, 1986, as scheduled.

Sincerely,

Clair Effingham
Shipping Manager

Figure 13.3   Electronic mail reply

Facsimile Processing   Facsimile machines offer a specialized type of electronic mail service to companies needing to transmit *exact* copies of typed, handwritten, or graphic material immediately. One can think of the facsimile machine as a long-distance photocopier.

At 9:15 A.M. Central Standard Time, Hay's Accounting Department completes a word processed report detailing third-quarter revenues and expenditures for the company's European division and making fourth-quarter projections. Hay's European department heads have flown to the division headquarters in London for a meeting to begin at 4:00 P.M. London (Universal Standard) time, which corresponds to 10:00 A.M. CST.

The department heads *must* have the report in time for their meeting. To get the report across the Atlantic and into the executives' hands in 45 minutes, an Accounting Department secretary commands the word processor to print a copy of the document. The secretary then dials the London office on a telephone connected to a high-speed facsimile machine in the Chicago office. This same secretary places the report into the facsimile machine, which "reads" it for transmission over the telephone lines into another facsimile machine in the London office. Capable of making duplicates at faster than a page a minute, the London machine produces a complete accounting report copy in 15 minutes. A clerk in the London office then takes the report to a high-speed, collating photocopier in the same room. The photocopy machine makes enough reports for the department heads in 5 minutes. Within another 5 minutes, the clerk has stapled each copy and placed one report in front of each executive's place at the London conference room table in time for the meeting.

For companies that need to send many documents between distant locations immediately, purchasing or renting "fax" machines may offer economy as well as speed. The cost for sending the Hay accounting report, for example, was the price of the 15-minute Chicago-to-London direct-dial call plus the cost of paper and staples.

Business word processors are capable of letting employees mix written text on the same page with statistics and graphics. Hay's Accounting Department often uses this interactive capability. For instance, Accounting sends out frequent, one-page memos to all sales personnel. These memos keep sales staff abreast of revenues, expenses, and other financial data. The Accounting Department strives to keep each memo to a single page so that salespeople can tape these communications to their office walls for quick reference.

Word Processing Integrated with Other Computerized Business Operations

Agnes King, a staff accountant, is responsible for sending one of these memos on a quarterly basis. The memo specifies the percentage of total quarterly revenue for which each Hay United States sales region (East, Midwest, South, West) is responsible. The memo compares revenue from each region for the current quarter, as well as for the previous quarter and the same quarter one year ago.

King "builds" this memo in the same fashion every three months. She uses an accounting program to calculate each region's percentage of total revenue from previously entered dollar figures. The accounting program displays these percentages in spreadsheet fashion: a matrix of rows and columns.

After completing the percentage calculations, King uses another program to create a vertical bar chart displaying the revenue data in graphic form. By looking at the percentages and the bar graph, King then writes a brief memo announcing the subject of the communication and summarizing the data in written text. Figure 13.4 displays King's completed memo with word processing adjustments made automatically to accommodate both the spreadsheet and bar chart on one page.

A Few Words of Caution

Now that you have seen some of the many ways word processing technology speeds and improves business writing, a few words of caution are in order. By heeding this advice, you will insure that word processing supports your problem-solving efforts as efficiently as possible.

Do Your Own Proofreading

As we have mentioned several times in this book. the final responsibility for any piece of business writing rests with you, its author. Be certain that you proofread your document before transmitting it to a reader. Word processing programs such as the very useful spelling checkers can cut down on the number of errors you have to correct when you proofread. No program, though, has yet been invented that tells you what *you* mean to say.

Thus when the computerized dictionary sees the word *deceive* in one of your sentences, it will not flag it as an error. Because *deceive* is in the dictionary, the spelling checker will assume that it is the word you meant to write. Suppose, though, that you were a Hay Watch Company sales executive writing a letter to invite a long-time customer to tour the Chicago factory. Suppose, too, that you had meant to say, "We'll be delighted to see you at the main plant on the 26th. Hay Watch Company is always pleased to receive a long-time client." But you actually keyboarded, "We'll be delighted to see you at the main plant on the 26th. Hay Watch Company is always pleased to *deceive* a long-time client." If you simply used the dictionary program, printed out the letter, and mailed it without a final proofreading, you might find yourself wondering why your client never appeared or contacted you on the 26th—or ever again, for that matter.

Use the dictionary, punctuation, and other specialized programs by all means! Just make certain that you reserve the last proofreading for yourself.

Figure 13.4
Accounting and
graphic data
integrated with
memo

TO: All Hay Sales Staff
FROM: Agnes King, Accounting Department
SUBJECT: Third Quarter Sales Revenues by U.S. Region
DATE: October 15, 1986

Preliminary percentages for third-quarter sales revenues by U.S. region are now available. The
display below reports such percentages for this year's third quarter, as well as for this year's
second quarter and last year's third quarter.

Percent of U.S. Sales Revenue by Region

	Current Third Quarter	Current Second Quarter	Last Third Quarter
East	30	32	35
Midwest	32	34	37
South	20	18	16
West	18	16	12
Total	100	100	100

The bar chart below translates this data into graphic terms.

A East Last 3rd Q 35%
B East Cur. 2nd Q 32%
C East Cur. 3rd Q 30%
D Midw. Last 3rd Q 37%
E Midw. Cur. 2nd Q 34%
F Midw. Cur. 3rd Q 32%
G So. Last 3rd Q 16%
H So. Cur. 2nd Q 18%
I So. Cur. 3rd Q 20%
J West Last 3rd Q 12%
K West Cur. 2nd Q 16%
L West Cur. 3rd Q 18%

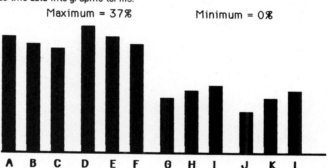

Maximum = 37%   Minimum = 0%

Note the decreased share of revenues from our East and Midwest regions from last quarter to this
quarter, as well as from last year's third quarter to this year's. Note, too, the corresponding
increases for our South and West regions. Since revenues are up in each region (see memo of
October 12, 1986), increased revenue shares for the South and West regions can be attributed to
particularly brisk sales in recent quarters. Overall, these percentages suggest that Sales is
achieving the regional balance hoped for by the executive board.

**Make Your Own
Decisions about
Style**

Word processing programs that claim to improve your style do exist. Generally they have a list of "tired" and "vague" words and phrases in their memories. When the program finds something from the list in your document, it alerts you to the fact and offers "fresh," "specific" alternatives. These suggestions are fine except for one thing. The program has no way of knowing what writer's image you have in mind for a particular writing problem. You may wish to use *some* of the lively words and phrases suggested by the program. However, only you should choose the words to soothe your angry customer or the phrases to discuss a touchy subject.

**Do Your Own
Thinking and
Writing**

Commercial programs that provide you with 5, 10, 20, 50, or more "standard" letter forms are now on the market. They simply require you to type names, addresses, and other personalizing information into various blanks that appear on the screen. These may be tempting when your time is short and your energy is low, but we urge you not to give up your power to think and express yourself and turn it over to the word processor. Once again, only you can define and analyze your writing problem. Only you can make the decisions necessary for creating an effective draft. And only you can revise and edit that draft so it achieves the objective you first set for it.

Summary

Word processing can help speed completion of writing tasks. A word processor may allow you to define and analyze a writing problem quickly. This technology enables you to draft rapidly because you can keyboard without having to worry about making mistakes. Automatic scrolling, blocking, reformatting, and saving let you complete large-scale revision efficiently. Other features, including adding, deleting, searching, finding, replacing, screen splitting, and spelling checking, help to speed small-scale editing. Instant centering, margin changes, justification, vertical spacing, and page numbering help prepare your document for transmittal.

Word processing and related technology make some specialized procedures physically possible or economically feasible. You can create form letters and memos that have the look of originals. You can communicate instantly within your company via networks and outside the company by electronic mail. Facsimile processing allows you to transmit lengthy documents long distances within minutes. You can mix text with statistics and computer graphics.

It is important to use word processing's capabilities judiciously. Retain ultimate control over your own proofreading and wording—indeed, your whole writing process. With these controls, you can use word processing technology to solve writing problems more efficiently and skillfully.

Writing Problems

Note: We recognize that some of you have access to word processors and some do not. Therefore, we have divided the exercises for this chapter into two sections: one group of problems for which a word processor is not required and a second group of problems requiring word processing equipment. Although we hope to have acquainted you with word processing if you were not already familiar with its benefits, *the main point in writing this chapter was to show how to use this technology to speed and improve application of the problem-solving approach to business writing.* The exercises that do require word processors have this meshing of technology with problem solving as their objective.

Problems for Which a Word Processor Is Optional or Not Needed

1. Visit the word processing center of a nearby firm. Use the letter writing techniques detailed in chapter 6 to request a tour. Ask your host whether he or she would show you how the company uses the word processing features described in this chapter. Follow up your visit with a thank-you note to your host and a short oral report to your class on your findings.

2. Visit a computer store. Use the letter writing techniques detailed in chapter 6 to ask the store's manager if and when you could see various word processing hardware and software the store recommends for business use. With your instructor's permission, invite the store to send a representative to demonstrate word processing equipment during a class session.

3. You work in the in-house marketing and advertising department of the Thomas Health and Beauty Aid Company. Thomas is introducing a new toothpaste with the following benefits: cinnamon flavoring, fluoride, low abrasiveness, pleasant taste, and a tough tube. Thomas will be distributing free samples in its test area. Your job is to prepare a form letter leaving blanks for personalized data (names and addresses of people who will receive the sample). Write the letter so that the word processor will be able to merge names and addresses into your text. Give the new toothpaste a name, and be certain to praise its virtues in your letter.

Problems Requiring a Word Processor

4. You handle consumer complaints for the Wells Athletic Equipment Company. A customer, Kate Johnson, has just written to complain

that her recently purchased barbells are cracked. She is also upset because the store where she purchased the weights will not honor her lifetime warranty. Having checked your company's files, you know Johnson never returned the warranty registration card enclosed in her new barbell set. Nor did she follow the repair procedure specified in the booklet, also included with each Wells product. The procedure requires the customer to contact an authorized Wells Athletic Equipment Repair Center, which the store where Johnson purchased the barbells is not. After you have defined and analyzed the writing problem, use a word processor to draft, revise, and print your letter of response to Johnson.

5. Both you and a classmate work for the same commercial coffee service. Your company leases coffee makers and sells packets of coffee to businesses for employee use. You are in charge of the company's eastern distribution network; your classmate heads the western distribution network. Each of you needs to write a memo to the distribution supervisors in each state in your territory. Each memo announces a meeting of state supervisors on October 30. The eastern meeting takes place in Pittsburgh and the western meeting in Denver. Both meetings have a five-item agenda that you and your classmate should make up. The overriding reason for each meeting is to get state distribution supervisors ready for the holiday season, when demand for coffee service rises sharply. After defining and analyzing the writing problem, one of you should use a word processor to draft, revise, and print the memo. The other should perform drafting, revision, and document preparation by hand or typewriter. After each of you has completed a memo, meet with your classmate. Make a list of similarities and differences in your memo writing experience—for example, how long it took to complete each problem-solving step, how many drafts you had to prepare, how you checked for typographical errors.

6. You are a bookkeeper for a branch office of a national chain of budget menswear stores. A company accountant at the headquarters office is in the process of compiling a report from data submitted by branch office bookkeepers. The accountant calls to say that you have forgotten to send a page of data on revenues, expenditures, and inventory from the shoe departments of the 10 stores served by your branch office. This page is stored in a file in your computer, which is tied to an electronic mail service. Use a commercial electronic mail service or the intracampus electronic mail facility of your school's computer to send the letter of transmittal that will accompany the missing data to the accountant. *Note:* Send the letter to yourself. If you have an electronic mail subscription of your own, use that; if your instructor has such a subscription, use that; if you have access to your school's computer intra campus electronic mail service, use that.

7. You have just learned of a job opening in your field. You are highly qualified for and interested in the position, but you do not have a resume to send. Use a word processor to compose and print out your current resume. Use any of the available special word processing print features to enhance the appearance of your resume tastefully.

8. Work together with two or three classmates to plan and stage a "word processing show" for your class. Ask classmates who own word processing equipment whether they would be willing to bring it to school and demonstrate its features. If several students do agree to bring equipment, the best way to do this is to set up "demonstration stations" around the classroom. Then have class members move from station to station while the demonstrations are taking place. As an alternative to using class time, you might reserve a dormitory function room for an evening show. If your school is primarily a commuter campus, you might ask for your instructor's help in reserving a student center function room for a lunchtime or evening demonstration. *Note:* For security's sake, insist that your demonstrators bring their equipment when the show starts, stay with it throughout the demonstration, and take it home as soon as the show is finished.

Extended Application

Take the topic on which you have been working since the extended application in chapter 1. Find out how companies and employees in industries and kinds of work related to your topic use word processing technology. You might write several companies a letter requesting such information and explaining why you wish to know about it. You can also consult your reference librarian for direction toward articles on word processing in your selected industry or work category. You might set up an interview with someone who works in your selected job. Perhaps you can even arrange to visit a company in an industry pertinent to your topic to view their word processing equipment in action.

CHAPTER 14

Dictating

ictation is a more efficient method of writing than the pen, the typewriter, or even the word processor. There are two modes of dictating. In the face-to-face method, a manager dictates a document to a secretary sitting across the desk. In machine dictation, the manager dictates a document into a recording device, and the secretary later replays the recording and types the document for the manager's signature.

The point we wish to stress is that dictation is as much a form of writing as sitting down with a legal pad and pencil. Only one part of the process changes. In traditional writing, you personally write out the words on the page; in dictation, someone else transcribes the words on paper for you. Everything else is essentially the same. You still have to perform all other acts of the writing process: profiling the reader, defining your objectives, organizing your thoughts, and revising and editing the rough draft of your dictation. However, dictation is a more efficient form of writing because it removes the drudgery of handwriting.

In business, dictating is becoming increasingly popular. (It is also becoming an increasingly valuable skill.) Many types of professionals dictate every day, including medical people, lawyers, police officers, sales people, and managers. Dictation increases productivity; it saves time.

This chapter presents reasons for developing the skill of dictating, acquaints you with the major kinds of dictation equipment, teaches you the fundamentals of effective dictating, and, finally, gives you practice in dictating.

Although face-to-face dictation is also common, we will discuss machine dictation exclusively. Nor will we debate which is more efficient, because each has advantages. The fact is, the vast majority of you will simply not have secretaries to whom to dictate your correspondence face-to-face, at least partly because changes in the work place are creating changes in the secretary's role. If you dictate, you will probably do so to a machine, so you should be prepared for that eventuality. Should you later have the dictation services of a secretary, you will not find it difficult to switch from machine to face-to-face dictation because the fundamentals are the same.

One advantage is that machine dictation does not require the transcriber to be present at the time of dictation. You can record the dictation at your convenience, and the transcriber can type it at his or hers, an even greater advantage considering that certain kinds of dictation equipment allow you to phone in your dictation 24 hours a day!

As you may have noticed, we use the term *transcriber* for *secretary*. Some support personnel who transcribe dictation are secretaries, but some are specialists in transcription. The term *transcriber* describes the employee's function more precisely.

Why You Should Learn to Dictate

Here are four good reasons for learning to dictate: (1) dictation saves time; (2) you can do it anywhere, anytime; (3) it is cost-effective; and (4) it is relatively easy to learn.

Dictating Saves Time   If the manager's most valuable resource is time, then dictation is one way to make the most of it. You should dictate not just letters and memos but reports and speeches—anything you write. Experts tell us to dictate reports and proposals that run as long as 100 pages. Imagine the time you could save by dictating rather than writing longhand a proposal of 50 pages. Imagine the time you could save over the years if you dictate your daily writing.

You Can Dictate Anywhere, Anytime   Dictation is flexible. With today's technology, you dictate almost anywhere, anytime: at the office, at home, in a hotel room, in a car (while someone else is driving), on a plane, or on a train.

Dictating Is Cost-Effective   On the average, dictating to a recording unit is about 25 percent less expensive than dictating face-to-face to a secretary. Imagine the savings over a period of time. How many letters and memos will you write in a month, a year, five years? How many letters and memos would a whole department or company generate over the same time? Dictation can save a great deal of money.

Dictating Is Relatively Easy to Learn   Dictation skills are not difficult to acquire; you don't have to take a lengthy course or research the matter extensively. Some dictation units come with recorded instructions. All units are accompanied by an operator's manual that contains brief instructions and sometimes exercises to get you started. Some vendors provide video cassettes to orient you to using their units.

Another way to learn is to ask a coworker, especially someone who would like to see you begin dictating, to demonstrate the use of the unit. Unfortunately, the chapter cannot include instructions on particular units, but it does include instructions on how to dictate once you have become familiar with your equipment.

Today's Dictation Equipment

First, we will explain how dictation equipment works: the standard features of all units, the most common recording media, and the process of transcription onto paper. Second, we will cover the three kinds of dictation units: portable, desk-top, and central dictation units.

How Dictation Equipment Works

Common Features on Dictation Units   Virtually every dictation unit has certain standard features that allow you to:

1. Record dictation
2. Pause during dictation to focus your thoughts or to interrupt dictating—for example, to answer the telephone
3. Play back dictation to review it for clarity and accuracy
4. Correct any errors in your original dictation
5. Indicate the end of each document, the end of your dictation, and instructions to the transcriber—for example, regarding format

The last item on the list brings us to an essential element in dictation: communicating effectively with your transcriber. Even when you write longhand, you must give certain instructions to the typist regarding, for example, spacing, indentation, and paragraphing. In dictation, you must give all instructions on the tape, vocally. You cannot expect your transcriber to phone you to ask whether Mr. Bodo's name is spelled with only one *d*. Interruptions such as that would defeat the efficiency of dictation.

The method used to communicate instructions to the transcriber is called **cueing**. Cueing allows you, the dictator, to include instructions at any point in the dictation. It allows you to indicate to the transcriber the location of an instruction, a mistake to be corrected, or the end of the document.

Cueing can take several forms. On some units you press a button that generates an electronic tone or a flicker of light on a display panel to indicate to the transcriber the location of special instructions and the beginning and ending of each recorded document. Other units have an odometer, a digital readout counter. When you begin dictating, you turn it on: as you insert an instruction to the transcriber, you note the number; when you finish dictating, you note the number again. Still other models use an index strip, which you mark to indicate the location of a special instruction.

Recording Media   Another important element in any dictation unit is the medium, that element upon which your dictation is recorded. For example, when you use a tape recorder, the medium is the cassette. Some common media in use in dictation systems today are, first, **standard cassettes**, which hold up to 120 minutes of dictation. Second, **microcassettes** and **minicassettes** are smaller than standard cassettes but hold up to 120 minutes of dictation; their popularity is growing. Third, the **endless loop magnetic tape** is enclosed in a tank and is automatically erased at regular intervals. It allows the transcriber to begin typing the dictation a few seconds after dictation begins.

The Role of the Transcriber   The transcriber could be located in your immediate vicinity; but if you work for a firm that has a word processing center, the transcriber may be located on another floor. The concept of the word processing center means that many secretarial services are centrally located in the firm or located at smaller centers around the firm. You may not even know personally the transcriber who types your document, because your line of communication with the word processing center will probably be through its supervisor.

Before the transcriber begins to type your dictation, he or she scans the medium to learn the document's length. Doing so allows the transcriber to set margins so that the finished document appears neatly arranged on the page. The transcriber also scans the document for the instructions you have recorded. In typing the document, the transcriber wears a headset that allows only the transcriber to hear your dictation. With a foot pedal attached to the dictation unit, the transcriber controls the speed of playback so that he or she can comfortably type as well as listen.

There are three kinds of dictation units: portable units, desk-top units, and central dictation units.

Kinds of
Recording Units

Portable Units   The growing popularity of portable units is largely due to their flexibility. They fit easily into your hand, and you can carry them in a pocket, purse, or briefcase. Figure 14.1 shows their convenient size. Portable units run on batteries. Most use microcassettes, minicassettes, or standard cassettes. The small size of these recording media is an advantage.

When you're out of town, for instance, you can easily mail them to your office for transcription.

Some units allow you to transmit your dictation at high speed over the telephone wires. For example, from out of town you phone a secretary in your office and play your prerecorded dictation over the phone at fast forward. The secretary records the dictation on a unit at the office and plays it back at a speed convenient for transcribing.

As noted earlier, portables are popular because of their flexibility. You can use them in the car, on a plane, in a motel or hotel room. Most portable models even pick up whispered dictation so you don't disturb others. At a conference, for instance, you can dictate brief notes on the speaker's presentation to your portable dictation unit. Should a business idea come to you away from the office, you can record it on a portable.

The portable unit is the simplest in design. Usually, one switch, operated by your thumb, controls all functions. That's recording, playback, fast forward, reverse, pause, cueing, stopping, and ejecting the cassette. This single-switch control feature allows you to hold your papers in one hand and operate the unit with your other hand. Cueing is handled in a variety of ways on portable units (odometer, index strip, or electronic tone).

Portable units are best for people who do not have a large volume of dictation and often dictate away from the office. For maximum effectiveness, many executives combine a portable unit with either a desk-top unit or access to a central system.

Desk-top Units   The portable unit can never be self-contained, because the recording medium—for example, the microcassette—must be transported to another unit for transcription. The desk-top unit, however, often combines dictation and transcription functions. You lose the portability of the smaller unit but gain other features; for example, many desk-top units allow you to phone in dictation.

In design, desk-top units differ more than do portable ones. The unit shown in figure 14.2, however, is representative. The corded microphone is in the cradle at the left side of the unit. The microphone has built-in controls that allow you to operate the unit with one hand while holding your notes with the other. There are three reasons a desk-top unit might meet your needs. First, your load of dictation may exceed the capacity of a portable unit, but it might not justify the purchase of a central dictation system. Second, although you might have access to your company's central dictation system, your personal volume of dictation might be too large for the system to accommodate. Third, a desk-top unit offers you a sense of privacy because it allows you to maintain complete control of your recording media.

Figure 14.2
Desk-top dictation
unit. (Source:
Dictaphone, A
Pitney Bowes
Company.)

Central Dictation Units   The smaller firm may prefer to supply its personnel with desk-top models, but the larger firm will frequently choose a
central dictation unit (also called the central system). This unit is often an
integral part of their word processing center, where perhaps 40 or more
transcribers support as many as 100 dictators.

The central system not only handles larger volumes of dictation but is
able to accommodate very different dictation loads from individuals.
Another important feature of central systems is their phone-in capacity,
often allowing dictators to phone in their dictation 24 hours a day from
anywhere in the world. Companies whose personnel travel a great deal or
are frequently away from the office often use a central system.

Access to a central dictation system is usually by telephone. You perform
all dictating functions—recording, cueing, editing—by pressing different
buttons on the phone. Figure 14.3 shows a business-size card one company
gives users. One side of the card tells you how to use the system; the other
side tells you what controls go with what pushbutton.

Many central systems feature taped instructions that help the dictator to
use the system. For example, a recorded voice may ask you to identify
yourself by using a prearranged code number. The voice may tell you when
to begin dictating, how to give instructions, how much recording time you
have left, or how to signal the word processing center supervisor that you
are dictating a confidential document. Some units have a feature that
automatically stops the tape when you stop speaking. Some central systems
allow you to indicate the priority of your dictation through the use of a
code.

CONTROLS

1 LISTEN	**2** RECORD	**3** SHORT REVIEW
4 PAUSE	**5** END	**6**
7 SKIP FORWARD	**8** CONTINUOUS REVERSE	**9** MANUAL DISCONNECT
* PASSCODE	**0** INTERCOM	**#** CASSETTE CHANGE

750-063   Printed in USA

LANIER

TO RETRIEVE MESSAGE:
1. Dial phone number. Wait for ready tone.
2. Touch "*" + passcode.
___ ___ ___ ___
3. Listen to messages and hang up.

TO CLOSE MESSAGES:
1. After listening to messages, wait for ready tone. Touch "5".

TO RECORD MESSAGE:
1. Dial phone number. To change mail box position, touch "#" + number.
2. When ready tone appears, touch "2" and record.
3. To pause, touch "4". Touch "2" to record again.
4. Upon completion, hang up. (In some areas, touch "9" to disconnect.)

MESSENGER™

Figure 14.3 Phone-in dictation instructions. (Source: Lanier Business Products, Inc.)

The Process of Effective Dictation

Dictation fits easily into the problem-solving approach to writing because it is simply writing without transcribing. We have some suggestions on how to adapt the problem-solving steps, especially analysis through outlining, to the process of writing via dictation. Finally, we will explain how to work cooperatively with a transcriber and how to follow standard dictating procedure.

Become familiar with the equipment at your work place. Read the user's manual; ask help from a coworker. Check to see whether the equipment comes with prerecorded instructions or whether the office has an instructional cassette or video cassette. Most vendors publish helpful pamphlets on how to dictate. If the office does not have such a pamphlet, you might write to request one from the vendor.

Ask your word processing center supervisor for instructional materials. Perhaps the center or your training department offers a short course in

Learning to Operate Your Equipment

dictating. Above all, practice dictating whenever you get a chance. If feasible, ask a word processing specialist in your company to evaluate your dictation, giving pointers on how to improve your technique.

Establish a Routine   Try to dictate your daily correspondence at a regular time—when you are alert in the morning is a good time. As far as possible, eliminate distractions while you're dictating—ask incoming calls to be stopped. (You can call back later.)

Gather All Necessary Materials   Collect the materials you will need for dictation. For example, gather the letters or memos you are responding to, price lists, catalogues, policy statements, or whatever you will refer to in dictation. If you are answering several memos or letters, number each one in the upper right-hand corner for easy reference. You may then introduce the documents you dictate as responses to the numbered pieces of correspondence. For example, "This is a memorandum in response to item number 4." Doing so will make for easy reference, and, if your transcriber is located close by, you can avoid having to dictate the addresses of your correspondents because the transcriber will have the numbered pieces of correspondence.

Follow the Four Problem-Solving Steps   Novice dictators tend to regard dictation more as speaking than writing, but the result of dictation is a document that will not be heard but *read*. Your reader will have none of the advantages of a listener in a conversation—no chance to respond immediately, ask questions, or even register reactions through facial expressions or body language. Nor will you have any immediate feedback from your reader. Therefore, view dictation as spoken *writing*. The four problem-solving steps apply to its development. You may need to adapt them to this medium, but you must keep them in mind if you are to dictate effectively.

Having assembled your materials, you are ready to do your pre-writing planning. You might perform these tasks quickly, but you should not skip them. Profile your reader. What special needs of this reader must you meet? What preconceptions of this reader must you consider? It should help if you imagine your reader seated across from your desk as you plan and dictate your message.

Define your objectives. Do you want to inform, persuade, or move your reader to action? Will this message be good or bad news? What tone do you wish to adopt? What image of yourself do you wish to convey?

Consider, however briefly, possible alternative strategies to achieve your objectives; then decide upon a strategy or plan to follow in dictating. How thoroughly you plan depends on whether you are dictating a rough draft or a final copy. If you are dictating a rough draft, not much planning may be needed or even desirable, because dictating can be a way to get all your ideas on a subject down on paper—to brainstorm, overcome writer's block, and get the actual writing started. Later you can use the transcribed document to "cut and paste" a final draft.

On the other hand, if you're dictating what will be substantially the document that goes out, you will want to do more planning, even if you do it quickly. You must identify the issues you will discuss and the order in which you will discuss them. Because plans for messages have already been covered, that material will not be repeated. But, having chosen a strategy—for example, a direct plan—you must organize your points to implement that strategy.

For dictating short memos and letters, you can plan as follows. If you are responding to a memo or a letter, reread it analytically. Underline or highlight key lines, for example, the statement of purpose, specific requests, indications of attitude, or deadline dates. Make notes in the margins.

Next list the points you intend to develop in your response. Jot them down in the order that they come to you just to get every important point down. Then study the list to determine the order in which you will treat these points. For example, will you use a chronological order or a logical one? Choose a plan and number each point accordingly.

For example, assume that you are a representative for a vendor of dictation equipment and you are responding to a request for information from a potential client. The client is the dean of the Business Administration College at a nearby university, Dr. Ruth Previn. She wants to know what kind of dictation equipment will best meet the needs of her college of some 25 instructors. Before you switch on your personal desk-top model, jot down the following list and then number the points in the order that you will develop them:

5. See enclosed brochure on Dicta-System III.
2. Faculty: 25 full-time and 18 part-time. Secretaries: 2 full-time and 5 part-time.
3. Dicta-System III increases productivity.
4. Central dictation unit probably appropriate.
6. Will take survey of their needs.
7. Request opportunity to make presentation. Arrange appointment.
1. Thank her and express confidence in outcome.

When you begin to dictate, take your points in numerical order—you'll save the time of having to rewrite them in logical order. If the list is short, you may not even have to number the items: looking at a list of four points, you can easily spot your opening idea. Dictate that point and draw a line through that item on the list, then move through the rest of the list.

If, on the other hand, the document you are dictating is several pages long and contains complicated thought and organization, you will need to make a formal outline. You will probably develop a topic outline in which you use phrases rather than sentences, which would slow you down and diminish the advantage of dictation—speed. Nonetheless, your analytical step will be fairly complex. Your objectives and knowledge of the task will tell you how much planning to do, whether a few minutes or hours. Failing to plan can lead you into rambling—straying from the important points— or into needlessly repeating yourself. Dictating with a plan will help you to be direct and concise.

Dictating

We will begin with general guidelines that apply to any form of dictation and follow with the standard operating procedure that most effective dictators follow.

Guidelines for Promoting Teamwork with Your Transcriber   In dictating, you have to consider the needs not only of your reader but of the transcriber as well. You may never see the transcriber of your document, but you must work efficiently with him or her. Develop the habit of consideration and courtesy for this professional. For example, if you know the transcriber's name, use it. If not, address him or her as "Secretary." We have several suggestions to increase teamwork.

Speak Distinctly   If you are dictating into a microphone, hold it three to five inches from your mouth. Do not breathe audibly into the microphone because doing so may distract the transcriber. Speak in a clear, distinct tone of voice—don't mumble! Speak deliberately—don't rush! Adopt a pace that is natural but a little slower than that of normal conversation. Pause at the ends of longer phrases and sentences to allow the transcriber to move easily through the dictation. If you pause for a few minutes to collect your thoughts, however, use the pause button to stop the recording. Long pauses in dictation make the transcriber's work tedious.

Make your pronunciation precise. Emphasize endings of verbs so that the transcriber gets the right verb tense. For example, stress the difference between "I have" and "I had," the difference between "she believes" and "she believed."

Avoid behavior that could impair the clarity of your speech. For example, don't chew gum, eat a snack, smoke a pipe, or chew on a pencil. Don't tap the mike with a pencil or your finger. If you sneeze or cough, you may have to rerecord that part of your message to make it clear.

Spell Out Problem Words   As you dictate, your transcriber cannot interrupt to ask you questions. Therefore you must carefully pronounce or spell words that sound alike. The following partial list will alert you to such words:

accede, exceed	farther, further
accept, except	incidence, incidents
access, excess	incite, insight

adapt, adept
addition, edition
advice, advise
affect, effect
all ready, already
allusion, illusion
assistance, assistants
aver, avert
bear, bare
believe, receive
born, borne
break, brake
canvas, canvass
cease, seize
cite, sight, site
coarse, course
comments, commence
commuter, computer
competent, compliment, complement
correspondents, correspondence
council, counsel, console
decent, descend, descent, dissent
defer, differ
deposition, disposition
device, devise
disapprove, disprove
disburse, disperse
dissolution, disillusion
elicit, illicit
eligible, illegible
enclose, inclose, impose
enforce, in force
era, error
exceed, accede
finally, finely
fiscal, physical
formally, formerly
forth, fourth

interment, internment
interstate, intrastate
its, it's
later, latter
legislator, legislature
loose, lose
material, matériel
medal, meddle, metal, mettle
miner, minor
Ms., Mrs., Miss
ordinance, ordnance
over, overt
parcel, partial
passed, past
persecute, prosecute
personal, personnel
perspective, prospective
poor, pore
practical, practicable
pray, prey
precede, proceed
precedence, precedents
principal, principle
quite, quiet
receipt, receive
reference, reverence
relief, relieve
residence, residents
respectfully, respectively
rite, right, write
stationery, stationary
suit, suite
their, there, they're
through, threw
to, too, two
whose, who's
your, you're

When you use one of these words or phrases in a context that can confuse the transcriber, spell out the word. In fact, spell out any word that might cause problems, for example, names. Many first names can be spelled in at least two ways: is it *Mary Ann, Maryann,* or *Mary Anne?* Last names can cause problems, too. Your authors happen to have names that can easily be misspelled. Is it *Schiff* or *Schif*, *McNally* or *MacNally*? Spell out technical words when you think the transcriber may not be familiar with them, for example, *prima facie*. Spell out uncommon words such as *monometalism*. Spell out company names, street names, and the names of cities, for example, Hackensack.

When you spell out words, use a phonetic alphabet, such as the one the telephone operators use, which follows:

A	Alice	N	Nellie
B	Bertha	O	Oliver
C	Charles	P	Peter
D	David	Q	Quaker
E	Edward	R	Robert
F	Frank	S	Samuel
G	George	T	Thomas
H	Henry	U	Utah
I	Ida	V	Victor
J	James	W	William
K	Kate	X	X-ray
L	Lewis	Y	Young
M	Mary	Z	Zebra

Dictate Unusual Capitalizations   You will not have to dictate the obvious capitalizations, such as the first letters in names of people, companies, streets, cities, and obvious titles, like *The Wall Street Journal*. But you will have to dictate the capital letters in headings and subheadings in a report and those in the title of an article, for example, "How to Cut Costs and Increase Productivity through Dictation." We cannot list all possible capitalizations that should be dictated, but if you think the transcriber might miss it, dictate it.

Indicate the capitalization *before* you dictate the word or phrase so the transcriber does not have to go back and retype the word. Indicate a single capitalization this way. Say "first letter cap" immediately before dictating a word, the first letter of which you want capitalized. For example, "Please contact an officer in [first letter cap] Accounting." If you want to capitalize the first letter of each word in a title, heading, or phrase, say "initial caps, please." For example, "In tomorrow's meeting we will explore the technique known as [initial caps, please] Management By Objectives." If you want to capitalize all the letters in a word or phrase, before you dictate it say "all caps, please." For example, "This sale [all caps, please] ENDS FRIDAY, MAY 18."

Dictate Unusual Punctuation   You do not have to dictate all punctuation, since your inflection will normally signal much punctuation to the transcriber, for example, periods and question marks. You don't have to dictate every comma, either. For instance, you would not need to dictate the commas that occur in this and the preceding sentence. But dictate any punctuation that the transcriber could miss. Some instances of the comma, such as this sentence contains, need to be dictated. To dictate a comma, just say the word *comma* at the point you wish the comma inserted. Dictate semicolons, colons, hyphens, dashes, and exclamation points. For example, "We must get hopping on this one! [exclamation point] Every day we lose—[dash] every hour—[dash] could mean the difference between meeting the deadline or missing it." Also dictate quotation marks, parentheses, and underlining. Use the signals that follow:

"Quote . . . unquote"

"Open parenthesis . . . close parenthesis"

"Begin underlining . . . stop underlining"

Dictate Paragraphing   Indicate paragraphs by saying "new paragraph." If you want other indentations, say so. For example, you would dictate the indented list in the previous paragraph by saying "indent list . . . stop indenting."

Dictate Numbers   Numbers require special attention. For example, don't say "first . . . second . . ." if you want "(1) . . . (2). . . . " You must say "one in parentheses . . . two in parentheses. . . ." Sound out longer numbers; for example, to dictate 5,412,730, say "that's five, comma, four-one-two, comma, seven-three-zero." Note that zero is sounded as "zero" and not as "oh."

Standard Operating Procedure for Dictating   The following steps represent standard operating procedure for effective dictating:

1. Identify yourself. Give your name, department, and telephone extension number. If you are dictating to a central dictation unit, you may have to give your account number as well. For example, "This is Gina Lowenstein, Purchasing Department, extension number 5416, account number 10-42-7550."

2. If you are dictating a series of items, indicate the number of each. For example, "This is item number 1." Also indicate the end of each item in the series by saying, for example, "End of item number 1." This practice makes it easier for the transcriber to locate the beginning and end of a document.

3. If this document is a high-priority item, indicate that. Some dictation equipment allows you to assign a priority code to the item. Otherwise, indicate to the transcriber that you need the item by a certain time. Or you may phone the word processing center to alert them to the priority of the item.

4. If the item is confidential, alert the center supervisor by phone or tell the transcriber so on the tape.

5. Indicate the form and approximate length of the item. Is it a letter, memo, report, wire, mailgram, or numbered form? Should the transcriber expect it to be half a page or three to four pages in length?

6. Indicate whether you wish to dictate a final copy or a rough draft. The spacing usually varies. Final copy is usually single-spaced, a rough draft double-spaced. The rough draft of a report, however, is usually triple-spaced.

7. In dictating a letter, indicate any change from the standard format. Most companies use one format for all letters, for example, the block style. (See chapter 6 for the different formats.) If you want your letter typed in the semiblock format, say so; otherwise, the transcriber will follow company practice.

8. If you want special stationery or paper, say so; otherwise, the transcriber will follow company practice. For example, normal practice may be to type a letter on company letterhead with one copy for the files. If you want your letter typed on plain white bond with two carbon copies, say so before the transcriber begins to type.

9. Dictate the heading of a letter or memo. In a letter, dictate the date if it is not the present day. Dictate the receiver's name (spelled out), title, and his or her company's name (spelled out) and address with zip code. Dictate the salutation, for example, "Dear Dr. Previn" or "Dear Ruth." In a memo, dictate the name of the receiver (spelled out, if necessary), his or her location in the company, your own name (spelled out, if necessary), the subject line, and the date if it is not the present day.

10. Dictate the body of the document, following the guidelines given previously about spelling out certain words, dictating punctuation, capitalizations, and the like.

11. In a letter or memo, dictate the closing material. In a letter, dictate the complimentary close, for example, "Sincerely," your name and title (*Mr., Ms., Mrs.,* or *Miss*), the distribution of copies (if applicable), and the number of enclosures. In a memo, dictate the distribution of copies (if applicable) and the number of enclosures.

12. In a letter, dictate any special mailing instructions. For example, do you want an attention line typed on the envelope? A special size of envelope? Do you want the letter to go by priority mail or special delivery?

13. If you want the document stored, say so. For example, if you want a copy of the letter stored on a disk or tape, tell the transcriber that and how long you want it stored.

14. Review your dictation and edit it as necessary. The method of making corrections will vary with the equipment. Consult the user's manual for the proper procedure. Edit with the following questions in mind:

- Have you dictated each phrase and statement so that the transcriber should have no difficulty understanding your dictation?

- Will each passage be clear to your reader?

- Have you repeated yourself unnecessarily?

- Is the tone of individual paragraphs appropriate or do some words or phrases convey the wrong connotations?

- Are any paragraphs too long—do they need breaking down? For example, if a single paragraph contains 8 to 10 sentences, could you break it into two paragraphs?

15. Thank the transcriber and signal the end of your dictation, using his or her name if you know it. Otherwise, say "Thank you, Secretary. End of dictation."

16. When the transcribed document is returned, proofread it for errors. Use the standard proofreader's marks given in figure 14.4 to correct mistakes. Make corrections in pencil to avoid the necessity of retyping if possible. If there are corrections, return the document to the transcriber. If not, mail it.

An example of a dictated letter, complete with instructions (in brackets) to the transcriber, follows. It happens to be the letter you might have dictated to Dr. Ruth Previn in response to her inquiry concerning dictation equipment for her staff.

Good morning, Secretary. This is Richard Peerless from the Sales Department, extension 5509, account number 135-452-3. This is a one-page letter, which I would like to have in tomorrow's mail. Please use full block format. I would like a copy for my file.

November 4, 1986

Dr. Ruth Previn [that's P as in Peter, r-e-v as in Victor, i-n]
Dean, College of Business Administration
Erie [that's E as in Edward, r-i-e] State University
Erie, OH 45217

Dear Dr. Previn [colon]:

Thank you for allowing [initial caps, please] Dictation Systems the opportunity to serve you [exclamation point]! I am confident that we have the products and expertise to increase the efficiency of your [y-o-u-r] college through [t-h-r-o-u-g-h] dictation.

[New paragraph] In our phone conversation [comma], you mentioned that your college of 25 [that's 2-5] full-time and 18 [that's 1-8] part-time instructors is served by 2 [that's the number 2] full-time and 5 [that's the number 5] part-time secretaries. As you pointed out [comma], that's an enormous burden on such a small staff. Yet with the equipment and training we can provide [comma], your [y-o-u-r] staff will be able to meet this challenge [dash]-- successfully.

[New paragraph] From our experience with similar organizations, Dr. Previn, I would recommend a central dictation unit [dash]-- the Dicta-System III [that's capital D as in David i-c-t-a hyphen, capital S as in Samuel, y-s-t-e-m, capital I, capital I, capital I]. I am enclosing an illustrated brochure that fully explains this state [hyphen] -of [hyphen] -the [hyphen] -art communications system [comma], complete with 24 [that's 2-4 hyphen] -hour telephone access from any telephone in the world.

[New paragraph] To assess your [y-o-u-r] needs most accurately [comma], I hope you will permit me to do a survey of the kinds and volume of paperwork originating from your [y-o-u-r] college. This confidential survey is completely without charge. It requires only about 15 [that's 1-5] minutes from each of your [y-o-u-r] people to fill in a survey form.

[New paragraph] I would also appreciate the chance to make a 30 [that's 3-0 hyphen] -minute slide [s-l-i-d-e] presentation to you and your [y-o-u-r] department. In it I will explain the unique advantages the Dicta-System can contribute to your college [semicolon]; I will also explain the training and continuing support we provide to our users.

[New paragraph] My secretary will call you to arrange a convenient time for the presentation.

Sincerely [comma],

Richard J. [as in James,] Peerless [P as in Peter, e-e-r-l-e-s-s]
Sales Representative

There will be one enclosure. End of dictation. Thank you, Secretary.

Figure 14.4
Proofreader's
marks

Proofreader's Marks

The italicized words below indicate the instruction conveyed by the particular proofreader's mark. Normally the marks are written both within the line and in one of the margins to signal the transcriber to look for a correction within the respective line.

Capitalize:
> Original: Send a copy of Dr. toshiba's book to Ms. Klein.   *cap*
> Revised: Send a copy of Dr. Toshiba's book to Ms. Klein.

Close up space:
> Original: Keep a copy for yourself.
> Revised: Keep a copy for yourself.

Delete:
> Original: Mail me me one at my home.
> Revised: Mail me one at my home.

Insert word(s):
> Original: Mail the book to her in a bag.   *jiffy*
> Revised: Mail the book to her in a jiffy bag.

Insert a space:
> Original: Congratulations on your promotion.   #
> Revised: Congratulations on your promotion.

Insert a comma:
> Original: We mailed your check Tuesday Mr. Gualdoni.
> Revised: We mailed your check Tuesday, Mr. Gualdoni.

Insert a semicolon:
> Original: We mailed your check Tuesday, Mr. Gualdoni you should
> receive it tomorrow.
> Revised: We mailed your check Tuesday, Mr. Gualdoni; you should
> receive it tomorrow.

Insert a colon:
> Original: We have enclosed a copy of the report please keep it con-
> fidential.
> Revised: We have enclosed a copy of the report: please keep it con-
> fidential.

Insert a period:
> Original: We mailed your check Tuesday, Mr. Gualdoni You should
> receive it tomorrow.
> Revised: We mailed your check Tuesday, Mr. Gualdoni. You should
> receive it tomorrow.

Figure 14.4
Continued

Insert a question mark:
    Original: Did you receive your copy of the proposal
    Revised: Did you receive your copy of the proposal?   ?

Insert an apostrophe:
    Original: I mailed the package to McAtees assistant.
    Revised: I mailed the package to McAtee's assistant.

Insert a hyphen:
    Original: We will hire a part time data entry clerk.
    Revised: We will hire a part-time data entry clerk.

Insert quotation marks:
    Original: "Keep the change, she said.
    Revised: "Keep the change," she said.

Lower case:
    Original: The entire Department is to be reorganized.   *l.c.*
    Revised: The entire department is to be reorganized.

New paragraph:
    Original: The advantages of dictation are many. Increased white-collar productivity is the first advantage. If we compare the time required to write out a single-page memo by hand with the time it takes to dictate the same memo, we see immediately the advantage of dictation. Let's look at the figures.
    Revised: The advantages of dictation are many. Increased white-collar productivity is the first advantage. If we compare the time required to write out a single-page memo by hand with the time it takes to dictate the same memo, we see immediately the advantage of dictation.
        Let's look at the figures.

No new paragraph:
    Original: The advantages of dictation are many. Increased white-collar productivity is the first advantage.   *Run in.*
        If we compare the time required to write out a single-page memo by hand with the time it takes to dictate the memo, we see immediately the advantage in dictation.
    Revised: The advantages of dictation are many. Increased white-collar productivity is the first advantage. If we compare the time required to write out a single-page memo by hand with the time it takes to dictate the memo, we see immediately the advantage in dictation.

Figure 14.4
Continued

Spell out:
    Original: We will complete the project in ③ days.   *sp*
    Revised: We will complete the project in three days.

Spelling error: *sp*
    Original: To keep your policy in affect, mail us a check.   *SP*
    Revised: To keep your policy in effect, mail us a check.

Transpose (letter or word):
    Original: Please our be guest for lunch.   *tr*
    Revised: Please be our guest for lunch.

Italics:
    Original: We <u>must</u> receive a phone call by Friday.   *ital*
    Revised: We *must* receive a phone call by Friday.

Summary

This chapter focuses on dictating to a dictation unit rather than to a secretary. In that context, you should view dictation as a form of *spoken writing*. It involves all the steps in the writing process but eliminates the act of transcribing the words onto paper. In business, the popularity of dictation is growing because it increases productivity. There are four reasons why you should learn to dictate: dictation saves time; you can do it almost anywhere, anytime; it is cost-effective; and it is relatively easy to learn.

All dictation units have certain standard features, such as a pause button, fast forward button, and playback button. They also allow you to erase parts of your dictation and insert revised passages. They use a device called cueing, which allows you to give instructions to the transcriber about how you want the document typed. They use a variety of recording media, such as cassettes, minicassettes, microcassettes, and magnetic tape.

There are three kinds of dictation units: portable, desk-top, and central units. Portable units, which are small enough to be held in the hand and carried in a briefcase, are especially useful for people who have to be away from the office frequently. Desk-top units accommodate more dictation than portables and often have phone-in capacity. Central dictation units handle still larger volumes of dictation and have phone-in capacity, often from anywhere in the world.

To dictate effectively, you must know how to operate your equipment. Equipment vendors and word processing centers often provide instructional materials. Equally important, you should follow the problem-solving steps in dictating. These steps need to be adapted to the dictation process, but they must still be there in essence if you are to become an effective dictator.

There are some general guidelines to follow in dictating. You must develop a sense of teamwork with your transcriber by speaking distinctly, spelling out problem words, and dictating unusual capitalizations, unusual punctuation, paragraphing, and numbers.

Finally, it is important to follow standard operating procedure in dictating. These procedures are reduced to 16 steps, such as identifying yourself to the transcriber, indicating the form of the document (memo or letter), and indicating any deviations from standard format.

Writing Problems

The following problems offer a variety of dictating experiences from simple to complex. Of course, when the problem calls for dictation, the presence of up-to-date dictation equipment will make the experience more meaningful. If dictation equipment is not conveniently at hand, however, students can bring personal tape recorders to class and perform the same exercises on the tape recorders.

1. Dictate your thoughts on any subject randomly. Describe somebody's outfit or the contents of somebody's purse or wallet. Then ask a classmate to critique your dictation. He or she should check such items as pace, clarity of pronunciation, and the presence of sound-alike words. Listen to your own dictation. Sometimes people are surprised by the way their recorded voice sounds. How distinct is your pronunciation? Does your speech tend to be rapid? Do you slur any consonants, for instance, a final *s* at the end of a verb (*sets*) or at the end of a plural noun (*articles*)?

2. To get the feel of dictation gradually, pick out any letter among the figures in chapter 6 for practice. Dictate the letter several times, specifying only capitalizations. When you feel that you have mastered capitalizations, begin dictating the letter again, this time only for the punctuation. After mastering punctuation, begin dictating the letter again, this time only for spelling. When you master spelling, try dictating the letter for *both* capitalizations and punctuation, then work at dictating capitalization, punctuation, and spelling together.

3. Interview someone who dictates regularly. Find out the variety of documents he or she dictates. Ask the person for tips on dictating, especially specific advice for a beginning dictator such as yourself.

Write a memorandum to your instructor explaining in detail the advice this experienced dictator has given you.

4. Visit a business equipment store that sells dictation equipment. Ask the salesperson to demonstrate the use of a portable or desk-top unit. Ask for literature about the lines of dictation equipment carried by the store. Write a memo to your instructor detailing your findings. With the permission of your instructor, write a letter to this salesperson inviting him or her to demonstrate equipment in a class period. Be sure to work out the details of the invitation with your instructor beforehand, for example, the possible class periods open for the demonstration.

5. Visit the word processing center of a large firm. Ask the supervisor beforehand for a tour of the center. Interview one of the transcribers. What advice does this person have for a beginning dictator? What does he or she consider most essential to effective teamwork between the author and the transcriber? Ask for a copy of any manual or literature they distribute to their clients within the firm. Report the substance of your conversation to your instructor in the form of a memo.

6. Assume the role of Dr. Ruth Previn, dean of the Business Administration College of Erie State University. Dictate a brief reply to the letter of the sales representative, Richard Peerless, given earlier in this chapter. Thank him for his prompt response to your inquiry about dictation equipment and tell him that you will work his presentation into the agenda of a regular college meeting. Meetings are held every Tuesday afternoon at 3:30 P.M. Suggest that he choose either March 3 or March 10 for his presentation, but tell him that due to the length of meetings you can give him only a maximum of 20 minutes' time. Ask him to let you know by February 28 whether he will be able to make one or the other meeting date.

7. Again, assuming the identity of Dr. Previn of the previous problem, dictate a memorandum to all members of the College of Business Administration. Tell them that Richard J. Peerless of Dictation Systems, Inc., will make a 20-minute presentation at the end of the regular college meeting on Tuesday, March 3. The meeting will, of course, begin at 3:30 P.M. and last till around 4:45. Mr. Peerless will discuss the advantages to professionals of using dictation equipment and the training and the support his company provides to the users of their equipment. The meeting will take place in the seminar room in Pfeifer Hall. There will be a question and answer period after the presentation. Include in the memo a persuasive appeal for all members of the college to remain for the presentation. Apply the problem-solving approach to dictating this memo.

8. Again as Dr. Previn in the preceding problems, dictate a brief memorandum to the secretary of the academic vice-president to reserve the seminar room in Pfeifer Hall for the meeting described in the previous problem. The secretary's name is Lawrence Landini; his address is the Academic Vice-President's Office, 501 Rudorf Hall. If the seminar room is not available at the time stated in the previous problem, ask him to notify you shortly. If you do not hear from him soon, you will assume that the reservation is in effect.

9. If your school has dictation equipment, your instructor may wish to devote a class period to demonstration. Either the instructor or a member of the college staff may conduct the demonstration. If there is time, individual students may dictate a short document—for example, a brief letter congratulating a classmate on being elected to student government—to be critiqued by either the instructor or the demonstrator for effective technique.

CHAPTER 15

Collaborative Writing

rom earlier chapters, you have learned that business often requires complex writing tasks. Such tasks may be so involved that only several people working together can bring sufficient expertise to them. This chapter explains **collaborative writing**. *To collaborate* is the act of "working with." The chapter begins by suggesting the benefits of collaborative writing to solving a particular problem and continues by detailing ways to define collaborative writing teams. From there we discuss how writing done in cooperation with others can proceed efficiently. The chapter concludes with a discussion of special problems raised by collaborative writing.

Purposes of Collaborative Writing

Having more than one person at work on a major writing project can bring the benefits of increased experience and knowledge to the task. Let's propose an instance where such expertise becomes crucial. A frozen food preparation company is considering introducing new products into the market. The company's current line of "traditional favorites" (apple pies and pizzas) has done well over the years. However, competitors are grabbing supermarket freezer space and with it an increased market share by introducing such popular products as croissants, meat-filled pastries, and pecan pies.

To get started in developing their own new entries in the field, management might assign personnel grouped into teams to write a memo that details ideas for new products. The teams might have a month to develop the report and present it to the vice-president for research and development (R & D).

By assigning teams, management can tap the skills of marketing and technical experts, for example. In addition, executives can introduce safeguards into the creative system to prevent potentially disastrous ideas from taking hold and gaining momentum before they can be properly analyzed. For example, it is conceivable that a single staffer might propose packaging of the company's apple pie filling in a plastic bag that is then inserted into a frozen crust, which is, in turn, boxed for sale. The rationale for such packaging would be to give the consumer the feeling of baking it himself or herself. Although such a change would nullify the company's strength, the production of ready-to-eat favorites, and would require an enormous conversion in production and promotion methods, it might win favor with an executive in a position to push it along at least into the consumer-testing phase. Creating ideas and developing them into a thoughtful memo thus becomes a serious rhetorical problem.

A collaborative writing team whose members can ask pointed questions about such a radical shift can prevent a rashly conceived document. Collaborators also share the work load, decreasing the chance that tight time constraints might result in an ill-considered major report. Checks on the quality of ideas proposed in writing and sharing of the work load are thus two goals of efficient collaboration. Achieving these aims requires careful definition of the writing team.

Defining the Writing Team

Collaborative writing requires two or more people to work closely together. We can define the makeup of that team by the collaborators' organizational relationships to one another.

Horizontal
Definition

When two or more workers at the same level of responsibility and power within a department work together on a writing project, their team is **horizontally defined**. On a chart of the company hierarchy, no team member's position appears at a higher level than any other's. In the frozen food example, this horizontally defined team might consist of two staff members of the research and development department.

Certain assumptions go along with the assignment of a horizontally defined team to a writing project. Each member of the team is expected to share equally in the work load, and each is expected to offer roughly equal numbers of ideas and suggestions. For all of us who have worked in small groups (two to eight people), such equality of effort and performance may not be the case. One lab partner may do more than another; one basketball team member may practice harder than another; one club member may take on a greater proportion of fund-raising effort than another.

We will deal later with means of making the effort and performance levels of all team members appropriate to the goal of the group—in this case to produce a memo acceptable to the manager(s) making the assignment. The key for horizontally defined groups, as for other types of writing teams, is to mesh individual strengths to improve team performance.

Instead of or in addition to assigning horizontally defined teams to develop ideas in writing, an R & D manager might ask a single subordinate to collaborate with him or her on a project. This relationship, in which power and responsibility are *not* equal, is said to be **vertical**. On a chart showing the company hierarchy, the team members would appear on different levels, one above the other (although not necessarily directly above).

Vertical Definition

Certain assumptions underlie such vertically defined writing teams: the subordinate team member will probably come up with ideas and "bounce them off" the superior for that person's acceptance, rejection, or modification. Also, the superior will almost certainly delegate most of the routine writing to the subordinate.

In reality, the superior may already have specific ideas in mind and want help expanding and/or refining those ideas. As for delegating work, many supervisors get to their positions through high individual achievement; once there they may continue to try to do it all themselves. In such a situation, the subordinate can feel like an outsider in the collaborative writing process. By following the procedures specified in this chapter, vertically defined teams can check potential problems such as these as they move toward their objectives—in this case, a memo that the superior member of the team can present to executives at an even higher level, perhaps even to the officer with the power to authorize new product development and testing.

With a decision as important to a company's fortunes as introduction of new products, people from different departments, especially technical departments, are almost certain to be involved in proposal development. For example, a biochemist and a marketing specialist might be assigned to the task of preparing one of the reports that will suggest new frozen food

Lateral Definition

products. This bringing together of people with different expertise and perspectives is a way to head off problems later. For example, whereas the biochemist might champion a line of frozen granola snacks, the marketer might see *frozen* and *natural* as mutually exclusive terms, a combination that consumers would simply not buy. Writing teams that include members who have similar levels of responsibility and power but are from clearly distinct departments or even from different companies (if a joint product venture is contemplated) are **laterally defined.**

Such writing teams present challenges of their own. Members often need to play down their varying backgrounds and compromise their concerns to agree on what is feasible. Additionally, there may be even greater disparity among team members' writing abilities when they come from different disciplines than there would be if they were all from the same department, as in horizontally defined collaboration. Meeting these challenges requires writing before the drafting of the memo even begins. Much of the rest of this chapter deals with those pre-writing tasks and how they can support efficient completion of the final memo.

Mixed Definitions of Collaboration

Major writing projects such as the frozen food company's rarely occur in a vacuum. Many people are involved, and painstaking care is taken to see that the finished document is the best possible one given the circumstances and nature of the company. A well-planned matrix of writing responsibilities can assist the idea development phase of the project by providing balance between staff enthusiasm for a new product(s) and executive caution based on the realities of the marketplace. To this end, the vice-president of research and development might assign three or more teams to prepare memos.

A horizontally defined team might consist of two staffers in the product development department. A vertically defined team might involve the head of the research department and two subordinates. A third team, laterally defined, could take in a chemist, a production specialist, and a marketing specialist. Together, these teams—all reporting to the vice-president of research and development—form a mixed-definition "superteam" whose goal is to present three memo reports that can then be distilled into one recommendation report to the company president.

Getting Started with Collaborative Writing

Knowing why we write collaboratively and understanding where we fit in with the other member(s) of the writing team are important. But these are simply preludes to getting started working together. We suggest two techniques for getting the work under way: (1) alternating writing responsibilities and (2) brainstorming.

We noted previously that one possible disruption to a writing team's efficient operation is the unequal distribution and completion of work on a particular project. The supervisor making assignments or the team members themselves need to avoid the disorder and bad feelings resulting when one or more group members fail to assume a fair share of the labor. This requires preparation of a written work schedule specifying how team members will alternate responsibilities. For example, in a vertically defined collaboration in which the head of the product development department and a staffer in that department work together, the following order of responsibilities may exist:

Alternating
Responsibilities

1. The department head prepares a *list* of potential new products for consideration.
2. The staffer prepares a *two-or-three-sentence written comment* about the feasibility of each of the items on the potential new products list.
3. After examining these comments, the department head develops a *revised list* of potential new products.
4. Once again, the staffer makes a *brief written comment* on each of the items on the department head's list.

This procedure can continue until the department head is satisfied with the revised list. At that point, with the fundamental ideas down on paper, the collaborators can continue their deliberations.

If the writing team is horizontally defined with three people working together, they might develop a system for alternating responsibilities in which each member develops ideas independently and then submits those ideas for the review of the two other collaborators. Then each member revises and expands upon the reviewed material. At a subsequent meeting, the collaborators mesh their ideas into a form usable for drafting the report itself. Figure 15.1 shows how the alternating pattern of responsibility might flow over the course of a writing project for such a horizontally defined, three-person writing team.

After specifying alternating responsibilities, everyone knows what to do and to whom materials need to be delivered. For example, in figure 15.1, all the staffers know that copies of their original lists of ideas for new products are to be given to each of the other members of the writing team. They know that a meeting will be scheduled after they have revised their individual product idea lists. They know this entire procedure will be repeated until the group either (1) is satisfied with the idea list, (2) runs up against a deadline and has to ask for more time, or (3) admits it cannot agree on how to proceed.

Another advantage to alternating responsibilities is that everyone involved gets structured feedback to ideas. In this advantage, however, lies one of the system's potential drawbacks. Sometimes a reviewer's negative remarks may discourage a creative, potentially viable idea. Additionally, the reviewing process itself may stall if one of the participants has trouble coming up with any ideas at all.

Such potential problems need not develop. Use of the techniques specified in chapter 2 (journals and interpretive note-taking) can get all collaborators' thoughts flowing. Having reviewers ask questions rather than offer criticisms of colleagues' ideas can assist in the improvement of those ideas. For instance, a team member might ask a cowriter, "How can you justify expansion to 'exotic' fruit pies such as elderberry, gooseberry, and huckleberry in light of the high cost of these fruits?" Such a question causes the proposer of the idea to reevaluate the thought, to substantiate the position, to modify it, or to abandon it. Such a question contrasts with a dogmatic statement, such as "The cost of 'exotic' fruit pies would be prohibitive; they simply won't work!"

The reviewer's job, then, is to provide a collaborator with carefully conceived questions that further thoughtful analysis of ideas, not to cut off the creative flow of thought and possibly cause hurt feelings in the bargain.

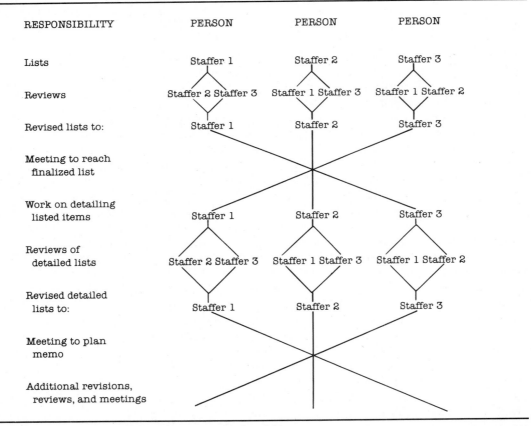

Figure 15.1 Flow chart of collaborative review and revision

Another way to get started in writing collaboratively is brainstorming. This requires the writing team, a laterally defined twosome of a marketing researcher and an R & D specialist, for example, to meet. Each person brings a pad and pencil to the meeting and spends the first 15 to 20 minutes of the session jotting down as many possibilities (in this case, ideas for new products) as possible. When the allotted time is up, the collaborators share their lists. As they look over the lists, they make no *evaluative comments*. They may only offer new ideas for addition to the list. From this process of jotting, sharing, and adding, the team emerges with an expanded list of possibilities. Only after this expanded list exists does discussion of individual items on the list begin.

Brainstorming

Discussion may occur in one of two ways: (1) oral discussion to narrow down the list to a manageable size at the time of the first meeting or (2) written review of the ideas with an eye toward narrowing them down at a subsequent meeting. Figure 15.2 shows how the individually brainstormed lists of the marketing researcher and the R & D specialist were expanded into a longer merged list and then refined into a single shorter list. Note that the written notes (in parentheses) are just a few words each. Such brevity is perfectly acceptable and desirable at this early stage, when the goal is to decide upon a few viable possibilities and then to pursue them.

In a subsequent meeting to discuss their revisions, each collaborator might offer reasons why particular items are no longer on his or her shorter list. The R & D specialist might justify exclusion of Greek pastries by jotting down the following problems: (1) need for honey and nuts, both high-cost ingredients; (2) lack of mass technology for baking these types of specialized, layered-dough products; (3) potential problems with freezing products for shipment and retail sale.

The marketing specialist might indicate a reservation about Greek-style pizza, which did not make the marketer's list—namely, because research indicates that not many people like olives. On the other hand, the marketer might note that there is little competition in specialty pizzas for the olive lover's niche in the market. As a result of these jottings and their discussion, the collaborators might decide to keep the pizza with olives on the new product possibility list but to remove the honey/nut/layered-dough pastries from consideration.

Brainstorming offers undeniable advantages in getting the collaborative writing process off to a good start: getting ideas flowing and providing the opportunity for creativity to result in a new and successful outcome. As with any system, though, there is a potential drawback to brainstorming as well. One member of the group may dominate, leading to a list that develops through force of personality rather than through soundness of ideas. By appointing a moderator whose job is to give each collaborator a chance to speak and make a case for particular ideas and by appointing a recorder (if no secretary is available) who takes notes, the team can insure that each idea

Figure 15.2
Revision of
brainstormed lists

Biochemist's List

1. Tacos
2. Egg rolls
3. Calzone
4. Croissants
5. Greek pastries

Marketer's List

1. Dutch apple pie
2. Apple crumb pie
3. Apple cake
4. Apple dumpling
5. Apple crisp

Brainstormed List

1. Tacos
2. Egg Rolls
3. Calzone
4. Croissants
5. Greek pastries
6. Dutch apple pie
7. Apple crumb pie
8. Apple cake
9. Apple dumpling
10. Apple crisp
----
11. Mexican style pizza (hot)
12. Greek style pizza (olives)
13. Hawaiian style sweet pizza (coconut and pineapple)
14. German apple cake
15. Hawaiian style apple pie (with coconut)

DECISIONS ON WHAT TO RETAIN AND WHY

Biochemist

Dutch apple pie
   (easy to add raisins and
   icing)
German apple cake
   (supplies all on hand)
Mexican style pizza
   (only needs meat and
   spices)
Greek style pizza
   (just needs olives)

Marketer

Greek pastries
   (open market)
Dutch apple pie
   (appeals as premium pie)
German apple cake
   (market as breakfast
   cake)
Mexican style pizza
   (strong market for
   Mexican food)

MEETING TO NEGOTIATE FINAL LIST OF FOUR ITEMS

Agreed upon: Dutch apple pie; German apple cake; Mexican style
              pizza.
Negotiated: Greek pastries deleted from final list because of expense
              of ingredients and mass production problems.
              Greek style pizza retained for final list because there is
              no competition in this specialty market.

expressed gets fair attention. When two people collaborate, the structures for insuring fair attention to each other's ideas can be more informal. Here it is each collaborator's responsibility to let the cowriter know when personality rather than ideas is becoming the deciding factor.

One other way to build safeguards into the process of getting started writing collaboratively is to combine the brainstorming and assigned responsibilities methods. In one such model, the writing team would begin with a brainstorming, idea-development session. Those ideas would then go through a series of reviews before being brought up again at a later meeting for further discussion. By mixing the two processes, the advantages of each—creativity for brainstorming and orderly analysis for alternating responsibilities—are preserved, and the potential drawbacks to getting collaborative writing started don't develop.

Keeping the Flow of Ideas Going

Once the collaborators have used writing to develop the ideas from which they will begin to draft their project, team members need to continue work in timely fashion. To do this, cowriters should: (1) set deadlines with defined responsibilities, (2) survey available clerical support, (3) schedule collaborative revision sessions, (4) insure stylistic consistency, and (5) facilitate individuals' work within the larger writing team.

Sometimes, the responsibility for working on the collaborative writing project will be all that staff members have to do over a period of time. At other times, the collaborative effort will be but one part of an employee's busy schedule. In either case, each team member must keep up with the assigned tasks to insure that work proceeds on schedule. To achieve this result, responsibilities must be defined and deadlines set. Setting deadlines may prevent writers from considering some promising tangents, but it is usually possible to construct a work schedule that allows some flexibility yet meets the project completion date. We suggest using the work schedule presented in chapter 1 as a model. Figure 15.3 depicts such a timetable for preparing a collaboratively written project.

In this table, we see the plans for the problem definition, analysis, decision making, drafting, and editing of Wilson and Smathers, a horizontally defined writing team from the frozen food company's research and development department. Note the amount of interaction between the two employees. Even though Wilson and Smathers have clearly defined responsibilities and individually specified deadlines, they meet at least four times while developing their report to the vice-president of research and development. Note, too, that these meetings are scheduled in advance, thus providing the collaborators with intermediate deadlines toward which they can

Setting Deadlines with Defined Responsibilities

direct their short-range efforts. Finally, the schedule specifies when things are to be typed and allows time for that task.

The next section deals with the importance of considering typing and other clerical needs as early and as carefully as possible.

Figure 15.3
Timetable for preparing a collaborative writing project

1. Defining the Problem
   - Preparing a statement of the problem
     2 days--Wilson and Smathers work together
   - Testing possibilities
     1 day--brainstorming by Wilson and Smathers together
     1 day--Wilson and Smathers revise lists separately
     1 day--Wilson and Smathers meet to reach final list

2. Analyzing the Problem
   - Reading and note taking
     7 days--Wilson and Smathers divide task; Wilson does reading on marketing involving foreign flair product lines; Smathers does reading on successful and unsuccessful frozen food company product line expansion
   - Interviewing
     2 days--Wilson interviews production staff
     2 days--Smathers interviews marketing staff

3. Decision Making
   - Organizing
     1 day--Wilson and Smathers meet to pool data into master file
     2 days--Wilson and Smathers meet to decide which data to retain, which to highlight, which to discard
   - Outlining
     2 days--Wilson and Smathers meet to outline memo to vice-president of research and development

4. Writing the Rough Draft
     1 day--Wilson and Smathers meet to codraft memo introduction
     2 days--Wilson and Smathers divide task; Wilson writes section on international cake line; Smathers writes section on international pizza line

5. Editing
     2 days--Wilson and Smathers exchange draft sections and revise

It is always important to know what help you can expect with typing, duplicating, collating, filing, and the other clerical support services vital to document production. However, in collaborative writing projects, the logistics of such support require thought. A secretary who usually gets a series of tasks from an individual or individuals may suddenly start receiving interdependent parts of a single project from the several people on the writing team. Instead of receiving a steady flow of work as people finish one job and move on to another, the secretary may receive nothing from the writing team until the members' drafts are completed and ready for their cowriters' reviews. At that time, as with Wilson and Smathers in figure 15.3, the secretary may receive two or more drafts, all to be completed and duplicated on short notice. When two or more people's drafts need merging into a single report, the task becomes even more complicated.

The actual merging of parts of the overall report is the team's responsibility. Making sense of the various handwritings, arrows, insertions, and cuttings and pastings of team members is both the team's and the typist's job. Clear indication of what goes where, clear marking of inserts (for example, "Insert this paragraph after the * on page 3"), clear verbal instructions, and taking the time to have the typist read back the memo to the collaborators *before* typing or word processing it can save major revision time that should be spent on proofreading the typed report.

Unfortunately, the necessary clerical support is sometimes lacking. A team may get no help until the typing of the final draft. In such a case, collaborators must negotiate and divide up tasks. The fastest typist should do the bulk of the typing. Other members should share the recording of notes at meetings, make their own handwritten drafts, and duplicate their own materials. A simple, written notation of duties should suffice:

Staffer 1: Types lists
            Types memo drafts

Staffer 2: Handwrites all meeting notes
            Duplicates meeting notes
            Collects data for all team members

Staffer 3: Handwrites all memo inserts
            Makes all handwritten revisions
            Duplicates memo drafts for all members
            Goes over revised, handwritten memo with final typist

Having such a *written* list may seem elementary, but it is vital in dividing tasks equitably and efficiently. Besides, such a list also provides a measure of accountability for each group member. There are no excuses about not knowing who was supposed to do what, no relegation of one member to role of recording secretary, no missed communications among group members or between the group and its typist.

Surveying
Available Clerical
Support

**Collaborative
Revision Sessions**

As important as taking another team member's draft home for review is, it is equally important that group members get together to revise their work collaboratively. Revision done communally has several advantages over revision done alone:

1. It offers each collaborator the chance to explain any debatable writing decisions—and to strive for a consensus on resolving disagreements.
2. It provides an opportunity for more than one person to suggest needed changes in a particular document.
3. It offers an early opportunity for collaborators to read their entire draft to see if it is logical and if it is written in a consistent style (for example, all active voice, third person, present tense) so it *sounds* like a team effort rather than the patched together work of several individuals.

The following draft of a product proposal for the frozen food company suggests some of the stylistic problems inherent in collaborative writing and some of the ways in which revising as a team can solve those problems. Our comments about the draft are bracketed.

Sample memo draft

Date: September 11, 1986

To: D. Davis, Vice-President for Research and Development

From: D. Smathers and S. Wilson

Subject: Proposed New Products

[First paragraph drafted by both Smathers and Wilson during a meeting.]

As your memo of August 1, 1986, specified, we are reporting on the results of our product proposal development efforts. Given the problem--to meet competitors' entrance into new frozen baked goods markets--we present the following recommendations:

[Second paragraph drafted by Smathers--note the use of passive voice, third person, and future tense.]

1. It is hoped that the company will add new dessert items to its baked goods line. Furthermore, it is suggested that these items be cakes rather than pies so that a wider range of consumer preferences will be reached. In particular, the proposal is made to add a "German Style Cinnamon Apple Cake" to the

line and to follow that with a "French Style Apple Croissant Cake." Those products will serve to provide a way into the croissant market and to the premium market for baked goods with an international flavor currently provided by local bakeries with respect to the cake and by specialty stores with respect to the croissants.

[Third paragraph drafted by Wilson--note the use of active voice, first person, and present tense.]

2. We also propose developing a new line of pizzas. These are competitive because they offer consumers a choice of our present mild-tasting product or the spicier new products we suggest. We should be able to market our new "International Pizza Line" with little difficulty: a Greek Style Pizza with olives, a Mexican Style Pizza with peppers, a Swiss Style Pizza with sharp, aged cheese. These new offerings provide us with the potential to increase our share of supermarket freezer space and to increase overall market share in the frozen pizza business at the same time.

[Concluding paragraph drafted collaboratively.]

Our recommendation, as you can see, is for a two-pronged attack. By expanding in the cake and pizza lines—our traditional strengths—we bring our experience and know-how to the marketplace. We also counter inroads made by our competitors and offer consumers new options in frozen food.

At the collaborative revision session, Smathers and Wilson might agree to (1) stick to the active voice, (2) write mainly in the first person, (3) use the present tense, (4) develop an opening paragraph that gets right to the point, and (5) draft a lead-in to their last paragraph that emphasizes their secondary point—that new products will require aggressive marketing. The revised memo might emerge:

Revised memo

Date: September 14, 1986

To: D. Davis, Vice-President for Research and Development

From: D. Smathers and S. Wilson

Subject: New Product Proposal

We are reporting on our proposal development. Given the problem--to meet competitors' entrance into new frozen baked goods markets--we make the following two-pronged recommendation:

We recommend that the company add new dessert items to its baked goods line. These items should be cakes rather than pies so that we can appeal to a wider range of consumer tastes. In particular, we urge product testing of a "German Style Cinnamon Apple Cake," followed by testing of a "French Style Apple Croissant Cake." These apple based products will provide a way into the premium baked goods markets currently dominated by local bakeries and by specialty croissant shops.

We also recommend developing a new line of pizzas. They are competitive because they offer customers a choice of our present mild-tasting product or spicier new products. We should be able to market our new "International Pizza Line" with great success. The "Greek Style Pizza with Olives," the "Mexican Style Pizza with Peppers," and the "Swiss Style Pizza with Sharp Cheese" give us the potential to increase our supermarket shelf space. Subsequently, we should be able to increase our overall market share in the pizza segment of the frozen food industry.

These products will require aggressive marketing. We would like to see the use of such techniques as product tie-ins and coupons. By expanding within the cake and pizza lines--our traditional strengths--we bring our expertise and know-how to the marketplace. We also counter inroads made by our competitors and offer old and new customers options in frozen food.

pb

Note that in this collaboratively revised memo, Smathers and Wilson retain only one passive construction: ". . . markets currently dominated by local bakeries and by specialty croissant shops." The cowriters keep to the present tense, and they use first person plural to refer to themselves, reserving third person ("*They* are competitive . . .") for their company and its products.

Stylistic Consistency

When merging drafts by two or more collaborators, it is also important to keep the level of vocabulary and sentence complexity balanced. If vocabulary in the first part of a document is highly technical, it should be the same in the rest of the document. For example, you should write "The cake line should garner 5 to 7 percent of the market within one year of being introduced. . . . The pizza line should gain 3 to 5 percent of the market within one year of introduction," *not* "The cake line should garner 5 to 7 percent of the market within one year of being introduced. . . . The pizzas should be an improvement over what we've got going now."

Try varying sentence length and complexity throughout your document, but only if all sentences communicate the information you want to convey. One portion of a document should not have mostly complex, lengthy sentences while another has mostly simple, almost "telegraphic" sentences.

Ask someone who does not know that the document was written collaboratively to read it and make comments on its style. If the reader makes no comments about inconsistency of reference, voice, vocabulary, or sentence structure, you can probably feel confident about the unity of the joint effort. If your reader does note such inconsistencies, meet with your collaborators to resolve those differences.

Even though you write collaboratively, you must do much work alone. This requires you to adopt certain techniques to insure that your shared work goes well:

Working Alone "Together"

1. *Telephone for clarification or help.* There are times when you simply need to ask your cowriter(s) a question: "What do you mean by a 'marketing concept'?" "Where do you think I might find sales figures on our competitors' specialty items?" "I forgot a paragraph in the draft you took to review. Can you insert it if I dictate it over the phone?"

2. *Write down your ideas and questions.* You may have questions about a cowriter's draft that you want to ask at tomorrow's scheduled meeting. Before you forget them, write down those questions. Keep a note pad nearby for those ideas that occur to you on your way to work, just before you go to sleep, or at other nonworking times.

3. *View your ideas objectively, and be prepared to defend those that have merit.* We have already spoken about the need to compromise when working on a collaborative writing project. But sometimes a compromise results in a final idea that is weaker than the result of accepting the idea of another team member or fighting for your own idea if you can present solid evidence that it is the best option. For example, if one staff member wishes to recommend that the food company introduce a line of donuts and a second staffer would like the new product to be apple cake, a *superficially* logical compromise might be to recommend a line of apple-filled donuts. But such a line may well lose money because of competition from fresh donut shops. In this case, accepting one collaborator's or the other's suggestion would be a wiser course. To insure the best possible decisions in a team writing project requires the willingness to speak up to defend your own ideas *and* the need to look objectively at those same ideas, realizing that they may not be accepted by colleagues.

4. *Listen to criticism.* The necessity for realistic appraisals leads to another requirement, the willingness to accept a collaborator's criticism, even if it is not what you wish to hear. Using a cowriter's good advice to improve the finished product is, after all, one of the reasons to collaborate.

5. *Spend time alone.* No matter how well things are going with collaborators, it is necessary at times to be alone so your thoughts can coalesce. Such introspection can provide the change of focus necessary to allow your most creative thoughts to come to consciousness. By being alone now and then, you can sometimes discover just the viewpoint that will assist in making the cooperative writing venture successful. Remember to have that pad and pen handy so those first-rate ideas survive until the next writing team meeting!

From Draft to Document—Collaboratively

Once the team members have merged their drafts and agreed upon revisions, it is time to edit the draft and prepare and transmit the final document.

Collaborative Editing Session

It is imperative that the writing team get together to answer a variety of questions. For instance, do all team members agree that the draft will produce the intended effect upon its reader? Taking a few moments to role play the intended reader's possible reactions to the document may highlight needed changes. Does one of the team members know of a term that the specified reader particularly dislikes? Are the transitions between paragraphs clear? What would be the effect of merging those two short sentences into one?

Have the collaborators consistently followed rules of usage? It is helpful to decide on a style manual beforehand and to make certain that each writer has one available for quick reference. Are punctuation and spelling accurate? Because a collaboratively written piece reflects upon all of the writers involved, it is every team member's responsibility to check over the entire draft for mechanical accuracy.

These are the sorts of editorial questions that cowriters need to ask. Only when you and your colleagues are satisfied that all of the necessary questions have been asked and answered is it time to consider preparation of the final document.

Preparing and Transmitting the Final Document

As noted previously, team members should have clearly defined responsibilities for making certain the revised document is typed accurately, proofread carefully, and duplicated in sufficient quantity. Proofreading can be made somewhat less time consuming when several people are involved. Be certain, however, that each collaborator proofreads the entire document. An error that slips through one member's proofreading "net" may be caught by another's. Use the techniques (such as reading aloud and reading the document backward) discussed in chapter 4, and the result should be a piece of good writing.

Similar care needs to be taken with duplication and collating of the document. Even when there is clerical support to do the actual duplication, even when there are machines to do collating, each member of the team should double-check the duplicated, collated document to make certain that every page has been included in its proper order and that every page is legible. It is frustrating for a reader to find that a page is missing or that one is difficult to read because of poor duplication. Collaborative writing offers the opportunity to insure that the quality of the document is high but also widens the sphere of responsibility when it is not.

One team member should take the document to its drop-off point for transmittal. This means seeing that it is packaged if necessary, gets to the mail drop, is picked up by the express mail service, is entered into the electronic mail terminal, or even is hand delivered to its reader.

One final note: each collaborator should retain at least one copy of the final document. Aside from insuring its existence if other copies are lost or destroyed, this policy insures that each collaborator will have a copy when it is needed to address responses from a reader.

Special Problems in Collaboration

The preceding sections have covered the process of developing a document collaboratively. There are many variations on the nature of this collaboration, and some call for prior thought on the part of writers.

Even though collaborative writing techniques have been illustrated, along with examples of two- or three-person teams working on a project, larger groups or committees can also apply the techniques successfully. Here are a few guidelines:

Writing in a Committee

An effective **committee chair** or **committee head** is crucial. Chairs will need to:

1. Do some of the writing and undertake other tasks done by consensus in smaller groups
2. Take charge of scheduling meetings and reminding committee members of meeting dates and times

3. Moderate group discussion leading to the sorts of assignments mentioned earlier in this chapter, for example, research, typing, duplication
4. Set up a system to make certain each committee member gets to review other members' drafts in a timely fashion
5. Communicate and clarify the revised draft to the final typist

The committee chair accepts the brunt of this organizing responsibility mainly because he or she is most likely to be the contact person for upper management. In this case, the weight of responsibility shifts. What had been equally distributed before now becomes weighted more toward one person. The committee chair may get more recognition than any other single committee member for a job well done—and more blame when things go wrong.

Don't misunderstand. Members of larger collaborative writing teams have responsibilities too! With a greater number of people involved, it is even more important that committee members meet deadlines for their assigned portion of a document draft. Each committee member must speak up at meetings to make certain the full benefit of the whole team's expertise is realized. Conversely, with so many people's time at a premium, committee members must exercise self-control, *not* going off on tangents and *not* arriving late for meetings. Committee members, like members of two- or three-person writing teams, must work for the overall good of the project. With these few cautions in mind, the larger writing team can use the same techniques that work so well for the smaller team.

Collaborative Writing by Mail

Particularly in large organizations, collaborators may be separated by hundreds or even thousands of miles. With face-to-face meetings not feasible, collaborators need to work out carefully the details of their cooperative venture. The telephone becomes an essential force assisting the writing process. If no face-to-face meetings are possible, collaborators should schedule their work by telephone. They can write and exchange a work schedule later, but the give-and-take afforded by telephone conversation— even conference calls—can prevent misunderstandings and missed deadlines later.

If the writing team is following the same steps in their work as specified in figure 15.3, they should add one or more day's time to each item on the schedule to allow for mailing drafts, reviews, and revisions to one another. If the writing team thinks this additional time may interrupt the flow of ideas or cause it to miss deadlines, collaborators may want to consider one of the overnight mail services that have proliferated in recent years.

If your organization does not have a mailroom or if the mail service within your organization is less than efficient, learn your company's overnight mail procedures and be certain that your collaborative project includes a budget for overnight mailing of documents. Regular first class mail may well be adequate. However, knowing that your written materials will arrive promptly is a comforting thought that will help your project maintain its momentum. This sense of momentum is a critical intangible in the collaborative writing process: with it, team members will feel enthusiastic about continuing their efforts; without it, members may become frustrated at the project's fitful, stop-and-start nature.

When working collaboratively by mail, overnight or otherwise, each team member should send any document or materials with a note of transmittal. This can be as simple as: "Dear Jane: My draft of the first part of our memo is enclosed. According to our schedule, I should receive back your reviews of it by next Monday, April 7. Please call me if you have any questions. I hope the weather is as pleasant out your way as it is around here. Best regards, Bill." Also, when sending your document, *always* retain your own copy! Finally, as noted in the section on working together "alone," jot down questions and ideas for your next talk with that collaborator.

Writing collaboratively by mail is not easy. It requires strict adherence to a schedule, total reliability in seeing that things are mailed out properly, and a bit of luck to be certain that the communication services upon which you depend work properly. However, with careful preparation and follow-through, collaboration by mail can produce some outstanding writing: communication that merges the perspectives of people in various locations to provide the best possible written thought on a problem.

Electronic mail is not really mail in the sense we know it. Rather, it is a computerized system for delivering writing over telephone lines. In collaborative writing, this is usually done in one of two ways. Hard copy (or paper) delivery involves keyboarding text into a terminal in city A and sending it electronically to another terminal in city B, where it is printed for use by a cowriter.

Collaboration via Electronic Mail

The other means for use of the electronic mail requires the cowriters to sit at terminals in their respective offices. They then keyboard text for immediate review and reaction. Writing team members can even combine a telephone with this interactive keyboarding to supplement the written text with conversation. After exchanging greetings, combined electronic mail (EM) and telephone conversations can go something like this one between Bill and Jane:

VIA PHONE: "Bill, I've got our draft introduction to the report on the screen."
"Right, Jane. Let me take a moment to read through it."

VIA EM: Draft—Report on Frozen Food Shelf Space:
Introduction: Many supermarkets are now stocking entire aisles of frozen pizzas and frozen desserts. Freezer space is at a premium and the two or three biggest purveyors of

these products are gaining supermarket shelf space quickly. Most are doing so through promotional techniques such as money-back offers or tie-ins to other products—for example, "Buy an apple pie and get 25 cents off a purchase of _____ brand vanilla ice cream." We suggest a different approach—introduction of new products related to our strengths in these areas to fill a niche in specialty areas of these markets—namely, premium apple-based desserts and more highly spiced pizzas.

VIA PHONE: "It looks good, Bill. Here are some stylistic suggestions. Let's make a hard copy to save the original, then I'll feed you some possible changes."

VIA EM: (Jane keyboards in changes): *purveyors* to *manufacturers*

VIA PHONE: "I agree, Jane. That's a more precise word."

VIA EM: (Jane keyboards in changes): *in these areas* is deleted

VIA PHONE: "I'll go along with eliminating *in these areas*. But can we replace it with something specific? Look at this."

VIA EM: (Bill keyboards): ". . . introduction of new products related to our traditional strengths to fill a niche . . ."

VIA PHONE: "O.K., Bill. That looks fine to me. Let's get on to the body of the report."

Bill and Jane continue until they have made revisions that please them both. Combining electronic mail with telephone conversation *is* an expensive collaborative technique, but it offers distant writers the chance to see drafts and revisions instantly and to offer or hear suggestions for further changes. In companies equipped to handle such technology, it becomes possible to improve materially the quality of collaborative writing traditionally done through the mails.

When Collaborators Disagree

In spite of the most careful efforts to insure efficient, harmonious working among collaborators, cowriters occasionally disagree with one another. Indeed, we would be suspicious of the effect of collaboration on projects in which there were never any disagreements. After all, the whole purpose of writing as a team is to bring more than one person's ability and expertise to a composing task.

What *is* critical is that you and your cowriters resolve these disagreements without impairing the overall efficiency of the collaborative effort. By planning ahead, such disagreements over the style or substance of what is being written can become forums for improving the quality of the finished product. To insure productive resolution of disagreements, you and your collaborators should use a written form that allows you to bring up opinions for discussion. Such a form contains space for specifying the nature of the disagreement and for writing down changes one collaborator would like another to accept.

QUESTIONS/DISAGREEMENTS OVER:
Ideas:
Writing style (wording, sentence types, and the like):
Editorial matters (items needing correction--punctuation, spelling, syntax):

(*Note:* In resolving disagreements over editorial matters, reference to a handbook such as the one appended to this text can prove a useful arbitration technique.) You should bring these forms to meetings and, if feasible, clip them to the draft documents themselves. Marginal numbers in the text can help speed the discussion process (number consecutively throughout the document). Then use the disagreement form to bring up questions or points of argument about a document. The introduction to the memo about new frozen foods that was presented earlier in this chapter shows how marginal numbers can be used:

Draft

Date: September 14, 1986

To: D. Davis, Vice-President for Research and Development

From: D. Smathers and S. Wilson

Subject: New Product Proposal

We are reporting on our proposal development. Given the problem--to meet competitors' entrance into new frozen baked goods markets--we make the following two-pronged recommendation: 1

We recommend that the company add new dessert items to its baked goods line. These items should be cakes rather than pies so that we can appeal to a wider range of consumer tastes. In particular, we urge product testing of a "German Style Cinnamon Apple Cake" followed by testing of a "French Style Apple Croissant Cake." These apple based   2
products will provide a way into the premium baked goods markets currently dominated by local bakeries and by specialty croissant shops.

We also recommend developing a new line of pizzas. These are competitive because they offer customers a choice of our present mild-tasting product or spicier new products. We should be able to market our new "International Pizza Line" with great success. The "Greek Style Pizza with Olives," the "Mexican Style Pizza with Peppers," and the "Swiss Style Pizza with Sharp Cheese" give us the potential to increase our supermarket shelf space. Subsequently, we should be able to increase our overall market share in the pizza segment of the frozen food industry.

These products will require aggressive marketing. We would like to see use of such techniques as product tie-ins and coupons. By expanding within the cake and pizza lines--our strengths--we bring our expertise and know-how to the marketplace. We also counter inroads made by our competitors and offer old and new customers options in frozen food.   4

pb

QUESTIONS/DISAGREEMENTS OVER:

Ideas: 1. I disagree on adding two new product lines. Why don't we focus our energies on only one?

                       3. What is the impact of product tie-ins on our bottom line?

Style: 4. Change "old and new" to "present and future."

Editorial matters: 2. Change "apple based" to "apple-based" (hyphen usage).

The team's deadline acts as the ultimate resolver of disagreements. All those involved must know that the need for compromise or even giving up will arise as the due dates for various segments of the project draw closer. With the sort of written medium for airing disagreements suggested here, you and your collaborators can express differences of opinion and still work to meet the needs of the writing team.

After Transmittal— Response, Credit, and Blame

While you are accountable for what happens in your areas of business responsibility, those lines of responsibility can blur when collaborators get together to write. After you have transmitted a collaboratively prepared document, who bears responsibility for its success or failure? How are questions about its content to be answered?

As with every other facet of writing in a team, a prearranged strategy for dealing with response can make such communication efficient and productive. For example, the product development team of the frozen food company might receive this response to its memo from the vice-president for research and development: "What makes you think we have the resources for new product development and marketing in such diverse areas as baked goods and specialty pizzas? Should our marketing strategy be regional? Have you any ideas on consumer testing or should we turn this part of product development over to an outside research firm?"

Answers to such questions may come from *one* designated representative of the team after consultation with collaboraors or can emerge from a meeting convened to draft a memo to answer the vice-president's questions. In the latter case, the collaborators follow the same idea development, drafting, revision, and document preparation functions as in preparation of the original memo. However, this time, the process will probably be condensed and take far less time than the preparation of the original report.

What if the vice-president's response is not simply in the form of questions for clarification? What if, instead, the vice-president finds the memo itself unacceptable because of such factors as an error in marketing research (for example, neglecting to mention a competitor who tried to market a specialty pizza and failed) or a negative response to the entire idea (for example, the vice-president believes that the company should move into entirely new product areas rather than broadening its base in specialty desserts and pizzas)? Whose fault is the failure of the report? The answer is clear. It's the fault of all the collaborators. Once names are affixed to a document, even if yours is only one of many, you take responsibility for its content.

Fortunately, the same applies to sharing credit when the document is a success. If the proposal is well received, its ideas test out, are developed, marketed, and increase the company's share of freezer space—*and if* consumers buy the product—team members can expect recognition for a job well done.

Thus, collaborative writing does not, as might first be thought, dilute responsibility. Rather, it heightens it. You are now responsible not only for yourself and to a superior but to a group of colleagues as well. You not only share in the group's writing successes but accept blame for its rhetorical failures. What's to be gained from all this effort to work together? As we've said before, the immediate reward is the knowledge that you've increased the odds of producing a better document than one person could produce.

Whether you are one member of a writing team or chair of a writing committee, no writing project should be transmitted until the entire collaborative team has given its general approval. Of course, some group members may not like certain facets of the completed document. But if there is not a general underlying consensus that the document as a whole accomplishes the task for which it was designed, the document should *not* be sent out.

Every project experiences the unexpected. With advance planning, some of those events can become, if not expected, then at least anticipated.

Planning for the Unexpected

- *Deadlines are missed.* Sometimes collaborators individually or as a team fail to meet deadlines. A simple solution to reduce this possibility is to build a cushion of extra days for various parts of the project into the timetable.

- *Documents are lost.* The mails or the garbage pail may accidentally swallow up your hard work. The simple solution is to make certain that every collaborator has at least one copy of the document and that a spare copy is stored some safe place other than the office(s) in which the collaborators work.

- *The nature of the project changes.* Your superior may inform you that you must take a different approach to your task or format the document in a way other than you had planned. To deal with this change, convene a meeting of the writing team to develop a revised plan and timetable. Work from the original timetable, making revisions directly onto the old copy. Then have the new schedule typed and distributed.

- *New evidence undercuts findings.* The proposers of the frozen cake and pizza products may suddenly discover that their largest competitors have introduced a new line of pizzas that include the same items proposed by the team. Once again, it will be necessary to reconvene and perhaps to have the superior present for evaluation and strategy discussions. This is not an unusual problem, given the pace at which commerce and technology move today.

Here are some additional guidelines for minimizing the possibility of unpleasant, unexpected occurrences that might jeopardize the success of the project:

1. Give your clerical support staff advance notice of work they will be receiving.
2. Make certain that all needed hardware (telephone lines, photocopiers, typewriters) is available and in working order.
3. Understand your mailing procedures clearly. This includes such things as the need for the new nine-digit zip codes.
4. Double-check each collaborator's schedule to be certain that all your people are available for meetings as needed.
5. Provide your superior(s) with regular progress reports of the team's work. This need be no more than a short memo stating what you have been doing and what remains to be done to complete the project. Such regular communication between the team and upper management can prevent any surprises arising from misunderstanding of what is expected of the collaborators or what is being done by them.

Remember that problem solving is a recursive process. Your writing will not progress in lockstep fashion from problem definition through final document preparation. With collaborative writing, expect even more digressions to refine work completed during prior phases of the writing project. If you plan for contingencies in the ways detailed, you will be able to keep these digressions to a minimum and improve the chances that those detours you must make will be productive rather than merely time-consuming.

Summary

Collaborative writing brings the experience and knowledge of two or more people to bear on a writing task. Writing teams may be defined horizontally to include writers at the same level of responsibility within the same department or vertically to involve subordinates and superiors. Laterally defined teams include writers from different departments. Many writing projects use a mixture of horizontally, vertically, and laterally defined teams.

Setting up a work schedule that alternates team members' responsibilities is one way to get collaborative writing started. Brainstorming, where team members meet to jot down as many ideas as possible on the writing task, is another method for beginning work.

By setting deadlines, surveying clerical support, scheduling collaborative revision sessions, insuring stylistic consistency, and helping individuals to work within the writing team, collaborators can keep ideas flowing. Collaborative editing sessions insure that the revised draft of a document meets the approval of the entire team. Clearly defined responsibilities for preparing and transmitting the final document help it to reach its reader efficiently.

Writing done by a committee requires an active committee chair and supportive committee members. Collaborators separated by long distances may have to work through the mails or via electronic mail. Whether distant or nearby, team members must have a plan for dealing with disagreements and for handling responses to their work. Finally, collaborators must know what to do if they miss a deadline, receive a sudden change in their assignment, or experience another snag in their work.

Earlier chapters stressed that successful business writing requires a commitment to ideas and to the process that transforms those ideas into effective communication. Conversely, we urge you not to put your name to any piece of writing to which you cannot honestly give your support. Be a supportive collaborator by doing your share to help develop the strongest possible document. This means a combination of hard work, responsibility, outspokenness, and willingness to compromise. The task may be difficult—to say nothing of being unfamiliar to those of you who have always thought of writing as a solitary venture—but the result will be worth it!

Writing Problems

1. A manufacturer of kitchen gadgets seeks new products to develop and market. Working with a classmate, brainstorm a list of 10 new products that might interest the manufacturer. Follow the procedures

specified in the chapter to arrive at your final list and include these written steps with the materials you turn in to your instructor:

   a. Two brainstormed lists of 10 products each (one list by each classmate)

   b. One pared-down list of 10 products agreed upon by both classmates

   c. A revised list of 5 products with a one-sentence description of each product

2. You and a classmate work for a local radio station. One of you is in charge of promotions (contests, concerts, special events) designed to boost the number of listeners tuning to your station. The other is an accountant concerned about how much the station is paying for these promotions. Working together, brainstorm a list of 10 promotions that will increase the number of listeners but not cost the station "too much money." Follow the procedures specified in this chapter to arrive at your final list and include these written steps with the material you submit to your instructor:

   a. Two brainstormed lists of 10 promotions each (one list by each classmate)

   b. One pared-down list of 10 promotions agreed upon by both classmates

   c. A revised list of 5 promotions with a one-sentence description of each promotion

3. You and two classmates work for an office furniture retailer, who has assigned you to a horizontally defined writing team. Your supervisor requires you to draft a report suggesting that the company either lease or purchase its own fleet of trucks to deliver furniture rather than continue to contract with a delivery company. You need to produce a schedule of responsibilities for completing the report. Model this schedule on the one presented in this chapter (figure 15.3).

4. You and two classmates work for a small company whose general manager wants your opinions on which overnight mail service to use for sending letters. Meet with your classmates to prepare a schedule of responsibilities for finding out which services offer the best rates and delivery times. Contact services directly, read their magazine advertisements, and speak to local business people who use such services. After agreeing with your classmates on which service to recommend and listing reasons why, collaboratively prepare a short memo to the general manager, including the following:

   a. A list of stylistic features (passive or active voice, first person included or excluded, technical vocabulary included or excluded) that you will use consistently throughout the memo

   b. A draft of the memo

   c. A revised version of the memo—the result of individual revision
      followed by a team meeting to make agreed-upon revisions

5. You and your classmate are frequent business travelers on a particular airline. Working together, prepare a letter to the airline. In your
   letter, specify services that the airline should add to make your travel
   easier. These services can be either already existing (such as business-
   class seating or frequent-flier discounts) or new ones that would be of
   particular interest to business people. In drafting the letter, *communicate with your classmate only in writing and/or by telephone.*

6. You and four or five classmates are regular readers of a particular
   business magazine or newspaper (you choose which publication).
   Form a committee to write a letter to the magazine or newspaper. Be
   certain to choose a chairperson to coordinate your efforts. In your
   letter, specify those features of the newspaper or magazine you particularly enjoy and mention features you would like to see expanded
   or added. Provide your instructor with these materials:
   a. Your revised list of features you would like to see
   b. The first draft of your letter
   c. A revised draft of your committee's letter ready for transmittal

Extended Application

Convene a "brain trust" of yourself and two classmates. Working together,
investigate possible improvements in aspects of the business for which you
have been preparing exercises since the end of chapter 1. For each of the
businesses you three are working with, develop:

a. A list of improvements
b. A schedule for preparing a memo to recommend those improvements to
   a superior
c. The short memo itself
d. A note to your instructor specifying the dates and times during which
   you worked on this exercise collaboratively

The Handbook

The Rationale behind This Handbook

This handbook provides a review of some basic and intermediate grammar. We are not attempting to cover all the uses of each topic listed. For example, under the heading of Commas, we have not listed *every* use of the comma but the ones we feel you will most likely need to review. And we have not included guidelines for using the period, hyphen, exclamation point, and parentheses. When you need more information on any topic of style, look up one of the many style manuals available in the reference section of your university library and your university bookstore. Careful attention to these details can help your documents make a positive impression.

How to Use the Handbook

A term printed in **boldface** has its own separate entry. You will find it listed in alphabetical order with the other general topics in the handbook.

Below are listed alphabetically all the topics treated in the handbook. Using this list will help you find related topics. For example, by looking up the entry **Punctuation,** you will find listed all entries relating to punctuation, providing you with a review of this subject. You can do the same thing with such subjects as **Sentence structure, Parts of speech,** and **Verb.**

Topics Covered in
the Handbook

Active voice	Noun
Adjective	Number, grammatical
Adverb	Numbers
Agreement	Parallelism
Antecedent	Participial phrase
Apostrophe	Participle
Appositive	Parts of speech
Brackets	Passive voice
Capitalization	Phrase
Clause	Plural/singular
Cliché	Possessives
Colon	Predicate
Comma	Preposition
Comma fault	Pronoun-antecedent agreement
Comma splice	Pronoun shift
Complement	Pronouns
Complex sentence	Punctuation
Compound sentence	Quotation marks with punctuation
Compound-complex sentence	Reference of pronouns
Conjunction	Relative clause
Contractions	Restrictive clause
Coordinate clause	Semicolon
Coordinating conjunction	Sentence fragment
Correlative conjunction	Sentence structure
Dangling modifier	Sentences, types of
Dash	Sequence of tenses
Dates, punctuation with	Simple sentence
Dependent clause	Singular/plural
Direct object	Subject-verb agreement
Ellipsis	Subject
Fragment	Subjunctive mood
Gerund	Subordinate clause
Imperative mood	Subordinating conjunction
Independent clause	Titles of documents
Infinitive	Transitive/intransitive verbs
Italics	Vague reference of pronouns
Nominative case of pronouns	Verb
Nonrestrictive clause	Voice of verbs

Active voice See **Voice of verbs.**

Topics Listed in
Alphabetical
Order

Adjective A word that modifies (describes) a **noun** or a **pronoun.** Examples of adjectives are underlined below:
A substantial increase
Moderate prices
A fortunate someone

Adverb A word used to modify (describe) a verb, an adjective, or another adverb. In the following examples, adverbs are underlined.
1. Adverb modifying a verb:
The rate clerk usually calculates the invoice amounts.
2. Adverb modifying an adjective:
The microcassette is very portable.
3. Adverb modifying another adverb:
The billing machine works but usually slowly.

Agreement This term refers to the coordination of **pronouns** with their **antecedents** and of **verbs** with their **subjects.**
1. Pronoun-antecedent agreement: Sometimes writers match up the wrong pronouns with antecedents. The objective is to match a singular pronoun with a singular antecedent and a plural pronoun with a plural antecedent. For example, a common mistake is to write, "Anyone can cash *their* check at the bursar's office." But *anyone* is singular; *their* is plural. The sentence should read, "Anyone can cash his or her check at the bursar's office."
2. Subject-verb agreement: Sometimes writers match up the wrong verbs with subjects. Singular subjects take singular verbs, plural subjects take plural verbs. For example, it would be incorrect to write: "None *have* tried." *None* is singular; *have* is plural. The sentence should read, "None has tried."

Antecedent Describes the word to which a pronoun refers. Take the following sentence as an example: "Ellen left the meeting before I could give the book to her." Since the pronoun *her* refers to Ellen, Ellen is the antecedent of her.

Apostrophe See **Contractions** and **Possessives.**

Appositive A word or phrase following a noun or pronoun that describes the noun or pronoun. It is set off by commas. An example of an appositive is the italic phrase in this sentence: "Meredith, *the department head,* has approved the request." See also **Comma.**

Brackets   In quotations, transcripts of meetings, and courtroom testimony, brackets are used to indicate insertions, corrections, or comments that are not a part of the original text. For example, courtroom testimony can be clarified by the following insertions: "I saw that lady [pointing to Thelma Godsey] administering first aid to the victim [pointing to Arnold Thelen]."

Capitalization   Capitalize the following terms:
1. Proper names.
Examples:
Sidney Livernois, the Panama Canal, the House of Representatives, Senator Susan Townshend, Newark, or the Heritage Life & Casualty Company.
2. Derivatives of proper names.
Examples:
British, Italian, Roman, Chinese, or Malayan. Some exceptions: french fries, venetian blinds, arabic numerals.
3. Names of organizations.
Examples:
the Department of Labor, the Bureau of Statistics, the New York Stock Exchange, the University of Illinois, the French Embassy, the Lions Club, or the United Methodist Church.
4. The names of members of organizations.
Examples:
a Democrat, a Rotarian, a Conservative, a Communist, or a Mason.
5. The names of countries and political subdivisions.
Examples:
the United States, the State of California, the Commonwealth of Virginia, Ontario Province, or the People's Republic of China.
6. The names of regions, localities, and geographic features.
Examples:
the Gulf States, the Midwest, the Badlands, the Deep South, the Mississippi Valley, or the Tropics.
7. Trademark names, variety names, and names of market grades and brands.
Examples:
Linotype, Plexiglas, Levi's, Loafer, Snow Crop, or Choice Lamb.
8. Historical periods.
Examples:
the Depression, the New Deal, the New Frontier, or the Middle Ages. Some exceptions: the nineteenth century, ancient Greece, the colonial period.
9. Titles of publications, papers, documents, acts, and laws.

Examples:
The Wall Street Journal, the Atlantic Charter, the Kentucky Revised Code, or the Equal Opportunity Act.
10. Titles preceding the name of the person.
Examples:
President Smith, Dr. Spilka, Professor Koch, or Mayor Daley.

Clause   A group of words containing a **subject** and a **predicate.**
Examples:
Warren types.
It may contain additional elements, such as a **direct object.**
Example:
Warren types 72 words a minute.
The clause may contain additional descriptive words and phrases.
Example:
Bleary-eyed, unshaven Warren types 72 words a minute on his old Smith-Corona typewriter.
The subject and the predicate of the clause may be a compound subject or a compound predicate.
Example:
Warren and Tillie type and write 72 words a minute.
There are two kinds of clauses—independent and dependent clauses. An *independent clause* expresses a complete thought and can thus stand alone as a sentence.
Example:
Warren types 72 words a minute.
A *dependent clause* does not express a complete thought, so it cannot stand alone as a sentence. A dependent clause usually begins with a **subordinate conjunction** such as *if, although, when,* or *since.*
Examples:
If Warren types 72 words a minute
Although Warren types 72 words a minute
When Warren types 72 words a minute

Cliché   A trite expression.
Examples:
Tried and true
Permit me to
Please advise
Getting ahead
State-of-the-art
Impact upon
Have input

Colon   The colon is used to:
1. Introduce a clause explaining the preceding clause.
Example:
Machine dictation can save you time and money: it is quicker and less expensive than dictating face-to-face to a secretary.
2. Introduce a list.
Example:
The company engaged in almost frantic hiring: managers, supervisors, technicians, secretaries, and clerks.
3. Separate titles from subtitles of books.
Example:
Management: A Communication Process.

Comma   Use commas:
1. To separate the items in a series.
Example:
We have bought a computer, software, and a printer.
2. To set off an introductory **phrase.**
Example:
In the first place, we have no written agreement with your firm.
3. To set off (before and after) **appositives** and titles abbreviated after proper names.
Examples:
Vern Predmore, C.P.A., will conduct the seminar.
Merle Aragon, the chief executive officer, addressed the meeting.
4. To set off parenthetical phrases occurring within the sentence.
Example:
Dale Karlin, on the other hand, offers an entirely different solution to the problem.
5. To set off **participial phrases** from the rest of the sentence, whether they come at the beginning or within the sentence.
Examples:
Working in sales, I meet many people.
I have, working in sales, met many people.
6. To separate short, closely related **independent clauses.**
Example:
Chris manages the store, Sam does the books.
7. To join the independent clauses in a **compound sentence.** The comma precedes the **conjunction.**
Example:
Our sales usually lag in March and April, but they make up for it in May, June, and July.
8. To set off a **dependent clause** preceding the main clause in a sentence.

Example:

When the morning mail arrives, you will sort it by department.

9. To set off **nonrestrictive clauses** or phrases from the rest of the sentence. A nonrestrictive clause or phrase is one that does not exclusively identify the term it modifies.

Examples:

Leigh Gilardi, the treasurer of Lotus Chemicals, addressed the group.

The topic of the speech, which occupied approximately 20 minutes, was governmental regulations in the chemical industry.

On the other hand, **restrictive clauses** or phrases—those that do exclusively identify the word they modify—are not set off by commas.

Examples:

The person who spoke last took up most of the meeting.

The topic that attracted the most attention was governmental regulations in the chemical industry.

10. To prevent misreading.

Example:

In Room 45, 26 clerks are manually posting the day's receipts.

Comma fault   Another term for **Comma splice.**

Comma splice   The comma splice is the error of joining two **independent clauses** with only a comma.

Example:

Our private practice begins to fall off around June, it begins to pick up again around January.

The simplest way to correct the comma splice is to add the appropriate **coordinating conjunction** (usually *and* or *but*) after the comma or use a semicolon.

Examples:

Our private practice begins to fall off around June, but it begins to pick up again around January.

Our private practice begins to fall off around June; it begins to pick up again around January.

Complement   Any element that complements or completes the thought or action described in the **predicate.** The element can be many things—a **direct object, predicate adjective, phrase, clause, noun,** or **pronoun.**

Examples of complements are underlined in these sentences:

Stacey discussed the possibility. (noun)

Lee seemed pleased. (adjective)

Jan stepped to the podium. (prepositional phrase)

The coordinator was she. (pronoun)

Complex sentence   See **Sentences, types of.**

Compound sentence   See **Sentences, types of.**

Compound-complex sentence   See **Sentences, types of.**

Conjunction   A word that joins words, **phrases,** or **clauses.** The conjunction *and* illustrates all three of these uses in the following example:
Vern <u>and</u> Dale [words], both at work and at play [phrases], are
close associates, <u>and</u> they have been that way for years [clauses].
There are three kinds of conjunctions:
1. Coordinating conjunctions: These join elements of equal importance. Examples of coordinating conjunctions are *and, but,* and *or.* The preceding example illustrates the function of a coordinating conjunction.
2. Subordinating conjunctions: These join a **dependent clause** to an **independent clause.** *Since, although, when,* and *if* are examples of subordinating conjunctions. Subordinating conjunctions introduce the **dependent clause.**
Example:
Since the company was founded, Lesley Cho has been its president.
3. Correlative conjunctions: These come in pairs and join words, phrases, or clauses of equal importance.
Examples:
either . . . or
neither . . . nor
both . . . and
whether . . . or
not only . . . but also
Example:
<u>Either</u> you will pass the exam, *or* you will not pass the course.

Contractions   A contraction uses an apostrophe to fuse a **pronoun** and a **verb** or to shorten a verb. The apostrophe stands for the omitted letters. For example, *she is* contracts to *she's,* with the apostrophe standing for the omitted letter *i,* and *cannot* becomes *can't.* Usually only two contractions cause writers any difficulty—*it's* and *they're*—because both contractions are similar to the possessive pronouns *its* and *their.* Simply remember that *its* is the possessive form, and *it's* is the contraction of *it is.* Similarly, *their* is the possessive form, and *they're* is the contraction of *they are.* When in doubt about a specific use, see whether substituting the pronoun *and* verb (*it is, they are*) makes sense in the sentence. If so, use the contraction. If not, use the possessive.

Coordinate clause   Another term for an **independent clause,** which is explained under the heading of **Clause.**

Coordinating conjunction   See **Conjunction.**

Correlative conjunction   See **Conjunction.**

Dangling and misplaced modifiers   Usually this error occurs when a phrase is incorrectly positioned in the sentence so that grammatically it modifies the wrong word. For example, take this sentence: "I saw a bus walking down the street." Grammatically, the sentence means that the bus was taking a walk because the phrase "walking down the street" is in a position to modify *bus.* To correct the error, put the misplaced modifier in position to modify the word it's supposed to. For example, "Walking down the street, I saw a bus." Often, what is being modified is missing from the sentence. For example, "To succeed in selling, self-confidence is essential" means that self-confidence is doing the selling. Revise the sentence to correct the mistake: "To succeed in selling, you need self-confidence."

Dash   Dashes are used:
1. To set off a parenthetical phrase within a sentence.
Example:
We immediately bought the major items—computer, software, and printer—necessary for word processing.
2. To emphasize a word or phrase at the end of a sentence.
Example:
We immediately bought the hardware and software necessary to begin word processing—our most pressing need.
3. To emphasize a word or phrase at the beginning of a sentence.
Example:
White-collar productivity—everybody is talking about it.
4. To set off a phrase that explains the words preceding it.
Example:
To begin word processing, you will need certain basic elements—a computer, software, and a printer.

Dates, punctuation with   Three styles are acceptable with dates:
5 May 1987
May 5, 1987
May 1987
Note how the first and last examples do not require commas.

Dependent clause   See **Clause.**

Direct object   When the **predicate** of the sentence or **clause** is in the **active voice,** the receiver of the predicate's action is called the direct object. The words underlined in the following examples are direct objects:
We immediately phoned her.
Hilary enjoys word processing.
The findings of the study support the hypothesis.
National Chemical promoted 11 executives last month.

Ellipsis   Used with quotations to indicate that part of the original quote has been omitted. Ellipsis points are three dots separated by spaces. Ellipsis can be used at the beginning of a quoted sentence.
Example:
". . . the price of Xilox shares has appreciated by 83 percent in the past decade."
Ellipsis can be used within the quoted sentence.
Example:
"In spite of the unfavorable market conditions, the price . . . has appreciated by 83 percent in the past decade."
Ellipsis points can be used at the end of the quoted sentence; the period ending the sentence supplies the fourth dot.
Example:
"In spite of the unfavorable market conditions, the price of Xilox shares has appreciated. . . ."

Fragment   See **Sentence fragment.**

Gerund   A verb form used as a noun and ending in *-ing*. The gerunds are underlined in the following examples.
Thinking is never easy.
Collecting the data takes most of the time.
I enjoy running.

Imperative mood   A verb form used to give directions or commands. The examples of the imperative mood are underlined here:
First call the bank.
Keep your canceled stub.

Independent clause   See **Clause.**

Infinitive   The *to* form of any **verb.** Infinitives take the place of nouns and modify other parts of a sentence.
Examples:
To think of a better plan—that's the task facing this committee.
She says it is going to snow.
Jim needs to analyze the situation.

Italics   On a typewriter or word processor, italics for words or titles of documents are indicated by underlining. For some appropriate titles to italicize, see **Titles of documents.**

Nominative case of pronouns   The same thing as the subjective case of pronouns, which is treated under **pronouns.**

Nonrestrictive clause   See **Comma.**

Noun   Refers to a person, place, or thing. Examples of nouns are:
machine
The President of the United States
The Wall Street Journal
The Pacific Stock Exchange
Helen Keller
Bakersfield, California
abstraction

Number, grammatical   Refers to the singularity or plurality specified by a term. When a term specifies one, it is *singular*; when it specifies more than one, it is *plural*. For example, *pen* specifies one pen; *pens* means more than one pen. *I* specifies one person; *we* indicates more than one. **Verbs, nouns,** and **pronouns** can be either singular or plural.

Numbers   The general rule for the use of numbers in business is to spell out the number if it is under 10 and to use arabic numerals if it is over 10.
Example:
"Five accounting firms" but "15 accounting firms."
However, if a series of numbers is used, some of which are below and some above 10, use arabic numerals throughout.
Example:
"The company has 14 accountants, 8 attorneys, and 6 computer programmers."
When you spell out a number, do not place the corresponding arabic numeral in parentheses behind it, except in legal documents. Note also that numerals are always used for percentages, but numbers are spelled out at the beginning of a sentence.
Example:
During the first quarter, sales were down 6 percent. Twenty percent of the managers cited one reason for this decrease.

Parallelism   Means expressing similar ideas in the same grammatical form. For instance, the following example uses three underlined **gerunds** that are parallel.

Keeping down costs, improving productivity, and developing new markets are ways of increasing profits.

Parallelism is faulty or fractured when the writer is inconsistent, using the same grammatical form for some similar ideas but not for others. For instance, the following example uses two gerunds followed by a noun instead of a third gerund.

Keeping down costs, improving productivity, and the development of new markets are ways of increasing profits.

Participial phrase   See **Participle.**

Participle   A **verb** form that modifies (describes) a **noun** or a **pronoun.** Most participles are either present or past tense. Here, examples of participles are underlined:

Working in sales, I meet many people. (present participle)

Having worked in sales, I have met many people. (past participle)

Notice how the **phrase** the participle introduces—called a *participial phrase*—is set off from the rest of the sentence by commas, even when it occurs in the middle of the sentence.

Example:

I have, working in sales, met many people.

Parts of speech   See **Adjective, Adverb, Conjunction, Gerund, Infinitive, Noun, Participle, Preposition, Pronouns**, and **Verb.**

Passive voice   See **Voice of verbs.**

Phrase   A group of related words that does not contain a **subject** and a **predicate.** Phrases beginning witb a **preposition** are called prepositional phrases.

Example:

In the car

Without a ticket

In front of the house

Phrases beginning with a **participle** are called participial phrases.

Examples:

Having put out the cat,

Thinking she was not coming,

Thoroughly beaten,

Note that a comma follows a participial phrase at the beginning of a sentence.

Plural/singular   See **Number, grammatical.**

Possessives   To form the possessive of a **noun** not already ending in *s*, add
an apostrophe followed by the letter *s*.
Example:
Gale's department
To form the possessive of a noun already ending in *s* or an *s* sound, add
the apostrophe without *s*.
Examples:
Alexis' department
Six weeks' pay
Fran Schmitz' department
To form the possessive of a *pronoun*, add the *s* without the apostrophe.
Examples:
The company must report its earnings.
The employees must see the program as theirs.

Predicate   The main **verb** of the **clause** or sentence. The following sen-
tences have their predicates underlined.
She delegates authority.
Getting a degree takes time.
When they hired me, they employed only five other salespersons.
In the last example, *hired* is the predicate of the **dependent clause;**
employed is the predicate of the **independent clause.**

Preposition   Prepositions connect **nouns** or **pronouns** to other elements
of the sentence. Hence they introduce phrases. They can best be de-
fined by example. Here are some prepositional phrases with the prep-
ositions underlined:
In the office, they use processors instead of typewriters.
Aside from the problem between the two managers
At the bank during office hours
Behind him and in front of her
To the buyer
The sale for last year's model

Pronoun-antecedent agreement   See **agreement.**

Pronoun shift   Sometimes a writer will begin using one viewpoint and
unconsciously shift to another. In the following example, the writer
begins by using the third-person viewpoint (*the customer service representative*) and shifts to second-person pronouns (*you*).
The customer service representative must never show irritation with
the customer, no matter how irritated the customer may be. The

dissatisfied customer may simply want someone to "take it out on" and since you represent the company, you're elected.

One viewpoint is not necessarily better than another: just be consistent—stick with the one adopted at the beginning. The following passage uses a consistent viewpoint.

The customer service representative must never show irritation with the customer, no matter how irritated the customer may be. The dissatisfied customer may simply want someone to "take it out on," and since the service representative obviously represents the company, he or she is elected.

Pronouns Words that can substitute for **nouns** or other pronouns. Take the following example: "Lee accepted the check and forwarded *it* to the bursar's office." The word *it* is a pronoun substituting for the noun *check*. Examples of various kinds of pronouns include the following:

I, me, myself, you, she, he, him, her, it, they, who, whom, anybody, some, somebody, none, any, that, which.

1. Pronoun case:

Six pronouns have case—that is, they change their form to suit their function in the sentence. Since pronouns can have two separate functions in a sentence—serving as subjects or as objects—they have two separate cases: the subjective case and the objective case. Below are the case forms of these pronouns:

Subjective case:

I, we, he, she, they, who

Objective case:

Me, us, him, her, them, whom

Thus the cases change with the functions as the following examples indicate:

I follow him; he follows her.

We treat them.

They find us.

She greets me.

Then there is the special case of *who* versus *whom*. This pronoun takes its case from its grammatical function in its own **clause.** If it is the subject of its own clause, it remains in the subjective case (*who*) no matter what comes before it.

Examples:

Give this letter to whoever is in charge.

(Whoever is the **subject** of its own clause.)

That is the person to whom I gave the letter.

(Whom is in the objective case, as the object of the preposition to.)

2. Reference of pronouns. See **Reference of pronouns.**

3. Shifts in pronoun viewpoint. See **Pronoun shift.**

Punctuation   See specific headings—**Apostrophe, Brackets, Colon, Comma, Comma fault, Comma splice, Dash, Ellipsis, Quotation marks with punctuation,** and **Semicolon.**

Quotation marks with punctuation   At the end of a quotation, place the comma or the final period *inside* the quotation marks.
Examples:
Gwyn said, "The answer is being decoded."
Explain the term "fiduciary."
Place other punctuation marks inside the quotation marks only if they are a part of the quoted words.
Examples:
We can do without that kind of "productivity"!
The boss answered with one word, "Productivity!"
She wrote, "When will you deliver it?"
Who wrote, "A penny saved is a penny earned"?
Colons and **semicolons** always go *outside* the quotation marks.
Example:
One of our ads says, "Welcome to our all-day sale!"; one of them says, "Welcome to our 24-hour sale!": the difference in wording could confuse customers.

Reference of pronouns   Describes the relationship between a **pronoun** and its **antecedent.** The pronoun *refers* to its antecedent. Take the following sentence: "I read the memo about the meeting and passed it along to Dale." The pronoun *it* refers to its antecedent, the noun *memo.* Sometimes, however, the writer fails to make clear which term is the antecedent of a pronoun, resulting in what is called a vague reference. Look at the following passage, for example:
The originator then calls the director of the Word Processing Center to alert the director that a confidential document is being dictated. This should take only a few minutes.
The reference of the pronoun *this* is vague, because it could refer to either of two antedecents: (1) the phone call to the director or (2) dictating the document. The writer should clarify the reference here by simply adding a phrase to the last sentence of the example: "This *phone call* should take only a few minutes."

Relative clause   When the first word of a **dependent clause** is a relative pronoun (*who, whom, whose, which,* or *that*), the clause is said to be relative. In the following sentences, the relative clauses are underlined:
The company of which I speak is B & D Enterprises.
The executive who directed that program has departed.
The organization that developed this concept is Eliason, Inc.

The new stationery, <u>which is yellow</u>, has not yet been delivered.

A relative clause can be a **restrictive clause** or a **nonrestrictive clause.** Those used in the preceding examples are restrictive, except for the last one.

Restrictive clause   See **Comma.**

Semicolon   The semicolon is used to:
1. Separate **independent clauses** not separated by a **coordinating conjunction** and a **comma.**

Example:

Shelley will coordinate the project; Stacey will write the proposal.

2. Separate independent clauses joined by certain words (called adverbial connectives or conjunctive adverbs) followed by a comma. These words include *accordingly, also, besides, consequently, furthermore, hence, however, indeed, moreover, nevertheless, otherwise, so, still, then, therefore, thus.*

Examples:

Shelley will coordinate the project; however, Stacey will write the proposal.

Lesley is the department's top salesperson; accordingly, her salary is the highest.

3. Separate independent clauses that contain internal commas.

Example:

Keeping down costs, increasing productivity, and developing new markets are important; research, testing, and development need our attention as well.

Sentence fragment   An incomplete sentence. Sometimes the use of an incomplete sentence is perfectly justifiable in context. The following examples could be considered acceptable fragments:

One word of caution.

Some examples, please!

On to the next chapter.

Not on your life!

Sometimes, important sentence elements are omitted, forcing the reader to guess at the missing element. Often the author intended the fragment to be part of the previous sentence but unthinkingly separated the fragment with a period.

Example:

The next day we began to sort the cards manually.

Using hours of valuable time.

To correct such an error, either add the element that will complete the sentence, or combine the two sentences.

Example:

The next day we began to sort the cards manually, using hours of valuable time.

Sentence structure   See **Sentences, types of, Subject, Predicate, Complement, Direct object, Indirect object, Clause, Phrase, Parallelism, Sentence fragment,** and **Dangling and misplaced modifiers.**

Sentences, types of   There are four types of sentences: the simple, compound, complex, and compound-complex sentence. They are described here:
1. The simple sentence: consists of a **subject, predicate,** and any modifiers and **complements** needed to express the thought. It is itself an **independent clause** with no **dependent clauses.**

Example:

Sidney, the company president, delegates virtually all authority.
2. The compound sentence: contains at least two independent clauses joined either by a **coordinating conjunction** with a **comma** or by a **semicolon.**

Examples:

Warren is the director of the Word Processing Department; Tillie is the manager of the Communications Department.

Warren is the director of the Word Processing Department, and Tillie is the manager of the Communications Department.

Warren is the director of the Word Processing Department; however, Tillie is the manager of the Communications Department.
3. The complex sentence: consists of at least one independent clause and at least one dependent clause.

Example:

While Warren was the director of the Word Processing Department [the dependent clause], Tillie was the manager of the Communications Department [the independent clause].
4. The compound-complex sentence: consists of at least two independent clauses and at least one dependent clause.

Example:

If I am not mistaken [the dependent clause], Warren is the director of the Word Processing Department [independent clause], and Tillie is the manager of the Communications Department [independent clause].

Sequence of tenses   See **Verb.**

Simple sentence   See **Sentences, types of.**

Singular/plural See **Number, grammatical.**

Subject-verb agreement See **Agreement.**

Subject In a **clause** or a sentence, it is the doer of the action described in the **predicate** verb when that verb is in the **active voice.** The subject is usually a noun or pronoun. Below are examples showing subjects underlined:

<u>Irene</u> presides.
<u>Accounting</u> is a rewarding career.
<u>Thinking of that</u> makes me angry.

The subject in a sentence or a clause is the receiver of the action of the predicate verb when that verb is in the **passive voice.** The following examples show subjects underlined:

<u>She</u> was elected president by the association.
<u>Thrift</u> is considered important.

Subjunctive mood The subjunctive mood applies to **verbs** describing states of being that are potential rather than actual or are contrary to fact. For example, take this statement: "If I *were* president, I would fire the Secretary of Commerce." It implies that the speaker is actually *not* president. Some of these potential states requiring the subjunctive are those of mere possibility, acquired right, and perceived obligation.

Examples of possibilities:
If I were
I would
I might
I could

Example of acquired right:
I may

Examples of perceived obligation:
I should
I ought to

Use *were* instead of *was* after *if, as if,* and *as though* when a prospect is contrary to fact or highly unlikely.

Examples:
If you were younger, you could enter the contest.
The new clerk acted as though she were the senior supervisor.

Subordinate clause Another term for a **dependent clause,** explained under the heading of **Clause.**

Subordinating conjunction See **Conjunction.**

Titles of documents   These are set off either by being italicized (indicated by underlining in typing) or by quotation marks. Here are general guidelines for determining how a given title should be set off. (1) Italicize the title of a document published by itself, as a unit. Thus italicize titles of books, periodicals, journals, and newspapers. (2) Use quotation marks for the title of a document published as part of a collection of documents. Thus use quotation marks for the titles of periodical or journal articles, newspaper articles, and essays. (3) Use quotation marks for the titles of unpublished documents, such as the titles of theses, dissertations, or speeches, as well as for the titles of television and radio programs.

Transitive/intransitive verbs   These two terms describe the relationship of a **verb** to its object. If the verb can take a **direct object,** it is transitive. Examples of transitive verbs are underlined below:
Dale sorts the mail.
Dale calls the mailroom.
If the verb cannot take a direct object and takes either no object or an **indirect object,** it is intransitive. Examples of intransitive verbs are underlined below:
Dale swims.
Dale swims at Sunlight Pool. [indirect object: at Sunlight Pool]

Vague reference of pronouns   See **Reference of pronouns.**

Verb   A word that expresses a state of being. Examples of verbs are *think, sing, is, calculate, have,* and *breathe.* Verbs delineate the time of an action by tense. The following list illustrates verb tenses:
Present: I think
Past: I thought
Past perfect: I had thought
Future: I will think
Future perfect: I will have thought
Keep verb tenses consistent, especially when dealing with an action completed in the past, for which you must use not only the past tense but also the past perfect tense. Note the following example: "Before I arrived, I *had thought* the job would be easy." Since *thinking* occurs before *arriving*, it must be put in the past perfect tense. Coordinating the tenses of different verbs is called maintaining the sequence of tenses. For more information about verbs, see **Voice of verbs, Transitive/intransitive verbs, Agreement, Imperative mood, Subjunctive mood, Participle, Gerund,** and **Predicate.**

Voice of verbs   Refers to the role of the **subject** in the sentence. The two voices are the active and the passive.

1. Active voice: In this case, the subject of the sentence performs the action.

Examples:

<u>Gale hired</u> Marion.

<u>Gale gave</u> it to Marion.

<u>Gale brought</u> Marion to work.

2. Passive voice: In this case, the subject of the sentence is acted upon.

Examples:

Marion <u>was hired</u> by Gale.

It <u>was given</u> to Marion by Gale.

Marion <u>was brought</u> to work by Gale.

Note that the passive voice does not have to indicate who performed the action; the passive can be used deliberately to conceal the doer of the action.

Examples:

Marion was hired. (By whom?)

It was given to Marion. (By whom?)

Marion was brought to work. (Who brought her?)

INDEX